I0132272

# MISSOURI PRIVATE LAND CLAIMS

# 1832

FINAL ADJUSTMENTS OF PRIVATE LAND CLAIMS IN MISSOURI, 1832

HOUSE OF REPRESENTATIVES DOCUMENT 1340

24TH CONGRESS — FIRST SESSION

1835

Heritage Books
2024

# HERITAGE BOOKS

*AN IMPRINT OF HERITAGE BOOKS, INC.*

## Books, CDs, and more—Worldwide

For our listing of thousands of titles see our website
at
www.HeritageBooks.com

A Facsimile Reprint
Published 2024 by
HERITAGE BOOKS, INC.
Publishing Division
5810 Ruatan Street
Berwyn Heights, MD 20740

House of Representatives Document 1340
24th Congress – First Session
1835

— Publisher's Notice —
In reprints such as this, it is often not possible to remove
blemishes from the original. We feel the contents of this
book warrant its reissue despite these blemishes and
hope you will agree and read it with pleasure.

International Standard Book Number
Paperbound: 978-0-7884-9403-1

24TH CONGRESS.] No. 1340. [1ST SESSION.

# FINAL REPORTS OF THE BOARD OF COMMISSIONERS ON PRIVATE LAND CLAIMS IN MISSOURI, UNDER THE ACT OF JULY 9, 1832.

COMMUNICATED TO THE SENATE DECEMBER 15, 1835.

GENERAL LAND OFFICE, *December* 10, 1835.

SIR: I have the honor to submit, herewith, for the consideration of the Senate, two bound volumes, containing the final reports of the Boards of Commissioners at St. Louis, under the act of July 9, 1832, entitled, " An act for the final adjustment of private land claims in Missouri," and of the act supplementary thereto, upon the claims to land in that State. One of the volumes contains their reports upon claims Nos. 256 to 345, inclusive, in the *first class,* and the other contains their reports upon claims Nos. 1 to 152, inclusive, except No. 20, which is stated to have been withdrawn by them, in the *second class.*

[For the report upon land claims, Nos. 1 to 142, see vol. 6, No. 1,173, February 5, 1834.

For report upon said claims, from Nos. 143 to 255 inclusive, see vol. 7, No. 1,336, March 3, 1835.]

As the voluminous character of these reports would prevent this office from making duplicate copies thereof for the two Houses of Congress, within a reasonable time, the original reports are now transmitted to the Senate, with a request that they may be placed in the possession of the House of Representatives, whenever the Senate shall have acted upon the subject.

It being very important that this office should be in possession of the *originals* of all the reports upon private land claims, I have to request that those now transmitted may be returned after the final action of Congress thereon.

With great respect, I have the honor to be, &c.

ETHAN A. BROWN.

The PRESIDENT *of the Senate of the United States.*

---

OFFICE OF THE RECORDER OF LAND TITLES, *St. Louis, Missouri, September* 30, 1835.

To HON. ETHAN ALLEN BROWN, *Commissioner of the General Land Office :*

SIR: The recorder and commissioners appointed under the act of Congress entitled " An act for the final adjustment of private land claims in Missouri," approved July 9, 1832, and the act supplementary thereto, approved March 2, 1833, beg leave to lay before you the result of their proceedings since the last report.

In prosecuting the examination of the claims, the commissioners have endeavored to confine themselves strictly to the duties prescribed by the laws under which they acted, which require of them " to examine all the unconfirmed claims to land in that State (Missouri), heretofore filed in the office of the said recorder, according to law, founded upon any incomplete grant, concession, warrant, or order of survey, issued by the authority of France or Spain, prior to the tenth day of March, one thousand eight hundred and four ; and to class the same so as to show, first, what claims, in their opinion, would in fact have been confirmed, according to the laws, usages, and customs of the Spanish government, and the practice of the Spanish authorities under them, at New Orleans, if the government under which said claims originated and continued in Missouri ; and, secondly, what claims in their opinion are destitute of merit, in law or equity, under such laws, usages, customs, and practice of the Spanish authorities aforesaid."

By an examination of the documentary evidence submitted with this and the former reports of the board, it may be readily seen that the practice under the French and Spanish authorities, with the usages and customs

T.49

T.48

T.47

T.46

Mississippi River

R. Jardogone

Missouri River

R.2          R.3          R.4          R.5

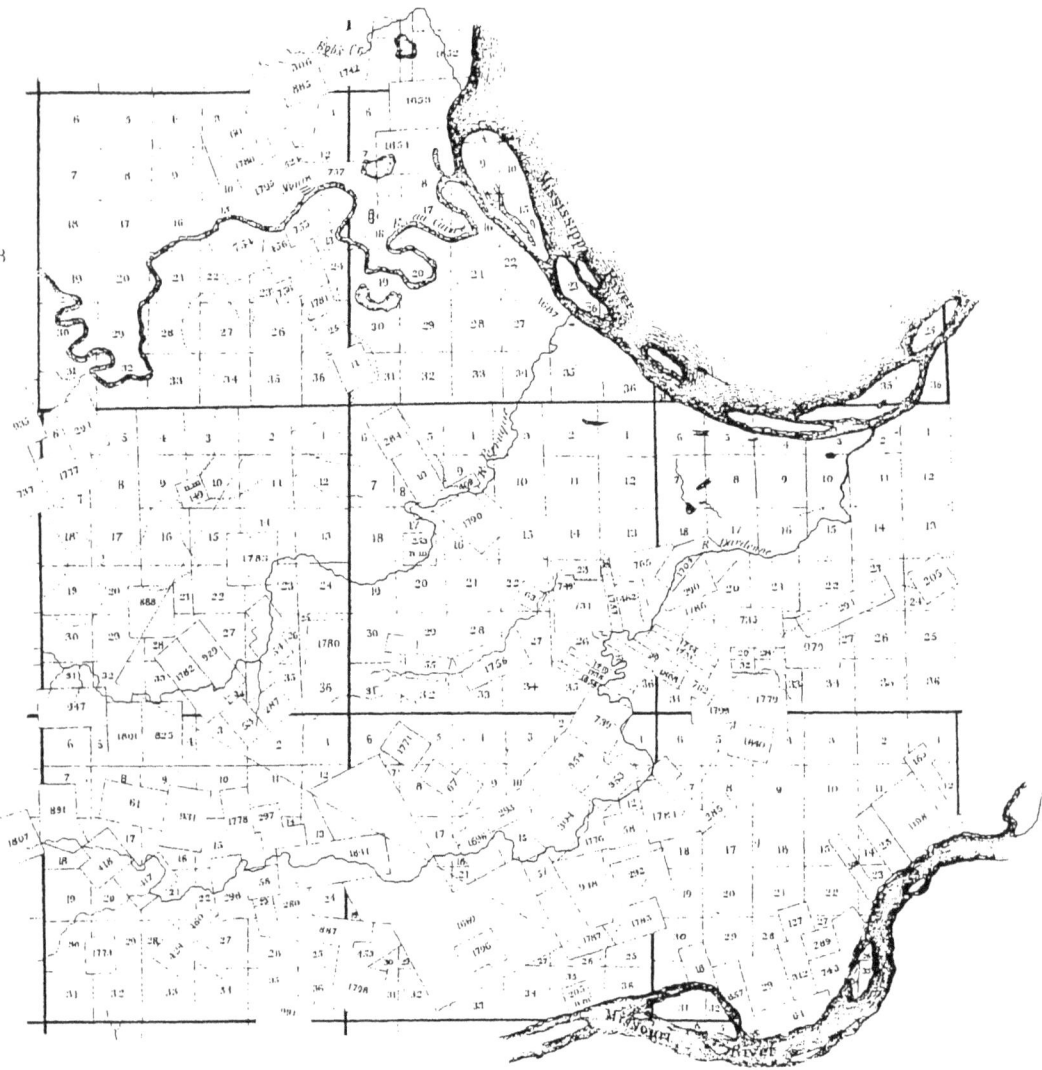

Scale of 200 chains to an inch

Surveyors Office,
St Louis 1st September 1845.

The above plat of Townships 46, 47 & 48 North Ranges 2,3 & 4 East of the 5th Principal Meridian
is conformable to the Township plats on file in this office

Geo: T. Langham, Surveyor of public lands

William Milburn chief clerk

from the first settlement of Louisiana to the time of its delivery to the authorities of the United States, has uniformly been, for those persons having the civil and military government of the provinces, commonly called lieutenant governors, sub-delegates, &c., to grant lands to the inhabitants, and to emigrants to the country, accompanied by an order of survey directed to the surveyor general; and if the duties of that officer did not permit to execute the survey with promptness, the grantee was permitted to take possession of the land as property vested, until such a time as a survey could be had. These concessions and orders of survey were made by the officers from a personal knowledge of the qualifications of the petitioners, or upon letters or certificates of the commandants of the posts within whose districts the applicants lived, and the land was situated. To perfect those incomplete titles, it was necessary for the parties interested to forward their concessions, together with plats and certificates of survey, to the governor or intendant general at New Orleans, who alone was competent to give the titles in form. The difficulty and expense of procuring a survey; the great distance from Upper Louisiana to New Orleans, together with the large amount which it cost to get a title completed; the scarcity of money among the settlers at that early day; and, last though not least, the indulgence uniformly extended to the inhabitants of the provinces by the French and Spanish governments; all, combined, have, in the opinion of the board, rendered the grantees, generally, too supine to take the necessary steps to procure perfect titles.

The confidence and security which the ancient inhabitants of Upper Louisiana had in those incomplete titles, is strongly evidenced by the fact of so few being perfected, even among those who had been in possession under their grants from twenty to forty years previous to the change of government; indeed the whole correspondence held between the governor or intendant general and the lieutenant governors of Upper Louisiana, which has come to the knowledge of the board, shows conclusively that it was assigned to the latter, as sub-delegates, to make the grants, and to the former to perfect the titles. This question has, however, been fully settled by the Supreme Court of the United States, in the case of Chouteau *et al. vs.* the United States; where the court declare the lieutenant governors to be, by virtue of their office, sub-delegates, with power to make grants. It is, perhaps, unnecessary to carry the argument further than it has been done, to sustain the principles which the board laid down as a ground of their report in 1833, to which you are again most respectfully referred, the same having governed in the decisions made on the claims which accompany the present; and it is no small degree of gratification to the members of the board, to find those principles sustained in their most important points, by the supreme judicial authority of the nation, so far as they have been called upon to decide; and it is confidently believed that the remaining points, of minor consideration, will be equally sustained by the same enlightened tribunal, whenever brought before them. In the case above cited, the court goes on to say, that "orders of survey made by the lieutenant governors of Upper Louisiana, are the foundation of title, and are capable of being perfected into complete titles; that they are property capable of being alienated, of being subject to debts; and is, as such, to be held as sacred and inviolate as other property." And, in the case of Charles D. Delassus, the court hold this language, in adverting to the treaty of cession: "The right of property then is protected and secured by the treaty, and no principle is better settled in this country, than that an inchoate title to land is property; independent of treaty stipulations, this right would be held sacred. The sovereign who acquires an inhabited territory acquires full dominion over it; but this dominion is never supposed to divest the vested right of individuals to property. The language of the treaty ceding Louisiana excludes every idea of interfering with private property, of transferring lands which have been severed from the royal domain. The people change their sovereign; their rights to property remain unaffected by the change."

The great difficulty the land claimants had to contend with, was the imputation of fraud cast upon their claims; the instructions of Mr. Gallatin, (the then Secretary of the Treasury,) of the 8th September, 1806, appear to have been founded upon a charge of that nature, and show the imperfect knowledge had at that early day, of the customs and regulations which governed in granting lands in the Spanish provinces. By those instructions, the whole burden of proof was thrown upon the claimant, and a failure in any one point decided the claim to be surreptitious. It was required of the claimant, by the former board, to give evidence of the verity of his papers; this was in many instances impracticable, from the absence of the officer, and the circumstance of no regular records having been kept. And it was further required to show the legal authority of the officer making the grant; this in no instance could be done, as the law of the country was the will of the sovereign, known only through the acts of the officer who represented him. No parol testimony was admitted to establish this fact, nor were there any written laws to be found; and the few letters of instructions which have since been filed in relation to the establishments in Upper Louisiana, were either rejected by or withheld from, the former board. Since the organization of the present board, its members have assiduously sought for the evidence to sustain the *general* charge of *fraud*, which has been made here and elsewhere, against the land claims. Their efforts in that respect have, for the most part, been unavailing; but it is believed they have, in some instances, saved the government from imposition; and it is their conviction that there are but few, if any, of the claims which have been placed in the first class, that would not stand the most rigid scrutiny of a court of justice, and will be found nothing more than what is strictly due to the claimants from the justice of Congress, and the plighted faith of the nation, given in a solemn treaty.

The policy of Spain with regard to her colonies in this country, was evidently of a most liberal and munificent character, and such as has ever characterized the policy of all other European nations towards their American colonies; none looked to their lands as a source of revenue, but distributed them liberally to the settlers; and he who encountered the losses, privations, and dangers, incident to making new establishments in the wilderness provinces in the New World, was considered as one possessing the strongest claims on the bounty of the government; it being a matter of much importance to the former governments of this country to strengthen, by a numerous population, their distant posts on the Mississippi and Missouri rivers, and give to them that permanency of character which would enable them to prevent the inroads of their British neighbors on the north, and hold in check the numerous bands of savages that molested them on every side.

The small number of the first emigrants to Upper Louisiana, and the warlike character of the surrounding tribes of Indians, compelled the pioneer settlers to establish themselves in villages, and to cultivate but small tracts in their immediate vicinity. Anticipating, at some future day, that their numbers would be sufficient to justify them in extending their settlements, they applied to the authorities and obtained grants for more remote tracts, which they looked upon as the future homes of their families, and some remuneration for the many dangers and privations encountered by them in making their first establishments in the country.

The present report includes ninety claims, which are placed in the first class, numbered from 256 to 345, inclusive, and are respectfully recommended for confirmation; and 152 claims which they have placed in the second class, numbered from 1 to 152, inclusive, not considering them possessed of sufficient merit to justify a report in their favor. The translations of the concessions and other documents appertaining to each class of claims, accompany this report, and are numbered to suit the particular transcripts to which they belong.

Previous to deciding upon the large claim of the heirs and legal representatives of Jacques Clamorgan, which is placed in the second class, No. 152, the board had recourse to all the documents in the different offices connected with the land department, having any connection with this claim, and find it to contain an area of about 80,000 acres, as exhibited by the accompanying plat marked A, within the bounds of which, or interfering with its lines, as designated on the plat, Zenon Trudeau, as lieutenant governor and sub-delegate, granted prior to the 3d day of March, 1797, (the date of the concession by him to Clamorgan,) fifteen hundred and twenty-four arpens, to seven different persons; and, subsequently, to eleven other individuals, twelve thousand and sixty-six arpens. Charles D. Delassus, during the term of his administration, viz. from August, 1799, to the 10th of March, 1804, granted to thirty-nine individuals, twenty-one thousand nine hundred and seventy-eight arpens; all of which have been confirmed by the former board of commissioners and recorder of land titles, with the addition of twenty-three thousand nine hundred and eighty acres, granted to fifty-six claimants, under the 2d section of the act of Congress of 1805, making the aggregate amount of about seventy-six thousand six hundred acres, confirmed by the government of the United States, within, or interfering with the claim now set up by the representatives of Clamorgan, as will be seen by reference to list marked B, obtained from the surveyor general's office at St. Louis, where the names and number of original claimants are set forth; and for the amount of lands entered, within the bounds of this claim, reference is made to list C, obtained from the register of the land office at St. Louis; and it is believed the present board have recommended other claims to the favorable consideration of Congress, which are located within the lines of this tract.

The great importance of this claim has induced the commissioners to make a careful examination of every fact in connection with it. The grants made by Trudeau prior and subsequent to the date of this to Clamorgan, the great number made by his successor Delassus, and the circumstance of the surveyor general having had no notice of the grant made to Clamorgan, as evidenced by his making, or causing to be made, surveys of nearly all the tracts granted, interfering with his claim, would seem to show that this grant to Clamorgan was not regarded by the officers of the Spanish government, or was abandoned by the claimant himself, soon after it was obtained.

The board take occasion to say that the concession, and the accompanying documents, which have been presented to them, give no evidence of being surreptitious, and they feel fully convinced that it was the intention of the government of the country to make the claimant compensation for his expenditures in maintaining a military force to protect the trade on the Missouri; but it is evident, from the subsequent acts of the same officer who made the grant, and his successor, that there must have been some further procedure in relation to the claim, which has not been brought to light before any of the tribunals of this government appointed for the adjustment of land titles; and it is further evidenced by the acts of the surveyor general of Upper Louisiana, (an officer known to be punctilious in the discharge of his duty,) that he never could have been notified by Clamorgan of his grant, or the surveys under his jurisdiction, subsequent to the date of this grant, would not have been permitted, and the lieutenant governor would have been notified by the surveyor of the interference of Clamorgan's grant with the seven claims previously granted and surveyed. These circumstances induce the board to believe that the claimant abandoned his claim, with the knowledge of the officers, to seek remuneration otherwise, or has been guilty of a neglect of his privileges under the grant, which would amount to a forfeiture. The board, therefore, could not recommend this claim for confirmation, believing that, had the government of Spain been continued over this country to this day, the tract, as designated, would not be confirmed to the claimants; but it is more than probable that, if the remuneration had not been made, which seems was intended by this grant, a location might be permitted in some part of the domain where it would not be prejudicial to others.

The board regrets to say, they have not been able to complete the investigation of all the claims in Missouri that the laws, under which they acted, made it their duty to examine. The prevalence of the cholera, and resignation of Mr. Updike, prevented a report being made the first year; and, subsequently, the resignation of Messrs. Linn and Harrison, and other unavoidable interruptions of the proceedings, left long intervals in which the board was not full; and being under the belief that it required the attendance of all its members to make decisions, little else was done in those intervals than to take testimony and prepare the transcripts from the old records.

There yet remains to be acted on about seven hundred claims within the State of Missouri, and it is respectfully but earnestly recommended to Congress to continue the investigations until the business is finally completed. This, we think, is due to the interests of both the state and general governments, as well as to that of the individuals immediately concerned. It should not be concealed, that the recent decisions of the Supreme Court have created much uneasiness among persons holding title to lands, under the United States, which are claimed by concessions and orders of survey under the French and Spanish governments. If we understand the decisions of the court correctly, the treaty of cession protects those claims as private property, and the United States are bound to perfect the incomplete grants made by the former governments. This being the case, we conceive it to present a subject of great and important consideration, calling for the early action of Congress. Appeals to the judiciary, by claimants, to establish their rights vested under a former government, and guaranteed by treaty, will seldom be forced upon them by the government of the United States, and certainly never, when Congress is properly informed on the subject.

The plan adopted by the board in making up the transcripts of the claims, exhibits, at one view, the whole subject, and will enable Congress to dispose of them according to their respective merits.

It is a work of much time and labor to trace the claims through the old records, which are voluminous and defective in their arrangement; but it is thought by the board, that all the claims within the State of Missouri which have been recorded and not reported on, might be fully examined and classed in two years after the reorganization of the board, provided Congress should pass an act to that effect.

JAMES H. RELFE,
FALKLAND H. MARTIN,
F. R. CONWAY.

No. 256.—*William McHugh, sr., claiming 640 acres.*

| No. | Name of original claimant. | Acres. | Nature and date of claim. | By whom granted. | By whom surveyed, date, and situation. |
|---|---|---|---|---|---|
| 256 | William McHugh, sr. | 640 | Settlement right. | | 1,320 arpens by John Harvey, D. S., 14th February, 1806; certified by A. Soulard, surveyor general, 21st February, 1806; Ramsay's creek, 45 miles N. W. of St. Charles. |

EVIDENCE WITH REFERENCE TO MINUTES AND RECORDS.

St. Louis, *December* 15, 1813.—James Morrison, assignee of William McHugh, sr., claiming 800 arpens of land on Bryan's, otherwise called Lost creek, county of St. Charles.

Frederick Dickson, duly sworn, says that witness saw claimant, McHugh, sr., inhabiting this tract of land in 1802, at which time he had corn for his use. In the following year, 1803, said McHugh, sr., raised good crops of corn, wheat, &c., and still inhabited the premises, and moved off to avoid the Indians, who made an inroad into the settlements in the fall of 1803. To the best of witness's recollection McHugh, sr., had a wife and eight children living with him in 1803. McHugh died two years, or about that time, having remained in the settlement until his death with his family, or that part thereof as escaped the scalping-knife, several of them having been killed by the Indians. (See Bates's minutes, page 78.)

(The following ought to have been entered first:)

*August* 7, 1807.—The board met pursuant to adjournment. Present: the Hon. John B. C. Lucas, Clement B. Penrose, and Frederick Bates.

James Morrison, assignee of William McHugh and wife, claiming 1,320 arpens of land, under the second section of the act of Congress of March 2, 1805, produces a deed from said McHugh and wife, dated April 23, 1803, and a plat and certificate of survey, dated February 14, 1806, and certified February 21, same year.

Jonathan Bryant, being duly sworn, says that he knows the above claim, and that William McHugh settled on it in 1801, and lived in a camp until some time in July of the same year; planted about two acres of corn and tended it; and that he and the greatest part of his family was taken sick and moved away; and that he had a wife and nine children at that time.

William Ewing, duly sworn, says that the said McHugh had some of his cattle killed by the Indians, and the witness says he saw the Indians carrying away some beef that they had killed, at the same time, and that he was living in the house with said McHugh, and that he was alarmed, and believed that the said McHugh and the rest of his family were also; that in consequence they all moved off, and that they were ten or twelve miles beyond any other settlement, and that the said McHugh had three children killed by the Indians at the place of his last removal, about the year 1804. Laid over for decision. (See book No. 3, page 54.)

*December* 2, 1809.—Board met. Present: John B. C. Lucas and Frederick Bates, commissioners.

James Morrison, assignee of William McHugh, claiming 1,320 arpens of land. (See book No. 3, page 54.) It is the opinion of the board that this claim ought not to be granted. (See book No. 4, page 218.)

*July* 6, 1833.—L. F. Linn, esq., appeared, pursuant to adjournment.

William McHugh, sr., alias McGue, claiming 640 acres, joining the tract of William Ramsay, sr., on Ramsay's lick.

Ira Cottle, being duly sworn, says that he well knew McHugh; that he had a considerable large family; that he had a house and a truck-patch on said piece of land, adjoining Ramsay's lick; that McHugh was on said piece of land in 1803, and that his children were killed on said place, by the Indians, in 1804. (See No. 6, page 215.)

*February* 15, 1834.—F. R. Conway, esq., appeared, pursuant to adjournment.

William McHugh, sr., by his assignee, James Morrison, claiming 640 acres of land, situate about forty-five miles northwest of St. Charles. (See record-book B, page 369; book F, page 112; recorder's minutes, page 78; Bates's decisions, page 33.)

Produces a survey of 1,320 arpens, executed by John Harvey, D. S., dated February 14, 1806, and certified by Antoine Soulard on February 21, 1806.

Nathaniel Simonds, being duly sworn, says that he is fifty-eight years of age; that he became acquainted with the original claimant, McHugh, in the spring of the year 1802, and knows the tract claimed; that in May or June of the year 1803, he was on said tract, and saw corn, potatoes, cabbages, and such vegetables as was usual at that time to plant, growing on said place. He does not now recollect how much was then in cultivation, but supposes there were some four, five, or six acres, which were enclosed by a fence. There was a cabin and smoke-house on the place at the time above mentioned. He further says, that McHugh had at that time eight or ten children; that this settlement was about fifteen miles from the main settlement; that the neighboring Indians were considered hostile; that there had been Indian signs seen near McHugh's; a cow beast had been killed, as supposed by them, and this deponent had gone there to aid McHugh to collect his stock and remove his family to the main settlement, which they did immediately; that in September, 1804, the Indians killed three of the sons of said McHugh; that said McHugh continued to reside in the country until his death, which took place about the year 1809 or 1810. (See book No. 6, page 499.)

*October* 8, 1834.—The board met pursuant to adjournment. Present: F. R. Conway, J. S. Mayfield, J. H. Relfe, commissioners.

In the case of William McHugh, alias McGue, claiming 640 acres of land. (See book No. 6, page 215.)

The testimony here below was taken by G. A. Harrison, late commissioner, under a resolution of the board, passed May 13, 1833.

Clarksville, *May* 24, 1833.—James Burnes, being duly sworn, upon his oath says, that at least two years before a change of government, and at the same time that William Ramsay came to that place, said McHugh cultivated a place on McHugh's creek; that after Ramsay was driven off by the Indians, about 1804, said McHugh was put in possession of said Ramsay's land, by Ramsay, as he supposes; that said McHugh had at that time a wife and nine children.

Joseph McCoy, being duly sworn, upon his oath says, that having heard the above testimony of James Burnes, the same is in all things substantially true, as he believes and recollects. (See book No. 7, page 20.)

*June 8, 1835.*—The board met pursuant to adjournment. Present: F. R. Conway, J. H. Relfe, commissioners.

William McHugh, sr., claiming 640 acres of land. (See book No. 6, page 215; No. 7, page 20.)

The board are of opinion that 640 acres of land ought to be granted to the said William McHugh, sr., or to his legal representatives, according to possession. (See book No. 7, page 168.)

JAMES H. RELFE,
F. R. CONWAY.

I have examined the transcript of the above claim, and concur in the decision.

F. H. MARTIN.

---

No. 257.—*William Ramsay, sr., claiming 748 arpens 8 perches.*

| No. | Name of original claimant. | Arpens. | Nature and date of claim. | By whom granted. | By whom surveyed, date, and situation. |
|---|---|---|---|---|---|
| 257 | William Ramsay, sr. | 748 8 pr. | Settlement right. | | John McKinney, D. S. 20th February, 1806; received for record by A. Soulard, surveyor general, February, 1806. |

EVIDENCE WITH REFERENCE TO MINUTES AND RECORDS.

*December 5, 1811.*—Board met. Present: John B. C. Lucas, Clement B. Penrose, and Frederick Bates, commissioners.

William Ramsay, claiming 748 arpens 68 (8) perches of land, district of St. Charles. Produces record of a plat of survey, dated February 20, 1806, certified February, 1806.

It is the opinion of the board that this claim ought not to be granted. (See No. 5, page 485.)

*March 26, 1835.*—F. R. Conway, esq., appeared, pursuant to adjournment.

William Ramsay, sr., claiming 748 arpens 8 perches of land, situate on Ramsay's creek. (See record-book B, page 239; minutes, No. 5, page 485.)

The following testimony was taken in Clarksville, on May 24, 1833, by A. G. Harrison, then one of the commissioners:

Ralph H. Flaugherty, duly sworn, says, that before the change of government took place, William Ramsay was living on a tract of land on a creek called Ramsay's creek, named after the claimant; that said Ramsay's family, while living there, having been taken sick, he left there and came down to witness's father's house, where he stayed some time. Witness says he does not recollect certainly the precise time that Ramsay was in possession of said land, but is sure it was before the change of government took place. At the time that Ramsay was in possession of said land, he, the said Ramsay, had a wife and five children.

James Burnes, being duly sworn, upon his oath says, that at least two years before the change of the Spanish to the American government, he knew the said William Ramsay cultivated a farm on what is now called Bryan's creek; that on said creek there is a spring called Ramsay's lick, which is on the above tract of land; that said Ramsay had houses, stables, and a field of at least twenty acres; was in the habit of selling corn to the neighborhood. That one Bryan also lived on said creek, near the above, from whom said creek took its name; that said creek is frequently mistaken for another creek higher up, called Ramsay's creek, where said Ramsay made a hunting-camp, and split some rails; that at the time of the possession aforesaid, said Ramsay had a wife and several children; that said land is about ten or eleven miles below Clarksville, and about two miles and a half above where said Bryan's creek empties into King's lake; that witness has frequently been at Ramsay's house, and would be able now to identify the place.

Joseph McCoy, being duly sworn, upon his oath says, that before the change of the Spanish government he was quite a youth, and lived near where Troy now stands, about sixteen or seventeen miles from the land above described; that he does not recollect ever to have been at Ramsay's before the change of government, but often heard it said that the said Ramsay lived at a place on the creek now called Bryan's creek, near a Mr. Bryan, who gave name thereto; that he has since frequently seen the improvements of said Ramsay. He further says that he has frequently heard many persons call said creek Ramsay's creek, through mistake, as he supposes, from the circumstance of Ramsay's lick being thereon; that Ramsay's creek is higher up, where he understands Ramsay made a hunting-camp, and split some rails; that Bryan's creek is even yet frequently mistaken for Ramsay's creek; that he has often been called on to know if he could show certain lands on Ramsay's creek, (so expressed by the inquirer;) that in course of conversation he would ascertain it was on Bryan's creek, (now so called,) and that he knew the places well. That Bryan's creek was by them called Ramsay's creek, but he always called another creek higher up Ramsay's creek.

Jonathan Bryant, being duly sworn, says that, in 1801, at what is called Ramsay's lick, on Bryan's creek, William Ramsay, sr., settled and cultivated a tract of land, made some improvements, as building cabins, clearing ground, &c., and left there in company with witness on account of sickness, in 1801, and left a man by the name of McHugh to take care of the place.

Joshua Stogsdill, being duly sworn, says that William Ramsay, sr., lived on and cultivated a place on Bryan's creek, in 1801 or 1802; that witness lived with said Ramsay on said place about eight weeks, at the time said Ramsay's family was sick, and left there a few days before the death of his wife; that said Ramsay had about fifteen or twenty acres of corn, stables, and other buildings on said place.   (See book No. 7, page 105.)

The following testimony was taken and entered on the minutes, on the 6th of July, 1833, but was not then transcribed, the agent for claimant having entered this claim, by mistake, for 1,100 arpens, which quantity was not found of record:

*July* 6, 1833.—L. F. Linn, commissioner, appeared, pursuant to adjournment.

William Ramsay, sr., by his legal representatives, claiming 1,100 (748 8 perches) arpens of land, situated on Ramsay's lick.

Ira Cottle, being duly sworn, says that he knew William Ramsay, sr., in 1802; that he then was cultivating land on Bryan's creek, at the saline, since called after him, Ramsay's lick; that said Ramsay cultivated on a grand scale, had a considerable stock, had quite a large farm, and was strong handed; that he understood, and believes, that, about the year 1804, he is not now certain of the year, there were several families killed in Mr. Ramsay's neighborhood; that McHugh's family were killed, and this was the cause of Ramsay's leaving said place.   (See book No. 6, page 214.)

*June* 8, 1835.—The board met, pursuant to adjournment.   Present: F. R. Conway, J. H. Relfe, commissioners.

William Ramsey, sr., claiming 748 arpens and 8 perches of land.   (See book No. 6, page 214; No. 7, 105.)

The board are of opinion that 748 arpens and 8 perches of land ought to be granted to the said William Ramsey, sr., or to his legal representatives, according to the survey.   (See book No. 7, page 169.)

JAMES H. RELFE,
F. R. CONWAY.

I have examined the transcript of the above claim, and concur in the decision.

F. H. MARTIN.

---

No. 258.—*Benjamin Gardiner, claiming 750 arpens.*

| No. | Name of original claimant. | Arpens. | Nature and date of claim. | By whom granted. | By whom surveyed, date, and situation. |
|---|---|---|---|---|---|
| 258 | Benjamin Gardiner. | 750 | Settlement right. | | Daniel Boon, D. S. 24th February, 1806. Received for record by Soulard, February 28, 1806. On the Missouri. |

EVIDENCE WITH REFERENCE TO MINUTES AND RECORDS.

*November* 19, 1811.—Board met.   Present: John B. C. Lucas, Clement B. Penrose, and Frederick Bates, commissioners.

Benjamin Gardiner, heirs of, claiming 750 arpens of land, situate in Missouri, district of St. Charles, produces record of a plat of survey, dated 24th, and certified 28th February, 1806.

It is the opinion of the board that this claim ought not to be granted.   (See book No. 5, page 426.)

*January* 27, 1835.—F. R. Conway, esq., appeared, pursuant to adjournment.

Benjamin Gardiner, by his heirs, claiming 750 arpens of land.   (See record-book B, page 255; minutes, No. 5, page 426.)

Jonathan Bryan, being duly sworn, says that he is in the 76th year of his age; that he came to this country in the year 1800, in company with Benjamin Gardiner, in whose right the above tract is claimed; that he knows the tract claimed; that Gardiner built a cabin on the place in the latter part of the year 1801, and moved in it in that year; that in the year 1802 he raised a crop of corn on the place, he thinks about five acres.   The said Gardiner had no wife; his sister lived with and kept house for him.   Witness thinks he continued to occupy the place about one year; he was in the habit of hunting and trapping; that he made three trips of from four to six months each.   He started on a fourth trip, and was taken sick and returned to the settlement, and died in the year 1805; that said Gardiner raised a crop of corn at Samuel Watkins's, in the year 1801, about five miles from the place claimed.   (See book No. 7, page 94.)

*March* 9, 1835.—F. R. Conway, esq., appeared, pursuant to adjournment.

Benjamin Gardiner, claiming 750 arpens of land.   (See No. 7, page 94.)   Isaac Darst, being duly sworn, says that he is in the 46th year of his age; that he was well acquainted with Benjamin Gardiner, and knows the tract of land claimed; that Gardiner was neighbor to witness's father; that he settled the place claimed in the year 1802, and in that year, or in 1803, he, witness, saw corn growing on the said place; that Gardiner had at that time some eight or ten acres enclosed, and about half that quantity under cultivation in corn. Gardiner went out frequently on hunting expeditions.   The last trip he made he was taken sick while out, was brought into the settlement, and died in a short time thereafter.   Witness was present at his death.   He was a single man, and appeared to be above the age of 21 years at the time he settled the place, and was well thought of by his neighbors.   (See No. 7, page 101.)

*March* 27, 1835.—F. R. Conway, esq., appeared, pursuant to adjournment.

Benjamin Gardiner, claiming 750 arpens.   The following testimony was taken in June, 1833, by A. G. Harrison, esq., then one of the commissioners:

Joshua Stogsdill, duly sworn, says that, in the year 1802 or 1803, he passed by a place in Darst's bottom, on the Missouri river, which place Benjamin Gardiner was then improving; that said Gardiner had on said place a cabin and several acres of cleared ground, and was living there at the time mentioned; that said Gardiner left there shortly afterward, and David Bryant succeeded him, in 1803, and cultivated and improved the same place.

John Manly, being duly sworn, says that witness came to the country in the spring of 1804, and that Benjamin Gardiner had settled the fall before in Darst's bottom, on the Missouri; that he had a small piece of cleared ground on said place and a cabin; that he resided there about two years, and that said Gardiner told witness that he had sold his claim on that place to David Bryant. (No. 7, page 109.)

*May* 7, 1835.—The board met, pursuant to adjournment. Present: F. R. Conway, James H. Relfe, commissioners.

In the case of Benjamin Gardiner, claiming 750 arpens of land. (See book No. 7, pages 93, 101, and 109.)

William Hays, being duly sworn, says he is near 54 years of age; that he knows of Benjamin Gardiner, the claimant, clearing several acres of land on the tract now claimed, in the year 1802, and in the same year said Gardiner had a potato patch, and planted and raised a crop of corn. Deponent thinks said Gardiner had in that year about seven acres under fence. This tract claimed is situated on the north side of the Missouri river, between the said river and the lands of Daniel M. Boon and of John Linsay. Witness further says, he does not know of said Gardiner cultivating said land for more than one year; he followed hunting, was a single man, and appeared at that time to be upward of twenty years of age. In the year 1801, claimant lived on the land of one Samuel Watkins, and there raised a crop of corn, his sister, a widow, living at that time with him. (See book No. 7, page 143.)

*June* 8, 1835.—The board met, pursuant to adjournment. Present: F. R. Conway, J. H. Relfe, commissioners.

Benjamin Gardiner, claiming 750 arpens of land. (See book No. 7, pages 93, 101, 109, and 143.)

The board are of opinion that 750 arpens of land ought to be granted to the said Benjamin Gardiner, or to his legal representatives, according to possession. (See book No. 7, page 169.)

JAMES H. RELFE,
F. R. CONWAY.

I have examined the transcript of the above claim, and concur in the decision.

F. H. MARTIN.

---

### No. 259.—*George Girty, claiming* 640 *acres.*

| No. | Name of original claimant. | Acres. | Nature and date of claim. | By whom granted. | By whom surveyed, date, and situation. |
|-----|---------------------------|--------|---------------------------|------------------|----------------------------------------|
| 259 | George Girty. | 640 | Settlement right. | | Near town of St. Charles. |

EVIDENCE WITH REFERENCE TO RECORDS AND MINUTES.

St. Louis, *December* 31, 1813.—The legal representatives of George Girty, claiming 640 acres of land, county of St. Charles, near the town.

George K. Spencer, duly affirmed, says, that in 1799 he was at the house of Girty on this tract; he then inhabited the tract with his family at that time, and cultivated the same; continued to inhabit and cultivate until the year 1801, when he removed, after having, as witness believes, raised a crop on this tract. Almost every year to this time, this tract has been inhabited and cultivated by others. Witness believes that the representatives of Peché inhabited and cultivated this tract in 1803, and throughout that year, including December 20. (Bates's minutes, page 134.)

*July* 6, 1838.—L. F. Linn, esq., appeared, pursuant to adjournment.

George Girty, by his legal representatives, claiming 640 acres of land near the village of St. Charles. (See Bates's minutes, page 134; Bates's decisions, page 37.)

Ira Cottle, duly sworn, says that he knew said Girty; he thinks it was about the year 1800; that said Girty then lived about half a mile from the village of St. Charles; that he had a house and lived there with his family, and had several children; that said Girty resided there some time. Deponent does not recollect how long, and then went on the Dardenne, where he died. (See book No. 6, p. 216.)

*March* 26, 1835.—F. R. Conway appeared, pursuant to adjournment.

George Girty, claiming 640 acres of land. (See book No. 6, page 216.)

The following testimony was taken by A. G. Harrison, esq., in May, 1833:

Ralph H. Flaugherty, duly sworn, says, that in the winters of 1799 and 1800, he saw George Girty in a habitation about a mile west of St. Charles; that, at that time, he had a house and a field of about five or six acres improved around the house; he had also fruit-trees planted on the place, and that he knew the said Girty to live there two or three years after the time he first saw him. He had been living there some time before witness saw him, judging from the appearance of the improvements; that said Girty, at the time witness first saw him, had a wife and five or six children, perhaps more.

Peter Teague, being duly sworn, says, that to the best of his knowledge, in the month of June, 1798, George Girty was living on a place about half a mile or three quarters of a mile northwest of St. Charles; that he had a small improvement on it with some fruit-trees, and that he lived there about three, four, or five years, cultivating the same, and had a wife and five children.

Noel John Prieur, being duly sworn, says that George Girty lived on, and cultivated a piece of land near a mile west of St. Charles; that said Girty had a field of about four acres, a house and an orchard on said place; that the time spoken of was before the change of government, and that he remained there three or four years; that he left said place, as witness now recollects, before the change of government, and moved on Dardenne, where he made an improvement; that said Girty told witness he had a concession for his place on Dardenne; that said place of Girty is in what are now the commons of St. Charles. (See book No. 7, page 107.)

*June* 8, 1835.—The board met, pursuant to adjournment. Present: F. R. Conway, J. H. Relfe, commissioners.

George Girty, claiming 640 arpens of land. (See book No. 6, page 216; No. 7, page 107.)

The board are of opinion that 640 acres of land ought to be granted to the said George Girty, or to his legal representatives, according to possession ; the same having been inhabited and cultivated before Delassus granted an increase to the common of St. Charles, which is now said to embrace this claim.  (See book No. 7, page 170.)

JAMES H. RELFE,<br>F. R. CONWAY.

I have examined the transcript of the above claim, and concur in the decision.

F. H. MARTIN.

---

No. 260.—*John Rourke, claiming 756 arpens.*

| No. | Name of original claimant. | Arpens. | Nature and date of claim. | By whom granted. | By whom surveyed, date, and situation. |
|---|---|---|---|---|---|
| 260 | John Rourke. | 756 | Settlement right | | James Mackay, D. S, December 16, 1805. Received for record February, 1806, by A. Soulard, S. G.; on river Dardennes, St. Charles. |

EVIDENCE WITH REFERENCE TO MINUTES AND RECORDS.

*December* 9, 1811.—Board met.  Present : John B. C. Lucas, Clement B. Penrose, and Frederick Bates, commissioners.

John Rourke, claiming 756 arpens of land, situate on Dardenne, district of St. Charles ; produces record of a plat of survey, dated 16th December, 1805, certified February, 1806.

It is the opinion of the board that this claim ought not to be granted.  (See book No. 5, page 490.)

St. Louis, *December* 29, 1813.—John Rourke, claiming 756 arpens of land, on Dardenne, in county of St. Charles.

William Dum, duly sworn, says that in June or July, 1802, saw this tract, and saw rails mauled and ground cleared.  In 1803 saw corn growing, fences and cabin ; did not at those times know that this was Rourke's claim ; was afterward informed so.  (See Bates's minutes, page 131.)

*March* 27, 1835.—F. R. Conway appeared, pursuant to adjournment.

John Rourke, by his legal representatives, claiming 756 arpens of land on river Dardenne.  (See record-book D, page 256 ; commissioners' minutes, book No. 5, page 490 ; Bates's minutes, page 131.)

The following testimony was taken in May, 1822, by A. G. Harrison, esq., then one of the commissioners :

Ralph H. Flaugherty, being duly sworn, says that he knew John Rourke ; that said Rourke lived on Dardenne, on a tract of land which he claimed, just below Arend Rutgers ; that at the time witness saw him living there, he had a cabin, and a small field around it in cultivation ; that to the best of witness's recollection, the time that Rourke lived there was about the last of the reign of the Spanish government, or shortly after.  (No. 7, page 108.)

*June* 8, 1835.—The board met, pursuant to adjournment.  Present : F. R. Conway, J. H. Relfe, commissioners.

John Rourke, claiming 756 arpens of land.  (See book No. 7, page 108.)

The board are of opinion that 640 acres of land ought to be granted to the said John Rourke, or to his legal representatives, to be taken within the original survey.  (See book No. 7, page 170.)

JAMES H. RELFE,<br>F. R. CONWAY.

I have examined the transcript of the above claim, and concur in the decision.

F. H. MARTIN.

---

No. 261.—*Mordicai Bell, claiming 350 arpens.*

To Don Charles Dehault Delassus, *Lieutenant Governor and Commander-in-chief of Upper Louisiana, &c. :*

Mordicai Bell, a Roman Catholic, has the honor to represent that, with the consent of your predecessor, he came over to this side, (of the Mississippi,) where he has selected a piece of land in his Majesty's domain, on the south side of the Missouri.  This being considered, he supplicates you to have the goodness to grant him, at the same place, for the support of his family, the quantity of three hundred and fifty arpens of land in superficie.  The petitioner having the means necessary to improve a farm, and having no other views but to live as a peaceable and submissive cultivator, hopes to obtain the favor he solicits.

St. Andre, *January* 21, 1800.

his<br>MORDICAI × BELL.<br>mark.

Be it forwarded to the lieutenant governor, with the information that the statement hereabove is true, and that the petitioner deserves the favor which he solicits.

St. Andre, *January* 21, 1800.

SANTIAGO MACKAY.

St. Louis of Illinois, *January* 29, 1800.

In consequence of the information of the commandant of St. Andrew, Don Santiago Mackay, I do grant to the petitioner the tract of land of three hundred and fifty arpens in superficie, which he solicits, provided it is not prejudicial to any person; and the surveyor, Don Antonio Soulard, shall put the interested in possession of the said quantity of land he asks for, in the place indicated; and this being executed, he shall make out a plat, delivering the same to the party, together with his certificate, in order to serve him to obtain the concession and title in form from the intendant general, to whom alone belongs, by royal order, the distributing and granting all classes of land belonging to the royal domain.

CARLOS DEHAULT DELASSUS.

Recorded, No. 12.                                                                MACKAY.

St. Louis, *April* 15, 1835.

I certify the above and foregoing to be truly translated from the original.

JULIUS DE MUN, *T. B. C.*

| No. | Name of original claimant. | Arpens. | Nature and date of claim. | By whom granted. | By whom surveyed, date, and situation. |
|---|---|---|---|---|---|
| 261 | Mordicai Bell. | 350 | Concession; 29th January, 1800. | C. Dehault Delassus. | James Mackay, D. S., January 21, 1806; recorded by Soulard, surveyor general, January 27th, 1806. |

EVIDENCE WITH REFERENCE TO MINUTES AND RECORDS.

*October* 10, 1811.—Board met. Present: John B. C. Lucas, Clement B. Penrose, and Frederick Bates, commissioners.

Amos Stoddard, assignee of James Mackay, assignee of Mordicai Bell, claiming 350 arpens of land, situate near the town of St. Louis, district of St. Louis, produces a plat of survey, dated 21st January, 1806, certified 27th January, 1806. Conveyance from Bell to Mackay, dated 29th May, 1804; from Mackay to claimant, dated 26th September, 1805.

It is the opinion of the board that this claim ought not to be confirmed. (See No. 5, page 359.)

*March* 30, 1835.—F. R. Conway, Esq., appeared, pursuant to adjournment.

Mordicai Bell, by the legal representatives of Amos Stoddard, claiming 350 arpens of land, situate in the grand prairie, near St. Louis. (See record-book A, page 93; book D, page 361; and minute-book No. 5, page 359.)

Produces a paper purporting to be an original concession from Carlos Dehault Delassus, dated January 29, 1800. Also, deed of conveyance from Mordicai Bell to James Mackay, and deed from said Mackay to Amos Stoddard.

M. P. Le Duc, being duly sworn, says that the signature to the concession is in the proper handwriting of Charles Dehault Delassus. Witness further says that, in the year 1804, he went, in company with Major Stoddard and several other gentlemen, to the place now claimed, and from that time the said place has always been called Stoddard's mound. (See book No. 7, page 110.)

*June* 8, 1835.—The board met, pursuant to adjournment. Present: F. R. Conway, J. H. Relfe, commissioners.

Mordicai Bell, claiming 350 arpens of land. (See book No. 7, page 110.)

The board are of opinion that 350 arpens of land ought to be confirmed to the said Mordicai Bell, or to his legal representatives, according to the survey on record, in book D, page 362. (See book No. 7, page 170.)

JAMES H. RELFE,
F. R. CONWAY.

I have examined the transcript of the above claim, and concur in the decision.

F. H. MARTIN.

No. 262.—*Antoine Lamarche, claiming* 750 *arpens.*

| No. | Name of original claimant. | Arpens. | Nature and date of claim. | By whom granted. | By whom surveyed, date, and situation. |
|---|---|---|---|---|---|
| 262 | Antoine Lamarche. | 750 | Settlement right. | | John Harvey, D. S., December 20, 1805; received for record, February 27, 1806, by A. Soulard, S. G.; District of St. Charles. |

EVIDENCE WITH REFERENCE TO MINUTES AND RECORDS.

*November* 23, 1811.—Board met. Present: J. B. C. Lucas, Clement B. Penrose, and Frederick Bates, commissioners.

Antoine Lamarche, claiming 750 arpens of land, situate on Lamarche's creek, district of St. Charles; produces record of a plat of survey, dated December 20, 1805, and certified February 27, 1806.

It is the opinion of the board that this claim ought not to be granted. (See book No. 5, page 444.)

*March* 31, 1835.—F. R. Conway, esq., appeared, pursuant to adjournment.

Antoine Lamarche, by his legal representatives, claiming 750 arpens of land on Lamarche's creek, in St. Charles county. (See record-book B, page 264; book No. 5, page 444.)

The following testimony was taken in May, 1833, by A. G. Harrison, then one of the commissioners:

Pierre Palardi, being duly sworn, says that he knew Antoine Lamarche; that said Lamarche lived on and cultivated a tract of land on Lamarche's run, four or five years, under the Spanish government; that at that time he had a wife and four children. The land spoken of is in St. Charles county.

Etienne Quenelle, being duly sworn, says that, having heard read the evidence of Pierre Palardi, as above, he knows the same facts, and makes the same his own.

Ralph H. Flaugherty, being duly sworn, says that he knew the said Lamarche; that he lived on a tract of land on a creek now called Lamarche's creek, under the Spanish government, as witness believes; that he had a house and a field on said land; that he had a wife and several children at that time. (See No. 7, page 111.)

June 8, 1835.—The board met, pursuant to adjournment. Present: F. R. Conway, J. H. Relfe, commissioners.

Antoine Lamarche, claiming 750 arpens of land. (See book No. 7, page 111.)

The board are of opinion that 750 arpens of land ought to be granted to the said Antoine Lamarche, or to his legal representatives, according to the survey on record in book B, page 264. (See No. 7, page 171.)

JAMES H. RELFE,
F. R. CONWAY.

I have examined the transcript of the above claim, and concur in the decision.

F. H. MARTIN.

---

No. 263.—*Samuel Holmes, claiming 840 arpens.*

| No. | Name of original claimant. | Arpens. | Nature and date of claim. | By whom granted. | By whom surveyed, date, and situation. |
|-----|---------------------------|---------|---------------------------|------------------|----------------------------------------|
| 263 | Samuel Holmes. | 840 | Settlement right. | | Daniel M. Boon, D. S., February 24, 1806. Received for record by Soulard, surveyor general, February 28, 1806. |

EVIDENCE WITH REFERENCE TO MINUTES AND RECORDS.

*November* 20, 1811.—Board met. Present: John B. C. Lucas, Clement B. Penrose, and Frederick Bates, commissioners.

Samuel Holmes, claiming 840 arpens of land, situate in Peruque, district of St. Charles. Produces record of plat of survey, dated February 24, and certified February 28, 1806.

It is the opinion of the board that this claim ought not to be granted. (See No. 5, page 432.)

*March* 31, 1835.—F. R. Conway, esq., appeared, pursuant to adjournment.

Samuel Holmes, by his legal representatives, claiming 840 arpens of land on Peruque. (See minute-book, No. 5, p. 432; record-book B, page 252.)

The following testimony was taken in May, 1833, by A. G. Harrison, esq., then one of the commissioners:

Etienne Quenelle, being duly sworn, says that he knew Samuel Holmes lived on Peruque from his first recollection, and that he, witness, is forty-seven or forty-eight years old; that Holmes lived there a long time before the change of government; that he had a wife and children.

Joseph Chartran, being duly sworn, says that he knew said Holmes; that he lived on the north side of Peruque, under the Spanish government; that he had a wife and three children. He had an orchard on the place, and was well fixed.

Daniel Keathly, being duly sworn, says that, in the month of November, 1803, he met with Samuel Holmes, who was then a stranger to witness; that said Holmes requested witness to show him some land to settle on; that witness took him on Peruque, somewhere about half-way from the mouth to the head of it; that said Holmes commenced immediately to make improvements on the land which witness had showed to him; built a cabin on the same, and cultivated said land. (See book No. 7, page 112.)

*June* 8, 1835.—The board met, pursuant to adjournment. Present: F. R. Conway, J. H. Relfe, commissioners.

Samuel Holmes, claiming 840 arpens of land. (See book No. 7, page 112.)

The board are of opinion that 640 acres of land ought to be granted to the said Samuel Holmes, or to his legal representatives, to be taken within the original survey. (See book No. 7, page 171.)

JAMES H. RELFE,
F. R. CONWAY.

I have examined the above transcript, and concur in the decision.

F. H. MARTIN.

---

No. 264.—*Vincent Lafoix and Nicholas Plante, claiming 416 arpens.*

St. Genevieve, *January* 17, 1797.

To Don Francis Valle, *Captain and Civil and Military Commandant of the post of St. Genevieve.*

Sir: The undersigned have the honor to represent that they wish to obtain from you a tract of land on a branch of the river establishment, commonly called La fourche à Duclos, (Duclos's fork,) in which place each of your petitioners has selected eight arpens in width by forty arpens in length, to begin ten arpens below a cave which is on the bank of said river, and the forty arpens to be taken ascending the said river; for which (tracts) the petitioners ask of you, sir, to grant them a concession in full property for them and their heirs, and they will pray for your preservation and prosperity.

his
VINCENT × LAFOIX.
mark.

his
NICOLAS × PLANTE.
mark.

St. Louis, *November* 13, 1797.

The surveyor of this jurisdiction, Don Antonio Soulard, shall put Messrs. Vincent Lafoix and Nicolas Plante in possession of the land they ask for in the foregoing petition; and afterward he shall make out a plat and certificate of his survey, and the whole shall be sent back to us to be forwarded to the commandant general of the province, for him to determine definitively upon the concession of the said land.

ZENON TRUDEAU.

Don Antonio Soulard, *Surveyor General of the settlements of Upper Louisiana.*

St. Louis of Illinois, *May* 17, 1798.

I certify that, on the 15th of December of last year, (by virtue of the foregoing decree of the lieutenant governor of these settlements of Illinois, Don Zenon Trudeau,) I went on the land of Vincent Lafoix and Nicolas Plante, in order to survey the same, conformably to their demand of two hundred and twenty-four arpens in superficie, which measurement was taken in presence of the proprietors with the perch of Paris of eighteen feet in length, according to the custom adopted in this province of Louisiana, and without regard to the variation of the needle, which is 7° 30' east, as evinced by the preceding figurative plat. The said land is situated at about nine miles west of the post of St. Genevieve, and bounded as follows: to the N. E. and N. W. by vacant lands of his Majesty's domain; to the S. W. by lands of Michael Placette; and to the S. E. by the banks of the river establishment. In testimony whereof, I do give these presents, together with the foregoing figurative plat, on which are indicated the dimensions and the natural and artificial limits which surround the same.

ANTONIO SOULARD, *Surveyor General.*

St. Louis, *April* 14, 1835.

I certify the above and foregoing to be truly translated from the original papers filed in this case.

JULIUS DE MUN, *T. B. C.*

| No. | Name of original claimant. | Arpens. | Nature and date of claim. | By whom granted. | By whom surveyed, date, and situation. |
|---|---|---|---|---|---|
| 264 | Vincent Lafoix and Nicolas Plante. | 416 | Concession, November 13, 1797, for 640 arpens. | Zenon Trudeau. | 224 arpens, by A. Soulard, December 15, 1797. Certified by same May 17, 1798. On river establishment. |

EVIDENCE WITH REFERENCE TO MINUTES AND RECORDS.

*April* 3, 1835.—F. R. Conway, esq., appeared, pursuant to adjournment.

Vincent Lafoix and Nicolas Plante, by their legal representatives, claiming 640 arpens of land, situate on the waters of establishment. (See record-book C, page 72; Bates's decisions, page 65, wherein 224 arpens of said claim are confirmed.)

Produces a paper purporting to be an original concession from Zenon Trudeau, dated November 13, 1797; also a plat and certificate of survey for 224 arpens. Said survey was made on December 15, 1797, and certified on May 17, 1798, by Antoine Soulard.

M. P. Le Duc, duly sworn, says that the signature to the concession is in the proper handwriting of Zenon Trudeau, then lieutenant governor, and that the signature to the plat and certificate of survey is in the proper handwriting of Antoine Soulard, surveyor general.

The following testimony was taken on May 4, 1833, in St. Genevieve county, by L. F. Linn, esq., then one of the commissioners:

John Baptiste Vallé, aged about 72 years, being first duly sworn, as the law directs, deposeth and saith, that he was well acquainted with the said Nicolas Laplante, alias Plante, and Vincent Lafoix, and that they and each of them at the date of the grant, were citizens and residents in the then province of Upper Louisiana, and that they continued to be citizens and residents till the time of their death; that he knows the grantees made sugar on the place at an early day.

J. B. VALLÉ.

Sworn to and subscribed before me, this 4th day of May, 1833.

L. F. LINN, *Commissioner.*

(No. 7, page 115.)

*June* 8, 1835.—The board met, pursuant to adjournment. Present: F. R. Conway, J. H. Relfe, commissioners.

Vincent Lafoix and Nicolas Plante, claiming 640 arpens of land. (See book No. 7, page 115.)

The board are of opinion that 416 arpens of land ought to be confirmed to the said Vincent Lafoix and Nicolas Plante, or to their legal representatives, extending the survey already made to the above quantity of 640 arpens. (See book No. 7, page 171.)

JAMES H. RELFE,
F. R. CONWAY.

I have examined the transcript of the above claim, and concur in the decision.

F. H. MARTIN.

No. 265.—*John Stewart, claiming 640 acres.*

| No. | Name of original claimant. | Acres. | Nature and date of claim. | By whom granted. | By whom surveyed, date, and situation. |
|---|---|---|---|---|---|
| 265 | John Stewart. | 640 | Settlement right. | | Survey on record, without date or signature. |

EVIDENCE WITH REFERENCE TO MINUTES AND RECORDS.

*April 4, 1835.*—F. R. Conway, esq., appeared, pursuant to adjournment.

John Stewart, claiming 640 acres of land, situate in the district of St. Genevieve. (See record-book C, page 510.)

The following testimony was taken by F. R. Conway, esq., at Potosi:

John McNeal deposeth and saith that, in the fall season of the year 1802, he stayed all night with John Stewart, and that said Stewart had raised his cabins some short time before; one was a very large cabin of good logs, much larger and higher than any built at that time, and the other a small cabin of the usual size, adjoining the large one; witness ate supper and breakfast with said Stewart. In the summer of 1803, witness passed a night, and ate supper and breakfast with the said Stewart, and then saw a field of good-looking corn growing near claimant's house, and witness told claimant that he had a large field of good corn; the said Stewart replied that it might not be as large as I thought, and asked me how much I supposed there was. I told him I supposed there was eight or ten acres. He said no, there is but six or seven acres in corn. Witness further says, that Moses Austin told him that the said John Stewart was entitled to land from the Spanish government, as one of said Austin's followers. Said Stewart's field was under good fence, and witness thinks, from the part he saw, that it was generally made of split rails. The said Stewart claims 640 acres of land, and witness never heard that he claimed any other land for his head or improvement right.

                                     JOHN T. McNEAL.

Sworn to and subscribed before me, at Potosi, Missouri, this 8th day of May, 1834.

                                     F. R. CONWAY.

(See No. 7, page 116.)

*June 8, 1835.*—The board met, pursuant to adjournment. Present: F. R. Conway, J. H. Relfe, commissioners.

John Stewart, claiming 640 acres of land. (See book No. 7, page 116.)

The board are of opinion that 640 acres of land ought to be granted to the said John Stewart, or to his legal representatives, according to possession. (See book No. 7, page 171.)

                                     JAMES H. RELFE,
                                     F. R. CONWAY.

I have examined the transcript of the above claim, and concur in the decision.

                                     F. H. MARTIN.

---

No. 266.—*William Meek, claiming 500 arpens.*

To Don CHARLES DEHAULT DELASSUS, *Lieutenant-Colonel, attached to the stationary regiment of Louisiana, Commander-in-chief of Upper Louisiana, &c.*

William Meek, a Roman Catholic, has the honor to represent that, with the permission of the government, he came over to this side, where he has selected a tract of land in the domain of his Majesty, for the purpose of making a plantation; therefore, he supplicates you to have the goodness to grant him, at the place he has selected, a tract of land corresponding to the number of his family, which is composed of himself, his wife, and six children. The petitioner, having sufficient means to improve a piece of land, and having no other views but to live as a peaceable and submissive cultivator of the soil, hopes to deserve the favor he solicits.

St. ANDRE, *June 4, 1803.*

                                     his
                             WILLIAM × MEEK,
                                   mark.

Be it forwarded to the lieutenant governor, together with the information that the above statement is true, and that the petitioner is worthy to obtain the favor he solicits.

St. ANDRE, *June 4, 1803.*

                                     ST. YAGO MACKAY.

                         ST. LOUIS OF ILLINOIS, *June 8, 1803.*

In consequence of the information given by Don Santiago Mackay, commandant of the post of St. André, by which the number (of persons) composing the family of the petitioner is proven, the surveyor, Don A. Soulard, shall put him in possession of five hundred arpens of land in superficie, in the place asked for, said quantity corresponding to the number of his family, conformably to the regulation made by the governor general of the province, and afterward the interested shall have to solicit the title of concession in form from the intendant general, to whom alone belongs, by royal order, the distributing and granting of all classes of lands in the royal domain.

                                     CARLOS DEHAULT DELASSUS.

I certify the above and foregoing to be truly translated from book B, page 198, of record in this office.
JULIUS DE MUN, *T. B. C.*

| No. | Name of original claimant. | Arpens. | Nature and date of claim. | By whom granted. | By whom surveyed, date, and situation. |
|---|---|---|---|---|---|
| 266 | William Meek. | 500 | Concession, June 8, 1803. | Carlos Dehault Delassus. | James Mackay, D. S. November 14, 1803; received for record by A. Soulard, S. G., Feb. 27, 1806; on the Missouri. |

EVIDENCE WITH REFERENCE TO MINUTES AND RECORDS.

*April* 1, 1835.—F. R. Conway, esq., appeared pursuant to adjournment.

William Meek, by his legal representatives, claiming 500 arpens of land on the Missouri. (See record-book B, page 198.)

The following testimony was taken in June, 1833, by A. G. Harrison, then one of the commissioners:

John Manly, being duly sworn, says that he came with said Meek to this country; that said Meek settled on a place on the Missouri, about four miles above the mouth of Chorette; that witness, in the spring of 1804, assisted said Meek in clearing ground and putting in a crop on said place; that a short time after putting in the crop, said Meek took sick and died. (See book No. 7, page 113.)

*June* 9, 1835.—The board met, pursuant to adjournment. Present: F. R. Conway, J. H. Relfe, commissioners.

William Meek, claiming 500 arpens of land. (See book No. 7, page 113.)

The board are of opinion that this claim ought to be confirmed to the said William Meek. or to his legal representatives, according to the survey recorded in book B, page 198, in the recorder's office. (See book No. 7, page 172.)

JAMES H. RELFE,
F. R. CONWAY.

I have examined the transcript of the above claim, and concur in the decision.

F. H. MARTIN.

No. 267.—*Jacob Wise, claiming* 37½ *acres.*

| No. | Name of original claimant. | Acres. | Nature and date of claim. | By whom granted. | By whom surveyed, date, and situation. |
|---|---|---|---|---|---|
| 267 | Jacob Wise. | 37½ | Settlement right. | | John Stewart, D. S. February 26, 1806; received for record February 26, 1806. Mine à Breton. |

EVIDENCE WITH REFERENCE TO MINUTES AND RECORDS.

*December* 23, 1811.—Board met. Present: John B. C. Lucas, Clement B. Penrose, and Frederick Bates, commissioners.

Jacob Wise, claiming 37½ acres of land, situate adjoining Mine à Breton, district of St. Genevieve. Produces a plat of survey, dated February 26, and certified February 28, 1806. Produces also permission to settle, sworn to by Joseph Decelle, syndic.

The following testimony in this claim, taken from testimony perpetuated and attested by two of the commissioners, October 24, 1808:

Francis Thibault, sworn, says that Jacob Wise cultivated the land claimed, nine or ten years ago, and ever since; built a house the first year, and was rented to Mr. Decelle for two years; has not since been inhabited, but has always been used as a barn; claimant lived adjoining the tract with one Charles Bequette; claimant is a single man.

The board remark that no kind of testimony suggests or makes it appear that the land claimed includes a lead mine. It is the opinion of the board that this claim ought not to be granted, claimant not having inhabited the same on December 20, 1803. (See book No. 5, page 535.)

*April* 7, 1835.—F. R. Conway, esq., appeared, pursuant to adjournment.

Jacob Wise, claiming 37½ acres of land, situate at Mine à Breton. (See record-book B, page 242; book No. 5, page 535.)

The following testimony was taken at Potosi, by F. R. Conway, esq., on the 8th day of May, 1834:

John McNeal, being duly sworn, deposeth and saith that, in the years 1803 and 1804, Jacob Wise, then a laboring man, was a resident in this country, and had some acres of land in cultivation, with a comfortable cabin thereon, the whole enclosed with a good fence; that said Wise claimed the same as a donation from the Spanish government; and witness never heard of his claiming any other head right than the one above mentioned, which will fully appear from the records of surveys recorded in the year 1806, in St. Louis.

JOHN T. McNEAL.

Sworn to and subscribed before me, at Potosi, Washington county, this 8th day of May, 1834.

F. R. CONWAY.

(See book No. 7, page 119.)

*June 9, 1835.*—The board met, pursuant to adjournment.  Present: F. R. Conway, J. H. Relfe, commissioners.

Jacob Wise, claiming 37¼ acres of land.  (See book No. 7, page 119.)

The board are of opinion that this claim ought to be granted to the said Jacob Wise, or to his legal representatives, according to the survey recorded in book B, page 242, in the recorder's office.  (See book No. 7, page 172.)

JAMES H. RELFE,<br>F. R. CONWAY.

I have examined the above transcript, and concur in the decision.

F. H. MARTIN.

### No. 268.—*Zachariah Dowty, claiming 450 arpens.*

| No. | Name of original claimant. | Arpens. | Nature and date of claim. | By whom granted. | By whom surveyed, date, and situation. |
|---|---|---|---|---|---|
| 268 | Zachariah Dowty. | 450 | Settlement right. | | |

EVIDENCE WITH REFERENCE TO MINUTES AND RECORDS.

*October 6, 1808.*—Board met.  Present: the honorable Clement B. Penrose and Frederick Bates, commissioners.

In the claim of the heirs of Zachariah Dowty, and his wife, deceased, claiming 450 arpens of land on Hubble's creek, district of Cape Girardeau.  (See page 54 of the reported testimony of the mission to the lower districts.)

It being asserted that the testimony heretofore taken was false, the board examined the following witnesses on the part of the United States:

Alexander Summers, sworn, says that Elizabeth Dowty, about the year 1800, built a camp on said tract, and that he, witness, ploughed a small piece of ground on the same for her, and sowed turnips.  Says that he has seen the place every year since, and that nothing has been done on the same by her, her representatives, or any other person for her.

John Weaver, sworn, says that he has known the land claimed about seven years; that there never has been anything done on it by Elizabeth Dowty or her representatives since that time.  (See book No. 3, page 281.)

*November 26, 1810.*—Board met.  Present: John B. C. Lucas, Clement B. Penrose, and Frederick Bates, commissioners.

Zachariah Dowty, heirs of, claiming 450 arpens of land situate on the waters of Hubble's creek, district of Cape Girardeau, produces to the board an affidavit of permission to settle from Louis Lorimier, commandant, dated June 3, 1808.  The following testimony in the foregoing claim, taken at Cape Girardeau, June 2, 1808, by Frederick Bates, commissioner, by authority from the board:

John Summers, sr., duly sworn, says that this land was improved and settled in 1800 or 1801, built a cabin, cleared, enclosed, and cultivated a small spot, cultivated and inhabited in the year 1803, and ever since; upward of twenty acres in cultivation, a peach orchard.  Elizabeth Dowty died, and was buried on the premises.  (See also No. 3, page 281.)

It is the opinion of the board that this claim ought not to be granted.  (See No. 5, page 12.)

*April 8, 1835.*—F. R. Conway, esq., appeared, pursuant to adjournment.  Zachariah Dowty, claiming 450 arpens of land, situate on Hubble's creek.  (See record-book E, page 239; minutes No. 3, page 281; No. 5, page 12.)

The following testimony was taken in June, 1834, by James H. Relfe, commissioner:

Alexander Summers, being duly sworn, states that he was well acquainted with the widow and family of Zachariah Dowty, formerly of the district of Cape Girardeau, in the province of Upper Louisiana, now State of Missouri.  He first became acquainted with them in the fore part of the year 1800 or 1801; they then resided on the waters of Hubble's creek, in said district, and inhabited and cultivated land on the same; they built a cabin in the same year, that is, in 1800 or 1801, which year this affiant is not positive.  They continued to live on said place up to the death of the said widow.

ALEXANDER SUMMERS.

Sworn to and subscribed before me, this 30th June, 1834.
(See No. 7, page 120.)

JAMES H. RELFE.

*June 9, 1835.*—The board met, pursuant to adjournment.  Present: F. R. Conway, J. H. Relfe, commissioners.

Zachariah Dowty, claiming 450 arpens of land.  (See book No. 7, page 120.)

The board are of opinion that this claim ought to be granted to the said Zachariah Dowty, or to his legal representatives, according to possession.  (See book No. 7, page 173.)

JAMES H. RELFE,<br>F. R. CONWAY.

I have examined the transcript of the above claim, and concur in the decision.

F. H. MARTIN.

### No. 269.—*Jane Logan, claiming 800 arpens.*

| No. | Name of original claimant. | Arpens. | Nature and date of claim. | By whom granted. | By whom surveyed, date, and situation. |
|---|---|---|---|---|---|
| 269 | Jane Logan. | 800 | Settlement right. | | On White Waters, Cape Girardeau |

EVIDENCE WITH REFERENCE TO MINUTES AND RECORDS.

*April 9, 1835.*—F. R. Conway, esq., appeared, pursuant to adjournment.

Jane Logan, claiming 800 arpens of land. (See record-book F, page 13 ; Bates' decisions, page 99.)

The following testimony was taken in Cape Girardeau county, by J. H. Relfe, commissioner :

John Rodney, being sworn, states that he was well acquainted with Jenny or Jane Logan ; he first became acquainted with her in 1802 ; she then lived in what was called the district of Cape Girardeau. She lived on Hubble's creek in said district, where she inhabited and cultivated a place. This was in the years 1802, '3, and '4, and she continued to live on the same for a number of years afterward. She had then children living with her at the time mentioned. There were also fruit-trees on said place, which is distant about nine miles south of the present town of Jackson.

JOHN RODNEY.

Sworn to and subscribed before me, this 30th of June, 1834.

JAMES H. RELFE.

(See book No. 7, page 121.)

*June 9, 1835.*—The board met, pursuant to adjournment. Present: F. R. Conway, J. H. Relfe, commissioners.

Jane Logan, claiming 800 arpens of land. (See book No. 7, page 121.)

The board are of opinion that 640 arpens of land ought to be granted to the said Jane Logan, or to her legal representatives, according to possession. (See book No. 7, page 173.)

JAMES H. RELFE,
F. R. CONWAY.

I have examined the transcript of the above claim, and concur in the decision.

F. H. MARTIN.

No. 270.—*Benjamin Tennel, claiming 800 arpens.*

| No. | Name of original claimant. | Arpens. | Nature and date of claim. | By whom granted. | By whom surveyed, date, and situation. |
|---|---|---|---|---|---|
| 270 | Benjamin Tennel. | 800 | Settlement right. | | On Castor creek, Cape Girardeau. |

EVIDENCE WITH REFERENCE TO MINUTES AND RECORDS.

*April 9, 1835.*—F. R. Conway, esq., appeared, pursuant to adjournment.

Benjamin Tennel, claiming 800 arpens of land on Castor creek, Cape Girardeau. (See record-book F, page 135 ; Bates's decisions, page 104.)

The following testimony was taken in the county of Washington, by James H. Relfe, commissioner :

Samuel Campbell deposeth and saith, that he was at the residence of Benjamin Tennel, on the waters of the St. François river, in the then district of St. Genevieve, province of Upper Louisiana, now county of Madison, State of Missouri, in the fall of 1803 ; he found him residing in a comfortable cabin. In the course of the winter he cleared upward of ten acres of ground, and, in the spring of the year 1804, planted said ten acres of ground in corn. Deponent further says he has been acquainted with said plantation from the time it was taken possession of, in the year 1803, until the present time, and it has been regularly possessed and occupied by said Benjamin Tennel, and his legal representatives, ever since. Deponent further says he was present at New Bourbon when Benjamin Tennel obtained permission from the commandant to settle on the domain, and never knew Tennel to claim any other land in this country.

SAMUEL CAMPBELL.

Sworn to and subscribed before me, this 3d July, 1834.

JAMES H. RELFE.

(See book No. 7, page 121.)

*June 9, 1835.*—The board met, pursuant to adjournment. Present: F. R. Conway, J. H. Relfe, commissioners.

Benjamin Tennel, claiming 640 acres of land. (See book No. 7, page 121.)

The board are of opinion that 640 acres of land ought to be granted to the said Benjamin Tennel, or to his legal representatives, according to possession. (See book No. 7, page 173.)

JAMES H. RELFE,
F. R. CONWAY.

I have examined the transcript of the above claim, and concur in the decision.

F. H. MARTIN.

No. 271.—*Julius Wickers, claiming 600 arpens.*

| No. | Name of original claimant. | Arpens. | Nature and date of claim. | By whom granted. | By whom surveyed, date, and situation. |
|---|---|---|---|---|---|
| 271 | Julius Wickers. | 600 | Settlement right. | | On the St. Francis. |

EVIDENCE WITH REFERENCE TO MINUTES AND RECORDS.

*April 9, 1835.*—F. R. Conway, esq., appeared, pursuant to adjournment.

Julius Wickers, claiming 600 arpens of land on the St. Francis river. (See record-book F, page 142; Bates's decisions, page 105.)

The following testimony was taken in Washington county, by James H. Relfe, commissioner:

Personally appeared Samuel Campbell, who deposeth and saith, that he was well acquainted with Julius Wickers in the year 1803; that early in the summer of said year he raised a cabin, cleared and cultivated a turnip-patch, and the following winter he extended his clearing, planted and cultivated a field of at least eight acres of corn in the spring of the year 1804; and said Julius Wickers, and his legal representatives, have continued to occupy said tract of land ever since. Deponent further says he lived in the neighborhood of Wickers for twenty-four years, was present when the commandant at New Bourbon gave said Wickers permission to settle on the public domain, and never knew of said claimant making claim to any other land.

SAMUEL CAMPBELL.

Sworn to and subscribed before me, this 3d of July, 1834.

JAMES H. RELFE.

(See book No. 7, page 122.)

*June 9, 1835.*—The board met, pursuant to adjournment. Present: F. R. Conway, J. H. Relfe, commissioners.

Julius Wickers, claiming 600 arpens of land. (See book No. 7, page 122.)

The board are of opinion that 600 arpens of land ought to be granted to the said Julius Wickers or to his legal representatives, according to possession. (See book No. 7, page 173.)

JAMES H. RELFE,
F. R. CONWAY.

I have examined the transcript of the above claim, and concur in the decision.

F. H. MARTIN.

---

No. 272.—*Louis Aubuchon, claiming 400 arpens.*

To Don CHARLES DEHAULT DELASSUS, *Lieutenant Governor of Upper Louisiana, &c.:*

SIR: Louis Aubuchon has the honor to represent to you that he would wish to establish himself in the upper part of this province, where he has been residing for several years. Therefore, he has recourse to the goodness of this government, praying that you will be pleased to grant him a piece of land of 800 arpens in superficie, to be taken in the King's domain, in the place which will appear most advantageous to the interest of the petitioner, who presumes to expect this favor of your justice.

ST. LOUIS, *January 8, 1800.*

his
LOUIS × AUBUCHON.
mark.

ST. LOUIS OF ILLINOIS, *January 10, 1800.*

Whereas, we are assured that the petitioner possesses sufficient means to improve the land he solicits —— [omission]—— if it is not prejudicial to any person, and the surveyor, Don Antonio Soulard, shall put the interested in possession of the quantity of land he asks, in a vacant place of the royal domain; and this being executed, he shall make out a plat, delivering the same to the party, together with his certificate, in order to serve him to obtain the title in form from the intendant general, to whom alone belongs, by royal order, the distributing and granting all classes of lands, etc.

CARLOS DEHAULT DELASSUS.

OFFICE OF THE RECORDER OF LAND TITLES, *St. Louis, May 11, 1835.*

I certify the above to be truly translated from book C, page 195, of record in this office.

JULIUS DE MUN, *T. B. C.*

| No. | Name of original claimant. | Arpens. | Nature and date of claim. | By whom granted. | By whom surveyed, date, and situation. |
|---|---|---|---|---|---|
| 272 | Louis Aubuchon. | 800 | Concession, 10th January, 1800. | C. Dehault Delassus. | John Stewart, D. S. 18th February, 1806. Received for record by A. Soulard, surveyor general, 27th February, 1806. |

EVIDENCE WITH REFERENCE TO MINUTES AND RECORDS.

*June 25, 1806.*—The board met, agreeably to adjournment. Present: the honorable Clement B. Penrose and James L. Donaldson, esquires.

James Hewitt, assignee of Antoine Dejarlais, who was assignee of Louis Aubuchon, claiming 800 arpens of land, situate at Belleview, district aforesaid, produces a concession from Charles D. Delassus to said Louis Aubuchon, dated January 10, 1800; a survey of said land dated 18th and certified 27th February, 1806; a deed of transfer by said Aubuchon to Antoine Dejarlais, dated November 22, 1804, and another deed of transfer from said Antoine Dejarlais to claimant, dated February 18, 1805.

William Reede, being duly sworn, says that in the spring of 1805, claimant came to his house; that he settled the said tract of land, built a house, raised a crop on the same that year, and has actually inhabited and cultivated it to this day ; that he had then a wife, four children, and a slave.

The board reject this claim, and observe that claimant purchased said concession for $500, and has actually paid $410 of the same. (See book No. 1, page 360.)

*August 28, 1810.*—Board met. Present : John B. C. Lucas, Clement B. Penrose, and Frederick Bates, commissioners.

James Hewitt, assignee of Antoine Dejarlais, assignee of Louis Aubuchon, claiming 800 arpens of land. (See book No. 1, page 360.) It is the opinion of the board that this claim ought not to be confirmed. (See No. 4, page 479.)

*April 24, 1835.*—The board met, pursuant to adjournment. Present : F. R. Conway, James H. Relfe, commissioners.

Louis Aubuchon, claiming 800 arpens of land, on waters of Big river, district of St. Genevieve. (See record-book C, page 195 ; minutes, book No. 1, page 360 ; No. 4, page 479.)

The following testimony was taken before L. F. Linn, commissioner, on May 7, 1833 :

John T. McNeal, of lawful age, being first duly sworn as the law directs, states that he well knows James Hewitt, and that he held his claim under some Frenchman, but the name he does not recollect ; the above claim lies on the waters of Big river, Belleview, Washington county. Hewitt occupied the above land in the year 1804, in April, as well as this deponent recollects, and raised a crop of corn there on that year. Hewitt resided on said land until the year 1813 or 1814, when he died, and his family has continued to reside on said land ever since. Hewitt left a wife and several children.

JOHN T. McNEAL,
L. F. LINN, *Commissioner.*

John Stewart, being first duly sworn in the above case, states that on February 18, in the year 1806, at the instance of James Hewitt, he surveyed a Spanish concession granted to Louis Aubuchon, for 800 arpens of land, lying in the Belleview settlement, now in Washington county. He states the above survey to be butted and bounded as follows, to wit : beginning at a white oak on a line of William Davis's grant, thence south 63 west, 40 acres, crossing Hazle creek to a branch of Big river to a Spanish oak ; thence north 27 west, 20 acres, crossing Hazle creek to a Spanish oak ; thence south 63 east, 40 acres, to a hickory ; thence south 27 east, 20 acres, to the beginning, including his improvement ; all which will fully appear by reference to the plat in the recorder's office, St. Louis. This deponent further states, that he was legally appointed and authorized to make the survey aforesaid, and when he made the same, James Hewitt was living on the land. The family of said Hewitt still live upon said tract of land. James Hewitt handed him the original concession to make the survey from, and this deponent returned the same with the plat of survey to the proper officer in accordance with his duty as surveyor. As to the concession being for 800 arpens, this deponent is not quite certain, but supposes so, inasmuch as he surveyed out, under the Aubuchon concession, 800 arpens.            JOHN STEWART.

Sworn to and subscribed May 7, 1833.

L. F. LINN, *Commissioner.*

(See book No. 7, page 130.)

*June 9, 1835.*—The board met, pursuant to adjournment. Present : F. R. Conway, J. H. Relfe, commissioners.

Louis Aubuchon, claiming 800 arpens of land. (See book No. 7, page 130.)

The board are of opinion that this claim ought to be confirmed to the said Louis Aubuchon, or to his legal representatives, according to the survey of record in book C, page 195, in the recorder's office. (See book No. 7, page 174.)

JAMES H. RELFE,
F. R. CONWAY.

I have examined the transcript of the above claim, and concur in the decision.

F. H. MARTIN.

---

No. 273.—*Silas Fletcher, claiming 300 arpens.*

NAMES OF INDIVIDUALS WHO ARE TO SETTLE IN TYWAPITY BOTTOM, WITH THE PERMISSION OF THE COMMANDANT OF NEW MADRID.

Silas Fletcher, his wife, two boys, and two girls, 300 arpens.

Mr. Story shall survey the lands of each inhabitant named in the above list, conformably to the quantities therein expressed, in the places selected by them, provided it is five leagues below Cape Girardeau, and he shall leave as commons about a mile square, on a bayou emptying into the Mississippi.

Given at New Madrid, the 22d of May, 1801.

HENRY PEYROUX.

OFFICE OF THE RECORDER OF LAND TITLES, *St. Louis, May* 11, 1835.

I certify the above to be truly extracted and translated from a list of twenty-one individuals, on which list said Silas Fletcher is number 13, to be found in book E, page 271, of record in this office.

JULIUS DE MUN, *T. B. C.*

| No. | Name of original claimant. | Arpens. | Nature and date of claim. | By whom granted. | By whom surveyed, date, and situation. |
|-----|---------------------------|---------|---------------------------|------------------|----------------------------------------|
| 273 | Silas Fletcher. | 300 | Order of survey, 22d May, 1802. | Henry Peroux, commandant of New-Madrid. | Tywapity ; New Madrid. |

EVIDENCE WITH REFERENCE TO MINUTES AND RECORDS.

*November* 19, 1811.—Board met.  Present: John B. C. Lucas, Clement B. Penrose, and Frederick Bates, commissioners.

Silas Fletcher, claiming 300 arpens of land, situate in Tywapity, district of New Madrid.  Produces record of an order of survey from Henry Peroux, commandant, dated May 22, 1801.

It is the opinion of the board that this claim ought not to be confirmed.  (See No. 5, page 425.)

*April* 24, 1835.—The board met, pursuant to adjournment.  Present: F. R. Conway, James H. Relfe, commissioners.

Silas Fletcher, claiming 300 arpens of land.  (See record-book E, page 271; book No. 5, page 425.)

The following testimony was taken before James H. Relfe, one of the commissioners:

Catharine Griffey, formerly Catharine Finley, states that her husband, Charles Finley, was in the military expedition to New Madrid, in the then province of Upper Louisiana, now State of Missouri, under the Spanish government; that some time previous to the year in which said expedition took place, she and her husband moved to and settled in the district of New Madrid, in said province.  There was a contest between Peyroux, the commandant at New Madrid, and Lorimier, the commandant at Cape Girardeau, as to whose district they were in.  In the year they moved to said province, one Fletcher, whose given name she understood was Silas, lived on what was called the Big lake, which runs near Matthews' prairie, in said province; he and his family lived there in a little cabin; she cannot recollect as to the balance of his improvement.

her<br>CATHARINE × GRIFFEY.<br>mark.

Sworn to and subscribed this 9th April, 1835.

JAMES H. RELFE, *Commissioner*.

(See book No. 7, page 135.)

*June* 9, 1835.—The board met, pursuant to adjournment.  Present: F. R. Conway, J. H. Relfe, commissioners.

Silas Fletcher, claiming 300 arpens of land.  (See book No. 7, page 135.)

The board are of opinion that 300 arpens of land ought to be granted to the said Silas Fletcher, or to his legal representatives, according to possession.  (See book No. 7, page 174.)

JAMES H. RELFE,<br>F. R. CONWAY.

I have examined the transcript of the above claim, and concur in the decision.

F. H. MARTIN.

---

No. 274.—*Malachi Jones, claiming* 790 *acres*.

NEW MADRID, *January* 12, 1802.

On a list of families arrived at Tywapity for the purpose of settling themselves, said list presented to Mr. Henry Peyroux on the 12th of January, 1802, by Mr. Reason Bowie, the following is written: "Malachi Jones, his wife, and four negroes."  And below is written: "Mr. ———, the syndic, is authorized by me to put the families here above named in possession of the lands lately abandoned at Tywapity, by several inhabitants of this district."

HENRY PEYROUX.

NEW MADRID, *July* 10, 1804.

I, the undersigned, civil commandant of New Madrid for the United States, certify that the above extract is conformable to the original, deposited in the archives of this commandancy by Mr. Jesse Masters, on the 14th of last June, conformably to the proclamation of the first civil commandant of this Upper Louisiana.  I have delivered the present certificate at the request of Mr. Edward Robertson.

PIERRE ANTOINE LAFORGE,<br>*Civil Commandant*.

ST. LOUIS, *May* 11, 1835.

I certify the above to be truly translated from record-book B, page 311.

JULIUS DE MUN, *T. B. C.*

| No. | Name of original claimant | Acres. | Nature and date of claim. | By whom granted. | By whom surveyed, date, and situation. |
|---|---|---|---|---|---|
| 274 | Malachi Jones. | 790 | Permission to settle, 12th January, 1802. | Henry Peyroux, commandant of New-Madrid. | John Wilbourn, D. S. 28th February, 1806.  Received for record by A. Soulard, S. G. 27th February, 1806. |

EVIDENCE WITH REFERENCE TO MINUTES AND RECORDS.

*November* 20, 1811.—Board met.  Present: John B. C. Lucas, Clement B. Penrose, and Frederick Bates, commissioners.

John Nicholas Shrum, assignee of Malachi Jones, claiming 790 acres of land, situate at Tywapity, district of Cape Girardeau, produces record of a permission to settle from Henry Peyroux, commandant, dated January 12, 1802; record of a plat of survey, dated February 28, 1806, certified February 27, 1806; record of transfer from Jones to claimant, dated October 4, 1803.

It is the opinion of the board that this claim ought not to be granted.  (See No. 5, page 437.)

*April* 27, 1835.—James H. Relfe, esq., appeared, pursuant to adjournment.

Malachi Jones, by his legal representative, Nicholas Shrum, claiming 790 acres of land. (See record-book B, page 311; minutes, book No. 5, page 437.)

The following testimony was taken in June, 1833, by L. F. Linn, commissioner:

*June* 11, 1833.—George Hacker being sworn, says that, in the year 1802, he passed Nicholas Shrum's improvement on the Mississippi river, in the district of New Madrid. He became acquainted with the said Nicholas in the year 1804. This affiant has understood that the said Nicholas purchased his improvement from one Malachi Jones.                                                                 GEORGE HACKER.

Sworn to and subscribed, this 11th June, 1833.

L. F. LINN, *Commissioner.*

The following testimony was taken before James H. Relfe, commissioner, in Scott county:

Thomas Fletcher, being sworn, states that he came to the province of Upper Louisiana in the year 1803; in that year he passed up the Mississippi river, and recollects passing Shrum or Shum's point, on said river, about ten or twelve miles above the mouth of Ohio river, in said province; there was an improvement on the point, which he was told belonged to Nicholas Shum or Shrum; there was a cabin on said place, and some three or four acres cultivated in corn at the time, in 1803; the place is still called Shum's point. This affiant recollects seeing and conversing with the said Shum at the time mentioned, and hearing him brag of what a fine place his was at the said point.

THOMAS FLETCHER.

Bridget Lane states that she married and settled in the province of Upper Louisiana about three years before the Americans took possession of the country. She well recollects Nicholas Shum or Shrum, a resident of said province. She knew him in early times in the country, the year she cannot recollect. He used to pass her house in going to his place on the Mississippi river, called Shum's or Shrum's point. The place is still called Shum's point.

her
BRIDGET × LANE.
mark.

Sworn to and subscribed, this 9th May, 1835.

JAMES H. RELFE, *Commissioner.*

(See book No. 7, page 137.)

*June* 10, 1835.—The board met, pursuant to adjournment. Present: F. R. Conway, J. H. Relfe, commissioners.

Malachi Jones, claiming 790 acres of land. (See book No. 7, p. 137.)

The board are of opinion that 640 acres of land ought to be granted to the said Malachi Jones, or to his legal representatives, to be taken within the original survey, recorded in book B, page 311, in the recorder's office.

(See book No. 7, page 175.)                                           JAMES H. RELFE,
F. R. CONWAY.

I have examined the transcript of the above claim, and concur in the decision.

F. H. MARTIN.

---

No. 275.—*John Baldwin, claiming* 400 *arpens.*

| No. | Name of original claimant. | Arpens. | Nature and date of claim. | By whom granted. | By whom surveyed, date, and situation. |
|-----|---------------------------|---------|--------------------------|------------------|----------------------------------------|
| 275 | John Baldwin. | 400 | Settlement right. | | |

EVIDENCE WITH REFERENCE TO MINUTES AND RECORDS.

*November* 1, 1811.—Board met. Present: John B. C. Lucas, Clement B. Penrose, and Frederick Bates, commissioners.

John Baldwin, claiming 400 arpens of land, produces to the board list B, on which claimant is No. 12, situate in the district of Cape Girardeau. It is the opinion of the board that this claim ought not to be granted. (See minute book No. 5, page 391.)

*April* 28, 1835.—The board met, pursuant to adjournment. Present: James H. Relfe, F. R. Conway, commissioners.

John Baldwin, claiming 400 arpens of land, situate in the district of Cape Girardeau. (See list B, in record-book B, page 324; minute-book No. 5, page 391.)

The following testimony was taken before L. F. Linn, commissioner:

STATE OF MISSOURI, *County of Cape Girardeau:*

*May* 11, 1833.—James Wilborn, who is about fifty-three years old, has known the said John Baldwin between thirty-five and forty years ago. The said John Baldwin moved to the district of Cape Girardeau in the fall of 1803, and settled in Tywapity bottom. He knows that the said John cleared land in the fall of 1803, in said bottom, and set out a nursery of fruit-trees; he also lived on said land at the same time. The next season, 1804, he planted corn and raised a crop. The said John was a married man; had a wife and four children at the time he made the said improvement. The said John Baldwin has lived ever since, and now resides, in the district of Cape Girardeau.

JAMES WILBORN.

Sworn to and subscribed, May 11th, 1833, before me,

L. F. LINN, *Commissioner.*

(See book No. 7, page 139.)

*June* 10, 1835.—The board met, pursuant to adjournment.   Present: F. R. Conway, J. H. Relfe, commissioners.

John Baldwin, claiming 400 arpens of land.   (See book No. 7, page 139.)

The board are of opinion that 400 arpens of land ought to be granted to the said John Baldwin, or to his legal representatives, according to possession.   (See book No. 175.)

JAMES H. RELFE,
F. R. CONWAY.

I have examined the transcript of the above claim, and concur in the decision.

F. H. MARTIN.

---

No. 276.—*Charles Sexton, claiming 300 arpens.*

| No. | Name of original claimant. | Arpens. | Nature and date of claim. | By whom granted. | By whom surveyed, date, and situation. |
|---|---|---|---|---|---|
| 276 | Charles Sexton. | 300 | Concession to 164 inhabitants, January 30, 1803. No. 48. 300 arpens. List A. | Carlos Dehault Delassus. | 300 acres, by Edward F. Bond, December 3, 1805. Received for record by A. Soulard, surveyor general, February 28, 1806. |

EVIDENCE WITH REFERENCE TO MINUTES AND RECORDS.

*May* 18, 1809.—Board met.   Present: John B. C. Lucas, Clement B. Penrose, commissioners.

Charles Sexton, claiming 350 arpens, 95 perches of land, situate on White Waters, district of Cape Girardeau, produces to the board as a special permission to settle, list A, on which claimant is No. 48, for 300 arpens, a plat of survey dated December 3, 1805, certified to be received for record February 28, 1806, by Antoine Soulard, surveyor general.

The following testimony in the foregoing claim, taken at Cape Girardeau, June 4, 1808, by Frederick Bates, commissioner:

Daniel Brant, duly sworn, says, that claimant made a small improvement in the year 1803, but did not inhabit; this improvement being afterward taken by the survey of Ezekiel Able, the surveyor laid out a tract for claimant in the woods adjoining the lands of the said Ezekiel, which has never been improved.   Laid over for decision.   (See book No. 4, page 61.)

*March* 8, 1810.—Board met.   Present: John B. C. Lucas and Clement B. Penrose, commissioners.

Charles Sexton, claiming 350 arpens 95 perches of land.   (See book No. 4, page 61.)   It is the opinion of the board that this claim ought not to be granted.   (See book No. 4, page 293.)

*April* 29, 1835.—The board met, pursuant to adjournment.   Present: J. H. Relfe, F. R. Conway, commissioners.

Charles Sexton, claiming 300 arpens of land, situate in district of Cape Girardeau.   For survey of 300 arpens, see record book B, page 303.   For list A, on which claimant is No. 48, see book B, page 320.   Also, minutes, book No. 4, pages 61 and 293.   For concession, see Joseph Thompson, jr.'s claim, decision No. 202.

The following testimony was taken in October, 1833, before L. F. Linn, esq., then one of the commissioners:

Daniel Brant states that he was on the Indian expedition to New Madrid, in the province of Upper Louisiana, in 1802, which was performed by order of the Spanish authorities at Cape Girardeau.   Amongst others who served a tour on said campaign, was Charles Sexton, who acted as drummer.   He lived in Cape Girardeau district, and was absent from home about six weeks; the men were promised land by the Spanish general and commandant, for serving on said expedition.

his
DANIEL x BRANT.
mark.

Sworn to and subscribed, October 18, 1833.

L. F. LINN, *Commissioner.*

(See book No. 7, p. 140.)

*June* 10, 1835.—The board met, pursuant to adjournment.   Present: F. R. Conway, J. H. Relfe, commissioners.

Charles Sexton, claiming 300 arpens of land.   (See book No. 7, page 140.   For concession, see claim No. 202.)

The board are of opinion that this claim of 300 arpens ought to be confirmed to the said Charles Sexton, or to his legal representatives, according to the concession, to be taken within the original survey, recorded in book B, page 303, in recorder's office.   (See book No. 7, page 175.)

JAMES H. RELFE,
F. R. CONWAY.

I have examined the transcript of the above claim, and concur in the decision.

F. H. MARTIN.

No. 277.—*Hugh Criswell, claiming* 101 *arpens and* 31 *perches.*

| No. | Name of original claimant. | Arpens. | Nature and date of claim. | By whom granted. | By whom surveyed, date, and situation. |
|---|---|---|---|---|---|
| 277 | Hugh Criswell. | 101 31 p. | Concession to 164 inhabitants, January 30, 1803, No. 139, for 100 arpens. List A. | Carlos Dehault Delassus. | B. Cousin, D. S., February 3, 1806; recorded February 13, 1806, by Soulard, S. G., eight miles W. N. W. from Cape Girardeau. |

EVIDENCE WITH REFERENCE TO MINUTES AND RECORDS.

*May* 18, 1809.—Board met. Present: John B. C. Lucas, Clement B. Penrose, commissioners.

Hugh Criswell, claiming 101 arpens 31 perches of land, situate on Randall's creek, district of Cape Girardeau. Produces to the board as a special permission to settle, list A, on which claimant is No. 139, for 100 arpens; a plat of survey, dated February 3, 1806, certified February 13, same year. Laid over for decision. (See book No. 4, page 60.)

*March* 8, 1810.—Board met. Present: John B. C. Lucas, Clement B. Penrose, commissioners.

Hugh Criswell, claiming 101 arpens 31 perches of land. (See book No. 4, page 60.)

It is the opinion of the board that this claim ought not to be granted. (See book No. 4, page 293.)

*May* 8, 1835.—The board met, pursuant to adjournment. Present: F. R. Conway, J. H. Relfe, commissioners.

Hugh Criswell, by his heirs and legal representatives, claiming 640 acres of land, situate on the waters of Randall's creek, Cape Girardeau county. (For survey of 101 arpens 31 perches, see record-book B, page 287. For list A, on which claimant is No. 139, for 100 arpens, see book B, page 323; minutes, book No. 4, pages 60 and 293. For concession, see claim No. 202.)

The following testimony was taken before L. F. Linn, commissioner, in October, 1833:

STATE OF MISSOURI, *county of Cape Girardeau:*

Daniel Brant, who is 59 years old, states that he moved to and settled in the district of Cape Girardeau, Upper Louisiana, in the year 1798; that he was and still is well acquainted with Hugh Criswell, of said district; that he knows of the said Hugh inhabiting and cultivating a place on the waters of Randall's creek, adjoining one Anthony Randall, in said district, in the year 1802. The said Criswell cultivated corn and other grain on said place, in said year 1802. The said Criswell had a cabin and about 7 acres of land cleared on said place, in said year 1802. He also had a family, consisting of a wife and three children. This affiant knows that the said Criswell continued to inhabit and cultivate said place for several years after the time mentioned above, but the precise number of years he cannot recollect. This affiant has frequently heard the Spanish commandant, Don Louis Lorimier, say that he wanted the people to settle close together, in order to protect themselves from the Indians; and if they could not get land enough where they lived, they should have it elsewhere.

DANIEL x BRANT.<br>
his<br>
mark.

Sworn to and subscribed, this 18th of October, 1833.

LEWIS F. LINN, *Commissioner.*

(See book No. 7, page 144.)

*June* 10, 1835.—The board met, pursuant to adjournment. Present: J. H. Relfe, F. R. Conway, commissioners.

Hugh Criswell, claiming 640 acres of land. (See book No. 7, page 144.)

The board are of opinion that 101 arpens 31 perches of land ought to be confirmed to the said Hugh Criswell, or to his legal representatives, according to the original survey recorded in book B, page 287, in the recorder's office. (See book No. 7, page 176.)

JAMES H. RELFE,<br>
F. R. CONWAY.

I have examined the transcript of the above claim, and concur in the decision.

F. H. MARTIN.

No. 278.—*Reuben Baker, claiming* 640 *acres.*

| No. | Name of original claimant. | Acres. | Nature and date of claim. | By whom granted. | By whom surveyed, date, and situation. |
|---|---|---|---|---|---|
| 278 | Reuben Baker. | 640 | Settlement right. | | John Hawkins, D. S., February 10, 1806; received for record by A. Soulard, surveyor general, February 27, 1806; in Boisbrulé, district of St. Genevieve. |

EVIDENCE WITH REFERENCE TO MINUTES AND RECORDS.

*October* 22, 1808.—Board met.  Present : Hon. Clement B. Penrose and Frederick Bates.

Reuben Baker, claiming 640 acres of land, situate in the district of St. Genevieve, produces to the board a survey of the same, dated February 10th, 1806, certified to be received for record February 27th, 1806.

Christopher Barnhart, sworn, says that claimant inhabited said tract in February, 1801, and occasionally inhabited it that year ; never saw any crop on said place.  Laid over for decision. (See book No. 3, page 314.)

*June* 21, 1810.—Board met.  Present : John B. C. Lucas, Clement B. Penrose, and Frederick Bates, commissioners.

Reuben Baker, claiming 640 acres of land.  (See book No. 3, page 314.)

It is the opinion of the board that this claim ought not to be granted.  (See No. 4, page 399.)

*May* 12, 1835.—The board met, pursuant to adjournment.  Present : James H. Relfe, F. R. Conway, commissioners.

Reuben Baker, claiming 640 acres of land.  (See record-book B, page 230 ; book No. 3, page 314 ; No. 4, page 399.)

The following testimony was taken before L. F. Linn, esq., in May, 1833, in Cape Girardeau county :

John Greenwalt states that he was acquainted with Reuben Baker very shortly after witness came to the country, in 1798 ; that previous to the year 1804, as witness verily believes, and according to the best of his recollection, the said Reuben Baker was settled on a piece of ground fronting on the Mississippi, in Boisbrule bottom ; had a cabin built on it, and had a nursery of peach and apple trees growing on said place ; that previous to 1804, claimant had made his garden and had raised corn, pumpkins, and other vegetables, on the land claimed ; and witness well recollects of said Reuben Baker continuing to live on said land for several years subsequent to 1804, and continuing to occupy and cultivate it until he sold his settlement right.

JOHN × GREENWALT.<br>his<br>mark.

Sworn and subscribed, May 6th, 1833.

L. F. LINN, *Commissioner.*

(See book No. 7, page 148.)

*June* 10, 1835.—The board met, pursuant to adjournment.  Present : J. H. Relfe, F. R. Conway, commissioners.

Reuben Baker, claiming 640 acres of land.  (See book No. 7, page 148.)

The board are of opinion that 640 acres of land ought to be granted to the said Reuben Baker, or to his legal representatives, according to the survey recorded in book B, page 230, in the recorder's office.  (See book No. 7, page 176.)

JAMES H. RELFE,<br>F. R. CONWAY.

I have examined the transcript of the above claim, and concur in the decision.

F. H. MARTIN.

---

No. 279.—*Sophia Bolaye, claiming* 150 *arpens.*

To Don ZENON TRUDEAU, *Lieutenant Colonel of the stationary regiment of Louisiana, Lieutenant Governor and Commander-in-chief of the western part of Illinois :*

SIR : Sophia Bolaye, residing in the village of Carondelet, has the honor to represent that she had begun to clear a piece of land, in order to build a house and make a plantation. on a tract situated on river Aux Gravois, between the Marameck and the village of St. Louis ; that she had all the timber prepared for a house, and even began a field, but having been frightened by the reports which have gone abroad of the bad intentions of the Indians, she then retired with her family to the village of Carondelet.  Now, she would wish to return and settle with her family upon the said plantation, therefore she claims of your goodness that you will please grant her a concession of ten arpens in front, at the distance of half a league from the junction of said river Aux Gravois with the river Des Peres ; the said ten arpens ascending in a straight line, five arpens on each side of the said river Aux Gravois, the length of fifteen arpens, which will make the quantity of one hundred and fifty arpens of land in superficie.  She only waits for your decision in order to go and settle herself on said place, and to work thereon with security, and to continue the improvements already begun.

This being considered, may it please you, sir, to grant to the petitioner, at the distance of half a league from the mouth of the said river Aux Gravois, the quantity of ten arpens, five on each side of the river, by fifteen in depth, in ascending the said river in a straight line.  The petitioner shall never cease to pray for your preservation.

ST. LOUIS, this 28th *June,* 1796.

her<br>SOPHIE BOLAYE, × not knowing how to sign.<br>mark,

ST. LOUIS, *June* 3, 1796.

In case that the land asked for belongs to the King's domain, the surveyor of this jurisdiction shall put the petitioner in possession of the quantity of arpens she asks in the manner designated, in order to deliver to her the concession in form, after the plat and certificate of survey are made out.

TRUDEAU.

ST. LOUIS, *May* 25, 1835.

Truly translated from the original, filed before the board of commissioners.

JULIUS DE MUN, *T. B. C.*

| No. | Name of original claimant. | Arpens. | Nature and date of claim. | By whom granted. | By whom surveyed, date, and situation. |
|---|---|---|---|---|---|
| 279 | Sophia Bolaye. | 150 | Concession, June 3, 1796. | Z. Trudeau. | On river Gravois. |

EVIDENCE WITH REFERENCE TO RECORDS AND MINUTES.

*May* 14, 1835.—The board met, pursuant to adjournment. Present: F. R. Conway, J. H. Relfe, commissioners.

Sophia Bolaye, claiming 150 arpens of land, situate on river Gravois. (See record-book E, page 327; Bates's decisions, page 91.)

Produces a paper purporting to be original concession from Zenon Trudeau, dated June 3, 1796. Also, the deposition of Philip Fine, taken August 13, 1819, before Joseph Charless, J. P.

M. P. Leduc, duly sworn, says that the signature to the concession or order of survey is in the proper handwriting of the said Trudeau.

TERRITORY OF MISSOURI, *County of St. Louis:*

Philip Fine, of the township of St. Louis, in said county, being duly sworn, upon his oath declares and says, that he well knows the tract described in the annexed petition of Sophia Bolaye, and has known it for at least forty years past, and that Sophia Bolaye, about thirty years ago, opened the ground, planted corn and potatoes, and built a house on said tract.

his<br>
PHILIP  ×  FINE.<br>
mark.

Sworn to and subscribed, this 13th day of August, 1819, before me, a justice of the peace in and for the county aforesaid.

JOS. CHARLESS, *J. P.*

(See book No. 7, page 152.)

*June* 10, 1835.—The board met, pursuant to adjournment. Present: J. H. Relfe, F. R. Conway, commissioners.

Sophia Bolaye, claiming 150 arpens of land. (See book No. 7, page 152.)

The board are of opinion that this claim ought to be confirmed to the said Sophia Bolaye, or to her legal representatives, provided the land belonged to the domain at the date of the concession. (See book No. 7, page 176.)

JAMES H. RELFE,<br>
F. R. CONWAY.

I have examined the transcript of the above claim, and concur in the decision.

F. H. MARTIN.

---

No. 280.— *William Easom, claiming 800 arpens.*

| No. | Name of original claimant. | Arpens. | Nature and date of claim. | By whom granted. | By whom surveyed, date and situation. |
|-----|---------------------------|---------|---------------------------|------------------|---------------------------------------|
| 280 | William Easom. | 800 | Settlement right. | | |

EVIDENCE WITH REFERENCE TO MINUTES AND RECORDS.

ST. LOUIS, *April* 28, 1813.—William Easom, claiming 800 arpens of land, county of St. Genevieve, on waters of St. Francis.

William Johnson, duly sworn, says that claimant inhabited and cultivated this tract in the winter of 1803, and continued there, as witness believes, till Christmas of that year, and by him or others constantly to this time. (See Bates's minutes, page 42.)

ST. LOUIS, *December* 24, 1813.—Wm. Easom. (See minutes, page 42.) Thompson Crawford, duly sworn, says that claimant, Easom, left his tract about 1st December, 1803, and never returned. John Sinclair was not inhabiting the cabins built by Patterson, and for a time inhabited by Easom, as early as 25th December, 1803. Easom cultivated the lands adjoining the cabins built by Patterson in 1803, and lived in them from some time in May till 1st December, 1803. Witness thinks that James Campbell lived in those cabins on 20th December, 1803, and is certain that he did on the 25th.

William Dillon, duly sworn, says that claimant moved into the settlement, in the month of May, 1803, and soon thereafter established himself on a tract on Cedar creek. When claimant moved there, there were already two cabins on the premises, built by one Patterson in the summer or fall of 1802. Patterson left the place in the winter following the building of the cabins, made no cultivation that witness knows of, that is to say, on last of 1802, or beginning of 1803. Thinks Easom went there in June, and left it some time in December, 1803. John Sinclair established himself on lands in this neighborhood, perhaps on the opposite of the creek from the cabins already spoken of, in December, 1803; this was a few days before the 20th of that month, as witness thinks. John Sinclair has inhabited and cultivated this tract from that to the present time. This establishment of Sinclair was opposite and near the cabins built by Patterson, and into which Easom went in the month of May or June, 1803, which cabins are the same which Sinclair has occupied since some time in the winter of 1803 and 1804. It is the opinion of the witness that there is sufficient vacant land extending back from the creek as the front line of two tracts, for a survey on each side of 640 arpens, though the quantity could not be made up of good land on either, nor perhaps half the quantity.

Joshua Edwards, duly sworn, says that David Patterson came to these lands in 1802, latter part of the summer, and raised turnips, and having built two cabins, left the place in the following winter, and left the improvement with James Campbell for sale. In spring of 1803, Easom came out and agreed with James Campbell for the place; went on it, planted corn with the assistance of witness. Easom fell sick, he became dissatisfied with the place, and sold to Samuel Campbell, and left it early in the month of December, 1803. James Campbell, brother of Samuel Campbell, lived in the cabins on 20th December, 1803. When Easom left this place he left some pot-metal which had been his, but knows not whether he had sold it, but as he moved on pack-horses he could not very well take such articles. James Campbell told this witness that he had sold the improvement whereon Easom had lived, and where he, James Campbell, was then living, to John Sinclair, for a horse; this was in January or February, 1804. John Sinclair took possession of the cabins in February or March, 1804, and has continued to inhabit and cultivate the premises ever since to this time. John Sinclair was established on the creek, opposite to the cabins, about 17th December, 1803. Where Sinclair first settled, an improvement had, before that time, been made by James Campbell, and sold by Campbell to Sinclair; he afterward purchased of same James Campbell on the opposite side. (See Bates's minutes, pages 105 and 106.)

St. Louis, *December* 25, 1813.—William Johnson, duly sworn, says, in explanation of his testimony given 28th April last, he did by no means intend to say that claimant was on the premises December 20, 1803, as that was a fact that he could not know, as he was not on the tract himself on that day; had seen him there in the summer, and had heard conversation in neighborhood that he remained there till some time in the winter, and the belief formerly expressed by me was not pretended to be founded on my own certain knowledge. (See Bates's minutes, page 112.)

*April* 8, 1835.—F. R. Conway, esq., appeared, pursuant to adjournment.

William Easom, claiming 800 arpens of land on the St. Francis river. (See record-book F, page 98; Bates's minutes, pages 42, 105, 106, and 112; Bates's decisions, page 31.)

The following testimony was taken in Madison county, by James H. Relfe, commissioner:

Samuel Campbell deposeth and saith, that he saw William Easom in possession of a tract of land on the waters of the St. Francis river in the spring of the year 1803; he had a house in which he lived, a kitchen, and about four acres of corn in cultivation, which said Campbell saw gathered the following fall by said William Easom.

SAMUEL CAMPBELL.

Sworn to and subscribed before me, this 28th of June, 1834.

JAMES H. RELFE.

*May* 23, 1835.—F. R. Conway, esq., appeared, pursuant to adjournment.

William Easom, claiming 800 arpens of land. (See book No. 7, page 120.)

The following testimony was taken in October, 1833, by L. F. Linn, commissioner:

STATE OF MISSOURI, *County of Madison:*

Thompson Crawford, aged about forty-seven years, being duly sworn, as the law directs, deposeth and saith that he well knew William Easom, the original claimant; that he came to this country, then the province of Upper Louisiana, in the spring of 1803. Witness also knows the land claimed, and knows that claimant settled thereon and made a crop in 1803. There were two cabins built on the place. Claimant fenced in, cleared, and cultivated three or four acres. Claimant remained on the place till some time in the year 1804, when he removed, and that the said land has been actually improved, inhabited, and cultivated ever since. Claimant had a wife and one child.

THOMPSON CRAWFORD.

Sworn to and subscribed before me, this 23d October, 1833.

L. F. LINN, *Commissioner.*

(See book No. 7, page 157.)

*June* 11, 1835.—The board met, pursuant to adjournment. Present: F. R. Conway and J. H. Relfe, commissioners.

William Easom, claiming 800 arpens of land. (See book No. 7, pages 120 and 157.)

The board are of opinion that 640 acres of land ought to be granted to the said William Easom, or to his legal representatives, according to possession. (See book No. 7, page 177.)

JAMES H. RELFE,
F. R. CONWAY.

I have examined the transcript of the above claim, and concur in the decision.

F. H. MARTIN.

---

No. 281.—*John Taylor, claiming 481 acres and 8 poles.*

| No. | Name of original claimant. | Acres. | Poles. | Nature and date of claim. | By whom granted. | By whom surveyed, date, and situation. |
|---|---|---|---|---|---|---|
| 281 | John Taylor. | 481 | 8 | Settlement right. | | B. Cousin, D. S., 6th December, 1805, countersigned A. Soulard, surveyor general; on Hubble's creek, Cape Girardeau. |

EVIDENCE WITH REFERENCE TO MINUTES AND RECORDS.

*May* 1, 1809.—Board met. Present: Clement B. Penrose and Frederick Bates, commissioners.

John Taylor, claiming five hundred and sixty-two arpens seventy-three and a half perches of land, situate on Hubble's and Randall's creek, district of Cape Girardeau, produces to the board, as a special permission to settle, list B, on which claimant is No. 20, for five hundred and fifty arpens, (this claim interfering with the foregoing William Hand,) a plat of survey, dated December 6, 1805, signed B. Cousin, countersigned Antoine Soulard, surveyor general.

The following testimony in the foregoing claim, taken at Cape Girardeau, June 2, 1808, by Frederick Bates, commissioner.

Samuel Pew, sworn, says he knows the land, lives near it, has passed through it, and knows of no cultivation on the premises in 1803.

David Patterson, sworn, says that he knew this tract of land, and was acquainted with it before Taylor moved to it, and verily believes that there was no improvements on the premises in the year 1803. At this time there is a good square log-house, stable, kitchen, smoke-house, and ten or —— acres in cultivation. Laid over for decision. (See book No. 4, page 31.)

*March* 14, 1810.—Board met. Present: John B. C. Lucas, Clement B. Penrose, and Frederick Bates, commissioners.

John Taylor, claiming five hundred and sixty-two arpens seventy-three and a half perches of land. (See book No. 4, page 31.) It is the opinion of the board that this claim ought not to be granted. (See book No. 4, page 297.)

*May* 27, 1835.—F. R. Conway, esq., appeared, pursuant to adjournment.

John Taylor, by his legal representatives, claiming six hundred and forty acres of land, situate on Hubble's creek, in Cape Girardeau county. (See record-book B, page 337, where this claim is entered for four hundred and eighty-one acres and eight poles. (Book No. 4, pages 31, 297.)

The following testimony was taken before L. F. Linn, commissioner, in June and October, 1833:

STATE OF MISSOURI, *County of Cape Girardeau:*

Richard Waller, being sworn, says he knew John Taylor well. He first became acquainted with him in 1802, in the district of Cape Girardeau, where the said John Taylor then lived, and continued to live up to the time of his death, ten or fifteen years ago. He saw him settled on a place in said district, in the year 1803, had built a house to live in, and had cleared some land. He had a wife and several children, number not recollected.

                                                                RICHARD WALLER.
Sworn and subscribed before me, June 11, 1833.

                                                                L. F. LINN, *Commissioner.*

Hugh Criswell is about sixty-seven years old; he was well acquainted with the said John Taylor. He knew the said Taylor in this country, district of Cape Girardeau, in the year 1803; he was then a farmer, and inhabited and cultivated land in said district. He improved his head right of settlement claim in the year 1803, in the said district, and lived on it until the time of his death, which happened some time about the year 1814. This affiant knows that he built a house in Spanish times, and set out peach and apple trees for an orchard. He had a wife, three boys, and two girls, that this affiant recollects.

                                                                      his
                                                           HUGH  ×  CRISWELL,
                                                                     mark.
Sworn and subscribed, this 11th June, 1833.

                                                                L. F. LINN, *Commissioner.*

William Williams states that he moved to, and settled in the district of Cape Girardeau, Upper Louisiana, in the year 1799; that he was well acquainted with John Taylor, deceased, formerly of said district. To the best of his recollection, the said Taylor moved to, and settled in said district in the year 1802. In the next year (that is in 1803) he moved to a place on the waters of Hubble's creek, about three miles northeast of the present town of Jackson, opened land, and raised a crop on the same, in said year 1803. This affiant also assisted the said Taylor in building a dwelling-house on said place, in said year. The said Taylor had a family at the time, consisting of himself, his wife, and four or five children. The said Taylor had an apple orchard very early on said place, but the year when he set it out, this affiant cannot state. The said Taylor lived on the said place up to the time of his death, some six or eight years after he settled. The said place is now owned by one John Cross.

                                                                WILLIAM WILLIAMS.
Sworn to and subscribed, October 16, 1833.

                                                                L. F. LINN, *Commissioner.*

(See book No. 7, page 160.)

*June* 11, 1835.—The board met, pursuant to adjournment. Present: F. R. Conway, J. H. Relfe, commissioners.

John Taylor, by his legal representatives, claiming four hundred and eighty-one acres and eight poles of land. (See book No. 7, page 160, where this claim is entered for six hundred and forty acres.) The board are of opinion that four hundred and eighty-one acres and eight poles of land ought to be granted to the legal representatives of the said John Taylor, deceased, according to the survey recorded in book B, page 337. (See book No. 7, page 178.)

                                                                JAMES H. RELFE,
                                                                F. R. CONWAY.

I have examined the transcript of the above claim, and concur in the decision.

                                                                F. H. MARTIN.

---

No. 282.—*Louis Buyat and others, claiming a special location.*

To Don FRANCIS VALLE, *Captain of Militia, and civil and military Commandant of the post of St. Genevieve:*

The undersigned have the honor to represent that they wish you would grant them a concession for the land immediately adjoining the forty arpens (lots) granted opposite the Little Hills, to end at the foot of the hill near Prairie à Gautier, and bounded on the two sides by the two forks of Gaboury river, without prejudice, however, to those who might have concessions on the said lands. Their gratitude shall have no bounds, and will always be equal to the very great respect with which they are, sir, your very humble and obedient servants,

LOUIS BUYAT,
JOSEPH LALUMANDIERE,
JOSEPH <sup>his</sup> × BEQUETTE,
<sub>mark.</sub>
LALUMANDIERE,
JEAN <sup>his</sup> × LALUMANDIERE,
<sub>mark.</sub>
J. M. PEPIN,
HIPPOLITE ROBERT,
GIROUARD,
J. BAPTISTE <sup>his</sup> × TAUMURE,
<sub>mark.</sub>
AUGUSTE <sup>his</sup> × AUBUCHON,
<sub>mark.</sub>
LOUIS <sup>his</sup> × CARRON,
<sub>mark.</sub>
DUFOUR, <sup>his</sup> ×
<sub>mark.</sub>
VITALE BEAUVAIS.

St. Louis, *September* 1, 1797.

The surveyor of this jurisdiction, Don Antonio Soulard, shall put the petitioners in possession of the land they ask for, in the foregoing petition, at the end of the lands, (of 40 arpens;) after which he shall make out a plat and certificate of his survey, and the whole shall be remitted to us, in order to send them to the governor general of the province, for him to determine definitively upon the concession of the said land.

ZENON TRUDEAU.

St. Louis, *May* 30, 1835.

I certify the above to be a true translation of the original, filed in this office.

JULIUS DE MUN, *T. B. C.*

| No. | Name of original claimant. | Arpens. | Nature and date of claim. | By whom granted. | By whom surveyed, date, and situation. |
|-----|---------------------------|---------|--------------------------|------------------|----------------------------------------|
| 282 | Louis Buyat and twelve others. | | Concession, 1st September, 1797. | Zenon Trudeau. | Special location between the two forks of the river Gaboury. |

EVIDENCE WITH REFERENCE TO MINUTES AND RECORDS.

*December* 10, 1811.—Board met. Present: John B. C. Lucas, Clement B. Penrose, and Frederick Bates, commissioners.

Louis Buyat and others, claiming a tract of land, situate between the two forks of river Gaboury, and adjoining the 40-arpen lots near Prairie à Gautier, district of St. Genevieve, produce record of a concession from Zenon Trudeau, lieutenant governor, dated September 1, 1797.

It is the opinion of the board that this claim ought not to be confirmed. (See book No. 5, page 508.)

*May* 29, 1835.—The board met, pursuant to adjournment. Present: F. R. Conway, J. H. Relfe, commissioners.

Louis Buyat and twelve others, claiming a tract of land, situate between the two forks of river Gaboury, and adjoining the 40-arpen lots near Prairie Gautier. (See No. 5, page 508.)

Produce a paper purporting to be an original concession from Zenon Trudeau, dated September 1, 1797.

The following testimony was taken in June, 1833, by L. F. Linn, commissioner:

STATE OF MISSOURI, *county of Saint Genevieve*:

Jean Baptiste Vallé, aged about seventy-two years, being duly sworn as the law directs, deposeth and saith that he was well acquainted with each and every of the petitioners and concessionees, and that each and every of them, at the date of the concession, were citizens and residents in the then province of Upper Louisiana, and that those who are dead continued citizens and residents till their death; and that those who are living are still citizens and residents of the country. This witness further says that he was well acquainted with Zenon Trudeau, who was lieutenant governor of Upper Louisiana at the date of the concession; that he has often seen him write, and that the name and signature to the concession from said Zenon Trudeau to the said thirteen concessionees, is in the proper handwriting of the said Zenon Trudeau. And this deponent further says that the claimants made a common field on the same, and actually cultivated the same for several years.

J. BAPTISTE VALLÉ.

Sworn and subscribed before me, this 17th June, 1833.

L. F. LINN, *Commissioner.*

(See book No. 7, page 162.)

*June* 12, 1835.—The board met, pursuant to adjournment. Present: F. R. Conway, J. H. Relfe, commissioners.

Louis Buyat, Hippolite Robert, Joseph Lalumandiere, Girouard, J. Baptiste Taumure, Joseph Béquette, Auguste Aubuchon, Jean Lalumandiere, Lalumandiere, Louis Carron, Vitale Beauvais, Dufour, and J. M. Pepin, claiming a special location between the two forks of the river Gaboury. (See book No. 7, page 162.)

The board are of opinion that this claim ought to be confirmed to the said Louis Buyat and to the above-named twelve individuals, or to their legal representatives, according to the petition and concession. (See book No. 7, page 279.)

JAMES H. RELFE,
F. R. CONWAY.

I have examined the transcript of the above claim, and concur in the decision.

F. H. MARTIN.

No. 283.—*Dennis Sullivan, claiming 350 arpens.*

| No. | Name of original claimant. | Arpens. | Nature and date of claim. | By whom granted. | By whom surveyed, date, and situation. |
|---|---|---|---|---|---|
| 283 | Dennis Sullivan. | 300 | Concession to 164 inhabitants. 30th January, 1803. List A, No. 94. | | B. Cousin, D. S., 30th December, 1805. Countersigned, A. Soulard, S. G.; on Byrd's creek, Cape Girardeau. |

EVIDENCE WITH REFERENCE TO MINUTES AND RECORDS.

*May* 18, 1809.—Board met. Present: John B. C. Lucas, Clement B. Penrose, commissioners.

Dennis Sullivan, claiming 350 arpens 93⅓ perches of land, situated on Byrd's creek, district of Cape Girardeau, produces to the board as a special permission to settle, list A, on which claimant is No. 94, for 300; plat of survey, dated December 30, 1805, signed B. Cousin, countersigned Antoine Soulard, surveyor general.

The following testimony in the foregoing claim, taken at Cape Girardeau, June 4, 1808, by Frederick Bates, commissioner:

John McCarty, duly sworn, says that claimant came to Louisiana in the year 1802, and worked at the blacksmith business for two years; since which he has taught a school; no improvement. Laid over for decision. (See book No. 4, page 57.)

*March* 2, 1810.—The board met. Present: John B. C. Lucas, Clement B. Penrose, and Frederick Bates, commissioners.

Dennis Sullivan, claiming 350 arpens 93⅓ perches of land. (See book No. 4, page 57.) It is the opinion of the board that this claim ought not to be granted. (See No. 4, page 288.)

*May* 29, 1835.—The board met, pursuant to adjournment. Present: F. R. Conway, J. H. Relfe, commissioners.

Dennis Sullivan, by his legal representatives, claiming 640 acres of land, situate in the district of Cape Girardeau. (See record-book B, page 320 for list A, on which claimant is No. 94, for 300 arpens, and same book, page 337, for survey. See also No. 4, pages 54 and 288.)

The following testimony was taken in October, 1833, before L. F. Linn, commissioner:

Jonathan Buis states that, in the fall of 1802, after his return from a visit to New Orleans, he saw and knew Dennis Sullivan or O'Sullivan, in the district of Cape Girardeau, Upper Louisiana, now State of Missouri, where the said O'Sullivan resided and continued to reside up to the time of his death, which took place some time after the change of government. The said Dennis was a mechanic, a blacksmith by trade, which business he pursued and carried on in different places in the said district. This affiant frequently heard the Commandant Lorimier say that mechanics were not required to settle and improve their lands.

JONATHAN BUIS.

Sworn and subscribed to, October 17, 1833.

L. F. LINN, *Commissioner.*

Moses Byrd also states that he was well acquainted with the said Dennis Sullivan, who came to the district of Cape Girardeau, Upper Louisiana, in 1801 or 1802. The said Dennis was a blacksmith by trade, which occupation he continued to follow in different parts of said district up to the time of his death, which occurred after the change of government, the precise year he does not recollect.

MOSES BYRD.

Sworn and subscribed to before me, in Cape Girardeau county, October 17, 1833.

L. F. LINN, *Commissioner.*

(See book No. 7, page 163.)

*June* 12, 1835.—The board met, pursuant to adjournment. Present: F. R. Conway, J. H. Relfe, commissioners.

Dennis Sullivan, claiming 300 arpens of land. (See book No. 7, page 163, where this claim is entered for 640 acres. For concession, see Joseph Thompson, jr.'s claim, decision No. 202.)

The board are of opinion that 300 arpens of land ought to be confirmed to the said Dennis Sullivan, or to his legal representatives, according to the concession. (See book No. 7, page 179.)

JAMES H. RELFE,
F. R. CONWAY.

I have examined the transcript of the above claim, and concur in the decision.

F. H. MARTIN.

No. 284.—*Curtis Wilbourn, claiming* 600 *arpens.*

| No. | Name of original claimant. | Arpens. | Nature and date of claim. | By whom granted. | By whom surveyed, date, and situation. |
|-----|---------------------------|---------|---------------------------|------------------|----------------------------------------|
| 284 | Curtis Wilbourn. | 600 | Settlement right. | | |

EVIDENCE WITH REFERENCE TO MINUTES AND CLAIMS.

*November* 1, 1811.—Board met. Present: John B. C. Lucas, Clement B. Penrose, and Frederick Bates, commissioners.

Curtis Wilbourn, claiming 600 arpens of land, situated in the district of Cape Girardeau, produces to the board list B, on which claimant is No. 10.

It is the opinion of the board that this claim ought not to be granted. (See book No. 5, page 391.)

*June* 1, 1835.—The board met, pursuant to adjournment. Present: F. R. Conway, James H. Relfe, commissioners.

Curtis Wilbourn, by his legal representatives, claiming 640 acres of land, situated in the former district of Cape Girardeau. (See record-book B, page 324, for list B, on which claimant is No. 10, for 600 arpens; minute-book No. 5, page 391.)

The following testimony was taken before L. F. Linn, commissioner, in June, 1833:

STATE OF MISSOURI, *County of Cape Girardeau:*

John Baldwin knew said Curtis. He came to the district of Cape Girardeau in the year 1803, and settled in Tywapity in the fall of said year; he built a house in fall or winter of 1803, and immediately commenced clearing land, and in 1804 he raised corn and other things on said place. This affiant saw his permission to settle on the books of Lorimier. Claimant was a married man, had a wife and six children, five sons and one daughter. The said Curtis was killed some six or eight years ago. This affiant has understood and believes that all his children are dead except two, who are the actual claimants.     JOHN BALDWIN.

Sworn and subscribed to, this 11th day of June, 1833.

L. F. LINN, *Commissioner.*

(See minute-book No. 7, page 165.)

*June* 12, 1835.—The board met, pursuant to adjournment. Present: F. R. Conway, J. H. Relfe, commissioners.

Curtis Wilbourn, claiming 600 arpens of land. (See book No. 7, page 165, where this claim is entered for 640 acres.)

The board are of opinion that 600 arpens of land (it being the quantity claimed on record) ought to be granted to the said Curtis Wilbourn, or to his legal representatives, according to possession. (See book No. 7, page 179.)

JAMES H. RELFE,
F. R. CONWAY.

I have examined the transcript of the above claim, and concur in the decision.

F. H. MARTIN.

No. 285.—*Alexander Butner* or *Burton, claiming* 300 *arpens.*

| No. | Name of original claimant. | Arpens. | Nature and date of claim. | By whom granted. | By whom, surveyed, date, and situation. |
|-----|---------------------------|---------|---------------------------|------------------|-----------------------------------------|
| 285 | Alexander Butner or Burton. | 300 | Settlement right. | | |

EVIDENCE WITH REFERENCE TO MINUTES AND RECORDS.

*November* 1, 1811.—Board met. Present: John B. C. Lucas, Clement B. Penrose, and Frederick Bates, commissioners.

Alexander Butner or Burton, claiming 300 arpens of land, situate in the district of Cape Girardeau, produces to the board list B, on which claimant is No. 38.

It is the opinion of the board that this claim ought not to be granted. (See book No. 5, page 392.)

*June* 1, 1835.—The board met, pursuant to adjournment. Present: F. R. Conway, James H. Relfe, commissioners.

Alexander Butner or Burton, claiming 300 arpens of land, situated in the district of Cape Girardeau. (See record book B, page 324, for list B, on which claimant is No. 38, for 300 arpens; minutes, book No. 5, page 392.)

The following testimony was taken before L. F. Linn, commissioner, in June, 1833:

STATE OF MISSOURI, *County of Cape Girardeau:*

Philip Young, being duly sworn, deposeth and saith that he was acquainted with the abovenamed Alexander Butner or Burton; that he settled a place on the waters of Caney creek, in the year 1802, and that he raised a crop of corn on said place in the year 1803, and that he continued to reside on and cultivate the same in 1804, and probably 1805. And further, this deponent states that he resided within about two miles from the said Alexander Burton during the time above stated.     PHILIP YOUNG.

Sworn to and subscribed, June 11, 1833.

L. F. LINN, *Commissioner.*

(See book No. 7, page 165.)

*June* 12, 1835.—The board met, pursuant to adjournment. Present: F. R. Conway, J. H. Relfe, commissioners.

Alexander Butner or Burton, claiming 300 arpens of land. (See book No. 7, page 165.)

The board are of opinion that 300 arpens of land ought to be granted to the said Alexander Butner or Burton, or to his legal representatives, according to possession. (See book No. 7, page 179.)

JAMES H. RELFE,
F. R. CONWAY.

I have examined the transcript of the above claim, and concur in the decision.

F. H. MARTIN.

---

### No. 286.—*Guillaume Bizet, claiming 40 arpens.*

On the said day (7th February, 1769), upon the demand of Guillaume Bizet, inhabitant, we have granted and do grant to him, in full property, for him, his heirs or assigns, a tract of land situated at the Cul de Sac of the Grand prairie, containing one arpent in width by forty in depth, joining on one side the land of Bacannet, on the other side to that of Kiery Desnoyers, on condition to establish the said land in one year and a day, and that it will be subject to public charges, and others which it may please his Majesty to impose.

At St. Louis, on the said day and year.                    ST. ANGE LABUXIERE.

St. Louis, *June* 12, 1835.

I certify the above to be truly translated from Livre Terrien, page 21, of record in the recorder's office.

JULIUS DE MUN, *T. B. C.*

| No. | Name of original claimant. | Arpens. | Nature and date of claim. | By whom granted. | By whom surveyed, date, and situation. |
|---|---|---|---|---|---|
| 286 | Guillaume Bizet. | 40 | Concession, February 7, 1769. | St. Ange. | |

EVIDENCE WITH REFERENCE TO MINUTES AND RECORDS.

*June* 2, 1835.—The board met, pursuant to adjournment. Present: F. R. Conway and James H. Relfe, commissioners.

Guillaume Bizet, by his legal representatives, claiming 40 arpens of land, situated in the Cul de Sac of Grand prairie. (See Livre Terrien, book No. 1, page 21; book F, page 155.)

Pierre Gueret, duly sworn, says that he is fifty-seven years of age; that he knows the tract claimed; that he owned land near the said tract, and that he has perfect recollection of having seen the late Jean Baptiste Provencher (who had married the widow of Guillaume Bizet, the original grantee) in possession of the tract now claimed, and that said Provencher cultivated the same for many years, but how long he cannot say. Witness further says that said Provencher did cultivate said land while under the government of Francisco Perez, or Zenon Trudeau, or may be under both, he is not positive, but he is certain that it was before Mr. Delassus was lieutenant governor. (See book No. 7, page 166.)

*June* 12, 1835.—The board met, pursuant to adjournment. Present: F. R. Conway and J. H. Relfe, commissioners.

Guillaume Bizet, claiming 40 arpens of land. (See book No. 7, page 165.)

The board are of opinion that this claim ought to be confirmed to the legal representatives of the said Guillaume Bizet, deceased, according to the concession. (See book No. 7, page 180.)

JAMES H. RELFE,
F. R. CONWAY.

I have examined the transcript of the above claim, and concur in the decision.

F. H. MARTIN.

---

### No. 287.—*James Wilbourn, claiming 300 arpens.*

| No. | Name of original claimant. | Arpens. | Nature and date of claim. | By whom granted. | By whom surveyed, date, and situation. |
|---|---|---|---|---|---|
| 287 | James Wilbourn. | 300 | Settlement right. | | |

EVIDENCE WITH REFERENCE TO MINUTES AND RECORDS.

*November* 1, 1811.—Board met. Present: John B. C. Lucas, Clement B. Penrose, and Frederick Bates, commissioners.

James Wilbourn, claiming 300 arpens of land, situate in the district of Cape Girardeau, produces to the board list B, on which claimant is No. 11. It is the opinion of the board that this claim ought not to be granted. (See minute-book No. 5, page 391.)

*January* 8, 1834.—F. R. Conway, esq., appeared, pursuant to adjournment.

James Wilbourn, by his legal representatives, claiming 640 acres of land, in the late district of Cape Girardeau. (See book No. 5, page 391; book P, 324.)

John Baldwin, aged about sixty-two years, is well acquainted with the said James Wilbourn; the said James came to the district of Cape Girardeau, in the fall of 1803, and settled in Tywapity bottom; he built a cabin as soon as he arrived, that is, in the winter of 1803; as soon as he built he commenced opening a farm, and in 1804 he raised corn and other things on said improvement. This affiant has seen the permission of the said James to settle, on the books of Cousin, at Cape Girardeau. The said James was, at the time of the settling of this country, a married man, with a wife and one child.

JOHN BALDWIN.

Sworn to and subscribed, this 11th day of June, 1833.

L. F. LINN, *Commissioner.*

(See book No. 6, page 450.)

*April 27, 1835.*—James H. Relfe, esq., appeared, pursuant to adjournment.

In claim of James Wilbourn, claiming 640 acres of land, (see book No. 6, page 450,) the following testimony was taken by James H. Relfe, commissioner, in Scott county:

Bridget Lane, widow, stated that she moved to and settled in the district of New Madrid, then province of Upper Louisiana, now State of Missouri, about three years before the Americans took possession of said province. The Christmas, a year after she had moved, James Wilbourn, also, came to the country, and his father's family eat dinner with us. The same winter, or next spring, the said James Wilbourn made a settlement and improvement in Tywapity bottom, in said province. He built a very good little cabin, made a garden, and planted seed which he brought from Georgia with him. This affiant recollects he sowed some sowerdock and she scolded him for it. He had a smart little strip in cultivation. He had a wife and one child; said Wilbourn has lived in the country ever since.

her
BRIDGET × LANE.
mark.

Sworn to and subscribed, this 9th April, 1835.

JAMES H. RELFE, *Commissioner.*

*June 12, 1835.*—The board met, pursuant to adjournment. Present: F. R. Conway, J. H. Relfe, commissioners.

James Wilbourn, claiming 300 arpens of land. (See book No. 6, page 450, where this claim is entered for 640 acres.)

The board are of opinion that 300 arpens of land (it being the quantity claimed on record) ought to be granted to the said James Wilbourn, or to his legal representatives, according to possession. (See book No. 7, page 180.)

JAMES H. RELFE,
F. R. CONWAY.

I have examined the transcript of the above claim, and concur in the decision.

F. H. MARTIN

---

No. 288.—*Israel Dodge, claiming 7,056 arpens.*

To Don CHARLES DEHAULT DELASSUS, *Lieutenant Colonel, attached to the stationary regiment of Louisiana, and Lieutenant Governor of the upper part of the same province:*

Israel Dodge, father of a numerous family and (*owner*) of several slaves, having erected in the country several mills, distilleries, breweries, &c., and having exercised his industry in a blameless manner, hopes that you will be pleased to make him partake of the favors which the government grants with generosity to all those who come to fix themselves under the domination of his Majesty, and particularly to those who, by their labor, have deserved his regard. Therefore, full of confidence in your justice, he has the honor to supplicate you to have the goodness to grant to him in full property, for establishing an extensive stock farm, one league of land in superficie, or 7,056 arpens, to be taken in a vacant part of the domain, at his choice, and in the manner most convenient to his views. Your petitioner, having more than the means necessary to make the establishment contemplated, and this quantity of land having almost always been granted in such cases, without difficulty, by the government, hopes that his known conduct, his character, his submission and fidelity to the laws, will be motives which will contribute, in part, to the accomplishment of his wishes. In so doing, you will do justice.

ISRAEL DODGE.

ST. GENEVIEVE, *December 5, 1800.*

We, the undersigned, commandant of the post of New Bourbon, do certify to the lieutenant governor of Upper Louisiana, that the concession for one league (square of land) asked by the petitioner, in a vacant place, not already conceded to any person, and being a part of the King's domain, is indispensably necessary to him for the purpose of establishing a grazing farm, in order to feed and maintain the great number of cattle he owns, which it is impossible for him to do on his lands, they being all situated on barren hills; besides, the establishments so useful to the public, such as mills, distilleries, and breweries, which the petitioner has had erected in this post, at a great expense, are great inducements to grant him the favor which he solicits.

Done at New Bourbon, December 8, 1800.

P. DELASSUS DE LUZIERE.

ST. LOUIS OF ILLINOIS, *December 11, 1800.*

Having examined the foregoing statement, together with the information given by the commandant of the post of New Bourbon, captain of militia, Don Pedro Delassus de Luziere, and considering that the petitioner is one of the most ancient inhabitants of this country, I do grant to him and his heirs the land which he solicits, provided it is not to the prejudice of any person; and the surveyor, Don Antonio Soulard, shall put the interested in possession of the quantity of land he asks in the place indicated, and this being executed, he shall make out a plat, delivering the same to the party, together with his certificate, in order to serve him to obtain the concession and title in form from the intendant general, to whom alone belongs, by royal order, the distributing and granting all classes of land belonging to the royal domain.

CARLOS DEHAULT DELASSUS.

Truly translated from the original.

JULIUS DE MUN, *T. B. C.*

ST. LOUIS, *August 14, 1834.*

No. 288.—*Israel Dodge, claiming 7,056 arpens.*

| No. | Name of original claimant. | Arpens. | Nature and date of claim. | By whom granted. | By whom surveyed, date, and situation. |
|---|---|---|---|---|---|
| 288 | Israel Dodge. | 7,056 | Concession, December 11, 1800. | Carlos Dehault Delassus. | Unlocated. |

EVIDENCE WITH REFERENCE TO MINUTES AND RECORDS.

*November* 14, 1811.—Board met.   Present: John B. C. Lucas, Clement B. Penrose, and Frederick Bates, commissioners.

Israel Dodge, claiming 7,056 arpens of land, district of St. Genevieve, produces the record of a concession from Charles D. Delassus, L. G., dated December 11, 1800.

It is the opinion of the board that this claim ought not to be confirmed.   (See minutes, book No. 5, page 407.)

*November* 15, 1833.—The board met, pursuant to adjournment.   Present: L. F. Linn, A. G. Harrison, F. R. Conway, commissioners.

Israel Dodge, claiming 7,056 arpens of land.   (See record-book E, page 219; No. 5, page 407.)   Produces a paper purporting to be an original concession from Carlos Dehault Delassus, dated December 11, 1800.

M. P. Leduc, duly sworn, says that the signature to the above concession is in the true handwriting of said Carlos Dehault Delassus.   (See book No. 6, page 338.)

*June* 13, 1835.—The board met, pursuant to adjournment.   Present: F. R. Conway, J. H. Relfe, commissioners.

Israel Dodge, claiming 7,056 arpens of land.   (See book No. 6, page 338.)

The board are of opinion that this claim ought to be confirmed to the said Israel Dodge, or to his legal representatives, according to the concession.   (See book No. 7, page 181.)

JAMES H. RELFE,
F. R. CONWAY.

I have examined the transcript of the above claim, and concur in the decision.

F. H. MARTIN.

No. 289.—*Agnew Massey, claiming 248 arpens.*

| No. | Name of original claimant. | Arpens. | Nature and date of claim. | By whom granted. | By whom surveyed, date, and situation. |
|---|---|---|---|---|---|
| 289 | Agnew Massey. | 248 | Settlement right. | | |

EVIDENCE WITH REFERENCE TO MINUTES AND RECORDS.

*June* 28, 1809.—Board met.   Present: John B. C. Lucas, Clement B. Penrose, and Frederick Bates, commissioners.

Agnew Massey, claiming 300 arpens of land, situate in Tywapity, district of New Madrid, produces to the board a certified list of permission to settle, formerly given, No. 1369, on which claimant is No. 248.

The following testimony in the foregoing claim was taken at New Madrid, June 16, 1808, by Frederick Bates, commissioner:

Edward Mathews, duly sworn, says that, in the spring of 1802, claimant built a cabin, and inhabited and cleared, enclosed and cultivated, a few acres; he left the premises in the fall of that year; since which time it has neither been inhabited nor cultivated.   Claimant had a wife and one child.   Laid over for decision.   (See book No. 4, page 108.)

*December* 12, 1810.—Board met.   Present: John B. C. Lucas, Clement B. Penrose, and Frederick Bates, commissioners:

Agnew Massey, claiming 300 arpens of land.   (See book No. 4, page 108.)   It is the opinion of the board that this claim ought not to be granted.   (See book No. 5, page 26.)

*January* 21, 1834.—F. R. Conway, esq., appeared, pursuant to adjournment.

Agnew Massey, by his legal representatives, claiming 640 acres of land, situate in Prairie St. Charles, alias Mathews' prairie.   (See book E, page 194; book No. 4, page 108; No. 5, page 26.)

STATE OF MISSOURI, *County of Cape Girardeau:*

George Hacker being sworn, says he was well acquainted with Agnew Massey, who resided in the district of New Madrid; he first knew him in April, 1802, in Prairie St. Charles, in said district, where he inhabited and cultivated land; he had cleared land which was in cultivation, and built a dwelling-house, &c.   He had a wife, one son, and one daughter.

GEORGE HACKER.

Sworn and subscribed to, June 11, 1833.

L. F. LINN, *Commissioner.*

I do hereby swear that I came to and settled in Prairie St. Charles, in Scott county, and State of Missouri, in the spring of 1802, and that some time within the said year I saw and became acquainted with Agnew Massey, who built a small cabin, without any other improvement, and left it in a few months.

DANIEL STRINGER.

Sworn and subscribed to before me, a justice of the peace for Byrd township, in Cape Girardeau, county and State of Missouri, this 15th day of October, 1833.

A. H. BREWARD.

Sworn to, and signature acknowledged, October 15, 1833.

L. F. LINN, *Commissioner.*

This day personally appeared before me, Lewis F. Linn, one of the commissioners appointed, &c., Robert Giboney, of lawful age, who being duly sworn, deposeth and saith that he emigrated to the district of Cape Girardeau, then under the Spanish government, in the year 1797; that, in the year 1804 and 1805, as well as this affiant recollects, in an arrangement made between Agnew Massey and this affiant's brother, about going to Mathews' prairie and bringing his (said Massey's) horses to the saline on the Mississippi, then in the district of St. Genevieve, that this affiant went for his brother, and drove Massey's horses to the saltworks as above; the compensation for the above labor was paid in salt, but how much this affiant does not recollect.

ROBERT GIBONEY.

L. F. LINN, *Commissioner.*

(See book No. 6, page 478.)

*April 25, 1835.*—James H. Relfe, esq., appeared, pursuant to adjournment.

In the case of Agnew Massey, claiming 640 acres of land, (see book No. 6, page 478,) the following testimony was taken before James H. Relfe, commissioner, in Scott county:

Elizabeth Smith states on her oath, that she moved to and settled in Mathews's prairie, province of Upper Louisiana, now State of Missouri, in the year 1804. In the month of May or June of that year she saw the improvement of Agnew Massey in said prairie; from the appearance of the place, she supposes it was in cultivation the year previous; the fence-rails looked old, as if they had been made several years before. There appeared to be two or three acres under fence, which had been in cultivation.

her
ELIZABETH × SMITH.
mark.

Also, Daniel Stringer being sworn, states that in 1803 he knew Agnew Massey in Mathews's prairie, in the province of Upper Louisiana. In that year he was at the house of the said Massey, in said prairie; he had a family. This affiant does not recollect as to the size of his improvement. He lived in a log cabin, which was the common kind of houses in the country at that time. He had in that year ground enclosed; how much witness cannot state.

DANIEL STRINGER.

Sworn to and subscribed, this 10th April, 1835.

JAMES H. RELFE, *Commissioner.*

(See No. 7, page 138.)

*June 13, 1835.*—The board met, pursuant to adjournment. Present: F. R. Conway and J. H. Relfe, commissioners.

Agnew Massey, claiming 248 arpens of land. (See book No. 6, page 478, where this claim is entered for 640 acres. No. 7, page 138.)

The board are of opinion that 248 arpens of land (it being the quantity claimed on record) ought to be granted to the said Agnew Massey, or to his legal representatives, according to possession. (See book No. 7, page 181.)

JAMES H. RELFE,
F. R. CONWAY.

I have examined the transcript of the above claim, and concur in the decision.

F. H. MARTIN.

---

No. 290.—*Joseph Doublewye, claiming 640 arpens.*

| No. | Name of original claimant. | Arpens. | Name and date of claim. | By whom granted. | By whom surveyed, date, and situation. |
|-----|----------------------------|---------|-------------------------|------------------|-----------------------------------------|
| 290 | Joseph Doublewye. | 640 | Settlement right. | | On the waters of St. Francis river. |

EVIDENCE WITH REFERENCE TO MINUTES AND RECORDS.

*August 2, 1813.*—Joseph Doublewye's legal representatives, claiming 800 arpens of land on the waters of St. Francis, county of Cape Girardeau.

David Ferrell, duly sworn, says that claimant, Doublewye, had a man on this tract in 1803 and 1804, working for him, and living on the land, himself being occasionally there. Said tract has been inhabited and cultivated to this time. (See recorder's minutes, page 47.)

*December 15, 1813.*—The representatives of Joseph Doublewye, claiming 800 arpens of land, on the waters of the river St. Francis, in the county of Cape Girardeau, on the interference of Charles Peyton and Henry Burning.

Robert A. Logan, duly sworn, says that he has lived on the river St. Francis, in the district or county of Cape Girardeau, for upward of ten years, to wit, September, 1803; has constantly resided there, and is, and has been very well acquainted with the settlers on the river, and with those on the waters of the river St. Francis, within the county of Cape Girardeau, and that he, said witness, never either knew or heard of a man of the name of Joseph Doublewye within the said settlements, as an improver of lands. Witness further says that, in April, 1804, a cabin was *raised* by a man said to have been employed by E. Able on lands in the neighborhood of improvements subsequently made by C. Peyton and others; but at that time there were no immediate neighbors. In the fall of that year said man covered the cabin; this cabin never was inhabited, and a few years thereafter was burnt down. In the year 1806, a man of the name of Hillhouse built a cabin, inhabited and cultivated a tract of land in the neighborhood of said cabin; the dwelling of Hillhouse was about half a mile distant therefrom. Since Hillhouse's establishment, the place improved by him has been constantly inhabited and cultivated to this time. Witness understands that Peyton's and Burning's claims are derived from Hillhouse.

Francis Clark, duly sworn, says that in April or May, 1804, witness went to the settlements on the river St. Francis in the then district of Cape Girardeau; was pretty generally acquainted with the people of that river and its waters in said county, and never knew or heard of Joseph Doublewye either improving or claiming lands therein, until the entry of his notice. Thomas Ring told this witness that he, Ring, had built a cabin for E. Able on the waters of the river St. Francis, in 1804. (See recorder's minutes, page 78.)

*December* 28, 1833.—F. R. Conway, esq., appeared, pursuant to adjournment.

Joseph Doublewye, alias Deblois, by his legal representatives, claiming 640 acres of land, situate on the waters of St. Francis, county of Madison. (See record-book F, page 50; recorder's minutes, pages 47 and 78.)

STATE OF MISSOURI, *county of Madison*.

Samuel Campbell, aged about 68 years, being duly sworn as the law directs, deposeth and saith, that he was well acquainted with Joseph Deblois, the original claimant; that he was one of the old settlers of the country, then the province of Upper Louisiana; witness also knows the land claimed, and knows that the claimant settled on the same in the summer of 1803, and actually built a house thereon, and cleared and fenced in several acres of land. Claimant hired one Thomas Ring to help him do the work, for which he paid Ring $40, which was valued between the parties by this witness. Witness also knows that the claimant inhabited the house in the fall and winter of 1803 and 1804, and that in the spring of 1804, the claimant planted corn, made a garden, and cultivated the land. In the summer, the Osage Indians made a break in the settlements, and drove the claimant, with many others, from their farms; but witness knows that claimant returned in the fall and gathered his corn, and then returned to the place and again inhabited the house; and that the claimant and others under him, from thenceforward for several successive years, continued to inhabit and cultivate the same place, and extend his improvements; the claimant had a family, or a wife and two children, and the said tract of land has been continually inhabited and cultivated ever since.

SAMUEL CAMPBELL.

Sworn to and subscribed before me, this 23d day of October, 1833.

L. F. LINN, *Commissioner*.

Also came John Clements, a witness, aged 53 years, who, being duly sworn, deposeth and saith, that he knows the land claimed; that it was always called Deblois's land or improvement; witness saw Thomas Ring at work there in the fall of 1803, in building a house or cabin, and was told by Ring that it was for the claimant; witness also saw the horse which claimant paid Ring for his labor done on the said place; witness also saw corn standing on the place in the fall of 1804; the house was fenced in by the land cleared, and that was the land that was in corn; witness saw afterward one Hillhouse, or Hillis, on the place, and understood that he was there by permission of Deblois.

JOHN x CLEMENTS.
his
mark.

Sworn to and subscribed before me, this 23d October, 1833.

L. F. LINN, *Commissioner*.

And also came John L. Pettit, a witness, aged about 51 years, who, being duly sworn, deposeth and saith, that he knew the original claimant in this country as a citizen and resident, since the year 1801. Witness had a conversation with the commandant of the post, in 1801, in which conversation the commandant told the witness that claimant had his permission to settle on land; that claimant was entitled to land, being a mechanic, a carpenter, and at work for the government at St. Genevieve. Claimant was one of the old settlers in the country.

JOHN L. PETTIT.

Sworn to and subscribed before me, this 23d October, 1833.

L. F. LINN, *Commissioner*.

(See book No. 6, page 420.)

*June* 13, 1835.—The board met, pursuant to adjournment. Present: F. R. Conway, and J. H. Relfe, commissioners.

Joseph Doublewye, alias Deblois, claiming 640 acres of land. (See book No. 6, page 420.)

The board are of opinion that this claim ought to be granted to the said Joseph Doublewye, alias Deblois, or to his legal representatives, according to possession. (See book No. 7, page 181.)

JAMES H. RELFE,
F. R. CONWAY.

I have examined the transcript of the above claim, and concur in the decision.

F. H. MARTIN.

---

No. 291.—*Antoine V. Bouis, claiming 1,000 arpens.*

ST. LOUIS OF ILLINOIS, *November* 11, 1796.

*To the Lieutenant Governor*.

Antonio Vincent Bouis, sub-lieutenant of the militia of this town of St. Louis of Illinois, and residing in the same, with due respect, and in the best manner possible, has the honor to represent to you, that he wishes to establish a plantation for the increase of agriculture, and wanting lands for that purpose, as also to raise cattle, he humbly supplicates you to be pleased to grant to him, in fee simple, for him and his heirs, or others who may represent his right, twenty-five arpens of land in front by forty in depth, in the place where Emilian Yosty has got his plantation, joining him, and continuing, in a straight line, on the side where passes the road to St. Charles of Missouri, and running, for depth, to the hills, the petitioner obliging himself to leave the said road free, and subjecting himself to what the laws prescribe in this particular.   Favor which he hopes to deserve of your known justice.

his<br>
DON ANTONIO  ×  VINCENT.<br>
mark.

St. Louis of Illinois, <i>November</i> 11, 1796.

The surveyor of this jurisdiction shall put this party [omission in the original] of the quantity of land in the place and in the shape solicited by him, provided it be vacant, and not prejudicial to any one.

ZENON TRUDEAU.

St. Louis, <i>July</i> 27, 1833.   Truly translated.

JULIUS DE MUN.

| No. | Name of original claimant | Arpens. | Nature and date of claim. | By whom granted. | By whom surveyed, date, and situation. |
|---|---|---|---|---|---|
| 291 | Antoine V. Bouis. | 1,000 | Concession, 11th November, 1796. | Zenon Trudeau. | |

EVIDENCE WITH REFERENCE TO MINUTES AND RECORDS.

*July* 23, 1807.—The board met, pursuant to adjournment.   Present: Hon. John B. C. Lucas, Clement B. Penrose, and Frederick Bates, esquires.

The same (Antoine V. Bouis) claims 1,000 arpens of land, situate on the river Missouri, district of St. Louis, produces a concession from Zenon Trudeau, dated 11th November, 1794 (1796).   It being suggested that the claims of Joseph Williams and Robert Young interfered in this claim, ordered, by the board, that this claim will be taken up for further examination on Thursday next, and that the claimant give notice of the day to the said persons, at least four days previous thereto.   (See book No. 3, page 7.)

*July* 30, 1807.—The board met, agreeably to adjournment.

Antoine V. Bouis, claiming 1,000 arpens, situate on the river Missouri.   This case is proceeded on in pursuance of an order of the 23d inst.   The claimant files a caveat against Jacques Chovan.   The claim of Joseph Williams interfering with the above 1,000 arpens tract, the board went into an investigation of the same.

Nicholas Lecompte, sworn, says that, about the year 1795, he was put in possession, and had his land surveyed by one Bouvet, and the deponent produced a plat of survey of his land, dated February 20, 1795.

McDaniel, the agent of Joseph Williams, motioned the board for a postponement of this case after hearing testimony.   Ordered, by the board, that the same be postponed until January 29, 1808, if not on Sunday, and if on Sunday, until the next day.

James Mackay, duly sworn, says he is acquainted with the survey of Williams, and that about the year 1798, he saw the said Joseph Williams on his land, and that the same had been inhabited and cultivated ever since.

Robert Owen, sworn, says that the first improvement made on the aforesaid land was by Joseph Williams, about eleven years ago.   And witness further says that, in the spring of the year, after the first improvement was made, it was inhabited, and has been inhabited and cultivated ever since; and that, in the year 1800, there was about fifteen or eighteen acres under cultivation.

The agent of the United States declares that he believes the concession and survey of the aforesaid Joseph Williams's land are both antedated; whereupon the board require further proof.

Nicholas Lecompte, duly sworn, says that Joseph Williams informed him, at the time he came to work on the land he now claims, that he had a concession for 400 arpens, to include the land he was then improving; he also says that John Louis Mark settled on land in this neighborhood in the spring of 1796.

Robert Owen, sworn, says, about eleven years ago he was in the quarters of the late Spanish officer, M. Trudeau, where there were several persons present, among others, a certain John L. Mark, who made application for a tract of land adjoining or in the neighborhood of N. Lecompte.   M. Trudeau replied that he had already made concessions adjoining Lecompte to A. V. Bouis, and to Joseph Williams, and was doubtful whether there remained any vacant land.

Robert Young, sworn, says that, about the year 1800, James Mackay surveyed the land on which Joseph Williams now lives, and the deponent further says that he carried the chain, but whether by regular appointment or not, he does not now recollect.   The tract, as surveyed by Mackay, contained, as well as this deponent now recollects, 800 arpens.   The board are satisfied as to the dates of the concession and survey aforesaid.

Christopher Sharls, sworn, says that Zenon Trudeau gave his father a grant to settle on the land which A. V. Bouis now claims, and that, after working there some time, he received an order from said Trudeau to remove from said land, otherwise he would lose his labor, as A. V. Bouis's claim was older than that of the deponent's father.   This took place about ten or eleven years ago; in consequence of said order, the deponent's father removed from said land, and that Robert Young afterward settled on Williams's land, at the place from which this deponent's father had removed.

Antoine Soulard, sworn, says that Antoine V. Bouis often applied to him to survey his land, before a survey on Williams's land was made; that various circumstances prevented his compliance with this request; and the deponent further says that the decision of Gayoso, respecting those claims, took place after the surveys of Williams and others were made.   (See minutes No. 3, pages, 16, 17, and 18.)

*January* 29, 1808.—The board met, pursuant to adjournment.   Present: Hon. John B. C. Lucas, Clement B. Penrose, and Frederick Bates.

The contending claims of Antoine Vincent Bouis, for 1000 arpens of land, situate on the river Missouri, and of Joseph Williams, for 800 arpens, referred for decision on this day, at a board held on the 30th of July, 1807, page 16.

Jean Louis Marc, duly sworn, says that at least twelve years ago, during the time that Don Zenon Trudeau was lieutenant governor of Upper Louisiana, he (the deponent) applied to him for a tract of land, situate between

Emilian Yosti and Nicholas Lecompte; the lieutenant governor replied, that he believed he had already granted the said land to Antoine Vincent Bouis; the deponent being informed, by several other persons, that the said land did belong to Antoine Vincent Bouis, he went to him, and agreed with him to settle on the said land for three or four years, as the tenant of said Bouis, and that said Vincent Bouis was to let him have three or four arpens of said land, if he complied with his contract, and that said Vincent Bouis verbally agreed to give the deponent ten or twelve head of cows, and from sixteen to twenty sows; this agreement took place in the fall, and that, in the spring following, he, the deponent, went on said tract of land, and built a small cabin, and made sugar; and that, in the following spring, he built a good cabin on the land between Yosti and Lecompte, on a place which he supposed would be vacant, and that, in case he was on the land of Antoine Vincent Bouis, he would get land from said Bouis, but should it be vacant, he would hold it in his own right: made and fenced in a field of about three arpens, and continued on it about twenty months; further says, that Vincent Bouis never complied with his contract, but told him that his time was still going on; that said Vincent Bouis's stock was scattered about in the rushes and could not collect them; that when the lines should be run he would allow him the land according to contract; that during the time he was settled on said land, a man by the name of Shultz went and cut house logs on said tract, and that the deponent gave notice of it to A. V. Bouis, and that said Bouis applied to the lieutenant governor, Zenon Trudeau, and obtained an order, forbidding the said Shultz from cutting logs on said land. Further says, that his house was on the road of the Indians to their hunting ground, and that his wife was frequently insulted by them; he therefore left the house and went near to St. Charles, expecting to return when there should be other settlers near the place which he had left; says that he went a voyage up the Missouri, and when he returned, found trees marked on said land; says that at the time he made said settlement he considered himself as the tenant of Antoine V. Bouis; further says, that about seven or eight months after he had settled with his family in his large cabin, Joseph Williams came and settled near him. Deponent says, that while settled on said land, he raised corn, tobacco, and garden stuff; had raised nothing when said Williams made his settlement, it not being planting time, but had fenced in his field.

*Question by agent of Williams.* Do you expect to receive from Vincent Bouis the four acres of land contracted for?

*Answer.* I know nothing of it; but if Mr. Vincent Bouis gets the land, I suppose it to be just that I should have some land for the twenty months I lived on it. (See book No. 3, page 177.)

*February* 1, 1808.—Board met, pursuant to adjournment. Present: Hon. John B. C. Lucas, Clement B. Penrose, and Frederick Bates.

The contending claims of Antoine V. Bouis, for 1,000 arpens of land, and of Joseph Williams, for 800 arpens, before the board.

Louis Braseau, duly sworn, says that he saw Jean Louis Marc making sugar at the bottom of a hill, near the road from St. Louis to St. Charles, about ten or eleven years ago; the said Jean Louis Marc told the deponent, at that time, that he was working on the land of Antoine V. Bouis; deponent further saith, that he knows that Jean Louis Marc was making sugar between the settlements of Emilian Yosti and Nicholas Lecompte, and that there was a cabin built on said place, in which said Jean Louis then lived.

Robert Owens, duly sworn, says that Joseph Williams made the first improvement by one year, but don't know who built the first cabin; further says that Williams made his improvement eleven years ago last spring, or eleven years this spring, but thinks it is twelve years this spring coming.

John Richardson, duly sworn, says that he came to this country in the year 1797, and settled within six miles of Williams; had his washing done at Williams' house; saw corn growing in the field ever since occupied by Williams, same year; that he knows the place where Jean Louis Marc made his improvement; that at that time no improvement was made by said Jean Louis

*Question by the agent of Antoine V. Bouis.* Do you know Jean Louis Marc?

*Answer.* I do not.

*Question by same.* Do you know how long since Williams built the first house on the place where he now lives?

*Answer.* I cannot say.

*Question by same.* Was there any building on the land in 1797?

*Answer.* Nothing more than a camp.

*Question by same.* Did Williams and his family live on the land in 1797?

*Answer.* Yes, they did.

*Question by same.* How far from said land did Williams' wife reside?

*Answer.* About three or four miles.

*Question by agent of Williams.* What do you understand by a man and his family?

*Answer.* I understand he and all his concerns.

*Question by same.* How large are the apple-trees on said land?

*Answer.* I saw them in blossom last year.

*Question by same.* How long did Mrs. Williams remain in the house where she did your washing, before she moved on to the place where Williams made his improvements?

*Answer.* A very short time, not past three or four months.

Antoine Soulard, duly sworn

*Question by agent of Joseph Williams.* Did you, in pursuance of an order of Don Zenon Trudeau, lieutenant governor of Upper Louisiana, dated the 26th of August, 1796, put Joseph Williams in possession of a tract of land?

*Answer.* Yes, I did.

*Question by same.* Where is that land situated?

*Answer.* On the south side of the road from St. Louis to St. Charles, about thirty arpens from the Missouri river, and is the same land described in a survey made the 10th of April, 1800, and certified the 10th of May, 1803.

*Question by same.* Did you at any time put Antoine Vincent Bouis in possession of a tract of land, in pursuance to an order of Don Zenon Trudeau, lieutenant governor of Upper Louisiana, dated the 11th of November, 1796?

*Answer.* No, I did not; but I went on to the place to put said Bouis in possession, but the obstacles I met with prevented it.

*Question by the same.* What were those obstacles?

*Answer.* In setting out from Yosti's corner, in presence of Lafoucade, agent for A. V. Bouis, and Williams being also present, said Williams told him that if he run that line he would take all his, the said Williams', improvement; which proceeding took p'ace before Williams' survey was made; deponent further says that he ran a line from Yosti's corner, about twelve or fourteen arpens in length; he then became convinced that in running said survey, he would take in the improvement of said Wil'iams; and seeing the concessions of Williams was older than the concession of A. V. Bouis, and that said Williams was established on the land, he therefore did not proceed to the survey required by said Bouis; further says, that there was no settlement made on said Bouis' land, at that time, to his knowledge, and that nothing of the kind was claimed by the agent of said Bouis; further says, that he does not remember to have had any conversation with Lafoucade, the agent of Bouis, concerning any settlement on the land of said Bouis.

*Question by the agent of Antoine V. Bouis.* Who first applied to you to make a survey?

*Answer.* Williams applied first, because I had his concession in my hands before that of A. V. Bouis.

*Question by same.* Why did you proceed to the survey of Antoine V. Bouis' land before that of Williams?

*Answer.* I did not proceed to the survey for A. V. Bouis before that of Williams; I went to survey both of them, provided there should be vacancy sufficient; and finding there was not vacancy enough, I referred the parties to the lieutenant governor.

*Question by the board.* Do you know, of your own knowledge, when you ran the assaying line, that said Williams had been settled on said place for several years before?

*Answer.* Yes.

*Question by same.* Was the time when said Williams delivered his concession into your hands, near the time that it bears date?

*Answer.* Very near.

On motion of the agent of A. V. Bouis, this case is postponed until this day two weeks. (See book No. 3, page 180.)

*March* 14, 1808.—Board met, pursuant to adjournment. Present: Hon. John B. C. Lucas, Clement B. Penrose, and Frederick Bates.

This being the day given to the contending claimants, Antoine V. Bouis and Joseph Williams, for a hearing, and to receive the answers of Christopher Shultz, on interrogatories filed 15th February last, the same were this day returned and filed. Laid over for decision. (Book No. 3, page 188.)

*October* 2, 1809.—Board met. Present: John B. C. Lucas, Clement B. Penrose, and Frederick Bates, commissioners.

Antoine V. Bouis, claiming 1,000 arpens of land, situate on the river Missouri. (See book No. 3, page 16, 177, 180, and 188.)

Joseph Brazeau, being duly sworn, says that he saw Louis Marc making sugar upon said land, fifteen or sixteen years ago, perhaps less, but long since; that the land upon which the sugar was made, he understood to be the property of Antoine V. Bouis; further says, that Louis Marc had a cabin thereon, but does not know how long he continued there.

The board order a survey to be made of this claim, at the expense of Antoine V. Bouis; to be made as nearly conformable as may be to the concession, so as to include the improvements made by Jean Louis Marc, and not to interfere with the survey ordered for Joseph Williams in this book, page 174, or any other land legally surveyed, except the survey heretofore surveyed for said Joseph Williams. And the board further order that the said survey of Antoine V. Bouis be made at the same time that the survey ordered for Joseph Williams is made. Ordered by the board, that the clerk of this board transmit to the principal deputy surveyor of this Territory, a copy of the orders of this board, for the surveys in both the claims of Antoine V. Bouis and Joseph Williams, and that the said surveyor survey or make return thereof in two weeks from this day. (See book No, 4, page 175.)

*November* 1, 1809.—Board met. Present: John B. C. Lucas, Clement B. Penrose, Frederick Bates, commissioners.

Antoine V. Bouis, claiming 1,000 arpens of land, situate on the Missouri district of St. Louis. (See book No. 1, page 78; book No. 3, pages 177, 180, and 188; book No. 4, page 175.)

It is the opinion of a majority of the board that this claim ought not to be confirmed. Clement B. Penrose, commissioner, voting for the confirmation thereof. (See book No. 4, page 184.)

*July* 8, 1833.—L. F. Linn, esq., appeared, pursuant to adjournment.

Antoine V. Bouis, by his legal representative, F. V. Bouis, claiming twenty-five by forty arpens of land, situate near Yosti's plantation, in the Missouri bottom, on the road leading from St. Louis to St. Charles, (special location.) (See record-book C, page 204; minutes No. 4, pages 175 and 184.) Produces a paper, purporting to be an original concession from Zenon Trudeau, dated 11th November, 1796.

M. P. Leduc, duly sworn, says that the decree and signature to the same are in the proper handwriting of said Zenon Trudeau. (See book No. 6, page 220.)

*June* 13, 1835.—The board met, pursuant to adjournment. Present: F. R. Conway, J. H. Relfe, commissioners.

A. V. Bouis, claiming 1,000 arpens of land. (See book No. 6, page 220.)

The board are of opinion that this claim ought to be confirmed to the said A. V. Bouis, or to his legal representatives, according to the concession. (See book No. 7, page 181.)

JAMES H. RELFE,
F. R. CONWAY.

I have examined the transcript of the above claim, and concur in the decision.

F. H. MARTIN.

---

No. 202.—*Andre Chevalier, claiming 400 arpens.*

To Don CHARLES DEHAULT DELASSUS, *Lieutenant Colonel in the armies of his Catholic Majesty, and Lieutenant Governor of Upper Louisiana:*

Andre Chevalier, jr., humbly supplicates and has the honor to represent to you that, being on the point of settling himself, he desires to make and improve a plantation, and wishes that you would grant and concede to him a concession of 400 arpens in superficie, to be taken in a vacant place of the domain. The petitioner hopes to obtain this favor, being the son of one of the most ancient inhabitants of this place, and also able to improve his plantation and raise cattle thereon. In so doing, he shall never cease to pray for the conservation of your days.

Done at New Bourbon, October 1, 1799.

his
ANDRE  ×  CHEVALIER.
mark.

We, the undersigned, commandant of New Bourbon, do certify to the lieutenant governor of Upper Louisiana, that the petitioner is worthy to obtain the concession he solicits for, as much on account of the length of time his family has been settled in the upper part of this colony, and their honesty, as also because he has no other profession to support himself but that of a farmer, which he has practised with advantage since his youth.

Done in New Bourbon, October 4, 1799.

PEDRO DELASSUS DE LUZIERE.

St. Louis of Illinois, *October* 18, 1799.

In consequence of the information given by the commandant of the post of New Bourbon, Captain Don Pedro Delassus de Luziere, and considering that the petitioner is the son of one of the most ancient inhabitants of this country, and that he possesses sufficient means to improve the land he solicits, I do grant to him and his heirs the land he solicits, provided it is not to the prejudice of anybody; and the surveyor, Don Antonio Soulard, shall put the party interested in possession of the quantity of land he asks for, in a vacant place in the King's domain; and this being executed, he shall make out a plat, delivering the same to said party, with his certificate, in order to serve to him to obtain the concession and title in form from the intendant general, to whom alone corresponds the distributing and granting all classes of lands of the royal domain.

CARLOS DEHAULT DELASSUS.

The present original title of concession has been recorded, and its compared copy deposited in the archives of this post of New Bourbon, under No. 20.                                                                 D. L.

St. Louis, *July* 24, 1833.  Truly translated.

JULIUS DE MUN, *T. B. C.*

| No. | Name of original claimant. | Arpens. | Nature and date of claim. | By whom granted. | By whom surveyed, date, and situation. |
|-----|----------------------------|---------|---------------------------|------------------|----------------------------------------|
| 292 | Andre Chevalier. | 400 | Concession, 18th October, 1799. | C. Dehault Delassus. | |

EVIDENCE WITH REFERENCE TO MINUTES AND RECORDS.

*Sittings at* St. Genevieve, *June*, 1806.—Camille Delassus, assignee of Andrew Chevalier, claiming 400 arpens of land, produces an unlocated concession from Charles D. Delassus, dated the 18th of October, 1799, and a deed of transfer, dated the 19th of May, 1804.

The board require proofs of the date of said concession, and of the age of said Andrew Miller (Chevalier). Rejected.  (See book No. 2, page 25.)

*September* 28th, 1810.—Board met.  Present: John B. C. Lucas and Clement B. Penrose, commissioners.

Camille Delassus, assignee of Andrew Chevalier, claiming 400 arpens of land.  (See book No. 2, page 25.) It is the opinion of the board that this claim ought not to be confirmed.  (See book No. 4, page 515.)

*July* 6, 1833.—L. F. Linn, esq., appeared, pursuant to adjournment.

Andre Chevalier, by his legal representatives, claiming 400 arpens of land.  (See record-book B, page 511; minutes, book No. 2, page 25; No. 4, page 515.)  Produces a paper purporting to be an original concession from Carlos Dehault Delassus, dated October 18th, 1799, preceded by a recommendation from Pierre Delassus Deluziere, commandant of New Bourbon.

M. P. Leduc, being duly sworn, says that the signature to the concession is in the proper handwriting of Carlos Dehault Delassus, and that the recommendation and the signature affixed to it is in the proper handwriting of Pierre Delassus Deluziere, then commandant of New Bourbon.  (See book No. 6, page 213.)

*June* 15, 1835.—The board met, pursuant to adjournment.  Present: F. R. Conway and J. H. Relfe, commissioners.

Andre Chevalier, claiming 400 arpens of land.  (See book No. 6, page 213.)

In this case the following certificate was sworn to, and signature acknowledged, before L. F. Linn, commissioner:

I certify that it is not in my power to survey Andre Chevalier's survey between now and the 1st of March.  Given under my hand, February the 24th, 1806.

THOMAS MADDIN.

Sworn to, and signature acknowledged, May 11th, 1833.

L. F. LINN, *Commissioner.*

The board are of opinion that this claim ought to be confirmed to the said Andre Chevalier, or to his legal representatives, according to the concession.  (See book No. 7, page 183.)

JAMES F. RELFE,
F. R. CONWAY.

I have examined the transcript of the above claim, and concur in the decision.

F. H. MARTIN.

---

No. 293.—*Joseph Silvain, claiming 250 arpens.*

To Don Charles Dehault Delassus, *Lieutenant Colonel, attached to the stationary regiment of Louisiana, and Lieutenant Governor of Upper Louisiana.*

Joseph Silvain, a Roman Catholic and French Canadian, has the honor to represent to you that, having resided for some time in Cape Girardeau, where he has resolved to settle himself, he would wish to obtain, in said place, a concession of two hundred and fifty arpens of land for himself, his wife, and one child; if you were pleased to grant this favor, which he expects of your justice and for which he shall never cease to pray Heaven for your preservation.

Cape Girardeau, *October* 18, 1799.

his
JOSEPH ×  SILVAIN.
mark.

We, commandant of the post of Cape Girardeau, do inform the lieutenant governor that the land demanded and occupied by the petitioner is a part of his Majesty's domain, and that himself has all the qualifications required to obtain the favor which he solicits.

L. LORIMIER.

Cape Girardeau, *October* 10, 1799.

St. Louis of Illinois, *December* 15, 1799.

Whereas by the information given by the commandant of the post of Cape Girardeau, Don Luis Lorimier, the number of persons composing the family of the petitioner is ascertained, the surveyor, Don Antonio Soulard, shall put him in possession of two hundred and fifty arpens of land in superficie, in the place asked for, said quantity corresponding to the number of his family, according to the regulations of the governor general of this province; and afterward the party interested shall have to solicit the title of concession in form from the intendant general of these provinces, to whom alone belongs, by order of his Majesty, the distributing and granting all classes of lands of the royal domain.

CARLOS DEHAULT DELASSUS.

St. Louis, *February* 6, 1834.  Truly translated.

JULIUS DE MUN, *T. B. C.*

| No. | Name of original claimant. | Arpens. | Nature and date of claim. | By whom granted. | By whom surveyed, date, and situation. |
|---|---|---|---|---|---|
| 293 | Joseph Silvain. | 250 | Concession, 15th December, 1799. | C. Dehault Delassus. | |

EVIDENCE WITH REFERENCE TO MINUTES AND RECORDS.

*December* 9, 1811.—Board met.  Present: John B. L. Lucas, Clement B. Penrose, and Frederick Bates, commissioners.

Joseph Silvain, claiming 250 arpens of land, situate in district of Cape Girardeau.  Produces record of a concession from Delassus, L. G., dated December 15, 1799.

It is the opinion of the board that this claim ought not to be confirmed.  (See No. 5, page 499.)

*December* 5, 1833.—F. R. Conway, esq., appeared, pursuant to adjournment.

Joseph Silvain, claiming 250 arpens of land.  (See record-book E, page 27; book No. 5, page 499.)

Produces a paper purporting to be an original concession from Charles Dehault Delassus, dated December 15, 1799.

M. P. Leduc, duly sworn, says that the signature in the recommendation is in the true handwriting of Louis Lorimier, commandant of Cape Girardeau, and the signature to the concession is in the proper handwriting of Carlos Dehault Delassus.  (See book No. 6, page 365.)

*June* 15, 1835.—The board met, pursuant to adjournment.  Present: F. R. Conway and J. H. Relfe, commissioners.

Joseph Silvain, claiming 250 arpens of land.  (See book No. 6, page 365.)

The board are of opinion that this claim ought to be confirmed to the said Joseph Silvain, or to his legal representatives, according to the concession and to possession.  (See book No. 7, page 183.)

JAMES H. RELFE,
F. R. CONWAY.

I have examined the transcript of the above claim, and concur in the decision.

F. H. MARTIN.

---

No. 294.—*Jacob Neal, claiming 800 arpens.*

To Don F. Valle, *Captain and civil and military Commandant of the post of St. Genevieve of Illinois, &c.:*

Jacob Neal, being among the number of families to which the government has permitted to settle in this country, in consequence of the demand made by Mr. Moses Austin, as appears by the certificate of the said Austin here annexed, has the honor to represent that, being desirous to make a plantation in order to support his numerous family, composed of himself, his wife, and nine children, and also to establish a gunpowder manufactory, which article will be most advantageous to this colony, he would wish to have a certain quantity of land; therefore, the said petitioner applies to your goodness, and to the generosity of the government which you represent in this district, praying that you be pleased to grant to him, his heirs or assigns, a concession of 800 arpens of land in superficie, situated on the bank of the river called Mine à Breton, at about two leagues below the settlement at the said Mine.  In doing which you will do justice.

JACOB NEAL.

St. Genevieve, *November* 20, 1799.

Having examined the foregoing petition, we do refer it to the lieutenant governor, for him to determine what he shall think fit.

F'COIS VALLÉ.

St. Genevieve, *November* 22, 1799.

St. Louis of Illinois, *November* 29, 1799.

In consequence of the official order of the Baron de Carondelet, dated March 15, in the year 1797, granting lands to all those who have come to this country with Mr. Moses Austin, the party interested shall prove, before the commandant of St. Genevieve, in whose jurisdiction he resides, the number of persons composing his family, and afterward, the surveyor, Don Antonio Soulard, shall put him in possession of 200 arpens of land in superficie for the husband and wife, 50 for each child, and 20 for each negro, and the whole not to exceed 800 arpens for one single owner, as it is ordered by the regulation of the governor general of the province. And this being executed, the interested shall have to solicit the title of concession in form from the intendant general of these provinces, to whom alone corresponds, by order of his Majesty, the distributing and granting all classes of lands belonging to the royal domain.

CARLOS DEHAULT DELASSUS.

St. Louis, August 24, 1833.  Truly translated.

JULIUS DE MUN, T. B. C.

| No. | Name of original claimant. | Arpens. | Nature and date of claim. | By whom granted. | By whom surveyed, date, and situation. |
|---|---|---|---|---|---|
| 204 | Jacob Neal. | 800 | Concession, 29th November, 1799. | Carlos D. Delassus. | On Mine à Breton creek. |

EVIDENCE WITH REFERENCE TO MINUTES AND RECORDS.

*August 23, 1833.*—The board met, pursuant to adjournment. Present, L. F. Linn, A. G. Harrison, F. R. Conway, commissioners.

Jacob Neal, by his legal representatives, claiming 800 arpens of land, situated on the waters of the river or creek of Mine à Breton. (See book C, page 497.)

Produces a paper purporting to be an original concession from Carlos Dehault Delassus, dated the 29th day of November, 1799.

The following testimony was taken before Lewis F. Linn, esq., one of the commissioners:

STATE OF MISSOURI, *County of St. Genevieve:*

John B. Vallé, aged about 72 years, being duly sworn, as the law directs, deposeth and saith, that he was well acquainted with François Vallé; that he has often seen him write; that the said François Vallé was commandant of the post and district of St. Genevieve, in the year 1799, and that the name, signature, and writing to the recommendation for said grant, dated as aforesaid, is the proper name and signature, and in the proper handwriting of the said François Vallé, the commandant as aforesaid. And this deponent further says that he was well acquainted with Charles Dehault Delassus; that he has often seen him write; that he was the lieutenant governor of the province of Upper Louisiana in the year 1799, and that the name, signature, and handwriting to the said concession from him to the said Jacob Neal, dated the 29th day of November, in the year 1799, is the proper name and signature, and in the proper handwriting of the said Charles Dehault Delassus. Sworn to and subscribed before me, L. F. Linn, one of the commissioners appointed, &c., this 4th day of May, 1833.

J. B. VALLÉ.
L. F. LINN, *Commissioner.*

And also came John T. McNeal, a witness, aged about 70 years, who being duly sworn, as the law directs, deposeth and saith, that he was well acquainted with Jacob Neal, the original claimant; that he saw him in this country, then called the province of Upper Louisiana, in the year 1799; that he was then a citizen and resident in the country; had a wife and nine children; that he understood he had obtained a grant for land from the Spanish government, situate on the creek or river of Mine à Breton; that he understood it to be the intention of the said Neal to erect a powder mill on the land granted, but that before he could carry the same into effect he died. Sworn to and subscribed before me, Lewis F. Linn, commissioner, this 8th day of May, 1833.

JOHN T. McNEAL.
L. F. LINN, *Commissioner.*

(See book No. 6, page 249.)

*June 15, 1835.*—The board met, pursuant to adjournment. Present: F. R. Conway and J. H. Relfe, commissioners.

Jacob Neal, claiming 650 arpens of land. (See book No. 6, page 249, where this claim is entered for 800 arpens.)

The board are of opinion that 650 arpens of land ought to be confirmed to the said Jacob Neal, or to his legal representatives, according to the concession and number of persons composing his family. (See book No. 7, page 183.)

JAMES H. RELFE.
F. R. CONWAY.

I have examined the transcript of the above claim, and concur in the decision.

F. H. MARTIN.

No. 205.—*Pierre Dumais, claiming 1,000 arpens.*

CAPE GIRARDEAU, *January 6, 1800.*

To Don CHARLES DEHAULT DELASSUS, *Lieutenant Governor of Upper Louisiana, &c. :*

SIR: Pierre Dumais has the honor to represent to you that, having resided in this province since his infancy, he would wish to make therein an establishment; therefore he has recourse to the bounty of this government, praying that you may be pleased to grant to him a tract of vacant land, of 1,000 arpens in superficie, to be taken in the district of Cape Girardeau, in the place called the Old Cape, adjoining a tract of land belonging to Mr. Louis Lorimier. Favor which the petitioner presumes to expect of your justice.

PIERRE DUMAIS.

CAPE GIRARDEAU, *January 9, 1800.*

We, commandant of the post of Cape Girardeau of Illinois, have the honor to inform the lieutenant governor that the statement of the petitioner is true, and that we believe him worthy to obtain the concession which he solicits, and which is a part of his Majesty's domain.

LOUIS LORIMIER.

ST. LOUIS OF ILLINOIS, *January 23, 1800.*

In consequence of the information given by the commandant of the post of Cape Girardeau, Don Louis Lorimier, by which it appears that the petitioner possesses means more than sufficient to obtain the concession which he solicits, I do grant, to him and his heirs, the land he solicits, provided it is not prejudicial to any person ; and the surveyor, Don Antonio Soulard, shall put the party interested in possession of the quantity of land he asks, on the designated spot of the royal domain ; and this being executed, he shall make out a plat of his survey, delivering the same to said party, with his certificate, in order that it shall serve to him to obtain the concession and title, in form, from the intendant general, to whom alone belongs, by royal order, the distributing and granting all classes of lands belonging to the royal domain,

CARLOS DEHAULT DELASSUS.

ST. LOUIS, *February 6, 1834.*—Truly translated.

JULIUS DE MUN, *T. B. C.*

| No. | Name of original claimant. | Arpens. | Nature and date of claim. | By whom granted. | By whom surveyed, date, and situation. |
|---|---|---|---|---|---|
| 295 | Pierre Dumais. | 1,000 | Concession, January 23, 1800. | Carlos Dehault Delassus. | Near the Old Cape, district of Cape Girardeau. |

EVIDENCE WITH REFERENCE TO MINUTES AND RECORDS.

*November* 14, 1811.—Board met.  Present: John B. C. Lucas, Clement B. Penrose, and Frederick Bates, commissioners.

Peter Mainard, assignee of Peter Dumais, claiming 1,000 arpens of land, situate near Old Cape, district of Cape Girardeau.  Produces the record of a concession from C. D. Delassus, lieutenant governor, dated 23d January, 1800 ; a transfer from Dumais to claimant, dated 20th May, 1806.

It is the opinion of the board that this claim ought not to be confirmed.  (See book No. 5, page 416.)

*December* 5, 1833.—F. R. Conway, esq., appeared, pursuant to adjournment.

Pierre Dumais, by his legal representative, claiming 1,000 arpens of land, situate at the place called the Old Cape Girardeau.  (See record-book E, page 27 ; No. 5, page 416.)  Produces a paper, purporting to be an original concession from Charles Dehault Delassus, dated 23d January, 1800.

M. P. Leduc, duly sworn, says that the signature to the recommendation is in the proper handwriting of Louis Lorimier, commandant of Cape Girardeau, and the signature to the concession is in the proper handwriting of Carlos Dehault Delassus.  (See book No. 6, page 364.)

*June* 15, 1835.—The board met, pursuant to adjournment.  Present: F. R. Conway, J. H. Relfe, commissioners.

Pierre Dumais, claiming 1,000 arpens of land.  (See book No. 6, page 364.)

The board are of opinion that this claim ought to be confirmed to the said Pierre Dumais, or to his legal representatives, according to the concession.  (See book No. 7, page 183.)

JAMES H. RELFE,
F. R. CONWAY.

I have examined the transcript of the above claim, and concur in the decision.

F. H. MARTIN.

---

No. 296.—*Samuel Neal, claiming 200 arpens.*

To Don FRANCIS VALLE, *Captain and civil and military Commandant of the post of St. Genevieve, &c. :*

ST. GENEVIEVE, *November 22, 1799.*

Samuel Neal, one among the number of families to whom the government has permitted to establish themselves in this country, in consequence of the demand made by Mr. Moses Austin, as appears by the certificate of the said Austin, dated 17th instant, laid before you by Jacob Neal, has the honor to represent that, wishing to improve a plantation, in order to cultivate grain and other things, he has recourse to your goodness and to the generosity of the government which you represent in this district, for the purpose of obtaining for him, his heirs or assigns, a concession of 240 arpens of land in superficie, situated on the bank of the river called Mine à Breton, at about two leagues and a half below the settlement at the said Mine.  In doing which you will do justice.

SAMUEL NEAL.

ST. GENEVIEVE, *November 22, 1799.*

Having examined the foregoing petition, we do forward it to the lieutenant governor, in order for him to determine what he shall think fit.

FRANCOIS VALLE.

ST. LOUIS OF ILLINOIS, *November 29, 1799.*

In consequence of the official order of the Baron de Carondelet, dated March 15, 1797, granting lands to all those who have come to this country with Mr. Moses Austin, the party interested shall prove before the commandant of St. Genevieve, in whose jurisdiction he resides, the number of persons composing his family, and afterward the surveyor, Don Antonio Soulard, shall put him in possession of 200 arpens of land in superficie, for the husband and wife, 50 for each child, and 20 for each negro; the whole not to exceed 800 arpens for one single proprietor, as it is ordered by the regulation of the governor general of the province. And this being executed, the interested shall have to solicit the title of concession in form, from the intendant general of this province, to whom alone corresponds, by order of his Majesty, the distributing and granting of all classes of lands belonging to the royal domain.

CARLOS DEHAULT DELASSUS.

St. Louis, *August* 24, 1833. Truly translated.

JULIUS DE MUN, *T. B. C.*

| No. | Name of original claimant. | Arpens. | Nature and date of claim. | By whom granted. | By whom surveyed, date, and situation. |
|---|---|---|---|---|---|
| 296 | Samuel Neal. | 200 | Concession, November 29, 1799. | Carlos Dehault Delassus. | On Mine à Breton creek. |

EVIDENCE WITH REFERENCE TO MINUTES AND RECORDS.

*August* 23, 1833.—The board met, pursuant to adjournment. Present: L. F. Linn, A. G. Harrison, F. R. Conway, commissioners.

Samuel Neal, by his legal representatives, claiming 800 arpens of land, situate on the waters of the creek of Mine à Breton. (See record-book C, page 498.)

Produces a paper purporting to be an original concession from Carlos Dehault Delassus, dated November 29, 1799.

The following testimony was taken before L. F. Linn, esq., one of the commissioners:

John B. Vallé, aged about 72 years, being duly sworn, as the law directs, deposeth and saith that he was well acquainted with François Vallé; that he has often seen him write; that he was the commandant of the post and district of St. Genevieve in the year 1799; and that the name and signature and handwriting to the recommendation to the lieutenant governor, dated the 22d day of November, in the year 1799, is the proper handwriting of the said François Vallé. And this deponent further says, that he was well acquainted with Charles Dehault Delassus; that he has frequently seen him write; that the said Delassus was the lieutenant governor of the province of Upper Louisiana in the year 1799, and that the name, signature, and handwriting to the concession from him to the said Samuel Neal, dated the 29th day of November, in the year 1799, is the proper name, signature, and in the proper handwriting of the said Charles Dehault Delassus.

Sworn to and subscribed before me, L. F. Linn, one of the commissioners, &c., this 4th day of May, 1833.

J. B. VALLE,

L. F. LINN, *Commissioner.*

And also came John T. McNeal, a witness aged about 70 years, who being duly sworn, as the law directs, deposeth and saith that he was well acquainted with Samuel Neal, the original grantee; that he was a citizen and resident in the province of Upper Louisiana in the year 1799; that he understood he had obtained a grant for land from the Spanish government, and that he had prepared and started to make an improvement thereon; that he was informed the land granted was on the waters of Mine à Breton creek or river; that he labored with the said Samuel Neal in the furnace of Moses Austin.

Sworn to and subscribed before me, Lewis F. Linn, commissioner, this 8th day of May, 1833.

JOHN T. McNEAL.

L. F. LINN, *Commissioner.*

(See minutes, book No. 6, page 247.)

*June* 15, 1835.—The board met, pursuant to adjournment. Present: F. R. Conway, J. H. Relfe, commissioners.

Samuel Neal, claiming 200 arpens of land. (See book No. 6, page 247, where this claim is entered for 800 arpens.)

The board are of opinion that 200 arpens of land ought to be confirmed to the said Samuel Neal, or his legal representatives, according to the concession. (See book No. 7, page 184.)

JAMES H. RELFE,

F. R. CONWAY.

I have examined the transcript of the above claim, and concur in the decision.

F. H. MARTIN.

---

No. 297.—*Jean B. Lamarche, claiming* 800 *arpens.*

To Mr. ZENON TRUDEAU, *Lieutenant Colonel and Lieutenant Governor of the western part of Illinois and dependencies, &c.*.

SIR: J. B. Lamarche, residing in St. Louis, wishing to establish himself on the banks of the Missouri, supplicates you to be willing to grant to him a piece of vacant land, of six arpens in front, situated between Mr. Chartrand on one side, and François Janis on the other, by forty (arpens) in depth, having for boundary on one end the Missouri, and on the other Mr. Yosty. Favor which is expected from you by one who shall never cease to pray most sincerely for your prosperity.

J. B. x LAMARCHE.
his
mark.

St. Louis, *November* 18, 1798.

St. Louis, *November* 18, 1798.

The piece of land asked for, of six arpens in front by forty arpens in depth, being vacant on account of the abandonment made of it by one Water, who absconded from this jurisdiction, Mr. B. Lamarche may locate himself there and improve the same ; and the surveyor of this jurisdiction shall make out the survey, in order to serve to obtain the concession of the governor general ; whom I inform that the said B. Lamarche is a Canadian, a married man, an inhabitant of the country, and a mechanic, having all the qualifications required to obtain this concession.

ZENON TRUDEAU.

Don Antonio Soulard, *Surveyor General of the settlements of Upper Louisiana :*

I do certify that a tract of land of 800 arpens in superficie, was measured, the lines run, and bounded, in favor and in presence of Gregorio Sarpy, by virtue of the power given by him for this purpose to the deputy surveyor. Said land belonged originally to B. Lamarche, as appears by the title here annexed, which has been presented to me by the said Gregorio Sarpy, a creditor of the said original owner, who absconded from this country some years ago.

The said land was measured with the perch of the city of Paris, of eighteen French feet, lineal measure of the same city, conformably to the custom of measuring land in this province. This land is situated at about twenty-four miles southwest of St. Louis, and bounded on its four sides by vacant lands of the royal domain. The survey and measurement were made without regard to the variation of the needle, which is 7° 30′ east, as appears by the foregoing figurative plat, on which are described the dimensions, courses of the lines, and other boundaries, &c. The survey was made by virtue of the decree of the lieutenant governor, Don Zenon Trudeau, dated November 18, 1798, here annexed. In testimony whereof, I do give the present certificate, with the foregoing figurative plat, drawn conformably to the survey executed by the deputy surveyor, John Terry, on the 12th of January, 1804, who signed the minutes to which I certify.

St. Louis, *April* 15, 1804.    ANTONIO SOULARD, *Surveyor General.*

St. Louis, *August* 8, 1833.    Truly translated from book C, page 263.

JULIUS DE MUN.

| No. | Name of original claimant. | Arpens. | Nature and date of claim. | By whom granted. | By whom surveyed, date, and situation. |
|---|---|---|---|---|---|
| 297 | Jean B. Lamarche. | 240 | Concession for 240 arpens, November 18, 1798. | Z. Trudeau. | Survey of 800 arpens by John Terry, D. S., January 12, 1804 ; certified by Soulard, April 15, 1804 ; 24 miles S. W. of St. Louis. |

EVIDENCE WITH REFERENCE TO MINUTES AND RECORDS.

*September* 19, 1806.—The board met, agreeably to adjournment. Present : Hon. John B. C. Lucas and Clement B. Penrose, esq.

John B. Lamarche, claiming 6 by 40 arpens of land, situate on the Missouri, to be bounded on each side by one Chartrand and François Janis, and in the rear by Emilian Yosti. Produces a concession from Zenon Trudeau, dated November 18, 1798, and a survey of said quantity, taken on the river Marameck, in consequence of the above described tract having previously been surveyed by another person, the said survey without date.

Toussaint Cerre, being duly sworn, says that the said claimant actually inhabited the said tract of land as surveyed on the Marameck, about 7 or 8 years ago. Rejected. (See No. 2, page 15.)

*September* 27, 1810.—Board met. Present : John B. C. Lucas, Clement B. Penrose, and Frederick Bates, commissioners.

Gregoire Sarpy, assignee of John Baptist Lamarche, claiming 800 arpens of land. (See book No. 2, page 15, for the claim of John Baptist Lamarche.) It is the opinion of the board that this claim ought not to be confirmed. (See book No. 4, page 512.)

*July* 8, 1833.—L. F. Linn, esq., appeared, pursuant to adjournment.

Jean B. Lamarche, by Alexander McNair's legal representatives, claiming 800 arpens of land, originally granted by Zenon Trudeau, to said Lamarche, on November 18, 1798. (See record-books D, page 345, and C, page 263. Minutes No. 2, page 15 ; No. 4, page 512.) Produces sheriff's deed. (See book No. 6, page 223.)

*June* 15, 1835.—The board met, pursuant to adjournment. Present : F. R. Conway, J. H. Relfe, commissioners.

Jean B. Lamarche, claiming 240 arpens of land. (See book No. 6, page 223, where this claim is entered for 800 arpens.) The board are of opinion that 240 arpens of land, which is the quantity asked for in the petition, ought to be confirmed to the said Jean B. Lamarche, or to his legal representatives, according to the concession, to be taken within the survey of record in book C, page 263, in the recorder's office. (See book No. 7, page 184.)

JAMES H. RELFE,
F. R. CONWAY.

I have examined the transcript of the above claim, and concur in the decision.

F. H. MARTIN.

No. 298.—*J. P. Cabanné, claiming* 2,000 *arpens.*

St. Louis, *November* 11, 1799.

To Don Charles Dehault Delassus, *Lieutenant Colonel, attached to the stationary regiment of Louisiana, and Lieutenant Governor of the upper part of the same province :*

Sir : J. Pre. Cabanné, father of a family, residing in this town, and since several years in this province of

Louisiana, has the honor to represent to you that, considering the dangers to which one is exposed in the fur trade, which is decreasing every day, and viewing agriculture as the only secure and certain means of procuring an independent existence, he hopes that you will be pleased to treat him with the same goodness and generosity that all the subjects of his Majesty have found in you : therefore, not having yet received any concession, he has the honor to supplicate you to have the goodness to grant to him, in full property, a tract of land of 2,000 arpens in superficie, to be taken in a vacant place of his Majesty's domain, on the north side of the Missouri. This favor shall be one link more to bind him to the soil he inhabits, and will increase in him, if possible, the sentiments of fidelity and devotedness he bears to the government under which he has found all the advantages which can make a Frenchman, whom the revolution has exiled from his country, forget all the evils he has formerly experienced ; and you will do justice.

CABANNÉ.

St. Louis of Illinois, November 12, 1799.

Considering that the petitioner has been settled in this country since a long time, and whereas we are assured that he possesses sufficient means to improve the lands which he solicits, I do grant to him and his heirs the land he solicits, provided that it is not to the prejudice of any one, and the surveyor, Don Antonio Soulard, shall put the party interested in possession of the quantity of land he asks, in a vacant place of the royal domain ; which being executed, he shall make out a plat of his survey, delivering the same to said party with his certificate, in order to serve to him to obtain the concession and title in form from the intendant general, to whom alone corresponds, by royal order, the distributing and granting all classes of lands of the royal domain.

CARLOS DEHAULT DELASSUS.

St. Louis, August 6, 1833.

Truly translated from the Spanish record of concessions, book No. 2, pages 44 and 45.

JULIUS DE MUN.

| No. | Name of original claimant. | Arpens. | Nature and date of claim | By whom granted. | By whom surveyed, date, and situation. |
|---|---|---|---|---|---|
| 298 | Jean P. Cabanné. | 2,000 | Concession, Nov. 12, 1779. | Carlos Dehault Delassus | Unlocated. |

EVIDENCE WITH REFERENCE TO MINUTES AND RECORDS.

*October* 7, 1808.—Board met. Present : Hon. Clement B. Penrose and Frederick Bates, commissioners.

J. P. Cabanné, claiming 2,000 arpens of land, to be taken on any vacant land, produces to the board a notice of said claim to the recorder, dated May 31, 1808, in which he states his concession to have been lost; produces to the board a registry of the same in book No. 2, marked B, page 44, lodged in the recorder's office.

Claimant, sworn, says that he has not the concession in his hands at present ; does not know where it is, and believes it to be lost.

Antoine Soulard, sworn, says that, about the year 1800, he had the concession of claimant in his possession, and then recorded it in the registry, as before stated, in book No. 2, marked B, page 44. Laid over for decision. (See minutes, book No. 3, page 283.)

*June* 18, 1810.—Board met. Present : John B. C. Lucas, Clement B. Penrose, and Frederick Bates, commissioners.

Jeane Pierre Cabanné, claiming 2,000 arpens of land. (See book No. 3, page 283.) It is the opinion of the board that this claim ought not to be confirmed. The board, on examining the registry referred to in this claim, to wit, book No. 2, marked B, find several concessions of subsequent dates to the one referred to, page 44 ; in the pages of the book preceding that number, and particularly in page 43, one dated 31st March, 1803 ; and, also, on examining the said alleged registry, (book No. 1, page 27,) the board find a concession dated 21st November, 1803. (See book No. 4, page 386.)

*July* 8, 1833.—L. F. Linn, esq., appeared, pursuant to adjournment.

J. P. Cabanné, claiming 2,000 arpens of land. (See record-book D, page 180. Minutes No. 3, page 283 ; No. 4, page 386. Spanish record of concessions, No. 2, page 44. See book No. 6, page 221.)

*June* 15, 1835.—The board met, pursuant to adjournment. Present : F. R. Conway, J. H. Relfe, commissioners.

John P. Cabanné, claiming 2,000 arpens of land. (See book No. 6, page 221.)

The board are of opinion that this claim ought to be confirmed to the said John P. Cabanné, or to his legal representatives, according to the concession. (See book No. 7, page 185.)

JAMES H. RELFE,<br>F. R. CONWAY.

I have examined the transcript of the above claim, and concur in the decision.

F. H. MARTIN.

No. 299.—Jean Marie Cardinal, claiming 40 arpens.

Don FRANCISCO CRUZAT, *Lieutenant-Governor of the Settlements of Illinois :*

Having examined the statement contained in the foregoing memorial, dated August 27th, 1777, and the demand of John Mary Cardinal, inhabitant of this town of St. Louis, in which he represents that he has not a quantity of land sufficient to make the sowings necessary for the maintenance of his family, I have granted, and do grant to him, in fee simple, for him and his heirs, a tract of land of two arpens in width by twenty in length, situated in the prairie called the White-ox prairie ; bounded on one side by the (land) of Lewis Biponet, behind by a branch that comes down from the hills, and on the two other sides by land not yet granted, on condition to establish said land in one year from this day, his Majesty reserving the right to dispose of the same, as being his domain, in case of utility to his royal service.

Given in St. Louis of Illinois, August 28, 1777.

FRANCISCO CRUZAT.

ANTONIO SOULARD, *Ex-Surveyor General of this Upper Louisiana for his Majesty:*

We do certify to all whom it may concern, that the foregoing title is conformable to the original, recorded on page 12, of book No. 3, of the ancient titles of concessions in this Upper Louisiana, under my charge; which copy I have delivered at the request of Mr. Louis Labaume, he being the purchaser of said land by virtue of a certified copy of a juridical deed of sale, which he communicated to us, and executed to him in St. Charles, for the said property, before Captain Mackay, commandant of the settlements on the Missouri, dated July 26th, 1804. Which (certificate) I have delivered in order that it may serve and be available to the (party) interested, as in right, before all competent authorities and tribunals.

ANTONIO SOULARD.

St. Louis, *August 5, 1804.*

JULIUS DE MUN.

St. Louis, *May 7, 1833.*

| No. | Name of original claimant. | Arpens. | Nature and date of claim. | By whom granted. | By whom surveyed, date, and situation. |
|-----|---------------------------|---------|---------------------------|------------------|----------------------------------------|
| 299 | Jean Marie Cardinal. | 40 | Concession, August 28, 1777. | Francisco Cruzat. | James Mackay, D. S, February 10, 1806. Received for record, February 28, 1806. A. Soulard, S. G., White-ox prairie. |

EVIDENCE WITH REFERENCE TO MINUTES AND RECORDS.

*February 21, 1809.*—Board met. Present: John B. C. Lucas, Clement B. Penrose, and Frederick Bates, commissioners.

The claim of Louis Lebaume, assignee of François (Jean) Maria Cardinal, being taken up by the board, and a vote being taken thereon, it is the opinion of the board that said claim ought not to be confirmed; this claim, for the major part, being included within the claim of the widow and representative of Antoine Morin, this day confirmed to them. (See book No. 3, page 485.)

*March 25, 1833.*—F. R. Conway, esq., appeared, pursuant to adjournment.

Jean Maria Cardinal, by L. Lebaume's legal representatives, claiming 40 arpens of land in White-ox prairie. (See book D, page 296. Livre terrien, No. 3, page 12. Book F, page 184. Minutes, No. 3, page 485.) Produces a copy of a duly-registered concession granted by Francisco Cruzat, bearing date August 28, 1777, taken from said livre terrien; also a certificate of Soulard, dated August 5, 1804; also, a copy of a survey of said land, certified by M. P. Leduc; also a copy of a deed from the heirs of Cardinal to Lebaume, dated July 26, 1804, certified by James Mackay, commandant of St. Charles.

M. P. Leduc, duly sworn, says that the signature to the above-mentioned papers are in the proper and respective handwriting of the above-mentioned individuals who signed them. (See book No. 6, page 150.)

*July 8, 1833.*—L. F. Linn, esq., appeared, pursuant to adjournment.

In the case of Jean Marie Cardinal, claiming 40 arpens of land. (See page 150 of this book, No. 6.) Claimant produces a paper purporting to be a plat and certificate of survey, dated February 28, 1806, by Antoine Soulard.

M. P. Leduc, duly sworn, says that the signature to said plat and certificate is in the proper handwriting of said Antoine Soulard. (See book No. 6, page 219.)

*June 15, 1835.*—The board met, pursuant to adjournment. Present: F. R. Conway and J. H. Relfe, commissioners.

Jean Marie Cardinal, claiming 40 arpens of land. (See book No. 6, pages 150 and 219.)

The board are of opinion that this claim ought to be confirmed to the said Jean Marie Cardinal, or to his legal representatives, according to the concession. (See book No. 7, page 185.)

JAMES H. RELFE,
F. R. CONWAY.

I have examined the transcript of the above claim, and concur in the decision.

F. H. MARTIN.

---

*No. 300.—Widow Dodier, claiming 120 arpens.*

St. Louis, *May 23, 1772.*

I, the undersigned, Martin Duralde, by virtue of the power in me vested by Don Pedro Piernas, captain of infantry and lieutenant governor of the settlements and other parts dependent of the Spanish government of Illinois, at the request of the inhabitants of this post of St. Louis, asking that the dimensions, courses of the lines, and boundaries of the lands, they own in the vicinity of said post be determined by a competent person, authorized to that effect, declare to all those whom it may concern, that, at the request of each of the said inhabitants, during the fall of the year 1770, and the springs of the years 1771 and 1772, (of which I neither state the months nor the days, the operations (of survey) having been made at different times, and not in succession,) in relation to those who have possessions distant from one another and situated in various places,) and, namely, at the desire of the widow Dodier, I purposely went from my dwellings, situated in the above said post of St. Louis, on a tract of land of three arpens in width by forty others in length, to her belonging, part of it ploughed and the rest untilled, situated in the prairie beyond the mound called Lagrange, and adjoining immediately to that (the land) of Mr. Debrusseau, and on the other side to that of said Debrusseau, on the two other sides to the King's domain, in order to survey the same with my instrument and a chain of forty-five feet in length, which length taken four times just makes the arpent used in this country, which has one hundred and eighty feet on each side. In the execution of which survey I was accompanied by the said proprietor and by her said most immediate neighbor, in order to serve as assisting witnesses, and to indicate exactly the true situation of their respective concessions. I succeeded in surveying the same, and had it bounded, in my presence, with stones at its four angles, (extremities,) after having measured it on its lines of width and length; which first two parallels, that is to say, in width, run between north one quarter northwest and the north, or, more exactly, deviate from the north toward the west, five degrees; and the two others, that is to say, in length, also parallels, run west one quarter northwest, or, rather, deviate from the west toward the north, eleven degrees fifteen minutes, without regard to the variation of the compass which may exist, making, consequently, in directing the sight from the point of departure toward the courses indicated, an acute angle of seventy-three degrees forty-five minutes, allowance being made for the differences caused by the unevenness of the land and inclination of the lines toward one another, relatively to the horizontal perpendiculars, which always serve to their true measures, as well on the width as on the length. And I do attest the same with my signature, and with the unanimous consent of all the proprietors here above named, (in livre terrien, No. 2,) assembled at present, with the approbation of the said Don Pedro Piernas, in the government-house, in order to serve mutually as witnesses and affirm the facts, some with their signatures and others with their declarations, not knowing how to sign, in presence of Don Pedro Piernas, the aforesaid lieutenant governor, and Don Louis St. Ange de Bellerive, formerly a captain, and lately commandant of this said post, both serving, to wit: the last named to certify with his signature, that, in his said capacity, and by virtue of the power with which he was vested, to have granted, either by titles or verbally, the above-described tracts of land, in the name of his Majesty; and the said Mr. Piernas to approve, confirm, and ratify, (also with his signature in his capacity of actual lieutenant governor, by which he is vested with the same power of granting,) the possessions already granted by the said St. Ange, and specified in the foregoing register, containing sixty-eight written pages, this inclusive, which I remit in the archives of this government, in order to be therein preserved forever, and serve, in case of need, of surety, authenticity and attestation in behalf of all therein stated.

MARTIN DURALDE.

| | |
|---|---|
| LACLEDE LIGUEST, | AMABLE GUION, |
| HUBERT, | BECQUET, |
| DODIE, | SARPY, |
| A. CONDE, | COTTEE. |
| RENE KIERCEREAU, | |

ST. ANGE PEDRO PIERNAS.

ST. LOUIS, *October* 31, 1834.

Truly translated from livre terrien, No. 2, pages 1, 2, 38, 39, 67 and 68.

JULIUS DE MUN, *T. B. C.*

NOTE.—The following is written on the margin of page 38: Reunited to the King's domain on account of having been abandoned since a long time.

TRUDEAU.

*June* 4, 1793.

JULIUS DE MUN, *T. B. C.*

| No. | Name of original claimant. | Arpens. | Nature and date of claim. | By whom granted. | By whom surveyed, date, and situation. |
|---|---|---|---|---|---|
| 300 | Widow Dodier. | 120 | Concession, May 23, 1772. | St. Ange and Piernas. | Martin Duralde, May 23, 1772; in the prairie beyond the Grange de Terre (Big Mound.) |

EVIDENCE WITH REFERENCE TO MINUTES AND RECORDS.

*November* 14, 1811.—Board met. Present: John B. C. Lucas, Clement B. Penrose, and Frederick Bates, commissioners.

Louis Labeaume, assignee of Margaret Becquette, widow of Dodier, and others, heirs of François M. Mette. Widow Dodier, claiming three arpens by forty, situate prairie adjoining the town of St. Louis. Produces a concession from St. Ange and Piernas, L. G., dated 23d May, 1772; record of transfer from said widow and others, to claimant, dated the 18th August, 1806. In the margin of the concession is written, " Réunie au domaine du Roi pour les avoir abandonnées depuis long tems. St. Louis, ce 4 Juin, 1793." (Reunited to the King's domain for having abandoned them since a long time. St. Louis, June 4, 1793.)

It is the opinion of the board that this claim ought not to be confirmed. (See minutes, No. 5, page 414.)

*June* 8, 1833.—F. R. Conway, esq., appeared, pursuant to adjournment.

Widow Dodier, by Louis Labeaume's representatives, claiming three by forty arpens of land. (See record-book D, pages 306, 307, and 308; Minutes, No. 5, page 414.) Produces livre terrien, No. 2, page 38, and a copy of the same; also deed from the heirs of said Dodier to L. Labeaume. (See minutes No. 6, page 174.)

*June* 15, 1835.—The board met, pursuant to adjournment. Present: F. R. Conway, J. H. Relfe, commissioners.

Widow Dodier, claiming 120 arpens of land. (See book No. 6, page 174.)

The board are of opinion that this claim ought to be confirmed to the said widow Dodier, or to her legal representatives, according to the survey in livre terrien, book No. 2, page 38. (See book No. 7, page 185.)

JAMES H. RELFE,
F. R. CONWAY.

I have examined the transcript of the above claim, and concur in the decision.

F. H. MARTIN.

---

No. 301.—*William Hartly, claiming 650 arpens.*

To Don CHARLES DEHAULT DELASSUS, *Lieutenant-Colonel, attached to the stationary regiment of Louisiana, and Lieutenant Governor of Upper Louisiana:*

St. Louis, *January* 14, 1800.

Wm. Hartly, Roman Catholic, has the honor to represent to you that he came to this country about three years ago, with the intention to settle himself in the same; that for that purpose he obtained the permission of your predecessor, Don Zenon Trudeau, with his promise of a concession for a tract of land. In consequence he returned to America (the United States) in order to bring his family immediately, but a serious disease having obliged him to delay his departure, he could not get here as soon as he would have wished. He hopes of your justice that you will be pleased to take his demand into consideration, and grant to him a concession for a tract of land corresponding to the number of his family, which consists of himself, his wife, and nine children. Which (land) he has chosen at about six leagues in the N. W. of this town, St. Ferdinand, and near the plantation of Mr. Yosty, in the same settlement. The petitioner having no other views but to live as a peaceable and submissive cultivator (of the soil,) hopes to deserve the favor which he claims of your kindness.

his
WM. × HARTLY.
mark.

St. Louis of Illinois, *January* 14, 1800.

In consequence of the official note sent to us by Don Antonio Soulard, surveyor general of this Upper Louisiana, under date of this same day and month, by which he certifies to the number of persons composing the family of the petitioner, and to other corresponding circumstances, the same surveyor, Don Antonio Soulard, shall put him in possession of 650 arpens of land in superficie, in the place where he asks the same; said quantity being proportionate to the number of persons composing his family, according to the regulation of the governor general of this province. And this being executed, the party interested shall have to solicit the title of concession in form, from the intendant general of these provinces, to whom alone corresponds, by order of his Majesty, the distributing and granting all classes of lands of the royal domain.

CARLOS DEHAULT DELASSUS.
MACKAY.

(Recorded No. 66.)

St. Louis, *April* 12, 1833.—Truly translated.

JULIUS DE MUN.

| No. | Name of original claimant. | Arpens. | Nature and date of claim. | By whom granted. | By whom surveyed, date, and situation. |
|---|---|---|---|---|---|
| 301 | William Hartly. | 650 | Concession, January 14, 1800. | Carlos Dehault Delassus. | |

EVIDENCE WITH REFERENCE TO MINUTES AND RECORDS.

*November* 20, 1811.—Board met. Present: John B. C. Lucas, Clement B. Penrose, and Frederick Bates, commissioners.

James Mackay, assignee of John Long, assignee of William Hartly, claiming 650 arpens of land, situate in Missouri, district of St. Louis, produces record of concession from Charles D. Delassus, lieutenant governor, dated January 14, 1800; record of a transfer from Hartly to Long, dated February 10, 1801; record of a transfer from Long to claimant, dated February 8, 1805.

It is the opinion of the board that this claim ought not to be confirmed. (See book No. 5, page 434.)

*March* 21, 1833.—F. R. Conway, esq., appeared, pursuant to adjournment, being authorized to receive evidence by a resolution of this board, taken 9th instant.

William Hartly, by his legal representatives, claiming 650 arpens of land. (See book C, page 480; minutes, No. 5, page 434; Bates' decisions, book No. 2, page 34.) Produces a paper, purporting to be an original concession, dated January 14, 1800, from Carlos Dehault Delassus.

M. P. Leduc, duly sworn, says that the signature is in the proper handwriting of said C. D. Delassus. (See book No. 6, page 134.)

*June* 15, 1835.—The board met, pursuant to adjournment. Present: F. R. Conway, J. H. Relfe, commissioners.

William Hartly, claiming 650 arpens of land. (See book No. 6, page 134.)

The board are of opinion that this claim ought to be confirmed to the said William Hartly, or to his legal representatives, according to the concession. (See book No. 7, page 185.)

JAMES H. RELFE,
F. R. CONWAY.

I have examined the transcript of the above claim, and concur in the decision.

F. H. MARTIN.

No. 302.—*Absalom Kennison, claiming 640 acres.*

| No. | Name of original claimant. | Acres. | Nature and date of claim. | By whom granted. | By whom surveyed, date, and situation. |
|---|---|---|---|---|---|
| 302 | Absalom Kennison. | 640 | Settlement right. | | |

EVIDENCE WITH REFERENCE TO MINUTES AND RECORDS.

*November* 20, 1811.—Board met.  Present: John B. C. Lucas, Clement B. Penrose, and Frederick Bates, commissioners.

Absalom Kennison, claiming 640 arpens of land, situate in Bois-brule, district of St. Genevieve, produces notice to the recorder.

It is the opinion of the board that this claim ought not to be granted. (See minute-book No. 5, page 442.)

*January* 31, 1834.—F. R. Conway, esq., appeared, pursuant to adjournment.

Absalom Kennison, by his legal representatives, claiming 640 acres of land, situate in Bois-brule bottom, Perry county.  (See record-book E, page 241; minute-book No. 5, page 442.)

The following testimony was taken before L. F. Linn, commissioner:

Claimant produces, in support of said claim, Thomas Allen as a witness, who, being duly sworn, deposes and says that he emigrated to this State, then known as the Territory of Upper Louisiana, in the spring of 1797, and settled in the Bois-brule bottom, in Perry county, where he has had his home, and resided ever since.  This deponent was well acquainted with the said Absalom Kennison, deceased, and he well recollects that said Kennison moved to and settled in the said Bois-brule bottom in the year 1799, on a place at or near the hill bounding said bottom; and that he continued to reside there for several years; that he well recollects that, in the year 1803, he had on said place a considerable field, he thinks not less than ten or twelve acres, cleared, fenced, and cultivated, and had built a dwelling-house thereon, in which he resided with his family, and other out-buildings, such as were usual in the country at that time.  This deponent further states that the place, so settled and improved by the said Absalom Kennison, deceased, is now covered by other claims, and that the same are held, as he believes, and as is generally understood in the neighborhood, by those deriving title to the same from the government; and that the said Absalom Kennison continued to reside in the country until the time of his death, which was, as he thinks, about the year 1816.

                                                              his
                                               THOMAS  ×  ALLEN.
                                                             mark.
OCTOBER 25, 1833.                              L. F. LINN, *Commissioner.*

Elizabeth Locherd, also being sworn, testifies and says that she came to this country, then Upper Louisiana, in the spring of 1800, and settled in the edge of Bois-brule bottom aforesaid, and that very shortly after her arrival she was at the house of Absalom Kennison, senior, deceased, where he resided with his family, described in the foregoing deposition of Thomas Allen, and continued to visit there frequently, having been the neighbor of the said Kennison in Kentucky, and being also a neighbor here; and that the said Kennison had a considerable field enclosed and cultivated, previous to and in the year 1803, and saw corn and other things growing in said field.

                                                             her
                                             ELIZABETH  ×  LOCHERD.
                                                            mark.
OCTOBER 25, 1833.                              L. F. LINN, *Commissioner.*

Hezekiah P. Harris, being sworn, testifies and says that, in the summer of 1804, he well recollects the said Absalom Kennison inviting him to assist him in reaping wheat, at the place described in the foregoing depositions of Thomas Allen and Elizabeth Locherd, and that he accordingly went and assisted in reaping, and that the said Kennison was then residing there with his family, and had a considerable improvement, more, he should think, than twelve acres.

                                               H. P. HARRIS.
OCTOBER 25, 1833.                              L. F. LINN, *Commissioner.*

(See book No. 6, page 491.)

*June* 16, 1835.—The board met, pursuant to adjournment.  Present: F. R. Conway, J. H. Relfe, commissioners.

Absalom Kennison, claiming 640 acres of land.  (See book No. 6, page 491.)

The board are of opinion that 640 acres of land ought to be granted to the said Absalom Kennison, or to his legal representatives, according to possession.  (See book No. 7, page 186.)

                                               JAMES H. RELFE,
                                               F. R. CONWAY.

I have examined the transcript of the above claim, and concur in the decision.

                                               F. H. MARTIN.

No. 303.—*Jacob Miller, claiming 300 acres.*

| No. | Name of original claimant. | Acres. | Nature and date of claim. | By whom granted. | By whom surveyed, date, and situation. |
|---|---|---|---|---|---|
| 303 | Jacob Miller. | 300 | Settlement right. | | James Boyd, D. S. Received for record by A. Soulard, S. G. |

EVIDENCE WITH REFERENCE TO MINUTES AND RECORDS.

*February* 11, 1809.—Board met.  Present: Hon. John B. C. Lucas, Clement B. Penrose, and Frederick Bates.

Jacob Miller, claiming 350 arpens of land, situate in White Water, district of Cape Girardeau, produces to the board, as a certificate of permission to settle, list B, on which said claimant is No. 32, and a plat of survey signed by B. Cousin, and signed by Antonio Soulard, as received for record.

Joseph Niswanger, being duly affirmed, says that claimant settled in the year 1804, cleared five or six acres, built a cabin.  In the same or following year, claimant sold the improvement, and removed to another tract which he had purchased, which latter has an enclosure and cultivation of about ten acres, a cabin and stable.  Inhabitation and cultivation to the present day.  Claimant has a wife and one child.  Laid over for decision  (See book No. 3, page 467.)

*December* 22, 1809.—Board met.  Present: John B. C. Lucas, Clement B. Penrose, and Frederick Bates, commissioners.

Jacob Miller, claiming 350 arpens of land.  (See book No. 3, page 467.)  It is the opinion of the board that this claim ought not to be granted.  (See book No. 4, page 235.)

*January* 30, 1834.—F. R. Conway, esq., appeared, pursuant to adjournment.

Jacob Miller, by his legal representatives, claiming 300 acres of land, situate in the county of Cape Girardeau.  (See record-book B, page 292; minute-book No. 3, page 467, and No. 4, page 235.)

STATE OF MISSOURI, *Cape Girardeau county:*

Personally appeared before L. F. Linn, one of the commissioners, &c., Isaac Miller, of lawful age, who being duly sworn, deposeth and saith that his father, John Miller, emigrated to the upper province of Louisiana, now State of Missouri, in the month of October, in the year 1803; that this affiant and the above-named Jacob Miller, an elder brother, moved with him; that in the same year application was made to the Spanish commandant of the post of Cape Girardeau, Louis Lorimier, for a grant of land for each of them, and the said commandant granted to John Miller 800 arpens, and to this affiant and Jacob Miller 300 arpens each, and that the application for these grants was made for the express purpose of permanently settling on and improving the same, they all being farmers and cultivators of the soil; that they all settled on and cultivated those said grants of land; that the grants made to this affiant and John Miller, were confirmed to them by a former board of commissioners.  The grant to Jacob Miller, the elder brother, was not confirmed, for some cause to this affiant unknown.  This deponent further states that Jacob Miller made valuable improvements on the same—dwelling-houses, out-houses, orchards, &c.; the dwelling-house was built in the year 1803, the other buildings immediately afterward, either late in the fall of 1803, or in the beginning of the year 1804, witness does not positively recollect which.  Witness further states claimant commenced preparing ground for cultivation in 1803, and in the year 1804 raised a crop of corn, vegetables, &c.

ISAAC MILLER.

Sworn to and subscribed, October 19, 1833.

L. F. LINN, *Commissioner.*

Joseph Niswanger, of lawful age, being sworn, deposeth and saith that he was intimately acquainted with the above-named Jacob Miller; that he knows he emigrated to this country in the year 1803, perhaps in the month of September or October; that the said Jacob Miller immediately commenced clearing land and preparing for a crop, and raised a crop in the year 1804, and continued to cultivate his farm till he moved away, many years after; the time he left his farm not recollected, probably the year 1820.

his
JOSEPH × NISWANGER.
mark.

Sworn to and subscribed, October 19, 1833.

L. F. LINN, *Commissioner.*

(See No. 6, page 489.)

*June* 16, 1835.—The board met, pursuant to adjournment.  Present: F. R. Conway, J. H. Relfe, commissioners.

Jacob Miller, claiming 300 acres of land.  (See book No. 6, page 489.)

The board are of opinion that this claim ought to be granted to the said Jacob Miller, or to his legal representatives, according to the survey.  (See book No. 7, page 186.)

JAMES H. RELFE,
F. R. CONWAY.

I have examined the transcript of the above claim, and concur in the decision.

F. H. MARTIN.

---

No. 304.—*John Greenwalt, jr., claiming 640 acres.*

| No. | Name of original claimant. | Acres. | Nature and date of claim. | By whom granted. | By whom surveyed, date, and situation. |
|---|---|---|---|---|---|
| 304 | John Greenwalt, jr. | 640 | Settlement right. | | |

EVIDENCE WITH REFERENCE TO MINUTES AND RECORDS.

*June,* 1806.—The same, (Israel Dodge,) assignee of John Greenwalt, claiming under the second section a tract of land situate on the waters of Bois-brule, produces a deed of transfer executed by the aforesaid John Greenwalt, dated October 27, 1804.

Camille Lassus, being duly sworn, says that the said Greenwalt had obtained a permission to settle from Pierre de Luziere.

Thomas Maddin, being also sworn, says that the said Greenwalt had a concession for said land ; that he, the witness, surveyed the same by virtue of said concession ; that the same was bought by one Hayden, but, witness believes, never cultivated.   The board reject this claim.   (See book No. 2, page 23.)

*September* 28, 1810.—Board met.   Present : John B. C. Lucas and Clement B. Penrose, commissioners.

Israel Dodge, claiming as an assignee of John Greenwalt, —— arpens of land.   (See book No. 2, page 23.)

It is the opinion of the board that this claim ought not to be granted.   (See book No. 4, page 514.)

*January* 29, 1834.—F. R. Conway, esq., appeared, pursuant to adjournment.

John Greenwalt, jr., by his legal representatives, claiming 640 acres of land situated on Bois-brule creek, Perry county.   (See record-book E, page 218 ; minute-book No. 2, page 23, and No. 4, page 514.)

Claimant produces, in support of said claim, John Greenwalt, the father of said settler, who states that his son John improved a place on Bois-brule creek, in the bottom of the same name, now in Perry county, and State of Missouri, adjoining to a tract of land of Jones Newsom on one side, and John Morgan on the other side ; that he settled on said place as early as the winter of 1803 and 1804 ; that he built a cabin on it, and cleared a piece of ground, and planted fruit trees thereon, previous to the summer of 1804, in which summer he raised corn and all other vegetables usual to be raised.   On the ground he had 30 —— cleared.   This deponent knows the above facts, because he lived with his son at the same time ; that his said son was then more than twenty-five years of age, and doing for himself.

his

JOHN × GREENWALT.

mark,

*October* 25, 1833.

L. F. LINN, *Commissioner.*

John Kennison, being sworn, states that he knows as to the correctness of the above statement of John Greenwalt, and of the house built and improvement made as stated in the above deposition, frequently passing the place in the summer of 1804, the said John Greenwalt, jr., then residing there and improving, and had the same in corn and other things, as stated in the foregoing deposition, and the place is yet known in the neighborhood by the name of John Greenwalt's improvement.

JOHN KENNISON.

*October* 25, 1833.

L. F. LINN, *Commissioner.*

(See book No. 6, page 488.)

*June* 16, 1835.—The board met, pursuant to adjournment.   Present : F. R. Conway and J. H. Relfe, commissioners.

John Greenwalt, jr., claiming 640 acres of land.   (See book No. 6, page 488.)

The board remark that the testimony given by Thomas Maddin, before the former board of commissioners, has no relation to this claim, but refers to the claim of John Greenwalt, sr., recorded in book B, page 201, and confirmed by Bates to Clement Hayden, assignee of said Greenwalt, sr.   (See Bates's decisions, page 64.)

The board are of opinion that 640 acres of land ought to be granted to the said John Greenwalt, jr., or to his legal representatives, according to possession.

JAMES H. RELFE,<br>F. R. CONWAY.

I have examined the transcript of the above claim, and concur in the decision.

F. H. MARTIN.

No. 305.—*William Thompson, claiming* 640 *acres.*

| No. | Name of original claimant. | Acres. | Nature and date of claim. | By whom granted. | By whom surveyed, date, and situation. |
|---|---|---|---|---|---|
| 305 | Wm. Thompson. | 640 | Settlement right. | | E. F. Bond, D. S., Feb. 14, 1806 ; received for record by A. Soulard, S. G., Feb. 23, 1806. (Survey of 790 acres.) |

EVIDENCE WITH REFERENCE TO MINUTES AND RECORDS.

*December* 10, 1811.—Board met.   Present : John B. C. Lucas, Clement B. Penrose, and Frederick Bates, commissioners.

William Thompson, claiming 790 acres of land, situate in the district of Cape Girardeau, produces record of a plat of survey, dated 14th February, and certified 28th February, 1806.   It is the opinion of this board that this claim ought not to be granted.   (See book No. 5, page 505.)

*January* 10, 1834.—F. R. Conway, esq., appeared, pursuant to adjournment.

William Thompson, by his legal representatives, claiming 640 acres of land, situate on Hubble's creek, county of Cape Girardeau.   (See record-book B, page 303 ; book No. 5, page 505.)

STATE OF MISSOURI, *County of Cape Girardeau, ss:*

William Williams states that he is aged about 58 or 59 ; that he moved to, and settled in the district of Cape Girardeau, Upper Louisiana, in 1799 ; that he was well acquainted with one William Thompson ; he knows that the said Thompson had an improvement on the waters of Randle's creek, in said district, in the year 1800 or 1801 ; the said Thompson had corn growing on said place in the year 1801 ; and this affiant, from the best of his recollection, states that the said Thompson occupied said place up to the year 1802. There was something like two or three acres of land cleared on said place, at the time mentioned above.

WILLIAM WILLIAMS.

Sworn to and subscribed, October 16, 1833.

L. F. LINN, *Commissioner.*

(See book No. 6, page 454.)

*June* 16, 1835.—The board met, pursuant to adjournment.  Present: F. R. Conway, J. H. Relfe, commissioners.

William Thompson, claiming 648 acres of land.   (See book No. 6, page 454.)

The board are of opinion that 640 acres of land ought to be granted to the said William Thompson, or to his legal representatives, to be taken within the survey recorded in book B, page 303.  (See book No. 7, page 187.)

JAMES H. RELFE,
F. R. CONWAY.

I have examined the transcript of the above claim, and concur in the decision.

F. H. MARTIN.

---

No. 306.—*John Murphy, claiming 550 arpens.*

To Don CHARLES DEHAULT DELASSUS, *Lieutenant Governor and Commander-in-chief of Upper Louisiana, &c.:*

John Murphy, a Roman Catholic, has the honor to represent to you, that with the permission of the government, he is settled on this side of the Mississippi since several years, having made choice of a piece of land in the domain of his Majesty, in order to make a farm; therefore he supplicates you to have the goodness to grant to him, at the said place, a tract of land corresponding to the number of persons in his family, which consists of himself, his wife, and seven children.  The petitioner having the means to improve a farm, and no other views but to live as a submissive cultivator, hopes to obtain the favor which he solicits of your justice.

ST. ANDRE, *November* 18, 1799.

                                                              his
                                    JOHN  ×  MURPHY.
                                                             mark.

ST. ANDRE, *November* 18, 1799.

Be it forwarded to the lieutenant governor, with the information that the foregoing statement is true, and that the petitioner deserves the favor demanded.         SANTYAGO MACKAY.

ST. LOUIS OF ILLINOIS, *November* 25, 1799.

In consequence of the information given by Don Santyago Mackay, commandant of the settlement of St. Andre, by which the number of persons composing the family of the petitioner is proven, the surveyor, Don Antonio Soulard, shall put him in possession of five hundred and fifty arpens of land in superficie, in the place where he asks the same; said quantity corresponding to the number of his family, according to the regulations of the governor general of the province; and this being executed, the party interested shall have to solicit the title of concession in form from the intendant general of the same province, to whom alone belongs, by royal order, the distributing and granting all classes of lands belonging to the royal domain.

CARLOS DEHAULT DELASSUS.

ST. LOUIS, *October* 18, 1834.—Truly translated from record-book C, pages 80 and 81.

JULIUS DE MUN, *T. B. C.*

TERRITORY OF LOUISIANA, *District of St. Louis:*

I do certify that the above plat represents 550 arpens (or 470 acres 15 poles) and surveyed by James Richardson, deputy surveyor, the 20th of present month, at the request of Josiah Park, by virtue of a Spanish concession granted to John Murphy, who has no other claim of land on record in my office.  I have recorded the above in book E, fol. 27, No. 27.   At St. Louis, the 24th February, 1806.

ANTOINE SOULARD, *Surveyor General, Territory of Louisiana.*

ST. LOUIS, *October* 18, 1834.—Truly copied from record-book C, page 81.

JULIUS DE MUN, *T. B. C.*

MY DEAR MACKAY:  In consequence of the promise I made to one John B. Morfy, under date of 18th March, of this year, the commandant has no objection to grant him the 550 arpens of land which said Morfy asked me.   At present the only difficulty is to know the limits of the land he has selected, and whether it really is vacant; after ascertaining the facts, you may make out his petition, together with the information, and his decree will be immediately granted.

This letter has been directed to me on the 10th of September, 1799, by Don Zenon Trudeau, who forgot to sign it.                                                  SANTYAGO MACKAY.

I certify the above letter to be truly translated from record-book C, p. 80.

JULIUS DE MUN, *T. B. C.*

JUNE 16, 1835.

| No. | Name of original claimant. | Arpens. | Nature and date of claim. | By whom granted. | By whom surveyed, date, and situation. |
|-----|---------------------------|---------|---------------------------|------------------|---------------------------------------|
| 306 | John Murphy, | 550 | Concession, November 25, 1799. | C. Dehault Delassus. | James Richardson, D. S., February 20, 1806.  Certified by Soulard, S. G., February 24, 1806.  On Fifi's creek. |

*October* 19, 1808.—The board met. Present: the Hon. John B. C. Lucas, Clement B. Penrose, and Frederick Bates.

Josiah Park, assignee of John Murphy, claiming 550 arpens of land, situate on Fifi's creek, district of St. Louis. Produces to the board a concession for the same, from Don Carlos Dehault Delassus, lieutenant governor, to John Murphy, dated 25th November, 1799; also a plat and certificate of survey, dated 20th, and certified 24th of February, 1806; a deed of conveyance from said Murphy and wife to claimant, dated 27th June, 1805; also an official letter from Zenon Trudeau, lieutenant governor, to James Mackay, in which it is stated that as soon as said Murphy shall choose a spot, it shall be granted to him, dated 10th September, 1799.

James Mackay sworn, says that the official letter stated above was received by him near the time it bears date. Laid over for decision. (See minutes, book No. 3, page 305.)

*June* 20, 1810.—Board met. Present: John B. C. Lucas, Clement B. Penrose, and Frederick Bates, commissioners.

Josiah Park, assignee of John Murphy, claiming 550 arpens of land. (See book No. 3, page 305.) It is the opinion of the board that this claim ought not to be confirmed. (See minutes, book No. 4, page 396.)

*July* 2, 1833.—The board met, pursuant to adjournment. Present: L. F. Linn, F. R. Conway, commissioners.

John Murphy, by his assignee, Josiah Park, claiming 550 arpens of land, on the waters of Fifi's creek, county of St. Louis. (See record-book C, page 80 and following; minutes No. 3, page 305; No. 4, page 396; records of grants in St. Charles and St. Andre, No. 15.)

Hartley Lanham, being duly sworn, says that he has known the said Josiah Park, the present claimant, for upward of thirty years, and that in 1806, on the return of the witness to this country from a journey to Kentucky, the said Josiah Park was inhabiting and improving the above-mentioned tract of land; that he had a stock of horses, cattle, hogs, &c.; that the said tract has been cultivated by, through, and for him, ever since. (See minutes, book No. 6, page 209.)

*June* 17, 1835.—The board met, pursuant to adjournment. Present: F. R. Conway, J. H. Relfe, commissioners.

John Murphy, claiming 550 arpens of land. (See book No. 6, page 209.)

The board are of opinion that this claim ought to be confirmed to the said John Murphy, or to his legal representatives, according to the survey recorded in book C, page 81. (See book No. 7, page 188.)

JAMES H. RELFE,
F. R. CONWAY.

I have examined the transcript of the above claim, and concur in the decision.

F. H. MARTIN.

---

No. 307.—*William Morrison, claiming 750 arpens.*

To Don CHARLES DEHAULT DELASSUS, *Lieutenant Colonel, attached to the stationary regiment of Louisiana, and Commander-in-chief of Upper Louisiana:*

William Morrison, a Roman Catholic, has the honor to represent to you, that he has come over to this side with the permission of the government, and has made choice of a tract of land on a vacant place; therefore he has the honor to supplicate you to have the goodness to grant to him, at the said place, the quantity of land corresponding to the number of persons in his family, which is composed of himself, his wife, and eleven children. The petitioner having the means necessary to make a plantation, and having no other views but to live as a peaceable and submissive cultivator of the soil, hopes to obtain the favor which he solicits of your justice.

WM. MORRISON.

St. Andre, *June* 1, 1803.

Be it forwarded to the lieutenant governor, informing him at the same time that the above statement is true, and that the petitioner deserves the favor he solicits.

SANTYAGO MACKAY.

St. Andre, *June* 1, 1803.

St. Louis of Illinois, *June* 9, 1803.

In consequence of the information given by Don Santyago Mackay, commandant of the settlement of St. Andre, confirming the number of persons composing the family of the petitioner, the surveyor, Don Antonio Soulard, shall put him in possession of seven hundred and fifty arpens of land in superficie, in the place he asks; the said quantity corresponds with the number of his family, according to the regulation of the governor of the said province, to whom alone belongs, by royal order, the distributing and granting all classes of lands of the royal domain.

CARLOS DEHAULT DELASSUS.

St. Louis, *August* 18, 1834. Truly translated from the original.

JULIUS DE MUN, *T. B. C.*

| No. | Name of original claimant. | Arpens. | Nature and date of claim. | By whom granted. | By whom surveyed, date, and situation. |
|---|---|---|---|---|---|
| 307 | William Morrison. | 750 | Concession, June 9, 1803. | C. Dehault Delassus. | |

*November* 27, 1811.—Board met. Present: John B. C. Lucas, Clement B. Penrose, and Frederick Bates, commissioners.

George Washington Morrison, assignee of William Morrison, claiming 750 arpens of land, situate in the district of St. Charles, produces record of a concession from Charles D. Delassus, L. G., dated June 9, 1803.

It is the opinion of the board that this claim ought not to be confirmed.  (See No. 5, page 456.)

*July* 8, 1834.—The board met, pursuant to adjournment.  Present: J. H. Relfe and F. R. Conway, commissioners.

William Morrison, by his legal representatives, claiming 750 arpens of land.  (See record-book C, page 470 ; minute-book No. 5, page 456.)

Produces a paper purporting to be an original concession from Carlos Dehault Delassus, dated June 9, 1803.

M. P. Leduc, duly sworn, says that the signature to the said concession is in the proper handwriting of said Carlos Dehault Delassus.  (See minute-book No. 7, page 1.)

*June* 17, 1835.—The board met, pursuant to adjournment.  Present: F. R. Conway and J. H. Relfe, commissioners.

William Morrison, claiming 750 arpens of land.  (See book No. 7, page 1.)

The board are of opinion that this claim ought to be confirmed to the said William Morrison, or to his legal representatives, according to the concession.  (See book No. 7, page 189.)

JAMES H. RELFE,<br>
F. R. CONWAY.

I have examined the transcript of the above claim, and concur in the decision.

F. H. MARTIN.

---

### No. 308.—*Solomon Bellen, claiming 350 arpens.*

To Don CHARLES DEHAULT DELASSUS, *Lieutenant Governor and Commander-in-chief of Upper Louisiana:*

Solomon Bellen, a Roman Catholic, has the honor to represent that, with the permission of the government, he is going to settle on a tract of land in his Majesty's domain, and on the south side of the Missouri, therefore he supplicates you to have the goodness to grant to him, at the said place, three hundred and fifty arpens of land in superficie.  The petitioner, possessing the means necessary to make a farm, and having no other views but to live as a peaceable and submissive cultivator of the soil, hopes to obtain the favor he solicits of your justice.

ST. ANDRE, *December* 5, 1800.

Be it forwarded to the commander-in-chief, with the information that the above statement is true, and that the petitioner deserves to obtain the favor which he solicits.

ST. ANDRE, *December* 5, 1800.

SANTYAGO MACKAY.

ST. LOUIS OF ILLINOIS, *December* 11, 1800.

In consequence of the information given by the commandant of St. Andre, Don Santyago Mackay, I do grant to the petitioner the tract of land of three hundred and fifty arpens in superficie, which he solicits, provided it is not to the prejudice of any person ; and the surveyor, Don Antonio Soulard, shall put the party interested in possession of the said quantity of land demanded, in the place designated ; and this being executed, he shall make out a plat, delivering the same to said party, together with his certificate, in order to serve to him to obtain the concession and title in form from the intendant general, to whom alone belongs the distributing and granting all classes of lands of the royal domain.

CARLOS DEHAULT DELASSUS.

Recorded, No. 14.

MACKAY.

ST. LOUIS, *August* 19, 1834.—Truly translated from the original.

JULIUS DE MUN, *T. B. C.*

| No. | Name of original claimant. | Arpens. | Nature and date of claim. | By whom granted. | By whom surveyed, date, and situation. |
|---|---|---|---|---|---|
| 308 | Solomon Bellen. | 350 | Concession, Dec. 11, 1800. | C. Dehault Delassus. | |

#### EVIDENCE WITH REFERENCE TO MINUTES AND RECORDS.

*June* 16, 1834.—The board met, pursuant to adjournment.  Present: J. S. Mayfield and F. R. Conway, commissioners.

Solomon Bellen, by his legal representatives, claiming 350 arpens of land, situate on river Gravois, in the county of St. Louis.  (See record-book E, page 357.)  Produces a paper purporting to be an original concession from Carlos Dehault Delassus, dated 11th December, 1800.

M. P. Leduc, duly sworn, says that the signature to said concession is in the proper handwriting of said Carlos Dehault Delassus.  (See minute-book No. 6, page 530.)

*June* 17, 1835.—The board met, pursuant to adjournment.  Present: F. R. Conway and J. H. Relfe, commissioners.

Solomon Bellen, claiming 350 arpens of land.  (See book No. 6, p. 130.)

The board are of opinion that this claim ought to be confirmed to the said Solomon Bellen, or to his legal representatives, according to the concession.  (See book No. 7, page 189.)

JAMES H. RELFE,<br>
F. R. CONWAY.

I have examined the transcript of the above claim, and concur in the decision.

F. H. MARTIN.

### No. 309.—*Paschal Detchmendy, claiming 7,056 arpens*

To Don CHARLES DEHAULT DELASSUS, *Lieutenant Colonel, attached to the stationary regiment of Louisiana, and Lieutenant Governor of the upper part of the same province:*

Paschal Detchmendy, a Frenchman, residing since several years in St. Genevieve, has the honor to represent to you that, with the aid of the government, he has succeeded in getting in operation the first saw-mill that ever was in the country; which mill has been of the greatest assistance in all the undertakings of individuals; and wishing, more than ever, to turn his industry as much to his advantage as to that of his fellow-citizens, he has in contemplation the establishing of a stock farm, on a large scale, so as to enable him to have, in the said St. Genevieve, a slaughter-house, which will not fail to furnish meat all the year round, at a moderate price; having also the project to establish a tan-yard, when the sale of his cattle shall have procured him a sufficient quantity of hides; he presumes again to hope, in this circumstance, for the protection and assistance of the authorities, in order to obtain the concession of an insulated tract of land suitable to the execution of his undertaking, giving you the assurance that, in case the government was to send troops in this upper part of Louisiana, he would furnish the rations of meat in a way to be relied upon, and at a lower price than anybody else. Therefore, he has the honor to supplicate you to have the goodness to condescend to grant him, in a vacant part of the domain, at his choice, a league (square) of land in superficie, or 7,056 arpens; considering that this same quantity has always been granted, without difficulty, in the posts of Opelousas and Atacapas, to all those who had the means to establish stock farms, and it being well known to you that I can comply with all that is required in such a case; that the Illinois are as susceptible to have such establishments as any other post in this province; the petitioner has the honor to hope that you will be pleased to do justice to the demand of a faithful subject, who is grateful for the bounties which have been heaped upon him, in a country, in the bosom of which he has forgotten his past adversities and misfortunes.

P. DETCHMENDY.

ST. LOUIS, *December 27, 1799.*

ST. LOUIS OF ILLINOIS, *December 28, 1799.*

Whereas, we are assured that the petitioner possesses sufficient means to improve the land which he solicits, I do grant to him and his heirs the land he solicits, provided it is not prejudicial to anybody; and the surveyor, Don Antonio Soulard, shall put the party interested in possession of the quantity of land he asks, in the place designated; and that being executed, he shall make out a plat of his survey, delivering the same to said party with his certificate, in order that it shall serve to him to obtain the concession and title, in form, from the intendant general, to whom alone belongs, by royal order, the distributing and granting all classes of lands of the royal domain.

CARLOS DEHAULT DELASSUS.

Registered at the request of the party interested, in book No. 2, folios 11 and 12.

SOULARD.

Truly translated, St. Louis, February 22, 1834, from book D, page 109, of record in the recorder's office.

JULIUS DE MUN, *T. B. C.*

| No. | Name of original claimant. | Arpens | Nature and date of claim. | By whom granted. | By whom surveyed, date, and situation. |
|-----|---------------------------|--------|---------------------------|------------------|----------------------------------------|
| 309 | P. Detchmendy. | 7,056 | Concession, 28th December, 1799. | C Dehault Delassus. | Unlocated. |

EVIDENCE WITH REFERENCE TO MINUTES AND RECORDS.

*November* 14, 1811.—Board met. Present: John B. C. Lucas, Clement B. Penrose, and Frederick Bates, commissioners.

William Morrison, assignee of Paschal Detchmendy, claiming 7,056 arpens of land, district of St. Genevieve. Produces records of concession from Charles D. Delassus, L. G., dated 28th December, 1799; a transfer from Detchmendy to claimant, dated 29th December, 1806.

It is the opinion of the board that this claim ought not to be confirmed. (See No. 5, page 414.)

*December* 12, 1835.—F. R. Conway, esq., appeared, pursuant to adjournment.

Paschal Detchmendy, by his legal representatives, claiming 7,056 arpens of land. (See book D, page 109; minutes, No. 5, page 414.)

Produces an original petition to Congress; a letter of P. Detchmendy to Soulard, dated 14th February, 1804; also a letter from Thomas Maddin, deputy surveyor, to Antoine Soulard; also testimony of Soulard, taken before F. M. Guyol, justice of the peace, on the 7th day of December, 1818. On the back of Thomas Maddin's letter to Soulard, dated 14th February, 1804, is the following testimony:

Thomas Maddin, being duly sworn, as the law directs, says that the signature to the within letter is in his handwriting, and that the facts stated in said letter are just and true.

THOMAS MADDIN.

Sworn to and subscribed before me, this 11th May, 1833.

L. F. LINN, *Commissioner.*

On the 28th day of October, 1818, before me, Joseph Bogy, one of the justices of the peace of the county of St. Genevieve, in the Missouri Territory, personally appeared Thomas Maddin, esq., of the said county, who being duly sworn, according to law, deposeth and saith that, in the beginning of February, 1804, he, as deputy for Antoine Soulard, the Spanish surveyor general of the upper part of the province of Louisiana, received instructions from the said surveyor to make a survey for Mr. Paschal Detchmendy, of the said now county, then district, of St. Genevieve, of a tract of land, granted to him by the Spanish commandant, of several thousand arpens, but the exact quantity he does not now recollect; that, in company with the said Paschal Detchmendy, he, the deponent, in consequence of such orders, went to a place now called Bellevue, in the now county of Washington, in the said territory, and in the then district of St. Genevieve, for the purpose of making the said survey; that when they were there, and preparing to make the same, they were met by a number of armed men, at least ten, who, by force, and with threats of personal violence, prevented him from doing so; in consequence of which he was obliged to leave the ground, and desist from his operations. The same armed persons even following them some distance, for fear, as he then thought, and now thinks, that he and the said Detchmendy should return to survey the said tract of land. And the deponent further saith, that the said survey would then have been made, if he had not been opposed in the manner as above mentioned; and that the said survey was so attempted to be made on or about the middle of the said month of February, in the said year, and before the possession of the country was had by the United States. And lastly, the deponent saith that he does not think, nor does he now believe the said survey could at any time thereafter have been made, and that any further attempts to have done so would have been attended with the like danger of personal violence and opposition.

THOMAS MADDIN.

Sworn to and subscribed the day and year within, before me

JOSEPH BOGY, J. P.

Sworn to, and signature acknowledged before me, May 11, 1833.

L. F. LINN, *Commissioner.*

John B. Vallé, aged about 70 years, being duly sworn, as the law directs, deposeth and saith that he was well acquainted with the said Charles Dehault Delassus; that he was the lieutenant governor of the province of Upper Louisiana, in the year 1799, and this deponent further says that he was, and still is well acquainted with the said Paschal Detchmendy, the original claimant; that he was a citizen and resident in the province of Upper Louisiana before and in the year 1799, and that he has continued a citizen and resident ever since, and still is so; that, at the date of the grant aforesaid, the said Paschal Detchmendy was a man of considerable property; that he had a family and slaves; was active and enterprising, having built a mill, and improved other property in the country.

J. B. VALLÉ.

Sworn to and subscribed before me, this 27th May, 1833.

L. F. LINN, *Commissioner.*

(See book No. 6, page 378.)

*October* 8, 1834.—The board met, pursuant to adjournment. Present: F. R. Conway, J. S. Mayfield, J. H. Relfe, commissioners.

In the case of Paschal Detchmendy, claiming 7,056 arpens of land, (see book No. 6, page 378,) the following testimony was taken by James H. Relfe, commissioner:

STATE OF MISSOURI, *County of Washington:*

Personally appeared before James H. Relfe, one of the commissioners for the adjustment of private land claims in the State of Missouri, John Stewart, who deposeth and saith that, in the month of November, 1805, he was appointed deputy surveyor, under Antoine Soulard, for all operations to be made in the settlement of Bellevue, which appointment and instructions from James Wilkinson, is herewith exhibited. In obedience to instructions, he called on Mr. Maddin for a report of such claims as had been surveyed by him within the district now assigned to this deponent; in reply to which, a communication was received, dated December 9, 1805, stating Mr. Bates's and Mr. Stodard's (Strother's) were the only claims surveyed by him which lay within the bounds assigned to this deponent. No application was ever made for the survey of the claim of Paschal (now Morrison's) nor does deponent recollect to have heard of the claim until after the expiration of the time allowed for the survey of the private land claims. In executing the surveys of private land claims in Bellevue, deponent made a survey for William Reed, sr., adjoining the land of Moses Bates, which has been confirmed; also a tract for William Reed, jr., adjoining the land of Edward Johnson, which is now before the board of commissioners; also a survey for Joseph Reed, sr., adjoining the land of Robert Reed, which has been confirmed; and a tract for Joseph Reed, jr., adjoining to and south of the land of Joseph Reed, sr., which is now before the board of commissioners for their action, and which will more particularly appear by reference to the plats and field notes returned by deponent to the proper office, in the months of January and February, 1806. Deponent further says, that the said William Reed, sr., William Reed, jr., Joseph Reed, sr., and Joseph Reed, jr, were four different persons, inhabiting and cultivating the four different tracts named, when the surveys were made. Deponent says he removed to Upper Louisiana from the State of Kentucky, in the year 1800, and established himself in Mine à Breton, and has continued to reside in the district of country now called Washington county, ever since. It was his practice to hunt for some distance round the mines, and he believes himself to have been one of the first Americans who discovered the valley of land now called Bellevue, and it was through his information and advice the first settlements were made by the Reeds and others, in the year 1803. For a considerable time after the commencement of the settlements around the mines, it was dangerous for families to live remote from each other, on account of the Indians, who, if they could find a small party of whites, would beat them severely, and rob them of their horses and other property. As late as the year 1808, the Osage Indians made an incursion in Bellevue, and drove off between twenty-five and thirty horses, or nearly all the work-horses in the settlement.

JOHN STEWART.

Sworn to and subscribed before me, this 25th June, 1834.

JAMES H. RELFE, *Commissioner.*

STATE OF MISSOURI, *County of Washington:*

Personally appeared before James H. Relfe, one of the commissioners, &c., John T. McNeal, who deposeth and saith that, in the year 1797, he arrived in the province of Upper Louisiana, and the following year took up his residence at Mine à Breton; that he was well acquainted with the country now called Bellevue, at the time of its settlement by the Reeds and others. At its first settlement it was called Big lick, but late in the year 1803, deponent understood an old Frenchman, of influence at the mines, gave it the name of Bellevue, which it has retained ever since. And deponent further states he never heard of the claim of Paschal, now attempted to be established by Morrison, until after the settlements and surveys of the lands of the Reeds, Bates, Strothers, and others; nor until the attempt of Mr. Maddin to survey the claim, when the settlers drove them off, and would not permit the survey to be made, to include their settlements, as the deponent understood.

JOHN McNEAL.

Sworn to and subscribed before me, this 21st day of June, 1834.

JAMES H. RELFE.

(See book No. 7, page 25.)

*Letter of Thomas Maddin to A. Soulard.*

St. Genevieve, *February* 14, 1804.

Dear Sir: I have just returned from surveying at the mines for Mr. Choteau, and the inhabitants of the old mines. The division lines between each person's share, I have not yet run, as I find it necessary to have the whole of the proprietors there at the time of the divisions being made. While in that country, I called on Mr. Auston respecting Doctor Watkins's survey, who seemed to find it not consistent with the interest of the Doctor to lay it on that place, nor does not seem to have any other place in view. I told him there was but eight hundred acres surveyed there; should you want it surveyed there, let me know your intentions respecting it, and will have it done as soon as possible; if not, let me know if the land may be surveyed for others. From the mines I went with Mr. Paschal to survey his concession at Bellevue. On my arrival at Wm. Reed's, I found several armed men there, who, without any provocation, behaved very insolent, and declared themselves and country entirely out of the possession of the Spanish government, and that if I surveyed any land within nine miles of that place, they would break, kill, and slay all before them. I have been many times in the course of the night apprehensive for Mr. Paschal, myself, and compass. I hope you will not think that I tell you through any enmity that I think Mr. Auston is at the head of this business, as he called Thomas Rush out of my company, who says that at that time Mr. Auston proposed to him to join the company at Bellevue; that now was the time for him to save his land, and if they could keep the land from being surveyed, he would engage him his land, with other circumstances too tedious to mention. The French people here in general are very much displeased at the rebellious and ungenerous proceedings of those people, who, I think, if ordered, will be willing to assist in bringing them to punishment, the which, if Mr. Lasource does not order, I do not expect we will be able to survey much more. It seems hard to see this rebellious crew have their intentions fulfilled in that manner, and go unpunished, and am, dear sir, with compliments to Madam Soulard,

Your humble servant,    THOMAS MADDIN.

I have made my complaint to Mr. Vallé, who sends it to the governor.

Mr. Anthony Soulard.

St. Louis, *June* 17, 1835.—The above letter is truly copied from the original filed in this office.

JULIUS DE MUN, *T. B. C.*

*June* 17, 1835.—The board met, pursuant to adjournment. Present: F. R. Conway, J. H. Relfe, commissioners.

Paschal Detchmendy, claiming 7,056 arpens of land. (See book No. 6, page 378.)

The board are of opinion that this claim ought to be confirmed to the said Paschal Detchmendy, or to his legal representatives, according to the concession. (See book No. 7, page 189.)

JAMES H. RELFE,
F. R. CONWAY.

I have examined the transcript of the above claim, and concur in the decision.

F. H. MARTIN.

---

No. 310.—*Baptiste Aumure, claiming 240 arpens.*

To Don Francis Valle, *Captain of Militia, and Civil and Military Commandant of the post at St. Genevieve of Illinois:*

Sir: The undersigned has the honor to represent to you that he wishes to establish a plantation; therefore he humbly prays that you will condescend to grant to him a concession of six arpens in front by forty in depth, on the right bank of the south fork of river Lafourche. In so doing, petitioner shall never cease to pray for the preservation of your days.

his
BAPTISTE × AUMURE.
mark.

St. Genevieve, *June* 22, 1797.

St. Louis, *November* 13, 1797.

The surveyor of this jurisdiction, Don Antoine Soulard, shall put Mr. Baptiste Aumure in possession of the land demanded in the foregoing petition, and afterward he shall make out a plat and certificate of his survey, the whole to be remitted to us, in order to have it forwarded to the commander-in-chief of the province, for him to determine definitively upon the concession of the said land.

ZENON TRUDEAU.

St. Louis, *August* 19, 1834. Truly translated from the original.

JULIUS DE MUN, *T. B. C.*

| No. | Name of original claimant. | Arpens. | Nature and date of claim. | By whom granted. | By whom surveyed, date, and situation. |
|---|---|---|---|---|---|
| 310 | Baptiste Aumure, alias Taumure. | 240 | Concession, 13th November, 1797. | Zenon Trudeau. | |

### EVIDENCE WITH REFERENCE TO MINUTES AND RECORDS.

*December* 10, 1811.—Board met. Present: John B. C. Lucas, Clement B. Penrose, and Frederick Bates, commissioners.

Baptiste Taumure, claiming six by forty arpens of land, situate on the river Lafourche, district of St. Genevieve; produces record of a concession from Zenon Trudeau, L. G., dated 13th November, 1797.

It is the opinion of the board that this claim ought not to be confirmed. (See book No. 5, page 507.)

*April* 8, 1834.—F. R. Conway, esq., appeared, pursuant to adjournment.

Baptiste Aumure, alias Taumure, by his heirs and legal representatives, claiming 240 arpens of land, situate on the south fork of the river Lafourche, county of St. Genevieve. (See book No. 5, page 507; book D, page 42.)

Produces a paper purporting to be an original concession from Zenon Trudeau, dated November 13, 1797.

Bernard Pratte, aged about 60 years, being duly sworn, deposes and says that he was personally acquainted with the original grantee, Baptiste Aumure or Taumure; that he was a citizen of, and resident in, the province of Upper Louisiana, at the date of the grant in the year 1797. Witness was also well acquainted with Zenon Trudeau, and knows that he was lieutenant governor of the province of Upper Louisiana, in the year 1797. And witness further knows the handwriting of said Zenon Trudeau, from having seen him write, and knows that the name and signature of the said Zenon Trudeau to the original concession or order of survey, is the proper name and signature, and in the proper handwriting of the said Zenon Trudeau. (See book No. 6, page 514.)

*June* 17, 1835.—The board met, pursuant to adjournment. Present: F. R. Conway, J. H. Relfe, commissioners.

Baptist Aumure or Taumure, claiming 240 arpens of land. (See book No 6, page 514.)

The board are of opinion that this claim ought to be confirmed to the said Baptiste Aumure or Taumure, or to his legal representatives, according to the concession. (See book No. 7, page 190.)

JAMES H. RELFE,
F. R. CONWAY.

I have examined the transcript of the above claim, and concur in the decision.

F. H. MARTIN.

---

No. 311.—*Priscilla Estep, claiming* 800 *arpens.*

| No. | Name of original claimant. | Arpens. | Nature and date of claim. | By whom granted. | By whom surveyed, date, and situation. |
|---|---|---|---|---|---|
| 311 | Priscilla Estep. | 800 | Settlement right. | | |

### EVIDENCE WITH REFERENCE TO MINUTES AND RECORDS.

*December* 29, 1812.—Priscilla Estep, claiming 800 arpens of land, county of St. Louis, on S. E. side of Big river. Produces notice.

John Wideman, duly sworn, says that he saw claimant at work on this tract in 1802; the year after, saw flax growing on same piece of ground. She lived on this tract in the year 1804; witness saw growing on it in that year. In the year 1803, she had a child certainly, perhaps in 1802. Saw no camp or cabin in 1802. (See recorder's (Bates's) minutes, page 33.)

*March* 18, 1834.—F. R. Conway, esq., appeared, pursuant to adjournment.

Priscilla Estep, by her legal representatives, claiming 800 arpens of land, situated S. E. side of Big river. (See record-book E, page 356; Bates's minutes, page 33; Bates's decisions, page 30.)

John Stewart, being duly sworn, says that he is in the 73d year of his age; that in the year 1803, he saw claimant living on the land claimed; she had then a cabin and cotton-patch, and some gardening in vegetation; that she came to the country at the same time with her father, James Rogers; that he, witness, first saw them in this country in the year 1801. Witness further says, that he carried cotton to her to spin; that she was an industrious woman, and that she lived and died in the neighborhood of witness. (See book No. 6, page 509.)

*July* 5, 1834.—F. R. Conway, esq., appeared, pursuant to adjournment.

In the case of Priscilla Estep, claiming 800 arpens of land. (See book No. 6, page 509.)

Samuel Harrington, duly sworn, says that the said Priscilla Estep did arrive in this country with her husband, in the year 1801 or 1802, in company with five or six families; that witness afterward saw the said Priscilla Estep several times, and knows she lived on Big river, but never saw her improvement; that said Priscilla had two children, and that she was an industrious, hard-working woman; that about three years after their arrival, her husband abandoned and left her, and went down the Mississippi. (See book No. 6, page 542.)

*June* 17, 1835.—The board met, pursuant to adjournment. Present: F. R. Conway, J. H. Relfe, commissioners.

Priscilla Estep, claiming 800 arpens of land. (See book No. 6, page 509.)

The board are of opinion that 640 acres of land ought to be granted to the said Priscilla Estep, or to her legal representatives, according to possession. (See book No. 7, page 190.)

JAMES H. RELFE,
F. R. CONWAY.

I have examined the transcript of the above claim, and concur in the decision.

F. H. MARTIN.

---

No. 312.—*Adrien Langlois, claiming* 1,500 *arpens.*

To Don CARLOS DEHAULT DELASSUS, *Lieutenant Governor of Upper Louisiana, &c.:*

ST. GENEVIEVE, *October* 4, 1799.

SIR: Adrien Langlois has the honor to represent to you that, having emigrated, at the solicitation of Mr. Lassus de Luziere, to this Upper Louisiana, where he has resided a long time with Mr. Lorimier, and with Mr.

Peyroux; and having acquired by his labor and industry a great number of cattle, and sufficient property to establish a farm, he wishes to settle himself in this country; therefore he has recourse to the goodness of this government, praying that you will be pleased to grant to him a tract of land of 1,500 arpens in superficie, to be taken on the Flintstone hill, district of New Bourbon, between the plantation of Mr. Israel Dodge and that of Mr. Lassus de Luziere; favor which the petitioner presumes to expect of your justice.

                                                                                        LANGLOIS.

We, the undersigned, civil and military commandant of the post and district of New Bourbon, do certify to the lieutenant governor of Upper Louisiana, that the statement made in the above petition is sincere, exact, and. true. We do particularly attest, as it is asserted by the petitioner that he has been induced by us to emigrate from the United States, and to come to settle in Illinois; and that he has well and honestly conducted himself when he was living with Messrs. Lorimier and Peyroux, as well as with Mr. Menard, whose affairs he has yet the management of, on this side; that he is married, and owns a great many cattle, and with his means he is well able to improve the concession he solicits, which evidently belongs to the King's domain.

Done in New Bourbon, October 7, 1799.

                                                                    P'RE DELASSUS DE LUZIERE.

                                                ST. LOUIS OF ILLINOIS, *October* 24, 1799.

In consequence of the information given by the captain of the post of New Bourbon, Don Pr. Lassus de Luziere, by which it appears to me that the petitioner possesses sufficient means to obtain the concession which he solicits, I do grant to him and his heirs the land he solicits, provided it is not prejudicial to anybody, and the surveyor, Don Antonio Soulard, shall put .the party interested in possession of the quantity of land he asks, in the place designated, belonging to the royal domain; and this being executed, he shall make out a plat of his survey, delivering the same to said party, with his certificate, in order to serve him to obtain the concession and title in form from the intendant general, to whom alone corresponds, by royal order, the distributing and granting all classes of lands of the royal domain.

                                                                CARLOS DEHAULT DELASSUS.

                                                            ST. LOUIS, *September* 9, 1833.

Truly translated from a paper purporting to be a copy of the original concession.

                                                                JULIUS DE MUN. *T. B. C.*

| No. | Name of original claimant. | Arpens. | Nature and date of claim. | By whom granted. | By whom surveyed, date, and situation. |
|-----|----------------------------|---------|---------------------------|------------------|----------------------------------------|
| 312 | Adrien Langlois. | 1,500 | Copy of concession, October 24, 1799. | C. Dehault Delassus. | Near New Bourbon. |

EVIDENCE WITH REFERENCE TO MINUTES AND RECORDS.

*November* 25, 1811.—Board met. Present: John B. C. Lucas, Clement B. Penrose, and Frederick Bates, commissioners.

Adrien Langlois, claiming 1,500 arpens of land, district of St. Genevieve, produces a notice to the recorder. The concession stated in said notice is not found of record.

It is the opinion of the board that this claim ought not to be confirmed. (See book No. 5, page 451.)

*August* 28, 1833.—Board met, pursuant to adjournment. Present: A. G. Harrison, F. R. Conway, commissioners.

Adrien Langlois, by his heirs and legal representatives, claiming 1,500 arpens of land, situate district of St. Genevieve.

The original concession, in this case, is not produced, the same, as is stated, being lost, destroyed, or mislaid, by time and accident; but claimant produces a copy thereof, dated October 24, 1799, by Charles Dehault Delassus; also, a copy of the recommendation of Pierre Delassus de Luziere; also, a plat of survey, from the register's office, to show that the same has been reserved from sale, &c. (For notice in the recorder, see book E, page 238; No. 5, page 451.)

The following testimony was taken before L. F. Linn, esq., one of the commissioners:

STATE OF MISSOURI, *County of St. Genevieve:*

Paschal Detchmendy, aged 71 years, being duly sworn, as the law directs, deposeth and saith that he was well acquainted with Adrien Langlois; that he was a resident in this country in the year 1796, when he (the deponent) came to the country, and that he continued to reside in the country for many years before and after the country was purchased by the United States; that he never saw the original concession relied on, but that he always understood he had a grant or concession for land within a few miles of the town of St. Genevieve. And he further states, that he saw the said Langlois at work on the said land, which, he understood, had been granted to him; that there was a house and field thereon; and that the same was always claimed by him during his lifetime, and by his representatives ever since.

                                                                        P. DETCHMENDY.

Sworn to, &c., this 29th day of October, 1832.

                                                            L. F. LINN, *Commissioner.*

And also came Bartholomew St. Gemme, aged 58 years, who, being also sworn, as the law directs, deposeth and saith that he has examined the above and foregoing deposition of Paschal Detchmendy, and that he personally knows substantially the same facts.

                                                            BARTHOLOMEW ST. GEMME.

Sworn to, &c., this 29th day of October, 1832.

                                                            L. F. LINN, *Commissioner.*

(See book No. 6, page 258.)

*April 2, 1835.*—F. R. Conway, esq., appeared, pursuant to adjournment.

In the case of Adrien Langlois, claiming 1,500 arpens of land. (See book No. 6, page 258.)

Claimant produces a paper purporting to be the original concession from Carlos Dehault Delassus, dated 24th October, 1799.

M. P. Leduc, duly sworn, says the signature to the concession is in the proper handwriting of the said Carlos Dehault Delassus. (See book No 7, page 114.)

*June 17, 1835.*—The board met, pursuant to adjournment. Present: F. R. Conway, J. H. Relfe, commissioners.

Adrien Langlois, claiming 1,500 arpens of land. (See book No. 6, page 258.)

The board are of opinion that this claim ought to be confirmed to the said Adrien Langlois, or to his legal representatives, according to the concession. (See book No. 7, page 190.)

JAMES H. RELFE,
F. R. CONWAY.

I have examined the transcript of the above claim, and concur in the decision.

F. H. MARTIN.

---

### No. 313.—*Thomas Powers, claiming 650 arpens.*

To Don CARLOS DEHAULT DELASSUS, *Lieutenant Governor and Commander-in-chief of Upper Louisiana, &c. :*

ST. ANDRE, *January* 31, 1800.

Thomas Powers, a Roman Catholic, has the honor to represent that he has settled himself on this side (of the Mississippi,) on his Majesty's domain, with the permission of the government ; therefore, he supplicates you to grant him the quantity of six hundred and fifty arpens of land in superficie, said quantity being necessary to include water and timber sufficient for a farm. The petitioner having the means to improve a plantation, and having no other views but to live as a cultivator, submissive to the laws, hopes to deserve the favor he solicits of your goodness and justice.

his
THOMAS × POWERS.
mark.

ST. ANDRE, *January* 31, 1800.

Be it forwarded to the commander-in-chief, together with the information that the above statement is true, and that the petitioner deserves the favor he solicits.

SANTYAGO MACKAY.

ST. LOUIS OF ILLINOIS, *February* 9, 1800.

In consequence of the information given by the commandant of St. Andre, Don Santyago Mackay, I do grant to the petitioner the tract of land of six hundred and fifty arpens in superficie, which he solicits, provided it is not prejudicial to any person ; and the surveyor, Don Antonio Soulard, shall put the party interested in possession of the said quantity of land asked for, in the place indicated ; and this being executed, he shall make out a plat, delivering the same to said party, together with his certificate, in order to serve him to obtain the concession and title in form from the intendant general, to whom alone belong the distributing and granting all classes of lands of the royal domain.

CARLOS DEHAULT DELASSUS.

ST. LOUIS, *July* 20, 1835.

I certify the above and foregoing to be duly translated from the original filed in this office.

JULIUS DE MUN, *T. B. C.*

| No. | Name of original claimant. | Arpens. | Nature and date of claim. | By whom granted. | By whom surveyed, date, and situation. |
|---|---|---|---|---|---|
| 313 | Thomas Powers. | 650 | Concession, 9th February, 1800 | Carlos Dehault Delassus. | James Mackay, D. S., 22d February, 1806 ; received for record, 27th February, 1806, by A. Soulard, surveyor general ; district of St. Louis, on the river St. John. |

EVIDENCE WITH REFERENCE TO MINUTES AND RECORDS.

*December* 6, 1811.—Board met. Present: John B. C. Lucas, Clement B. Penrose, and Frederick Bates, commissioners.

Thomas Powers, claiming 650 arpens of land, situate on river St. John, district of St. Louis, produces a record of a petition dated 31st January, 1800, and a concession annexed to the same without date, from Delassus, L. G., for 650 arpens ; record of a plat of survey dated 22d February, 1806, certified 27th February, 1806.

It is the opinion of the board that this claim ought not to be confirmed. (See book No. 5, page 477.)

*June* 18, 1835.—The board met, pursuant to adjournment. Present: F. R. Conway, J. H. Relfe, commissioners.

Thomas Powers, by his legal representatives, claiming 650 arpens of land. (See record-book B, 266 ; minutes, book No. 5, page 477.)

Produces a paper purporting to be an original concession, (the date of which has been omitted on record,) from Charles Dehault Delassus, dated 9th February, 1800 ; a plat of survey by James Mackay, D. S., dated 22d February, 1806, and received for record by A. Soulard, surveyor general, 27th February, 1806.

M. P. Leduc, duly sworn, says that the signature to the concession is in the proper handwriting of the said Carlos Dehault Delassus, and that the signature to the plat of survey is in the proper handwriting of the said Antoine Soulard.   (See book No. 7, page 191.)

*August* 17, 1835.—The board met, pursuant to adjournment.   Present : F. R. Conway, J. H. Relfe, F. H. Martin, commissioners.

Thomas Powers, claiming 650 arpens of land.   (See book No. 7, page 191.)

The board are unanimously of opinion that this claim ought to be confirmed to the said Thomas Powers, or to his legal representatives, according to the concession and survey.   (See book No. 7, page 216.)

JAMES H. RELFE,<br>F. R. CONWAY,<br>F. H. MARTIN.

---

No. 314.—Ludwell Bacon, claiming 1,000 arpens.

To Don CARLOS DEHAULT DELASSUS, *Lieutenant Governor and Commander-in-chief of Upper Louisiana, &c. :*

Ludwell Bacon, a Roman Catholic, and father of a family, has the honor to represent that, with the permission of the government, he came over on this side of the Mississippi, where he has selected a tract of land in his Majesty's domain, in the district of St. Louis ; therefore, he supplicates you to have the goodness to grant him, at the same place, one thousand arpens of land in superficie, said quantity being necessary for the employment of his slaves and his other means.   The encouragement which this beneficent government has always given to industry, induces the petitioner to hope that you will please grant him the favor he solicits of your justice.

LUDWELL BACON.

ST. ANDRE, *December* 6, 1802.

Be it forwarded to the lieutenant-governor, together with the information that the above statement is true, and that the petitioner deserves to obtain the favor he solicits.

SANTYAGO MACKAY.

ST. ANDRE, *December* 6, 1802.

ST. LOUIS OF ILLINOIS, *December* 14, 1802.

In consequence of the information given by the commandant of St. Andre, Don Santyago Mackay, I do grant to the petitioner the tract of land of one thousand arpens in superficie, which he solicits, provided it is not prejudicial to any person ; and the surveyor, Don Antonio Soulard, shall put the party interested in possession of the said quantity of land asked for, in the place indicated ; and this being executed, he shall make out a plat, delivering the same to said party, together with his certificate, in order to serve him to obtain the concession and title in form from the intendant general, to whom alone belongs the distributing and granting all classes of lands of the royal domain.

CARLOS DEHAULT DELASSUS.

Registered, No. 7.

MACKAY.

ST. LOUIS, *July* 20, 1835.

I certify the above and foregoing to be truly translated from the original filed in this office.

JULIUS DE MUN, *T. B. C.*

| No. | Name of original claimant. | Arpens. | Nature and date of claim. | By whom granted. | By whom surveyed, date, and situation. |
|---|---|---|---|---|---|
| 314 | Ludwell Bacon. | 1,000 | Concession, 14th December, 1802. | C. Dehault Delassus. | |

EVIDENCE WITH REFERENCE TO MINUTES AND RECORDS.

*October* 18, 1811.—Board met.   Present: John B. C. Lucas, Clement B. Penrose, and Frederick Bates, commissioners.

Rufus Eaton and William Russell, assignees of Ludwell Bacon, claiming 1,000 arpens of land, situate on Big Manito creek, district of St. Charles, produce a concession from Delassus, L. G., dated 14th December, 1802 ; a transfer from Bacon to claimants, dated 27th April, 1807.

It is the opinion of the board that this claim ought not to be confirmed.   (See No. 5, page 378.)

*June* 18, 1835.—The board met, pursuant to adjournment.   Present : F. R. Conway, James H. Relfe, commissioners.

Ludwell Bacon, by his legal representatives, claiming 1,000 arpens of land.   (See record-book E, page 315 ; book No. 5, page 378 ; and Bates's decisions, page 91.)

Produces a paper purporting to be an original concession from Carlos Dehault Delassus, dated 14th December, 1802 ; a plat of survey signed William Russell, and dated August 18, 1812.

M. P. Leduc, duly sworn, says that the signature to the concession is in the proper handwriting of the said Carlos Dehault Delassus.   (See book No. 7, page 192.)

*August* 17, 1835.—The board met, pursuant to adjournment.   Present : F. R. Conway, J. H. Relfe, and F. H. Martin, commissioners.

Ludwell Bacon, claiming 1,000 arpens of land.   (See book No. 7, page 192 )

A majority of the board are of opinion that this claim ought to be confirmed to the said Ludwell Bacon, or to his legal representatives, according to the concession.   James H. Relfe, commissioner, dissenting.   (See book No. 7, page 216.)

JAMES H. RELFE,<br>
F. R. CONWAY,<br>
F. H. MARTIN.

No. 315.— *George Pursley, claiming 800 arpens.*

| No. | Name of original claimant. | Arpens. | Nature and date of claim. | By whom granted. | By whom surveyed, date, and situation. |
|---|---|---|---|---|---|
| 315 | George Pursley. | 800 | Settlement right. | | |

EVIDENCE WITH REFERENCE TO MINUTES AND RECORDS.

*October* 28, 1808.—Board met.   Present: Hon. Clement B. Penrose, and Frederick Bates.

William Russell, assignee of George Pursley, claiming 1,100 arpens of land, situate on the waters of Point Labadie creek, district of St. Louis, produces to the board a notice to the recorder, and a deed of transfer from George Pursley to claimant, dated 2d September, 1807.

Aaron Colvin sworn, says that George Pursley, seven years ago, built a cabin on the tract claimed, and commenced clearing some ground, but never finished it; he knows of nothing else being done on the land by or for him, said Pursley.

Ambrose Boles, sworn, says that George Pursley was living on the tract claimed in April, 1803, had a garden fenced in, and something growing in it, when he was driven off by the Indians.   For permission to settle, see Mackay's list.   Laid over for decision.   (See book No. 3, page 336.)

*April* 16, 1810.—Board met.   Present: John B. C. Lucas, and Frederick Bates, commissioners.

William Russell, assignee of George Pursley, claiming 1,100 arpens of land.   (See book No. 3, page 336.) The following testimony in the foregoing claim, transcribed from the rough minutes, as perpetuated by the board on the 17th January, 1810:

Peter Pritchett, duly sworn, says that Pursley inhabited and cultivated the land claimed, in the spring of 1803: that he, witness, saw vegetables growing at that time on said land; that on or about the 3d of April, same year, the Indians killed a man by the name of Ridenhour in the same settlement; that the settlement, in consequence of said Ridenhour being killed, broke up.   Witness says that George McFall, by permission of said Pursley, inhabited said land in the fall of said year; that Pursley's family, in the year 1803, consisted of his wife and four or five children.   Witness says that the inhabitants generally returned to the settlement in the fall of 1803.

It is the opinion of the board that this claim ought not to be granted.   (See book No. 4, page 323.)

*St. Louis, December* 19, 1813.—William Russell, assignee of George Pursley, claiming 800 arpens of land, said to be on the waters of Point Labadie creek, county of St. Louis, produces deed from Pursley, dated 2d of September, 1807.   (Recorded in book D, page 322.)

Thomas Gibson, duly sworn, says that George Pursley raised a house on this tract in 1802, in the fall.   In the spring of 1803 he moved on the tract and cultivated it.   In that year, 1803, this settlement was broken up by an inroad of the Indians.   A small field was in cultivation when the Indians drove him away.   McFall, when the danger ceased, went upon this tract under Pursley, by purchase or permission.   Thinks it was in the fall following, to wit, fall of 1803.   The winter succeeding the term of McFall's taking possession, said McFall inhabited the premises.

John McMickle, duly sworn, says that he was at McFall's on this tract in 1804.   Said McFall was making sugar.   At that time there was a good cabin inhabited by McFall.   There was ground clear and fenced at that time.   Said tract has been inhabited and cultivated for six years past, constantly.   (See Bates's minutes, page 83.)

*June* 18, 1835.—The board met, pursuant to adjournment.   Present: F. R. Conway, J. H. Relfe, commissioners.

George Pursley, by his legal representatives, claiming 800 arpens of land, situate on Point Labadie creek. (See record-book D, page 323, for notice of 1,100 arpens; book E, for notice for abandoning over 800 arpens; minutes, book No. 3, page 336; No. 4, page 323; Bates's minutes, page 24, where the same is "not granted." See book No. 7, page 192.)

*August* 17, 1835.—The board met, pursuant to adjournment.   Present: F. R. Conway, J. H. Relfe, F. H. Martin, commissioners.

George Pursley, claiming 800 arpens of land.   (See book No. 7, page 192.)

The board are unanimously of opinion that 640 acres of land ought to be granted to the said George Pursley, or to his legal representatives, according to possession.   (See book No. 7, page 217.)

JAMES H. RELFE,<br>
F. R. CONWAY,<br>
F. H. MARTIN.

No. 316.—*Ephraim Musick, claiming 800 arpens.*

| No. | Name of original claimant. | Arpens. | Nature and date of claim. | By whom granted. | By whom surveyed, date, and situation. |
|---|---|---|---|---|---|
| 316 | Ephraim Musick. | 800 | Settlement right. | | |

EVIDENCE WITH REFERENCE TO MINUTES AND RECORDS.

*August* 31, 1812.—Peter Jump and Ephraim Musick, contending claims.

Monday, the 21st of September next, assigned as the day of hearing. Service of a copy hereof on the adverse party ten days previously to the hearing, or publication in the Missouri Gazette for two preceding weeks, will be deemed sufficient notice. (See Bates's minutes, page 1.)

St. Louis, *September* 21, 1812.—Present: Frederick Bates, commissioner.

This being the day set for the hearing testimony in the contending claims of Peter Jump and Ephraim Musick, the said Peter Jump appeared with his witnesses.

Peter Jump, claiming 80 arpens of land on Feefee creek, in district of St. Louis, adjoining the tract purchased by said Jump from Ephraim Musick and one Campbell, by virtue of having actually inhabited and cultivated the same.

Absalom Link, duly sworn, says that it is about five or six years since claimant went on the adjoining lands, which he purchased of Ephraim Musick, and has constantly, since that time, cultivated the land claimed; raised, planted trees, apple, peach, and cherry, and built houses.

*Question by Peter Jump.* Do you know of Ephraim Musick, or any other person than claimant, having actually settled this tract?

*Answer.* I know of no other than yourself.

*Question by claimant.* Where was E. Musick actually residing when he cultivated the land claimed?

*Answer.* He lived on lands which he is understood to have purchased of Joseph Williams.

Lewis Williams, being duly sworn, says that the land claimed was cultivated in the year 1801, by E. Musick; that said land came into possession of claimant by virtue of a deed from E. Musick, given in 1807, and that claimant has had undisturbed possession thereof ever since; that he has two buildings on said tract, and said land cultivated every year since 1801 to the present day. Corn, grass, orchards, &c., are now growing; that the houses in which he first lived were on the line; some on outside. I never knew an actual settler on the place except claimant.

*Question by William Russell, for Musick, to Absalom Link.* 1st, How long since Peter Jump came to Louisiana?

*Answer.* Five or six years.

*Question 2, by Russell.* Who did the first cultivation on tract claimed?

*Answer.* Does not certainly know; but the land was in E. Musick's possession, and supposes that the first cultivation was either by him or for him.

*Question 3.* When did E. Musick first come into possession?

*Answer.* Before 1803, but how long does not know.

*Question 4.* How long since E. Musick left the possession of said tract?

*Answer.* Five or six years.

*Question 5.* Do you or do you not know that E. Musick cultivated said tract before 1803, and till 1806, every year?

*Answer.* Believes that he did cultivate every year from before 1803, till he left it, probably in 1806.

*Question 1—to Lewis Williams.*

*Answer.* Six years this fall.

*Question 2.* Same answer.

*Question 3.* Answer. In 1801.

*Question 4.* Same answer.

*Question 5.* Do you or do you not know that E. Musick cultivated said tract from 1801 till 1806, every year.

*Answer.* I believe he did, or had it cultivated.

It is the admission of the parties that E. Musick gave other lands in lieu of the lands in question. At the margin is the following: Not granted—Jump's claim not granted. (See Bates's minutes, pages 1 and 2.)

*June* 19, 1835.—The board met, pursuant to adjournment. Present: F. R. Conway, J. H. Relfe, commissioners.

Ephraim Musick, by his legal representatives, claiming 800 arpens of land, situate on the waters of Feefee's creek. (See record-book C, page 319; Bates's minutes, pages 1 and 2; Bates's decisions, page 27. See book No. 7, page —.)

*August* 17, 1835.—The board met, pursuant to adjournment. Present: F. R. Conway, J. H. Relfe, F. H. Martin, commissioners.

Ephraim Musick, claiming 800 arpens of land. (See book No. 7, page 193.)

The board are unanimously of opinion that 640 acres of land ought to be granted to the said Ephraim Musick, or to his legal representatives, according to possession. (See book No. 7, page 217.)

JAMES H. RELFE,
F. R. CONWAY,
F. H. MARTIN.

---

No. 317.— *Thomas P. Bedford, claiming 800 arpens.*

| No. | Name of original claimant. | Arpens. | Nature and date of claim. | By whom granted. | By whom surveyed, date, and situation. |
|-----|---------------------------|---------|---------------------------|------------------|----------------------------------------|
| 317 | Thomas P. Bedford. | 800 | Settlement right. | | |

EVIDENCE WITH REFERENCE TO MINUTES AND RECORDS.

St. Louis, *December* 24, 1813.—Thomas P. Bedford's representatives claiming 800 arpens, St. Genevieve, not exceeding seven miles from the town. Thomas Maddin, duly sworn, says that this tract was inhabited and cultivated by Joseph Frederick before 1800, and afterward by one named Bedford. For several years after Bedford, no person inhabited ; it was sold by the commandant to satisfy the debts of Bedford, when Girouard became the purchaser, about 1801 or 1802, since which it is believed to have remained in the possession of Girouard or his representatives. Laporte, who married the widow Girouard, has cultivated for a few of the last years.

At the margin, " Not granted." (See Bates's minutes, page 109.)

*June* 19, 1835.—The board met, pursuant to adjournment. Present : F. R. Conway, J. H. Relfe, commissioners.

Thomas P. Bedford, claiming 800 arpens of land, situate about seven miles from St. Genevieve. (See record-book E, page 335 ; Bates's minutes, page 109 ; Bates's decisions, page 35. See book No. 7, page 193.)

*August* 17, 1835.—The board met, pursuant to adjournment. Present : F. R. Conway, J. H. Relfe, F. H. Martin, commissioners.

Thomas P. Bedford, claiming 800 arpens of land. (See book No. 7, page 193.)

The board are unanimously of opinion that 640 acres of land ought to be granted to the said Thomas P. Bedford, or to his legal representatives, according to possession. (See book No. 7, page 217.)

> JAMES H. RELFE,
> F. R. CONWAY,
> F. H. MARTIN.

---

No. 318.—*Joab Line, claiming 750 arpens.*

PERMISSION.

Joab Line, formerly an inhabitant of Tennessee, United States of America, has a wife called Jeany, two children, and two young orphans, relations of his said wife ; 5 horses, 11 head of horned cattle, 9 hogs, and sundry articles of household furniture and farming utensils. He is a farmer by profession.

I, the undersigned Joab Line, certify that I am ready to take the oath of fidelity to his Catholic Majesty, and to swear that my wife is legitimate ; that the cattle and effects above mentioned do belong to us in common, and that we profess the Roman Apostolic and Catholic religion.

> JOAB LINE.

New Bourbon, *December* 1, 1800.

In consequence of the foregoing declaration, and having received the oath above mentioned, from the said Joab Line, we may receive him among the number of the inhabitants of our district, and do give him leave to establish himself about the north fork of the river St. Francis, and there to make search for a piece of vacant land belonging to the King's domain, and afterward to ask the concession of the intendant of the province, in order to make his plantation.

Done by us, commandant of New Bourbon, on the 6th of December, 1800.

> P. DELASSUS DE LUZIERE.

St. Louis, *July* 20, 1835.

Truly translated from record-book B, page 95.

> JULIUS DE MUN, *T. B. C.*

| No. | Name of original claimant. | Arpens. | Nature and date of claim. | By whom granted. | By whom surveyed, date, and situation. |
|---|---|---|---|---|---|
| 318 | Joab Line. | 750 | Settlement right. | | |

EVIDENCE WITH REFERENCE TO MINUTES AND RECORDS.

*September* 9, 1806.—Joab Line, claiming under the second section of the act, 400 arpens of land situate on the western fork of the river St. Francis, district of St. Genevieve, produces a permission to settle from Pierre D. de Luziere, dated 6th December, 1800.

Michael Hart, being duly sworn, says that claimant settled a tract of land in the spring of 1801, on the waters of river St. Francis ; that the said tract is distant about four miles from said river ; that he raised two crops on the same, to wit, in 1801 and 1802, but did not actually inhabit the same ; that in the fall of 1802, he sowed a crop which witness believes he did not gather ; that in the beginning of the winter of that year he left his house, his wife having eloped from him. Had about sixteen or seventeen arpens under fence ; that when absent he still kept on said tract his goods, furniture, and stock, and would often call to see to the same ; that he the witness was present when a survey of one Murphy, taken by virtue of a concession, took in said improvement ; that claimant objected to the same, threatening to sue him, but all without effect ; that when said survey took place, he had a crop of grain in his fields.

James Cunningham, being also duly sworn, says that he saw the above claimant in full possession of said land, in the spring of 1802 ; that he remained so until the year following, when the survey of said Murphy, by virtue of the aforesaid concession, took in all his improvement, to about three arpens ; and also, that his house was surveyed in and taken possession of. He claims no other land in his own name in the Territory, and had, on the 20th December, 1803, a wife.

The board reject this claim. (See book No. 2, page 29.)

*May* 2, 1810.—Board met. Present : John B. C. Lucas, Clement B. Penrose, and Frederick Bates, commissioners.

Joab Line, claiming 400 arpens of land. (See book No. 2, page 29.)

The board, on examining the record of this claim in book B, page 95, find the quantity claimed to be one hundred arpens. It is the opinion of the board that this claim ought not to be granted. (See book No. 4, page 344.)

St. Louis, *November* 6, 1813.—Joab Line, claiming 750 arpens of land, county of St. Genevieve, on and adjoining waters of Wolf creek.

NOTICE.—John Smith, duly sworn, says he, witness, was on this tract in spring of 1803 ; saw claimant on the premises. He had a cabin as a dwelling-house, a kitchen, &c. Witness's business there was to bring away a load of corn. which he supposes claimant had raised the year before. Saw at this time wheat growing which had been sowed the fall before ; witness also saw a good garden on the premises. At this time saw cornstalks still in the fields. Saw evidences of the cultivation of tobacco also. Also saw a nursery of fruit-trees on this tract. After-ward, during the year 1803, witness occasionally passed this improvement, and generally saw claimant inhabiting the house, and saw that the garden was cultivated, but as the fields lay in an opposite direction from the road, has no particular recollection as to them. (At the margin :) "Not granted. Claim decided by late board. Interfer-ence with Murphy." (See Bates's minutes, page 66.)

*July* 19, 1835.—The board met, pursuant to adjournment. Present : F. R. Conway. J. H. Relfe, commis-sioners.

Joab Line, claiming 750 arpens of land on Wolf creek, St. Genevieve. (See book E, page 341. For notice for 100 arpens, see book B, page 95 ; commissioners' minutes, book No. 2, page 20 ; No. 4, page 344 ; Bates's minutes, page 66 ; Bates's decisions, page 32. See book No. 7, page 193.)

*August* 18, 1835.—The board met, pursuant to adjournment. Present : F. R. Conway, J. H. Relfe, F. H. Martin, commissioners.

Joab Line, claiming 750 arpens of land. (See book No. 7, page 193.)

The board are unanimously of opinion that 750 arpens of land ought to be granted to the said Joab Line, or to his legal representatives, according to possession. (See book No. 7, page 217.)

JAMES H. RELFE,
F. R. CONWAY,
F. H. MARTIN.

No. 319.— *Walter Smoot, claiming 800 arpens.*

| No. | Name of original claimant. | Arpens. | Nature and date of claim | By whom granted. | By whom surveyed, date, and situation. |
|-----|---------------------------|---------|--------------------------|------------------|----------------------------------------|
| 319 | Walter Smoot. | 800 | Settlement right. | | |

EVIDENCE WITH REFERENCE TO MINUTES AND RECORDS.

ST. LOUIS, *December* 29, 1835.—William Russell, assignee, John Donnohue, assignee Walter Smoot, claiming 800 arpens of land, Cape Cinqhommes, in county of St. Genevieve, produces transfers not authenticated.

James McLean, duly sworn, says the first improvement was made on this tract in 1801. Witness saw it again about 15th December, 1803 ; Walter Smoot was then inhabiting premises. At this time witness also saw corn standing in a field of two or three acres. No cultivation since. Smoot is believed to have removed soon thereafter. Witness did not see this tract for four or five years thereafter, when some fences and peach-trees were remaining. (At the margin :) "Not granted." (See Bates' minutes, page 128.)

*June* 19, 1835.—The board met, pursuant to adjournment. Present : F. R. Conway, J. H. Relfe, com-missioners.

Walter Smoot, by his legal representatives, claiming 800 arpens of land, county of St. Genevieve. (See record-book F, pages 260 and 261 ; Bates's minutes, page 128 ; Bates's decisions, page 21.) (See No. 7, page 194.)

*August* 18, 1835.—The board met, pursuant to adjournment. Present : F. R. Conway, J. H. Relfe, F. H. Martin, commissioners.

Walter Smoot, claiming 800 arpens of land. (See book No. 7, page 194.)

The board are unanimously of opinion that 640 acres of land ought to be granted to the said Walter Smoot or to his legal representatives, according to possession. (See book No. 7, page 218.)

JAMES H. RELFE,
F. R. CONWAY,
F. H. MARTIN.

No. 320.—*Abraham Randall, claiming 300 arpens.*

| No. | Name of original claimant. | Arpens. | Nature and date of claim. | By whom granted. | By whom surveyed, date, and situation. |
|-----|---------------------------|---------|--------------------------|------------------|----------------------------------------|
| 320 | Abraham Randall. | 300 | Concession to 164 in-habitants, January 30, 1803. List A, No. 52. | Carlos Dehault Delassus. | 778 arpens, 29 perches, by ————. February 2, 1806. Received for rec-ord by Antonio Soulard, February 13, 1806. |

EVIDENCE WITH REFERENCE TO MINUTES AND RECORDS.

*February* 20, 1809.—Board met. Present : John B. C. Lucas, Clement B. Penrose, and Frederick Bates, commissioners.

Abraham Randall, claiming 778 arpens, 29 perches, of land, situate on Hubble and Randall's creek, district of

Cape Girardeau, produced to the board, as a special permission to settle, list A, on which claimant is No. 52 ; a plat of survey dated 2d March, 1805, and certified 13th February, 1806.

The following testimony, in the above claim, taken by Frederick Bates, commissioner, by authority from the board, at Cape Girardeau, May 30, 1808 :

Thomas Bull, duly affirmed, says that said land was first improved by the establishment of a cabin by witness' brother-in-law, who abandoned the same in two or three months as public lands.   In 1801 or 1802, Peter Bellen took possession of and lived in the said cabin for a short time, who, in 1803, left the same ; after which, claimant made a settlement in 1804, repaired the roof of the cabin and planted peach-trees, who has ever since inhabited and cultivated the premises.   About seven or eight acres now in cultivation.   Claimant has a wife and two children.

The following testimony taken as aforesaid, May 31, 1808 :

John Abernathie, duly sworn, says that when Peter Bellen left the premises, in September, 1803, he offered for sale merely his labor on this land, disclaiming all right to the soil, intending to place, or having previously placed, his head-right on or near White-water.

Medad Randall, duly sworn, says Peter Bellen left premises with an intention to keep a stock for witness. Some little time after this, claimant observed to Bellen that he wished to settle on this tract thus abandoned ; Bellen replied, that he might do so, for that he, Bellen, had no claim to it ; he was welcome.   Laid over for decision.   (See book No. 3, page 477.)

*December* 22, 1809.—Board met.   Present : John B. C. Lucas, Clement B. Penrose, and Frederick Bates, commissioners.

Abraham Randall, claiming 778 arpens, 29 perches, of land.   (See book No. 3, page 477.)

It is the opinion of the board that this claim ought not to be granted.   (See book No. 4, page 235.)

*June* 19, 1835.—The board met, pursuant to adjournment.   Present : F. R. Conway, J. H. Relfe, commissioners.

Abraham Randall, claiming, by his legal representatives, 778 arpens, 29 perches, of land, situate on Hubble and Randall's creek.   (For list A, on which claimant is No. 52 for 300 arpens, see record-book B, page 320. For survey of 778 arpens, 29 perches, see book B, page 333 ; minutes, book No. 3, page 477 ; No. 4, page 325. See book No. 7, page 194.)

*August* 18, 1835.—The board met, pursuant to adjournment.   Present : F. R. Conway, J. H. Relfe, F. H. Martin, commissioners.

Abraham Randall, claiming 300 arpens, 0 perches, of land.   (See book No. 7, page 194.)

The board are unanimously of opinion that 300 arpens of land ought to be confirmed to the said Abraham Randall, or his legal representatives, according to the concession and list A, on which claimant is No. 52, for 300 arpens.   For concession and list A, see Joseph Thompson, jr.'s claim, decision No. 202.   (See No. 7, page 218.)

                                        JAMES H. RELFE,
                                        F. R. CONWAY,
                                        F. H. MARTIN.

-------

### No. 321.—*François Lacombe, claiming 400 arpens.*

To Don ZENON TRUDEAU, *Lieutenant Governor, Captain in the stationary regiment of Louisiana, and Commander-in-chief of the western part of Illinois :*

SIR : François Lacombe, inhabitant of Carondelet, has the honor to supplicate you to condescend to grant him a concession for a tract of land of ten arpens in front by forty in depth, situated on river Aux Gravois ; the said land to be bounded on the upper side by the line of one Hugh Grim's land, and on the two other sides by the King's domain ; favor which he expects of your justice.

The petitioner will observe to you that this land has already been granted to one Macfatte, and the said Macfatte having absconded and abandoned the same, it returns to the King's domain.

                                        FRANCOIS LACOMBE.
ST. LOUIS, *November* 26, 1797.
                                        ST. LOUIS, *November* 26, 1797.

The surveyor of this jurisdiction shall put the petitioner in possession of the land he asks, provided it be vacant, and is not prejudicial to any person, in order that, after the survey is made, he may solicit the concession from the commander general.                   ZENON TRUDEAU.

                                        ST. LOUIS, *October* 7, 1803.

We, special surveyor of this Upper Louisiana, do certify that, at the time when the land of Mr. Pre. Didier was surveyed, Mr. François Lacombe had not given us any knowledge of the title he obtained by the above decree.                                   SOULARD.

                                        ST. LOUIS, *October* 8, 1803.

Having seen the above certificate, and whereas the party interested has delayed until now to have a survey made for the land granted to him by my predecessor, it cannot hereafter be surveyed, unless said party shall content himself of vacant parts of the domain, without any possibility in him to alter anything to surveys already made.

                                        CARLOS DEHAULT DELASSUS.

                                        ST. LOUIS, *July* 20, 1835.

I certify the above and foregoing to be truly translated from the original filed in this office.

                                        JULIUS DE MUN, T. B. C.

| No. | Name of original claimant. | Arpens. | Nature and date of claim. | By whom granted. | By whom surveyed, date, and situation. |
|---|---|---|---|---|---|
| 321 | François Lacombe. | 400 | Concession, November 26, 1797.  Order of survey, October 8, 1803. | Zenon Trudeau, Carlos Dehault Delassus. | |

EVIDENCE WITH REFERENCE TO MINUTES AND RECORDS.

St. Louis, *October 6, 1813.*—Charles Sanguinet, claiming 400 arpens of land as assignee of François Lacombe (on vacant lands), produces notice; also concession from Zenon Trudeau, lieutenant governor, dated November 26, 1797; copy of a deed from Lacombe to claimant, dated December 7, 1808.

Antoine Soulard, being duly sworn, says that he knows perfectly well that Zenon Trudeau, lieutenant governor, gave this concession at the time it bears date.

Gregoire Sarpy, duly sworn, says that witness, some years before the cession of this country to the United States, put his own papers generally into the hands of Antoine Soulard. When he received them afterward, the papers appertaining to this claim are supposed to have been misplaced among them, as they were for a long time mislaid, and afterward found among them (this deponent's papers.) Lacombe was an inhabitant of this county for twenty-six years. (At the margin :) "Not confirmed." (See Bates's minutes, page 61.)

*June 25, 1835.*—F. R. Conway, esq. appeared, pursuant to adjournment.

François Lacombe, by his legal representatives, claiming 400 arpens of land, situated on river Gravois. (See record-book F, page 143; Bates's minutes, page 61; Bates's decisions, page 32.)

Produces a paper purporting to be an original concession from Zenon Trudeau, dated November 26, 1797.

M. P. Leduc, duly sworn, says that the signature to the concession is in the proper handwriting of the said Zenon Trudeau. (See book No. 7, page 198.)

*August 18, 1835.*—The board met, pursuant to adjournment. Present: F. R. Conway, J. H. Relfe, F H. Martin, commissioners.

François Lacombe, claiming 400 arpens of land. (See book No. 7, page 198.)

The board are unanimously of opinion that this claim ought to be confirmed to the said François Lacombe, or to his legal representatives, according to the order of survey by Charles Dehault Delassus. (See book No. 7, page 218.)

JAMES H. RELFE,
F. R. CONWAY,
F. H. MARTIN.

---

No. 322.—*Jean Harvin, claiming 600 arpens.*

Don CHARLES DEHAULT DELASSUS, *Lieutenant Governor of Upper Louisiana:*

Sir: Jean Harvin has the honor to represent to you that, having resided since several years in this province, he would wish to make a settlement in the same; therefore he has recourse to the goodness of this government, praying that you will please grant him a tract of land of six hundred arpens in superficie, to be taken on the vacant lands on the King's domain, in the place which will appear to him most suitable to his interest. The petitioner presumes to expect this favor of your justice.

his
JEAN  ×  HARVIN.
mark.

St. Genevieve, *September 8, 1800.*

We, the undersigned, captain, civil and military commandant of the post of New Bourbon of Illinois, do certify and attest to Don Carlos Dehault Delassus, lieutenant colonel in the armies of his Catholic Majesty, and lieutenant governor of Upper Louisiana, that Mr. Harvin, who presents the foregoing petition, is worthy, under all points of view, to obtain the concession of six hundred arpens of land which he solicits, in a vacant place of the King's domain; the said Harvin having a great number of cattle, and means sufficient to settle and improve his farm, and being a very honest man and a good farmer.

Done in New Bourbon, September 12, 1800.

PRE. DELASSUS DE LUZIERE.

St. Louis of Illinois, *September 22, 1800.*

In consequence of the information given by the captain of the post of New Bourbon, Don Pedro Delassus de Luziere, by which it appears that the petitioner has more than the means necessary to obtain the concession he solicits, I do grant to him and his heirs the land he solicits, provided it is not prejudicial to any person, and the surveyor, Don Antonio Soulard, shall put the party interested in possession of the quantity (of land) he asks, in a vacant place of the royal domain; and this being executed, he shall make out a plat, delivering the same to said party, together with his certificate, in order to serve him to obtain the concession and title in form from the intendant general, to whom alone belongs, by royal order, the distributing and granting all classes of lands of the royal domain.

CARLOS DEHAULT DELASSUS.

St. Louis, *July 18, 1835.*—I certify the above and foregoing to be truly translated from the original filed in this office.

JULIUS DE MUN, *T. B. C.*

| No. | Name of original claimant. | Arpens. | Nature and date of claim. | By whom granted. | By whom surveyed, date, and situation. |
|---|---|---|---|---|---|
| 322 | Jean Harvin. | 600 | Concession, September 22, 1800. | Carlos Dehault Delassus. | |

EVIDENCE WITH REFERENCE TO MINUTES AND RECORDS.

*June* 30, 1835.—F. H. Martin, esq., appeared, pursuant to adjournment.

Jean Harvin, by his legal representatives, claiming 600 arpens of land, situate in Bois-brule bottom, district of St. Genevieve.  (See book of record E, page 226.)

Produces a paper purporting to be an original concession from Carlos Dehault Delassus, dated September 22, 1800.

M. P. Leduc, duly sworn, says that the signature to the concession is in the proper handwriting of the said Carlos Dehault Delassus.

Françoise Dany, duly sworn, says that she is upward of 59 years of age; that in the year 1803 she was on the tract claimed; that in said year she saw on said place a dwelling-house and several outbuildings, wherein said Harvin lived with his family, composed of himself, his wife, and four children; that Harvin had a field, but witness does not recollect how many arpens were then enclosed.  There was a good garden, and said Harvin had a good stock of horses and cattle.  (See book No. 7, page 200.)

*August* 18, 1835.—The board met, pursuant to adjournment.  Present: F. R. Conway, J. H. Relfe, F. H. Martin, commissioners.

Jean Harvin, claiming 600 arpens of land.  (See book No. 7, page 200.)

The board are unanimously of opinion that this claim ought to be confirmed to the said Jean Harvin, or to his legal representatives, according to the concession.  (See book No. 7, page 218.)

JAMES H. RELFE,
F. R. CONWAY,
F. H. MARTIN.

---

No. 323.—*Alexis Maurice, claiming 400 arpens.*

Don CARLOS DEHAULT DELASSUS, *Lieutenant Governor of Upper Louisiana, &c.*:

SIR: Alexis Maurice, residing in this Upper Louisiana since several years, has the honor to represent to you that he would wish to establish himself therein; therefore he has recourse to the goodness of this government, praying that you would be pleased to grant him a tract of land of four hundred arpens in superficie, to be taken on the vacant lands of his Majesty, in the place which will appear most suitable to the interest of your petitioner, who presumes to expect this favor of your justice.

his
ALEXIS × MAURICE.
mark.

ST. GENEVIEVE, *May* 5, 1800.

We, the undersigned, captain, civil and military commandant of the post and district of New Bourbon of Illinois, do certify to Don Charles Dehault Delassus, lieutenant governor of Upper Louisiana, that Mr. Alexis Maurice, who has presented the foregoing petition, is a very good man, an excellent mechanic and farmer, and worthy, under all points of view, to obtain from the government the concession of 400 arpens of land he asks for, in a vacant place of the King's domain, and that he is able, with his means and cattle, to improve the same.

Done in New Bourbon, 12th May, 1800.

PRE. DELASSUS DE LUZIERE.

ST. LOUIS OF ILLINOIS, *May* 24, 1800.

In consequence of the information given by the captain of the post of New Bourbon, Don Pedro Delassus de Luziere, and it appearing to me that the petitioner has more than the means necessary to obtain the concession he solicits, I do grant to him and his heirs the land he solicits, provided it is not prejudicial to any person, and the surveyor, Don Antonio Soulard, shall put the party interested in possession of the quantity of land he asks, in a vacant place of the royal domain; and this being executed, he shall make out a plat delivering the same to said party, together with his certificate, in order to serve him to obtain the concession and title in form from the intendant general, to whom alone belongs the distributing and granting all classes of lands of the royal domain.

CARLOS DEHAULT DELASSUS.

ST. LOUIS, *July* 18, 1835.

I certify the above and foregoing to be truly translated from the original filed in this office.

JULIUS DE MUN, *T. B. C.*

| No. | Name of original claimant. | Arpens. | Nature and date of claim. | By whom granted. | By whom surveyed, date, and situation. |
|---|---|---|---|---|---|
| 323 | Alexis Maurice. | 400 | Concession, May 24, 1800. | Carlos Dehault Delassus. | |

EVIDENCE WITH REFERENCE TO MINUTES AND RECORDS.

*November* 27, 1811.—Board met.  Present: John B. C. Lucas, Clement B. Penrose, and Frederick Bates, commissioners.

Peter Menard, assignee of Alexis Maurice, claiming 400 arpens of land, situate district of St. Genevieve, produces notice to the recorder.  It is the opinion of the board that this claim ought not to be confirmed.  (See book No. 5, page 460.)

*June 30, 1835.*—F. H. Martin, esq., appeared, pursuant to adjournment.

Alexis Maurice, claiming 400 arpens of land, situate Bois-brule, district of St. Genevieve.  (See book No. 5, page 460; record-book E, page 266.)

Produces a paper purporting to be an original concession from Carlos Dehault Delassus, dated May 24, 1800. M. P. Leduc, duly sworn, says that the signature to the concession is in the proper handwriting of the said Carlos Dehault Delassus.  (See book No. 7, page 201.)

*August 18, 1835.*—The board met, pursuant to adjournment.  Present: F. R. Conway, J. H. Relfe, and F. H. Martin, commissioners.

Alexis Maurice, claiming 400 arpens of land.  (See book No. 7, page 201.)

The board are unanimously of opinion that this claim ought to be confirmed to the said Alexis Maurice, or to his legal representatives, according to the concession.  (See book No. 7, page 218.)

JAMES H. RELFE,
F. R. CONWAY,
F. H. MARTIN.

---

No. 324.—*Joseph Belcour, claiming 400 arpens.*

Don CHARLES DEHAULT DELASSUS, *Lieutenant Governor of Upper Louisiana, &c.:*

ST. GENEVIEVE, *March 9, 1800.*

SIR : Joseph Belcour has the honor to represent to you that, having resided since several years in this country, he would wish to settle in the same, and make an establishment; therefore he has recourse to the goodness of this government, praying that you be pleased to grant him a tract of land of four hundred arpens in superficie, to be taken upon the vacant lands of the King's domain, in the place which will appear most convenient and most advantageous to the interest of your petitioner, who presumes to expect this favor of your justice.

his
JOSEPH  ×  BELCOUR.
mark.

We, the undersigned, civil and military commandant of the post of New Bourbon, of Illinois, do certify to the lieutenant governor of Upper Louisiana, that the petitioner is a perfectly honest man, a good workman, who has cattle and means sufficient to well stock and improve the farm of 400 arpens of land, for which he solicits a concession in a vacant place of the King's domain.

Done in New Bourbon, March 12, 1800.

PR. DELASSUS DE LUZIERE.

ST. LOUIS OF ILLINOIS, *March 18, 1800.*

In consequence of the information given by the captain of the post of New Bourbon, Don Pr. Delassus de Luziere, by which it appears that the petitioner has more than the means necessary to obtain the concession he solicits, I do grant to him and his heirs the land he solicits, provided it is not prejudicial to any person, and the surveyor, Don Antonio Soulard, shall put the interested in possession of the quantity of land he asks, in a vacant place of the King's domain; and this being executed, he shall make out a plat of his survey, delivering the same to the party, together with his certificate, in order to serve him to obtain the title in form from the intendant general, to whom alone belongs, by royal order, the distributing and granting all classes of lands of the royal domain.

CARLOS DEHAULT DELASSUS.

ST. LOUIS, *July 16, 1835.*

I certify the above and foregoing to be truly translated from the original.

JULIUS DE MUN, *T. B. C.*

| No. | Name of original claimant. | Arpens. | Nature and date of claim. | By whom granted. | By whom surveyed, date, and situation. |
|---|---|---|---|---|---|
| 324 | Joseph Belcour. | 400 | Concession, March 18, 1800. | Carlos Dehault Delassus. | |

EVIDENCE WITH REFERENCE TO MINUTES AND RECORDS.

*December 1, 1808.*—Board met.  Present: Hon. John B. C. Lucas, Clement B. Penrose, and Frederick Bates, commissioners.

Joseph Belcour, claiming 400 arpens of land, situate district of St. Genevieve, by concession (as is alleged in his notice) from Don Carlos Dehault Delassus, lieutenant governor, dated March 18, 1800.

Archibald Huddleston, sworn, says that about nine or ten years ago, he saw claimant working on the place claimed at two different times, near a cabin in which he saw claimant's clothes; that the said land was cultivated for the four following years.  Laid over for decision.  (See book No. 3, page 387.)

*July 12, 1810.*—Board met.  Present: John B. C. Lucas, Clement B. Penrose, and Frederick Bates, commissioners.

Joseph Belcour, claiming 400 arpens of land.  (See book No. 3, page 387.)

It is the opinion of the board that this claim ought not to be confirmed.  (See book No. 4, page 481.)

*June 30, 1835.*—F. H. Martin, esq., appeared, pursuant to adjournment.

Joseph Belcour, claiming 400 arpens of land, situate Bois-brulé, district of St. Genevieve.  (See record-book E, page 226; Commissioners' minutes, book No. 3, page 387; No. 4, page 481.)

Produces a paper purporting to be an original concession from Carlos Dehault Delassus, dated March 18, 1800.  M. P. Leduc, duly sworn, says that the signature to the concession is in the proper handwriting of the said Carlos Dehault Delassus.  (See book No. 7, page 201.)

*August* 18, 1835.—The board met, pursuant to adjournment.   Present: F. R. Conway, J. H. Relfe, F. H. Martin, commissioners.

Joseph Belcour, claiming 400 arpens of land.   (See book No. 7, page 201.)

The board are unanimously of opinion that this claim ought to be confirmed to the said Joseph Belcour, or to his legal representatives, according to the concession.   (See book No. 7, page 219.)

JAMES H. RELFE,<br>
F. R. CONWAY,<br>
F. H. MARTIN.

---

No. 325.—*Henry O'Hara, claiming* 1,000 *arpens.*

| No. | Name of original claimant. | Arpens. | Nature and date of claim. | By whom granted. | By whom surveyed, date, and situation. |
|---|---|---|---|---|---|
| 325 | Henry O'Hara. | 1,000 | Settlement right. | | |

EVIDENCE WITH REFERENCE TO MINUTES AND RECORDS.

*July* 2, 1835.—F. R. Conway, esq., appeared, pursuant to adjournment.

Henry O'Hara, by his legal representatives, claiming 1,000 arpens, situate on Grand Glaize, district of St. Louis.   (See record-book D, page 166.)

Claimant refers to commissioners' minutes, book No. 4, page 148, for testimony of Antoine Vachard, dit Lardoise, in the case of Charles Vallé, claiming 320 arpens, to wit:

*August* 2, 1809.—Board met.   Present: John B. C. Lucas, Clement B. Penrose, and Frederick Bates, commissioners.

Henry O'Hara, the heirs and representatives of, claiming 320 arpens of land, situate in Grand Glaize, district of St. Louis, as assignee of Louis Robert, who was assignee of Charles Vallé, produces, &c.

Antoine Vachard, dit Lardoise, duly sworn, says that about 22 years ago, he saw Louis Robert residing on the land claimed; that said Louis Robert built a small cabin, made a small improvement, and resided there a short time; that when Louis Robert first went on the land, there was a small cabin already built, and a small improvement, which witness understood to have been made by Charles Vallé.   Witness lived a neighbor to Henry O'Hara, who inhabited and cultivated a tract of land adjoining this claim, and also cultivated on this claim; that O'Hara was settled there before deponent went to live there as a neighbor, and said O'Hara continued to inhabit and cultivate, as before stated, all the time deponent lived there, which was about six years.   The two tracts of land were separated by a small run coming from two springs near the Mississippi.   Witness left said neigborhood about 21 years ago.   Witness, O'Hara, and other neighbors abandoned their lands because the Indians were troublesome, and killing some of them.   Says that he went to reside in said settlement about 26 years ago.   On witness being asked whether Louis Robert left the settlement at the time he, witness, went to reside there, answers that he believes he did in the following year, but the time has been so long he does not remember dates.   There were no other settlers but witness, Little Billy, and Henry O'Hara.   (See book No. 4, page 148.)

*July* 7, 1835.—F. R. Conway, esq., appeared, pursuant to adjournment.

In the case of Henry O'Hara, claiming 1,000 arpens of land.   (See book No. 7, page —.)

Baptiste Dominé, duly sworn, says, that he is 85 years of age; that during the Spanish government, under either Manuel Perez or Zenon Trudeau, witness saw the said O'Hara living on a tract of land situate between the river Joachim and the Little Rock, on the Mississippi.   Claimant had on said piece of land a dwelling-house, out-houses, a field, and a fine orchard.

Charles Vachard, duly sworn, says that he is about 63 years of age; that, during the Spanish government, he saw claimant on a piece of land situated on the Mississippi, about one mile and a half below the Joachim; that he had a large field, in which he raised corn, wheat, &c.; also had a fine orchard.   Witness's brother lived near O'Hara's improvement, and witness was often on said O'Hara's plantation; the said O'Hara had a large family, and that he was driven away from his place by the Indians.   Witness further says that he cannot state exactly how long said O'Hara remained on said land, but when witness went to reside with his brother, O'Hara had settled his place several years before, and witness remained seven or eight years with his said brother, during which time said O'Hara continued to inhabit and cultivate said place.

Pierre Chouteau, sr., duly sworn, says that, in the year 1778 or 1779, as he was coming from St. Genevieve in a boat, he was obliged, on account of the ice drifting in the Mississippi, to unload his boat, and put his goods in one Charles Vallé's house; that Henry O'Hara had a plantation adjoining that of said Vallé.   Witness knew said O'Hara for many years, having transacted business with him during the time O'Hara remained on said place, which was at least for ten consecutive years.   Witness further says that, after the attack of the Indians on the settlements, in the year 1780, all the settlers were called in by the lieutenant governor, and said O'Hara among the rest; that said Henry O'Hara, sometime afterward, sold his plantation, which was situated below the Little Rock, near the Grand Glaize.   Witness does not recollect whether it was ever cultivated afterward.   (See book No. 7, page 210.)

*August* 19, 1835.—The board met, pursuant to adjournment.   Present: F. R. Conway, J. H. Relfe, F. H. Martin, commissioners.

Henry O'Hara, claiming 1,000 arpens of land.   (See book No. 7, page 210.)

The board are unanimously of opinion that 1,000 arpens of land ought to be granted to the said O'Hara, or his legal representatives, according to possession.   (See book No. 7, page 222.)

JAMES H. RELFE,<br>
F. R. CONWAY,<br>
F. H. MARTIN.

No. 326.—*Gabriel Cerré claiming* 400 *arpens.*

To the BARON DE CARONDELET, *Governor General of Louisiana, &c.:*

Gabriel Cerré, a merchant of this town, has the honor to represent that, having, since a long time, heard it mentioned that there was a lead mine on the right bank of Marameck river, at about sixty leagues from its mouth, the petitioner made all the exertion in his power to discover the same. An American residing in this country, offered to show him the said mine for the sum of $200; for which sum he would abandon to the petitioner and his heirs all his pretensions to the said discovery. To these conditions the petitioner legally consented, and having gone on the spot to examine whether such mine existed, he actually found some indications, which determined him to pay, according to his promise, the sum agreed upon, to the said American, although it is yet uncertain that the said mine can defray the petitioner of his disbursement and the works he intends to have done, which would become absolutely onerous to him if any one was permitted to work on said place. Therefore, the supplicant humbly prays your excellency to grant him a concession for the said mine, of 20 arpens in front by 20 arpens in depth, taking for centre the said discovered mine, in order for him to work, make the necessary establishments, and maintain the number of cattle required for the working of the same; favor which he hopes to obtain of your goodness.

CERRÉ.

St. Louis, *March* 29, 1796.

I am satisfied that the lead mine above solicited belongs to his Majesty's domain, and that the granting of it is not prejudicial to any person; on the contrary, its being worked by Don Gabriel Cerré, who is industrious, and who owns a number of slaves, and employs many hired white men, will be very advantageous to our settlements.

ZENON TRUDEAU.

NEW-ORLEANS, *April* 25, 1796.

The surveyor, Don Antonio Soulard, shall locate, and put the party in possession of, the 20 arpens of land in front, by the depth of 20, including in the centre the lead mine which has been discovered, which may be worked by said party exclusively, provided it is vacant and does not cause any prejudice to the adjoining neighbors, he having to maintain the roads necessary for the public intercourse and transit. Under which considerations the operations of survey shall be made out, and remitted to me, in order to provide the interested with the corresponding title in form.

EL BARON DE CARONDELET.

NEW-ORLEANS, *April* 25, 1796.

I send back to you, with a favorable decree, the memorial of Don Gabriel Cerré, merchant and inhabitant of St. Louis, in which he solicits a concession for a lead mine discovered lately at 60 leagues from the mouth of the river Marameck, and which you sent me, together with your official letter, No. 246.

May God preserve you many years.

EL BARON DE CARONDELET.

Sr. Don ZENON TRUDEAU.

*Don Antonio Soulard, Surveyor General of Upper Louisiana:*

I do certify that, on the 25th of January, of this present year, (by virtue of the annexed decree of his excellency, the governor general of these provinces, the Baron de Carondelet, dated April 25, 1796,) I went on the land of Don Gabriel Cerré, in order to survey the same according to his demand of 400 arpens in superficie; this measurement was made in presence of the interested, by virtue of the power he gave me to that effect, with the perch of Paris, of 18 feet in length, conformably with the custom adopted in this province of Louisiana, and without regard to the variation of the needle, which is 7° 30′ E., as appears from the foregoing figurative plat. This land is situated on the left bank of the river Marameck, and at about 75 miles, more or less, from this town of St. Louis, and is bounded on the E. N. E., N. N. W., and S. S. E., by vacant lands of the royal domain, and on the W. S. W. by the left bank of the river Marameck. In testimony whereof, I do give these presents, together with the preceding figurative plat, on which are noted the dimensions, and the natural and artificial boundaries which surround said land.

ANTONIO SOULARD, *Surveyor General.*

St. Louis of Illinois, *January* 28, 1800.

St. Louis, *July* 22, 1835.

I certify the above and foregoing to be truly translated from book A, page 246, of record in the recorder's office.

JULIUS DE MUN, *T. B. C.*

| No. | Name of original claimant. | Arpens. | Nature and date of claim. | By whom granted. | By whom surveyed, date, and situation. |
|-----|---------------------------|---------|---------------------------|------------------|----------------------------------------|
| 326 | Gabriel Cerré. | 400 | Concession, April 25, 1796. | Baron de Carondelet. | Antonio Soulard, S. G. January 25, 1800; certified by same, January 28, 1800. On the left bank of the Marameck, about 75 miles from St. Louis. |

EVIDENCE WITH REFERENCE TO MINUTES AND RECORDS.

*December* 21, 1805.—The board met, agreeably to adjournment. Present: Hon. John B. C. Lucas, Clement B. Penrose, and James L. Donaldson, esquires.

In the case of James Richardson, claiming under a concession from Zenon Trudeau, for 400 arpens of land, including a lead mine, under the date of April 25, 1796, granted to one Gabriel Cerré for certain considerations therein mentioned, which said concession is confirmed to the said Gabriel Cerré by the Baron de Carondelet.

In support of his claim, the said James Richardson produced the said concession, so confirmed as aforesaid, together with a certificate of survey for said 400 arpens, dated January 28, 1800, and a bill of sale of said 400 arpens of land, under the date of October 20, 1802, executed by Anthony Soulard to the said James Richardson; an act of partition of the property of the above-named Gabriel Cerré, dated June 19, 1802, was also produced, whereby it appears the said 400 arpens of land had fallen to the portion of the said Anthony Soulard, as heir to the estate of the above-named Gabriel.

Whereupon the board confirms to the said James Richardson his said 400 arpens, as per the concession and certificate of survey aforesaid. (See commissioners' minutes, book No. 1, page 12.)

*December* 20, 1811.—Board met. Present: John B. C. Lucas, Clement B. Penrose, and Frederick Bates, commissioners.

Clement B. Penrose, commissioner, retired from the board in consequence of his having become interested in this claim since the decision of the former board.

James Richardson, claiming under Gabriel Cerré, 400 arpens of land. Produces a petition signed Gabriel Cerré, directed to Baron de Carondelet, governor general, praying for a concession for 400 arpens of land, including a mine; an information from Zenon Trudeau, L. G., dated March 29, 1796; an official letter from Baron de Carondelet to Zenon Trudeau, L. G., dated April 25, 1796; a concession from Baron de Carondelet, governor general, for the same, dated April 25, 1796; a plat of survey of the same, dated January 25, 1800, certified January 28, 1800; an extract of an act of partition of the estate of Gabriel Cerré, by which it appears that the said 400 arpens of land fell to the share of Antoine Soulard, in right of his wife, as heir of Catharine Giard, deceased, in her lifetime the wife of Gabriel Cerré.

Frederick Bates, commissioner, forbears giving an opinion. It is the opinion of John B. C. Lucas, commissioner, that this claim ought not to be confirmed. (See book No. 5, page 522.)

*July* 2, 1835.—F. R. Conway, esq., appeared, pursuant to adjournment.

Gabriel Cerré, by his legal representatives, claiming 400 arpens of land, situate on the Marameck. (See record-book A, page 246; Minutes, book No. 1, page 12; No. 5, page 522. See book No. 7, page 203.)

*August* 19, 1835.—The board met, pursuant to adjournment. Present: F. R. Conway, J. H. Relfe, and F. H. Martin, commissioners.

The board are unanimously of opinion that this claim ought to be confirmed to the said Gabriel Cerré, or to his legal representatives, according to the concession. (See book No. 7, page 222.)

JAMES H. RELFE,
F. R. CONWAY,
F. H. MARTIN.

---

No. 327.—*Robert McCay, claiming 320 arpens.*

NEW ORLEANS, *April* 27, 1802.

*Sor. Intendant General:*

Don Roberto McCay, captain of militia in the post of New Madrid, with due respect to your lordship, represents that, wishing to establish a cowpen in the district of Cape Girardeau, he hopes of your lordship's goodness, that you will condescend to grant him, in said place, one thousand arpens of land, on which he may form such an establishment; for which favor he will be forever grateful for your lordship's beneficence and justice.

ROBERTO McCAY.

Be it laid before the fiscal.

NEW ORLEANS, *April* 28, 1802.

El Sor. Don Juan Ventura Morales, principal accountant of the army, intendant per interim of the royal treasury of the provinces of Louisiana and Western Florida, has decided on the above, and put his flourish to it, (lo rubrico,) together with the assessor general.

CARLOS XIMENES.

NEW ORLEANS.

On the same day, I gave notice of the above to Don Roberto McCay, to which I certify.

XIMENES.

On the said day, I made it known to, and laid it before, the sor. fiscal of the royal treasury, to which I certify.

XIMENES.

NEW ORLEANS, *May* 5, 1802.

The fiscal of the royal treasury, after taking cognizance of the petition of the captain of militia, Don Roberto McCay, who asks a concession of one thousand arpens of land at Cape Girardeau, for the purpose of establishing a cowpen thereon, says that he is of opinion that the tribunal can notify the commandant of said district to give the said quantity of land belonging to the royal domain, provided it is not prejudicial to the surrounding neighbors, and that after the plat and corresponding certificate of survey is made out by the special surveyor of those settlements, the said documents be returned to this intendancy in order to deliver to the petitioner the title in form, conformably to what is stipulated in the regulation made on these matters.

GILBERTO LEONARD.

(Auto:) Be the decree made.

NEW ORLEANS, *May* 6, 1802.

El Sor. Don Juan Ventura Morales, principal accountant of the army, intendant *per interim* of the royal treasury of these provinces of Louisiana and Western Florida, has given his decision on the above, and put his flourish to it (lo rubrico), together with the assessor general.

CARLOS XIMENES.

NEW-ORLEANS.

On the same day, I gave notice of it to Don Roberto McCay, to which I certify.

XIMENES.

On the said day, I communicated the same to the fiscal of the royal treasury, to which I certify.

XIMENES.

Having taking congnizance of the foregoing, considering that on account of the distance, the petitioner cannot present the necessary documents, according to the regulation ; and whereas, by the same, no more than eight arpens in front, by forty in depth, ought to be granted to him, he shall be made acquainted with it, and if he is satisfied with said quantity, this decree, certified, be delivered to him, in order that, presenting the same to the sub-delegate, he shall order, after giving notice to the adjoining neighbors, the survey and plat to be made, and sent here for the purpose of making the corresponding title.

For the asesoria, ten reals.

JUAN VENTURA MORALES.
MANL. SERRANO, *Attorney.*

NEW ORLEANS, *May* 7, 1802.

El Sor. Don Juan Ventura Morales, principal accountant of the army, intendant per interim of these provinces of Louisiana and Western Florida, and sub-delegate of the superintendency general, gave his decree, and signed it in accordance with the attorney, Don Manuel Serrano, assessor general of this intendancy.

CARLOS XIMENES.

RECORDER'S OFFICE, *St. Louis, July* 26, 1835.

I certify the above and foregoing to be truly translated from the original filed in this office.

JULIUS DE MUN, *T. B. C.*

| No. | Name of original claimant. | Arpens. | Nature and date of claim. | By whom granted | By whom surveyed, date, and situation. |
|---|---|---|---|---|---|
| 327 | Robert McCay. | 320 | Order of survey, 7th May, 1802. | Juan Ventura Morales. | |

#### EVIDENCE WITH REFERENCE TO MINUTES AND RECORDS.

*December* 3, 1810.—Board met. Present : John B. C. Lucas, Clement B. Penrose, and Frederick Bates, commissioners.

Robert McCay, claiming 320 arpens of land, situate in the district of Cape Girardeau, produces to the board a concession from Juan Ventura Morales, intendant general, dated May, 1802. It is the opinion of the board that this claim ought not to be confirmed. (See book No. 5, page 17.)

*June* 24, 1835.—F. R. Conway, esq., appeared, pursuant to adjournment.

Robert McCay, by his legal representatives, claiming 320 arpens of land, in the district of Cape Girardeau. (See record-book E, page 125 ; book No. 5, page 17 ; Bates's decisions, page 10, where the same is " not confirmed.")

Produces a paper purporting to be an original order of survey, signed by Juan Ventura Morales, acting intendant, Manuel Serrano, assessor general, dated May 7, 1802.

The following testimony was taken on the 28th of May and the 15th of October, 1833, before L. F. Linn, esq., then one of the commissioners :

STATE OF MISSOURI, *County of Cape Girardeau :*

Joseph Bogy, aged about 51 years, being duly sworn, as the law directs, deposeth and saith that he was well acquainted with Juan Ventura Morales, who was intendant, per interim, in 1802, at New Orleans : that he has often seen him write, and that the signature of the said Morales to the concession or grant appended to the original petition of the said McCay, is the proper name and signature, and in the proper handwriting of the said Juan Ventura Morales. Deponent was also well acquainted with Manuel Serrano, who was the counsellor, attorney, or legal adviser, under the Spanish government, in 1802, and that the signature to the grant aforesaid is the proper name and signature, and in the proper handwriting of the said Manuel Serrano. And this deponent further says that he knew Robert McCay, the original grantee ; that he was an officer under the Spanish government, but the exact year he does not remember.

JOSEPH BOGY.

Sworn to and subscribed before me, this 28th day of May, 1833.

L. F. LINN, *Commissioner.*

John Friend, a witness, aged fifty-two years, being duly sworn, as the law directs, deposeth and saith, that he came to this country (then the province of Upper Louisiana) in the year 1799, in the fall of that year ; that he became acquainted in that year with Robert McCay, who was then a citizen and resident in New Madrid ; that said Robert McCay has, from the year 1799 to the present time, remained and continued a citizen and resident of the country, and still is so.

his
JOHN x FRIEND.
mark.

Sworn to and subscribed before me, this 15th day of October, 1833.

L. F. LINN, *Commissioner.*

(See book No. 7, page 197.)

*August* 19, 1835.—The board met, pursuant to adjournment.  Present: F. R. Conway, J. H. Relfe, F. H. Martin, commissioners.

Robert McCay, claiming 320 arpens of land.  (See book No. 7, page 197.)

The board are unanimously of opinion that 320 arpens of land ought to be confirmed to the said Robert McCay, or to his legal representatives, according to the order of survey.  (See No. 7, page 223.)

JAMES H. RELFE,
F. R. CONWAY,
F. H. MARTIN.

No. 328.—*Joseph Mottard, claiming 1,340 arpens.*

To Don CARLOS DEHAULT DELASSUS, *Colonel in the royal armies, and Lieutenant Governor of Upper Louisiana*:

ST. LOUIS, *January* 20, 1804.

Calvin Adams, an inhabitant of this town of St. Louis of Illinois, in the most legal manner, and with the respect due to you, represents that, on the 7th of November, 1800, he purchased of Mr. Patrick Lee about seven arpens of land, situated at the place called Le Cul de Sac; said tract formerly belonging to Mr. Joseph Mottard. As the said land has not been surveyed, the petitioner implores your justice that you will condescend to order the surveyor of this Upper Louisiana to survey the same, and make out a figurative plat for the satisfaction of your petitioner, who hopes to deserve this favor of you; whose life may the Almighty preserve many years.

CALVIN ADAMS.

ST. LOUIS OF ILLINOIS, *January* 20, 1804.

Be it transmitted to Don Antonio Soulard, in order that he executes the same.

DELASSUS.

ST. LOUIS, *September,* 3, 1834.—Truly translated from record-book B, page 480.

JULIUS DE MUN, *T. B. C.*

| No. | Name of original claimant. | Arpens. | Nature and date of claim. | By whom granted. | By whom surveyed, date, and situation. |
|---|---|---|---|---|---|
| 328 | Joseph Mottard. | 1,340 | Settlement right. | | James Mackay, D. S., 16th November, 1805.  Recorded by Soulard, surveyor general, 16th January, 1806.  Cul de Sac, Grande Prairie. |

EVIDENCE WITH REFERENCE TO MINUTES AND RECORDS.

*September* 9, 1806.—The board met, agreeably to adjournment.  Present: Hon. John B. C. Lucas and James L. Donaldson, esq.

Calvin Adams, assignee of Patrick Lee, who was assignee of Joseph Mottard, claiming, under the 2d section of the act, 1,340 arpens of land, situate on Mill creek, district of St. Louis, produces a survey of the same, dated 16th of November, 1805; a deed of transfer, executed before commandant, by Joseph Mottard to said Patrick Lee, dated the 7th November, 1800; and another deed of transfer, executed also before the commandant, by said Patrick Lee to claimant, dated the 22d August, 1803.

Auguste Chouteau, being duly sworn, says that the said Joseph Mottard had no family; that the said tract of land was settled about twelve years ago by one Cotard, for said Mottard; that the same was actually inhabited and cultivated until the year 1800; that it was well improved; said Mottard had on the same a house and outhouses.  The board reject this claim for want of actual inhabitation and cultivation, on the 20th day of December, 1803.  (See minutes, book No. 1, page 524.)

*October* 25, 1808.—Board met.  Present: Hon. Clement B. Penrose and Frederick Bates.

Calvin Adams, assignee of Patrick Lee, assignee of Joseph Mottard, claiming 1,340 arpens of land, situate on Mill creek, district of St. Louis.  David Musick produces a deed of conveyance from said Adams and wife to him, dated 22d January, 1808; said deed on file.  Laid over for decision.  (See No. 3, page 323.)

*June* 25, 1810.—Board met.  Present: John B. C. Lucas, Clement B. Penrose, and Frederick Bates, commissioners.

Calvin Adams, assignee of Patrick Lee, assignee of Joseph Mottard, claiming 1,340 arpens of land.  (See book No. 1, page 524; No. 3, page 323.)  It is the opinion of the board that this claim ought not to be granted.  On comparing the plats of survey, this land appears to be within the tract claimed as the common of St. Louis.  (See book No. 4, page 405.)

*July* 8, 1833.—F. L. Linn, esq, appeared, pursuant to adjournment.

Joseph Mottard, by Calvin Adams' legal representatives in the name of said Adams, and as assignee of Patrick Lee, who was assignee of Joseph Mottard, claiming 1,340 arpens of land, on Mill creek, near the city of St. Louis.  (See record-book B, page 480; Minutes, No. 1, page 524; No. 3, page 323, and No. 4, page 405.)

Produces a paper purporting to be a translation of a concession, sworn to and subscribed by Peter Provenchere.

Louis Dubreuil, being duly sworn, says that forty years ago there was, to his knowledge, people working under Mottard on said piece of land; that he, several times, wrote accounts for his father, for produce which his said father had bought from said plantation; that Mottard had there some cattle; that said place was occupied for a long time by one Cotard, under Mottard; and deponent often went on said place to see said Cotard; and that said place continued to be occupied by or under Mottard till his death, which happened a short time prior to the change of government.

Peter Chouteau, sr., duly sworn, says that 42 or 43 years ago, Joseph Mottard was cultivating said land, and had one Cotard on said place as his agent; that said land was cultivated till Mottard's death; that after his death a mulatto man lived on said place; that at Mottard's death said tract was sold, and, deponent thinks, was bought by Patrick Lee; that Mottard cultivated said land for 10 or 12 consecutive years, by himself or through him. Deponent further says that the said tract did not interfere with the commons.

Alexander Bellissime, being duly sworn, says that he has been in this country these 45 years; that when he arrived in this country, the said Mottard was inhabiting and cultivating said tract of land; that deponent often went on said place to see said Mottard, who had there an orchard bearing fine apples; and that the place continued to be cultivated by or under Mottard, till very near the time of the taking of possession of the country by the American government. (See book No. 6, page 216.)

*July* 7, 1835.—F. R. Conway, esq., appeared, pursuant to adjournment. In the case of Joseph Mottard, claiming 1,340 arpens of land. (See book No. 6, page 216.)

Pascal L. Cerré, duly sworn, says that he knew Mottard's plantation from the year 1787 to 1791, and from 1794 till the change of government; that said plantation, as cultivated by or under said Mottard, was, to his perfect knowledge, outside of the St. Louis common.

Michel Marli, duly sworn, says that he is 56 years of age; that he knew Mottard's plantation for 40 years; that the fences of the common went to Mottard's field and thence run toward Riviere des Peres, leaving said Mottard's farm onside of the said common. Witness further says that he rented said plantation for two years, from Calvin Adams; this was about 15 years ago. Witness does not know of any other improvement made in that neighborhood.

Charles Vachard, being duly sworn, says that he has known Mottard's plantation for a great many years; that he, witness, cultivated the same for two or three years; that it was outside of the common, and he can yet show where the fence of the common was laid, leaving said plantation entirely outside of said common. Witness never knew of any other improvement in that vicinity. (See book No. 7, page 213.)

*August* 20, 1835.—The board met, pursuant to adjournment. Present: F. R. Conway, J. H. Relfe, F. H. Martin, commissioners.

Joseph Mottard, claiming 1,340 arpens of land. (See book No. 6, page 217; No. 7, page 213.)

The board are unanimously of opinion that 280 arpens of land (it being the quantity ordered to be surveyed by the lieutenant governor) ought to be confirmed to the said Joseph Mottard, or to his legal representatives, according to the said order of survey. (See book No. 7, page 224.)

                                                                    JAMES H. RELFE,
                                                                    F. R. CONWAY,
                                                                    F. H. MARTIN.

No. 329.—*Curtis Morris, claiming* 746 *arpens,* 75 *perches.*

| No. | Name of original claimant. | Arpens. | Nature and date of claim. | By whom granted. | By whom surveyed, date, and situation. |
|---|---|---|---|---|---|
| 329 | Curtis Morris. | 746 75 per. | Settlement right. | | John Stewart, D. S., January 6, 1806. Received for record February 26, 1806, by A. Soulard, S. G. |

EVIDENCE WITH REFERENCE TO MINUTES AND RECORDS.

*June* 27, 1806.—The board met, agreeably to adjournment. Present: Hon. Clement B. Penrose, and James L. Donaldson, esq.

Curtis Morris, claiming, as aforesaid (under the 2d section of the act), 746 arpens, 75 perches, of land, situate in Bellevue settlement, produces a survey of the same, taken January 22, and certified February 27, 1806.

Benjamin Crow, being duly sworn, says that the claimant improved the said tract of land in the year 1804, built a house on the same, raised a crop in 1805, and had, December 20, 1803, a wife.

The board reject this claim. (See No. 1, page 376.)

*September* 1, 1810.—The board met. Present: John B. C. Lucas, Clement B. Penrose, and Frederick Bates, commissioners.

Curtis Morris, claiming 746 arpens, 75 perches, of land. (See book No. 1, page 376.) Produces to the board a certificate of permission to settle; on file.

It is the opinion of the board that this claim ought not to be granted. (See book No. 4, page 483.)

*December* 16, 1833.—F. R. Conway, esq., appeared, pursuant to adjournment.

Curtis Morris, by his legal representatives, claiming 746 arpens, 75 perches, of land, situated in Bellevue settlement. (See record-book B, page 227; Minutes, book No. 1, page 376; No. 4, page 482.)

STATE OF MISSOURI, ss:

*The State of Missouri to any two justices of the peace within and for the county of Washington, greeting:*

Know ye, that, in confidence of your prudence and fidelity, I do require, and authorize, and command you to cause to come before you, James Bear, John Swan, J. T. McNeal and Mary McNeal his wife, Joseph McMaurtry, Samuel Bridge, and Bernard Rogan, and each of them examine upon their respective corporeal oath, to be by you, or one of you, administered, touching their knowledge of anything that may relate to the cultivation, inhabitation, and claiming of the southwest quarter of section No. 18, township No. 35, in range No. 2 east of the said 5th principal meridian, by Thomas Morrow and William Inge, and of William Hinge, prior to the twelfth day of April, 1814; and also to the cultivation, inhabitation, and claiming of the said land by Curtis Morris, in order to perpetuate the remembrance of the said facts, on behalf of William Hudspeth, under Airs Hudspeth. And having reduced to writing, in the English language, or the language of the deponents, the depositions so by you taken as aforesaid, you send the same, certified by you, sealed up and directed, together with this writ, to the clerk of the circuit court of Washington county, wherein the said lands are said to be situated, with all convenient speed.

Given under my hand and seal, in Washington county, this 25th day of June, A. D. 1827.

WILL. C. CARR.  [l. s.]

COUNTY OF WASHINGTON :

Be it remembered that, in pursuance of a commission from the honorable William C. Carr, judge of the third district in the state of Missouri, directed to two justices of the peace, in the county and state aforesaid, and agreeably to an advertisement in the *Missouri Republican*, by William Hudspeth and Airs Hudspeth, we, the undersigned, William Hinkson and Andrew Goforth, two justices of the peace, in the county aforesaid, have met at the house of Andrew Goforth, esq., in the township of Bellevue, on the 9th day of October, A. D. 1827, and proceeded to take the depositions of witnesses as named in the aforesaid commission, touching their knowledge of the facts as contained in the aforesaid commission, and proceeded to take the depositions of witnesses, as follows, to wit :

James Bear, of lawful age, being produced and sworn according to law, upon his corporeal oath deposeth and saith :

*Question by A. W. Hudspeth, agent for William and Airs Hudspeth.* Did you know of Thomas Morrow and William Inge inhabiting and cultivating on the S. W. quarter section, No. 18, in township No. 35, N., range 3, E. of the 5th principal meridian ; and also at the same time a part of the S. E. quarter section No. 13, township No. 35, N., range 2, E. of the 5th principal meridian ?

*Answer by deponent.* I was knowing to Thomas Morrow settling on the S. E. quarter section, No. 13, (agreeably to the surveying,) in township 35, N., range 2, E. of the 5th principal meridian. There was a piece of ground cleared on the same, part of which improvement is included in the S. W. quarter of section No. 18, township 35, N., range 3, E. of the 5th principal meridian.

*Question by same.* In what year did Thomas Morrow settle there ?

*Answer by deponent.* As well as I recollect, it was in the fall of 1811 or 1812.

*Question by same.* Did you ever hear Thomas Morrow say that William Inge was his partner ?

*Answer by deponent.* I did.

*Question by same.* Did you know of any ground being cultivated, in 1812 or 1813, on one or both of the above-named quarter sections ?

*Answer by deponent.* Yes ; there was corn raised on the improvement that was included on both of the above-named quarter sections.

*Question by same.* Who did the labor that raised that corn ?

*Answer by deponent.* I do not know.

*Question by same.* Do you know of Jacob Mahon working for Thomas Morrow and William Inge, on said improvement, in 1812 or 1813 ?

*Answer by deponent.* I saw Jacob Mahan working with Thomas Morrow at the distillery on that place.

*Question by same.* Did you understand from Thomas Morrow or William Inge that the aforesaid improvement belonged to them ?

*Answer by deponent.* I do not recollect.

*Question by same.* Did you know who claimed and occupied the improvement in the spring of 1814 ?

*Answer by deponent.* I do not recollect.

JAMES BEAR.

Sworn and subscribed before us, on the 10th day of October, 1827, at the place and within the hours first aforesaid.

A. GOFORTH,    } *Justices of the Peace.*
WM. HINKSON, }

Joseph McMurtry, of lawful age, being produced and sworn according to law, upon his corporeal oath deposeth and saith :

*Question by A. W. Hudspeth.* In what year did Curtis Morris settle and improve the place whereon Daniel Phelps now lives ?

*Answer by deponent.* In 1805, Curtis Morris married, and the next morning he started, as he said, to fix a house where Daniel Phelps now lives, to live in ; further, I do not know whether Curtis Morris had any improvement on that place before that time or not.

*Question by same.* Did you know of Walter Crow cultivating the land now in question in 1803 or 1804 ?

*Answer by deponent.* I was there in 1803 and saw an improvement, and Walter Crow told me that he made an improvement there.

*Question by Timothy Phelps.* Do you know who claimed the place in 1804 ?

*Answer by deponent.* I do not recollect.

And further this deponent saith not.

JOSEPH McMURTRY.

Sworn to and subscribed before us, on the 10th day of October, 1827, at the place and between the hours first aforesaid.

G. GOFORTH,    } *Justices of the Peace.*
WM. HINKSON, }

Sworn to, and signature acknowledged, May 9th, 1833.

L. F. LINN, *Commissioner.*

John T. McNeal, of lawful age, being produced, and after being duly sworn according to law, upon his corporeal oath deposeth and saith :

*Question by A. W. Hudspeth.* Do you know when Curtis Morris first settled on, and inhabited and cultivated the place whereon Daniel Phelps and Timothy Phelps now live ?

*Answer by deponent.* I do not know.

*Question by same.* Were you acquainted with Curtis Morris in the year 1801 ?

*Answer by deponent.* Yes, I was.

*Question by same.* Where did Curtis Morris make his home in the summer of 1804?

*Answer by deponent.* In the forepart of the summer he made his home at William Ashbrook's.

*Question by same.* Did you ever hear Curtis Morris say that he raised a crop on Ananias McCay's plantation, or in that neighborhood, in the [omission] of 1804?

*Answer by deponent.* I am not certain.

*Question by same.* How far do you think William Ashbrook lived, in the summer of 1804, from the place in question?

*Answer by deponent.* I suppose it to be about six miles.

*Question by same.* In what year and month did Curtis Morris marry?

*Answer by deponent.* Agreeably to my recollection, about the last of January, 1805.

*Question by Timothy Phelps.* When did you assist Curtis Morris to build a cabin on the place in question?

*Answer by deponent.* In February or March, 1804.

*Question by A. W. Hudspeth.* Was the cabin made ready for the reception of a family, and in what situation was the cabin prepared in 1804?

*Answer by deponent.* It was raised to the eave-bearers the day I assisted, and I do not recollect that I was on the place any more in that year.

*Question by Timothy Phelps.* Where was the place in question situated, and by whose claims was it bounded?

*Answer by deponent.* It was situated on the south side of Cedar creek, and bounded by Benjamin Strother's claim on the north, by Walter Crow's on the west, by Benjamin Crow's on the southwest, and by Bernard Ragin's on the south.

*Question by Timothy Phelps.* Did you understand by Curtis Morris that he claimed that improvement, at the time you helped him to build the cabin?

*Answer by deponent.* Yes, I did.

*Question by A. W. Hudspeth.* Did you know of Curtis Morris making any other improvement on the place in question, in the year 1804, except the part of cabin aforesaid?

*Answer by deponent.* I do not.

And furthermore this deponent saith not.                                                  JOHN T. McNEAL.

Sworn and subscribed to, before us, on the 11th day of October, at the place and between the hours first aforesaid.

A. GOFORTH,
WM. HINKSON,  } *Justices of the Peace.*

Sworn to, and signature acknowledged, May 9, 1833.

L. F. LINN, *Commissioner.*

[Here follows the certificate of the two justices of the peace, A. Goforth and William Hinkson, dated 12th October, 1827, and also the certificate of John Jones, clerk of the circuit court, and ex-officio recorder, dated 3d November, 1827.]

THE STATE OF MISSOURI, *County of Wayne:*

Deposition of witness examined on the 4th day of October, in the year of our Lord 1827, between the hours of 8 o'clock in the forenoon and 7 o'clock in the afternoon of that day, in the township of Kelly, at the dwelling-house of Joseph Pain in the county aforesaid, in pursuance of an order from the Hon. William C. Carr, judge of the third judicial district, to any two justices of the peace in the county of Wayne. Ordered, that the deposition of Jacob Mahan be taken to perpetuate the remembrance of facts on the part, and in behalf of William Hudspeth and Airs Hudspeth, relating to the improving, cultivating, and inhabiting of an improvement lying and being on the waters of Cedar creek, in Bellevue township, in the county of Washington, and State of Missouri, now claimed by the aforesaid W. Hudspeth and A. Hudspeth as a pre-emption right. And now, at this day, Jacob Mahan, of lawful age, being produced, sworn, and examined, deposeth and saith as follows:

*Question by A. Hudspeth.* Were you ever employed by Thomas Morrow and William Inge to work and improve a tract of land in Bellevue township, in the county of Washington and State of Missouri?

*Answer by Jacob Mahan.* I was employed by Thomas Morrow, and I considered Thomas Morrow and William Inge in partnership, and I was employed to work on and build a still-house on the said improvement, lying and being near the forks of Saline and Cedar creeks.

*Second question.* In what year, and how long were you employed by Thomas Morrow?

*Answer.* I began to work with him the last week in November, 1812, and continued with him five months, and assisted him in planting corn in the month of May following, in the same place.

*Question.* Did you consider Morrow and Inge in co-partnership at the time you were employed by Morrow?

*Answer.* I did, for they both frequently told me they were in co-partnership.

*Question.* Do you know who succeeded Morrow and Inge on the aforesaid improvement?

*Answer.* Yes, in the year, 1814, the third week in February, I was employed by Inge to go out and take possession of the improvement for him, and carry on the work for him, and I continued for him one month to attend the still-house, and raised a crop of corn for myself the following season, but considered the land to belong to Inge.

*Question.* Did Inge pay you for your services done in the years 1812 and 1813?

*Answer.* Yes, he agreed to pay me all, and some time afterward he paid me part, and denied the partnership, and refused to pay me the balance after Morrow left the country.

*Question.* Did you understand that Morrow intended to return to this country when he went away?

*Answer.* When I parted with Morrow he told me he would come back.

*Question.* Did you understand what became of Morrow?

*Answer.* I did not.

*Question.* Do you know if Inge and Morrow built a mill on Cedar creek?

*Answer.* Yes, in the time of my work for Morrow, a few days before my time was out, Morrow commenced building a mill on Cedar creek, and from that time till I came out to take possession for Inge, the mill was grinding.

*Question.* Do you know the section this improvement is on, or who joins it, and who occupied the improvement last, and how far was the improvement from the said mill?

*Answer.* I do not know the sectional lines, but it laid near south of Benjamin Strother's confirmation claim, and east of Daniel Phelps' claim, and east of the great road leading from Mine à Breton through Bellevue ; and when I was at the place last, I saw an old man there, who was called Hudspeth, and told me he lived there. The improvement was about twenty-five rods from the mill, on Cedar creek.

*Question by Timothy Phelps.* Since Morrow left the country, did you not frequently hear Inge deny the partnership between him and Morrow ?

*Answer.* Yes, I did.

*Question.* Did you not make a demand of upward of $100 for services rendered and corn made use of on that place, in consequence of Wm. Inge denying the partnership between him and Morrow ?

*Answer.* Yes, I did.

*Question.* Did not Morrow leave this country with the express declaration of going to the Spanish country in February, 1814 ?

*Answer.* Yes, he did.

And further, this deponent saith not. Given under my hand, this 14th day of October, in the year of our Lord 1827.

JACOB MAHAN. [L. S.]

[Here follows the certificate of the two justices, Isaac Kelly and Joseph Pain, same date as above, and also the certificate of John Jones, clerk of the circuit court, and *ex-officio* recorder, dated November 5, 1827.]

The following testimony was taken before L. F. Linn, commissioner :

Nancy Gregg, of lawful age, being first duly sworn, deposeth and saith that she was acquainted with Curtis Morris before his marriage. Curtis Morris married the sister of this deponent, and during the courtship the acquaintance with him was formed. At that time, this affiant does believe the house or place of residence of said Curtis Norris was at William Ashbrook's, and this deponent never has understood that Curtis Morris changed his place of residence until after he was married to the sister of affiant, as aforesaid. Curtis Morris, after he was married, removed to a place about two miles distant from deponent's father's place of residence, which is the same now claimed by heirs of Daniel Phelps as Curtis Morris's settlement right, situated in Bellevue township, Washington county.

NANCY GREGG.

*May 9, 1833.*                              L. F. LINN, *Commissioner.*

John T. McNeal, of lawful age, being first sworn, according to law, to give evidence in this behalf, deposeth and saith that, in the year 1811 or 1812, Thomas Morrow was in possession of an improvement in Bellevue, on the south side of Cedar creek ; it was near a mill that was owned by said Morrow ; this mill broke, and Morrow built another dam, and removed the mill upon land that was considered as public. Morrow continued in the occupancy of the said improvement until, this deponent believes, in the year 1813, when William Inge purchased out Thomas Morrow, and continued in the occupancy thereof, until Samuel Morrison purchased said mill and improvement. There was also a distillery on the improvement. This deponent knows positively that there was cultivation on said improvement, to wit, corn and potatoes, in the year 1813, and does believe that the same was inhabited as well as cultivated in the year 1812.

JOHN T. McNEAL.
L. F. LINN, *Commissioner.*

John Stuart, of lawful age, being produced and sworn, deposeth and saith that he, this affiant, was a surveyor by lawful appointment, and that, agreeably to his authority, he surveyed, in 1806, in the month of January or February, 638 acres and 56 poles of land for Curtis Morris, who then lived on the place where Timothy Phelps now lives, claimed by the heirs of Daniel Phelps and Curtis Morris ; at that time there was a small turnip-patch, or improvement like a turnip-patch, at that place, and Walter Crow and Curtis Morris agreed to divide, and did divide, the said truck-patch between them, and then Curtis Morris agreed, and made his beginning at or near the spring where the said Timothy now makes use of for family use, running north, 65 east, 2 poles ; thence north, 26 poles ; thence north, 65 east, 120 poles ; thence south, 70 east, 60 poles ; thence north, 70 east, 140 poles ; thence east, 100 poles ; thence south, 217 poles ; thence around to the beginning, agreeably to a plat hereunto annexed, bounded by Robert Reed, Bernard Rogan, Benjamin Crow, and Walter Crow. This original survey left a piece of vacant land up and down Cedar creek, situated in the southeast quarter of section No. 13 in t. 35 north, r. 2 east, on which the mill now owned by A. W. Hudspeth, and the seat that is said to be where Morrow and Inge did build a mill is situated ; and the forge seat, with a part of the improvement of the said Hudspeth, as the representative of the said Morrow and Inge, and Inge individually, is situated on the then vacant part of the southwest fractional part of section No. 18, in t. 35 N., in range 3 east of the 5th principal meridian, in the county of Washington, in Bellevue township. The strip of vacant land was about 48 poles wide ; the whole of which vacant land, original survey, will more fully appear by reference to the plat hereunto annexed. This deponent further says that he does not intend to say that the turnip-patch, above spoken of, was the only improvement on the land, for there were undoubtedly other improvements on the land, and corn had been raised on the land.

JOHN STEWART.

Sworn to and subscribed, May 14, 1833.

L. F. LINN, *Commissioner.*

(See book No. 6, page 385.)

*October* 8, 1834.—The board met, pursuant to adjournment. Present : F. R. Conway, J. S. Mayfield, J. H. Relfe, commissioners.

In the case of Curtis Morris, claiming 746 arpens, 75 perches, of land. (See book No. 6, page 385.) The following additional testimony was taken by James H. Relfe, commissioner, on the 5th July, 1834 :

STATE OF MISSOURI, *County of Washington:*

Personally appeared before James H. Relfe, one of the commissioners for the adjustment of private land claims, John Paul, who deposes and says, he is 67 years of age, or about that, and came to Mine à Breton, in the district of St. Genevieve, province of Upper Louisiana, in the year 1802, and continued to reside there until, in the month of March, in the year 1804, when he removed to Bellevue, in the same district and province. Deponent says he became acquainted with Curtis Morris in the year 1803 or 1804, in Mine à Breton, but at which period deponent is unwilling to say, but it was in the fall of the year. Said Morris resided with William Ashbrook, and continued to live with him until the end of the year 1804, and until he was married to Polly Crow, which he believes was in the latter end of the year 1804, or beginning of 1805. Witness continued to reside in Bellevue for two crop seasons, and never knew of any other Curtis Morris than the one first named, and resided about half a mile from Mr. Ashbrook's, with whom Curtis Morris resided, when he, deponent, moved to Bellevue.

JOHN PAUL.

Sworn and subscribed before me, this 5th day of July, 1834.

JAMES H. RELFE, *Commissioner.*

STATE OF MISSOURI, *County of Washington :*

Personally appeared before James H. Relfe, one of the commissioners for the adjustment of private land claims, Martha Paul, who deposes and says she is 63 years of age, and answers to the following interrogatories :

*Question* 1. Where did you reside in the year 1802 and 1803 ?

*Answer.* In Mine à Breton, district of St. Genevieve, province of Louisiana.

*Question* 2. Where did you reside in 1804?

*Answer.* In Bellevue, in the same district and province, on Big River.

*Question* 3. Did you know Curtis Morris in 1804 ?

*Answer.* I did know him ; he came to the country and resided with William Ashbrook, and, to the best of my knowledge, resided with him that summer and fall. Deponent saw said Morris working with William Ashbrook, ploughing corn in that year. Witness resided between half a mile and a mile from the residence of said Ashbrook ; and said Curtis Morris continued to reside with Ashbrook until after his marriage, to the best of her recollection, to Polly Crow, daughter of Benjamin Crow.

*Question* 4. How long did you continue to reside in Bellevue, and did you know of any other man named Curtis Morris in that neighborhood, during your residence ?

*Answer.* I resided three years in Bellevue, and never knew but the one man named Curtis Morris.

her
MARTHA  ×  PAUL.
mark.

Sworn to and subscribed before me, this 5th of July, 1834.

JAMES H. RELFE.

(See book No. 7, page 12.)

The following testimony in this case was sworn to, and signatures acknowledged, before L. F. Linn, commissioner :

STATE OF MISSOURI, *Washington county :*

Be it remembered, that on this 10th day of January, 1832, the following persons appeared before me, Henry Shurlds, a justice of the peace in and for said county :

Martin Ruggles, aged 57 years and upward, being duly sworn, deposeth and saith that he was at the place in now Washington county, commonly called and known, as he believes, as the claim of Curtis Morris, some time in the month of August or September, 1804, at which time he saw a cabin or log-house, about 12 or 14 feet square, at said place, and saw corn growing at the same time and place, supposed to be two or three acres ; the corn then appeared to be full grown ; there was no person at the cabin at the time, and it had the appearance of being inhabited, and the same has been inhabited and cultivated ever since.

MARTIN RUGGLES.

Subscribed and sworn to the day and year aforesaid.

HENRY SHURLDS, *J. P.*

Sworn to and signature acknowledged before me, this 7th day of May, 1833.

L. F. LINN, *Commissioner.*

John T. McNeal, aged 68 years and upward, being duly sworn, deposeth and saith that he assisted Curtis Morris in raising a cabin or log-house, on the claim of said Morris, in the month of February or first of March, 1804, which claim is situated in what is now called Washington county, aforesaid ; that he saw Morris living on the same, in the summer of the same year, and dined with him, he, Morris, having cooked dinner for them. There was, at the time the cabin was built, an enclosure at the same place, of an acre, perhaps, or upward, and a Mr. Reed went to the enclosure, and brought from thence some turnips, of which witness partook. He saw cornstalks, he thinks, standing in the same enclosure, but from the length of time, he cannot be entirely certain, and the place has been inhabited and cultivated ever since.

JOHN T. McNEAL.

Subscribed and sworn to by John T. McNeal, who is personally known to me, the day and year first aforesaid.

HENRY SHURLDS, *J. P.*

Sworn to, and signature of John T. McNeal acknowledged before me, this 7th day of May, 1833.

L. F. LINN, *Commissioner.*

James Johnson, aged 43 years and upward, being duly sworn, deposeth and saith that in July or August, 1804, he saw a small piece of ground cleared on the claim commonly called the claim of Curtis Morris, on which there was at the time corn growing, and he believes the same has been inhabited and cultivated ever since.

JAMES JOHNSON.

Subscribed and sworn to, the day and year first aforesaid.

HENRY SHURLDS, *J. P.*

Sworn to, and signature of James Johnson acknowledged before me, this 7th day of May, 1833.

L. F. LINN, *Commissioner.*

(See book No. 7, page 23.)

*April* 21, 1835.—The board met, pursuant to adjournment. Present : F. R. Conway, James H. Relfe, commissioners.

In the case of Curtis Morris, claiming 746 arpens, 75 perches, of land. (See book No. 6, page 385.) The following testimony was taken before James H. Relfe, commissioner :

STATE OF MISSOURI, *County of Washington :*

Personally appeared before James H. Relfe, one of the commissioners for the final adjustment of land claims in Missouri, John T. McNeal, who testifies and says, in explanation of testimony heretofore taken on the claim of Curtis Morris to land in the county aforesaid, he wishes to be understood, when having said " that Robert Reed or Mr. Reed went into the lot or field, or turnip-patch, and brought in some turnips of which he, deponent, partook," that said Reed brought the turnips from the hole where they had been put for preservation through the winter ; that the turnips had been gathered from the piece of ground in which they were buried ; and there still was to be seen at that time, viz., in February or March, 1804, turnips growing in said enclosure, which had all the appearance, and I have no hesitation in saying, had been raised from cultivation the fall previous, on the said piece of ground, and which said land has continued in the possession and cultivation of the said Curtis Morris and his representatives to this day.

JOHN T. McNEAL.

Sworn to and subscribed, this 9th of January, 1835.

JAMES H. RELFE, *Commissioner.*

(No. 7, page 131.)

*October* 23, 1834.—The board met, pursuant to adjournment. Present : F. R. Conway, J. S. Mayfield, J. H. Relfe, commissioners.

In the case of Curtis Morris, claiming 746 arpens, 75 perches, of land. (See book No. 6, page 385.) The board are of opinion that justice to the claimants requires that an order should be made to take the deposition of Walter Crow and others residing in the Territory of Arkansas, and that the party to whom said order shall be made shall give notice to the other, of the time and place of taking the same ; which said depositions shall be sealed, certified, and returned to the board, in pursuance of the law in such cases, on or before the 9th day of July next. (See book No. 7, page 46.)

STATE OF MISSOURI, *County of St. Louis :*

CITY OF ST. LOUIS, *Commissioners' office, November* 18, 1834.—In pursuance of the annexed order and resolution of the board of commissioners, bearing date the 23d of October, 1834, any two justices of the peace, within and for the county of Hempstead, in the Territory of Arkansas, are hereby commissioned and empowered to cause to come before them, at such time and place as they may think convenient, Walter Crow and others, and them examine, *de bene esse,* touching their knowledge of the cultivation, possession, and improvement of the land claimed by Daniel Phelps, assignee of Curtis Morris ; which said examination of such witnesses shall be taken upon oath or affirmation, and the same reduced to writing, and returned to this board, annexed to the above order and commission for taking the same. Given under our hands and seals, this the day and year first above written.

JAMES S. MAYFIELD,
JAMES H. RELFE,
F. R. CONWAY.

The justices who may take the testimony in pursuance of the within order, will please to forward it by mail, directed to the recorder of land titles, St. Louis, Missouri. It is required of Mr. Hudspeth or Mr. Phelps to advance the amount of charge for postage and any fees that may accrue.

JAMES H. RELFE, *Commissioner of Private Land Claims.*

*July* 2, 1835.—F. R. Conway, esq., appeared, pursuant to adjournment.
The following testimony, in Curtis Morris' claim, was received by mail :

TERRITORY OF ARKANSAS, *Hempstead County, ss. :*

Depositions of witnesses produced, sworn and examined, on the 12th day of June, 1835, between the hours of eight o'clock in the forenoon and six in the afternoon of that day, in the clerk's office, in the town of Washington, county of Hempstead, Territory of Arkansas, before Birkett D. Jett and Henry Dixon, two justices of the peace within and for the county aforesaid, in pursuance of an order of the honorable board of commissioners appointed for the final adjustment of private land claims in Missouri, passed on the 23d day of October, 1834, authorizing the claimants for the land claimed by Curtis Morris or his legal representatives, to take the deposition of Walter Crow and others, residing in the Territory of Arkansas, it appearing to us that the notice had been given to the adverse claimant, agreeably to the order of the board :

Walter Crow, of lawful age, being first duly sworn, deposeth and saith :

*Question by James McLaughlin, agent for A. W. Hudspeth.* Do you know Curtis Morris's settlement right in Bellevue, Washington county, State of Missouri ?

*Answer.* I do.

*Question by same.* When was it made ?

*Answer.* In the year 1804.

*Question by same.* When was it inhabited and cultivated by Morris ?

*Answer.* In the year 1805 he moved on it and cultivated it.

*Question by same.* Do you or do you not know, from information obtained from Curtis Morris, whether he improved and settled said place for himself or another ?

*Answer.* I heard Curtis Morris say, some time after he settled on the place aforesaid, that he settled it for himself, although it had been said he settled it for James Austin.

*Question by same.* Have you knowledge when he first claimed in his own name ?

*Answer.* I have not.

*Question by same.* When did he finish his cabin fit for the reception of his family ?

*Answer.* He removed into his cabin early in the year 1805, perhaps in the month of January or February.

*Question by same.* Did Walter Crow have an improvement in 1804, at the spring where Curtis Morris settled, and did he cultivate it in that year, hold his land by it, and take it within his lines when confirmed, and did he sell it to Daniel Phelps ?

*Answer.* He had an improvement in 1804, but did not cultivate it in that year, and did hold his land by it. When his land was confirmed, and lines run, they left out a part of his own improvement, and took in a part of said Morris's improvement. He sold a part of said land to Daniel Phelps, and that part included his original improvement.

*Question by same.* Did Curtis Morris cultivate or inhabit it before his marriage?

*Answer.* I do not know.

*Question by same.* Were you frequently at that place in the year 1804?

*Answer.* I do not recollect being on the place but once in that year, and then saw Morris there carrying on work and building a house.

*Question by same.* Did the original lines of Curtis Morris take in the improvement and mill made by Thomas Morrow and William Inge, and Jacob Mahan, for Inge, and now claimed by A. W. Hudspeth, on Cedar creek, in Bellevue, aforesaid?

*Answer.* I do not know.

*Question by same.* Where did Curtis Morris make his home in 1804?

*Answer.* I do not certainly know, but am impressed with the belief that it was with William Ashbrook, about five miles from the improvement aforesaid.

*Question by the justices.* Do you know of Curtis Morris, or any one for him, having performed any labor on the land mentioned, prior to the 20th of December, 1803?

*Answer.* I do not.

And further this deponent saith not.                                      WALTER CROW.

Subscribed and sworn to before the undersigned, two justices of the peace within and for the county of Hempstead, Arkansas Territory, at the place, and on the day, and between the hours aforesaid. Given under our hands and seals this 12th day of June, A. D., 1835.

                                      HENRY DIXON, *J. P.*
                                      BIRKETT D. JETT, *J. P.*

James L. McLaughlin, being of lawful age, and first duly sworn, deposeth and saith:

*Question.* Do you know the land settled by Curtis Morris, and now claimed by the representatives of Daniel Phelps, in Bellevue, Washington county, State of Missouri?

*Answer.* I do.

*Question.* When did said Morris first settle, inhabit, and cultivate the same; and what do you know about it?

*Answer.* In the forepart of 1804, I saw said Morris working on the aforesaid land, building a cabin, which he then raised about as high as a man's shoulders, which cabin he finished, I think, early in 1805. I frequently passed in 1804, and said unfinished cabin is all I recollect seeing until 1805. Mr. Morris married, I think, the 9th of January, 1805, and soon after removed to said cabin, and cultivated it in that year.

*Question.* Do you know of Curtis Morris, or any person for him, having performed any labor upon the land mentioned, prior to the 20th day of December, 1803?

*Answer.* I do not.

And further this deponent saith not, being no further interrogated.

                                      JAMES L. McLAUGHLIN.

Subscribed and sworn to before the undersigned, two justices of the peace within and for the county of Hempstead, Arkansas Territory, at the place, and on the day, and between the hours aforesaid.

Given under our hands and seals, this 12th day of June, A. D. 1835.

                                      HENRY DIXON, *J. P.*
                                      BIRKETT D. JETT, *J. P.*

THE UNITED STATES OF AMERICA, *Territory of Arkansas, County of Hempstead, ss.:*

I, James W. Finley, deputy clerk for Allen M. Oakley, clerk of the Hempstead county court, do hereby certify that Henry Dixon and Birkett D. Jett, whose names are affixed to the foregoing depositions, are duly commissioned, and acting justices of the peace in and for the county and territory aforesaid, and that, as such, due faith and credit is and ought to be given to all their official acts.

In testimony whereof, I have hereunto set my hand as clerk, and affixed the seal of said county, at Washington, this 12th day of June, 1835, and of the independence of the United States the 59th.

                                      JAMES W. FINLEY, *Deputy for Allen M. Oakley, Clerk.*

(See No. 7, page 203.)

*July 8, 1835.*—The board met, pursuant to adjournment. Present: F. R. Conway, J. H. Relfe, commissioners.

In the case of Curtis Morris, claiming, &c., (see book No. 6, page 385,) the following testimony was taken before James H. Relfe, commissioner:

STATE OF MISSOURI, *Washington county:*

Personally appeared before James H. Relfe, one of the commissioners for the adjustment of private land claims, Elijah Gragg, who, on his oath, deposeth and saith that, in about the year 1816 or 1817, he was conversing with Curtis Morris on the subject of his land claim in Bellevue, and asked him why he sold his land so cheap. He replied, he never thought it would be confirmed, as it was not settled in time. As well as deponent recollects, Phelps gave three hundred dollars for the claim.

                                      ELIJAH GRAGG.

Sworn to and subscribed, this 6th of July, 1835.

                                      JAMES H. RELFE, *Commissioner.*

(See book No. 7, page 215.)

*August 21, 1835.*—The board met, pursuant to adjournment. Present: F. R. Conway, J. H. Relfe, F. H. Martin, commissioners.

Curtis Morris, claiming 746 arpens and 75 perches of land. (See book No. 6, page 385; No. 7, pages 12, 26, 46, 131, 203, and 215.)

The board are unanimously of opinion that 746 arpens and 75 perches of land ought to be granted to the said Curtis Morris, or to his legal representatives, according to the survey executed by John Stewart, on the 6th of January, 1806, and recorded in book B, page 227, in the recorder's office. (See book No. 7, page 225.)

                                      F. H. MARTIN,
                                      F. R. CONWAY.

No. 330.—*John L. Pettit, claiming 640 acres.*

| No. | Name of original claimant. | Acres. | Nature and date of claim. | By whom granted. | By whom surveyed, date, and situation. |
|---|---|---|---|---|---|
| 330 | John L. Pettit. | 640 | Settlement right. | | On waters of St. Francis, county of Madison. |

EVIDENCE WITH REFERENCE TO MINUTES AND RECORDS.

*December* 30, 1833.—F. R. Conway, appeared, pursuant to adjournment.

John L. Pettit, claiming 640 acres of land, situate on the waters of St. Francis river, county of Madison. (See record-book F, page 13 ; Bates's decisions, page 97.)

STATE OF MISSOURI, *County of Madison :*

John Clements, aged about 53 years, being duly sworn as the law directs, deposeth and saith that he was well acquainted with the original claimant, who, he believes, first came to this country in the year 1801, and was sent back by his father to Kentucky to transact his business ; that the witness also knows the land claimed, and knows that the father of the said John L. Pettit, together with a negro boy of the said claimant, for the use and benefit of the said John, settled on, improved, and cultivated the said land in the years 1803 and 1804 ; there was a house built on the land, and in the year 1804, there was fenced in, cleared, and actually cultivated in corn and other things, about eight or ten acres ; the father of said John informed this witness that this building, improvement, and cultivation, was for the said John, his son, as he had sent his son back to the State of Kentucky to wind up his business there ; and that the negro boy, who was then at work, was the property of the said John. Witness also knows that the said John returned to this country and still resides here, and that the land claimed has been actually inhabited and cultivated ever since.   Witness also worked on the land and hewed house logs, and understood from the father, who was, he understood, acting as agent for the claimant, that the logs, house, and improvements, were for the use and benefit of the claimant, he being absent on business as aforesaid.

his<br>
JOHN  x  CLEMENTS.<br>
mark.

Sworn to and subscribed before me, this 22d October, 1833.

L. F. LINN, *Commissioner.*

Also came John Reaves, a witness, aged about seventy-three years, who, being also duly sworn, deposeth and saith that he was well acquainted with the original claimant ; that he came to this country, then the province of Upper Louisiana, in the year 1801 or 1802.   Witness also knows the land claimed, and knows that the same was actually settled on in the year 1803 ; there was then a house and other buildings on the land at that time, and the house, he believes, is still standing, being cedar timber ; that Benjamin Pettit, the father of claimant, lived on the land in 1803, and raised a crop thereon ; there were some eight or ten acres under fence, cleared and in actual cultivation, and the same land was still inhabited and cultivated in 1804, and further improvements made.   Witness also knows, from the information of Benjamin Pettit, the father, that this was the claim of John Pettit, and said he was laboring and fixing the place for and under John L. Pettit, his son, whom he had sent back to Kentucky to finish and wind up his business there, and that in this way they had exchanged work ; witness knows that the claim was filed for John L. Pettit in his name, by his father, for witness was present and paid the fees for recording ; that some time afterward John L. Pettit returned to this country, and has remained herein to the present time, and is still a citizen, and that the said tract of land has been from time to time inhabited and cultivated ever since, and still is.   Witness also knows that while the father was at work on the place for John, that the negro man of John was also there at work on the place.

his<br>
JOHN  x  REAVES.<br>
mark.

Sworn to and subscribed before me, this 23d October, 1833.

L. F. LINN, *Commissioner.*

(See book No. 6, page 425.)

*August* 21, 1835.—The board met, pursuant to adjournment.   Present : F. R. Conway, J. H. Relfe, F. H. Martin, commissioners.

John L. Pettit, claiming 640 acres of land.   (See book No. 6, page 425.)

The board are unanimously of opinion that 640 acres of land ought to be granted to the said John L. Pettit or to his legal representatives, according to possession.   (See book No. 7, page 225.)

JAMES H. RELFE,<br>
F. R. CONWAY,<br>
F. H. MARTIN.

---

No. 331.—*Peggy Jones, now Peggy Carter, claiming 640 acres.*

| No | Name of original claimant. | Acres. | Nature and date of claim. | By whom granted. | By whom surveyed, date, and situation. |
|---|---|---|---|---|---|
| 331 | Peggy Jones, now Peggy Carter. | 640 | Settlement right. | | |

EVIDENCE WITH REFERENCE TO MINUTES AND RECORDS.

*July* 8, 1834.—The board met, pursuant to adjournment. Present: J. H. Relfe, F. R. Conway, commissioners.

Peggy Jones, now Peggy Carter, claiming 640 acres of land, situate on Grand Glaize.

Pascal L. Cerré, duly sworn, says that when the former board of commissioners was sitting, the said Peggy Jones came to St. Louis to file her claim before said board; that he, witness, went with said claimant to give testimony in her behalf; that after she had filed her claim, witness was sworn and gave his testimony; that claimant being required to give more testimony, she went back to her settlement for witnesses, but having met with an accident, (a fall from her horse,) she was prevented from coming back for a long while; that Clement B. Penrose, one of the commissioners, meeting the witness some time afterward, asked him the reason why the said Peggy Jones had not come back with her witnesses. Deponent further says that, prior to the change of government, he was several times on the land claimed, and saw cabins, and a field under cultivation; claimant had also horses and cattle; that said Peggy Jones lived there with her husband and children; that said place lies south of Little-Rock creek, west of Samuel Wilson's tract, and bounded east by the Sulphur spring, at the distance of about twenty miles from St. Louis; that said place was much exposed to incursions of the Osage Indians. (See book No. 7, page 4.)

*August* 21, 1835.—The board met, pursuant to adjournment. Present: F. R. Conway, J. H. Relfe, F. H. Martin, commissioners.

Peggy Jones, now Peggy Carter, claiming 640 acres of land. (See book No. 7, page 4.)

The board are unanimously of opinion that 640 acres of land ought to be granted to the said Peggy Jones, now Peggy Carter, or to her legal representatives, according to possession. (See book No. 7, page 226.)

JAMES H. RELFE,<br>F. R. CONWAY,<br>F. H. MARTIN.

No. 332.—*William Janes, claiming 620 arpens, 27 perches.*

| No. | Name of original claimant. | Arpens | Nature and date of claim. | By whom granted. | By whom surveyed, date, and situation. |
|---|---|---|---|---|---|
| 332 | William Janes. | 620 27 p. | Settlement right. | | John Stewart, D. S., February 20, 1806. Received for record by A. Soulard, S. G., February 27, 1806. Bellevue settlement. |

EVIDENCE WITH REFERENCE TO MINUTES AND RECORDS.

*June* 27, 1808.—Board met, on application of a claimant. Present: the Hon. John B. C. Lucas and Clement B. Penrose.

William Janes, claiming 620 arpens, 27 perches, of land, district of St. Genevieve, Bellevue settlement, produces to the board a plat of survey, dated February 20, 1806, certified to be received for record, February 27, 1806, by Antoine Soulard.

Elisha Baker, sworn, says that in 1805, claimant had a cabin on the land, and has inhabited and cultivated the same ever since; raised a crop in 1805. Laid over for decision. (See No. 3, page 214.)

*June* 6, 1810.—Board met. Present: John B. C. Lucas, Clement B. Penrose, and Frederick Bates, commissioners.

William Janes, claiming 620 arpens, and 27 perches, of land. (See book No. 3, page 214.)

It is the opinion of the board that this claim ought not to be granted. (See No. 4, page 368.)

*May* 13, 1835.—The board met, pursuant to adjournment. Present: F. R. Conway and James H. Relfe, commissioners.

William Janes, by his legal representatives, claiming 640 acres of land in Bellevue settlement. (See record-book B, page 235; book No. 3, page 214; No. 4, page 368.)

The following testimony was taken in Washington county, by L. F. Linn, esq., in May, 1833:

STATE OF MISSOURI, *County of Washington:*

John T. McNeal, aged about 70 years, being duly sworn as the law directs, deposeth and saith that he was well acquainted with William Janes, the original claimant; that he improved the tract of land claimed in the year 1803, and continued on the same in 1804. Witness saw a cabin on said land in 1804, and in the winter of 1804 and '5, he was on the place, and saw the cornstalks standing there, which must have been the cornstalks of the crop of 1804. There were several acres under fence, and witness believes said Janes continued to live on said land till the year 1807, when he left the country.

JOHN T. McNEAL.

Sworn and subscribed, May 6, 1833.

L. F. LINN, *Commissioner.*

(See book No. 7, page 150.)

*August* 21, 1835.—The board met, pursuant to adjournment. Present: F. R. Conway, J. H. Relfe, and F. H. Martin, commissioners.

William Janes, claiming 620 arpens, and 27 perches, of land. (See book No. 7, page 150.)

The board are unanimously of opinion that 620 arpens, and 27 perches, of land, ought to be granted to the said William Janes, or to his legal representatives, according to possession and survey. (See No. 7, page 226.)

JAMES H. RELFE,
F. R. CONWAY,
F. H. MARTIN.

### No. 333.—*Alexander Colman, claiming 800 arpens.*

| No. | Name of original claimant. | Arpens. | Nature and date of claim. | By whom granted. | By whom surveyed, date, and situation. |
|---|---|---|---|---|---|
| 333 | Alexander Colman. | 800 | Settlement right. | | Old Mines. |

EVIDENCE WITH REFERENCE TO MINUTES AND RECORDS.

St. Louis, *November 28, 1812.*—Alexander Colman, claiming 800 arpens of land, old Mines, district of St. Genevieve.

Bernard Colman, duly sworn, says that said tract was inhabited and cultivated in 1803, and continually to this day. Single man in 1803. (See Bates's minutes, page 18.)

*April 10, 1835.*—F. R. Conway, esq., appeared, pursuant to adjournment.

Alexander Colman, claiming 800 arpens, at the Old Mines. (See record-book F, page 391; Bates's minutes, page 18. See No. 7, page 124.)

*August 22, 1835.*—The board met, pursuant to adjournment. Present: F. R. Conway, J. H. Relfe, and F. H. Martin, commissioners.

Alexander Colman, claiming 800 arpens of land. (See book No. 7, page 124.)

The board are unanimously of opinion that 640 acres of land ought to be granted to the said Alexander Colman, or to his legal representatives, but not to interfere with the Old Mine concessions. (See book No. 7, page 227.)

JAMES H. RELFE,
F. R. CONWAY,
F. H. MARTIN.

### No. 334.—*J. B. Vallé, claiming 20,000 arpens.*

To Don Zenon Trudeau, *Lieutenant Governor of the western part of Illinois:*

The undersigned, John Baptiste Vallé, supplicates you very humbly, and has the honor to represent that, having a numerous family, and wishing to provide for their maintenance, being owner of a prodigious number of cattle of all kinds, he desires to have lands in proportion, not only for agricultural purposes, but also for pasturage; therefore, the petitioner has recourse to your authority, sir, praying you will please grant him, in full property, a concession for twenty thousand arpens of land in superficie, to be taken in a vacant place of his Majesty's domain. This favor the petitioner hopes to receive from the generosity of the government which you represent, and he shall not cease to pray for the preservation of your precious life.

J. B. VALLÉ.

St. Genevieve, *February 15, 1797.*

Don Zenon Trudeau, *Lieutenant Governor of the western part of Illinois:*

The surveyor, Don Antonio Soulard, shall survey, in favor of the interested, the twenty thousand arpens of land in superficie, which he solicits, in the place above mentioned, and (le entregara proceso verbal de su apeo) he shall deliver to him a plat and certificate of his survey, in order that, together with this decree, it will serve him as a title for his property, until the corresponding title in form be delivered to him by the general government.

ZENON TRUDEAU.

St. Louis, *February 19, 1797.*

RECORDER'S OFFICE, *St. Louis, May 4, 1835.*

I certify the above and foregoing to be a true translation from the original filed in this office.

JULIUS DE MUN, *T. B. C.*

| No. | Name of original claimant. | Arpens. | Nature and date of claim. | By whom granted. | By whom surveyed, date, and situation. |
|---|---|---|---|---|---|
| 334 | Jean B. Vallé. | 20,000 | Concession, Feb. 19, 1797. | Zenon Trudeau. | |

EVIDENCES WITH REFERENCE TO MINUTES AND RECORDS.

*April 24, 1835.*—Board met, pursuant to adjournment. Present: F. R. Conway, James H. Relfe, commissioners.

John Baptiste Vallé, claiming 20,000 arpens of land, by virtue of a concession from Zenon Trudeau. (See record-book E, page 199.)

Produces a paper purporting to be an original concession from Zenon Trudeau, dated February 19, 1797.

The following testimony was taken by James H. Relfe, commissioner, in St. Genevieve:

Bartholomew St. Gemme, aged about sixty years, being duly sworn, deposeth and saith that he was well acquainted with Zenon Trudeau; that he was lieutenant governor of Upper Louisiana, in the year 1797, at the date of the concession. He further says that he is acquainted with the handwriting of the said Zenon Trudeau; that he has often seen him write, and that the signature to the said concession is in the proper handwriting of the said Zenon Trudeau. This witness further says that he well knows the said John B. Vallé, the claimant; that he was, long before the date of the grant, and after the date of the grant, a citizen and resident in the then province of Upper Louisiana, and that he has continued a citizen and resident ever since; and the said Vallé, at the date of the grant, was the father of a family large and numerous; that he had a large quantity of slaves, and a very large stock of horses, cattle, and other animals; that his family and connections were large and respectable; that he acted as the commandant of the post, and was held in high estimation and repute by the Spanish government.

BARTHOLOMEW ST. GEMME.

Sworn to and subscribed, April 22, 1835, before

JAMES H. RELFE, Commissioner.

(See book No. 7, page 129.)

*August* 22, 1835.—The board met, pursuant to adjournment. Present: F. R. Conway, J. H. Relfe, F. H. Martin, commissioners.

John B. Vallé, claiming 20,000 arpens of land. (See book No. 7, page 129.)

The board are unanimously of opinion that this claim ought to be confirmed to the said John B. Vallé, or to his legal representatives, according to the concession. (See book No. 7, page 227.)

JAMES H. RELFE,<br>F. R. CONWAY,<br>F. H. MARTIN.

---

No. 335.—James Brown, claiming 640 acres.

| No. | Name of original claimant. | Acres. | Nature and date of claim. | By whom granted. | By whom surveyed, date, and situation. |
|-----|----------------------------|--------|---------------------------|------------------|----------------------------------------|
| 335 | James Brown. | 640 | Settlement right. | | John Stewart, D. S., February 8, 1806. Received for record by Soulard, S. G., February 27, 1806. |

EVIDENCE WITH REFERENCE TO MINUTES AND RECORDS.

*June* 27, 1806.—The board met, agreeably to adjournment. Present: Hon. Clement B. Penrose and James L. Donaldson, esquire.

James Brown, claiming, under the second section of the act of Congress, 748 arpens, 68 perches, of land, situate in Bellevue, district of St. Genevieve, produces a survey of the same, dated the 8th, and certified 27th February, 1806.

Elisha Baker, being duly sworn, says that he, the witness, was on the said tract of land early in the year 1804; that the same was then actually inhabited, and bore the marks of its having been cultivated the year before; and, further, that it has been actually inhabited and cultivated to this day. Had, on the 20th day of December, 1803, a wife and child.

The board reject this claim. (See minutes, No. 1, page 376.)

*September* 1, 1810.—Board met. Present: John B. C. Lucas, Clement B. Penrose, and Frederick Bates, commissioners.

James Brown, claiming 748 arpens, 68 perches, of land. (See book No. 1, page 376.)

It is the opinion of the board that this claim ought not to be granted. (See book No. 4, page 482.)

*December* 7, 1833.—F. R. Conway, esq., appeared, pursuant to adjournment.

James Brown, by his heirs and legal representatives, claiming 640 acres of land in Bellevue settlement, county of Washington. (See book No. 1, page 376; No. 4, page 482; record-book B, page 349.)

STATE OF MISSOURI, *County of Washington:*

John T. McNeal, aged about 70 years, being duly sworn, as the law directs, deposeth and saith that he was well acquainted with James Brown, the original claimant; that he came to this country in 1803; that he also knows the land claimed, and that the claimant settled on it in the spring of the year 1804; that he built a house and made an improvement in 1804; and, he believes, had a garden that year, and there were several acres cleared that year; that the same James Brown continued to inhabit and cultivate the same some two or three years, and then sold to George Smurls; Smurls then took possession, and continued thereon till he sold to John Stewart, who then took the same into possession, and continued on the same till he sold to Rudolf Hoverstick, and that the said Hoverstick continued on the same till he sold to Samuel Hunter, who went on the premises, and remained thereon till he died; that said James Brown, when he settled on the place, had a wife and one child.

JOHN T. McNEAL.

Sworn to and subscribed before the commissioner, this 9th day of May, 1833.

L. F. LINN, Commissioner.

And also came John Stewart, a witness, aged 64 years, who, being duly sworn, as the law directs, deposeth and saith, that he was well acquainted with James Brown, the original claimant; that he first saw him in 1803; he had a wife and one or two children; that he first saw him on the land claimed in the fall of 1804; that he had raised a crop there in that year; he had a house on the land at the time, and some cleared land, some few acres; and, he thinks, the next year he traded off the land; then witness surveyed the land in the year 1806, made a plat of survey, and returned the same to the proper officer for record, and that the recording fees were paid.

JOHN STEWART.

Sworn to and subscribed before me, this 9th day of May, 1833.

L. F. LINN, Commissioner.

John Stewart, being further sworn, deposeth and saith that James Brown and his wife resided at Squire Boher's at the time he, James Brown, was building and making his improvement before he moved, and this was in the year 1804 that he was building and improving on the land; then Brown moved on the land in 1804.

JOHN STEWART.<br>L. F. LINN, Commissioner.

(See No. 6, page 369.)

*April 24, 1835.*—The board met, pursuant to adjournment. Present: F. R. Conway, J. H. Relfe, commissioners.

In the case of James Brown, claiming 640 acres of land, (see book No. 6, page 369,) the following testimony was taken before James H. Relfe, commissioner:

STATE OF MISSOURI, *County of Washington:*

Personally appeared before James H. Relfe, one of the commissioners for the adjustment of private land claims in Missouri, William Davis, sr., who deposeth and saith that, in the fall of the year 1809, witness, with James Brown and others, were on Black-river hunting-land, when James Brown informed witness that he, said Brown, had been employed by Joseph Bear, or Barr, to build a cabin on a tract of land in Bellevue, held by said Barr as assignee of —— Cordor, and, after having built the cabin, he moved into it, and kept possession of the land, until it was confirmed to Barr; believing he had as much right as Barr had to it, while in possession of the land, he sold the west half of the tract to one Saul Hewitt, the same which Samuel Hunter possessed at the time of his death. Deponent says he knows it to be the same land which has been confirmed to the legal representatives of —— Corder, who are now in possession of the same, one King now living in the cabin which Brown informed witness he built.

his<br>WILLIAM × DAVIS.<br>mark.

Sworn to, this 18th December, 1834.

JAMES H. RELFE, Commissioner.

(See book No. 7, page 132.)

*July 8, 1835.*—The board met, pursuant to adjournment. Present: F. R. Conway, J. H. Relfe, commissioners.

The following testimony was taken before James H. Relfe, commissioner, in Washington county:

Zachariah Goforth deposeth and saith that he came in the settlement of Bellevue, in the county of Washington, in the Territory of Missouri, in the month of March, 1804; that, in the month of July or August following, a certain James Brown came to the neighborhood, and established himself in a camp about three miles west of the present village of Caledonia, where deponent's father lived; that the said Brown lived in this camp some short time, and then erected a small cabin. Deponent has no recollection of any cultivation on said place, as made by claimant, Brown, that fall. As well as deponent recollects, the next season, viz., in 1805, Brown built a cabin for Joseph Barr, and, when it was finished, moved into it. This is the same improvement which was confirmed to John Corder's representatives. About the time Brown moved into the cabin built on Corder's place, he sold the cabin he first built to one Saul or Solomon Hewitt.

Z. GOFORTH.

Sworn to and subscribed, this 30th June, 1835.

JAMES H. RELFE, Commissioner.

(See book No. 7, page 214.)

*August 22, 1835.*—The board met, pursuant to adjournment. Present: F. R. Conway, J. H. Relfe, F. H. Martin, commissioners.

James Brown, claiming 640 acres of land. (See book No. 6, page 369; No. 7, pages 132 and 214.)

The board are unanimously of opinion that 640 acres of land ought to be granted to the said James Brown, or to his legal representatives, according to the survey. (See book No. 7, page 227.)

JAMES H. RELFE,<br>F. R. CONWAY,<br>F. H. MARTIN.

---

No. 336.—Louis Giguiere, claiming 800 arpens.

To Don CARLOS DEHAULT DELASSUS, *Lieutenant Governor of Upper Louisiana:*

SIR: Louis Giguiere has the honor to represent to you that he would wish to form an establishment in the upper part of this province, where he has been residing for some time; having a family, he has recourse to your goodness, praying you to be pleased to grant to him a tract of land of 800 arpens in superficie, to be taken on the vacant lands of his Majesty's domain, in the manner which will appear most convenient to the interest of your petitioner, who presumes to hope this favor of your justice.

his<br>LOUIS × GIGUIERE.<br>mark.

ST. LOUIS, *June 11, 1800.*

Decree.

ST. LOUIS OF ILLINOIS, June 13, 1800.

Whereas we are assured that the petitioner possesses sufficient means to improve the lands which he solicits, I do grant to him and his heirs the land he solicits, provided it is not prejudicial to anybody, and the surveyor, Don Antonio Soulard, shall put the interested (party) in possession of the quantity of land he asks, in a vacant place of the royal domain; which being executed, he shall make out a plat of (his) survey, delivering the same to the party, with his certificate, in order to enable him to obtain the title in form from the intendant general, to whom alone corresponds, by royal order, the distributing and granting all classes of lands, &c.

CARLOS DEHAULT DELASSUS.

St. Louis, *April* 27, 1833.

Truly translated from a copy certified by Antonio Soulard, surveyor general of the Territory of Louisiana, under date of February 26, 1806.

Record of concession, book No. 2, page 67 and 68.

JULIUS DE MUN.

| No. | Name of original claimant. | Arpens. | Nature and date of claim. | By whom granted. | By whom surveyed, date, and situation. |
|---|---|---|---|---|---|
| 336 | Louis Giguiere. | 800 | Concession, June 13, 1800. | C. Dehault Delassus. | |

EVIDENCE WITH REFERENCE TO MINUTES AND RECORDS.

*November* 20, 1811.—Board met. Present: John B. C. Lucas, Clement B. Penrose, and Frederick Bates, commissioners.

Louis Labeaume, assignee of Peter Lord, assignee of Lewis Giguiere, claiming 800 arpens of land, situate in Richwood, district of St. Genevieve. Produces record of a concession from C. D. Delassus, lieutenant governor, dated June 13, 1800; record of a plat of survey certified by Soulard, March 15, 1808; record of a transfer from Giguiere to Lord, dated January 12, 1805; record of a transfer from Lord to claimant, dated July 18, 1806. It is the opinion of the board that this claim ought not to be confirmed. (See book No. 5, p. 438.)

*March* 25, 1833.—F. R. Conway, esq., appeared, pursuant to adjournment.

Lewis Giguiere, by L. Labeaume's representatives, claiming 800 arpens of land. (See book D, page 298; Minutes No. 5, page 438; Spanish record of concession, No. 2, page 67.) Produces a paper purporting to be a certified copy of a concession granted to said Giguiere by Charles D. Delassus, dated June 13, 1800, and certified by Antoine Soulard; also, deed from Giguiere to Peter Lord, dated January 12, 1805; also, deed from said Lord to Labeaume, dated July 18, 1806.

M. P. Leduc, duly sworn, says that the certificate and signature affixed to it are in the proper handwriting of said Antoine Soulard, as registered in book No. 2, pages 67 and 68 of record in the office of recorder of land titles.

Albert Tyson, duly sworn, says that he had once in his possession three concessions, among which was the original of the above-mentioned copy; that on his way from Cold Water to this place, his pocket-book, containing the three concessions aforesaid, was lost. Witness further says that, in 1806, he went on said land, and it was then inhabited and cultivated, and has been so ever since, having now between 40 and 50 acres under cultivation. (See book No. 6, page 140.)

*August* 26, 1835.—The board met, pursuant to adjournment. Present: F. R. Conway, J. H. Relfe, and F. H. Martin, commissioners.

Louis Giguiere, claiming 800 arpens of land. (See book No. 6, page 140.)

The board are unanimously of opinion that this claim ought to be confirmed to the said Louis Giguiere, or to his legal representatives, according to the concession. (See book No. 7, page 243.)

JAMES H. RELFE,
F. R. CONWAY,
F. H. MARTIN.

---

No. 337.—*F. M. Benoit, claiming* 800 *arpens.*

To Don CARLOS DEHAULT DELASSUS, *Lieutenant Governor of Upper Louisiana:*

SIR: F. M. Benoit has the honor of representing to you that, having resided in this province since a long time, he wishes to settle himself and form an establishment in the same; therefore, he has recourse to the kindness of this government, praying you to be pleased to grant to him a tract of land of eight hundred arpens in superficie, to be taken on the vacant lands of the King's domain, in the place which shall appear most advantageous and most convenient to the interest of your petitioner; who presumes to expect this favor of your justice.

F. M. BENOIT.

St. Louis, *August* 12, 1800.

St. Louis of Illinois, *August* 14, 1800.

Whereas we are assured that the petitioner possesses sufficient means to improve the lands which he solicits, I do grant to him and his heirs the lands he solicits, provided it is not prejudicial to any person, and the surveyor, Don Antonio Soulard, shall put the (party) interested in possession of the land he asks, in a vacant place of the royal domain; which being executed, he shall make out a plat of his survey, delivering the same to said party, with his certificate, in order to enable him to obtain the title in form from the intendant general, to whom alone corresponds, by royal order, the distributing and granting all classes of lands, &c.

CARLOS DEHAULT DELASSUS.

Registered at the request of the interested. (Book No. 2, folios 31 and 32, No. 22.)

SOULARD.

St. Louis, *April* 29, 1833. Truly translated.

JULIUS DE MUN.

| No. | Name of original claimant. | Arpens. | Nature and date of claim. | By whom granted. | By whom surveyed, date, and situation. |
|---|---|---|---|---|---|
| 337 | F. M Benoit. | 800 | Concession, Aug. 14, 1800. | C. Dehault Delassus. | |

EVIDENCE WITH REFERENCE TO MINUTES AND RECORDS.

*October* 18, 1811.—Board met. Present: John B. C. Lucas, Clement B. Penrose, and Frederick Bates, commissioners.

Albert Tyson, assignee of Louis Labeaume, assignee of François M. Benoit, claiming 800 arpens of land, situate in Richwood, district of St. Genevieve, produces a concession from Charles D. Delassus, Lieutenant Governor, dated August 14, 1800. Plat of survey signed John Feney, certified by Ant. Soulard, March 15, 1808; a transfer from Benoit to Labeaume, dated March 5, 1805, from Labeaume to claimant, dated September 19, 1807. It is the opinion of the board that this claim ought not to be confirmed. (See book No. 5, page 331.)

*March* 25, 1833.—F. R. Conway, esq., appeared, pursuant to adjournment.

François M. Benoit, by L. Labeaume's legal representative, claiming 800 arpens of land. (See book D; Minutes, No. 5, page 381.) Produces a paper purporting to be an original concession from Carlos Dehault Delassus, dated August 14, 1800; also, a deed from said Benoit to Labeaume, dated March 5, 1805.

M. P. Leduc, duly sworn, says that the signature to the said concession is in the proper handwriting of said Carlos Dehault Delassus. (See book No. 6, page 140.)

*August* 26, 1835.—The board met, pursuant to adjournment. Present: F. R. Conway, J. H. Relfe, and F. H. Martin, commissioners.

F. M. Benoit, claiming 800 arpens of land. (See book No. 6, page 140.)

The board are unanimously of opinion that this claim ought to be confirmed to the said F. M. Benoit or to his legal representatives, according to the concession. (See book No. 7, page 243.)

JAMES H. RELFE,
F. R. CONWAY,
F. H. MARTIN.

---

No. 338.—*Israel Dodge, claiming 1,000 arpens.*

To Don CHARLES DEHAULT DELASSUS, *Lieutenant Colonel, attached to the stationary regiment of Louisiana, and Lieutenant Governor of the upper part of the same province:*

Israel Dodge, an ancient inhabitant of the country, has the honor to represent to you that he had obtained leave of Monsieur le Chevalier de Bourbon, in consequence of the verbal permission given by your predecessor, Don Zenon Trudeau, to select, on the domain, a tract of vacant lands suitable to his views; for that purpose he took the necessary steps, and discovered, more than one year ago, the tract of land represented in the above figurative plat. He hopes, therefore, that you will be pleased to grant to him, in full property, the quantity of 1,000 arpens of land in superficie, to be taken in the same manner as described in his figurative plat, and at the place designated, as follows: In a bottom situated between the fork of the St. Francis, called Gaboré's fork, and the fork called *Des Loups* (Wolves' fork), in such a way as to include a spring which discharges a part of its waters in a branch which empties into Wolves' fork; at the said above-mentioned spring there is a tree, commonly called by Americans *dogwood*, and marked I. D. The said land is situated at about two and a half or three miles north of the Hunter's path, which crosses Wolves' fork and the Gaboré river, at about twenty-five miles W. S. W. of the post of New Bourbon.

The petitioner expects of your justice, in case you are pleased to grant his demand, that you will condescend to empower him to give to his lines any other directions than those designated in the above figurative plat, should it be judged more advantageous to his interest, considering that the directions demanded are the result of a mere guess-work, subject to many errors.

The petitioner, full of confidence in your justice, and in the generosity of the government, to which he has always given proofs of his fidelity, hopes that you will be pleased to do justice to his demand, in a manner favorable to the accomplishment of his views.

NEW BOURBON, *October* 15, 1799. ISRAEL DODGE.

We, the undersigned, commandant of the post of New Bourbon of Illinois, do certify to Don Charles Dehault Delassus, lieutenant colonel, attached to the stationary regiment of Louisiana, and lieutenant governor of the upper part of the said colony of Louisiana, that the statement made in the foregoing petition is very exact, sincere, and true; we do certify, besides, that the petitioner is one of the most honest inhabitants of our post, who has often signalized his zeal for the King's service, and that of the colony; in short, we do attest that the said petitioner has erected, at a very great expense, several establishments, such as mills, breweries, distilleries, and others, which are of the most precious utility to the inhabitants of this section of the country; and that under these several heads he is worthy, in all points of view, to obtain the concession which he solicits.

Done at New Bourbon, October 20, 1799. PIERRE DELASSUS DE LUZIERE.

ST. LOUIS OF ILLINOIS, *October* 25, 1799.

Cognizance being taken of the statement made in the foregoing petition, as also of the information of the commandant of the post of New Bourbon, the captain of militia, Don Pedro Delassus de Luziere, considering the numerous family of the petitioner, and that he is one of the first Americans who settled in this country, and that he has more than the means and number of hands (population) necessary to obtain the concession which he solicits, I do grant to him and his heirs the land which he solicits, provided it is not prejudicial to anybody; and the surveyor, Don Antonio Soulard, shall put the party interested in possession of the quantity of land he asks, in the place designated. The alterations solicited in the directions (of the lines) described in the figurative plat, may be effected, because in either way it cannot be prejudicial to any one who holds a title of prior date than this one; and this being executed, he shall make out a plat, delivering the same to said party, with his certificate, in order to serve to him to obtain the concession and title in form from the intendant general, to whom alone belongs, by royal order, the distributing and granting all classes of lands of the royal domain.

CARLOS DEHAULT DELASSUS.

I notify the party interested, that I have cause to believe that the tract of land mentioned in his petition is already settled; this might lead into difficulties which it would be better to avoid, by asking of the lieutenant governor the permission to take the same quantity of land in any vacant part of the domain.

ST. LOUIS, *December* 15, 1799. SOULARD.

ST. LOUIS OF ILLINOIS, *December* 16, 1799.

In consequence of the above information, we authorize the party interested to take the same quantity of land in any other vacant part of the domain, to which the surveyor of this Upper Louisiana, Don Antonio Soulard, shall have to conform himself.

DELASSUS.

Truly translated from book E, pages 220 and 221, of record in the recorder's office.

JULIUS DE MUN, *T. B. C.*

ST. LOUIS, *February* 20, 1834.

| No. | Name of original claimant. | Arpens. | Nature and date of claim. | By whom granted. | By whom surveyed, date and situation. |
|-----|---------------------------|---------|---------------------------|------------------|---------------------------------------|
| 338 | Israel Dodge. | 1,000 | Concession, October 25, 1799. | C. Dehault Delassus. | |

EVIDENCE WITH REFERENCE TO MINUTES AND RECORDS.

*December* 6, 1833.—F. R. Conway, esq., appeared, pursuant to adjournment.

Israel Dodge, by his legal representatives, claiming 1,000 arpens of land, produces record of a concession from Carlos Dehault Delassus, dated 25th October, 1799. (See record-book E, page 220. See book No. 6, page 366.)

*August* 26, 1835.—The board met, pursuant to adjournment. Present: F. R Conway, J. H. Relfe, and F. H. Martin, commissioners.

The board are unanimously of opinion that this claim ought to be confirmed to the said Israel Dodge, or to his legal representatives, according to the concession. (See book No. 7, page 243.)

JAMES H. RELFE,
F. R. CONWAY,
F. H. MARTIN.

No. 339.—*Walter Fenwick, claiming 10,000 arpens.*

*To the Lieutenant Governor of Upper Louisiana:*

Walter Fenwick has the honor to represent that, having come over to this side of Illinois with the consent and recommendation of the governor-general, the Baron de Caroudelet, in order to make an extensive establishment; therefore he has visited the country and found a vacant tract at the place commonly called La Mine a la Motte, at the distance of about fifteen leagues from the village of St. Genevieve, said place belonging to his majesty's domain, and being fit for cultivation, and at the same time advantageous for the purpose of raising cattle, which are very much needed in the country, and the petitioner being able to draw from the United States all kind of cattle, it might become, in a little while, profitable to him and advantageous to the whole colony. For this consideration, and that of being a new settler, who has become encouraged by the generous offers of government, and his projects requiring an extensive tract of land, as well for cultivation as to establish a stock farm, the petitioner supplicates you very humbly to grant to him, in full property, *ten* thousand arpens of land in superficie, at the said place of Mine a la Motte. In doing which, he shall never cease to pray for your happiness and prosperity.

ST. GENEVIEVE, *August* 14, 1796.

WALTER FENWICK.

ST. LOUIS, *August* 23, 1796.

The surveyor, Don Antonio Soulard, shall survey, in favor of the party interested, the ten thousand arpens of land which he solicits in the said place of Mine a la Motte, and he shall deliver to him a plat and certificate of survey, in order that, together with the present decree, they shall serve as a title to his property until the corresponding title be made out by the general government, in which he shall have to apply for greater formality.

ZENON TRUDEAU.

*September* 2, 1833.—Truly translated.

JULIUS DE MUN, *T. B. C.*

NOTE.—In the tenth line from the bottom, on the other side, the word *ten* was originally written *huit* (eight) and afterward altered into *dix* (ten.)

JULIUS DE MUN, *T. B. C.*

| No. | Name of original claimant. | Arpens. | Nature and date of claim. | By whom granted. | By whom surveyed, date, and situation. |
|-----|---------------------------|---------|---------------------------|------------------|----------------------------------------|
| 339 | Walter Fenwick. | 10,000 | Concession, August 23, 1796. | Zenon Trudeau. | Mine a la Motte, district of St. Genevieve. |

EVIDENCE WITH REFERENCE TO MINUTES AND RECORDS.

*November* 14, 1811.—Board met. Present: John B. C. Lucas, Clement B. Penrose, and Frederick Bates, commissioners.

Walter Fenwick, claiming 10,000 arpens of land, situated near Mine a la Motte, district of St. Genevieve, produces record of a concession from Zenon Trudeau, L. G., dated the 23d August, 1796.

It is the opinion of the board that this claim ought not to be confirmed. (See minutes, No. 5, page 422.)

*August* 24, 1833.—The board met, pursuant to adjournment. Present: L. F. Linn, A. G. Harrison, F. R. Conway, commissioners.

Walter Fenwick, by his legal representatives, claiming 10,000 arpens of land, situated near Mine a la Motte. (See book No. 5, page 422; records, book D, pages 41 and 43.) Produces a paper purporting to be an original concession from Zenon Trudeau, dated August 23, 1796.

The following testimony was taken before L. F. Linn, esq., one of the commissioners:

STATE OF MISSOURI, *County of St. Genevieve:*

John Baptiste Vallé, sr., being duly sworn as the law directs, deposeth and saith that he is about 72 years of age; that he was well acquainted with Zenon Trudeau; that he was the lieutenant governor of the province of Upper Louisiana in the year 1796; and this deponent further states that he is well acquainted with the name, signature, and handwriting of the said Zenon Trudeau; that he has often seen him write, and that the name, signature, and handwriting, to the said concession from Zenon Trudeau, to said Walter Fenwick, for the quantity of 10,000 arpens of land, dated the 23d day of August, in the year 1796, is the proper name, signature, and handwriting of the said Zenon Trudeau. And the deponent further says that he was well acquainted, personally, with Walter Fenwick, the grantee: that the said Walter Fenwick was, at the date of the grant, a citizen and resident in the then province of Upper Louisiana, and had been for some time before; and that the said Fenwick continued to be a citizen and resident until the time of his death, which the deponent believes was some time in the year 1811 or '12; and that the signature to the petition is in the proper handwriting of the said Walter Fenwick. Sworn to and subscribed before me, L. F. Linn, one of the commissioners appointed to investigate and report on land claims in Missouri, this 4th day of May, 1833.

J. BAPTISTE VALLÉ.

(See book No. 6, page 251.)                L. F. LINN, *Commissioner.*

*November* 17, 1834.—The board met, pursuant to adjournment. Present: F. R. Conway, J. H. Relfe, and J. S. Mayfield, commissioners.

Walter Fenwick, claiming 10,000 arpens of land. (See book No. 6, page 251.)

The board are unanimously of opinion that the above claim is destitute of merit, an alteration being apparent in the original concession on file, as noted in the translation of said concession; the word *huit* (eight) in the original having been altered into *dix* (ten). (See book No. 7, page 68.)

JAMES S. MAYFIELD,
JAMES H. RELFE,
F. R. CONWAY.

*August* 26, 1835.—The board met, pursuant to adjournment. Present: F. R. Conway, J. H. Relfe, and F. H. Martin, commissioners.

Walter Fenwick, claiming 10,000 arpens of land. (See book No. 6, page 251; No. 7, page 68.)

On motion, the board agreed to reconsider the decision made on this claim, on the 17th of November, 1834, and, on a re-examination of the original concession, find that the alteration above spoken of is *not* made in the concession, but in the petition; and the words "*diez mil arpanes*" (ten thousand arpens) in the concession, are fairly written, it is believed, in the proper handwriting of the lieutenant governor, Zenon Trudeau, and that the alteration in the *petition* must have been made anterior to the granting of the concession.

The board, therefore, rescind their former decision in this case, and are unanimously of opinion that this claim of 10,000 arpens of land ought to be confirmed to the said Walter Fenwick, or to his legal representatives, according to the concession. (See book No. 7, page 244.)

JAMES H. RELFE,
F. R. CONWAY,
F. H. MARTIN.

No. 340.—*Peter Burns, sr., claiming* 640 *acres.*

| No. | Name of original claimant. | Acres. | Nature and date of claim. | By whom granted. | By whom surveyed, date, and situation. |
|-----|---------------------------|--------|--------------------------|------------------|----------------------------------------|
| 340 | Peter Burns, sr. | 640 | Settlement right. | | On the waters of St. Francis river, county of Madison. |

EVIDENCE WITH REFERENCE TO MINUTES AND RECORDS.

*December* 27, 1833.—F. R. Conway, esq., appeared, pursuant to adjournment.

Peter Burns, sr., by his legal representatives, claiming 640 acres of land, situate on the waters of St. Francis river, county of Madison. (See record-book F, page 53; Bates's decisions, page 102.)

STATE OF MISSOURI, *County of Madison:*

John Mathews, a witness, aged about 62 years, being duly sworn as the law directs, deposeth and saith, that he was well acquainted with Peter Burns, sr.; that this witness came to this country in the year 1800; that Peter Burns, sr., came to this country, then the province of Upper Louisiana, in the year 1804; that he settled on the tract of land in the summer of 1804; that he had a house on the land, and lived in it with his family, which was a wife and some seven or eight children; that he saw some land open on the place, and that there was something growing thereon, but whether corn, potatoes, or turnips, he does not recollect; that there was a small field of two or three arpens opened at the time, and he is sure some cultivation was done in the year 1804; that said

Peter Burns, sr., remained on the place several years, and then was scared or run off by the Osage Indians, who drove them into the settlements, where the family remained; that the Indians did, at that time, frighten the people, and committed several depredations on the waters of the St. Francis, and forced the people for safety to come into the settlements.

JOHN MATHEWS.

Sworn to and subscribed before me, this 31st of May, 1833.

L. F. LINN, *Commissioner.*

Also came John Clements, a witness, aged 53 years, who being duly sworn as the law directs, deposeth and saith, that he was well acquainted with the original claimant; that he came to this country in the year 1803, to the best of his recollection, or early in the year 1804; witness also knows the land claimed, and that shortly afterward he settled on the land, built a house, fenced in and cleared several acres of land, and cultivated the same in corn, tobacco, cotton, vegetables, and common garden; and that the land has been generally inhabited and cultivated ever since the settlement was begun, shortly after he came to the country.

JOHN ×<sup>his</sup> CLEMENTS.
<small>mark.</small>

Sworn and subscribed, this 21st of October, 1833.

L. F. LINN, *Commissioner.*

Also came Thompson Crawford, a witness, aged about 47 years, who being duly sworn as the law directs, deposeth and saith, that he was well acquainted with the original claimant; that he came to this country in the spring of 1804; witness also knows the land claimed, and knows that the claimant inhabited, improved, and cultivated the same in the year 1804; that he built a house thereon, and lived on the same, and that the land has been actually inhabited and cultivated ever since.

THOMPSON CRAWFORD.

Sworn to and subscribed, this 22d of October, 1833.

L. F. LINN, *Commissioner.*

And also came John Reaves, a witness, aged about 73 years, who, being duly sworn, deposeth and saith that he knew the original claimant, who came in this country, he believes, in 1802; that the claimant was here in 1803, and then witness became acquainted with him, from which time witness and claimant lived neighbors. Witness also knows the land claimed, and that the claimant settled on the same early in the spring of 1804, having built a house, and moved into the same on the land in the winter of 1803 and 1804; and that in 1804 he cleared, fenced in, and cultivated several acres in corn and other things necessary for a family. In the summer or spring of 1804, the Osage Indians made a break on the settlement and drove off the settlers, particularly the women, and in the fall claimant returned and gathered his crop, and the said tract of land has been, from time to time, inhabited and cultivated ever since.

JOHN ×<sup>his</sup> REAVES.
<small>mark.</small>

Sworn to and subscribed before me, this 23d of October, 1833.

L. F. LINN, *Commissioner.*

(See book No. 6, page 416.)

*September* 19, 1833.—The board met, pursuant to adjournment. Present: F. R. Conway, J. H. Relfe, and F. H. Martin, commissioners.

Peter Burns, sr., claiming 640 acres of land. (See book No. 6, page 416.)

The board are unanimously of opinion that 640 acres of land ought to be granted to the said Peter Burns, sr., or to his legal representatives, according to possession. (See book No. 7, page 245.)

JAMES H. RELFE,
F. H. MARTIN,
F. R. CONWAY.

---

No. 341.—*William Reed, jr., claiming 727 arpens.*

| No. | Name of original claimant. | Arpens. | Nature and date of claim. | By whom granted. | By whom surveyed, date, and situation. |
|-----|---------------------------|---------|---------------------------|------------------|----------------------------------------|
| 341 | William Reed, Jr. | 727 | Settlement right. | | John Stewart, D. S., February 26, 1806; received for record by Soulard, S. G., February 27, 1806, in Bellevue, district of St. Genevieve. |

EVIDENCE WITH REFERENCE TO MINUTES AND RECORDS.

*June* 26, 1806.—The board met, pursuant to adjournment. Present: Hon. Clement B. Penrose and James L. Donaldson, esquires.

William Reed, jr., claiming 727 arpens of land, situate at Bellevue, district of St. Genevieve, produces survey of the same, taken the 26th, and certified 27th February, 1806.

John Lewis, being duly sworn, says that he always understood from the neighbors of the claimant, that he had obtained a permission to settle from some persons authorized to grant the same; that he arrived in the country in November, 1803, settled said land in 1804, worked on the same occasionally, living then with his father-in-law; and further, that he was a single man, and of the age of 21 years and upward.

The board rejected this claim. (See No. 1, page 369.)

*December* 3, 1807.—The board met, agreeably to adjournment. Present: Hon. J. B. C. Lucas, C. B. Penrose, and Frederick Bates.

William Reed, jr., claiming 727 arpens of land, situate in Bellevue, district of St. Genevieve, produces a survey of the same, dated as above.

William Murphy, being duly sworn, says that he was present when old William Reed obtained permission to settle himself, and friends, and connections, on vacant land, from Mr. De Luziere, late commandant of New Bourbon, in 1798 or 1799; and that witness always understood that said William Reed was brother's son of said William Reed, sr.

Joseph Reed, being duly sworn, says that claimant built a cabin on said tract in 1804, and moved in the same in 1805, and lived in it ever since.

John Lewis, being also sworn, says that claimant raised a crop on said tract in 1806 or 1807. Laid over for decision. (See book No. 3, page 125.)

*April* 20, 1810.—Board met. Present: John B. C. Lucas, Clement B. Penrose, and Frederick Bates, commissioners.

William Reed, jr., claiming 727 arpens of land. (See book No. 1, page 369; No. 3, page 125.) It is the opinion of the board that this claim ought not to be granted. (See No. 4, page 335.)

*November* 30, 1833.—F. R. Conway, esq., appeared, pursuant to adjournment.

William Reed, jr., claiming 727 arpens of land. (See record-book B, page 454; book No. 1, page 369; No. 3, page 125; and No. 4, page 336.)

The following testimony was taken before L. F. Linn, commissioner:

State of Missouri, *County of Washington:*

Be it remembered that, on the 10th day of January, 1832, before me, Henry Shurlds, a justice of the peace within and for said county, the following persons appeared:

John T. McNaill, aged 68 years and upward, being duly sworn, deposeth and saith that, some time in the fall of the year 1804, he called at Jacob Job's, who was then living with his family on what was called William Reed, junior's claim, in now Washington county aforesaid; that he was living in a cabin, and had a crop of corn growing, and he understood from said Reed that Job was living there by his (Reed's) consent. In 1805, Job moved off, and Reed moved into the same place, and continued there until 1815 or 1816, as well as he remembers; and the place has been inhabited and cultivated ever since.

JOHN T. McNAILL.

Subscribed and sworn to by John T. McNaill, who is personally known to me.

HENRY SHURLDS, *J. P.*

Sworn to, and signature acknowledged, May 6th, 1833.

L. F. LINN, *Commissioner.*

Potosi, Washington County, *May* 6, 1833.

Personally appeared before L. F. Linn, commissioner, Mr. John Stewart, deputy-surveyor, under General Wilkinson, who, after being duly sworn, deposes and says, that he surveyed this tract of land for William Reed, jr., in the year 1806; that there was a good cabin and corn-crib on said place; there was corn in the crib, a field cleared, and there was reason, from appearances, to believe said place was in cultivation for two crops.

JOHN STEWART.

Sworn to and subscribed on the day above written.

L. F. LINN, *Commissioner.*

(No. 6, page 351.)

*September* 19, 1835.—The board met, pursuant to adjournment. Present: F. R. Conway, J. H. Relfe, and F. H. Martin, commissioners.

William Reed, jr., claiming 727 arpens of land. (See book No. 6, page 350.)

The board are unanimously of opinion that 727 arpens of land ought to be granted to the said William Reed, jr., or to his legal representatives, according to possession and survey. (See No. 7, page 245.)

JAMES H. RELFE,
F. H. MARTIN,
F. R. CONWAY.

No. 342.—*William Davis, claiming 640 acres.*

| No. | Name of original claimant. | Acres. | Nature and date of claim. | By whom granted. | By whom surveyed, date, and situation. |
|-----|---------------------------|--------|---------------------------|------------------|----------------------------------------|
| 342 | William Davis. | 640 | Settlement right. | | John Stewart, D. S., 18th February, 1806. Survey of 338 arpens. Received for record by A. Soulard, S. G., 27th February, 1806. In Bellevue settlement. |

EVIDENCE WITH REFERENCE TO MINUTES AND RECORDS.

*November* 13, 1811.—Board met. Present: John B. C. Lucas, Clement B. Penrose, and Frederick Bates, commissioners.

William Davis, claiming 338 arpens of land and 7 perches, situate in Bellevue, district of St. Genevieve, produces a notice to recorder; a plat of survey, dated 18th February, 1806, certified 27th February, 1806.

It is the opinion of the board that this claim ought not to be granted. (No. 5, page 404.)

*December* 13, 1833.—F. R. Conway, esq., appeared, pursuant to adjournment.

William Davis, by his legal representatives, claiming 640 acres of land, (originally filed for a less quantity,) situate in Bellevue settlement, county of Washington. (See record-book B, page 453; Minutes, No. 5, page 404.)

STATE OF MISSOURI, *County of Washington:*

John Stewart, being duly sworn, deposeth and saith that he was called on by John Little, who claimed under the same William Davis, to survey the tract of land here claimed, which he said was granted to said Davis by the Spanish government, and that this deponent surveyed the same in January or February, 1806, and returned the plat of survey to the proper officer, and the recording fees were paid; that when he surveyed the same there was a good improvement on the same, and some houses, and that the house and improvements had the appearance of being some two or more years old.

JOHN STEWART.

Sworn to and subscribed before me, this 9th day of May, 1833.

L. F. LINN, *Commissioner.*

And also came John T. McNeal, a witness, aged about 70 years, who, being duly sworn, deposeth and saith that he is acquainted with the tract of land claimed; that in the year 1805 he saw one John Little on the same, in the spring of the year: that the house and improvements had the appearance of having been made the year before. Said Little told this witness that he had purchased the land of a man of the name of Davis, who, he said, had procured a Spanish right for the same, and that he knows said Little continued on the same land for several years, and raised several crops.

JOHN T. McNEAL.

Sworn to and subscribed before me, this 9th of May, 1833.

L. F. LINN, *Commissioner.*

And also came Uriah Hull, a witness, aged about 56 years, who, being duly sworn, deposeth and saith that he knew John Little; that he, Little, was on this tract of land in the summer of 1804; that he raised a crop on the land that year; that there was a cabin on the land, in which he lived; that he had a wife and several children.

URIAH HULL.

Sworn to and subscribed before me, this 10th day of May, 1833.

L. F. LINN, *Commissioner.*

(See minutes, book No. 6, page 381.)

*September* 19, 1835.—The board met, pursuant to adjournment. Present: F. R. Conway, James H. Relfe, and F. H. Martin, commissioners.

William Davis, claiming 338 arpens and 7 perches of land. (See book No. 6, page 381, where this claim is entered for 640 acres.)

The board are unanimously of opinion that 338 arpens and 7 perches of land ought to be granted to the said William Davis, or to his legal representatives, according to possession and survey. (See book No. 7, page 245.)

JAMES H. RELFE,
F. H. MARTIN,
F. R. CONWAY.

---

No. 343.—*Thompson Crawford, claiming 600 arpens.*

| No. | Name of original claimant. | Arpens. | Nature and date of claim. | By whom granted. | By whom surveyed, date, and situation. |
|-----|---------------------------|---------|---------------------------|------------------|----------------------------------------|
| 343 | Thompson Crawford. | 600 | Settlement right. | | On the waters of St. Francis river. |

EVIDENCE WITH REFERENCE TO MINUTES AND RECORDS.

*December* 28, 1813.—Thompson Crawford, claiming 600 arpens of land, on waters of river St. Francis, county of St. Genevieve.

Joshua Edwards, duly sworn, says claimant came out to St. Francis settlement, in May, 1803, and lived that year with his father, (being sick,) and has been in that settlement ever since, except occasional short absences. (See recorder's minutes, page 117.)

*December* 28, 1833.—F. R. Conway, esq., appeared, pursuant to adjournment.

Thompson Crawford, claiming 640 acres of land, situate on the waters of the St. Francis, county of Madison. (See record-book F, page 91; recorder's minutes, page 117; Bates's decisions, page 36.)

STATE OF MISSOURI, *County of Madison:*

John Mathews, aged about 62 years, being duly sworn as the law directs, deposeth and saith that he is well acquainted with the claimant, Thompson Crawford; that he has known him from the year 1803, early in the spring of that year; that he was then grown up, and, this witness believes, was working for himself; that this witness, about that time, hired him to work for him; that he believes the claimant lived at his father's, and this land claimed lies adjoining the lands then occupied by his father; that shortly afterward the claimant settled on this land claimed, built a house, and commenced to improve and cultivate the same, and has continued to improve, inhabit, and cultivate the same ever since, and still resides thereon.

JOHN MATHEWS.

Sworn to and subscribed before me, this 31st day of May, 1833.

F. L. LINN, Commissioner.

Also came Samuel Campbell, a witness, aged about 68 years, who, being duly sworn, deposeth and saith that he was well acquainted with the original claimant; that he came to this country, then the province of Upper Louisiana, in the spring of the year 1803; witness also knows the land claimed, and further knows that the claimant settled on, inhabited, improved, and cultivated the same in the year 1804; that the land settled on, improved, and cultivated, was about one mile from his father's, where his father then lived; and this witness believes it was the same land now claimed; and that he knows the land was inhabited, improved, and cultivated by the claimant till within some eight years since, when witness went off from this place, but the same may have been continually inhabited, improved, and cultivated, during even those eight years, for all the witness knows, as he was absent.

SAMUEL CAMPBELL.

Sworn to and subscribed before me, this 21st October, 1833.

L. F. LINN, Commissioner.

(See No. 6, page 425.)

*September* 19, 1835.—The board met, pursuant to adjournment. Present: F. R. Conway, J. H. Relfe, and F. H. Martin, commissioners.

Thompson Crawford, claiming 600 arpens of land. (See book No. 6, page 423, where this claim is entered for 640 acres.)

The board are unanimously of opinion that 600 arpens of land ought to be granted to the said Thompson Crawford, or to his legal representatives, according to possession. (See book No. 7, page 245.)

JAMES H. RELFE,<br>F. H. MARTIN,<br>F. R. CONWAY.

---

No. 344.—Dawalt Critz, claiming 200 acres and 53 poles.

| No. | Name of original claimant. | Acres. | Nature and date of claim. | By whom granted. | By whom surveyed, date, and situation. |
|---|---|---|---|---|---|
| 344 | Dawalt Critz. | 200 53 poles. | Settlement right. | | Plat signed B. Cousin; countersigned Antonio Soulard, S. G. |

EVIDENCE WITH REFERENCE TO MINUTES AND RECORDS.

*January* 3, 1834.—F. R. Conway, esq., appeared, pursuant to adjournment.

Dawalt Critz, by his legal representatives, claiming 640 acres of land. (See record-book B, page 292.)

STATE OF MISSOURI, *County of Cape Girardeau :*

George F. Bollinger, aged about 60 years, being duly sworn, as the law directs, deposeth and saith that he was well acquainted with the said Dawalt Critz, the original claimant; that the claimant came to this country, then the province of Upper Louisiana, now State of Missouri, in the year 1802; that he was a cripple, and unable to go about much; that Daniel Bollinger applied to, and obtained permission or grant from Louis Lorimier, Spanish commandant of the district, for him to settle; that said Critz selected the land claimed, which the witness also knows; that the land was actually cultivated in the year 1804, and had the same surveyed, and has been actually cultivated ever since; that valuable improvements were made on the same, such as a good dwelling-house, out-houses, barn, stables, and orchards.

GEORGE F. BOLLINGER.

Sworn to and subscribed, October 19, 1833.

L. F. LINN, Commissioner.

(See book No. 6, page 441.)

*September* 19, 1835.—The board met, pursuant to adjournment. Present: F. R. Conway, J. H. Relfe, and F. H. Martin, commissioners.

Dawalt Critz, claiming 200 acres and 53 poles of land. (See book No. 6, page 441, where this claim is entered for 640 acres.)

The board are unanimously of opinion that 200 acres and 53 poles of land ought to be granted to the said Dawalt Critz, or to his legal representatives, according to the survey recorded in book B, page 292. (See book No. 7, page 246.)

JAMES H. RELFE,<br>F. H. MARTIN,<br>F. R. CONWAY.

No. 345.—*Pierre Tornat dit Lajoie, claiming 600 arpens.*

| No. | Name of original claimant. | Arpens. | Nature and date of claim. | By whom granted. | By whom surveyed, date, and situation. |
|---|---|---|---|---|---|
| 345 | Pierre Tornat dit Lajoie. | 600 | Settlement right. | | On the Marameck. |

EVIDENCE WITH REFERENCE TO MINUTES AND RECORDS.

*June 26, 1833.*—Board met, pursuant to adjournment. Present: L. F. Linn, F. R. Conway, commissioners.

Pierre Tornat dit Lajoie, by his legal representatives, claiming 600 arpens of land, situate on the Marameck, by settlement right. (See book F, page 137; Bates's decisions, page 104.)

Produces in evidence a sworn certificate of James Mackay, sworn to and subscribed before Jeremiah Connor, a justice of the peace; also a certificate of Francis Roy, dated August 23, 1819, sworn before F. M. Guyol, a justice of the peace. (See minutes, No. 6, page 189.)

*Francis Roy's certificate.* Before me, F. M. Guyol, a justice of the peace for the county of St. Louis, appeared personally Francis Roy, of the village of Carondelet, county of St. Louis, Missouri Territory, and made oath on the holy evangelist, that the plantation in Lejoie's bottom, on the north side of the Marameck, and in said Missouri Territory, and claimed as a settlement right by Mary Ann Chatillon Tornat, widow and representatives of Peter Tornat or Turnat dit Lajoie, deceased, has been inhabited and cultivated by and for the said Peter Tornat or Turnat, about twenty years ago, to my knowledge, and is still inhabited and cultivated by the said widow Mary Ann and her children.

his<br>
FRANCIS × ROY.<br>
mark.

Sworn to and subscribed before me, this 23d day of August, 1819.

F. M. GUYOL, *J. P.*

*Mackay's certificate.* Before me, Jeremiah Connor, esq., a justice of the peace for the county and township of St. Louis, came and appeared personally James Mackay, of Carondelet county, and township aforesaid, who made oath on the holy evangelist, that the plantation in Lajoie's bottom, on the north side of the Marameck river, in the county of St. Louis, and Territory of Missouri, claimed as a settlement right by Marie Ann Chatillon Tornat dit Lajoie, widow of Peter or Pierre Tornat dit Lajoie, or Lacheway, deceased, has been inhabited and cultivated by and for the said Peter Tornat dit Lajoie, some years prior to the year 1803, and that year also, and is still in actual habitation and cultivation by the said Maria Ann and her children; and that said Peter, nor his said widow, ever got any grant for land from the Spanish government, except a verbal permission to settle on said plantation; and that this is the real state of the above said claim, to the best of his knowledge.

JAMES MACKAY.

Sworn to and subscribed before me, the 25th October, 1819.
(See book No. 6, page 189.)

JEREMIAH CONNOR, *J. P.*

*June 15, 1835.*—The board met, pursuant to adjournment. Present: F. R. Conway, J. H. Relfe, commissioners.

Pierre Tornat dit Lajoie, claiming 600 arpens of land. (See book No. 6, page 189.)

The board are of opinion that this claim ought not to be granted. (See book No. 7, page 185.)

JAMES H. RELFE,<br>
F. R. CONWAY.

*July 7, 1835.*—In the case of Pierre Tornat, claiming 600 arpens of land. (See book No. 6, page 189.)

David Fine, duly sworn, says that he is about 71 years of age; that he came to this country in 1802, and settled a place in 1803, about three miles from the land claimed; that in 1804 he went on the tract claimed, and there saw two men, Gigniere and Baudouin, working on said land; they lived in a cabin which appeared to be an old one. Witness further says there was an enclosure of two or three arpens, and as well as he can recollect, there were some fruit-trees planted, and some of them are yet standing; that said Lajoie moved on said place, he thinks, in 1806, and lived there till his death; that after Lejoie's death his widow left the place for about one year, and having married one St. John, came back to said place, and lived there till the said St. John's death, which happened about ten or eleven years ago. Witness believes there must be now under cultivation about 40 or 45 acres.

Pascal L. Cerré, duly sworn, says that, several years before the change of government, under Mr. Delassus, he saw Gigniere and Baudouin living in a camp made with clapboards, and working on said piece of land for and under Pierre Tornat dit Lajoie, who had hired them by the year; that said two men had, before the cession to the United States, a small field of three or four arpens, in which they raised corn and tobacco, and had apple-trees planted; that said Lajoie moved to said place with his family in 1806 or 1807, and continued to inhabit and cultivate the same until his death. Witness further says, that said Lajoie was an excellent and very industrious farmer; that this land is situated on the north side of the Marameck, about two miles below John Boli's ferry, opposite the little Saline, and bounded on one side by the river Marameck, and on the other by Mrs. Boli's line. Lajoie's house was about twenty-five arpens from the banks of the river. (See book No. 7, page 208.)

*September 19, 1835.*—The board met, pursuant to adjournment. Present: F. R. Conway, James H. Relfe, and F. H. Martin, commissioners.

Pierre Tornat dit Lajoie, claiming 600 arpens of land. (See book No. 6, page 189; No. 7, page 208.)

The board rescind their former decision on this claim, (see book No. 7, page 185;) further testimony in behalf of said claim having been given since said decision.

The board are unanimously of opinion that six hundred arpens of land ought to be granted to the said Pierre Tornat dit Lajoie, or to his legal representatives, according to possession. (See book No. 7, page 246.)

JAMES H. RELFE,<br>
F. R. CONWAY,<br>
F. H. MARTIN.

REPORTS

*Of the Board of Commissioners at St. Louis, under the act of the 9th of July, 1832, and the act supplementary thereto, in relation to the claims to lands in the State of Missouri, upon claims No. 1 to No. 152, inclusive (except No. 20), in the Second Class.*

Class 2. No. 1.—*Louis Lorimier, claiming 1,000 arpens.*

To Don CARLOS DEHAULT DELASSUS, *Lieutenant Colonel in the armies of his Catholic Majesty, Lieutenant Governor and Commander-in-chief of Upper Louisiana, &c. :*

The undersigned has the honor to represent to you that, intending to build a saw-mill on a creek which runs through his concession at Cape Girardeau, and the mill-seat being situated so near his lower line that a grantee contiguous to him on that side might easily make the water flow back to his mill, and thereby cause him considerable injury; he has also the honor to observe to you that, when his land was surveyed, it was found, in running the lines conformably to his demand, (granted by a decree,) that the improvements of several inhabitants whose concessions were of a later date, were included in the said survey, and the petitioner, in order not to put them to any inconvenience, had the directions of the lines altered, depriving himself in this way of more than a thousand arpens of the best land, to take in exchange stony lands, unfit for cultivation. In compensation of this sacrifice, and, besides, in order to secure the peaceable enjoyment of his intended mill, the petitioner prays you, sir, to grant to him the tract of vacant lands which is situated to the south of and adjoining his concession, and containing twenty arpens in front on the river, extending in depth to the concession of Mr. E. Robertson. The petitioner shall never cease to pray for the preservation of your days and your prosperity.

CAPE GIRARDEAU, *July* 10, 1800.                           L. LORIMIER.

The petitioner shall have recourse to the intendant of these provinces, whom we inform that the petitioner, on account of his usefulness and the zeal he has shown in the royal service before and since he is commandant of the post of Cape Girardeau, besides being an excellent husbandman, appears to us to be worthy of the favor which he solicits ; and further, that his project of building a mill shall be of the greatest utility to the public. His lordship will determine as he thinks fit.

ST. LOUIS, *July* 31, 1800.

                                                    CARLOS DEHAULT DELASSUS.

ST. LOUIS, *May* 31, 1833.   Truly translated.

                                                    JULIUS DE MUN.

| No. | Name of original claimant. | Arpens. | Nature and date of claim. | By whom granted. | By whom surveyed, date, and situation. |
|-----|---------------------------|---------|--------------------------|------------------|----------------------------------------|
| 1 | Louis Lorimier. | 1,000 | Recommendation to the Intendant, 31st July, 1800. | Carlos Dehault Delassus. | Cape Girardeau. |

EVIDENCE WITH REFERENCE TO MINUTES AND RECORDS.

*May* 25, 1809.—Board met. Present: John B. C. Lucas, Clement B. Penrose, and Frederick Bates, commissioners.

Louis Lorimier, claiming 1,000 arpens of land ; produces to the board a petition to Don Carlos Dehault Delassus, lieutenant governor, and a recommendation from said Delassus to the intendant, dated 31st July, 1800. Laid over for decision. (See book No. 4, page 74.)

*March* 22, 1810.—Board met. Present: John B. C. Lucas, Clement B. Penrose, and Frederick Bates, commissioners.

Louis Lorimier, claiming 1,000 arpens of land. (See book No. 4, page 74.) It is the opinion of the board that this claim ought not to be confirmed. (See book No. 4, page 302.)

*March* 16, 1833.—The board met, pursuant to adjournment. Present: L. F. Linn, A. G. Harrison, and F. R. Conway, commissioners.

Louis Lorimier, sr., by his legal representatives, claiming 1,000 arpens of land by way of extension of a former concession. (See book E, pages 22 and 23 ; Minutes, No. 4, pages 74 and 302.) Produces a document signed Charles D. Delassus, dated 31st July, 1800.

Pierre Menard, duly sworn, says that the signature to said document is in the handwriting of Carlos Dehault Delassus, and the signature to the petition is in the handwriting of Louis Lorimier, sr. (See book No. 6, page 128.)

*November* 11, 1833.—The board met, pursuant to adjournment. Present: L. F. Linn, A. G. Harrison, and F. R. Conway, commissioners.

In the case of Louis Lorimier, claiming 1,000 arpens of land. (See page 128, No. 6.)

Pierre Menard, duly sworn, says that he was well acquainted with the said Louis Lorimier ; that he dealt largely with him ; witness believes that in 1803 or 1804, said Lorimier began to build a saw and grist mill ; that, if some one had possessed the land below his mill, he might easily have rendered said mill useless, by backing the water ; that the whole tract claimed was subject to overflowing. (No. 6, page 317.)

*November* 17, 1834.—The board met, pursuant to adjournment. Present: F. R. Conway, J. H. Relfe, and J. S. Mayfield, commissioners.

Louis Lorimier, claiming 1,000 arpens of land. (See book No. 6, page 128.)

The board cannot take cognizance of this claim, there being no concession, warrant, or order of survey. (See book No. 7, page 67.)

                                                    JAMES S. MAYFIELD,
                                                    JAMES H. RELFE,
                                                    F. R. CONWAY.

Class 2. No. 2.—*Louis Coyteux, claiming 400 arpens.*

To Don CHARLES DEHAULT DELASSUS, *Lieutenant Colonel in the armies of his Catholic Majesty, and Lieutenant Governor of Upper Louisiana:*

Louis Coyteux, jr., very humbly supplicates, and has the honor to represent to you, that, desiring to make and improve a plantation, he would wish that you would grant to him, for that purpose, the quantity of 400 arpens of land in superficie, to be taken in a vacant place of the domain. The petitioner, being born a subject of his Catholic Majesty, hopes to obtain this favor; in so doing, he shall never cease to pray for the conservation of your days.

Done at New Bourbon, October 5, 1799.

his<br>LOUIS × COYTEUX.<br>mark.

CAMILLE DELASSUS, witness to the mark.

We, the undersigned, commandant of the post of New Bourbon, do certify to the lieutenant governor of Upper Louisiana that the petitioner is worthy to obtain the concession which he asks, as much on account of the important services his father has rendered in his capacity of commissary of police for the district of Bois-brulé, as because the said petitioner has no other way of supporting himself but that of farming.

Done at New Bourbon, October 10, 1799.

P'RE DELASSUS DE LUZIERE.

ST. LOUIS OF ILLINOIS, *October* 18, 1799.

In consequence of the information given by the commandant of the post of New Bourbon, Captain Don P're Delassus de Luziere, and considering that the petitioner is the son of one of the old inhabitants of this country, and that he possesses sufficient means to improve the lands which he solicits, I do grant to him and his heirs the land which he solicits, provided it is not to the prejudice of any other person, and the surveyor, Don Antonio Soulard, shall put the party interested in possession of the quantity of land he asks, in a vacant place of the King's domains; and this being executed, he shall make out a plat of his survey, delivering the same to said party, with his certificate, in order to serve to him to obtain the concession and title in form from the intendant general, to whom corresponds the distributing and granting all classes of lands belonging to the royal domain.

CARLOS DEHAULT DELASSUS.

No. 17.—Deposited the title of concession of a piece of land granted to Louis Coyteux, jr., registered under the number 17.

ST. LOUIS, *July* 24, 1833. Truly translated.

JULIUS DE MUN.

| No. | Name of original claimant. | Arpens. | Nature and date of claim. | By whom granted. | By whom surveyed, date, and situation. |
|-----|----------------------------|---------|---------------------------|------------------|----------------------------------------|
| 2 | Louis Coyteux, jr. | 400 | Concession, 18th October, 1799. | Carlos Dehault Delassus. | |

EVIDENCE WITH REFERENCE TO MINUTES AND RECORDS.

*July* 5, 1833.—L. F. Linn, esq., appeared, pursuant to adjournment.

Louis Coyteux, jr., by his legal representatives, claiming 400 arpens of land, produces a paper purporting to be an original concession from Carlos Dehault Delassus, dated 18th October, 1799, with a recommendation from Pierre Delassus de Luziere, commandant of New Bourbon, dated 8th October, 1799; the whole headed by a petition from said Coyteux.

By the recommendation, it appears that the commandant of New Bourbon recommends the said Coyteux as worthy to obtain the grant which he asks for, as well on account of the signal services of his father, in the capacity of commissioner of police of the canton of Bois-brulé, as because the suppliant has no other means of subsistence but that of a cultivator. Also, the following endorsement is found on the back of the title-papers: No. 17. *Dépôt des titres de concession d'une terre accordée au Sieur Louis Coyteux fils, enregistrés sous le No.* 17. (The title of concession for a piece of land granted to Louis Coyteux, jr., has been deposited and registered under No. 17.) Also, *Rejected for want of a plat of survey.*

J. L. DONALDSON, *Recorder, St. Louis.*

M. P. Leduc, duly sworn, says that the signature to the concession is in the proper handwriting of Carlos Dehault Delassus; that the signature to the recommendation is in the proper handwriting of Pierre Delassus de Luziere, commandant of New Bourbon; that the signature to the endorsement, by J. L. Donaldson, is in the proper handwriting of said Donaldson, then recorder of land-titles in St. Louis. Deponent further says that it appears, by said endorsement, that the said Donaldson rejected the recording of said claim for want of a plat of survey. (See book No. 6, page 210.)

*November* 17, 1834.—The board met, pursuant to adjournment. Present: F. R. Conway, J. H. Relfe, and J. S. Mayfield, commissioners.

Louis Coyteux, claiming 400 arpens of land. (See book No. 6, page 210.)

The board cannot take cognizance of this claim, there being no registry of the same. (See book No. 7, page 67.)

JAMES S. MAYFIELD,<br>JAMES H. RELFE,<br>F. R. CONWAY.

Class 2. No. 3.—*François Coyteux, jr., claiming 400 arpens.*

To Don CHARLES DEHAULT DELASSUS, *Lieutenant Colonel in the armies of his Catholic Majesty, and Lieutenant Governor of Upper Louisiana :*

François Coyteux, jr., humbly supplicates, and has the honor to represent that, being desirous of making a plantation, he would wish that you would grant to him, for that purpose, the quantity of four hundred arpens of land, to be taken in a vacant part of the domain. The petitioner hopes to obtain this favor, being born a subject of his Catholic Majesty.

In so doing, he shall never cease to pray for the preservation of your days.

Done at New Bourbon, October 5, 1799.

his
FRANCOIS × COYTEUX, fils.
mark.

CAMILLE DELASSUS, witness of the mark.


We, the undersigned, commandant of the post of New Bourbon, do certify to the lieutenant governor of Upper Louisiana, that the petitioner is worthy to obtain the concession which he solicits, as well on account of the eminent services of his father in the capacity of commissary of the police for the canton of Bois-Brulé, as that the said petitioner does not know or exercise any other profession for his support but that of a farmer.

Done at New Bourbon, October 10, 1799.

P're DELASSUS DE LUZIERE.


ST. LOUIS OF ILLINOIS, *October* 18, 1799.

In consequence of the information given by the commandant of the post of New Bourbon, Captain P're Delassus de Luziere, and considering that the petitioner is the son of one of the ancient inhabitants of this country, and that he possesses sufficient means to improve the land he solicits, I do grant to him and his heirs the land which he solicits, provided it is not to the prejudice of anybody, and the surveyor, Don Antonio Soulard, shall put the party interested in possession of the quantity of land he asks, in a vacant place of the King's domain ; and this being executed, he shall make out a plat, delivering the same to said party, together with his certificate, in order to serve him to obtain the title and concession in form from the intendant general, to whom belongs the distributing and granting all classes of lands belonging to the royal domain.

CARLOS DEHAULT DELASSUS.

ST. LOUIS, *August* 19, 1834. Truly translated from the original.

JULIUS DE MUN, *T. B. C.*

| No. | Name of original claimant. | Arpens. | Nature and date of claim. | By whom granted. | By whom surveyed, date, and situation. |
|---|---|---|---|---|---|
| 3 | François Coyteux, jr. | 400 | Concession, 18th October, 1799. | Carlos Dehault Delassus. | Unlocated. |

EVIDENCE WITH REFERENCE TO MINUTES AND RECORDS.

*July* 8, 1834.—The board met, pursuant to adjournment. Present: J. H. Relfe, F. R. Conway, commissioners.

François Coyteux, jr., by his legal representatives, claiming 400 arpens of land, produces a paper purporting to be an original concession from Carlos Dehault Delassus, dated 18th October, 1799. (On the back of said concession the following was written : " Rejected for want of a plat of survey. J. L. Donaldson. Rec. St. Louis.")

M. P. Leduc, duly sworn, says that the signature to said concession is in the proper handwriting of the said Carlos Dehault Delassus. (See book No. 7, page 5.)

*November* 17, 1834.—The board met, pursuant to adjournment. Present: F. R. Conway, J. H. Relfe, and J. S. Mayfield, commissioners.

François Coyteux, jr., claiming 400 arpens of land. (See book No. 7, page 5.)

The board cannot take cognizance of this claim, there being no registry of the same. (See book No. 7, page 67.)

JAMES S. MAYFIELD,
JAMES H. RELFE,
F. R. CONWAY.

————


Class 2. No. 4.—*Hippolite Bolon, claiming 720 arpens.*

Don CARLOS DEHAULT DELASSUS, *Colonel in the armies of his Catholic Majesty, and formerly Lieutenant Governor of Upper Louisiana :*

We do certify to all those whom it may concern that, in the year 1799, we required Mr. Hippolite Bolon to come forthwith to this place to fix his residence, in order to fulfil the functions of interpreter to the Indian nations ; that he came, and has lived in this place all the time that our command lasted, until the delivery of this province to France.

In testimony whereof, we have signed the present certificate, in St. Louis of Illinois, October 23, 1804.

CARLOS DEHAULT DELASSUS.

ST. LOUIS, *September* 9, 1833. Truly translated.

JULIUS DE MUN.

*Hippolite Bolon, claiming 720 arpens.*

| No. | Name of original claimant. | Arpens. | Nature and date of claim. | By whom granted. | By whom surveyed, date, and situation. |
|-----|---------------------------|---------|---------------------------|------------------|----------------------------------------|
| 4 | Hippolite Bolon. | 720 | Settlement right. | | Bois-Brulé, on the Mississippi, 682 acres, by John Hawkins, D. S, February 15, 1806. Received for record by Soulard, S. G., February 27, 1806. |

EVIDENCE WITH REFERENCE TO MINUTES AND RECORDS.

*October* 24, 1808.—Board met. Present: Hon. Clement B. Penrose and Frederick Bates.

Israel Dodge, assignee of Hippolite Bolon, claiming 682 acres of land, situate Bois Brulé, district of St. Genevieve, produces to the board a plat of survey, dated February 15, 1806, certified to be received for record February 27, 1806 ; also the sale of a concession, provided it shall be found in the archives of the post of St. Genevieve, for 18 acres in front by 40 in depth. Sale dated April 25, 1805.

Alexander McConshow, sworn, says that ten years ago he rented from Hippolite Bolon a sugar camp, on the tract claimed, and worked it for four or five years.

Joseph Tucker, sworn, says that in 1799 he saw said Bolon in a camp on the tract claimed. Laid over for decision. (See book No. 3, page 320.)

*June* 22, 1810.—Board met. Present: John B. C. Lucas, Clement B. Penrose, and Frederick Bates, commissioners.

Israel Dodge, assignee of Hippolite Bolon, claiming 682 acres of land. (See book No. 3, page 320.)

It is the opinion of the board that this claim ought not to be granted. (See No. 4, page 402.)

*August* 20, 1833.—The board met, pursuant to adjournment. Present: A. G. Harrison, F. R. Conway, commissioners.

Hippolite Bolon, by his legal representatives, Israel Dodge and Rufus Easton, claiming 18 arpens of land in front by 40 arpens in depth, situated at Bois-Brulé, adjoining the land of Mr. Patterson. (See book C, page 492 ; Minutes, No. 3, page 320 ; No. 4, page 402.)

Produces a notice to the recorder, dated July 17, 1807 ; also a certificate of the late lieutenant governor, Charles Dehault Delassus. (See No. 6, page 260.)

*November* 17, 1834.—The board met, pursuant to adjournment. Present: F. R. Conway, J. H. Relfe, J. S. Mayfield, commissioners.

Hippolite Bolon, claiming 720 arpens of land. (See book No. 6, page 260.)

The board are unanimously of opinion that this claim ought not to be granted, the said Hippolite Bolon having a concession of record in book A, page 94, in the recorder's office. (See book No. 7, page 68.)

JAMES S. MAYFIELD,
JAMES H. RELFE,
F. R. CONWAY.

Class 2.   No. 5.—*Louis Desnoyers, claiming 800 arpens.*

| No. | Name of original claimant. | Arpens. | Nature and date of claim. | By whom granted. | By whom surveyed, date, and situation. |
|-----|---------------------------|---------|---------------------------|------------------|----------------------------------------|
| 5 | Louis Desnoyers. | 800 | Settlement right. | | On the little Marameck. |

EVIDENCE WITH REFERENCE TO MINUTES AND RECORDS.

*February* 4, 1813.—Louis Desnoyer's legal representatives, claiming 800 arpens of land, on little Marameck, county of St. Louis. (See notice, record-book F, page 96.)

Louis Courtois, duly sworn, says that, about twenty-eight years ago, Louis Desnoyers inhabited and cultivated this tract of land for about two or three consecutive years; Louis Desnoyers had then a wife and two children. (See recorder's minutes, page 40.)

On the margin the following is written : " Not granted."

*August* 12, 1833.—The board met, pursuant to adjournment. Present: L. F. Linn, A. G. Harrison, F. R. Conway, commissioners.

Louis Desnoyers, by his legal representatives, claiming 800 arpens of land. (See book F, page 96 ; Recorder's minutes, page 40.)

Laurent Reed, duly sworn, says that Louis Desnoyers cultivated said land about forty years ago, and continued to inhabit and cultivate the said tract of land for about five or six years consecutively, when he was plundered and driven away by the Indians. (See book No. 6, page 242.)

*November* 17, 1834.—The board met, pursuant to adjournment. Present: F. R. Conway, J. H. Relfe, and J. S. Mayfield, commissioners.

Louis Desnoyers, claiming 800 arpens of land. (See book No. 6, page 242.)

The board are unanimously of opinion that this claim ought not to be granted, the said Louis Desnoyers having had a concession, recorded in book C, page 438, in the recorder's office. (See book No. 7, page 68.)

JAMES S. MAYFIELD,
JAMES H. RELFE,
F. R. CONWAY.

Class 2.  No. 6.—*Regis Loisel, claiming* 44,800 *arpens.*

To Mr. CHARLES DEHAULT DELASSUS, *Lieutenant Colonel of the stationary regiment of Louisiana, and Lieutenant Governor of Upper Louisiana, &c. :*

SIR: Regis Loisel has the honor to submit that, having made considerable sacrifices in the Upper Missouri Company, in aiding to the discoveries of Indian nations in that quarter, in order to increase commerce hereafter, as also to inculcate to those different nations favorable sentiments toward the government, and have them devoted to the service of his Majesty, so as to be able to put a stop to the contraband trade of foreigners who, scattering themselves among those Indians, employ all imaginable means to make them adopt principles contrary to the attachment they owe to the government.  The petitioner has also furnished, with zeal, presents, in order to gain the friendship of those different nations, for the purpose to disabuse them of the errors insinuated to them, and to obtain a free passage through their lands and durable peace.  The petitioner, intending to continue on his own account the commerce which his partners have abandoned in that quarter, hopes that you will be pleased to grant to him, for the convenience of his trade permission to form an establishment in Upper Missouri, where he will build a fort, about seven leagues higher up than the great bend (grand detour), distant about four hundred leagues from this town, and which shall be situated on the said Missouri, between the river known under the name of Rivière du vieux Anglais (river of the old Englishman), which empties itself in the said Missouri, on the right side of it, in descending the stream, and lower down than Cedar island, and the river known under the name of Rivière de la Côte de Medecine (river of the medicine bluff), which is on the left side, in descending the stream, and higher up than Cedar island ; which island is at equal distance from each of the two rivers above named.  That place being the most convenient for his operations, as well in the Upper as in the Lower Missouri, and it being indispensable to secure to himself the timber in an indisputable manner, he is obliged to have recourse to your goodness, praying that you will be pleased to grant to him a title of concession in full property for him, his heirs or assigns, for the extent of land situated along the banks of the said Missouri, and comprised between the river called the Old Englishman's, and the one called the Medicine bluff, here above mentioned, by the depth of one league in the interior, on each side of the Missouri, and including the island known by the name of Cedar island, as also other small timbered islands.  In granting his demand, he shall never cease to render thanks to your goodness.

REGIS LOISEL.

ST. LOUIS OF ILLINOIS, *March* 20, 1800.

ST. LOUIS OF ILLINOIS, *March* 25, 1800.

Whereas it is notorious that the petitioner has made great losses, when in the company he mentions, and as he continues his voyages of discoveries conformably to the desire of the government, which are the cause of great expenses to him ; and it being necessary for the commerce of peltries with the Indians, that forts should be constructed among those remote nations, as much to impress them with respect, as to have places of deposit for the goods and other articles which merchants carry to them, and particularly for those of the petitioner : for these reasons I do grant to him and his successors the land which he solicits, in the same place where he asks, provided it is not to the prejudice of anybody ; and the said land being very far from this post, he is not obliged to have it surveyed at present ; but, however, he must apply to the intendant general, in order to obtain the title in form from said intendant, because to him belongs, by order of his Majesty, the granting of all classes of lands belonging to the royal domain.

CARLOS DEHAULT DELASSUS.

At the request of Mr. James Clamorgan, I do certify to have copied the part of the course of the river Missouri, comprised in the above plat, from a chart of the said river which I have in my possession, and to have drawn the plat of the land granted to Mr. Regis Loisel, deceased, by the lieutenant governor, Don Charles Dehault Delassus, under date of March 25, 1800, as near as possible conformable to the tenor of said title.  The said land extends, on its front, 4¾ French leagues of 30 to the degree, or thereabouts, and on its depth, 5½ of those same leagues, which will give a total superficie of upward of 26 leagues ; of which quantity, deducting about half for the course of the river Missouri, it reduces the superficie of the said land to about 14 leagues.  The said grant is situated at about 1,200 miles from the mouth of the said river, and between the 107th and 106th degrees of the longitude of London, and 44 degrees of latitude.  In testimony whereof, I have delivered the present (plat) to the party interested, to serve to him to prove his claim, where needed.

ANTOINE SOULARD, *Surveyor General in Territory of Louisiana.*

ST. LOUIS, *November* 20, 1805.

*July* 27, 1833.  Truly translated.

JULIUS DE MUN.

| No. | Name of original claimant. | Arpens. | Nature and date of claim. | By whom granted. | By whom surveyed, date, and situation. |
|---|---|---|---|---|---|
| 6 | Regis Loisel. | 44,800 | Concession, March 25, 1800. | Charles Dehault Delassus. | On the Missouri, about 1,200 miles from its mouth. |

EVIDENCE WITH REFERENCE TO MINUTES AND RECORDS.

*August* 22, 1806.—The board met, pursuant to adjournment.  Present: Hon. John B. C. Lucas, Clement B. Penrose, and James L. Donaldson.

The same (Jacques Clamorgan), assignee of Regis Loisel, claiming a tract of land or island on the Missouri.  Produces a concession for the same from Charles D. Delassus, dated March 25, 1800, and a figurative plan of the same, dated November 20, 1805.

Antoine Tabeau, being duly sworn, says that the said land is situate up the Missouri ; that, in the year

1802, he, the witness, went up the said river with the said Regis Loisel, who built a four-bastion fort of cedar, the whole at his own expense, and without any assistance from government ; that the year following, to wit, in 1803, they again went up together, when the said Loisel ascended with witness about sixty-five leagues higher up ; made a garden and large field; and further that he, the witness, never heard of said Loisel having a concession for the land.

Auguste Chouteau, being also duly sworn, says that the aforesaid fort was begun in 1800.

The board reject this claim, and require further proof. (See book No. 1, page 484.)

*September* 14, 1810.—Board met. Present : John B. C. Lucas, Clement B. Penrose, and Frederick Bates, commissioners.

Jacques Clamorgan, assignee of Regis Loisel, claiming 151,162 arpens and 85 perches of land. (See book No. 1, p. 484.) It is the opinion of the board that this claim ought not to be confirmed. (See book No. 4, p. 500.)

*July* 8, 1833.—L. F. Linn, esq., appeared, pursuant to adjournment.

Regis Loisel, by Jacques Clamorgan's representatives, claiming 44,800 arpens of land, situate at Cedar Island, on the Missouri. (See record book C, page 172 ; Minutes, No. 1, page 484 ; No. 4, page 500.)

Produces a paper purporting to be an original concession from Carlos Dehault Delassus, dated March 25, 1800 ; also, a plat certified by Antoine Soulard, and dated November 20, 1805 ; also, a copy of an adjudication of the said land to Jacques Clamorgan, certified by M. P. Leduc, the 7th of October, 1805 ; also, the affidavit of Antoine Tabeau and Pierre Dorion, taken before Charles Gratiot, judge of the court of common pleas.

M. P. Leduc, being duly sworn, says that the signature to the decree of concession is in the proper handwriting of Carlos Dehault Delassus; that the signature to said plat and certificate is in the proper handwriting of Antoine Soulard ; and that the signature to the adjudication is in the deponent's own handwriting. (See book No. 6, page 222.)

*November* 17, 1834.—The board met, pursuant to adjournment. Present : F. R. Conway, J. H. Relfe, and J. S. Mayfield, commissioners.

Regis Loisel, claiming 44,800 arpens of land. (See book No. 6, page 222.)

The board do not take cognizance of this claim, it being out of their jurisdiction. (See book No. 7, page 68.)

JAMES S. MAYFIELD,
JAMES H. RELFE,
F. R. CONWAY.

---

Class 2.    No. 7.—*Leo Fenwick, claiming* 500 *arpens.*

To Don Zenon Trudeau, *Lieutenant Governor of the western part of Illinois, and commandant of St. Louis :*

Leo Fenwick, from the State of Kentucky, professing the Roman Catholic religion, has the honor to represent to you, that having determined to come and settle himself in this country, he supplicates you to be willing to grant to him a concession of 500 arpens of land in superficie, situated between the river à la Pomme (Apple river), and the river à la Viand, alias the river of Cape St. Côme. The said Leo Fenwick pledging himself to build on and cultivate the same, in the time prescribed by the ordinance, and to conform himself to the laws and constitution of the kingdom, as a good, faithful, and loyal subject.

LEO FENWICK.

New Bourbon, *May* 26, 1797.

St. Louis, *June* 10, 1797.

The surveyor, Don Antonio Soulard, shall put this party in possession of the 500 arpens of land which he solicits, and the plat and certificate of survey being made out, he shall deliver them to him, in order to enable him to solicit the concession from the governor general of this province, whom I shall inform that the petitioner is a son of Joseph Fenwick, C. A. and R., whom his lordship has recommended, in order that lands should be granted to him, to his family, and to the settlers whom he should bring to establish themselves in this part of Illinois.

ZENON TRUDEAU.

St. Louis, *September* 2, 1833.   Truly translated.

JULIUS DE MUN.

| No. | Name of original claimant. | Arpens. | Nature and date of claim. | By whom granted. | By whom surveyed, date, and situation. |
|-----|---------------------------|---------|---------------------------|------------------|----------------------------------------|
| 7 | Leo Fenwick. | 500 | Concession, June 10, 1797. | Z. Trudeau. | On the Mississippi, between Apple Creek and Cape St. Côme Creek. |

EVIDENCE WITH REFERENCE TO MINUTES AND RECORDS.

*November* 14, 1811.—Board met. Present : John B. C. Lucas, Clement B. Penrose, and Frederick Bates, commissioners.

Leo Fenwick, claiming 500 arpens of land, situated as aforesaid, produces record of a concession from Zenon Trudeau, L. G., dated 10th June, 1797.

It is the opinion of the board that this claim ought not to be confirmed. (See book No. 5, page 423.)

*August* 26, 1833.—The board met, pursuant to adjournment. Present : L. F. Linn, A. G. Harrison, and F. R. Conway, commissioners.

Leo Fenwick, claiming 500 arpens of land, situated between the waters of Apple creek and Cape St. Côme. (See book No. 5, page 423 ; Records, book D, page 44.)

Produces a paper purporting to be an original concession from Zenon Trudeau, dated 10th of June, 1797.

The following testimony was taken before L. F. Linn. esq., one of the commissioners :

John B. Vallé, senior, aged about 72 years, who, being first duly sworn as the law directs, deposeth and saith, that said Zenon Trudeau was the lieutenant governor in the then province of Upper Louisiana, in the year

1797; that this deponent was well acquainted with his name, signature, and handwriting, having frequently seen him write, and that the name, signature, and handwriting, to the concession from him to Leo Fenwick, dated the 10th of June, 1797, for 500 arpens of land, is the proper handwriting, name, and signature, of the said Zenon Trudeau. And this deponent further saith that he was and is well acquainted with the said Leo Fenwick, the grantee, and that he was, at the date of the grant, a citizen and resident in the then province of Upper Louisiana, and that he has continued a citizen and resident ever since, and is still so (except when on a visit or for the purposes of education.)

Sworn to and subscribed before me, L. F. Linn, one of the commissioners for the settlement of land claims in Missouri, this 4th day of May, 1833.

J. B. VALLÉ.

(See No. 6, page 254.)

L. F. LINN, Commissioner.

*November* 17, 1834.—The board met, pursuant to adjournment. Present: F. R. Conway, J. H. Relfe, and J. S. Mayfield, commissioners.

Leo Fenwick, claiming 500 arpens of land. (See book No. 6, page 254.)

The board are unanimously of opinion that this claim is destitute of merit, an alteration being apparent in the original concession on file, as noted in the traslation of said concession; the name of river *à Brazeau* having been altered into that of river *à la Viande,* alias St. Côme, thus increasing the distance, for location of grant, several miles. (See book No. 7, page 68.)

JAMES S. MAYFIELD,<br>F. R. CONWAY,<br>JAMES H. RELFE.

*September* 19, 1835.—The board met, pursuant to adjournment. Present: F. R. Conway, J. H. Relfe, and F. H. Martin, commissioners.

Leo Fenwick, claiming 500 arpens of land. (See book No. 6, page 254.)

On request of the agent for claimant, the board agreed to reconsider this claim, and after a thorough re-examination, are unanimously of opinion to adhere to the decision taken on this claim in book No. 7, page 68, and add, as a further reason, that the conditions have not been complied with. (See book No. 7, page 247.)

F. R. CONWAY,<br>JAMES H. RELFE.

Class 2.   No. 8.—Ezekiel Fenwick, claiming 500 arpens.

To Don ZENON TRUDEAU, *Lieutenant Governor of the western part of Illinois, Commandant of St. Louis:*

Ezekiel Fenwick, a citizen of the State of Kentucky, professing the Roman Catholic religion, has the honor to represent to you that, having determined to come over to this side to establish himself, he supplicates you to be willing to grant him a concession of 500 arpens of land in superficie, situated between Apple river and river à la Viande, alias river St. Côme, engaging himself, the said Fenwick, to cultivate and build in the time prescribed by the ordinance, and to conform himself to the laws, customs, and constitution of the kingdom, as a good, loyal, and faithful subject.

NEW BOURBON, *May* 26, 1797.            EZEKIEL FENWICK.

ST. LOUIS, June 10, 1797.

The surveyor, Don Antonio Soulard, shall put the petitioner in possession of the 500 arpens of land which he solicits; and, after having made out a plat and certificate of the survey, he shall deliver it to said petitioner, in order to enable him to solicit the concession from the governor general, whom I shall inform that the petitioner is a son of Joseph Fenwick, the same whom his lordship has recommended, in order that land should be procured to him, his family, and to the C. A. and Roman settlers whom he would bring to settle in this part of Illinois.

ZENON TRUDEAU.

ST. LOUIS, *August* 13, 1834.  Truly translated from the original.

JULIUS DE MUN, T. B. C.

| No. | Name of original claimant. | Arpens. | Nature and date of claim. | By whom granted. | By whom surveyed, date, and situation. |
|---|---|---|---|---|---|
| 8 | Ezekiel Fenwick. | 500 | Concession, June 10, 1797. | Zenon Trudeau. | Between Apple creek and river St. Côme. |

EVIDENCE WITH REFERENCE TO MINUTES AND RECORDS.

*November* 14, 1811.—Board met. Present: John B. C. Lucas, Clement B. Penrose, and Frederick Bates, commissioners.

Ezekiel Fenwick, claiming 500 arpens of land, situate as aforesaid, (Apple creek, district of St. Genevieve,) produces record of a concession from Zenon Trudeau, lieutenant governor, dated 10th June, 1797.

It is the opinion of the board that this claim ought not to be confirmed. (See book No. 5, page 422.)

*November* 15, 1833.—The board met, pursuant to adjournment. Present: L. F. Linn, A. G. Harrison, and F. R. Conway, commissioners.

Ezekiel Fenwick, claiming 500 arpens of land, situated between Apple creek and river St. Côme. (See record-book D, page 44; Minutes, No. 5, page 422.) Produces a paper purporting to be an original concession from Zenon Trudeau, dated 10th June, 1797.

M. P. Leduc, duly sworn, says that the signature to the said concession is in the proper handwriting of the said Zenon Trudeau. (See book No. 6, page 339.)

*November* 17, 1834.—The board met, pursuant to adjournment. Present: F. R. Conway, J. H. Relfe, and J. S. Mayfield, commissioners.

Ezekiel Fenwick, claiming 500 arpens of land. (See book No. 6, page 339.)

The board are unanimously of opinion that this claim is destitute of merit, an alteration being apparent in the original concession on file, as noted in the translation of said concession, the name of river *à Brazeau* having been altered into that of river *à la Viande*, alias St. Côme ; thus increasing the distance, for location of grant, several miles. (See book No. 7, page 69.)

JAMES S. MAYFIELD,
F. R. CONWAY,
JAMES H. RELFE.

*September* 19, 1835.—The board met, pursuant to adjournment. Present: F. R. Conway, J. H. Relfe, and F. H. Martin, commissioners.

Ezekiel Fenwick, claiming 500 arpens of land. (See book No. 6, page 339.)

On request of the agent for claimant, the board agreed to reconsider this claim, and, after a thorough re-examination, are unanimously of opinion to adhere to the decision taken on this claim in book No. 7, page 69, and add as a further reason, that the conditions have not been complied with. (See book No. 7, page 247.)

F. R. CONWAY,
JAMES H. RELFE.

---

Class 2. No. 9.—*James Fenwick, claiming 500 arpens.*

To Don Zenon Trudeau, *Lieutenant Governor of the western part of Illinois, and Commandant of St. Louis :*

James Fenwick, from the State of Kentucky, professing the Roman Catholic religion, has the honor of representing to you that, having determined to come and settle himself in this country, he supplicates you to be willing to grant to him a concession of 500 arpens of land in superficie, situated between the river La Pomme (Apple river) and the river *à la Viande*, alias river St. Côme, the said James Fenwick pledging himself to cultivate and build on the same, in the time prescribed by the ordinance, and to conform himself to the laws and constitution of the kingdom, as a good, loyal, and faithful subject.

JAMES FENWICK.

New Bourbon, *May* 26, 1797.

St. Louis, *June* 10, 1797.

The surveyor, Don Antonio Soulard, shall put the party in possession of the 500 arpens of land which he solicits, and the plat and certificate of survey being made out, he shall deliver them to him in order to enable him to solicit the concession from the governor general of the province, who is hereby informed that the petitioner is a son of Joseph Fenwick, whom his lordship has recommended in order that lands in this western part of Illinois should be granted to him, his family, and to the C. A. and R. settlers whom he should bring with him.

ZENON TRUDEAU.

St. Louis, *August* 2, 1833. Truly translated.

JULIUS DE MUN.

| No. | Name of original claimant. | Arpens. | Name and date of claim. | By whom granted. | By whom surveyed, date, and situation. |
|---|---|---|---|---|---|
| 9 | James Fenwick. | 500 | Concession, June 10, 1797. | Zenon Trudeau. | On the Mississippi, between Apple creek and Cape St. Côme creek. |

EVIDENCE WITH REFERENCE TO MINUTES AND RECORDS.

*November* 14, 1811.—Board met. Present: John B. C. Lucas, Clement B. Penrose, and Frederick Bates, commissioners.

James Fenwick, claiming 500 arpens of land, situate as aforesaid. Produces record of concession from Zenon Trudeau, L. G., dated 10th June, 1797.

It is the opinion of the board that this claim ought not to be confirmed. (See book No. 5, page 423.)

*August* 24, 1833.—The board met, pursuant to adjournment. Present: L. F. Linn, A. G. Harrison, and F. R. Conway, commissioners.

James Fenwick, claiming 500 arpens of land, situated on the Mississippi, between Apple creek and Cape St. Côme creek, adjoining the land confirmed to George A. Hamilton. (See book No. 5, page 423 ; records, book D, page 44.)

Produces a paper purporting to be an original concession from Zenon Trudeau, dated June 10, 1797. No plat of survey is produced, but claimant states that the same was duly surveyed, and the plat returned to the proper office.

The following testimony was taken before L. F. Linn, esq., one of the commissioners :

State of Missouri, *County of St. Genevieve :*

William James, aged 56 years, being duly sworn, deposeth and saith, that he is well acquainted with the claimant, James Fenwick, otherwise called James J. Fenwick, from his infancy ; that the said James came to this country in the year 1797, and that he resided in this country and in the neighborhood of the land claimed ever since, that the tract of land claimed was settled on by Joseph Fenwick, father of the claimant, in the year

1800 or 1801, and that the said James lived with his father on the land at the time; that houses were built, fields cleared and fenced on the same, and that the said tract of land has been actually improved, inhabited, and cultivated ever since, and now is improved, inhabited, and cultivated.

Sworn and subscribed before me, L. F. Linn, one of the commissioners, &c., this 26th day of October, 1832.

WILLIAM JAMES.
L. F. LINN.

John Baptiste Vallé, sr., aged about 72 years, being duly sworn as the law directs, deposeth and saith that he is well acquainted with Zenon Trudeau, late lieutenant governor of Upper Louisiana; that he was lieutenant governor in the year 1797. This deponent further states, that he was and is well acquainted with the name, signature, and handwriting of the said Zenon Trudeau; that he has frequently seen him write; and that the name and signature to the concession from said Zenon Trudeau to the said James Fenwick, for 500 arpens of land, dated the 10th day of June, 1797, is the proper name and in the proper handwriting of the said Zenon Trudeau. And the deponent further says that he was well acquainted with Joseph Fenwick, the father of the grantee, and also with James Fenwick, the grantee; that they were citizens and residents in the province of Upper Louisiana, at the date of the grant, and that the said James (and his father till his death) have continued citizens and residents ever since.

Sworn to and subscribed before me, L. F. Linn, one of the commissioners, &c., this 4th day of May, 1833.

JOHN BAPTISTE VALLÉ.
L. F. LINN, Commissioner.

*November* 17, 1834.—The board met, pursuant to adjournment. Present: F. R. Conway, J. H. Relfe, and J. S. Mayfield, commissioners.

James Fenwick, claiming 500 arpens of land. (See book No. 6, page 252.)

The board are unanimously of opinion that this claim is destitute of merit, an alteration being apparent in the original concession on file, as noted in the translation of said concession; the name of river à *Brazeau* having been altered into that of river à *la Viande*, alias St. Côme, thus increasing the distance, for location of grant, several miles. (See book No. 7, page 69.)

JAMES S. MAYFIELD,
F. R. CONWAY,
JAMES H. RELFE.

*September* 19, 1835.—The board met, pursuant to adjournment. Present: F. R. Conway, J. H. Relfe, and F. H. Martin, commissioners.

James Fenwick, claiming 500 arpens of land. (See book No. 6, page 252.)

On request of the agent for claimant the board agree to reconsider this claim, and, after a thorough re-examination, are unanimously of opinion to adhere to the decision taken on this claim in book No. 7, page 69, and add, as a further reason, that the conditions have not been complied with.

F. R. CONWAY,
JAMES H. RELFE.

Class 2.   No. 10.—*Philip Bollinger, claiming 640 acres.*

| No. | Name of original claimant. | Acres. | Nature and date of claim. | By whom granted. | By whom surveyed, date, and situation. |
|---|---|---|---|---|---|
| 10 | Philip Bollinger. | 640 | Settlement right. | | On Whitewater, Cape Girardeau. |

EVIDENCE WITH REFERENCE TO MINUTES AND RECORDS.

*May* 1, 1809.—Board met. Present: Clement B. Penrose and Frederick Bates, commissioners.

Philip Bollinger, claiming 300 arpens of land, situate on Crooked creek, waters of Whitewater, district of Cape Girardeau, produces to the board as a special permission to settle, list A, on which claimant is No. 99. Laid over for decision. (See No. 4, page 33.)

*February* 19, 1810.—Board met. Present: John B. C. Lucas, Clement B. Penrose, and F. Bates, commissioners.

Philip Bollinger, claiming 300 arpens of land. (See book No. 4, page 32.) It is the opinion of the board that this claim ought not to be granted. (See No. 4, page 279.)

*January* 2, 1834.—F. R. Conway, esq., appeared, according to adjournment.

Philip Bollinger, by his legal representatives, claiming 640 acres of land, situate on Whitewater, county of Cape Girardeau. (See minutes, book No. 4, page 33 and 279; book B, page 293.)

Adam Statler, about 66 years of age, and William Bollinger, about 56 years of age, being duly sworn, deposeth and saith that, in the latter part of 1799, they emigrated to the then district of Cape Girardeau, Upper Louisiana, now county of Cape Girardeau, State of Missouri, where they have remained ever since; that at the same time with these affiants, the said Philip Bollinger emigrated to said district; that said Philip Bollinger, in the beginning of the year 1800, by the permission of the then Spanish commandant at that place, settled upon and actually inhabited a tract of land on the waters of Whitewater, in said district, and being so inhabitant and settled upon said land, said Philip Bollinger, in the said year 1800, cleared, growed, improved, and cultivated the ground on said tract of land, by fencing and raising corn thereon, and vegetables necessary for family use, and continued settled upon as an inhabitant of said tract of land (dwelling-houses and other buildings being erected thereon) during the years 1801, 1802, and 1803, to raise corn and the necessary vegetables for family use; that the said Philip Bollinger has, from the year first above named, continued to reside in the said Louisiana and Missouri, aforesaid.

his<br>
ADAM × STATLER.<br>
mark.<br>
his<br>
WILLIAM × BOLLINGER.<br>
mark.

Sworn to and subscribed, October 16, 1833.

L. F. LINN, Commissioner.

(See book No. 6, page 438.)

*November* 18, 1834.—The board met, pursuant to adjournment. Present: F. R. Conway, J. H. Relfe, and J. S. Mayfield, commissioners.

Philip Bollinger, claiming 640 acres of land. (See book No. 6, page 438.)

The board are unanimously of opinion that this claim ought not to be granted, the said Philip Bollinger having had a confirmation under a concession. (See commissioner's certificate, No. 227. See book No. 7, page 70.)

JAMES S. MAYFIELD,<br>
JAMES H. RELFE,<br>
F. R. CONWAY.

<hr>

Class 2. No. 11.—Daniel Bollinger, sr., claiming 640 acres.

| No. | Name of original claimant. | Acres. | Nature and date of claim. | By whom granted. | By whom surveyed, date, and situation. |
|---|---|---|---|---|---|
| 11 | D. Bollinger, sr. | 640 | Settlement right. | | James Boyd, D. S., signed B. Cousin, and countersigned Ant. Soulard. |

EVIDENCE WITH REFERENCE TO MINUTES AND RECORDS.

*May* 1, 1809.—Board met. Present: Clement B. Penrose and Frederick Bates, commissioners.

Daniel Bollinger, sr., claiming 372 arpens of land, situated on the Whitewater, district of Cape Girardeau, produces to the board, as a special permission to settle, list A, on which claimant is No. 161, a plat of survey of the same, signed B. Cousin, and countersigned 27th February, 1806, by Antoine Soulard, surveyor general. Laid over for decision. (See book No. 4, page 32.)

*February* 19, 1810.—Board met. Present: John B. C. Lucas, Clement B. Penrose, and Frederick Bates, commissioners.

Daniel Bollinger, sr., claiming 372 arpens of land. (See book No. 4, page 32.)

It is the opinion of the board that this claim ought not to be granted. (See book No. 4, page 279.)

*January* 1, 1834.—F. R. Conway, esq., appeared, pursuant to adjournment.

Daniel Bollinger, sr., by his legal representatives, claiming 640 acres of land, situated on Whitewater, county of Cape Girardeau. (See book No. 4, pages 32 and 279; Record-book B, page 279.)

Matthias Bollinger, being duly sworn, deposeth and saith that he, Matthias Bollinger, is aged about 64 years; that he emigrated in the year 1799, and came to the then district of Cape Girardeau, Upper Louisiana, now county of Cape Girardeau, State of Missouri, where he has ever since resided; that at the same time Daniel Bollinger, sr., came to said district with this affiant; that said Daniel Bollinger, in the year 1800, by permission of the then Spanish commandant at that place, with his family, settled upon and inhabited a tract of land on Whitewater, in said district, and being so inhabited and settled upon said land, he, said Daniel Bollinger, in said year 1800, cleared, improved, fenced, and cultivated the ground on said tract of land, planted, growed, and raised corn thereon, with the vegetables necessary for family use, and erected dwelling-houses and other buildings necessary for his family on said land; that the said Daniel Bollinger continued to inhabit and cultivate said tract of land, raising corn, grains, &c. thereon annually and each year on said tract of land, in the several years from said year 1800, and 1801, '2, '3 '4, and until 1808, and that said Daniel Bollinger still resides in this State.

MATTHIAS BOLLINGER.

Sworn and subscribed, October 17, 1833.

L. F. LINN, Commissioner.

(See book No. 6, page 435.)

*November* 18, 1834.—The board met, pursuant to adjournment. Present: F. R. Conway, J. H. Relfe, and J. S. Mayfield, commissioners.

Daniel Bollinger, claiming 640 acres of land. (See book No. 6, page 435.)

The board are unanimously of opinion that this claim ought not to be granted, the said Daniel Bollinger, sr., having had a confirmation under a concession. (See commissioner's certificate, No. 316; No. 7, book 7, p. 70.)

JAMES S. MAYFIELD,<br>
JAMES H. RELFE,<br>
F. R. CONWAY.

<hr>

Class 2. No. 12.—Paul Deguire, claiming 640 acres.

| No. | Name of original claimant. | Acres. | Nature and date of claim. | By whom granted. | By whom surveyed, date, and situation. |
|---|---|---|---|---|---|
| 12 | Paul Deguire. | 640 | Settlement right. | | On the waters of St. Francis river, co. of Madison. |

EVIDENCE WITH REFERENCE TO MINUTES AND RECORDS.

*March 26, 1813.*—Paul Deguire, claiming 800 arpens of land, between east fork of St. Francis river and Castor creek, county of St. Genevieve.

Gabriel Nicol, duly sworn, says that claimant had a sugar camp on this tract in 1804, and has made sugar every year to this time; built a cabin in 1804, and has inhabited it while he made sugar in subsequent years.

*April 3, 1813.*—Joseph Lafleur, sworn, says that claimant inhabited and cultivated this tract from and in the year 1803 to this time. (See recorder's minutes, page 41.)

*December 25, 1833.*—F. R. Conway, esq., appeared, pursuant to adjournment.

Paul Deguire, by his legal representatives, claiming 640 acres of land, situated on the waters of St. Francis river, county of Madison. (See recorder's minutes, page 41; Bates's decisions, page 30; Record-book F, page 95.)

STATE OF MISSOURI, *County of Madison:*

Nicholas Caillote Lachance, a witness, aged about 49 years, being duly sworn, deposeth and saith, that he has resided in this country about 43 or 44 years; that he is well acquainted with Paul Deguire, the original claimant; that he believes he was born in the country, then the province of Upper Louisiana. This witness also says that he knows the land claimed; that the claimant built a cabin on the same in the year 1803, and made sugar on the same; that he had a wife and four or five children at the time, and that the claimant continued to occupy the said cabin and lands for several years, and until one Charles L. Byrd pretended to have a concession therefor, and compelled the claimant to give up the same; that the said Deguire continued a citizen till the time of his death, and was a cultivator of the soil; that he always understood the claimant as claiming and owning this land, and that he only relinquished the possession from the threats of said Byrd.

his<br>NICHOLAS CAILLOTE × LACHANCE.<br>mark.

Sworn to before me, this 31st day of May, 1833.

L. F. LINN, *Commissioner.*

And also came François Caillote Lachance, aged about 66 years, and Michael Caillote Lachance, aged about 62 years, who, having severally heard the above deposition of Nicholas Caillote Lachance read and explained to them, say that they know the same facts, and that the statements and facts in said deposition contained are just and true.

F. CAILLOTE LACHANCE.<br>his<br>MICHAEL CAILLOTE × LACHANCE.<br>mark.

Sworn to and subscribed before me, this 31st day of May, 1833.

L. F. LINN, *Commissioner.*

(See book No. 6, page 410.)

*November 18, 1834.*—The board met, pursuant to adjournment. Present: F. R. Conway, J. H. Relfe, and J. S. Mayfield, commissioners.

Paul Deguire, claiming 640 acres of land. (See book No. 6, page 410.)

The board are unanimously of opinion that this claim ought not to be granted, the said Paul Deguire having had a confirmation under a concession. (See minutes, book No. 4, page 515. See book No. 7, page 70.)

JAMES S. MAYFIELD,<br>JAMES H. RELFE,<br>F. R. CONWAY.

---

Class 2.   No. 13.—*Thomas Ring, claiming 500 arpens.*

| No. | Name of original claimant. | Arpens. | Nature and date of claim. | By whom granted. | By whom surveyed, date, and situation. |
|---|---|---|---|---|---|
| 13 | Thomas Ring. | 500 | | | District St. Genevieve. |

EVIDENCE WITH REFERENCE TO MINUTES AND RECORDS.

*December 21, 1833.*—F. R. Conway, esq., appeared, pursuant to adjournment.

Thomas Ring, by his assignee, Camille Delassus, claiming 500 arpens of land, situate in the county of St. Genevieve. (See record-book F, page 97; Bates's decisions, page 103.)

Produces a paper purporting to be a copy of a deed of sale from Thomas Ring to Camille Delassus, dated 25th April, 1804, and certified by J. Baptiste Vallé, commandant of St. Genevieve. (See book No. 6, page 405.)

*November 18, 1834.*—The board met, pursuant to adjournment. Present: F. R. Conway, J. H. Relfe, and J. S. Mayfield, commissioners.

Thomas Ring, claiming 500 arpens of land. (See book No. 6, page 405.)

The board are unanimously of opinion that this claim ought not to be granted, the said Thomas Ring having had 640 acres granted to him. (See Bates's decisions, page 82. See book No. 7, page 70.)

JAMES S. MAYFIELD,<br>JAMES H. RELFE,<br>F. R. CONWAY.

Class 2.　No. 14.—*Joseph Thompson, sr., claiming* 640 *acres.*

| No. | Name of original claimant. | Acres. | Nature and date of claim. | By whom granted. | By whom surveyed, date, and situation. |
|---|---|---|---|---|---|
| 14 | Joseph Thompson, sr. | 640 | Settlement right. | | On Ramsay's creek, county of Cape Girardeau. |

EVIDENCE WITH REFERENCE TO MINUTES AND RECORDS.

*December* 31, 1833.—F. R. Conway, esq., appeared, pursuant to adjournment.

Joseph Thompson, sr., by his legal representatives, claiming 640 acres of land, situate on Ramsay's creek, county of Cape Girardeau. (See book F, page 146 ; Bates's decisions, page 105.)

John Abernethie, aged 71 years, being duly sworn, deposeth and saith that he came to the then district of Cape Girardeau, Upper Louisiana, now county of Cape Girardeau, in the year 1800, where he has ever since resided ; that in the year 1801 or 1802, Joseph Thompson, sr., came to said district, and with his family settled upon a tract of land in said district, by the permission of the then commandant, Louis Lorimier, at that place, and being so settled upon and inhabiting the said tract of land, continued thereon as such inhabitant during the year 1802 or 1803, and in said year improved, cleared, and cultivated said land ; made the necessary buildings, and planted, growed, and raised a crop of corn and the vegetables necessary for family use, during the season of the said year 1802. Further, that the said Joseph Thompson, sr., continued to reside with his family, and to be engaged in the cultivation of land, until the time of his death, which took place on his farm, on Ramsay's creek, in said district.

JOHN ABERNETHIE.

Sworn to and subscribed, October 18, 1833.

L. F. LINN, *Commissioner.*

John Rodney, of lawful age, being duly sworn, deposeth and saith that the tract of land of Joseph Thompson, sr., on which he resided at the time of his death, has been reserved from sale as a private unconfirmed land claim, by the register and receiver of the land district of Cape Girardeau, which tract of land is on Ramsay's creek, in Cape Girardeau county.

JOHN RODNEY.

Sworn to and subscribed, October 18, 1833.

L. F. LINN, *Commissioner.*

Ithamer Hubble, aged 71 years, being duly sworn, deposeth and saith that he first came, in 1797, to the then district of Cape Girardeau, Upper Louisiana, now county of Cape Girardeau, State of Missouri, where he has ever since resided ; that the aforesaid Joseph Thompson, sr., as early as the year 1801, with his family, came to said district, and in the year 1801 aforesaid, the said Joseph Thompson, with his family, settled upon and improved a tract of land in said county, by the permission of the then Spanish commandant ; made the necessary buildings thereon, cleared and fenced a part of said land, and in the said year 1801, so being an inhabitant of, and settled upon, said tract of land, he, said Joseph Thompson, in said year 1801, cultivated, planted, and raised a crop of corn thereon, of about fifteen acres ; that said Joseph Thompson, sr., lived in said district until the time of his death (with his family), which took place on his way from the town of Cape Girardeau to the place of his residence on his farm on Ramsay's creek, in said district ; that said Joseph Thompson left a number of heirs, who have ever since continued in the possession of said farm and tract of land on said Ramsay's creek, in the cultivation of the same.

　　　　　　　　　　　　　　　　　　　　　　　　　　　　　his
ITHAMER　×　HUBBLE.
　　　　　　　　　mark.

Sworn to and subscribed, October 18, 1833.

L. F. LINN, *Commissioner.*

Elijah Dougherty and Alexander Summers, being duly sworn, deposeth and saith that they were well acquainted with the said Joseph Thompson, sr., in his lifetime ; that they well recollect that, in the year 1801, the said Joseph Thompson, with his family, resided on a tract of land on Ramsay's creek, or waters of Ramsay's creek, in the said district of Cape Girardeau, mentioned in the foregoing depositions.

　　　　　　　　　　　　　　　　　　　　　　　　his
ELIJAH　×　DOUGHERTY.
　　　　　　　mark.
ALEXANDER SUMMERS.

Sworn to and subscribed, October 18, 1833.

L. F. LINN, *Commissioner.*

(See book No. 6, page 432.)

*November* 18, 1834.—The board met, pursuant to adjournment.　Present : F. R. Conway, J. H. Relfe, and J. S. Mayfield, commissioners.

Joseph Thompson, sr., claiming 640 acres of land. (See book No. 6, page 432.)

The board are unanimously of opinion that this claim ought not to be granted, the said Joseph Thompson, sr., having had a confirmation under a concession. (See commissioners' certificate, No. 240. See book No. 7, page 71.)

JAMES S. MAYFIELD,
JAMES H. RELFE,
F. R. CONWAY.

Class 2.    No. 15.—*Nicholas Lachance, claiming 640 acres.*

| No. | Name of original claimant. | Acres. | Nature and date of claim. | By whom granted. | By whom surveyed, date, and situation. |
|---|---|---|---|---|---|
| 15 | Nicholas Lachance. | 640 | Settlement right. | | On the waters of the St. Francis. |

EVIDENCE WITH REFERENCE TO MINUTES AND RECORDS.

*March* 26, 1813.—Nicholas Lachance, claiming 500 arpens of land, between the forks of St. Francis and Castor creek, county of St. Genevieve.

Gabriel Nichol, duly sworn, says that claimant built a cabin in 1803, and established a sugar camp, and made sugar every year to this time. (See recorder's minutes; Bates', page 41.) On the margin the following is written: "Not granted."

*December* 18, 1833.—F. R. Conway, esq., appeared, pursuant to adjournment.

Nicholas Lachance, alias Nicholas Caillote Lachance, claiming 640 acres of land, situate on the waters of St. Francis river. (See Bates's minutes, page 41; Bates's decisions, page 41; Record-book F, page 112.)

STATE OF MISSOURI, *County of Madison:*

Francis Caillote Lachance, aged about 66 years, being duly sworn as the law directs, deposeth and saith that he has resided in this country about 46 years; that he is well acquainted with the claimant, who came to this country, then the province of Upper Louisiana, about 43 or 44 years ago. This witness further says that he knows the land claimed; that the claimant settled on the same some thirty-one years, and while the country yet belonged to Spain; that he made a cabin on the same, and made sugar on the lands at that time; that, in one or two years after he built a cabin, the claimant moved and settled, and that he continued to claim the said land till one Charles L. Bird pretended that he had a concession for the land and compelled him to go off; that he has continued a citizen of the country and cultivator of the soil ever since.

F. CAILLOTE LACHANCE.

Sworn to and subscribed before me, this 31st day of May, 1833.

L. F. LINN, *Commissioner.*

And also came Michael Caillotte Lachance, a witness, aged about 62 years, who, after having heard the above and foregoing deposition of Francis Caillotte Lachance read and explained to him, deposeth and saith that he knows the same facts, and that the statements and facts contained therein are just and true.

his
MICHAEL CAILLOTE × LACHANCE.
mark.

Sworn to and subscribed before me, this 31st day of May, 1833.

L. F. LINN, *Commissioner.*

(See book No. 6, page 400.)

*November* 18, 1834.—The board met, pursuant to adjournment. Present: F. R. Conway, J. H. Relfe, and J. S. Mayfield, commissioners.

Nicholas Lachance, claiming 640 acres of land. (See book No. 6, page 400.)

The board are unanimously of opinion that this claim ought not to be granted, the said Nicholas Lachance having had a confirmation under a concession. (See minutes, book No. 4, page 515. See book No. 7, page 71.)

JAMES S. MAYFIELD,
JAMES H. RELFE,
F. R. CONWAY.

Class 2.    No. 16.—*John Helderbrand, claiming 200 arpens.*

| No. | Name of original claimant. | Arpens. | Nature and date of claim. | By whom granted. | By whom surveyed, date, and situation. |
|---|---|---|---|---|---|
| 16 | John Helderbrand. | 200 | Settlement right. | | |

EVIDENCE WITH REFERENCE TO MINUTES AND RECORDS.

*October* 13, 1808.—Board met. Present: Hon. Clement B. Penrose and Frederick Bates, commissioners.

Jonathan Helderbrand, assignee of Jesse Cain, assignee of Robert Owens, assignee of John Megar, claiming 200 arpens of land, situate on the Negro fork of the river Marameck, district of St. Louis, produces to the board a notice to the recorder, dated June 20, 1808; produces no assignment or transfers that the board thought they could receive as such.

William Bellen, sworn, says that about thirty years ago, John Helderbrand made an improvement on the land claimed, and inhabited and cultivated the same for five years, and then sold to John Megar, who, by his tenant, David Helderbrand, cultivated the same one year more.

Laid over for decision. (See book No. 3, page 296.)

*June* 19, 1810.—Board met. Present: John B. C. Lucas, Clement B. Penrose, and Frederick Bates, commissioners.

Jonathan Helderbrand, assignee of Jesse Cain, assignee of Robert Owens, assignee of John Megar, claiming 200 arpens of land. (See book No. 3, page 206.) It is the opinion of the board that this claim ought not to be granted. (See book No. 4, page 392.)

*February* 21, 1834.—F. R. Conway, esq., appeared, pursuant to adjournment.

Jonathan Helderbrand, (under John Helderbrand,) by his assignee, claiming 200 arpens of land, situate on the Negro fork of the river Marameck. (See record-book D, page 340 ; Minute-books No. 3, page 206 ; No. 4, page 392. See book No. 6, page 501.)

*November* 18, 1834.—The board met, pursuant to adjournment. Present : F. R. Conway, J. H. Relfe, and J. S. Mayfield, commissioners.

John Helderbrand, claiming 200 arpens of land. (See book No. 6, page 501.)

The board are unanimously of opinion that this claim ought not to be granted, the said John Helderbrand having had a grant of 400 arpens. (See commissioners' certificate No. 359. See book No. 7, page 71.)

JAMES S. MAYFIELD,<br>
JAMES H. RELFE,<br>
F. R. CONWAY.

---

Class 2.   No. 17.—John Payett, claiming 464 arpens.

| No. | Name of original claimant. | Arpens. | Nature and date of claim. | By whom granted. | By whom surveyed, date, and situation. |
|---|---|---|---|---|---|
| 17 | John Payett. | 464 | Settlement right. | | William Russell, D. S., January 21, 1806 ; certified February 21, 1806, by Antoine Soulard, S. G. ; on Negro fork of the Marameck. |

EVIDENCE WITH REFERENCE TO MINUTES AND RECORDS.

*August* 20, 1806.—The board met, agreeably to adjournment. Present : Hon. John B. C. Lucas, and Clement B. Penrose, esq.

John Payett, claiming under the second section of the act of Congress, 462 (464) arpens of land, situate on a fork of the waters of the Marameck, called the Negro fork, district of St. Louis, produces a survey of the same, dated the 21st January, and certified the 17th February, 1806.

James Richardson, being duly sworn, says that he knew the above claimant on the said tract of land, about fifteen years ago ; that he raised two crops on the same ; that, in the year 1790, he was driven away by Indians ; that he remained out until the year 1800, when he went back on said land ; that, in 1801, he planted a crop of corn, and was again driven away ; that some of the farmers were killed by the Indians in 1803 ; that although not residing on said land, he still continued the cultivating of the same, and raised four crops ; that, in the year 1805, he went again on said land, and has actually inhabited and cultivated it to this day. The board reject this claim. (See minute-book No. 1, page 482.)

*June* 18, 1810.—Board met. Present : John B. C. Lucas, Clement B. Penrose, and Frederick Bates, commissioners.

John Payett, claiming 462 (464) arpens of land. (See book No. 1, page 482.) It is the opinion of the board that this claim ought not to be granted. (See book No. 4, page 389.)

*February* 21, 1834.—F. R. Conway, esq., appeared, pursuant to adjournment.

John Payett, by his legal representatives, claiming 464 arpens of land, situate on Big river, (alias Negro fork,) of Marameck. (See record-book B, page 259 ; Minutes, book No. 1, page 482 ; No. 4, page 389.)

Abraham Helderbrand, being duly sworn, says that he is fifty-one years of age ; that, in 1802, he helped said Payett to raise a house on the land claimed ; that, in the fall of 1803, he passed by said place, and eat some melons which grew on said land, and saw a small patch of corn growing ; and, in the same fall, the Indians becoming troublesome, he moved to the Marameck settlement, about twelve miles below, and returned, as well as witness recollects, in the spring of 1805, and lived there till his death. Witness further says that his own farm lies about six miles from the land claimed, and that he has lived there for thirty-two years ; that he recollects that said Payett lived on the land claimed since he, witness, was about ten years old ; during which time the said Payett inhabited said place, except when compelled by the Indians, at different times, to leave the said place.

Jonathan Helderbrand, being duly sworn, says that he is in his fiftieth year ; that, in 1801 or 1802, he cannot say which of those years, he passed by said Payett's house, but did not see any white person ; there he found an Indian, with whom he passed the night in said Payett's house, the said Indian being a friendly one, and not an Osage ; that, in 1805, he saw the said Payett living on said place ; that he knows said Payett lived on the land claimed till his death ; that said Payett had a family consisting of his wife and several children, but does not recollect how many.

Jacob Payett, being duly sworn, says that he is forty-two years of age ; that, in 1801, John Payett went on said place, and planted some corn ; and, in 1802, he raised a house, but witness does not recollect whether said Payett moved there the same year, or in 1803 ; that, in the said year 1803, the said Payett was driven away by the Indians, and stayed away about two years, and then returned and lived on said place until he died ; witness further says that, at that time, the said Payett had a wife and eight or nine children ; that said Payett died about five years ago. (See book No. 6, page 501.)

*November* 18, 1834.—The board met, pursuant to adjournment. F. R. Conway, J. H. Relfe, and J. S. Mayfield, commissioners.

John Payett, claiming 464 arpens of land. (See book No. 6, page 501.)

The board are unanimously of opinion that this claim ought not to be granted, the said John Payett having had a confirmation by the former board. (See commissioners' certificate, No. 168. See book No. 7, page 71.)

> JAMES S. MAYFIELD,
> JAMES H. RELFE,
> F. R. CONWAY.

Class 2.    No. 18.—*John Scott, claiming 800 arpens.*

| No. | Name of original claimant. | Arpens. | Nature and date of claim. | By whom granted. | By whom surveyed, date, and situation. |
|---|---|---|---|---|---|
| 18 | John Scott. | 800 | Settlement right. | | On the waters of Dardenne. |

EVIDENCE WITH REFERENCE TO MINUTES AND RECORDS.

*June 25, 1834.*—The board met, pursuant to adjournment. Present : James S. Mayfield and F. R. Conway, commissioners.

John Scott, by his legal representatives, claiming 800 arpens of land, situate on the waters of Dardenne, county of St. Charles. (See book F, page 12 ; Bates's decisions, page 96.)

James Baldridge, being duly sworn, says that he is about fifty-eight years old ; that he thinks it was in 1800 that he helped said John Scott to make the first improvement on this tract ; that, in 1801, he, the deponent, lived part of his time with said Scott on the said place ; that Scott had then a house, and between ten and twelve acres cleared and in cultivation ; that said Scott lived on the place till his death ; that Scott's family has continued to live on said place, and are still living on the same.

John McConnell, duly sworn, says that he is in his fifty-second year ; that, late in the year 1799, he helped said John Scott to build a house on the land claimed, and, early in the year 1800, he assisted him in moving on the same ; that said Scott lived on said place, and, in the spring of 1800, he cleared and improved a field, and raised corn that same year ; that said Scott remained on the place till his death ; that his family continued to improve and enlarge the farm, and are still living on the same. Witness further says that he understood that this tract of land lies adjoining a tract confirmed to said John Scott, under Thomas Johnson, of 500 arpens.

John Howell, duly sworn, says that, in 1801, he laid the worm of a fence round a good large field on the land claimed ; that, in that same year, John Scott raised a crop in the field which deponent helped to fence in ; that said John Scott had a house, and his family was living there with him at the time ; that he had then four or five children. Deponent further says that, during the late war with the British and Indians, two of said John Scott's sons served as rangers during the whole war.

Michael Price, duly sworn, says that, in 1801, he was at John Scott's place, and he had then a good smart field, wherein corn was growing ; that John Scott was living there with his family, consisting of his wife and four or five children ; that said Scott had a good stock of horses, cattle, and hogs ; that, from the first settling of said place, Scott (and after his death his family) lived on, improved, and cultivated said place up to this day. (See book No. 6, page 534.)

*November 18, 1834.*—The board met, pursuant to adjournment. Present: F. R. Conway, J. H. Relfe, and J. S. Mayfield, commissioners.

John Scott, claiming 800 arpens of land. (See book No. 6, page 534.)

The board are unanimously of opinion that this claim ought not to be granted, the said John Scott having had a confirmation under a concession. (See commissioners' certificate No. 120. See book No. 7, page 71.)

> JAMES S. MAYFIELD,
> JAMES H. RELFE,
> F. R. CONWAY.

Class 2.    No. 19.—*Edward Mathews, claiming 640 acres.*

| No. | Name of original claimant. | Acres. | Nature and date of claim. | By whom granted. | By whom surveyed, date, and situation. |
|---|---|---|---|---|---|
| 19 | Edward Mathews. | 640 | Settlement right. | | Joseph Story, D. S., 5th of December, 1805. Received for record 27th February, 1806, by A. Soulard, S. G. |

EVIDENCE WITH REFERENCE TO MINUTES AND RECORDS.

*November 25, 1811.*—Board met. Present: John B. C. Lucas, Clement B. Penrose, and Frederick Bates, commissioners.

Edward Mathews, claiming 750 arpens of land, situate in the district of New Madrid, produces record of a plat of survey dated 19th December, 1805, certified 27th February, 1806.

It is the opinion of the board that this claim ought not to be granted. (See book No. 5, page 453.)

*January* 22, 1834.—F. R. Conway, esq., appeared, pursuant to adjournment.

Edward Mathews, by his legal representatives, claiming 640 acres of land, situate in Prairie St. Charles, alias Mathews's prairie, in Scott county. (See No. 5, page 453; Record-book A, page 465.)

STATE OF MISSOURI, *County of Cape Girardeau :*

Daniel Stringer states that he moved to and settled in the district of l'Anse-a-la-graisse, (New Madrid,) Upper Louisiana, in the year 1802; that he was well acquainted with Edward N. Mathews, who then, in 1802, resided in Prairie St. Charles, or Lorimier's prairie, in said district. This affiant knows that the said Edward inhabited and cultivated land in said prairie in the years 1802, 1803, and 1804; and that he continued to live in said prairie up to the time of his death, something better than a year ago. There was a double cabin on the land where the said Edward lived, in 1802, and a considerable improvement. The said Edward died on the said place, having a family, which still lives on said place.

DANIEL STRINGER,
L. F. LINN, *Commissioner.*

John Friend states that he moved to, and settled in, the district of l'Anse-a-la-graisse, (New Madrid,) Upper Louisiana, in 1799: that he was well acquainted with Edward Mathews. This affiant first became acquainted with the said Edward in the fall of 1801, who then resided in Prairie St. Charles, where he had settled in the spring of that year. This affiant knows that the said Edward inhabited and cultivated land in said prairie in the years of 1802, 1803, and 1804; and that he continued to live in said prairie up to the time of his death, which occurred something like twelve months ago. His children still live on said place, in said prairie.

JOHN × FRIEND.
his
mark.

Sworn to, and mark made in presence of

L. F. LINN, *Commissioner.*

*October* 15, 1833.
(See book No. 6, page 480.)

*November* 18, 1834.—Board met, pursuant to adjournment. Present: F. R. Conway, J. H. Relfe, and J. S. Mayfield, commissioners.

Edward Mathews, claiming 640 acres of land. (See book No. 6, page 480.)

The board are unanimously of opinion that this claim ought not to be granted. The said Edward Mathews had a confirmation. (See commissioners' certificate, No. 1038; Bates's decisions, page 18, for extension to 640 acres. See book No. 7, page 72.)

JAMES S. MAYFIELD,
JAMES H. RELFE,
F. R. CONWAY.

NOTE.—The claim numbered 20, has been withdrawn, having been so numbered inadvertently, it being a claim filed before this board, and found to be for an out-lot proven up before Recorder Hunt, and confirmed.

---

Class 2. No. 21.—*The inhabitants of St. Ferdinand, claiming 1,849¼ arpens.*

To Mr. BEAUROSIER DUNEGAND, *Commandant of the Militia of the Parish of St. Ferdinand :*

ST. FERDINAND, *August* 13, 1796.

The inhabitants of St. Ferdinand have the honor to represent that the Americans are taking concessions in the common, which is the only resource the said inhabitants have for the pasturage needed for this village; and the undersigned, apprehending that the Americans will ask for the only pasturage which now remains for our cattle, we unanimously claim your authority and your recommendation near Don Zenon Trudeau, lieutenant governor of the western part of Illinois, in order that he will please grant us a certain quantity of land to serve as commons for our cattle. The said commons to be taken south of the said village of St. Ferdinand, at the place called Latrappe, which adjoins the concession of Musick, the American, going north one league in length, and extending to the eastward one league in width, making one league square. Our cultivated lands being fenced in, and the concessions of the Americans bounding us on the other side, we have no other resource for the pasturage of our cattle but the land asked for. This being considered, may it please you to make our humble representations to the governor, that he will condescend to grant us our demand, and be convinced of our respectful submission, and we will unanimously pray for his preservation.

[Here follow the signatures or marks of 26 individuals.]

ST. LOUIS, *August* 16, 1796.

The commandant of St. Ferdinand will select the most proper place where to have commons of a sufficient extent for the said village, and shall make it known to us in order to deliver the concession.

ZENON TRUDEAU.

To Don ZENON TRUDEAU, *Lieutenant Governor and Commander-in-chief of the western part of Illinois, &c. :*

ST. LOUIS, *April* 1, 1797.

The inhabitants of St. Ferdinand have the honor to represent that, having asked you, through our commandant, Mr. Francis Dunegand, a concession for a common of one league square, you had authorized the said Dunegand to mark the place of the said common, and this being done, and it being essential to us to secure, for the benefit of the inhabitants of said village, the property of the said land, we have the honor to pray you to grant us the concession for the said common, as follows: the front to be on the river of the said settlement, beginning from the land of Mr. Musick, eighty-four arpens in depth, and having for boundary to the north the end of the lands of our village ; a favor which they hope to receive of your justice, as being absolutely necessary for the pasturage and maintenance of our cattle. Besides, the land demanded is not fit for cultivation ; and the said inhabitants shall never cease to pray for your happiness and prosperity.

F. DUNEGANT.

[Here are the marks of 54 individuals.]

Sr. Louis, *April* 1, 1797.

The surveyor of this jurisdiction, Don Antonio Soulard, shall set boundaries to a league square in the prairie, in order to form a common pasturage for the village of St. Ferdinand, provided it is not prejudicial to the plantations already granted, or to places suitable to make new ones, on account of the timber which might be convenient to those who may solicit them. The said common can be located but in places unfit for cultivation, for the want of water and timber.

ZENON TRUDEAU.

Sr. Louis of Illinois, *April* 15, 1797.

We, the undersigned, surveyor commissioned by the government, certify to all those whom it may concern, that this day, April 15, 1797, by virtue of the decree of the lieutenant governor, dated April 1, same year, we have been on a tract of land destined to serve as commons to the inhabitants of the village of St. Ferdinand, which is to have 84 arpens on the east line, and 70 on that of the north, where it meets the river of St. Ferdinand, which crosses said common almost diagonally. The superfice of said common making altogether 5,206¾ arpens and 1 perch. The said measurement was made in presence of the most notable inhabitants and adjoining neighbors, with the perch of the city of Paris, of 18 French feet in length, according to the usage and custom of this colony. The said common is situated to the eastward of the village of St. Ferdinand ; bounded to the north and west by the river St. Ferdinand ; to the south by the land of Israel Denton, and vacant lands of his Majesty's domain ; and to the east by the same vacant lands of his Majesty. And in order to enable the said inhabitants to prove their right, we have delivered to them these presents, together with the accompanying figurative plat, on which we have marked the natural and artificial limits, &c.

ANTONIO SOULARD.

Sr. Louis, *May* 13, 1835.

I certify the above and foregoing to be truly translated from record-book C, pages 488 and 489.

JULIUS DE MUN, *T. B. C.*

| No. | Name of original claimants. | Arpens. | Nature and date of claim. | By whom granted. | By whom surveyed, date, and situation. |
|---|---|---|---|---|---|
| 21 | The inhabitants of St. Ferdinand. | 1,849¼ | Concession for 7,056 arpens, 1st April, 1797. | Zenon Trudeau. | 5,206¾ arpens, by Antonio Soulard, 15th April, 1779, and certified same day. |

EVIDENCE WITH REFERENCE TO MINUTES AND RECORDS.

*August* 27, 1806.—The board met, agreeably to adjournment. Present : Hon. John B. C. Lucas and Clement B. Penrose, esq.

The inhabitants of the village of St. Ferdinand, to the number of fifty three, claiming, as commons, a league square, or 7,056 arpens, of land, situate at the aforesaid St. Ferdinand, produce a concession from Zenon Trudeau, dated April 1, 1797, and a survey of 5,206¾ arpens, taken and certified April 15, 1797.

John Bte. L. Collins, being duly sworn, says that he came to the said village about ten years ago ; that the said commons had been surveyed a few months prior to his arrival at that place ; that it is mostly prairie land, and is used as a pasture for the cattle of the inhabitants, and has always been used as such ; that the said land is absolutely unfit for cultivation, being mostly swamp, and part of the time under water ; and further, that he did, about eight years ago, see the aforesaid concession in the hands of Francis Dunegand, who was then the civil commandant of said village.

James Richardson, being also duly sworn, says that there is but very little or no wood on said land ; that about nine years ago he assisted Anthony Soulard in surveying said commons, and understood then that there was a concession for the same. The board reject this claim, and are satisfied that the said concession was granted at the time it bears date. (See book No. 1, page 497.)

*August* 20, 1811.—Board met. Present : Clement B. Penrose and Frederick Bates, commissioners.

Inhabitants of the village of St. Ferdinand, claiming 5,206¾ arpens of land. (See book No. 1, page 497.)

The board confirm to the inhabitants of the village of St. Ferdinand five thousand two hundred and six and three quarters arpens and one perch of land, as described in a plat of survey, certified April 15, 1797, and to be found of record in book C, page 489, of the recorder's office. (See book No. 5, page 322.)

*April* 16, 1833.—The board met, pursuant to adjournment. Present : A. G. Harrison, F. R. Conway, commissioners.

The inhabitants of St. Ferdinand, claiming 7,056 arpens of land, of which 5,206¾ arpens have been confirmed. (See book C, page 489 ; Minutes, book No. 1, page 497, and No. 5, page 322. See No. 6, page 156.)

*June* 8, 1835.—The board met, pursuant to adjournment. Present : F. R. Conway, J. H. Relfe, commissioners.

The inhabitants of St. Ferdinand, claiming 1,849¼ arpens of land, it being the balance of 7,506 arpens granted them for commons, of which 5,206¾ arpens have been confirmed. (See book No. 6, page 156.)

The board are of opinion that this claim ought not to be confirmed, the said inhabitants having had the said commons surveyed, conformably to the boundaries asked for in their petition, dated April 1, 1797, and the amount of said survey (5,206¾ arpens) having been confirmed by the former board of commissioners. (See book No. 7, page 169.)

JAMES H. RELFE,
F. R. CONWAY.

I have examined the transcript of the above claim, and concur in the decision.

F. H. MARTIN.

#### CONFLICTING CLAIMS.

Frederick Hyatt and Lewis Hume, for themselves, Reuben Musick, for himself, Joseph Tebeau, for himself, John Romaine, for himself, William Evans, for himself, and Dougald Pitzer, for himself, oppose and object to the confirmation of the additional claim for commons, in favor of the village of St. Ferdinand, in the county of St. Louis; and in support of their objection they state the following facts:

1. There has already been confirmed to the said village, on the claim for commons, a tract of land of five thousand acres or arpens, which is held without opposition or dispute. The claim now before the board, for an enlargement of the confirmation, is, as they are informed, based upon, or refers to a survey of such claim, made by the late John C. Sullivan, without any lawful authority, and which survey, they insist, is of no validity.

2. Each of the objectors is now the owner of lands within the said illegal survey, by regular and satisfactory titles from the United States. And they hereby offer to exhibit to the board the documentary evidence of their respective titles, according to the memorandum of their claims, which follows, viz.:

Frederick Hyatt and Lewis Hume own the following tracts within said claim and illegal survey:

1. The N. E. fractional quarter of sec. 25, in town. 47 N., range 6 E., 158 acres, evidenced by *patent*, dated June 10, 1824.

2. The W. half of N. W. quarter of sec. 30, town. 47, range 7 E., 78 acres and 22½ one-hundredths. Patent, November 10, 1830.

3. The S. W. fractional quarter sec. 25, town. 47 N., range 6 E., 16.80 acres. Patent, February 11, 1832.

4. The N. W. quarter of sec. 19, town. 47 N, range 7 E., 153.08 acres. Evidenced by the receipt of the receiver, dated December 27, 1831.

5. The N. E. quarter of sec. 24, town. 47 N., range 6 E., 121 acres. Received receipt December 26, 1831.

Reuben Musick owns the following tract: The S. E. quarter of sec. 24, in town. 47 N., range 6 E., 139.60. Evidenced by a patent, dated June 10, 1828. The enlarged claim of common and the illegal survey also conflict with the confirmed Spanish grant, in the name of John Brown, now owned and possessed by said Musick. The extent of the interference not precisely known.

William Evans owns the following tract: The S. W. quarter of sec. 19, in town. 47 N., range 7 E., 155.64 acres. Evidenced by the receiver's receipt, dated January 2, 1832.

Dougald Pitzer owns the following tract: The N. E. fractional quarter of sec. 19, town. 47 N., range 7 E., 159.92 acres. Receiver's receipt dated October 2, 1831.

John Romaine owns the following tract: The N. W. fractional quarter of sec. 36, in town. 47 N., range 6 E., 35 acres. Receiver's receipt dated October 18, 1832.

And Joseph Tebeau owns the following tracts: 1st. Lot No. 1, in the S. W. quarter of sec. 30, town. 47, range 7 east, 80 acres. Patent, November 10, 1830. 2d. Lot No. 2, in the S. W. quarter of sec. 30, town. 47 N., range 7 E., 81.40 acres. Receiver's receipt, September 14, 1832. 3d. The E. half of N. W. quarter of sec. 30, town. 47 N., range 7 east, 78 acres and 22½ one-hundredths. Receiver's receipt, August 5, 1829.

Upon the intrinsic demerits of the extended claim for commons, and upon the opposing titles above set forth, and now offered to be exhibited in proof, they respectfully insist that said claim ought not to be reported for confirmation.

Frederick Hyatt, Lewis Hume, Reuben Musick, William Evans, Dougald Pitzer, John Romaine, Joseph Tebeau, by their agent and attorney in fact,

EDWARD BATES.

---

Class 2. No. 22.—*Jerusha Edmondson, claiming 250 arpens.*

| No. | Name of original claimant. | Arpens. | Nature and date of claim. | By whom granted. | By whom surveyed, date, and situation. |
|---|---|---|---|---|---|
| 22 | Jerusha Edmondson. | 250 | Settlement right. | | On the west fork of Spring creek, district of St. Genevieve. |

#### EVIDENCE WITH REFERENCE TO MINUTES AND RECORDS.

St. Louis, *December* 24, 1812.—The interfering claims of S. Thompson, Burwell J. Thompson, assignees, &c., (of Michael Raber) and Jerusha Edmondson. This being the day assigned, the following witnesses were sworn on the part of J. Edmondson:

Green Jewitt, duly sworn, says he knows the land; that Michael Raber settled on the Joachim tract in the year 1801 or 1802, where he made one or two crops; knows not when he left it. In 1805, witness was at Raber's, on the land claimed; saw several cabins of different descriptions; crops growing, and from the appearance of the plantation, judges them to have been made at least a year previously. It was called Mr. Raber's plantation.

*Question by interfering claimant.* Was there a cabin on the Joachim tract when Mr. Raber went on it?

*Answer.* There was.

*Question.* Did you understand that Raber considered the Joachim tract as his head right?

*Answer.* I did understand that he had chosen it with that view.

*Question.* Did you, or did you not know that Raber and the adverse claimant were considered as man and wife, both on the Joachim tract and on the tract now claimed?

*Answer.* She was called Mrs. Raber: the witness had no positive information on the subject.

Witness says he knew John Tulk, a youth who lived in the family; does not recollect whether Tulk called the adverse claimant mother; he seemed to be acting under directions of M. Raber and J. Edmondson, as heads of families.

William Davis, duly sworn, says that he knows the tract claimed; heard J. Edmondson caution the adverse claimant against purchasing this tract, as she was the real proprietor of the land; helped the agent of Mr. Thompson to get in the corn, in fall 1811.

Samuel Thompson, one of the claimants, being duly sworn, says that he has used due diligence, and that it has been out of his power to procure the attendance of his witness. Ordered, that he be permitted to introduce the testimony hereafter, on giving ten days' previous notice to the adverse party. On the margin, the following is written: " Not granted."

(See Bates's minutes, page 30.)

*December* 23, 1834.—F. R. Conway, esq. appeared, pursuant to adjournment.

Jerusha Edmondson, by her legal representatives, claiming 250 arpens of land. (See book F, page 100; Bates's minutes, page 30; Bates's decisions, page 28.)

The following testimony was taken in May, 1833, before L. F. Linn, esq., then one of the commissioners:

John Stewart, aged about 74 years, being duly sworn, as the law directs, deposeth and saith, that he was well acquainted with the said Jerusha Edmondson; that her and one Michael Raber lived together on the tract of land claimed, in the year 1803, and raised a crop thereon in 1804; that there was a dwelling-house, kitchen, smoke-house, and other small houses, on the land; that there were several acres of land cleared, a good garden, and some fruit-trees planted. The houses had the appearance of being one or two years old; that he surveyed the land twice; once for said Michael Raber, and afterward for the said claimant, she claiming the land as hers; that said Raber and her had some difficulty, or quarrel, and both told this witness that they were not married to each other. He heard Jerusha say that the said Raber should not stay on the place, and he knows they separated and continued apart.

JOHN STEWART.

Sworn and subscribed before me, this 9th day of May, 1833.

L. F. LINN, Commissioner.

Israel McGready, aged about 55, being duly sworn, as the law directs, deposeth and saith, that he was well acquainted with Jerusha Edmondson; that she lived with one Michael Raber on the tract of land claimed; that she remained on the tract of land claimed after said Raber left her, and claimed the same as hers; that he has heard both the said Jerusha and Michael say they were not married; and that the tract of land claimed has been inhabited and cultivated ever since.

ISRAEL McGREADY.

Sworn and subscribed before me, this 9th day of May, 1833.

L. F. LINN, Commissioner.

Henry Pinkley, aged about 50 years, being duly sworn, as the law directs, deposeth and saith, that he was well acquainted with Jerusha Edmondson; that she lived on the tract of land claimed, and that one Michael Raber lived with her; that he was about to settle at or near the place claimed, and the said Jerusha forbid him to do so, as she said the land was hers; that the land, or place, was always called the place of Jerusha Edmondson by the people at large who spoke of the same; and that Michael Raber claimed land on the other side of the creek, about one half mile from this place claimed; that he had his buildings on the place he claimed, and not on the place claimed by Jerusha, on which this witness wanted to settle.

HENRY PINKLEY.

Sworn to and subscribed before me, this 9th day of May, 1833.

L. F. LINN, Commissioner.

John Stewart, being further sworn, deposeth and saith, that he knows that after the said Jerusha Edmondson and Michael Raber parted, the said Raber went off and left the said Jerusha in possession of the place, where she continued, claiming the same as her property; and the only way she could be got from the place was by the purchase of her right and interest, which, both Jerusha and Thompson told him, the said Thompson being the purchaser of her right.

JOHN STEWART.

Sworn to and subscribed before me, this 10th day of May, 1833.

L. F. LINN, Commissioner.

Uriah Hull, aged about 56 years, being duly sworn, as the law directs, deposeth and saith, that he knows the tract of land claimed; that the said Jerusha Edmondson and Michael Raber lived together on the same in the year 1804; that some time afterward, say five or six years, they separated, and the said Raber went off, leaving the said Jerusha Edmondson in the possession of the place; that she remained on the place for some time after Raber left her, and this witness understood she had sold her right to one or both of the Messrs. Thompson. This witness has since understood they were not married.

URIAH HULL.

Sworn to and subscribed before me, this 10th day of May, 1833.

L. F. LINN, Commissioner.

Benjamin Horine, being duly sworn, deposeth and saith, that he knew Jerusha Edmondson; that her and one Michael Raber lived together on the tract of land claimed, in the year 1804, and perhaps before that time; that the land was sometimes called Raber's, sometimes her's, and that the said Raber went off and left her in possession of the place, where she remained for sometime afterward.

BENJAMIN HORINE.

Sworn to and subscribed before me, this 11th day of May, 1833.

L. F. LINN, Commissioner.

The following testimony was taken in Washington county, by F. R. Conway, esq. :

John Stewart, being duly sworn, deposeth and saith that he has once before deposed before L. F. Linn, one of the commissioners, and wishes to amend the said deposition by adding the following facts : that toward the last of July or the first of August, 1804, he, said Stewart, was on, or at the place claimed by said Edmondson, and that there were several acres of land cleared and a good crop of corn growing, and that the said Jerusha Edmondson then told him that her and Michael Raber were not married, and that all the property belonged to her ; and that the said Raber sometime afterward told him that he and the said Jerusha were not married, and were not man and wife. And further states, that there were more than one house, a very comfortable cabin for a dwelling-house on the last of July or first of August, 1804, and that she always claimed the premises afterward until she sold.

JOHN STEWART.

Subscribed to and sworn the 5th of July, 1833.

F. R. CONWAY, *Commissioner*.

(See book No. 7, page 84.)

*June* 8, 1835.—The board met, pursuant to adjournment. Present : F. R. Conway, J. H. Relfe, commissioners.

Jerusha Edmondson, claiming 250 arpens of land. (See book No. 7, page 84.)

The board are of opinion that this claim ought not to be granted. The same 250 arpens being the same improvement claimed by, and included in a survey made for one Michael Raber, by John Stewart, deputy surveyor, on the 24th of February, 1806. The said Jerusha Edmondson living at that time with the said Raber, as his wife or mistress. (See book No. 7, page 169.)

JAMES H. RELFE,
F. R. CONWAY.

I have examined the transcript of the above claim, and concur in the decision.

F. H. MARTIN.

---

Class 2. No. 23.—*Joseph Chartran, sr., claiming 998 arpens.*

| No. | Name of original claimant. | Arpens. | Nature and date of claim. | By whom granted. | By whom surveyed, date, and situation. |
|---|---|---|---|---|---|
| 23 | Jos. Chartran, sr. | 998 | Settlement right. | | John McKinney, D. S., 1st February, 1806. Received for record by A. Soulard, S. G., February 25, 1806. On the Missouri. |

EVIDENCE WITH REFERENCE TO MINUTES AND RECORDS.

*July* 31, 1806.—Agreeably to adjournment, the Hon. John B. C. Lucas attended the board.

Joseph Chartran, claiming 998 arpens of land, situate on the river Chorette, district of St. Charles, produces a survey of the same, dated the 1st of February, 1805 (1806.)

Charles Tayon, being duly sworn, says that when he was commandant of St. Charles, the above claimant applied to him for permission to settle on vacant lands ; that he then submitted the said application to Zenon Trudeau, who told him he might grant the said permission ; that the said claimant settled the said tract of land in the year 1801, and did, prior to and on the 20th day of December, 1803, actually inhabit and cultivate the same ; and had then a wife and four or five orphan children entirely destitute of the means of subsistence, and looking up to claimant for the same.

The board grant the said claimant two hundred arpens of land, situate as aforesaid. (See No. 1, page 440.)

*August* 7, 1807.—The board met, agreeably to adjournment. Present : Hon. John B. C. Lucas, Clement B. Penrose, and Frederick Bates, esquires.

Joseph Chartran, claiming under the 2d section of the act of Congress of the 2d of March, 1805, 998 arpens of land, situate on the river Chorette, district of St. Charles, produces a survey of the same, dated 1st February, 1805.

John Baptiste Leauzon, being duly sworn, says that he knows the land claimed by the said Chartran, situated at the village Chorette ; that the land was settled by claimant, in the year 1801, and that he has continued to inhabit and cultivate the same ever since ; that the said claimant has generally had four orphan children with him, looking up to him for support, and whom he has treated with tenderness, and in every respect as a good father would treat his own ; that in 1803 he had three of them with him. (Laid over for decision. See book No. 3, page 54.)

*December* 1, 1809.—Board met. Present : John B. C. Lucas, Clement B. Penrose, and Frederick Bates, commissioners.

Joseph Chartran, claiming 998 arpens of land. (See book No. 1, page 440 ; book No. 3, page 54.)

It is the opinion of the board that this claim ought not to be granted. (See No. 4, page 218.)

*March* 27, 1835.—F. R. Conway, esq., appeared, pursuant to adjournment.

Joseph Chartran, by his legal representatives, claiming 998 arpens of land, on river Chorette. (See record-book B, page 219 ; Minutes, books No. 1, page 440 ; No. 3, page 54, and No. 4, page 218.)

The following testimony was taken in June, 1833, by A. G. Harrison, esq., then one of the commissioners :

John Mary Cardinal, being duly sworn, says that he knew said Chartran ; that he made a settlement and improvement on a tract of land on the upper part of Chorette ; that he had an orchard on the same tract ; that said improvement, settlement, &c., were made under the Spanish government about five or six years before the change of government ; that he was married at the time mentioned, and that he cultivated said place about a dozen years.

Charles Reille, being duly sworn, says that, having heard read the testimony of John Mary Cardinal, as above, that he testifies to the same facts in every particular as above, except that witness thinks said Chartran cultivated said land about fourteen years.  (See book No. 7, page 109.)

*June 8, 1835.*—The board met, pursuant to adjournment.  Present: F. R. Conway, James H. Relfe, commissioners.

Joseph Chartran, sr., claiming 998 arpens of land.  (See book No. 7, page 109.)

The board are of opinion that this claim cannot be granted, the said Joseph Chartran, sr., having had two concessions confirmed.  (See commissioners' certificates, Nos. 26 and 786.  See book No. 7, page 170.)

JAMES H. RELFE,<br>F. R. CONWAY.

I have examined the transcript of the above claim, and concur in the decision.

F. H. MARTIN.

Class 2.   No. 24.—*Pierre Palardie, claiming 1,000 arpens.*

| No. | Name of original claimant. | Arpens. | Nature and date of claim. | By whom granted. | By whom surveyed, date, and situation. |
|---|---|---|---|---|---|
| 24 | Pierre Palardie. | 1,000 | Settlement right. | | |

EVIDENCE WITH REFERENCE TO MINUTES AND RECORDS.

*December 6, 1811.*—Board met.  Present: John B. C. Lucas, Clement B. Penrose, and Frederick Bates, commissioners.

Pierre Palardie, claiming 1,000 arpens of land.  Produces notice to the recorder, district of St. Charles.  It is the opinion of the board that this claim ought not to be granted.  (See minutes, book No. 5, page 482.)

*March 31, 1835.*—F. R. Conway, esq., appeared, pursuant to adjournment.

Pierre Palardie, claiming 1,000 arpens of land, on the Dardenne.  (See record-book D, page 340; book No. 5, page 482.)

The following testimony was taken in May, 1833, by A. G. Harrison, esq., then one of the commissioners:

Gabriel Latreille, being duly sworn, says that he is well acquainted with said tract of land; that it is situated at the mouth of the Dardenne; that Palardie cut hay on said land to feed his cattle, with the intention of establishing himself on said place.  (See No. 7, page 113.)

*June 8, 1835.*—The board met, pursuant to adjournment.  Present: F. R. Conway, J. H. Relfe, commissioners.

Pierre Palardie, claiming 1,000 arpens of land.  (See book No. 7, page 113.)

The board are of opinion that this claim ought not to be granted.  (See book No. 7, page 171.)

JAMES H. RELFE,<br>F. R. CONWAY.

I have examined the transcript of the above claim, and concur in the decision.

F. H. MARTIN.

Class 2. No. 25.—*William Bates, claiming 640 acres.*

| No. | Name of original claimant. | Acres. | Nature and date of claim. | By whom granted. | By whom surveyed, date, and situation. |
|---|---|---|---|---|---|
| 25 | William Bates. | 640 | Settlement right. | | John Stewart, D. S., 3d February, 1806.  Received for record by A. Soulard, S. G., 27th February, 1806. |

EVIDENCE WITH REFERENCE TO MINUTES AND RECORDS.

*April 6, 1835.*—F. R. Conway, esq., appeared, pursuant to adjournment.

William Bates, claiming 640 acres of land, situate in the district of St. Genevieve.  (See record-book B, page 350.)

The following testimony was taken at Potosi, by F. R. Conway, esq.:

John T. McNeal, being duly sworn, deposeth and saith that, in the month of February, 1804, William Bates and he, witness, went in company where said Bates had made and laid the foundation of a house; there were some trees cut round, some brush-heaps made, and his name marked on a tree near the spring, and dated 1803; that said Bates claimed the same as his head right, as being one of Moses Austin's followers, as will fully appear on the original records of land titles under the Spanish government; that said William Bates claims 640 acres, and witness never heard of his selling or claiming any other land as his head right.

JOHN T. McNEAL.

Sworn to and subscribed before me, this 8th day of May, 1834, at Potosi, Missouri.

F. R. CONWAY.

(See book No. 7, page 117.)

*June* 8, 1835.—The board met, pursuant to adjournment. Present: F. R. Conway and J. H. Relfe, commissioners.

William Bates, claiming 640 acres of land. (See book No. 7, page 117.)

The board are of opinion that this claim ought not to be granted. (See book No. 7, page 172.)

JAMES H. RELFE,
F. R. CONWAY.

I have examined the transcript of the above claim, and concur in the decision.

F. H. MARTIN.

---

Class 2.   No. 26.—*Charles McDormet, claiming 640 acres.*

| No. | Name of original claimant. | Acres. | Nature and date of claim. | By whom granted. | By whom surveyed, date, and situation. |
|---|---|---|---|---|---|
| 26 | Charles McDormet. | 640 | Settlement right. | | John Hawkins, D. S. Received for record, by A. Soulard, S. G., 18th February, 1806. District of St. Genevieve. |

EVIDENCE WITH REFERENCE TO MINUTES AND RECORDS.

*April* 7, 1835.—F. R. Conway, esq., appeared, pursuant to adjournment.

Charles McDormet, claiming 640 acres of land, situate in the district of St. Genevieve. (See record-book B, page 245.)

The following testimony was taken by F. R. Conway, esq., at Potosi.

John T. McNeal, being duly sworn, deposeth and saith that, in the month of February, 1804, he, in company with William Bates, passed by what was called McDormet's improvement, where was the foundation of a house, some trees cut round, brush-heaps made, rails split, and a promising prospect for an improvement ; that the said McDormet has ever since claimed the same as his head right, as one of Moses Austin's followers, as will fully appear by having reference to the Spanish records, and claimant's name was marked on a sugar tree near the spring, dated 1803. Witness never heard of his claiming any other land under his head or improvement right.

JOHN T. McNEAL.

Sworn to and subscribed before me, this 8th day of May, 1834, at Potosi, Missouri.

(See Book No. 7, page 118.)

F. R. CONWAY.

*June* 8, 1835.—The board met, pursuant to adjournment. Present : F. R. Conway, J. H. Relfe, commissioners.

Charles McDormet, claiming 640 acres of land. (See book No. 7, page 118.)

The board are of opinion that this claim ought not to be granted. (See book No. 7, page 172.)

JAMES H. RELFE,
F. R. CONWAY.

I have examined the transcript of the above claim, and concur in the decision.

F. H. MARTIN.

---

Class 2.   No. 27.—*Louis Milhomme, claiming 620 acres.*

| No. | Name of original claimant. | Acres. | Nature and date of claim. | By whom granted. | By whom surveyed, date, and situation. |
|---|---|---|---|---|---|
| 27 | Louis Milhomme. | 620 | Settlement right. | | John Stewart, D. S., 4th Feb. 1806. Received for record, by A. Soulard, S. G., 28th Feb. 1806. Bellevue, district of St. Genevieve. |

EVIDENCE WITH REFERENCE TO MINUTES AND RECORDS.

*April* 10, 1835.—F. R. Conway, esq., appeared, pursuant to adjournment.

Louis Milhomme, claiming 620 acres of land, situate Bellevue. (See record-book B, page 249.)

The following testimony was taken in Washington county, by James H. Relfe, commissioner :

Personally appeared John T. McNeal, who deposeth and saith that he was well acquainted with Louis Milhomme, a laboring man, with a family, who resided in Mine à Breton, who had a house, and cultivated a garden and other improvements, in the years 1802, 1803, and 1804 ; and he never knew him to claim other lands.

JOHN T. McNEAL.

Sworn to and subscribed before me, this 21st June, 1834.

(See book No. 7, page 123.)

JAMES H. RELFE.

*June* 9, 1835.—The board met, pursuant to adjournment. Present : F. R. Conway, J. H. Relfe, commissioners.

Louis Milhomme, claiming 620 acres of land. (See book No. 7, page 123.)

The board are of opinion that this claim ought not to be granted, there being no proof of possession or cultivation, the only testimony given having reference to a town lot. (See book No. 7, page 173.)

JAMES H. RELFE,

F. R. CONWAY.

I have examined the transcript of the above claim, and concur in the decision.

F. H. MARTIN.

---

Class 2. No. 28.—Louis Lacroix, claiming 701 arpens.

| No. | Name of original claimant. | Arpens. | Nature and date of claim. | By whom granted. | By whom surveyed, date, and situation. |
|---|---|---|---|---|---|
| 28 | Louis Lacroix. | 701 | Settlement right | | John Stewart, D. S., 25th February, 1806. Received for record, by A. Soulard, S. G., 28th February, 1806; 701 arpens on Fourche à Courtois; 40 acres in Mine à Breton. |

EVIDENCE WITH REFERENCE TO MINUTES AND RECORDS.

*June 27, 1806.*—The board met, agreeably to adjournment   Present: Hon. Clement B. Penrose and James L. Donaldson, esq.

Louis Grinya and Francis Tibault, assignees of Louis Lacroix, claiming 701 arpens of land, situate at about three fourths of a mile of the Mine à Breton, district aforesaid, (of St. Genevieve,) produces a survey of the same, dated the 25th and certified the 28th February, 1806, together with a survey of 40 arpens, situate at the Mine à Breton, dated and certified as aforesaid.

Amable Partenais, being duly sworn, says that the aforesaid Louis Lacroix had, in 1802, a house built, and seven or eight arpens of land under fence in the aforesaid tract of 40 arpens; that he actually inhabited the same; that, in 1803, he planted a crop, which, together with the said improvement, he sold to claimants, who moved on the same in the month of October, 1803, and did, prior to, and on the 20th day of December, 1803, actually inhabit the same, having gathered the said crop.

The board reject this claim, for want of a permission to settle. (See book No. 1, page 379.)

*December 23, 1811.*—Board met. Present: John B. C. Lucas, Clement B. Penrose, and Frederick Bates, commissioners.

Louis Grinya and Francis Tibault, assignees of Louis Lacroix, claiming 40 arpens of land. (See book No. 1, page 379.)

The board remark that no kind of testimony suggests or makes it appear that the land claimed includes a lead mine.

It is the opinion of the board that this claim ought not to be granted. (See No. 5, page 534.)

*April 10, 1835.*—F. R. Conway, esq., appeared, pursuant to adjournment.

Louis Lacroix, claiming 701 arpens of land. (See minute-book No. 1, page 379; No. 5, page 534.)

The following testimony was taken in Washington county, by James H. Relfe, commissioner:

Personally appeared John T. McNeal, who deposeth and saith that he was well acquainted with Louis Lacroix, who lived in a house and cultivated a garden in Mine à Breton, in the years 1802 and 1803, and, like most others who lived at the mines, cultivated corn at some distance from the village; his field was on Big river. At that early day is was necessary to the safety of the inhabitants to live in the villages, to secure them from the attacks of savages, and for the convenience of working the mines. This deponent never knew Lacroix to claim any other lands.

JOHN T. McNEAL.

Sworn to and subscribed before me, this 21st of June, 1834.

JAMES H. RELFE, Commissioner.

(See book No. 7, page 124.)

*June 9, 1835.*—The board met, pursuant to adjournment. Present: F. R. Conway, J. H. Relfe, commissioners.

Louis Lacroix, claiming 701 arpens of land. (See book No. 7, page 124.)

The board are of opinion that this claim ought not to be granted, the said Louis Lacroix being one of the thirty-one inhabitants claiming each 400 arpens of land under the old mine concession. (See book No. 7, page 174.)

JAMES H. RELFE,

F. R. CONWAY.

I have examined the transcript of the above claim, and concur in the decision.

F. H. MARTIN.

---

Class 2. No. 29.—Nancy Ferguson, claiming 300 arpens.

| No. | Name of original claimant. | Arpens. | Nature and date of claim. | By whom granted. | By whom surveyed, date, and situation. |
|---|---|---|---|---|---|
| 29 | Nancy Ferguson. | 300 | Settlement right. | | |

EVIDENCE WITH REFERENCE TO MINUTES AND RECORDS.

*June* 21, 1809.—Board met.    Present : Clement B. Penrose and Frederick Bates, commissioners.

Nancy Ferguson, claiming 300 arpens of land, situate in Tywapity, district of New Madrid, produces to the board a certified list of permission to settle, formerly given, No. 1369, on which claimant is No. 298.

The following testimony in the foregoing claim, taken at New Madrid, June 15, 1808, by Frederick Bates, commissioner :

George Hacker, duly sworn, says that premises were improved in 1803 by splitting rails and clearing about an acre of ground ; no crop raised till the present year ; no inhabitation.    Laid over for decision.    (See No. 4, page 97.)

*December* 5, 1810.—Board met.    Present : John B. C. Lucas, Clement B. Penrose, and Frederick Bates, commissioners.

Nancy Ferguson, claiming 300 arpens of land.    (See book No. 4, page 97.)

It is the opinion of the board that this claim ought not to be granted.    (See book No. 5, page 22.)

*May* 1, 1835.—The board met, pursuant to adjournment.    Present : J. H. Relfe and F. R. Conway, commissioners.

Nancy Ferguson, by her heirs and legal representatives, claiming 300 arpens of land, situate in Tywapity, district of New Madrid.    (See record-book E, page 148 ; book No. 4, page 97 ; No. 5, page 22.)

The following testimony was taken before L. F. Linn, esq., in June, 1833 :

George Hacker, being sworn, says he is about 57 years old, and that he knew the said Nancy Ferguson well. She came to the district of New Madrid in the fall of 1802, and made an improvement in the winter of that year. The next season she planted corn and raised a crop on said land, where she also resided.   She had two children at that time.   She died in the year 1818, leaving her said two children, Elizabeth Northcut and John Johnson, as her sole heirs and legal representatives.   She inhabited and cultivated the said land in 1803, and had a permission to settle from Don Henry Peyroux, commandant of New Madrid.

GEORGE HACKER.

Sworn to and subscribed, this 11th day of June, 1833.

L. F. LINN, *Commissioner.*

(See book No. 7, page 141.)

*June* 9, 1835.—The board met, pursuant to adjournment.    Present : F. R. Conway and J. H. Relfe, commissioners.

Nancy Ferguson, claiming 300 arpens of land.    (See book No. 7, page 141.)

The board are of opinion that this claim ought not to be granted.    (See book No. 7, page 175.)

JAMES H. RELFE,
F. R. CONWAY.

I have examined the transcript of the above claim, and concur in the decision.

F. H. MARTIN.

---

Class 2.    No. 30.—*Urban Asherbraunner, claiming 350 arpens and 95 perches.*

| No. | Name of original claimant. | Arpens. | Nature and date of claim. | By whom granted. | By whom surveyed, date, and situation. |
|---|---|---|---|---|---|
| 30 | Urban Asherbraunner. | 350 95 per. | Settlement right. | | James Boyd, D. S. Received for record, 27th February, 1806, by A. Soulard, S. G.   On Castor creek, Cape Girardeau. |

EVIDENCE WITH REFERENCE TO MINUTES AND RECORDS.

*February* 20, 1809.—Board met.    Present : John B. C. Lucas, Clement B. Penrose, and Frederick Bates, commissioners.

Urban Asherbraunner, claiming 350 arpens 95 perches of land, situate on Castor creek, district of Cape Girardeau.   Produces to the board a plat of survey certified to be received for record 27th February, 1806, by Antoine Soulard, surveyor general.

The following testimony in the above claim, taken by Frederick Bates, commissioner, at Cape Girardeau, May 30, 1808 :

Daniel Asherbraunner, sworn, says that claimant improved a tract of land in the year 1800 ; that the survey of Philip Bollinger afterward took in the spring of the claimant, which induced him to abandon his improvement, and left the country in the following year ; he again returned in the year 1805, and in that year improved the premises now claimed ; settled in the following year, erected a cabin, a mill for the grinding of corn and wheat, and cultivated about three or four acres of land.    Claimant has continued to inhabit, cultivate, and improve, till the present day ; has a wife and one child.    Laid over for decision.    (See book No. 3, page 479.)

*December* 23, 1809.—Board met.    Present : John B. C. Lucas, Clement B. Penrose, and Frederick Bates, commissioners.

Urban Asherbraunner, claiming 350 arpens 95 perches of land.    (See book No. 3, page 479.)   It is the opinion of the board that this claim ought not to be granted.    (See book No. 4, page 238.)

*May* 7, 1835.—The board met, pursuant to adjournment.    Present : F. R. Conway, James H. Relfe, commissioners.

Urban Asherbraunner, claiming 350 arpens and 95 perches of land, situate on Castor creek, district of Cape Girardeau. (See record-book B, page 294, for survey of 300 acres; minutes, book No. 3, page 479; No. 4, page 238.)

The following testimony was taken before J. H. Relfe, commissioner, in Cape Girardeau county:

William Bollinger, sr., states that he moved to and settled in the district of Cape Girardeau, in the year 1801; that he was well acquainted with one Urban Asherbraunner, then a resident of said district. This affiant knows that the said Asherbraunner inhabited and cultivated a piece of land on Whitewater, in said district, in the year 1802. He had a house built on said place in said year, some trees were ——— and deadened on said place, at the time mentioned, by said Asherbraunner, who lived in this district upward of eighteen years. This improvement was made by the said Urban Asherbraunner, at the time mentioned, for his own use.

WILLIAM × BOLLINGER.<br>his<br>mark.

Sworn to and subscribed, this 7th April, 1835.

JAMES H. RELFE, Commissioner.

(See book No. 7, page 144.)

*June* 10, 1835.—The board met, pursuant to adjournment. Present: F. R. Conway and J. H. Relfe, commissioners.

Urban Asherbraunner, claiming 350 arpens 95 perches of land. (See book No. 7, page 144.)

The board are of opinion that this claim ought not to be granted. (See book No. 7, page 176.)

JAMES H. RELFE,<br>F. R. CONWAY.

I have examined the transcript of the above claim, and concur in the decision.

F. H. MARTIN.

---

Class 2.   No. 31.—Joseph Fenwick, claiming 800 arpens.

| No. | Name of original claimant. | Arpens. | Nature and date of claim. | By whom granted. | By whom surveyed, date, and situation. |
|---|---|---|---|---|---|
| 31 | Joseph Fenwick. | 800 | Settlement right. | | |

EVIDENCE WITH REFERENCE TO MINUTES AND RECORDS.

*May* 11, 1835.—The board met, pursuant to adjournment. Present: James H. Relfe, F. R. Conway, commissioners.

Joseph Fenwick, by his heirs and legal representatives, claiming 800 arpens of land. (See record-book E, page 271; Bates's decisions, page 93.)

The following testimony was taken before L. F. Linn, commissioner, on the 17th of June, 1833:

STATE OF MISSOURI, *County of St. Genevieve.*

John B. Vallé, aged about seventy-two years, being duly sworn as the law directs, deposeth and saith that he was well acquainted with the original claimant, Joseph Fenwick; that he came to this country, then the province of Upper Louisiana, in the year 1800, with a large and respectable family, and had considerable property; that the said Fenwick settled on the land claimed, made considerable buildings and improvements, and cultivated the same for some time, and that he then disposed of the same; that this tract of land has passed through several hands and to several claimants, but has always, from the time of the original settlement up to the present day, been actually inhabited and cultivated, and still is inhabited and cultivated.

J. B. VALLÉ.

Sworn to and subscribed before me, L. F. Linn, this 17th day of June, 1833.

L. F. LINN, Commissioner.

(See book No. 7, page 146.)

*June* 10, 1835.—The board met, pursuant to adjournment. Present: F. R. Conway, J. H. Relfe, commissioners.

Joseph Fenwick, claiming 800 arpens of land. (See book No. 7, page 146.)

The board are of opinion that this claim ought not to be granted, the said Joseph Fenwick having had lands confirmed to him. (See commissioners' certificate, No. 1243; Bates's decisions, page 57. See book No. 7, page 176.)

JAMES H. RELFE,<br>F. R. CONWAY.

I have examined the transcript of the above claim, and concur in the decision.

F. H. MARTIN.

---

Class 2.   No. 32.—Matthew Mullins, claiming 584 arpens 9 perches.

| No. | Name of original claimant. | Arpens. | Nature and date of claim. | By whom granted. | By whom surveyed, date, and situation. |
|---|---|---|---|---|---|
| 32 | Matthew Mullins. | 584 9 p | Settlement right. | | 500 acres; John Stewart, 5th Jan., 1806. Received for record, 25th February, 1806, by A. Soulard, surveyor general. |

*November* 25, 1811.—Board met. Present: John B. C. Lucas, Clement B. Penrose, and Frederick Bates, commissioners.

Matthew Mullins, claiming 745 arpens 68 perches of land, situate near Bellevue, district of St. Genevieve, produces record of a plat of survey, dated 5th January, and certified 25th February, 1806.

It is the opinion of this board that this claim ought not to be granted. (See book No. 5, page 454.)

*May* 12, 1835.—The board met, pursuant to adjournment. Present: James H. Relfe, F. R. Conway, commissioners.

Matthew Mullins, claiming 584 arpens 9 perches of land, near Bellevue settlement. (See record-book B, page 227; book No. 5, page 454.)

The following testimony was taken in Washington county, before F. R. Conway, esq.:

John Stewart, of lawful age, being first duly sworn, deposeth and saith that, in November, 1800, this affiant came to Mine à Breton, in the district of St. Genevieve, and was from that time for many years thereafter well acquainted with the above claimant, Matthew Mullins; that this affiant always understood from Moses Austin and others, that said Matthew was entitled to 400 arpens of land, on account of his having come to the Spanish country under Moses Austin, and in virtue of an understanding between Moses Austin and the Spanish authorities of the country, which will more at large appear by an examination of the records of the courts, in or about the year 1797, that being the year said Matthew came to the country, as this affiant has been informed. This affiant would further show, that Elias Bates was also a follower of Moses Austin, and obtained a gratuity of 400 arpens, upon the identical principles upon which Matthew claims his. In January or February, 1806, Matthew Mullins called upon affiant, who was legally authorized to make public surveys of land, to survey for him the above claim. This affiant having been instructed to survey for each land claimant 640 acres, accordingly surveyed for Matthew Mullins 640 acres of land in Bellevue, then district of St. Genevieve, now county of Washington, the plat whereof has been duly returned in order to its being recorded. Matthew Mullins showed the land which was surveyed, and pointed out to this affiant the beginning-corner of the same, which was accordingly fixed and established as such by this affiant, in virtue of his official duty as surveyor. And further, this deponent saith not.

                                                                          JOHN STEWART.

Sworn and subscribed before me, this 5th day of July, A. D. 1833.

                                                                          F. R. CONWAY.

(No. 7, page 147.)

*June* 10, 1835.—The board met, pursuant to adjournment. Present: F. R. Conway, J. H. Relfe, commissioners.

Matthew Mullins, claiming 584 arpens 9 perches of land. (See book No. 7, page 147.)

The board are of opinion that this claim ought not to be granted. (See book No. 7, page 176.)

                                                                          JAMES H. RELFE,
                                                                          F. R. CONWAY.

I have examined the transcript of the above claim, and concur in the decision.

                                                                          F. H. MARTIN.

---

Class 2.    No. 33.—*Charles McLane, claiming* 748 *arpens* 68 *perches.*

| No. | Name of original claimant. | Arpens. | Nature and date of claim. | By whom granted. | By whom surveyed, date, and situation. |
|-----|---------------------------|---------|--------------------------|-----------------|----------------------------------------|
| 33  | Charles McLane.           | 748 68 p. | Settlement right.       |                 | J. Stewart, D. S., February 15, 1806. Received for record Feb. 29, 1806, by Ant Soulard, S. G. In Bellevue settlement. |

*November* 25, 1811.—Board met. Present: John B. C. Lucas, Clement B. Penrose, and Frederick Bates, commissioners.

Charles McLane, claiming 748 arpens 68 perches of land, situated in Bellevue, district of St. Genevieve, produces record of a plat of survey, dated 15th, and certified 28th February, 1806.

It is the opinion of the board that this claim ought not to be granted. (See No. 5, page 454.)

*May* 15, 1835.—The board met, pursuant to adjournment. Present: F. R. Conway, J. H. Relfe, commissioners.

Charles McLane, claiming 748 arpens 68 perches of land, situated in Bellevue. (See record-book B, page 427; Minute-book No. 5, page 454.) Produces a plat of survey, executed by John Stewart, February 15, and received for record by A. Soulard, surveyor general, February 29, 1860. (See book No. 7, page 153.)

*June* 10, 1835.—The board met, pursuant to adjournment. Present: F. R. Conway, J. H. Relfe, commissioners.

Charles McLane, claiming 748 arpens 68 perches of land. (See book No. 7, page 153.)

The board are of opinion that this claim ought not to be granted. (See book No. 7, page 177.)

                                                                          JAMES H. RELFE,
                                                                          F. R. CONWAY.

I have examined the transcript of the above claim, and concur in the decision.

                                                                          F. H. MARTIN.

Class 2. No. 34.—*Louis Grenier, claiming 701 arpens.*

| No. | Name of original claimant. | Arpens. | Nature and date of claim. | By whom granted. | By whom surveyed, date, and situation. |
|---|---|---|---|---|---|
| 34 | Louis Grenier. | 701 | Settlement right. | | John Stewart, D. S., 25th February, 1806. Received for record, by Soulard, S. G., 28th February, 1806. On Fourche à Courtois, district of St. Genevieve. |

EVIDENCE WITH REFERENCE TO MINUTES AND RECORDS.

*May* 15, 1835.—The board met, pursuant to adjournment. Present: F. R. Conway, J. H. Relfe, commissioners.

Louis Grenier, claiming 701 arpens of land, situate on Fourche à Courtois, district of St. Genevieve. (See record-book B, page 225.)

The following testimony was taken by F. R. Conway, in July, 1833, in Washington county:

John Stewart, being duly sworn, deposeth and saith that he was well acquainted with Louis Grenier; that in the year 1803, the said Grenier was then a laboring man, living in a cabin in Mine à Breton. He had a garden, and in 1804 he cultivated some acres of land at said place; that in the year 1806, he called on witness to survey his land, but an old Spanish right on the east, a conditional line on the west, a claim on the south, and a Spanish concession on the north, confined him so close, witness could not get his complement of land, and surveyed the balance of his claim, in all 640 acres, about 18 miles, as witness supposes, from Mine à Breton, in woodland, not then claimed by any person; which survey witness made, returned the plat for record, and paid the recording fees.

JOHN STEWART.

Sworn to and subscribed before me, this 9th day of July, A. D., 1833.
(See minute-book No. 7, page 153.)

F. R. CONWAY.

*June* 10, 1835.—The board met, pursuant to adjournment. Present: F. R. Conway, James H. Relfe, commissioners.

Louis Grenier, claiming 701 arpens of land. (See book No. 7, page 153.)

The board are of opinion that this claim ought not to be granted. (See book No. 7, page 177.)

JAMES H. RELFE,<br>F. R. CONWAY.

I have examined the testimony of the above claim, and concur in the decision.

F. H. MARTIN.

---

Class 2. No. 35.—*Charles Becquette, claiming 606 acres.*

| No. | Name of original claimant. | Acres. | Name and date of claim. | By whom granted. | By whom surveyed, date, and situation. |
|---|---|---|---|---|---|
| 35 | Charles Becquette. | 606 | Settlement right. | | Survey on record, without date or signature. |

EVIDENCE WITH REFERENCE TO MINUTES AND RECORDS.

*May* 16, 1835.—The board met, pursuant to adjournment. Present: F. R. Conway and J. H. Relfe, commissioners.

Charles Becquette, claiming 606 acres of land, situate in Bellevue, district of St. Genevieve. (See record-book B, page 208.)

The following deposition was taken in Washington county, by F. R. Conway, esq.:

This day personally appeared before me, John Stewart, of lawful age, who deposeth and saith that, in the year 1803, Charles (otherwise called Charlot) Becquette was an inhabitant and resident in Mine à Breton, and cultivated some acres of land. In 1806, witness surveyed his improvement and the balance of the land, including in all 640 acres, agreeably to witness's instructions from the United States agent and commissioners; which survey I returned for record.

JOHN STEWART.

Sworn and subscribed before me, this 9th day of July, A. D., 1833.
(See book No. 7, page 154.)

F. R. CONWAY.

*June* 11, 1835.—The board met, pursuant to adjournment. Present: F. R. Conway and J. H. Relfe, commissioners.

Charles Becquette, claiming 606 acres of land. (See book No. 7, page 154.)

The board are of opinion that this claim ought not to be confirmed. (See book No. 7, page 177.)

JAMES H. RELFE,<br>F. R. CONWAY.

I have examined the transcript of the above claim, and concur in the decision.

F. H. MARTIN.

Class 2.  No. 36.—*Daniel Richardson, claiming 460 arpens.*

| No. | Name of original claimant. | Arpens. | Nature and date of claim. | By whom granted. | By whom surveyed, date, and situation. |
|---|---|---|---|---|---|
| 36 | Daniel Richardson. | 460 | Settlement right. | | John McKenny, D. S., 22d February, 1806. Received for record, 26th February, 1806, by A. Soulard, S. G. Point Labbadie, on the Missouri. |

EVIDENCE WITH REFERENCE TO MINUTES AND RECORDS.

*August* 7, 1806.—The board met, agreeably to adjournment.  Present: Hon. John B. C. Lucas and Clement B. Penrose, esq.

Daniel Richardson and John Caldwell, claiming, under the second section of the act of Congress, 460 arpens of land, situate on the Missouri, district of St. Louis, produces a survey of the same, dated the 22d, and certified 26th February, 1806.

James Stevens, being duly sworn, says that, in March, 1803, claimants did cut a few poles on said land, and were preparing to build and cultivate, but were prevented by the Indians.

The board reject this claim.  (See No. 1, page 444.)

*December* 6, 1811.—Board met.  Present: John B. C. Lucas, Clement B. Penrose, and Frederick Bates, commissioners.

Daniel Richardson, claiming 460 arpens of land, situate Point Labbadie, district of St. Louis, produces record of a plat of survey, dated 22d, and certified 26th February, 1806.

It is the opinion of the board that this claim ought not to be granted.  (See book No. 5, page 486.)

*May* 19, 1835.—F. R. Conway, esq., appeared, pursuant to adjournment.

Daniel Richardson, claiming 460 arpens of land, situate on the Missouri.  (See record-book B, page 346; minutes, book No. 1, page 444; No. 5, page 486.)

James Cowen, being duly sworn, says that, in the month of November next, he will be 54 years of age; that, in February, 1803, he settled in the neighborhood of claimant, and it was then reported that the said Daniel Richardson had then begun to improve the land claimed in the spring of said year, 1803, but witness did not see it himself.  The first time witness saw the said improvement, was in the fall of 1804, to the best of his recollection; there were, at that time, some rails split, house-logs cut, a small piece of land, about a quarter of an acre, enclosed with rails and poles, and a nursery of peach-trees planted in said enclosure.  Witness further says that, in the month of April, 1803, as well as he can recollect, the Indians made an incursion on their settlement, killed a man, burnt houses, and drove the settlers away.  Claimant was a single man, and boarded with one Stevens, whose land was adjoining that of said claimant.  (See book No. 7, page 155.)

*June* 11, 1835.—The board met, pursuant to adjournment.  Present: F. R. Conway, J. H. Relfe, commissioners.

Daniel Richardson, claiming 460 arpens of land.  (See book No. 7, page 155.)

The board are of opinion that this claim ought not to be granted.  (See book No. 7, page 178.)

JAMES H. RELFE,
F. R. CONWAY.

I have examined the transcript of the above claim, and concur in the decision.

F. H. MARTIN.

Class 2.  No. 37.—*Jerome Mattis, claiming 800 arpens.*

| No. | Name of original claimant | Arpens. | Nature and date of claim. | By whom granted. | By whom surveyed, date, and situation. |
|---|---|---|---|---|---|
| 37 | Jerome Mattis. | 800 | Settlement right. | | On the waters of the St. Francis river. |

EVIDENCE WITH REFERENCE TO MINUTES AND RECORDS.

*May* 22, 1835.—F. R. Conway, esq., appeared, pursuant to adjournment.

Jerome Mattis, by his legal representatives, claiming 800 arpens of land, situate on the waters of St. Francis river.  (See record-book F, page 146; Bates's decisions, page 105.)

The following testimony was taken in May, 1833, before L. F. Linn, commissioner:

STATE OF MISSOURI, *County of Madison:*

John Beeve, aged about 57 years, being duly sworn, as the law directs, deposeth and saith that he was well acquainted with Jerome Mattis; that he knew him to be a citizen and resident of this country, then the province of Upper Louisiana, some years before the year 1800, and that he continued to be a citizen of the country for many years afterward and until he died.  This witness further says that he knows the land claimed; that the claimant occupied the same in the year 1802 or 1803 ; that he built a camp on the same and made sugar there ; that the claimant continued to occupy the same, and made sugar there for several years ; that the claimant had a wife at the time.

his<br>
JOHN × BEEVE.<br>
mark.

Sworn and subscribed before me, this 31st day of May, 1833.

L. F. LINN, <i>Commissioner.</i>

(See book No. 7, page 156.)

*June* 11, 1835.—The board met, pursuant to adjournment.  Present : F. R. Conway, J. H. Relfe, commissioners.

Jerome Mattis, claiming 800 arpens of land.  (See book No. 7, page 156.)

The board are of opinion that this claim ought not to be granted ; claimant had a confirmation for 400 arpens. (See commissioners' minutes, book No. 4, page 515.  See book No. 7, page 178.)

JAMES H. RELFE,<br>
F. R. CONWAY.

I have examined the transcript of the above claim, and concur in the decision.

F. H. MARTIN.

---

Class 2.   No. 38.—Gasper Schell, claiming 640 acres.

| No. | Name of original claimant. | Acres. | Nature and date of claim. | By whom granted. | By whom surveyed, date, and situation. |
|---|---|---|---|---|---|
| 38 | Gasper Schell. | 640 | Settlement right. | | |

EVIDENCE WITH REFERNCE TO MINUTES AND RECORDS.

*May* 26, 1835.—F. R. Conway, esq., appeared, pursuant to adjournment.

Gasper Schell, claiming 640 acres of land, in the district of Cape Girardeau.  (See record-book F, page 146; Bates's decisions, page 105.)

The following testimony was taken in October, 1833, before L. F. Linn, commissioner :

STATE OF MISSOURI, *County of Cape Girardeau :*

Joseph Niswanger, of lawful age, being duly sworn, deposeth and saith he is well acquainted with Gasper Schell, the above claimant ; that he emigrated to this country, with his family, in the district of Cape Girardeau, in the latter part of the month of June or beginning of July, in the year 1804 ; that in the same year he moved on and settled the place where he now resides ; that said Schell has continued to inhabit and cultivate the same ever since ; that he has made valuable and lasting improvements on the same ; that his family consisted of a wife and seven or eight children.

his<br>
JOSEPH × NISWANGER.<br>
mark.

Sworn to and subscribed, October 17, 1833.

L. F. LINN, <i>Commissioner.</i>

George F. Bollinger, of lawful age, being sworn, deposeth and saith that he is well acquainted with the claimant, Gasper Schell ; that he emigrated to this country in the spring or summer of 1804 ; that some time after, he settled on the place where he now lives, and has resided there ever since ; that he has made valuable improvements on the same, to wit : a good dwelling-house, out-houses, barn, stables, mill, distillery, good orchard, &c.

GEORGE F. BOLLINGER.

Sworn to and subscribed, October 18, 1833.

L. F. LINN, <i>Commissioner.</i>

(See book No. 7, page 159.)

*June* 11, 1835.—The board met, pursuant to adjournment.  Present : F. R. Conway, J. H. Relfe, commissioners.

Gasper Schell, claiming 640 acres of land.  (See book No. 7, page 159.)

The board are of opinion that this claim ought not to be granted.  (See book No. 7, page 178.)

JAMES H. RELFE,<br>
F. R. CONWAY.

I have examined the transcript of the above claim, and concur in the decision.

F. H. MARTIN.

---

Class 2.   No. 39.—Peter Boyer, 639¾ acres and 12 perches.

| No. | Name of original claimant. | Acres. | Nature and date of claim. | By whom granted. | By whom surveyed, date, and situation. |
|---|---|---|---|---|---|
| 39 | Peter Boyer. | 639¾ 12 p. | Settlement right. | | Survey on record, without date or signature. West bank of the Old Mine creek. |

EVIDENCE WITH REFERENCE TO MINUTES AND RECORDS.

*August* 16, 1808.—Board met, on application of a claimant. Present: Hon. John B. C. Lucas and Frederick Bates.

Pierre Boyer, claiming 639¾ acres and 12 perches of land, situate on the west bank of the old Mine creek, district of St. Genevieve, produces to the board a notice of said claim to the recorder, dated 8th May, 1807; also a plat of the same, without date, and surveyor not named.

Jean Portell, sworn, says that claimant settled on said land in 1802, and has inhabited and cultivated the same to this day.

Laid over for decision. (See No. 3, page 226.)

*December* 30, 1811.—Board met. Present: John B. C. Lucas, Clement B. Penrose, and Frederick Bates, commissioners.

Peter Boyer, claiming 639¾ acres and 12 perches of land. (See book No. 3, page 226.)

It is the opinion of the board that this claim ought not to be granted. (See No. 5, page 547.)

*April* 10, 1835.—F. R. Conway, esq., appeared, pursuant to adjournment.

Peter Boyer, claiming 639¾ acres of land, situated on Old Mine creek. (See record-book C, page 509; minutes, No. 3, page 226; No. 5, page 547; Bates's decisions, page 75. See book No. 7, page 124.)

*June* 12, 1835.—The board met, pursuant to adjournment. Present: F. R. Conway, J. H. Relfe, commissioners.

Peter Boyer, claiming 639¾ acres. (See book No. 7, page 124.)

The board are of opinion that this claim ought not to be granted. The said Peter Boyer claims 400 arpens of land under the Old Mine concession. (See book No. 7, page 180.)

JAMES H. RELFE,<br>F. R. CONWAY.

I have examined the transcript of the above claim, and concur in the decision.

F. H. MARTIN.

---

Class 2.  No. 40.—*Charles Denné, claiming 750 arpens.*

| No. | Name of original claimant. | Arpens. | Nature and date of claim. | By whom granted. | By whom surveyed, date, and situation. |
|---|---|---|---|---|---|
| 40 | Charles Denné. | 750 | Settlement right. | | John Harvey, D. S., 22d February, 1806. Received for record, 26th February, 1806, by A. Soulard, surveyor general. On river Dardenne. |

EVIDENCE WITH REFERENCE TO MINUTES AND RECORDS.

*August* 7, 1806.—The board met, agreeably to adjournment. Present: Hon. John B. C. Lucas, and Clement B. Penrose, esq.

James Morrison, assignee of Charles Denné, claiming 750 arpens of land, situate on the river Dardenne, district of St. Charles, produces a survey of the same, dated the 22d, and certified the 26th February, 1806, and a deed of transfer, dated April 9, 1805.

Joseph Voisin, being duly sworn, says that the said Denné did, some time in July, 1803, begin the building of a house, and planted fruit-trees.

The board reject this claim. (See book No. 1, page 449.)

*September* 10, 1810.—Board met. Present: John B. C. Lucas, Clement B. Penrose, and Frederick Bates, commissioners.

James Morrison, assignee of Charles Denné, claiming 750 arpens of land. (See book No. 1, page 449.)

It is the opinion of the board that this claim ought not to be granted. (See book No. 4, page 494.)

*April* 5, 1834.—F. R. Conway, esq., appeared, pursuant to adjournment.

Charles Denné, by his legal representative, James Morrison, claiming 750 arpens of land, situate near Dardenne, under settlement right. (See record-book B, page 231; minute-books No. 1, page 449, and No. 4, page 494.)

Gabriel Latreille, duly sworn, says that he is 64 years of age; that he came to this country in the year 1793; he resided in St. Charles for the last 38 years; that, in the beginning of the year 1803, he went on the land claimed, in company with said Denné, who had then a cabin built and peach-trees planted, which appeared, by their growth, to have been planted two years before, and were in a piece of ground fenced in, of about half an arpen in superficie, the house standing outside of the fence; that said Denné was a single man, who lived with his brother-in-law, and went on his land to work without living on the same; that said Denné sold his improvement to James Morrison.

Claimant produces a plat of survey, dated 22d February, 1806, by John Harvey, D. S., and received for record by Soulard, S. G., 26th February, 1806. (See record-book No. 6, page 513.)

*October* 8, 1834.—The board met, pursuant to adjournment. Present: F. R. Conway, J. S. Mayfield, and J. H. Relfe, commissioners.

In the case of Charles Denné, claiming 750 arpens of land, (see book No. 6, page 513,) the following testimony was taken by James S. Mayfield, commissioner:

Andrew Zumalt, produced and sworn, on his oath states that he saw an improvement on the land mentioned, but does not recollect that he ever saw Mr. Denné at work on the land aforesaid; that the improvement mentioned was always called Denné's improvement, and at that time the said Denné was a single man; and further, that the said improvement consisted of the clearing of a small spot of ground, and enclosing the same, with the erection of a small building or hut on the same.   Deponent further states that said Denné was in possession of the land or improvement, two years or more, as he thinks, before the change of government.

his<br>
ANDREW  ×  ZUMALT.<br>
mark.

Sworn to this 3d day of July, 1834, at St. Charles.

(No. 7, page 17.)

JAMES S. MAYFIELD, Commissioner.

*June* 12, 1835.—The board met, pursuant to adjournment.   Present: F. R. Conway, J. H. Relfe, commissioners.

Charles Denné, claiming 750 arpens of land.   (See book No. 6, page 513 ; No. 7, page 17.)

The board are of opinion that this claim ought not to be granted.   (See book No. 7, page 180.)

JAMES H. RELFE,<br>
F. R. CONWAY.

I have examined the transcript of the above claim, and concur in the decision.

F. H. MARTIN.

---

Class 2.   No. 41.—Jean Baptiste Vallé and François Vallé, claiming 7,056 arpens.

*To his Lordship, the Intendant of the province of Louisiana, in his mansion at New Orleans:*

François Vallé, captain, civil and military commandant of the post of St. Genevieve of Illinois, and Jean Baptiste Vallé, his brother, captain of militia in the said post, supplicate very humbly, and have the honor to represent, that they have established and constructed, at a very great expense, two mills, one for grinding and the other for sawing, in the vicinity and between the posts of St. Genevieve and New Bourbon, which mills have been, till now, of the greatest utility to the numerous inhabitants of those two posts ; that, by a necessary consequence of the increase of population in those two places and in their districts, in the extent of which considerable clearings and falling of timber have been made, their saw-mill is on the eve of being abandoned, to the great prejudice of the public and of the petitioners, unless they promptly find the means to provide the necessary timber to keep their mill employed ; that, consequently, the petitioners have searched for a tract of land not yet conceded to any person, and belonging to the King's domain, upon which there should be pine-trees, it being the kind of timber more generally used for floors, and other carpenters' works, in the upper part of this colony ; that they have found such a tract, situated at the place called the Pinery of River aux Vases, having about one league in length on the two ridges of hills running along the south branch of the said River aux Vases, and adjoining the north branch of the said river.   The petitioners presume to flatter themselves of obtaining this concession of your goodness, my lord, because it is the only means to prevent the ruin of their said saw-mill, and of continuing to furnish to the daily wants of the public ; and that, besides, it is notorious that the greatest part of the soil in this tract is not suitable for any kind of cultivation, and they will prove, by an act drawn in due form before the commandant of New Bourbon in whose district the said land is situated, (according to the rules prescribed by the relation regulating to the demands of concessions,) that the land they solicit has never been granted to any one, and evidently belongs to the King's domain : therefore, the petitioners apply to you, and earnestly implore your goodness, justice, and authority, my lord, praying that you may be pleased to grant to them, their heirs and assigns, in full property. the concession of the above-mentioned tract of land, being a part of the Pinery of River aux Vases, extending about one league in length upon the two ridges of hills which run along the south branch of the said River aux Vases, and to join the north branch of said river, in order to use the pine and other timbers which are thereon for the works of their said saw-mill.   In so doing, my lord, the petitioners shall never cease to pray for the preservation of your days.

Done in St. Genevieve, August 11, 1801.

FRANCOIS VALLÉ,<br>
J. BAPTISTE VALLÉ.

NEW BOURBON, February 27, 1802.

We, the undersigned, commandant of the post of New Bourbon, do certify and attest to his lordship, the intendant of the province, that the statement in the foregoing petition is very exact, sincere, and true, and that it is very essential and important for the good of the public that the petitioners' saw-mill should not be stopped for want of timber, because it is the only one which furnishes to the daily wants of the inhabitants of St. Genevieve, of New Bourbon, and even of St. Louis : therefore, we, the said commandant, convinced of the good intentions of his lordship, the intendent, toward all that may tend to the welfare of the inhabitants of this country, authorize, liable to his lordship's approbation, the said petitioners, provisionally, and exclusively of any other, to use the pine and other timbers which may be found on that part of his Catholic Majesty's domains, for which they solicit a concession by the foregoing petition, in order to keep their said saw-mill constantly employed.

PIERRE DELASSUS DE LUZIERE.

The power of attorney made to the clergyman, Don Santiago Maxwell, and the accompanying documents, have been presented.   Be they all translated into the Spanish language by the interpreter, Don Pedro Derbigny, and, when it is done, let them be transmitted to the Fiscal.

MORALES.

ST. LOUIS, *July* 19, 1833.   Truly translated.

JULIUS DE MUN.

| No. | Name of original claimant. | Arpens. | Nature and date of claim. | By whom granted. | By whom surveyed, date, and situation. |
|---|---|---|---|---|---|
| 41 | Jean Baptiste Vallé and François Vallé. | 7,056 | Petition to the Intendant, 11th August, 1801, and order of said Intendant to have the papers translated. | | On the waters of River aux Vases. |

EVIDENCE WITH REFERENCE TO MINUTES AND RECORDS.

*June* 27, 1833.—The board met, pursuant to adjournment.  Present: L. F. Linn, F. R. Conway, commissioners.

Jean Baptiste Vallé and François Vallé, (the heirs and legal representatives of the latter,) claiming one league square of land, or 7,056 arpens, situate in the Pinery, on the waters of the River aux Vases, county of St. Genevieve.  (See record-book C, page 475.)  Produces a paper, purporting to be a petition from the said John B. Vallé and F. Vallé to the intendant of the province of Louisiana, dated 11th August, 1801, followed by a recommendation from Pierre Delassus de Luziere, commandant of New Bourbon, dated 27th February, 1802; and an order of Morales, the intendant, to have the papers translated into Spanish, and afterward presented to the Fiscal; also, a certificate signed by Thomas Eaddin, deputy surveyor, and others, certifying that the land demanded belongs to the King's domain.

STATE OF MISSOURI, *County of St. Genevieve:*

Bartholomew St. Gemme, aged about 59 years, being duly sworn, as the law directs, deposeth and saith that he was well acquainted with both the said J. B. Vallé and F. Vallé; that they were, for many years before the year 1801, and in the year 1801 and 1802, citizens and residents in the province of Upper Louisiana, and that the said J. B. Vallé is still a citizen and resident in the country, and that the said François Vallé continued a citizen and resident thereof till his death, and that his heirs and legal representatives have continued citizens and residents of the country ever since, and such of them as are living are still so.  This deponent further says that the said J. B. Vallé and F. Vallé both had large families of children, and many slaves, with other property; that they were active, enterprising, industrious, and useful citizens.  And this deponent further says, that he knows the claimants had a saw-mill in operation, as stated in the petition, in the years 1801 and 1802, and that it was useful to the public.  And this deponent further says that he was well acquainted with Pierre Delassus de Luziere; that he has seen him write, and that the said P. D de Luziere was the commandant of the post and district of New Bourbon, in the year 1802, and that the name and signature to the recommendation for said grant, dated the 27th of February, 1802, is the proper name and signature, and in the proper handwriting of the said Pierre Delassus de Luziere.  And this deponent further says, that the names of Thomas Maddin, François Janis, Fremon Delauriere, L. Largeau, and Pierre Delassus de Luziere, to the certificate by them signed, dated the 27th of February, 1802, are the proper names and signatures, and in the proper handwriting of the certifiers; that he has seen them write.

Sworn to and subscribed before me, Lewis F. Linn, commissioner, this 27th day of May, 1833.

B. ST. GEMME.

L. F. LINN, *Commissioner.*

(See minutes No. 6, page 196.)

*June* 13, 1835.—The board met, pursuant to adjournment.  Present: F. R. Conway, J. H. Relfe, commissioners.

Jean Baptiste Vallé and François Vallé, claiming 7,056 arpens of land.  (See book No. 6, page 196.)

The board have no jurisdiction on this claim, there being no concession, warrant, or order of survey.  (See book No. 7, page 182.)

JAMES H. RELFE,

F. R. CONWAY.

I have examined the transcript of the above claim, and concur in the decision.

F. H. MARTIN.

---

Class. 2.   No. 42.—*François Vallé, jr., claiming 7,056 arpens.*

*To his Lordship, the Intendant of the province of Louisiana, in his mansion at New Orleans:*

François Vallé, jr., officer of the militia of the post of St. Genevieve, and residing therein, humbly supplicates, and has the honor to represent to you that, having, until now, employed himself in working the lead mines, in which employment success is always uncertain, and wishing to have his activity and industry occupied in a more secure undertaking, that of a saw-mill has fixed his attention; and having visited several parts of the country, he has succeeded in finding a place fit and suitable for the erecting of a saw-mill, situated at the end of the pinery of River aux Vases, and consisting in one league square, extending along on the two ridges of hills of the north and south branches of said river, and adjoining, on the western side, the concession demanded by Messrs. François Vallé, sr., and Jean Baptiste Vallé, his brother.  The petitioner having procured an excellent workman, well versed in the construction of mills, and having already provided himself with the machinery necessary to erect a saw-mill in the place above mentioned, which he binds himself to build and establish immediately; he flatters himself so much the more to obtain this concession of your goodness, my lord, that it is a notorious truth that the said saw-mill shall be of the greatest utility to the public, and particularly to the inhabitants of St. Genevieve and New Bourbon, and, even of St. Louis; there remaining at the present but only Messrs. F. Vallé, sr., and J. B. Vallé's (his brother's) saw-mill, which is situated at St. Genevieve, and is insufficient to provide to the daily and urgent wants of the said inhabitants; and it is also equally notorious that the above-mentioned tract of land of one league square, for which the petitioner solicits a concession, belongs to his Catholic Majesty's domain, and has not been granted to any person.  Therefore, the said petitioner applies to you, my lord, praying that you will be pleased to grant to him, his heirs or assigns, in full property, a concession for the said league square of land, situate toward the end of the pinery of River aux Vases, such as it is here above designated, in order to erect thereon the said saw-mill, and to cut and use, for the work of the said mill, the pine-trees and other timbers which may be found on said tract, exclusively to any other persons.  In doing which, the petitioner shall never cease to pray for the preservation of your precious life.

ST. GENEVIEVE, *March* 10, 1802.

FRANCOIS VALLÉ, JR.

NEW BOURBON, *March* 13, 1802.

We, the undersigned, captain commandant of the post of New Bourbon, in whose district is situated the concession demanded by the petitioner, do certify to his lordship the intendant, that the statement in the foregoing petition is sincere, exact and true, and that the petitioner is worthy, under all points of view, to obtain the concession which he solicits.

PIERRE DELASSUS DE LUZIERE.

It has been presented, together with the power of attorney and accompanying documents. Let them be all translated by the interpreter, Don Pedro Derbigni, and when so translated, let them be laid before the Fiscal.

MORALES.

St. Louis, *July* 20, 1823.    Truly translated.

JULIUS DE MUN.

| No. | Name of original claimant. | Arpens. | Nature and date of claim. | By whom granted. | By whom surveyed, date, and situation. |
|-----|---------------------------|---------|--------------------------|------------------|----------------------------------------|
| 42  | François Vallé, jr.        | 7,056   |                          |                  | On River aux Vases, district of St. Genevieve. |

EVIDENCE WITH REFERENCE TO MINUTES AND RECORDS.

*December* 1, 1807.—The board met, pursuant to adjournment.  Present: Hon. John B. C. Lucas, Clement B. Penrose, and Frederick Bates, commissioners.

The same (Francis Vallé), claiming 7,056 arpens of land, situate in the district of New Bourbon, on the River aux Vases.

Produces a petition to Morales, the intendant general at New Orleans, for the above quantity of land, for the purpose of building a saw-mill, dated the 10th of March, 1802, together with a recommendation from Pierre D. de Luziere, commandant of the district of New Bourbon, to the said intendant general, stating that the claimant is worthy of the grant solicited ; also an order by the said Morales to Peter Derbigny, translator, to have the petition and recommendation translated, and then to be transmitted to the Fiscal for examination.

Thomas Dodge, being duly sworn, says that Francis Vallé, jr., began to build a mill and a cabin on said land in July, and finished it in November, 1802, and it was inhabited from that time until this day for claimant ; was cultivated in 1803, and ever since ; that the mill worked ever since it was completed, when there was a sufficiency of water.  Laid over for decision.  (Minutes, No. 3, page 107.)

*April* 17, 1810.—Board met.  Present: John B. C. Lucas, Clement B. Penrose, and Frederick Bates, commissioners.

François Vallé, claiming 7,056 arpens of land.  (See book No. 3, page 107.)

It is the opinion of the board that this claim ought not to be confirmed.  (Book No. 4, page 326.)

*June* 26, 1833.—The board met, pursuant to adjournment.  Present: L. F. Linn, F. R. Conway, commissioners.

François Vallé, jr., son of François Vallé, sr., deceased, claiming one league square, or 7,056 arpens of land, situate in the pinery, on the waters of the River aux Vases, or Muddy creek, in the county of St. Genevieve. (See record-book C, page 394 ; minutes No. 3, page 107 ; No. 4, page 326.)

Produces a paper purporting to be a petition to the intendant of Louisiana, dated 10th March, 1802, following which, is a recommendation, dated 13th March, 1802, signed by Pierre Delassus Deluzire, commandant of New Bourbon, and an order signed by Morales, the intendant general, to have the documents translated and presented to the Fiscal.   Also, a certificate, signed by Thomas Maddin, deputy surveyor, and others, before the commandant of New Bourbon, certifying that the land demanded belongs to the royal domain ; also a receipt of Maxwell, dated 13th March, 1802, for the above papers.

State of Missouri, *County of St. Genevieve:*

John Baptiste Vallé, sr., aged about 72 years, being duly sworn, as the law directs, deposeth and saith that he has often seen François Vallé, jr., write ; that he is well acquainted with him, and that the name and signature to the said petition, dated 10th March, 1802, is the name and signature and in the proper handwriting of the said François Vallé, jr.   And this deponent further says that he was well acquainted with Pierre Delassus de Luziere ; that he has often seen him write ; that he was commandant of the post and district of New Bourbon, in the year 1802, and that the name, and signature, and handwriting to the recommendation for said grant, dated 13th day of March, 1802, is the proper name and signature, and in the proper handwriting of the said Pierre Delassus de Luziere.   And this deponent further says that he is well acquainted with the tract of land claimed by the said François Vallé, jr., and that the said François Vallé, jr., the claimant, did, in the course of the year 1802, build and erect a water saw-mill on the head-waters of River aux Vases, on the said tract of land, for a grant of which he had petitioned, and that the said saw-mill was in complete operation in the spring of the following year, and continued in such operation until about the year 1812 or '13, when it was swept away by an extraordinary flood.   And this deponent further says that he knows that the said François Vallé, jr., his servants and workmen, resided at the said mill, on the said tract, at the time the said mill was in operation.   And further, this deponent says that, at the date of the application, and long before, the said François Vallé, jr., was a citizen and resident in this province of Upper Louisiana, and has continued and still is a citizen and resident in the province and in this county ; that he was born in the province.

Sworn to and subscribed before me, Lewis F. Linn, this 4th day of May, 1833.

J. B. VALLÉ,
L. F. LINN, *Commissioner.*

And also came John B. Vallé, jr, as a witness, aged about 49 years, who, being also sworn, as the law directs, deposeth and saith that he was in company with Mr. Thomas Maddin, deputy surveyor to Mr. Antoine Soulard, his Catholic Majesty's surveyor general, over the upper parts of the province of Louisiana, when he, the said Thomas Maddin, surveyed the said tract of land, of one league square, for the said François Vallé, jr., the claimant ; that he, this deponent, was employed as one of the chain carriers on the making of the said survey ; the exact time he does not now recollect.

Sworn to and subscribed before me, Lewis F. Linn, this 20th day of May, 1833.

J. B. VALLE, Jr.,
L. F. LINN, *Commissioner.*

(No. C, page 193.)

*June* 13, 1835.—The board met, pursuant to adjournment.  Present : F. R. Conway, J. H. Relfe, commissioners.

François Vallé, jr., claiming 7,056 arpens of land.  (See book No. 6, page 193.)

The board have no jurisdiction on this claim, there being no concession, warrant, or order of survey.  (See book No. 7, page 182.)

JAMES H. RELFE,<br>
F. R. CONWAY.

I have examined the transcript of the above claim, and concur in the decision.

F. H. MARTIN.

---

Class 2.  No. 43.—*John Ramsey, claiming 848 arpens.*

| No. | Name of original claimant. | Arpens. | Nature and date of claim. | By whom granted. | By whom surveyed, date, and situation. |
|-----|----------------------------|---------|---------------------------|------------------|----------------------------------------|
| 43  | John Ramsay.               | 848     | Settlement right.         |                  | John McHenry, D. S. Received for record, 28th Feb., 1806.  Ramsay's creek, district of St. Charles. |

EVIDENCE WITH REFERENCE TO MINUTES AND RECORDS.

*December* 6, 1811.—The board met.  Present : John B. C. Lucas, Clement B. Penrose, and Frederick Bates, commissioners.

John Ramsay, claiming 848 arpens 80 perches of land, district of St. Charles, produces record of a plat of survey, certified 28th February, 1806.

It is the opinion of the board that this claim ought not to be granted.  (See No. 5, page 485.)

*July* 6, 1833.—L. F. Linn, esq., appeared, pursuant to adjournment.

John Ramsay, by his legal representatives, claiming 848 arpens of land, situated on Sandy creek.  (See record-book B, page 345 ; minutes, No. 5, page 485.)

Ira Cottle, duly sworn, says that he knew John Ramsay, and that said Ramsay was married before the change of government.  (See minutes No. 6, page 216.)

*June* 15, 1835.—The board met, pursuant to adjournment.  Present : F. R. Conway, J. H. Relfe, commissioners.

John Ramsay, claiming 848 arpens of land.  (See book No. 6, page 216.)

The board are of opinion that this claim ought not to be granted.  (See book No. 7, page 282.)

JAMES H. RELFE,<br>
F. R. CONWAY.

I have examined the transcript of the above claim, and concur in the decision.

F. H. MARTIN.

---

Class 2.  No. 44.—*John Draper, claiming 747 arpens.*

| No. | Name of original claimant. | Arpens. | Nature and date of claim. | By whom granted. | By whom surveyed, date, and situation. |
|-----|----------------------------|---------|---------------------------|------------------|----------------------------------------|
| 44  | John Draper.               | 747     | Settlement right.         |                  | Joseph Cottle, D. S., 12th Feb., 1806.  Received for record, by Soulard, S. Gen., Feb. 27, 1806.  Bob's creek, St. Charles. |

EVIDENCE WITH REFERENCE TO MINUTES AND RECORDS.

*July* 12, 1806.—The board met, agreeably to adjournment.  Present : Hon. John B. C. Lucas, and James L. Donaldson, esq.

John Draper, claiming as aforesaid (under the 2d section of the act of Congress) 747 arpens of land, situate as aforesaid, (on the Dardenne, district of St. Charles,) produces a survey of the same, dated February 12th, 1806, and a certificate of permission to settle from James Mackay, dated 28th February, 1806.

Zadock Woods, being duly sworn, says that claimant settled said tract of land in 1803, built a house on the same, and enclosed a few arpens of the same ; that he was by profession a well-digger, and on the 20th day of December, 1803, of the age of 21 years and upward, and claims no other lands, in his own name, in the territory.

The board reject this claim.  (See minutes, book No. 1, page 400.)

*August* 19, 1811.—Board met.  Present : Clement B. Penrose and Frederick Bates, commissioners.

John Draper, claiming 747 arpens of land.  (See book No. 1, page 400.)  Certificate of permission stated to be produced, not found of record.  It is the opinion of the board that this claim ought not to be granted. (See book No. 5, page 319.)

*July* 6, 1833.—L. F. Linn, esq., appeared, pursuant to adjournment.

John Draper, by his legal representatives, claiming 747 arpens of land, situate on Bob's creek. (See record-book B, page 257; minutes, No. 1, page 400; No. 5, page 319.)

Ira Cottle, duly sworn, says that, some time in 1802, he knew John Draper having a house on Bob's creek; that Draper dug a well on said place. (See book No. 6, page 215.)

*June* 15, 1835.—The board met, pursuant to adjournment. Present: F. R. Conway, J. H. Relfe, commissioners.

John Draper, claiming 747 arpens of land. (See book No. 6, page 215.)

The board are of opinion that this claim ought not to be granted. (See book No. 7, page 182.)

JAMES H. RELFE,

F. R. CONWAY.

I have examined the transcript of the above claim, and concur in the decision.

F. H. MARTIN.

---

Class 2. No. 45.—*Bartholomew Richard, claiming 1,200 arpens.*

To Don ZENON TRUDEAU, *Lieutenant Colonel in the armies of his Majesty, and Commander-in-chief of Upper Louisiana :*

Bartholomew Richard humbly supplicates and has the honor to represent to you, that he would wish to settle in this colony and employ himself in agriculture, as a subject of his Catholic Majesty, if you were pleased to give him a share of the favors which are heaped by this government upon the inhabitants who cultivate the soil. Encouraged by this hope, the petitioner prays you, sir, to be pleased to grant him, in the district of Cape Girardeau, a concession of 1,200 arpens of land in superficie; favor which he expects of your justice.

B. RICHARD.

CAPE GIRARDEAU, *December* 12, 1798.

We, commandant of the post of Cape Girardeau, do inform the commander-in-chief of Upper Louisiana, that the petitioner, as well on account of his means as of his industry and the fair character he bears, deserves the concession which he solicits, as the same belongs to his Majesty's domain, and is not prejudicial to anybody; therefore, we are induced to recommend him particularly to the beneficence of the government.

L. LORIMIER.

CAPE GIRARDEAU, *December* 13, 1798.

ST. LOUIS OF ILLINOIS, *December* 20, 1798.

The surveyor, Don Antonio Soulard, shall put the party interested in possession of the land which he solicits, and afterward shall make out a plat and certificate of his survey, in order to serve to solicit the concession from the governor general of the province, who shall be informed that said land asked for is vacant, and that the petitioner conducts himself in such a manner as to deserve the favor which he solicits.

ZENON TRUDEAU.

ST. LOUIS, *February* 7, 1834. Truly translated.

JULIUS DE MUN, *T. B. C.*

| No. | Name of original claimant. | Arpens. | Nature and date of claim. | By whom granted. | By whom surveyed, date, and situation. |
|---|---|---|---|---|---|
| 45 | B. Richard. | 1,200 | Concession, 29th Dec., 1798. | Zenon Trudeau. | |

EVIDENCE WITH REFERENCE TO MINUTES AND RECORDS.

*December* 9, 1811.—Board met. Present: John B. C. Lucas, Clement B. Penrose, and Frederick Bates, commissioners.

Peter Menard, assignee of Peter Dumay, assignee of Bartholomew Richard, claiming 1,200 arpens of land, situated in the district of Cape Girardeau, produces record of a concession from Zenon Trudeau, dated 29th December, 1798.

It is the opinion of the board that this claim ought not to be confirmed. (See book No. 5, page 492.)

*December* 5, 1833.—F. R. Conway, esq., appeared, pursuant to adjournment.

Bartholomew Richard, claiming 1,200 arpens of land, situated in the district of Cape Girardeau. (See record-book E, page 26; minutes, No. 5, page 492.)

Produces a paper purporting to be an original concession from Zenon Trudeau, dated December 29, 1798.

M. P. Leduc, duly sworn, says that the signature to the recommendation is in the proper handwriting of Louis Lorimier, commandant of Cape Girardeau, and that the signature to the concession is in the proper handwriting of Zenon Trudeau.

ST. GENEVIEVE, *April* 29, 1835.

Personally appeared before me, one of the commissioners appointed, &c., Mr. Antoine Lachapelle, who, after being duly sworn, deposeth and saith that he knew that Mr. Bartholomew Richard inhabited and cultivated a tract of land in Cape Girardeau county, then Upper Louisiana, which tract of land was known by the name of the Old Cape; that he knew the said Richard to be an active, industrious, and worthy man; that the said Richard inhabited and cultivated said place at the Old Cape, in 1798 and 1799.

his

ANTOINE × LACHAPELLE.

mark.

L. F. LINN, *Commissioner.*

(See book No. 6, page 365.)

*June* 15, 1835.—The board met, pursuant to adjournment.    Present: F. R. Conway, J. H. Relfe, commissioners.

Bartholomew Richard, claiming 1,200 arpens of land.    (See book No. 6, page 365.)

The board are of opinion that this claim ought not to be confirmed, the said Richard having abandoned said land, which was afterward granted to Pierre Dumais, under a concession dated January 23, 1800.    (See book No. 7, page 184.)

JAMES H. RELFE,
F. R. CONWAY.

I have examined the transcript of the above claim, and concur in the decision.

F. H. MARTIN.

---

Class 2.    No. 46.—*Isidore Lacroix, claiming 6,000 arpens.*

To Mr. ZENON TRUDEAU, *Lieutenant Colonel of the stationary regiment of Louisiana, Lieutenant Governor of the western part of Illinois:*

Isidore Lacroix, merchant, of Michilimackinac, humbly supplicates and has the honor to represent that, desiring to fix his residence in your jurisdiction, therefore he has the honor to supplicate you to grant to him a lot which is convenient to him for the purpose of building a house, situated in his Majesty's domain, bounded on all sides by public roads, and containing 303 feet in depth by 240 in width ; said lot is situated half-way up the hill, in the direction of the village of St. Charles of Missouri, opposite the lot of one Cadieu.    He supplicates you also to grant to him a tract of arable land, of 10 arpens in width by 40 in depth, immediately following the lands already conceded, and near to Mr. François Duquette, at the Marais Croche.    He supplicates you furthermore to grant him 6 arpens in front, from the Marais Croche to the Missouri.    The petitioner presumes to hope, sir, that you will condescend to receive his demand, although he is a foreigner, with that generosity and goodness with which you have gained the esteem and affection of all those who have had the honor of applying to you.    It is with that confidence that the petitioner sends you the present petition ; he is persuaded that you will grant his demand.    He has the honor to be, with the greatest respect, sir, your very humble and very obedient servant,

LITTLE HILLS, ST. CHARLES, *January* 17, 1797.                              ISIDORE LACROIX.

ST. LOUIS, *January* 23, 1797.

I have the honor to inform the lieutenant governor that the lot demanded belongs to the King's domain, and is not prejudicial to any one ; that the vacant land between the line of Mr. Duquette and the Marais de Tems-clair also belongs to his Majesty's domain, and it is doubtful whether it contains 10 arpens ; that the land demanded at the Marais Croche has been reserved for the use of the prairie lands in the district of St. Charles.

CHARLES TAYON.

ST. LOUIS, *January* 23, 1797.

The surveyor of this jurisdiction, Don Antonio Soulard, shall put Mr. Isidore Lacroix in possession of the vacant lot of 240 feet in width by 300 in depth, situated in the village of St. Charles, as also of the space of vacant lands between Mr. Duquette and the Marais de Tems-clair, (Clear-weather swamp,) giving to the said tract forty arpens in depth.    As to the demand on the Marais Croche, (Crooked swamp,) it cannot be admitted.

ZENON TRUDEAU.

ST. LOUIS, *August* 9, 1833.    Truly translated from book C, page 281.

JULIUS DE MUN.

Don ANTONIO SOULARD, *Surveyor General of Upper Louisiana:*

I do certify that, on the 5th of December, 1799, (by virtue of the annexed decree of the lieutenant governor, Don Zenon Trudeau, dated January 23, 1797,) I went on the land of Don Isidore Lacroix, in order to survey the same, according to his demand, being 4,400 arpens in superficie.    This measurement was made in presence of Don Francisco Duquette, by virtue of the power given him by the proprietor to that effect, and of the adjoining neighbor, with the perch of Paris, of eighteen feet in length, according to the custom adopted in this province of Louisiana, and without regard to the variation of the needle, which is 7° 30′ E., as evinced by the foregoing figurative plat.    This land is situated in the Grand prairie called Prairie du Marais Croche, and at about six miles N. E. from the post of St. Charles, bounded on its three sides, N. E., S. E., and N. W., by vacant lands of the royal domain, and on its front S. W. by lands cultivated by the inhabitants of the town of St. Charles, which are called lands of the Grand prairie of the Crooked swamp.    In testimony whereof, I do give these presents, together with the foregoing figurative plat, on which are indicated the dimensions and the natural and artificial limits which surround said land.

ST. LOUIS OF ILLINOIS, *May* 30, 1803.                              ANTONIO SOULARD, *S. G.*

Augmentation of Mr. Duquette, at the Marais Tems-clair, (Clear-weather swamp,) district of St. Charles. Last survey of Mr. Duquette, 1,880 arpens.

*June* 28, 1805.                              JNO. HARVEY, *Deputy Surveyor.*

OFFICE OF THE RECORDER OF LAND TITLES, *St. Louis, May* 12, 1835.

I certify the above certificate of survey to be truly translated from book D, page 179, of record in this office.

JULIUS DE MUN, *T. B. C.*

| No. | Name of original claimant. | Arpens. | Nature and date of claim. | By whom granted. | By whom surveyed, date, and situation. |
|-----|---------------------------|---------|---------------------------|------------------|----------------------------------------|
| 46  | Isidore Lacroix.          | 6,000   | Concession for the vacant space between Duquette and the swamp, by 40 arpens in depth; 23d Jan., 1797. | Zenon Trudeau. | 4,400 arpens, by A. Soulard, December 5th, 1799; 6 miles northeast from St. Charles ; 1,880 arpens, by John Harvey, deputy surveyor, June 28, 1805, on Clearweather swamp. |

EVIDENCE WITH REFERENCE TO MINUTES AND RECORDS.

*August* 15, 1806.—The board met, agreeably to adjournment. Present: Hon. John B. C. Lucas and Clement B. Penrose, esq.

The same, (Francis Duquette,) assignee of the same, (Isidore Lacroix,) claiming 6,000 arpens of land, situate district of St. Charles, and adjoining the town, produces a petition for a tract contained within certain natural boundaries therein described; a certificate from Charles Tayon, the then commandant of St. Charles, stating his belief that the land petitioned for will not exceed ten arpens in width; a warrant of survey from Zenon Trudeau, dated January 23, 1797, for such a quantity as may be found in breadth between a tract, the property of said claimant and the Marais Tems-clair, by a depth of forty arpens, together with a survey of 4,400 arpens, taken December 5, 1799, and certified May 30, 1803; and a deed of transfer of the same, dated September 6, 1800.

Françoise Fabien, being duly sworn, says that the said tract of land was cultivated above nine years ago.

The board reject this claim, and remark that, from the papers on record, it appears that 400 arpens were intended to be granted by the aforesaid concession. (See book No. 1, page 464.)

*December* 5, 1809.—Board met. Present: John B. C. Lucas and Clement B. Penrose, commissioners.

Francis Duquette, assignee of Isidore Lacroix, claiming 6,000 arpens of land. (See book No. 1, page 464.)

It is the opinion of the board that this claim ought not to be confirmed. (See book No. 4, page, 225.)

*July* 8, 1833.—L. F. Linn, esq., appeared, pursuant to adjournment.

Isidore Lacroix's representatives, claiming 6,000 arpens of land, situated at Marais Tems-clair, county of St. Charles. (See book C, page 281; book D, page 178, two surveys; minutes, book No. 1, page 464; No. 4, page 225. See No. 6, page 224.)

*June* 15, 1835.—The board met, pursuant to adjournment. Present: F. R. Conway, J. H. Relfe, commissioners.

Isidore Lacroix, claiming 6,000 arpens of land. (See book No. 6, page 224.)

The board are of opinion that this claim ought not to be confirmed, claimant having had the lot in St. Charles confirmed, as also four hundred arpens of land, (see Bates's decisions, pages 59 and 53,) and no more being granted by the concession. (See book No. 7, page 184.)

JAMES H. RELFE,<br>
F. R. CONWAY.

I have examined the transcript of the above claim, and concur in the decision.

F. H. MARTIN.

---

Class 2. No. 47.—*John McCormack, claiming 1,000 arpens.*

| No. | Name of original claimant. | Arpens. | Nature and date of claim. | By whom granted. | By whom surveyed, date, and situation. |
|-----|---------------------------|---------|---------------------------|------------------|----------------------------------------|
| 47  | John McCormack.           | 1,000   | Settlement right.         |                  |                                        |

EVIDENCE WITH REFERENCE TO MINUTES AND RECORDS.

*November* 27, 1811.—Board met. Present: John B. C. Lucas, Clement B. Penrose, and Frederick Bates, commissioners.

Henry Cook, heir of McCormack, claiming 1,000 arpens of land, situate on Mill creek, district of St. Louis, produces a notice to the recorder.

It is the opinion of the board that this claim ought not to be granted. (See book No. 5, page 457.)

*March* 5, 1834.—F. R. Conway, esq., appeared, pursuant to adjournment.

John McCormack, by his heir at law, Henry Cook, claiming 1,000 arpens of land, situate on Mill creek, district of St. Louis, under a settlement right. (See record-book D, page 219; minute-book No. 5, page 457.)

James McRoberts, being duly sworn, says that he is upward of seventy years of age, and knows the tract claimed; that he came to this country in the year 1786, and resided on the east side of the Mississippi; that in the year 1789 he crossed to this, the west side of the Mississippi, for the first time, and passed by and saw this improvement; it then had the appearance of an old improvement; the stumps then looked old and were much decayed; the undergrowth had sprung up; the fences and buildings had been destroyed by fire; the place had not been cultivated for several years, as he understood, McCormack having died some years before; his widow had married again and moved off the place. Witness was informed that the place had been cultivated for some years before the death of McCormack. Witness passed frequently by this place in 1789, '90, and '91, and thinks it was the oldest improvement in that part of the country; he understood that there had been a mill built near this improvement by a man of the name of Thomas Tyler, who built it for the purpose of grinding for a few families; McCormack had charge of the mill; it was, however, soon washed away and never rebuilt. (See book No. 6, page 504.)

*June* 15, 1835.—The board met, pursuant to adjournment. Present: F. R. Conway and J. H. Relfe, commissioners.

John McCormack, claiming 1,000 arpens of land. (See book No. 6, page 504.)

The board are of opinion that this claim ought not to be granted. (See book No. 7, page 186.)

JAMES H. RELFE,<br>
F. R. CONWAY.

I have examined the transcript of the above claim, and concur in the decision.

F. H. MARTIN.

Class 2.   No. 48.—*James Bevins, claiming 200 arpens.*

| No. | Name of original claimant. | Arpens. | Nature and date of claim. | By whom granted. | By whom surveyed, date, and situation. |
|---|---|---|---|---|---|
| 48 | James Bevins. | 200 | Settlement right, | | |

EVIDENCE WITH REFERENCE TO MINUTES AND RECORDS.

*May* 8, 1809.—Board met.   Present: John B. C. Lucas, Clement B. Penrose, and Frederick Bates, commissioners.

James Bevins, claiming 200 arpens of land, situate on Whitewater, district of Cape Girardeau, produces to the board, as a special permission to settle, list B, on which claimant is No. 31.

The following testimony in the foregoing case, taken, as aforesaid, at Cape Girardeau, June 3, 1808, by Frederick Bates, commissioner:

Isaac Miller, duly sworn, says that this land was first settled in 1805, a cabin then built, and four or five acres enclosed and cultivated; constantly inhabited to this time; about 14 acres now in cultivation; no family. Laid over for decision.   (See No. 4, page 41.)

*February* 21, 1810.—Board met.   Present: John B. C. Lucas, Clement B. Penrose, and Frederick Bates, commissioners.

James Bevins, claiming 200 arpens of land.   (See book No. 4, page 41.)

It is the opinion of the board that this claim ought not to be granted.   (See book No. 4, page 283.)

*January* 10, 1834.—F. R. Conway, esq., appeared, pursuant to adjournment.

James Bevins, by his legal representatives, claiming 640 acres of land, situate on Whitewater, county of Cape Girardeau.   (See minutes, book No. 4, pages 41 and 283.)

STATE OF MISSOURI, *County of Cape Girardeau:*

Isaac Miller states that he moved to and settled in the district of Cape Girardeau, Upper Louisiana, now State of Missouri, in the year 1803; that he was well acquainted with one James Bevins, who also moved to and settled in said district, in said year 1803.   This affiant and the said Bevins, in the same year they arrived in the country, called on Lorimier, the Spanish commandant at Cape Girardeau, for land, and got permission to settle.   This affiant knows that the said James worked and made improvement on main Whitewater, in said district, in the winter of 1803, and raised corn thereon the next year, where he lived.   The said James died in the winter of 1804; the said place is now owned by the heirs of one John Miller.

                                                                             ISAAC MILLER.

Sworn to and subscribed, October 19, 1833.

                                                                             L. F. LINN, *Commissioner.*

(See book No. 6, page 455.)

*June* 16, 1835.—The board met, pursuant to adjournment.   Present: F. R. Conway, J. H. Relfe, commissioners.

James Bevins, claiming 200 arpens of land.   (See book No. 6, page 455, where this claim is entered for 640 acres.)

The board are of opinion that this claim ought not to be granted.   (See book No. 7, page 187.)

                                                                             JAMES H. RELFE,
                                                                             F. R. CONWAY.

I have examined the transcript of the above claim, and concur in the decision.

                                                                             F. H. MARTIN.

---

Class 2.   No. 49.—*Morris Young, claiming 300 arpens.*

| No. | Name of original claimant. | Arpens. | Nature and date of claim. | By whom granted. | By whom surveyed, date, and situation. |
|---|---|---|---|---|---|
| 49 | Morris Young. | 300 | Settlement right. | | James Boyd, D.S. No date. Countersigned A. Soulard. |

EVIDENCE WITH REFERENCE TO MINUTES AND RECORDS.

*May* 8, 1809.—Board met.   Present: John B. C. Lucas, Clement B. Penrose, and Frederick Bates, commissioners.

Morris Young, claiming 350 arpens 95 perches of land, situate on a fork of Byrd's creek, district of Cape Girardeau, produces to the board, as a special permission to settle, list B, on which claimant is No. 41, for 300 arpens, a plat of survey signed B. Causin, countersigned Antoine Soulard, S. G.   Laid over for decision.   (See No. 4, page 41.)

*February* 21, 1810.—Board met.   Present: John B. C. Lucas, Clement B. Penrose, and Frederick Bates, commissioners.

Morris Young, claiming 350 arpens of land.   (See book No. 4, page 41.)

It is the opinion of the board that this claim ought not to be granted.   (See book No. 4, page 282.)

*December* 24, 1833.—F. R. Conway, esq., appeared, pursuant to adjournment.

Morris Young, claiming 300 arpens of land, under a special permission to settle.   (See minutes No. 4, pages 41 and 282 ; record-book B, page 338.)

STATE OF MISSOURI, *County of Cape Girardeau :*

Personally appeared before L. F. Linn, one of the commissioners, George F. Bollinger and Moses Byrd, who, being duly sworn, deposeth and saith that they are well acquainted with Morris Young, the above-named claimant ; that said Young emigrated to this country in the year 1804 ; that he is a mechanic, a blacksmith by trade ; that he has resided in this country ever since, and followed his trade, and also cultivated or tilled the earth as a farmer.   And Moses Byrd, one of the deponents, further states that he was present at the commandant's, Louis Lorimier, in the year 1802 or '3, when Joseph Young, the brother of the claimant, applied to said commandant for a permission or grant for the above claimant, Morris Young.

GEORGE F. BOLLINGER,<br>MOSES BYRD.

Sworn to and subscribed, October 18, 1833.

L. F. LINN, *Commissioner.*

(See book No. 6, page 408.)

*June* 16, 1835.—The board met, pursuant to adjournment.   Present: F. R. Conway and J. H. Relfe, commissioners.

Morris Young, claiming 300 arpens of land.   (See book No. 6, page 408.)

The board are of opinion that this claim ought not to be granted.   (See book No. 7, page 187.)

JAMES H. RELFE,<br>F. R. CONWAY.

I have examined the transcript of the above claim, and concur in the decision.

F. H. MARTIN.

---

Class 2.   No. 50.—*David Reese, claiming 640 acres.*

| No. | Name of original claimant. | Acres. | Nature and date of claim. | By whom granted. | By whom surveyed, date, and situation. |
|---|---|---|---|---|---|
| 50 | David Reese. | 640 | Settlement right. | | William Johnson, 3d February, 1806.   Recorded by Soulard, 20th Feb., 1806. |

EVIDENCE WITH REFERENCE TO MINUTES AND RECORDS.

*May* 5, 1806.—The board met, agreeably to adjournment.   Present: Hon. Clement B. Penrose, and James L. Donaldson, esq.

David Reese, claiming, under the 2d section of the act, 240 arpens of land, situate on a fork of the river St. Francis, district aforesaid, produces a certificate of survey, dated 19th (20th) February, 1806.

Robert A. Logan, being duly sworn, says that claimant settled this tract of land, by his agent, Charles Logan, in 1803 ; that he moved on the same in the fall of 1805, and has actually inhabited and cultivated the same to this day ; was of the age of twenty-one years and upward on the 20th of December, 1803, and claims no other land in his own name in the territory.

The board reject this claim.   (See book No. 1, page 278.)

*August* 15, 1811.—Board met.   Present: Clement B. Penrose and Frederick Bates, commissioners.

David Reese, claiming 240 arpens of land.   (See book No. 1, page 278.)

It is the opinion of the board that this claim ought not to be granted.   (See book No. 5, page 309.)

*January* 4, 1834.—F. R. Conway, esq., appeared, pursuant to adjournment.

David Reese, by his legal representatives, claiming 640 acres of land, situate on the waters of the St. Francis.   (See book No. 1, page 278 ; No. 5, page 309 ; record-book B, page 469.)

STATE OF MISSOURI, *County of Cape Girardeau :*

Francis Clark, being duly sworn, says that he is well acquainted with David Reese ; first became acquainted with the said Reese early in the year 1804, in the district of Cape Girardeau, Upper Louisiana.   The said Reese was then living on the St. Francis river, in said district ; his improvement was small ; there were fruit-trees then growing on the said place ; the trees were of tolerable size, and looked as if they had been set out some time before ; the said place is still claimed by the said Reese, and there is a good house on it, and some ten or fifteen acres cleared.   The said place is situated on the St. Francis river, about twelve miles west of north of Greenville, Wayne county, Missouri.   There is no other old settler except himself, the deponent, and Mr. Pavrick, who is too old and infirm to come to Jackson, now living in the section of country where the above land is situated.

his<br>FRANCIS × CLARK.<br>mark.

Sworn to and mark made October 15th, 1833, in presence of

L. F. LINN, *Commissioner.*

(See No. 6, page 412.)

*June* 16, 1835.—The board met, pursuant to adjournment.   Present: F. R. Conway and J. H. Relfe, commissioners.

David Reese, claiming 640 acres of land.   (See book No. 6, page 442.)

The board are of opinion that this claim ought not to be granted.   (See book No. 7, page 187.)

JAMES H. RELFE,<br>F. R. CONWAY.

I have examined the transcript of the above claim, and concur in the decision.

F. H. MARTIN.

Class 2.   No. 51.—*Benjamin Pettit, jr., claiming 640 acres.*

| No. | Name of original claimant. | Acres. | Nature and date of claim. | By whom granted. | By whom surveyed, date, and situation. |
|---|---|---|---|---|---|
| 51 | Benjamin Pettit, jr. | 640 | Settlement right. | | On the waters of St. Francis river, Madison county. |

EVIDENCE WITH REFERENCE TO MINUTES AND RECORDS.

*November* 28, 1812.—Benjamin Pettit, jr.'s, representatives, claiming 640 acres of land, on St. Francis, district of Cape Girardeau.

Benjamin Pettit, sr., duly sworn, says that claimant settled this tract in 1803, and planted peach-trees. In this year claimant was taken sick and removed to house of witness, his father, and never returned, having died soon after; claimant had a wife and five children in 1803. (See recorder's minutes, page 17.)

*December* 26, 1833.—F. R. Conway, esq., appeared, pursuant to adjournment.

Benjamin Pettit, jr., by his legal representatives, claiming 640 acres of land, situate on the waters of St. Francis, county of Madison. (See record-book F, page 13; recorder's minutes, page 17; Bates's decisions, page 28.)

STATE OF MISSOURI, *County of Madison:*

John Clements, aged about fifty-three years, being duly sworn, as the law directs, deposeth and saith that he was well acquainted with the original claimant, Benjamin Pettit, jr., who was the son of Benjamin Pettit, sr., they both bearing the same name; that Benjamin Pettit, jr., had a wife and family; that he came to this country, then the province of Upper Louisiana, in the year 1803. Witness also knows the land claimed; he was with the claimant when he drove his wagon with his family on the land in the fall of 1803, and settled on the same; that claimant immediately built a cabin or house on the same, and resided thereon with his family till he became sick and afflicted, when he went near to his father's, where he died.

his<br>
JOHN  ×  CLEMENTS.<br>
mark.

Sworn to and subscribed before me, this 22d October, 1833.

L. F. LINN, *Commissioner.*

And also came Samuel Campbell, a witness, aged about sixty-eight years, who, after hearing the above and foregoing deposition read, deposeth and saith that he knows the same facts, and that the statements in the same are substantially correct and true.

SAMUEL CAMPBELL.

Sworn to and subscribed before me, this 22d October, 1833.

L. F. LINN, *Commissioner.*

Also came John L. Pettit, a witness, aged about fifty-one years, who, being duly sworn, as the law directs, deposeth and saith that he was well acquainted with the original claimant, who was his brother; that he had a wife and five children; that he came to this country, then the province of Upper Louisiana, in the fall of 1803; that he immediately moved on the land claimed (which he, witness, also knew) and settled on the same, built a house and lived therein till he became sick, when he made a temporary removal near to his father's, who was also called Benjamin Pettit, for the purpose of having better attendance during his sickness, when he died.

JOHN L. PETTIT.

Sworn to and subscribed before me, this 23d October, 1833.

L. F. LINN, *Commissioner.*

And also came John Reaves, a witness, aged about seventy-three years, who, being also duly sworn as the law directs, deposeth and saith that he was well acquainted with Benjamin Pettit, jr., the original claimant; that he came to this country, then the province of Upper Louisiana, in the year 1802 or 1803. Witness also knows the land claimed, and knows that the claimant actually settled on the same in the spring of 1803; built a cabin on the land, in which he resided with his family; claimant had some land fenced in and cleared in 1803, and a garden in cultivation on the same; the claimant continued to reside on the land till he became sick, when he was brought up by his father near himself, that he might be attended to during his sickness, as there was no person living near the place where he settled; and that, some time in the year 1804, claimant died. Witness knows the land was claimed for him by his father, Benjamin Pettit, sr., as he was present and paid the recording fees; and the witness also knows that the land claimed has always been called Benjamin Pettit, jr.'s place, and still is so; and witness also knows that the land claimed has been actually inhabited and cultivated ever since.

his<br>
JOHN  ×  REAVES.<br>
mark.

Sworn to and subscribed before me, this 23d October, 1833.

(See book No. 6, page 412.)

L. F. LINN, *Commissioner.*

*June* 16, 1835.—The board met, pursuant to adjournment. Present: F. R. Conway and J. H. Relfe, commissioners.

Benjamin Pettit, jr., claiming 640 acres of land. (See book No. 6, page 412.)

The board are of opinion that this claim ought not to be granted. (See book No. 7, page 188.)

JAMES H. RELFE,<br>
F. R. CONWAY.

I have examined the transcript of the above claim, and concur in the decision.

F. H. MARTIN.

Class 2.   No. 52.—*Robert Burns, claiming 640 arpens.*

| No. | Name of original claimant. | Acres. | Nature and date of claim. | By whom granted. | By whom surveyed, date, and situation. |
|---|---|---|---|---|---|
| 52 | Robert Burns. | 640 | Settlement right. | | On the waters of the St. Francis river, county of Madison. |

EVIDENCE WITH REFERENCE TO MINUTES AND RECORDS.

*December* 28, 1813.—Robert Burns, claiming 600 arpens of land, on the waters of river St. Francis, county of St. Genevieve.

Joshua Edwards, duly sworn, says that claimant came to the country in 1803, and remained in St. Francis till a short time ago, when he went to Black river to build a mill.   He made corn on the ground of other claimants from 1804 till lately.   (See recorder's minutes, page 117.)

*December* 27, 1833.—F. R. Conway, esq., appeared, pursuant to adjournment.

Robert Burns, by his legal representatives, claiming 640 acres of land on the waters of the St. Francis, county of Madison.   (See book F, page 53; recorder's minutes, page 117, and Bates's decisions, page 36.)

STATE OF MISSOURI, *County of Madison :*

John Matthews, aged about sixty-two years, being duly sworn as the law directs, deposeth and saith that he was well acquainted with the claimant, Robert Burns; that he came to this country, then the province of Upper Louisiana, in the year 1803, and that he continued a citizen and resident in the country till he died, about two years since.

JOHN MATTHEWS.

Sworn to and subscribed before me, this 31st day of May, 1833.

L. F. LINN, *Commissioner.*

And also came Thompson Crawford, a witness, aged about 47 years, who, being duly sworn, deposeth and saith, that he is well acquainted with Robert Burns, the original claimant; that he came to this country, then the province of Upper Louisiana, in the year 1803; witness also knows the land claimed, and also knows that the claimant settled on, improved, and cultivated the same in the years 1803 and 1804; that in 1804 claimant made a crop on the same, of corn and other things, and that he continued to inhabit and cultivate the same till the time of his death, a few years since.

THOMPSON CRAWFORD.

Sworn to and subscribed before me, this 21st October, 1833.

L. F. LINN, *Commissioner.*

(See book No. 6, page 419.)

*June* 16, 1835.—The board met, pursuant to adjournment.   Present: F. R. Conway, J. H. Relfe, commissioners.

Robert Burns, claiming 640 acres of land.   (See book No. 6, page 419.)

The board are of opinion that this claim ought not to be granted.   (See book No. 7, page 188.)

JAMES H. RELFE,
F. R. CONWAY.

I have examined the transcript of the above claim, and concur in the decision.

F. H. MARTIN.

---

Class 2.   No. 53.—*James Rogers, Jr., claiming 750 arpens.*

| No. | Name of original claimant. | Arpens. | Nature and date of claim. | By whom granted. | By whom surveyed, date, and situation. |
|---|---|---|---|---|---|
| 53 | James Rogers, jr. | 750 | Settlement right. | | Big river, fork of Merrimack. |

EVIDENCE WITH REFERENCE TO MINUTES AND RECORDS.

*June* 18, 1833.—F. R. Conway, esq., appeared, pursuant to adjournment.

James Rogers, jr., claiming 750 arpens of land, on Big river.   (See record-book E, page 356; Bates's decisions, page 94.)

Jacob Collins, duly sworn, says that he knows the land claimed, it being the same tract confirmed to Hugh McCullick, adjoining the one claimed by deponent; that he is well acquainted with claimant; that said claimant improved and cultivated the above mentioned tract, and raised corn thereon in 1802, to the best of his knowledge; that the said James Rogers stayed with him, the deponent, and did not build a house, he being a single man; that claimant had a clever little field, and raised sound corn.   (See minutes No. 6, page 177.)

*July* 5, 1834.—F. R. Conway, esq., appeared, pursuant to adjournment.

In the case of James Rogers, jr., claiming 758 arpens of land.   (See No. 6, page 177.)

Samuel Harrington, duly sworn, says that he is about 48 years of age; that he knew said James Rogers, jr., in the month of May, in the year 1801 or 1802, witness is not positive; that said Rogers came to this country at the time above mentioned, in company with five or six families, which, after resting a few weeks, scattered about Big river, and made settlements; that said Rogers lived in the same house with Jacob Collins, and worked his improvement, which was at a distance. Witness did not see said improvement at the time, saw it only one year after said improvement was made; that he then saw house, logs, trees deadened, and land ploughed, but does not recollect of having seen corn growing on the same, but he was told that claimant had raised corn there the year before; there was then three quarters of an acre, or may be an acre, cleared. Witness does not believe that the said tract was ever cultivated since. Witness further says that said improvement lies about half way between the improvement of said Jacob Collins and that of McCullick, being about 600 yards from each; that at the time witness saw said improvement, McCullick had not yet come to this country, that said McCullick arrived in the country in the year 1803. Further says that said Rogers was an active, industrious, hard-working man, who has ever since lived in the country, but witness never knew of his living on the place; that claimant had no family, being a single man. (See book No. 6, page 540.)

*June* 17, 1835.—The board met, pursuant to adjournment. Present: F. R. Conway, J. H. Relfe, commissioners.

James Rogers, jr., claiming 750 arpens of land. (See book No. 6, page 177.)

The board are of opinion that this claim ought not to be granted. (See book No. 7, page 188.)

JAMES H. RELFE,
F. R. CONWAY.

I have examined the transcript of the above claim, and concur in the decision.

F. H. MARTIN.

---

Class 2. No. 54.—*Reuben Middleton, claiming 640 acres.*

| No. | Name of original claimant. | Acres. | Nature and date of claim. | By whom granted. | By whom surveyed, date, and situation. |
|---|---|---|---|---|---|
| 54 | Reuben Middleton. | 640 | Settlement right. | | |

EVIDENCE WITH REFERENCE TO MINUTES AND RECORDS.

*October* 13, 1808.—The board met. Present: Hon. Clement B. Penrose and Frederick Bates, commissioners.

James Burns, assignee of Reuben Middleton, claiming 640 acres of land, situate at Bois-brulé, district of St. Genevieve, produces to the board a notice to the recorder, dated 27th June, 1808.

John Smith, senior, sworn, says that in the fall of the year 1804, Reuben Middleton cleared a small piece of ground on the land claimed, raised some turnips, and moved on the place, and inhabited and cultivated the same in 1805; and further, that said land has been inhabited and cultivated ever since.

Laid over for decision. (See book No. 3, page 293.)

*June* 19, 1810.—Board met. Present: John B. C. Lucas, Clement B. Penrose, and Frederick Bates, commissioners.

James Burns, claiming, as assignee of Reuben Middleton, 640 acres of land. (See book No. 3, page 293.)

It is the opinion of the board that this claim ought not to be granted. (See book No. 4, page 391.)

*January* 25, 1834.—F. R. Conway, esq., appeared, pursuant to adjournment.

Reuben Middleton, claiming 640 acres of land, situated in Bois-brulé bottom, district of St. Genevieve. (See record book E, page 212; minute book No. 3, page 293, and No. 4, page 391.)

Personally appeared before me, L. F. Linn, one of the commissioners appointed, &c., Mr. Thomas Allen, aged about 57 years, who, after being duly sworn, states that he was acquainted with Reuben Middleton; that said Middleton emigrated to the then province of Upper Louisiana and district of St. Genevieve, in the year 1800 or 1801, and settled in Bois-brulé bottom, near a creek of the same name. Deponent states that Middleton built a house in which he lived; he opened some land and cultivated it in potatoes, &c., perhaps two or three acres.

THOMAS x ALLEN.
his
mark.

*October* 25, 1833.

L. F. LINN, *Commissioner.*

Also, John Kennison appeared, who, after hearing the above deposition read, deposes and says, he believes and knows the statement above made by Mr. Allen to be true.

JOHN KENNISON.

*October* 25, 1833.

L. F. LINN, *Commissioner.*

(See book No. 6, page 483.)

*June* 17, 1835.—The board met, pursuant to adjournment. Present: F. R. Conway, J. H. Relfe, commissioners.

Reuben Middleton, claiming 640 acres of land. (See book No. 6, page 423.)

The board are of opinion that this claim ought not to be granted. (See book No. 7, page 188.

JAMES H. RELFE,
F. R. CONWAY.

I have examined the transcript of the above claim, and concur in the decision.

F. H. MARTIN.

Class 2.   No. 55.—*Joseph Dennis, claiming 640 acres.*

| No. | Name of original claimant. | Acres. | Nature and date of claim. | By whom granted. | By whom surveyed, date, and situation. |
|---|---|---|---|---|---|
| 55 | Joseph Dennis. | 640 | Settlement right. | | |

EVIDENCE WITH REFERENCE TO MINUTES AND RECORDS.

*November* 14, 1811.—Board met.   Present: John B. C. Lucas, Clement B. Penrose, and Frederick Bates, commissioners.

Joseph Dennis, claiming 250 arpens of land, situate district of Cape Girardeau, big bend of the Mississippi, produces notice to the recorder.

It is the opinion of the board that this claim ought not to be granted.   (See book No. 5, page 415.)

*January* 24, 1839.—F. R. Conway, esq., appeared, pursuant to adjournment.

Joseph Dennis, claiming 640 acres of land, situate on the Mississippi, in the county of Cape Girardeau. (See record book E, page 27; minute book No. 5, page 415.

STATE OF MISSOURI, *Cape Girardeau County:*

Personally appeared before L. F. Linn, one of the commissioners appointed, &c., Richard Waller, of lawful age, who, being sworn as the law directs, deposeth and saith that he was personally acquainted with Joseph Dennis; that he resided on the west bank of the Mississippi river, above the old cape, in what is called the big bend; that said Dennis had resided there some years, but how many this deponent cannot say; but in the year 1808, this deponent assisted to move said Dennis from said place to Illinois; that he had a dwelling-house erected, and a small farm opened on said place; that his family consisted of his wife and two children.

RICHARD WALLER.

Signed and sworn to in presence of

L. F. LINN, *Commissioner.*

JACKSON, *October* 15, 1833.
(See book No. 6, page 487.)

*June* 17, 1835.—The board met, pursuant to adjournment.   Present: F. R. Conway and J. H. Relfe, commissioners.

Joseph Dennis, claiming 640 acres of land.   (See book No. 6, page 487.)

The board are of opinion that this claim ought not to be granted.   (See book No. 7, page 189.)

JAMES H. RELFE,
F. R. CONWAY.

I have examined the transcript of the above claim, and concur in the decision.

F. H. MARTIN.

---

Class 2.   No. 56.—*Samuel Campbell, claiming 640 acres.*

| No. | Name of original claimant. | Acres. | Nature and date of claim. | By whom granted. | By whom surveyed, date, and situation. |
|---|---|---|---|---|---|
| 56 | Samuel Campbell. | 640 | Settlement right. | | On the waters of St. Francis river. |

EVIDENCE WITH REFERENCE TO MINUTES AND RECORDS.

*November* 30, 1812.—Samuel Campbell, claiming 800 arpens of land, on the waters of St. Francis, district of St. Genevieve.

Ezekiel Able, duly sworn, says that, in 1803, saw claimant's family inhabiting this tract, and that in 1804 they still lived on the land and raised a crop.   A wife and two children in 1803. ( See recorder's minutes, page 20.)

*August* 2, 1813.—Samuel Campbell, claiming 800 arpens of land.   (See minutes, 30th November last.)

David Terrell, duly sworn, says that claimant inhabited and cultivated this tract in 1803 and 1804, and till this time.   (See recorder's minutes, page 50.)

*December* 24, 1813.—Samuel Campbell.   (See minutes, pages 20 and 50.)   Claimant personally appears and disavows any intention of trespassing or claiming within the lines of James Hendley, as surveyed under concession of Z. Trudeau, dated 18th May, 1798, the plat recorded in book A, page 514; and engages that he will not, at any future time, demand or accept any part of the lands within the lines of said James Hendley, and relinquishes all claim which he may have heretofore had, or pretended to have, within said lines.   (See recorder's minutes, page 104.)

*December* 25, 1813.—Samuel Campbell.   (Pages 20, 50, and 104.)   Joshua Edwards duly sworn, says that Samuel Campbell lived, on 20th December, 1803, on the plantation of Benjamin Pettit, and remained there until next January following.   Witness understood, both from Pettit and claimant, Campbell, that he, Campbell, was the tenant of Pettit, having rented said plantation.   Previously to 20th December, 1803, witness never knew claimant to have lived one and a half or two miles below Captain Callaway's.   Witness went to that settlement in 1801, and never, until about eight months ago, heard of Campbell having a claim there.

Adam Johnson, duly sworn, says that Campbell lived on Matthew's place in the summer of 1803.

Thompson Crawford, duly sworn, says that Samuel Campbell lived at Pettit's place in 1803, in winter. Witness never before this time heard of Samuel Campbell's having a claim for land about one or two miles below Captain Callaway's. Witness went to that settlement in May, 1803; believes that Campbell did not, at any time that year, inhabit that place.

William Dillon, duly sworn, says that claimant, Campbell, did not inhabit the tract claimed on 20th December, 1803. When claimant left Pettit's place, witness believes, and it was the neighborhood belief, that he went to some of the settlements of the then district of Cape Girardeau; this was some time in the year 1804. (See recorder's minutes, page 110.)

*December* 26, 1833.—F. R. Conway, esq., appeared, pursuant to adjournment.

Samuel Campbell, claiming 640 acres of land, situate on the waters of St. Francis river, county of Madison. (See record-book F, page 89; recorder's minutes, pages 20, 50, 104, and 110.)

STATE OF MISSOURI, *County of Madison :*

John Clements, aged about 53 years, being duly sworn as the law directs, deposeth and says that he is well acquainted with Samuel Campbell, the original claimant; that he first saw him in this country, then the province of Upper Louisiana, in the spring of the year 1803. Witness also knows the land claimed, and also knows that the claimant settled on the land in the year 1803; built a house on the same, and had his family there residing; witness also knows that there was several acres of land fenced in and cleared, which were actually cultivated in the years 1803 and 1804, in corn and other things; and witness also knows that the said tract of land has been actually inhabited and cultivated ever since.

JOHN x CLEMENTS.
his
mark.

Sworn to and subscribed before me, this 22d November, 1833.

L. F. LINN, *Commissioner.*

Also, came Thompson Crawford, a witness, aged about 47 years, who being duly sworn, as the law directs, deposeth and saith that he is well acquainted with Samuel Campbell, the original claimant; that he was residing in this country, the province of Upper Louisiana, in the year 1803. Witness also knows the land claimed, and that the claimant settled on the same in the latter part of the spring, or early in the summer, of 1803. Claimant built a house on the same and moved into the same; claimant built a blacksmith shop also on the land, about the same time, and did work thereon for the people around him; claimant had a family, a wife, and one child. Claimant fenced in and cleared some three or four acres of land, which was actually cultivated in the years 1803 and 1804, in corn and other things necessary, and the said tract of land has been continually, from that time, inhabited and cultivated ever since.

THOMPSON CRAWFORD.

Sworn and subscribed before me, this 23d October, 1833.

L. F. LINN, *Commissioner.*

And also, came John Reaves, a witness, aged about 73 years, who being duly sworn, deposeth and saith, that he well knew the original claimant; that he found him a settler and cultivator of the soil in 1803, when witness came to this country; the witness also knows the land claimed; claimant was residing on the same in 1803; had a house and blacksmith shop, in which the witness worked in 1803 and 1804; claimant also lived there in 1804; there was a good large field under fence, cleared and in cultivation by the claimant, and the said tract of land has been continually inhabited and cultivated ever since.

JOHN x REAVES.
his
mark.

Sworn to and subscribed before me, this 23d of October, 1833.

L. F. LINN, *Commissioner.*

(No. 6, page 414.)

*June* 17, 1835.—The board met, pursuant to adjournment. Present: F. R. Conway, J. H. Relfe, commissioners.

Samuel Campbell, claiming 640 acres of land. (See book No. 6, page 414.)

The board are of opinion that this claim ought not to be granted, claimant being a tenant in the years 1803 and 1804. (See book No. 7, page 189.)

JAMES H. RELFE,
F. R. CONWAY.

I have examined the transcript of the above claim, and concur in the decision.

F. H. MARTIN.

Class 2. No. 57.—*Amable Patnotte, claiming 640 acres.*

| No. | Name of original claimant. | Acres. | Nature and date of claim. | By whom granted. | By whom surveyed, date, and situation. |
|---|---|---|---|---|---|
| 57 | Amable Patnotte. | 640 | Settlement right. | | John Stewart, D. S., 5th February, 1806. Received for record, 28th February, 1806, by A. Soulard, S. G |

EVIDENCE WITH REFERENCE TO MINUTES AND RECORDS

*December* 6th, 1811.—Board met. Present: John B. C. Lucas, Clement B. Penrose, and Frederick Bates, commissioners.

Amable Patnotte, claiming 748 arpens 68 perches of land, situate in Bellevue, district of St. Genevieve, produces record of a plat of survey, dated 5th February, 1806, and certified 28th February, 1806.

It is the opinion of the board that this claim ought not to be granted. (See book No. 5, page 477.)

*July* 9, 1834.—The board met, pursuant to adjournment. Present: J. S. Mayfield, J. H. Relfe, and F. R. Conway, commissioners.

Amable Patnotte, claiming 640 acres of land, situate in Bellevue settlement. (See record-book B, page 232; book No. 5, page 477.)

John Stuart, duly sworn, says that in 1802 claimant had a house and garden on the tract claimed, and that said claimant has ever since resided in this country.

The following testimony was taken before James H. Relfe, esq., on the 21st of last June:

STATE OF MISSOURI, *County of Washington :*

Personally appeared before James H. Relfe, one of the commissioners for the adjustment of private land claims in Missouri, John T. McNeal, who deposeth and saith that Amable Patnotte, a laboring man, lived in a cabin in Mine à Breton, and cultivated a garden and other improvements in the year 1800, and continued to reside there for some years after, and that he never knew him to claim any other lands.

JOHN T. McNEAL.

Sworn to and subscribed before me, this 21st June, 1834.

JAMES H. RELFE.

(See book No. 7, page 6.)

*October* 8, 1834.—The board met, pursuant to adjournment. Present: F. R. Conway, J. S. Mayfield, and J. H. Relfe, commissioners.

In the case of Amable Patnotte, claiming 640 acres of land, (see No. 7, page 6,) the following testimony was taken by James H. Relfe, commissioner:

STATE OF MISSOURI, *County of Washington :*

Personally appeared before James H. Relfe, one of the commissioners appointed, &c., Baptiste Plaget, who deposeth and saith he removed to Mine à Breton in the year 1808, and in the spring of the year 1809 removed to the Old Mine, in the then county of St. Genevieve, territory of Missouri, and was employed by Amable Patnotte to work on a tract of land and extend an improvement; from the appearance of the old improvement, deponent thinks it had been made five or six years previous to that time.

BAPTISTE  ×  PLAGET.<br>mark.

Sworn to and subscribed before me, this 28th July, 1834.

JAMES H. RELFE.

(See No. 7, page 29.)

*June* 17, 1835.—The board met, pursuant to adjournment. Present: F. R. Conway, J. H. Relfe, commissioners.

Amable Patnotte, claiming 640 acres of land. (See book No. 7, page 6.)

The board are of opinion that this claim ought not to be granted. (See book No. 7, page 189.)

JAMES H. RELFE,<br>F. R. CONWAY.

I have examined the transcript of the above claim, and concur in the decision.

F. H. MARTIN.

---

Class 2.    No. 58.— *William McHugh, jr., claiming 640 acres.*

| No. | Name of original claimant. | Arpens. | Nature and date of claim. | By whom granted. | By whom surveyed, date, and situation. |
|-----|---------------------------|---------|---------------------------|------------------|----------------------------------------|
| 58  | Wm. McHugh, jr.           | 640     | Settlement right.         |                  |                                        |

EVIDENCE WITH REFERENCE TO MINUTES AND RECORDS.

*St. Louis, December* 15, 1813.—James Morrison, assignee of William McHugh, sr., claiming 640 acres, as legal representatives of William McHugh, jr., at Sulphur spring or lick, near Bryan's creek, county of St. Charles.

Frederick Dickson, duly sworn, says that, in 1803, witness saw a cabin near the Sulphur spring, and also a small field in which vegetables, water-melons, &c. were cultivated. Witness went with claimant, McHugh, jr. on this tract in the fall of 1803, and dug potatoes, which witness has no doubt had been planted and cultivated by said William McHugh, jr. The tract and improvement went under his name and was considered as his property. McHugh, jr. was killed by the Indians in 1804. Perhaps the cabin was never completed. (See Bates's minutes, page 78.)

*April* 28, 1835.—The board met, pursuant to adjournment. Present: James H. Relfe, F. R. Conway, commissioners.

William McHugh, jr., by his legal representative, James Morrison, claiming 640 acres of land, situate near Bryan's creek, district of St. Charles. (See record-book F, page 112; Bates's minutes, page 78; Bates's decisions, page 33. See book No. 7, page 139.)

*June* 17, 1835.—The board met, pursuant to adjournment. Present: F. R. Conway, J. H Relfe, commissioners.

William McHugh, jr., claiming 640 acres of land. (See book No. 7, page 139.)

The board are of opinion that this claim ought not to be granted. (See book No. 7, page 190.)

JAMES H. RELFE,<br>F. R. CONWAY.

I have examined the transcript of the above claim, and concur in the decision.

F. H. MARTIN.

Class 2.  No. 59.—*Martin Thomas, claiming* 640 *acres.*

| No. | Name of original claimant. | Acres. | Nature and date of claim. | By whom granted. | By whom surveyed, date, and situation. |
|-----|----------------------------|--------|---------------------------|------------------|----------------------------------------|
| 59  | Martin Thomas.             | 640    | Settlement right.         | .                | James Boyd, D. S.  Countersigned Antonio Soulard, S. G.  On Whitewater. |

EVIDENCE WITH REFERENCE TO MINUTES AND RECORDS.

*February* 20, 1809.—Board met.  Present : John B. C. Lucas, Clement B. Penrose, and Frederick Bates, commissioners.

Martin Thomas, claiming 350 arpens of land and 95 perches, situate on Whitewater, district of Cape Girardeau, produces to the board as a special permission to settle, list B, on which claimant is No. 33, and a plat of survey certified to be received for record February 27, 1806, by Antonio Soulard, surveyor general.

The following testimony, taken by Frederick Bates, commissioner, at Cape Girardeau, in the above claim as aforesaid, May 31, 1808 :

Joseph Niswanger, affirmed, says that claimant, in 1806, enclosed about one-quarter acre of land, and planted turnip and apple seed.  Laid over for decision.  (See No. 3, page 481.)

*December* 29, 1809.—Board met.  Present : John B. C. Lucas, Clement B. Penrose, and Frederick Bates, commissioners.

Martin Thomas, claiming 350 arpens 95 perches of land.  (See book No. 3, page 481.)

It is the opinion of the board that this claim ought not to be granted.  (See book No. 4, page 241.)

*January* 3, 1834.—F. R. Conway, esq. appeared, pursuant to adjournment,

Martin Thomas, by his legal representatives, claiming 640 acres of land, situate on Little Whitewater, county of Cape Girardeau.  (See minutes, book No. 3, page 481 ; No. 4, page 241 ; record-book B, page 292.)

STATE OF MISSOURI, *County of Cape Girardeau :*

John Cotner, being duly sworn, states that he is well acquainted with Martin Thomas, who came to this district of Cape Girardeau, Upper Louisiana, in 1803, and had an improvement on Little Whitewater, in said district, in the fall of that year, at which time turnips were sowed.  Early the next spring this affiant worked on the said improvement, for the said Thomas, and assisted him in planting apple trees.  The said Thomas claimed and has owned ever since he occupied it in 1804.

                                                                          his<br>
                                                        JOHN  ×  COTNER.<br>
                                                                       mark.

Sworn to and subscribed, October 16, 1833.

L. F. LINN, *Commissioner.*

Joseph Niswanger states that he is well acquainted with the above Martin Thomas ; that he has read the foregoing statement of John Cotner, and knows the facts therein contained to be true.

                                                                          his<br>
                                                     JOSEPH  ×  NISWANGER.<br>
                                                                       mark.

Sworn before

L. F. LINN, *Commissioner.*

(See book No. 6, page 440.)

*April* 24, 1835.—The board met, pursuant to adjournment.  Present : F. R. Conway, J. H. Relfe, commissioners.

In the case of Martin Thomas, claiming 640 acres of land.  (See book No. 6, page 440.)

The following testimony was taken by James H. Relfe, Esq. :

Joseph Niswanger, jr. states that he is the son of Joseph Niswanger, sr. ; that he and his father moved to the province of Upper Louisiana, now State of Missouri, in 1799, where he has resided ever since.  He is the same person who gave a deposition before Mr. Commissioner Linn, in relation to Martin Thomas's unconfirmed land claim ; that he, this affiant, never gave testimony before any previous board, but he has heard his father, Joseph Niswanger, sr., say that he was a witness in said claim before one of the previous boards, and this affiant has no doubt of the fact.

JOSEPH NISWANGER, Jr.

Sworn to and subscribed before me,

JAMES H. RELFE, *Commissioner.*

*April* 6, 1835.—(See book No. 7, page 133.)

*June* 17, 1835.—The board met, pursuant to adjournment.  Present : F. R. Conway, J. H. Relfe, commissioners.

Martin Thomas, claiming 640 acres of land.  (See book No. 6, page 440 ; No. 7, page 133.)

The board are of opinion that this claim ought not to be granted.  (See book No. 7, page 190.)

JAMES H. RELFE,<br>
F. R. CONWAY.

I have examined the transcript of the above claim, and concur in the decision.

F. H. MARTIN.

Class 2.   No. 60.—*George Ayrey, claiming 750 arpens.*

| No. | Name of original claimant. | Arpens. | Nature and date of claim. | By whom granted. | By whom surveyed, date, and situation. |
|---|---|---|---|---|---|
| 60 | George Ayrey. | 750 | Settlement right. | | Daniel M. Boone, 24th February, 1806. Received for record by A. Soulard, S. G., 28th February, 1806. District of St. Charles. |

EVIDENCE WITH REFERENCE TO MINUTES AND RECORDS.

*October* 9, 1811.—Board met.  Present: John B. C. Lucas, Clement B. Penrose, and Frederick Bates, commissioners.

George Ayrey, claiming 750 arpens of land, situated in the district of St. Charles, produces a plat of survey, dated 24th February, and certified 26th (28th) February, 1806.

It is the opinion of the board that this claim ought not to be granted.  (See book No. 5, page 356.)

*May* 22, 1833.—F. R. Conway, esq., appeared, pursuant to adjournment.

George Ayrey, claiming 750 arpens of land.  (See record-book B, page 216, for plat of survey ; minutes No. 5, page 356.   See book No. 6, page 169.)

*October* 8, 1833.—The board met, pursuant to adjournment.  Present: F. R. Conway, J. S. Mayfield, and J. H. Relfe, commissioners.

George Ayrey, claiming 750 arpens of land.  (See book No. 6, page 169.)

The following testimony was taken before A. G. Harrison, commissioner, under a resolution passed by the board, on the 13th May, 1833 :

Isaac Vanbibber, sr., being duly sworn, says that Ayrey lived with William Ramsay, sr., before the change of government, and lived with him in 1800 ; and his claim adjoined, as witness understood, the claim of said Ramsay.

Joshua Stogsdill, being duly sworn, says that he, (witness,) in February, 1804, made for said Ayrey, on Lick branch, an improvement on a tract of land on said branch.  The improvements consisted in clearing ground and building a cabin ; that said Ayrey put in a crop on said place that year, as well as witness now recollects. (See book No. 7, page 19.)

*June* 17, 1835.—The board met, pursuant to adjournment.  Present: F. R. Conway, J. H. Relfe, commissioners.

George Ayrey, claiming 750 arpens of land.  (See book No. 6, page 169 ; No. 7, page 19.)

The board are of opinion that this claim ought not to be granted.  (See book No. 7, page 191.)

JAMES H. RELFE,<br>F. R. CONWAY.

I have examined the transcript of the above claim, and concur in the decision.

F. H. MARTIN.

---

Class 2.   No. 61.—*J. St. G. Beauvais, claiming 60 feet in circumference, &c.*

To Mr. HENRY PEROUSE DE LACOUDRENIERE, *Captain of Infantry, Civil and Military Commandant of the post of St. Genevieve :*

SIR : The undersigned has the honor of representing to you that, desiring to cross to this side to settle himself, and wishing to have his hands to work at Mine à Breton, if you were pleased to grant him a concession of sixty feet in circumference, around each hole where he may find mineral, the undersigned shall pray for your prosperity and conservation.

J. ST. G. BEAUVAIS.

ST. GENEVIEVE, *November* 19, 1788.

Be the present forwarded to Don Manuel Perez, captain of the stationary regiment of Louisiana, and lieutenant governor of this upper part, in order that he may be pleased to determine on the subject.

Given at St. Genevieve, 19th November, 1788.

PEROUSE DE LACOUDRENIERE.

Don MANUEL PEREZ, *Captain of the regiment of Infantry of Louisiana, Lieutenant Governor and Commandant of this western part and district of Illinois :*

Having seen the statement in the foregoing memorial, presented by Juan Bautista Senchem, bearing date the nineteenth of the present month and year, in which he solicits to come over to this Spanish side, to establish himself under the laws of his Catholic Majesty, in which consideration I have granted, and do grant, to him, in full property for him, his heirs, or others that may represent his right, the sixty feet in circumference, which he solicits at Mine à Breton, distant twenty or twenty-one leagues from St. Genevieve, on the same terms as he solicits, in order that he may work in said place ; being well understood that he is to verify the establishment of his family on this (Spanish) part.  Said lands remaining from this date subject to the public charges and others that his Majesty may be pleased to impose.

Given in St. Louis of Illinois, 27th September, 1788.

MANUEL PEREZ.

ST. LOUIS, *December* 12, 1832.  Truly translated.

JULIUS DE MUN.

*J. St. G. Beauvais, claiming 60 feet in circumference, &c.*

| No. | Name of original claimant. | Arpens. | Nature and date of claim. | By whom granted. | By whom surveyed, date, and situation. |
|-----|----------------------------|---------|---------------------------|------------------|----------------------------------------|
| 61  | St. G. Bauvais.            | 60 feet around each hole, &c. | Concession, 27th September, 1788. | M. Perez. |  |

EVIDENCE WITH REFERENCE TO MINUTES AND RECORDS.

*June* 20, 1806.—The board met, agreeably to adjournment. Present: Clement B. Penrose and James L. Donaldson, esquires.

The same, (St. Gemme Beauvais,) claiming some mine lands, situated Mine à Breton, district of St. Genevieve, produces a concession from Manuel Perez, granting claimant sixty feet in circumference around each hole wherein he might find ore; said concession dated November 22, 1788.

Baptist Vallé, being duly sworn, says that the claimant worked the said mines for about eight or ten years; that, having purchased a mine tract, he went to work the same; that everybody was at liberty of working the mine, and therefore entitled to sixty feet round the hole; so worked and continued to until an order was issued by government reducing the same to twelve feet square round the same.

The board reject this claim, and remark that the said concession is not duly registered. (See remark of the board at the bottom of this page, to wit:)

In the claim of the same, at the Mine à Breton, in this page, the board are of opinion that this concession vested in the claimant an incorporeal right to dig the mineral, not to affect the right of domain in the soil, which still remained in the Spanish government. (See book No. 1, page 317.)

*December* 21, 1811.—Board met. Present: John B. C. Lucas, Clement B. Penrose, and Frederick Bates, commissioners.

St. James Beauvais, claiming sixty feet in circumference around every hole where he may find mineral. (See book No. 1, page 316.)

It is the opinion of the board, (majority of,) that this claim ought not to be confirmed. Frederick Bates, commissioner, forbears giving an opinion. (See book No. 5, page 532.)

*December* 13, 1832.—F. R. Conway, esq., appeared, pursuant to adjournment.

St. Gemme Beauvais, claiming sixty feet in circumference around each hole, at Mine à Breton, where he may find mineral. (See book No. 1, page 316; No. 5, page 532; record-book C, page 456.)

Produces a paper purporting to be an original concession, from Manuel Perez, dated 27th November, 1788. (See book No. 6, page 74.)

*June* 17, 1835.—The board met, pursuant to adjournment. Present: F. R. Conway and J. H. Relfe, commissioners.

St. Gemme Beauvais, claiming sixty feet in circumference around each hole in which he may find mineral. (See book No. 6, page 74.)

The board are of opinion that this claim ought not to be confirmed. (See book No. 7, page 191.)

                                                                        JAMES H. RELFE,
                                                                        F. R. CONWAY.

I have examined the transcript of the above claim, and concur in the decision.

                                                                        F. H. MARTIN.

---

Class 2.    No. 62.—*Absalom Link, claiming 510 arpens.*

| No. | Name of original claimant. | Arpens. | Nature and date of claim. | By whom granted. | By whom surveyed, date, and situation. |
|-----|----------------------------|---------|---------------------------|------------------|----------------------------------------|
| 62  | Absalom Link.              | 510     | Settlement right.         |                  | James Mackay, 21st Nov., 1805, certified by Soulard, 25th January, 1806. On Whiteoak run, district of St. Louis. |

EVIDENCE WITH REFERENCE TO MINUTES AND RECORDS.

*November* 23, 1811.—Board met. Present: John B. C. Lucas, Clement B. Penrose, and Frederick Bates, commissioners.

Absalom Link, claiming 510 arpens of land, situate Whiteoak run, district of St. Louis, produces record of a plat of survey, dated 21st November, 1805, and certified 25th January, 1806.

It is the opinion of the board that this claim ought not to be granted. (See book No. 5, page 444.)

*June* 1, 1833.—F. R. Conway, esq., appeared, pursuant to adjournment.

Absalom Link, by his legal representative, William Ramsey, claiming 510 arpens of land, situated on Whiteoak run, district of St. Louis. (See minutes No. 5, page 444; book B, page 269.)

Produces a plat of survey by James Mackay, dated November 21, 1805, recorded by Soulard, January 26, 1806.

William Campbell, duly sworn, says that, in the spring of 1804, he saw on said place a small piece of ground enclosed, and the foundation of a cabin, as also, the name of Link carved on a tree; that said place was then considered as Absalom Link's land, under a settlement right.   (See book No. 6, page 172.)

*June* 13, 1833.—F. R. Conway, esq., appeared, pursuant to adjournment.

In the case of Absalom Link, claiming 510 arpens of land.   (See page 172 of this book.)

Sally Williams, duly sworn, says that she is in her 76th year; that she knows the claimant, Absalom Link; that in the year 1801 or 1802 he settled and improved a place adjoining that of her husband's, Joseph Williams; that one Robert Young, who had a grant prior to Link's improving said land, had the said Link's improvements included in his survey.   (See book No. 6, page 175.)

*July* 12, 1833.—The board met, pursuant to adjournment.   Present: L. F. Linn and F. R. Conway, commissioners.

In the case of Absalom Link, claiming 510 arpens.   (See pages 172 and 175 of this book.)

Lewis Musick, duly sworn, says that, at the latter end of 1803, or beginning or 1804, he was requested by the claimant to go with him on a piece of land which claimant wanted to improve; they went together, and said claimant laid the foundation of a cabin, deadened some trees, and cut his name on the bark of a tree; deponent further says, he heard that claimant had made an improvement, which had been taken away from him by a survey subsequently made, which induced claimant to make this new improvement.   (See book No. 6, page 232.)

*June* 17, 1835.—The board met, pursuant to adjournment.   Present: F. R. Conway and J. H. Relfe, commissioners.

Absalom Link, claiming 510 arpens of land.   (See book No. — pages 172, 175, and 232.)

The board are of opinion that this claim ought not to be granted.   (See book No. 7, page 191.)

JAMES H. RELFE,<br>
F. R. CONWAY.

I have examined the transcript of the above claim, and concur in the decision.

F. H. MARTIN.

---

Class 2.   No. 63.—*Peter Burell, claiming 2,000 arpens.*

| No. | Name of original claimant. | Arpens. | Nature and date of claim | By whom granted. | By whom surveyed, date, and situation. |
|-----|----------------------------|---------|--------------------------|------------------|----------------------------------------|
| 63  | Peter Burell.              | 2,000   | Settlement right.        |                  | South side of Marameck.                |

EVIDENCE WITH REFERENCE TO MINUTES AND RECORDS.

St. Louis, *October* 12, 1812.—Peter Burell, claiming 2,000 arpens of land on south side of Marameck.

John Helderbrand, duly sworn, says that about 33 or 34 years ago, Burell was inhabiting and cultivating this tract of land.   Witness purchased corn of said Burell; he had a considerably large field in cultivation; also a young orchard, beginning to bear fruit.   This claimant abandoned this tract, on account of Indian disturbances, soon after.   Burell had a wife and child.

John Cummings, sworn, 17th November, says Burell lived on and cultivated about five arpens on this tract, in 1781, and that he continued to inhabit and cultivate said tract for the three following years.   Witness believes that claimant was inhabiting and cultivating before 1781, but has no personal knowledge of the fact.   In the year 1784, witness went to Natchez, at which time said Burell was inhabiting and cultivating said tract.   (See Bates's minutes, page 7.   (At the margin: "Not granted.")

*June* 18, 1835.—The board met, pursuant to adjournment.   Present: F. R. Conway and J. H. Relfe, commissioners.

(Peter) Burell, by his legal representatives, claiming 2,000 arpens of land.   (See record-book B, page 325; Bates's minutes, page 7; Bates's decisions, page 27.   See book No. 7, page 192.)

*August* 17, 1835.—The board met, pursuant to adjournment.   Present: F. R. Conway, James H. Relfe, and F. H. Martin, commissioners.

Peter Burell, claiming 2,000 arpens of land.   (See book No. 7, page 192.)

The board are unanimously of opinion that this claim ought not to be granted, the said Peter Burell having had a tract of sixteen hundred arpens granted.   (See Bates's decisions, page 25.   See book No. 7, page 216.)

F. H. MARTIN,<br>
JAMES H. RELFE,<br>
F. R. CONWAY.

---

Class 2.   No. 64.—*Philip Robert, claiming 1,050 arpens.*

| No. | Name of original claimant. | Arpens. | Nature and date of claim. | By whom granted. | By whom surveyed, date, and situation. |
|-----|----------------------------|---------|---------------------------|------------------|----------------------------------------|
| 64  | Philip Robert.             | 1,050   | Settlement right.         |                  |                                        |

EVIDENCE WITH REFERENCE TO MINUTES AND RECORDS.

*December* 9, 1811.—Board met.   Present: John B. C. Lucas, Clement B. Penrose, and Frederick Bates, commissioners.

Philip Robert, claiming 1,050 arpens of land, situate in the district of St. Louis, produces notice to the recorder.

It is the opinion of the board that this claim ought not to be granted.   (See minute-book No. 5, page 492.)

St. Louis, *November* 30, 1812.—William Russell, assignee of Philip Robert, claiming 1,050 arpens of land, on the waters of Grand Glaize, district of St. Louis, produces notice; also, deed dated 23d August, 1809.

Frederick Connor, duly sworn, says that Robert lived on this tract in 1801, 1802, and 1803, during which time witness believes that he cultivated the same.   In 1803 witness knows that claimant had several children, perhaps three.

Benjamin Johnson, duly sworn, says that Robert had a wife and four children in 1803.   (See Bates's minutes, page 24.)   (At the margin is the following: "Not granted.")

*June* 18, 1835.—The board met, pursuant to adjournment.   Present: F. R. Conway, J. H. Relfe, commissioners.

Philip Robert, by his legal representatives, claiming 1,050 arpens of land on the waters of Grand Glaize. (See record-book F, page 39 ; minutes, book No. 5, page 492; Bates's minutes, page 24 ; Bates's decisions, page 29.   See book No. 7, page 193.)

*August* 15, 1835.—The board met, pursuant to adjournment.   Present: F. R. Conway, J. H. Relfe, F. H. Martin, commissioners.

Philip Robert, claiming 1,050 arpens of land.   (See book No. 7, page 193.)

The board are unanimously of opinion that this claim ought not to be granted, there being no proof of cultivation.   (See book No. 7, page 216.)

F. H. MARTIN,
JAMES H. RELFE,
F. R. CONWAY.

---

Class 2.   No. 65.—*John Daniel, claiming* 800 *arpens.*

| No. | Name of original claimant. | Arpens. | Nature and date of claim. | By whom granted. | By whom surveyed, date, and situation. |
|---|---|---|---|---|---|
| 65 | John Daniel. | 800 | Settlement right. | | |

EVIDENCE WITH REFERENCE TO MINUTES AND RECORDS.

St. Louis, *December* 29, 1813.—William Russell, assignee John Donnohue, assignee John Daniel, claiming 800 arpens of land on the waters of the Saline creek, county of St. Genevieve.   Produces unauthenticated transfers.

James McLean, duly sworn, says that he saw this tract 24th December, 1803, and observed that claimant Daniel had cut a considerable quantity of timber and mauled some rails, and collected logs for a cabin.   He had also cleared, fenced, and probably, from appearances, had cultivated a small spot as a garden.   At that time no cabin ; no person inhabiting.   Daniel told the witness that it was his improvement.   Witness saw a camp on the tract which had probably been inhabited.   (See Bates's minutes, page 128.)   (On the margin: "Not granted.")

*June* 19, 1835.—The board met, pursuant to adjournment.   Present: F. R. Conway, J. H. Relfe, commissioners.

John Daniel, by his legal representatives, claiming 800 arpens of land on the waters of Saline creek, county of St. Genevieve.   (See record-book F, pages 15 and 260 ; Bates's minutes, page 128; decisions, page 21.   See book Fo. 7, page 193.)

*August* 18, 1835.—The board met, pursuant to adjournment.   Present: F. R. Conway, J. H. Relfe, F. H. Martin, commissioners.

John Daniel, claiming 800 arpens of land.   (See book No. 7, page 193.)

The board are unanimously of opinion that this claim ought not to be granted.   (See No. 7, page 219.)

F. H. MARTIN,
JAMES H. RELFE,
F. R. CONWAY.

---

Class 2.   No. 66.—*Michael Raber, claiming* 748 *arpens.*

| No. | Name of original claimant. | Arpens. | Nature and date of claim. | By whom granted. | By whom surveyed, date, and situation. |
|---|---|---|---|---|---|
| 66 | Michael Raber. | 748 | Settlement right. | | John Stewart, D. S., 24th February, 1806.  Received for record, 27th February, 1806, by A. Soulard, S. G.  On the waters of Big river, St. Genevieve. |

EVIDENCE WITH REFERENCE TO MINUTES AND RECORDS.

*December* 6, 1811.—Board met.   Present: John B. C. Lucas, Clement B. Penrose, and Frederick Bates, commissioners.

Michael Raber, claiming 748 arpens of land, situate on Big river, district of St. Genevieve; produces record of a plat of survey, dated 24th of February, and certified 27th of February, 1806.

It is the opinion of the board that this claim ought not to be granted. (See book No. 5, page 485.)

St. Louis, *December* 27, 1813.—Michael Raber, claiming 748 arpens of land, on the waters of Big river, county of St. Genevieve.

John Tuck, duly sworn, says that he knows a tract of land cultivated by Raber, on the waters of Big river, (Spring creek); that in 1803, witness did some work on this place for claimant, to wit: made some small tents, camp, smoke-house; during the winter cleared some ground, lived on the premises, and early in spring had about six acres cleared and ready for cultivation; claimant came on the premises and inhabited the premises, and, together with this witness, (who worked for him,) cultivated the same. This tract is now greatly enlarged, and has been constantly, either by claimant or those deriving title from him, inhabited and cultivated to this time. (At the margin is the following: "Not granted; claimant has a settlement right on Joachim.") (See Bates's minutes, page 114.)

*June* 19, 1835.—The board met, pursuant to adjournment. Present: F. R. Conway, J. H. Relfe, commissioners.

Michael Raber, by his legal representatives, claiming 748 arpens of land, on the waters of Big river. (See record-book B, page 245; commissioners' minutes, book No. 5, page 485; Bates's minutes, page 114; Bates's decisions, page —. See book No. 7, page 194.)

*August* 18, 1835.—The board met, pursuant to adjournment. Present: F. R. Conway, J. H. Relfe, F. H. Martin, commissioners.

Michael Raber, claiming 748 arpens of land. (See book No. 7, page 194.)

The board are unanimously of opinion that this claim ought not to be granted, the said Michael Raber having had a settlement right granted to him. (See Bates's decisions, page 72; see book No. 7, page 219.)

F. H. MARTIN,<br>JAMES H. RELFE,<br>F. R. CONWAY.

Class 2.  No. 67.—*John Weldon, claiming 500 arpens.*

To Don CHARLES DEHAULT DELASSUS, *Lieutenant Colonel, attached to the stationary regiment of Louisiana, and Lieutenant Governor of Upper Louisiana:*

John Weldon, a Roman Catholic, has the honor to represent that he crossed over to this side (of the Mississippi) more than a year ago, and established himself on the north side of the Missouri, with the permission of your predecessor, Don Zenon Trudeau; therefore he has the honor to supplicate you to have the goodness to grant him, at the same place which he cultivates, the quantity of land corresponding to the number of his family, which is composed of himself, his wife, and six children. The petitioner having all the means necessary to improve a farm, and having no other views but to live as a peaceable and submissive cultivator of the soil, hopes to deserve the favor he claims of your justice.

St. ANDRE, *September* 5, 1799.

Be it forwarded to the lieutenant governor, informing him at the same time that the above statement is true, and that the petitioner is worthy of the protection of the government.

St. ANDRE, *September* 5, 1799.

SANTYAGO MACKAY.

St. LOUIS OF ILLINOIS, *September* 20, 1799.

In consequence of the information given by the commandant of St. Andre, Captain Don Santyago Mackay, the surveyor, Don Antonio Soulard, shall put the party interested in possession of 500 arpens of land in superficie, in the place where he asks the same; the said quantity corresponding to the number of his family, according to the regulation of the governor of this province; and this being executed, he shall make out a plat, delivering the same to said party, together with his certificate, in order to serve him to obtain the concession and title in form from the intendant general of these provinces, to whom alone belongs, by royal order, the distributing and granting all classes of lands of the royal domain.

CARLOS DEHAULT DELASSUS.

Don ANTONIO SOULARD, *Surveyor General of the settlements of Upper Louisiana:*

I certify that a tract of land of 500 arpens in superficie was measured, the lines run and bounded, for and in presence of John Weldon; it was measured with the perch of the city of Paris, of eighteen French feet in length, lineal measure of the said city, according to the custom adopted in this province. This land is situated on the river Missouri, above Bonhomme island, at twenty-four miles from St. Louis, (lindando por A. N. O. C. NE. y O. So.) bounded (on three sides) by vacant lands of the royal domain, and on the S. S. E. by the river Missouri. The said survey and measurement was made without regard to the variation of the needle, which is 7° 30′ E., as appears by the foregoing figurative plat, on which are noted the dimensions, courses of the lines, other boundaries, &c. Said survey was executed by virtue of the decree of the lieutenant governor and sub-delegate of the royal Fiscal, Don Carlos Dehault Delassus, under date of December 20, 1799, here annexed. In testimony whereof, I do give these presents, together with the preceding figurative plat, drawn conformably to the survey made by the deputy surveyor, Don Santyago Mackay, on the 17th of November, 1803, who signed on the minutes, to which I certify.

St. LOUIS OF ILLINOIS, *December* 27, 1803.

ANTONIO SOULARD, *Surveyor General.*

RECORDER'S OFFICE, *St. Louis, July* 21, 1835.

I certify the above and foregoing to be truly translated from record-book D, pages 108 and 109 of record in this office.

JULIUS DE MUN, *T. B. C.*

*John Weldon, claiming 500 arpens.*

| No. | Name of original claimant. | Arpens. | Nature and date of claim. | By whom granted. | By whom surveyed, date, and situation. |
|---|---|---|---|---|---|
| 67 | John Weldon. | 500 | Concession, 20th September, 1799. | C. Dehault Delassus. | James Mackay, 17th November, 1803. Certified by Soulard, 27th Dec., 1803. |

EVIDENCE WITH REFERENCE TO MINUTES AND RECORDS.

*April* 2, 1810.—Board met. Present: John B. C. Lucas, Clement B. Penrose, and Frederick Bates, commissioners.

John Weldon, claiming 500 arpens of land, situate district of St. Charles, produces to the board a notice of claim.

John Weldon, the claimant, personally appears before the board, and renounces all claim to certain land as surveyed in his name on the river Missouri; survey dated 17th November, 1803, certified 27th December, 1803, and recorded in book D, page 108, of the recorder's office.

Claimant produces also, as a permission to settle, a concession from Charles Dehault Delassus, lieutenant governor, to him, for 500 arpens, dated 20th December, (September,) 1799, recorded in book D, page 108, of the recorder's office.

The following testimony in the foregoing claim, transcribed from the rough minutes, as perpetuated by the board, on Friday, the 30th of March last:

John McConnell, sworn, says that the claimant inhabited a tract of land situate on the waters of the Darderine, about one or two miles from the habitation of Arund Rutgers, in the winter of 1802. In the spring following cultivated, and has continued to inhabit and cultivate said land ever since. Claimant had a wife and four children in 1802 and 1803.

It is the opinion of the board that this claim ought not to be granted. But the board do declare that they would have voted for the granting of 500 arpens, had this claim not have been embraced in the tract claimed by Arund Rutgers, under the first section of the act of 1805. (See commissioners' minutes, book No. 4, page 309.)

*June* 24, 1835.—F. R. Conway, esq., appeared, pursuant to adjournment.

John Weldon, by his legal representatives, claiming 500 arpens of land, district of St. Charles. (See record-book D, page 108; book No. 4, page 309. See book No. 7, page —.)

*August* 18, 1835.—The board met, pursuant to adjournment. Present; F. R. Conway, J. H. Relfe, F. H. Martin, commissioners.

John Weldon, claiming 500 arpens of land. (See book No. 7, page 196.)

The board are unanimously of opinion that this claim ought not to be confirmed, the said John Weldon having relinquished the same. (See book No. 7, page 219.)

F. H. MARTIN,
JAMES H. RELFE,
F. R. CONWAY.

---

Class 2. No. 68.—*Jonathan Vineyard, claiming 500 arpens.*

| No. | Name of original claimant | Arpens. | Nature and date of claim. | By whom granted. | By whom surveyed, date, and situation. |
|---|---|---|---|---|---|
| 68 | Jonathan Vineyard. | 500 | Settlement right. | | James Mackay, D.S., 27th December, 1805. Certified to be recorded on the 26th Jan., 1806, by A. Soulard, S. G. On Dubois creek, Franklin county. |

EVIDENCE WITH REFERENCE TO MINUTES AND RECORDS.

*August* 19, 1806.—Agreeably to adjournment, Hon. John B. C. Lucas attended the board and received testimony.

Jonathan Vineyard, claiming as aforesaid (under the second section of the act of Congress) 500 arpens of land, situate as aforesaid, produces a survey of the same, taken the 27th December, 1805, and certified the 27th (26th) January, 1806.

James Cowan, being duly sworn, says that claimant settled the said tract of land in September, 1804, and planted peach-stones; that he saw the same growing the spring following; that he came from Georgia, and did not arrive in the country until that time; and further, that he has actually inhabited and cultivated the same to this day. Had, when he arrived, a wife and two children.

The board reject this claim. (See book No. 1, page 475.)

*September* 14, 1810.—Board met. Present: John B. C. Lucas, Clement B. Penrose, and Frederick Bates, commissioners.

Jonathan Vineyard, claiming 500 arpens of land. (See book No. 1, page 475.) It is the opinion of the board that this claim ought not to be granted. (See book No. 4, page 499.)

*June* 29, 1835.—F. H. Martin, esq., appeared, pursuant to adjournment.

Jonathan Vineyard, claiming 500 arpens of land, situate in the district of St. Louis. (See record-book B, page 251; commissioners' minutes, No. 1, page 475; No. 4, page 499.)

John Pritchett, duly sworn, says that he is about 43 years of age; that in the beginning of the fall of 1804, he saw said Jonathan Vineyard inhabiting and cultivating the place claimed; that he had a temporary cabin wherein he lived with his wife, and, believes, two children. Witness thinks there was about half an acre fenced in with a brush fence, and may be, some rails; he saw turnips growing in said enclosure. Witness further says that the land lies on Dubois creek, about three or four miles from Washington, in Franklin county. (See book No.* 7, page 200.)

*August* 18, 1835.—The board met, pursuant to adjournment. Present: F. R. Conway, J. H. Relfe, F. H. Martin, commissioners.

Jonathan Vineyard, claiming 500 arpens of land. (See book No. 7, page 200.)

The board are unanimously of opinion that this claim ought not to be granted. (See book No. 7, page 219.)

F. H. MARTIN,<br>JAMES H. RELFE,<br>F. R. CONWAY.

---

Class 2.   No. 69.—*Jesse Raynor, claiming 640 acres.*

| No. | Name of original claimant. | Acres. | Nature and date of claim. | By whom granted. | By whom surveyed, date, and situation. |
|-----|---------------------------|--------|--------------------------|------------------|----------------------------------------|
| 69 | Jesse Raynor. | 640 | Settlement right. | | |

EVIDENCE WITH REFERENCE TO MINUTES AND RECORDS.

*November* 26, 1808.—Board met. Present: Hon. John B. C. Lucas, Clement B. Penrose, and Frederick Bates, commissioners.

Jesse Raynor, claiming 640 acres of land, situate on Sandy creek, district of St. Louis, produces to the board a notice to the recorder, dated 27th May, 1808.

William Jones, sworn, says that, about twenty-three or twenty-four years ago, Jesse Raynor had his stock on the land claimed, and built a cabin; and that his stock remained on the place one year.

Claimant declares that he has not resided in this territory since 1792. Laid over for decision. (See book No. 3, page 372.)

*August* 24, 1811.—Board met. Present: Clement B. Penrose and Frederick Bates, commissioners.

Jesse Raynor, claiming 748 arpens 68 perches of land. (See book No. 3, page 372.)

It is the opinion of the board that this claim ought not to be granted. (See book No. 5, page 337.)

*July* 1, 1835.—F. H. Martin, esq., appeared, pursuant to adjournment.

Jesse Raynor, claiming 640 acres of land, situate on Sandy creek, district of St. Louis. (See record-book D, page 165; minutes, book No. 3, page 372; No. 5, page 337. See book No. 7, page 202.)

*August* 19, 1835.—The board met, pursuant to adjournment. Present: F. R. Conway, J. H. Relfe, F. H. Martin, commissioners.

Jesse Raynor, claiming 640 acres of land. (See book No. 7, page 202.)

The board are unanimously of opinion that this claim ought not to be granted. (See book No. 7, page 223.)

F. H. MARTIN,<br>JAMES H. RELFE,<br>F. R. CONWAY.

---

Class 2.   No. 70.—*Philip Robert, claiming 1,097 arpens.*

| No. | Name of original claimant. | Arpens. | Nature and date of claim. | By whom granted. | By whom surveyed, date, and situation. |
|-----|---------------------------|---------|--------------------------|------------------|----------------------------------------|
| 70 | Philip Robert. | 1,097 | Settlement right. | | |

EVIDENCE WITH REFERENCE TO MINUTES AND RECORDS.

*December* 9, 1811.—Board met. Present: John B. C. Lucas, Clement B. Penrose, and Frederick Bates, commissioners.

Philip Robert, claiming 1,097 arpens of land, situate Marameck, district of St. Louis, produces notice to the recorder.

It is the opinion of the board that this claim ought not to be granted. (See book No. 5, page 492.)

*July* 1, 1835.—F. H. Martin appeared, pursuant to adjournment.

Philip Robert, by his legal representatives, claiming 1,097 arpens of land, situate on the waters of Grand Glaize, district of St. Louis. (See record-book E, page 234; book No. 5, page 492. See No. 7, page 202.)

*August* 19, 1835.—The board met, pursuant to adjournment. Present: F. R. Conway, J. H. Relfe, F. H. Martin, commissioners.

Philip Robert, claiming 1,097 arpens of land. (See book No. 7, page 202.)

The board are unanimously of opinion that this claim ought not to be granted. (See book No. 7, page 223.)

F. H. MARTIN,
JAMES H. RELFE,
F. R. CONWAY.

---

Class 2. No. 71.—*Thomas Jones, claiming 1,000 arpens.*

| No. | Name of original claimant. | Arpens. | Nature and date of claim. | By whom granted. | By whom surveyed, date, and situation. |
|---|---|---|---|---|---|
| 71 | Thomas Jones. | 1,000 | Settlement right. | | On Grand Glaize. |

EVIDENCE WITH REFERENCE TO MINUTES AND RECORDS.

*November* 20, 1811.—Board met. Present: John B. C. Lucas, Clement B. Penrose, and Frederick Bates, commissioners.

Thomas Tyler, assignee of Thomas Jones, claiming 1,000 arpens of land, situate on Grand Glaize, district of St. Louis, produces notice to the recorder, and record of transfer from Jones to claimant, dated 7th April, 1789.

It is the opinion of the board that this claim ought not to be granted. (See book No. 5, page 439.)

*July* 1, ——. —F. H. Martin, esq., appeared, pursuant to adjournment.

Thomas Jones, by his legal representatives, claiming 1,000 arpens of land on Grand Glaize creek, district of St. Louis. (See record-book D, page 165 ; minutes, book No. 5, page 439. See No. 7, page 202.)

*August* 19, 1835.—The board met, pursuant to adjournment. Present : F. R. Conway, J. H. Relfe, F. H. Martin, commissioners.

Thomas Jones, claiming 1,000 arpens of land on Grand Glaize. (See book No. 7, page 202.)

The board are unanimously of opinion that this claim ought not to be granted. (See No. 7, page 223.)

F. H. MARTIN,
JAMES H. RELFE,
F. R. CONWAY.

---

Class 2. No. 72.—*Thomas Jones, claiming 1,000 arpens.*

| No. | Name of original claimant. | Arpens. | Nature and date of claim. | By whom granted. | By whom surveyed, date, and situation. |
|---|---|---|---|---|---|
| 72 | Thomas Jones. | 1,000 | Settlement right. | | On Big river. |

EVIDENCE WITH REFERENCE TO MINUTES AND RECORDS.

*St. Louis, October* 13, 1812.—The legal representatives of Thomas Jones, claiming 1,000 arpens of land on Big river, district of St. Louis, produces notice.

John Helderbran, duly sworn, says that, more than thirty years ago, Thomas Jones settled on this tract of land, and inhabited and cultivated the same for two successive years, at which time the Indians becoming troublesome, several persons in that neighborhood moved away, Jones among others, as well as witness himself. When Jones lived on this tract of land he had a wife and six children with him ; also a son married and inhabiting elsewhere. (See Bates's minutes, page 6.)

Not granted. (See Bates's decisions, page 27.)

*July* 1, 1835.—F. H. Martin appeared, pursuant to adjournment.

Thomas Jones, by his legal representatives, claiming 1,000 arpens of land, on Big river, district of St. Louis. (See record-book E, page 326 ; Bates's minutes, page 6 ; Bates's decisions, page 27 ; No. 7, page 202.)

*August* 19, 1835.—The board met, pursuant to adjournment. Present : F. R. Conway, J. H. Relfe, and F. H. Martin, commissioners.

Thomas Jones, claiming 1,000 arpens of land on Big river. (See book No. 7, page 202.)

The board are unanimously of opinion that this claim ought not to be granted. (See book No. 7, page 223.)

F. H. MARTIN,
JAMES H. RELFE,
F. R. CONWAY.

---

Class 2. No. 73.—*John Gerard, claiming 320 arpens.*

| No. | Name of original claimant. | Arpens. | Nature and date of claim. | By whom granted. | By whom surveyed, date, and situation. |
|---|---|---|---|---|---|
| 73 | John Gerrard. | 320 | Settlement right. | | On Grand Glaize. |

EVIDENCE WITH REFERENCE TO MINUTES AND RECORDS.

*November* 20, 1811.—Board met. Present: John B. C. Lucas, Clement B. Penrose, and Frederick Bates, commissioners.

Thomas Tyler, assignee of John Gerrard, claiming 320 arpens of land, situate on Grand Glaize, district of St. Louis, produces record of transfer from Gerrard to claimant, dated 4th October, 1789.

It is the opinion of the board that this claim ought not to be granted.    (See book No. 5, page 430.)

*July* 1, 1835.—F. H. Martin appeared, pursuant to adjournment.

John Gerrard, by his legal representatives, claiming 320 arpens of land on Grand Glaize, district of St. Louis.  (See record-book D, page 165; minutes, book No. 5, page 430.  See book No. 7, page 202.)

*August* 19, 1835.—The board met, pursuant to adjournment.  Present: F. R. Conway, J. H. Relfe, and F. H. Martin, commissioners.

John Gerrard, claiming 320 arpens of land.  (See book No. 7, page 202.)

The board are unanimously of opinion that this claim ought not to be granted.  (See book No. 7, page 223.)

F. H. MARTIN,<br>JAMES H. RELFE,<br>F. R. CONWAY.

---

Class 2.    No. 74.—*James Swift, claiming* 640 *acres.*

| No. | Name of original claimant. | Acres. | Nature and date of claim. | By whom granted. | By whom surveyed, date, and situation. |
|---|---|---|---|---|---|
| 74 | James Swift. | 640 | Settlement right. | | |

EVIDENCE WITH REFERENCE TO MINUTES AND RECORDS.

*July* 7, 1835.—F. R. Conway, esq., appeared, pursuant to adjournment.

James Swift, by his legal representatives, claiming 640 acres of land in the district of St. Charles.  (See record-book D, page 333.)

Arthur Burns, duly sworn, says that he is about 52 years of age; that he came to this country while under the government of Zenon Trudeau; that before the change of government the said James Swift went on a piece of land which had been improved by one Boon; that said Swift built thereon a cabin, and cleared a small piece of land for the purpose of sowing turnips, but witness does not know whether the turnips were sowed.  Witness further says that said Swift being out of provisions, and the mosquitoes being very troublesome, he left said place about three weeks after he had first come there, and witness never knew that he returned to said place.  (See book No. 7, page 212.)

*August* 19, 1835.—The board met, pursuant to adjournment.  Present: F. R. Conway, J. H. Relfe, and F. H. Martin, commissioners.

James Swift, claiming 640 acres of land.  (See book No. 7, page 212.)

The board are unanimously of opinion that this claim ought not to be granted.  (See book No. 7, page 223.)

F. H. MARTIN,<br>JAMES H. RELFE,<br>F. R. CONWAY.

---

Class 2.    No. 75.—*Diego Maxwell, as Vicar General of Louisiana, claiming* 112,896 *arpens.*

To Don CARLOS DEHAULT DELASSUS, *Lieutenant Colonel in the royal armies and Lieutenant Governor of Upper Louisiana* :

Don Diego Maxwell, curate of St. Genevieve and vicar general of Illinois, with all the respect due to you, represents that the most excellent Duke De Alcudia, minister of state and universal despacho of the Indies, having manifested his desire that some Catholics from Ireland should come to settle themselves in this colony of Louisiana, knowing them to be faithful subjects, and affectionate to the Spanish government on account of their religion, as appears by the annexed letter of Don Thomas O'Ryan, chaplain of honor of his Majesty and confessor of the Queen, our lady, written to the petitioner in the English language, by order of his excellency, the above-named minister, the government engaging to have a church built for them in their settlement, and leaving to the judgment of the petitioner to solicit of the government the quantity of land of the royal domain, which he will think necessary for himself and the said settlers.  There being some vacant lands belonging to the domain, upon which no settlement has been made to this day, situated between Black river and the Currents, which are branches of White river, at the distance of from thirty to thirty-five leagues from this town, therefore the petitioner humbly supplicates that you will condescend to take the necessary measures in order to enable him to obtain from the government, in full property, the concession of four leagues square, making the quantity of 112,896 arpens of land in superficie, in the said place, and for afore-mentioned purpose; the petitioner having no other object but the advantage to his Majesty's service, and the salvation of the souls which shall be confided to his care.  He at the same time informs you that several of the above-mentioned Irish Catholics, induced by him, have already arrived from Ireland, and that many others are coming, and now on their way, with a part of his own family, not without great expenses and costs to your petitioner, for which he hopes to be remunerated by the government, and if not, by God and the gratitude of those poor people, for having rescued them from the British tyranny and persecution to which they were exposed on account of their religion.  This favor, solicited by the petitioner, he hopes to obtain from the generosity of the government which you represent in this part of the colony, as being conformable to the intentions of his Majesty, communicated by his minister.  Meanwhile, he will pray God to preserve your important life many years.

St. GENEVIEVE, *October* 15, 1799.                                             DIEGO MAXWELL.

St. Louis of Illinois, *November* 3, 1799.

(Visto de Illinois de esta peticion.) Supposed to be instead of, *having examined the statement in the above petition,* supported by the letter cited in the same, which has been presented to me by the petitioner; and whereas its contents are in accordance with the disposition of the governor general of these provinces, Don Manuel Gayoso de Lemos, (who permits the introduction of emigrants in this territory only to those who are really Catholics, A. and R.,) as appears by his order, dated New-Orleans, 3d of September, 1797; giving to the said letter all the consideration it deserves, inasmuch as its contents are derived from a wise disposition of his excellency, the minister of state, which will be, without doubt, of considerable advantage in increasing the population so necessary in these remote parts of his Majesty's domains, with a class of laborious inhabitants, to the satisfaction of the government. Therefore, according to the demand, I do grant to the petitioner four leagues square, or the quantity of 112,896 arpens of land in superficie, in the place he solicits, and for the object here above mentioned; and the surveyor general of this Upper Louisiana, Don Antonio Soulard, shall put him in possession of said quantity in the place mentioned, when requested by the (party) interested; which being executed, he shall make out a figurative plat of his (survey,) delivering the same to the party, with (his certificate,) in order to serve him to solicit the title in form from the intendant general of these provinces, to whom alone corresponds, by royal order, the distributing and granting of all classes of lands belonging to the royal domains.

CARLOS DEHAULT DELASSUS.

I, the undersigned, civil commandant of the post and district of New Bourbon, certify that the said title of concession is recorded, and the copy, compared with the original, is deposited in the archives of this post, and numbered 49.

PIERRE DELASSUS DE LUZIERE.

St. Louis, *June* 5, 1833. Truly translated from record-book B, pages 497 and 498.

JULIUS DE MUN.

| No. | Name of original claimant. | Arpens. | Nature and date of claim. | By whom granted. | By whom surveyed, date, and situation. |
|---|---|---|---|---|---|
| 75 | Diego Maxwell, as vicar general of Louisiana. | 112,896 | Concession, 3d November, 1799. | Carlos Dehault Delassus. | Wm. Johnson, D. S. Received for record, by Soulard, February 26, 1806. On the forks of Black river, 80 miles west of Cape Girardeau. |

EVIDENCE WITH REFERENCE TO MINUTES AND RECORDS.

*June* 28, 1806.—The board met, agreeably to adjournment. Present: Hon. Clement B. Penrose and James L. Donaldson, commissioners.

James Maxwell, vicar general of the province of Louisiana, claiming four leagues square, situate at the fork of Black river, district of St. Genevieve, produces a concession from Charles D. Delassus, dated November 3d, 1799, and a survey of 112,896 arpens, dated and certified the 9th February, 1806.

He also produces an affidavit of Pierre Delassus de Luziere, stating that he was present, in the beginning of 1800, at a conversation which took place between the aforesaid claimant and Charles D. Delassus, then lieutenant governor, when the latter inquired of said claimant where he intended to settle his large concession; does not recollect the answer; that a few days after, being at claimant's house, he saw, held, and read the aforesaid concession; a commission of vicar general of the province over the English and American settlers, signed Euge. de Llaguno, dated St. Lorenzo, 22d November, 1794;

A letter from the Bishop of Orleans, dated May 1st, 1799, requesting his attention, as vicar general, to the whole of the clergy of the province, and informing him that he had recommended him to the King;

A letter of instructions, founded upon a Spanish supreme consular state, at Madrid, directed to claimant through Lopez Armesto, secretary of the province, wherein the policy of government toward emigrants is explained, instructing the governor to grant them lands, and showing a desire that they might be converted to the Roman Catholic religion;

The consideration on which this grant was founded, being an obligation on the part of claimant to bring from Ireland Roman Catholic emigrants and form a settlement of the same. The claimant alleged as a reason for not having complied with said obligation, the then existing wars, and the subsequent prohibition of emigration from Ireland.

The board reject this claim, and are satisfied that it was granted at the time it bears date. (See book No. 1, page 384.)

*December* 7, 1807.—(See page 304, old minutes, *St. Genevieve.*)

James Maxwell, vicar general of the late province of Louisiana, claiming four leagues square, situated at the fork of Black river, in the district of St. Genevieve, produces a concession from Charles D. Delassus, dated November 3, 1799, and a survey of one hundred and twelve thousand eight hundred and ninety-six arpens, dated and certified the 9th day of February, 1806. Laid over for decision.

Owing to the record having been made up hastily, the above claim of James Maxwell was omitted; in order to supply this omission, we, two of the commissioners, have hereunto subscribed our names and attached the same to the records or minutes, Hon. C. B. Penrose being absent.

J. B. C. LUCAS,
FREDERICK BATES.

(See book No. 3, page 161.)

*May* 20, 1810.—Board met. Present: John B. C. Lucas, Clement B. Penrose, and Frederick Bates, commissioners.

James Maxwell, claiming four leagues square of land. (See book No. 1, page 384, annexed to book No. 3, page 161.)

On motion of John B. C. Lucas, commissioner, as follows, to wit: Whereas it appears, in the minutes of the former board, that the said board have remarked that they are satisfied that the said concession was granted at the time the same bears date, and inasmuch as it does not appear that any suggestion of fraud and antedate was made, either by the agent of the United States or any of the members of the board, which being the case, shows that no question did exist before said board, as to fraud or antedate, to which this decision, by way of remark, can apply ; and whereas any decision without question is in itself preposterous, and might be considered as officious ; therefore, resolved, that this remark and decision be rescinded. A question being taken on the motion, it was negatived ; and on a question being taken on the claim, it is the unanimous opinion of the board that this claim ought not to be confirmed. (See book No. 4, page 354.)

*March* 15, 1833.—The board met, pursuant to adjournment. Present : L. F. Linn, A. G. Harrison, F. R. Conway, commissioners.

Diego Maxwell, as vicar general of Louisiana, by the bishop of Missouri, his representative, claiming 112,896 arpens of land, or four leagues square. (See book B, page 497 ; minutes, No. 3, page 161 ; No. 4, page 354 ; and book No. 6, page 125.)

*August* 20, 1835.—The board met, pursuant to adjournment. Present : F. R. Conway, J. H. Relfe, F. H. Martin, commissioners.

Diego Maxwell, claiming 112,896 arpens of land. (See book No. 6, page 125.)

The board are unanimously of opinion that this claim ought not to be confirmed, the conditions not having been complied with. (See book No. 7, page 224.)

F. H. MARTIN,
JAMES H. RELFE,
F. R. CONWAY.

---

Class 2.    No. 76.—*James Craig, claiming 800 arpens.*

| No. | Name of original claimant. | Arpens. | Nature and date of claim. | By whom granted. | By whom surveyed, date, and situation. |
|---|---|---|---|---|---|
| 76 | James Craig. | 800 | Settlement right. | | Negro fork of Marameck. |

EVIDENCE WITH REFERENCE TO MINUTES AND RECORDS.

*November* 29, 1833.—F. R. Conway, esq., appeared, pursuant to adjournment.

James Craig, by his legal representative, Richard Everitt, claiming 800 arpens of land, on the Negro fork of the Marameck. (See record-book F, page 98 ; Bates's decisions, page 103.)

William Drenen, being duly sworn, says that he is 74 years of age ; that he was well acquainted with James Craig, the original claimant ; that, in the year 1801 or 1802, he is not positive which, said Craig, the original claimant, went on the tract claimed, cut house-logs, and planted peach and apple seed on the place. Witness does not think that Craig ever lived on the place, but was at that time, or shortly thereafter, a married man ; that Craig sold the place to the present claimant, who resided on the same until about two years ago, when he was forced to move off, in consequence of the United States selling the same. Witness knows that said Everitt resided on and cultivated the same for twenty-seven years. (See book No. 6, page 349.)

*August* 21, 1835.—The board met, pursuant to adjournment. Present : F. R. Conway, J. H. Relfe, and F. H. Martin, commissioners.

James Craig, claiming 800 arpens of land. (See book No. 6, page 349.)

The board are unanimously of opinion that this claim ought not to be granted. (See book No. 7, page 226.)

F. H. MARTIN,
JAMES H. RELFE,
F. R. CONWAY.

---

Class 2.    No. 77.—*James Summers, claiming 250 acres.*

| No. | Name of original claimant. | Acres. | Nature and date of claim. | By whom granted. | By whom surveyed, date, and situation. |
|---|---|---|---|---|---|
| 77 | James Summers. | 250 | Settlement right. | | On Whitewater, Cape Girardeau. |

EVIDENCE WITH REFERENCE TO MINUTES AND RECORDS.

*December* 9, 1811.—Board met. Present : John B. C. Lucas, Clement B. Penrose, and Frederick Bates, commissioners.

James Summers, claiming 250 acres of land, situate on Whitewater, district of Cape Girardeau. Produces notice to the recorder.

It is the opinion of the board that this claim ought not to be granted. (See No. 5, page 499.)

*April* 24, 1835.—The board met, pursuant to adjournment. Present : F. R. Conway, James H. Relfe, commissioners.

James Summers, claiming 250 acres of land on Whitewater, district of Cape Girardeau. (See record-book E, page 28; book No. 5, page 499.)

The following testimony was taken in June, 1833, by L. F. Linn, esq., then a commissioner:

Elijah Dougherty, being sworn, states that he has known the said James Summers ever since the year 1800; the said James then resided in the district of Cape Girardeau, where he has continued to live ever since. This affiant has seen the said James cultivating land, and improving the same, under the Spanish government, about the years 1801, 1802, 1803, and 1804, in the said district of Cape Girardeau, and knows of his cultivating land up to this time, June, 1833. Deponent does not know that the said James claimed the said land as his own.

ELIJAH <sup>his</sup> × <sub>mark.</sub> DOUGHERTY.

*June* 11, 1833.                                     L. F. LINN, *Commissioner.*

The following testimony was taken before James H. Relfe, commissioner:

STATE OF MISSOURI, *County of Cape Girardeau:*

Ithamar Hubble, being duly sworn, as the law directs, deposeth and saith, that he is aged about 73 years; that he is well acquainted with the claimant, James Summers; that he has known him ever since the year 1799; that, in that year, the said James Summers moved to, and settled in the district of Cape Girardeau, where he has resided ever since; that he was a farmer and cultivator of the soil; but this affiant does not know from his own knowledge that the said James had a grant. The said James, when he first came to this country, was a young man, without a family.

ITHAMAR <sup>his</sup> × <sub>mark.</sub> HUBBLE.

Sworn to and subscribed before me, this 6th day of April, 1835.

JAMES H. RELFE, *Commissioner.*

(See book No. 7, page 133.)

*August* 21, 1835.—The board met, pursuant to adjournment. Present: F. R. Conway, J. H. Relfe, F. H. Martin, commissioners.

James Summers, claiming 250 acres of land. (See book No. 7, p. 133.)

The board are unanimously of opinion that this claim ought not to be granted. (See book No. 7, page 226.)

F. H. MARTIN,<br>
JAMES H. RELFE,<br>
F. R. CONWAY.

---

Class 2. No. 78.—William Flynn, jr., claiming 200 arpens.

| No. | Name of original claimant. | Arpens. | Nature and date of claim. | By whom granted. | By whom surveyed, date, and situation. |
|---|---|---|---|---|---|
| 78 | William Flynn, jr. | 200 | Settlement right. | | Bois-brulé, St. Genevieve. |

EVIDENCE WITH REFERENCE TO MINUTES AND RECORDS.

*December* 3, 1807.—The board met, agreeably to adjournment. Present: Hon. John B. C. Lucas, Clement B. Penrose, and Frederick Bates.

William Flynn, jr., claiming 240 arpens of land, situated in Bois-brulé, in the district of St. Genevieve, produces in support of said claim, a notice to the recorder of land titles, dated 3d December, 1807.

William Flynn, sr., being duly sworn, says that, in the year 1804, to the best of his recollection, he assisted his son, the claimant, to clear about one quarter of an acre of land, and enclose the same, and also cultivated turnips thereon the same fall, but does not know whether the crop of turnips was taken off or gathered; does not know the age of his son exactly, but believes him to be 23 or 24 years of age at this time; nor does he know whether his son had permission to settle. Laid over for decision. (See No. 3, page 134.)

*August* 21, 1811.—Board met. Present: Clement B. Penrose and Frederick Bates, commissioners.

William Flynn, jr., claiming 240 arpens of land. (See book No. 3, page 134.)

It is the opinion of the board that this claim ought not to be granted. (See book No. 5, page 327.)

*May* 13, 1835.—The board met, pursuant to adjournment. Present: F. R. Conway, James H. Relfe, commissioners.

William Flynn, jr., claiming 200 acres of land in the district of St. Genevieve. (See record-book E, page 256; books No. 3, page 134, No. 5, page 327.)

The following testimony was taken in May, 1833, by L. F. Linn, commissioner:

John Greenwalt testifies and says, that he is about 68 years of age, and emigrated to Upper Louisiana in the spring of 1798, it being the spring after the high freshet of 1797, from which circumstance he is enabled to identify the time of his first coming to the country. Witness settled in Bois-brulé bottom, now in the county of Perry, and State of Missouri, where he has continued most of the time since. He further states, that the father of claimant, William Flynn, sr., emigrated to Louisiana, and settled with his family in Bois-brulé bottom aforesaid, as early as the year 1800, where he resided until the time of his death; that William Flynn, jr., the claimant, came with his father to the country, and was, as witness believes, about 20 years of age, being a man grown, and doing business for himself, and on his own account; that witness knows of claimant cultivating a piece of ground in Bois-brulé bottom, as early as the year 1804; that in the summer of 1804 claimant built a cabin, raised turnips and some vines on said land, and also, as he thinks, grew some corn on it, and then claimed, and has ever since claimed, the same as his settlement. Witness further states, that claimant continued to occupy said ground until 1807, when the same lay idle for two or three years, but that afterward, for several years, claimant rented it to men residing on it with their families for several years. Witness further states, that he has been a neighbor to claimant since his first coming to the country in 1800, and that he has uniformly understood from him, that the piece of ground above alluded to was the only land claimed by him as his settlement right, and that he has never had any lands confirmed to him.

JOHN <sup>his</sup> × GREENWALT.
<br>mark.

Sworn to and subscribed, May 6, 1833.

L. F. LINN, *Commissioner.*

(See book No. 7, page 150.)

*August* 21, 1835.—The board met, pursuant to adjournment.  Present: F. R. Conway, J. H. Relfe, and F. H. Martin, commissioners.

William Flynn, jr., claiming 200 acres of land.  (See book No. 7, page 150.)

The board are unanimously of opinion that this claim ought not to be granted.  (See book No. 7, page 226.)

F. H. MARTIN,
<br>JAMES H. RELFE,
<br>F. R. CONWAY.

---

Class 2.   No. 79.—*Antoine Vachard, dit Lardoise, claiming 640 acres.*

| No. | Name of original claimant. | Acres. | Nature and date of claim. | By whom granted. | By whom surveyed, date, and situation. |
|---|---|---|---|---|---|
| 79 | Antoine Vachard dit Lardoise. | 640 | Settlement right. | | |

EVIDENCE WITH REFERENCE TO MINUTES AND RECORDS.

St. Louis, *December* 31, 1813.—Antoine Vachard, dit Lardoise, claiming 640 acres of land, county of St. Louis, adjoining lands claimed by Henry O'Hara.

William Palmer, duly sworn, says that he knows a tract of land about a mile from the Joachim, and a mile from Glaize à Byet.  Claimant bought it twenty-seven or twenty-eight years ago, as witness then understood, of P. Vienentendre.  At that time this tract had a good house and garden picketed in, and the inhabitants were driven off about twenty-five years ago by the Indians.  Witness has not been there since.

Charles Vachard, duly sworn, says that witness, with claimant, resided on this place for six or seven following years, about twenty-five years ago.  Inhabiting and cultivating; left it on account of the Indians.  Claimant had this land by purchase, from Vienentendre.  (At the margin: "Not granted.")  (See Bates's minutes, page 133.)

*July* 7, 1835.—F. R. Conway, esq., appeared, pursuant to adjournment.

Antoine Vachard, dit Lardoise, by his legal representatives, claiming 640 acres, in the district of St. Louis.  (See record-book F, page 139; Bates's minutes, page 133; Bates's decisions, page 37.)

Baptiste Dominé, duly sworn, says that he is eighty-six years of age; that under the Spanish government he saw said Antoine Vachard inhabiting and cultivating a place between the Joachim creek and the Little rock; that there was a house on said place and a field; and witness, as he went and came from St. Genevieve, saw the said Vachard on said place for about four consecutive years.

Charles Vachard, duly sworn, says that he is about sixty-three years of age; that under the Spanish government, before Zenon Trudeau's time, witness's brother, Antoine Vachard, settled a place between the Joachim and the Little rock; that there was on said place a dwelling-house, a barn, and a field, in which said Antoine raised corn and wheat.  Witness thinks his brother lived at least ten years on said place, and was the last of the settlers who left that settlement on account of the Indians; this was several years before the change of government.  Witness says that Antoine Vachard never returned on said place, but remained in the country about New Madrid.  (See book No. 7, page ——.)

*August* 22, 1835.—The board met, pursuant to adjournment.  Present: F. R. Conway, J. H. Relfe, F. H. Martin, commissioners.

Antoine Vachard, claiming 640 acres of land.  (See book No. 7, page 211.)

A majority of the board are of opinion that this claim ought not to be granted, one John B. Olive having had a confirmation, under said Antoine Vachard, for a tract of 250 arpens in New Madrid.  (See commissioners' certificate, No. 631.)  F. R. Conway, commissioner, voted for granting 640 acres, on the ground that the tract confirmed to the above-named John B. Olive was sold by said Antoine Vachard prior to the act of Congress of 1805, and consequently was not claimed by him at the passage of that act.  (See book No. 7, page 227.)

F. H. MARTIN,
<br>JAMES H. RELFE,
<br>F. R. CONWAY.

---

Class 2.   No. 80.—*Louis Lamalice, claiming 800 arpens.*

To Don CARLOS DEHAULT DELASSUS, *Lieutenant Governor of Upper Louisiana:*

SIR: Louis Lamalice, dit Lemonde, has the honor to represent to you, that he would wish to form an establishment in this province, in which he resides since several years; therefore the petitioner prays you to grant to him a tract of land of eight hundred arpens in superficie, to be taken on the vacant lands of his Majesty's domain, in the place which will appear most convenient to his interest, a favor which the petitioner presumes to expect of your justice.

LOUIS <sup>his</sup> × LAMALICE.
<br>mark.

St. Louis, *November* 13, 1799.

St. Louis of Illinois, *November* 14, 1799.

Whereas we are assured that the petitioner possesses sufficient means to improve the land which he solicits, I do grant to him and his heirs the land he solicits, provided it is not prejudicial to any persons; and the surveyor, Don Antonio Soulard, shall put the party interested in possession of the quantity of land he asks, in a vacant place of the royal domain; which being executed, he shall make out a plat of his survey, delivering the same to said party, with his certificate, in order to enable him to obtain the concession and title in form from the intendant general, to whom alone corresponds, by royal order, the distributing and granting all classes of lands of the royal domain.

CARLOS DEHAULT DELASSUS.

Don Antonio Soulard, *Surveyor General of the settlements of Upper Louisiana:*

I do certify that a tract of land of two hundred arpens in depth by one hundred and forty arpens in front, or twenty-eight thousand arpens in superficie, was measured, the lines run and bounded, in the presence of Mr. Albert Tyson, duly appointed by the purchasers, Don Louis Labeaume and Don Santyago St. Vrain, as their agent. The said square of land is divided, as designated in the figurative plat, by dotted lines, indicating the place where each of the original owners is to be located, in thirty-five tracts of forty arpens of land in depth by 20 arpens in front, making 800 arpens in superficie, and each division is marked with the name of the original owner. (La superficie total de la tierra cae al angulo N. correspondiente al que va puesto al margen de cada memorial.) *The above, between parentheses, is supposed to have been written in lieu of—At the north angle of each of the said tracts is a number corresponding to the number put at the margin of each memorial*—in order to fix with clearness the situation of the respective tracts sold by each vendor, and facilitate to me the knowledge of the conditions contained in the different deeds of sale. The tracts bought by Don Louis Labeaume, twenty-one in number, make a superficie of 16,800 arpens, and are marked with L; and those purchased by Don St. Yago de St. Vrain, fourteen in number, are marked with an S, and make a superficie of 11,200 arpens.

The lines of division between each tract could not be run at the same time as those of the whole square, the deputy surveyor having fallen sick, and it could not be done afterward at the request of the (parties) interested, on account of the suspension of all surveys, until a new order, intimated to me by the captain of artillery of the United States of America, Don Amos Stoddard, first civil commandant of Upper Louisiana. The said survey was made with the perch of the city of Paris, of eighteen French feet, lineal measure of the same city, conformably to the agrarian measure of this province. This land is situated at about sixteen miles, more or less, west of the left bank of the river Mississippi, and at sixty-five miles north of this town of St. Louis. Bounded on its four sides as follows:* [*Note.*—The rest of this paper is torn and missing.]

St. Louis, *April* 30, 1833.—Truly translated from the original.

JULIUS DE MUN.

* To the N. N. W. in part by vacant lands of the royal domain and lands belonging to Don Antonio Soulard; to the S. S. E. in part by the said royal domain and lands belonging to Cerre Chouteau, jr.; to the W. S. W. by the said vacant lands; and lastly, to the E. N. E. by lands belonging to Don Santyago St. Vrain and Ambrosio Dorval, and on a small part, by lands of the royal domain. The said survey and measurement were made without regard to the variation of the needle, which is 7° 30′ E., as appears by the foregoing figurative plat, on which are noted the dimensions, courses of the lines, and other boundaries, &c. The said survey was executed by virtue of the decrees of the lieutenant governor and subdelegate of the royal Fiscal, Don Carlos Dehault Delassus, made in the years 1799, 1800, 1801, and 1802, which are here annexed, and to a part of which are subjoined the unauthenticated deeds of sale passed between the parties, the authenticated deeds being deposited in the archives of this government. In testimony whereof, I do give these presents, together with the foregoing figurative plat, drawn conformably to the survey executed by the deputy surveyor, James Rankin, on the 20th of February, of this present year, and who signed the minutes to which I certify.

ANTONIO SOULARD, *Surveyor General.*

St. Louis, *March* 28, 1804.

I certify the above to be truly translated from record-book C, page 349, of record, in the office of the recorder of land titles.

JULIUS DE MUN, *T. B. C.*

St. Louis, *August* 25, 1835.

| No. | Name of original claimant. | Arpens. | Nature and date of claim. | By whom granted. | By whom surveyed, date, and situation. |
|---|---|---|---|---|---|
| 80 | Louis Lamalice. | 800 | Concession, 18th November, 1799. | Carlos Dehault Delassus. | James Rankin, D. S., 20th February, 1804. Certified by Soulard, 28th March, 1804. Sixty-five miles north of St. Louis |

EVIDENCE WITH REFERENCE TO MINUTES AND RECORDS.

*October* 18, 1811.—The board met. Present: John B. C. Lucas, Clement B. Penrose, and Frederick Bates, commissioners.

Louis Labeaume, claiming 800 arpens of land, as assignee of Louis Lamalice, situate as above, produces a concession from Charles D. Delassus, lieutenant governor, dated 18th of November, 1799; a plat of survey as above; a certified extract of sale, made by Lamalice to claimant, dated 7th of November, 1803.

It is the opinion of the board that this claim ought not to be confirmed. (See book No. 5, page 365.)

*March* 25, 1833.—F. R. Conway, esq., appeared, pursuant to adjournment.

Louis Lamalice, alias Lemonde, by Louis Labeaume's legal representatives, claiming 800 arpens of land. See book C, pages 342 and 343; for survey, page 349; minutes, book No. 5, page 365.) Produces a paper purporting to be an original concession from Carlos Dehault Delassus, dated November 18, 1799. Also, a paper purporting to be an original plat of survey, (part of said paper torn and missing,) embracing thirty-five concessions of 800 arpens each, numbered from 1 to 35 inclusive, on which said Lamalice is No. 1; also, a certificate of transfer, signed M. P. Leduc, recorder.

M. P. Leduc, duly sworn, says that the signature to the concession is in the proper handwriting of Carlos Dehault Delassus, and that the torn original survey is in the proper handwriting of Antoine Soulard. (See book No. 6, page 142.)

*August* 24, 1835.—The board met, pursuant to adjournment. Present: F. R. Conway, J. H. Relfe, F. H. Martin, commissioners.

Louis Lamalice, claiming 800 arpens of land. (See book No. 6, page 142.)

After a careful examination of the testimony, and the various deeds of transfer on the claims numbered from —— to —— inclusive, the board have decided to place them in the second class, believing them to have been founded in an extensive scheme of speculation by the assignees, unknown to the governor, and that the ostensible object, the population of the country, was not intended to be complied with at the time of procuring the grant.

The board are unanimously of opinion that this claim ought not to be confirmed. (See book No. 7, page 228.)

F. H. MARTIN,
F. R. CONWAY,
JAMES H. RELFE.

---

Class 2.    No. 81.—*François Mottier, claiming 800 arpens.*

To Don CARLOS DEHAULT DELASSUS, *Lieutenant Governor of Upper Louisiana:*

SIR: François Mottier has the honor to represent to you that he would wish to form an establishment in the upper part of this province, where he has been residing since his infancy; therefore, he has recourse to your goodness, praying that you may be pleased to grant him a piece of land of eight hundred arpens in superficie, to be taken on the vacant lands of the King's domain, in the place which will appear most convenient to the interest of your petitioner, who presumes to expect this favor of your justice.

ST. LOUIS, *April* 14, 1800.                    FRANCOIS $\times$ MOTTIER.
                                                          his / mark.

ST. LOUIS OF ILLINOIS, *April* 18, 1800.

Whereas we are assured that the petitioner possesses sufficient means to improve the land which he solicits, I do grant to him and his heirs the land he solicits, provided it is not prejudicial to any person; and the surveyor, Don Antonio Soulard, shall put the interested in possession of the quantity of land he asks for, in a vacant place of the royal domain; and this being executed, he shall make out a plat, delivering the same to the party, together with his certificate, in order to serve to him to obtain the title in form from the intendant general, to whom alone belongs, by royal order, the distributing and granting all classes of lands, &c.

CARLOS DEHAULT DELASSUS.

ST. LOUIS, *April* 14, 1835.—I certify the above to be a true translation from the original.

JULIUS DE MUN, *T. B. C.*

| No. | Name of original claimant. | Arpens. | Nature and date of claim. | By whom granted. | By whom surveyed, date, and situation. |
|-----|---------------------------|---------|---------------------------|------------------|-----------------------------------------|
| 81 | François Mottier. | 800 | Concession, 18th April, 1800. | C. Dehault Delassus. | James Rankin, D. S., 20th Feb., 1804. Certified by Soulard, S. G., 24th March, 1804. 65 miles north of St. Louis, and about 17 from the Mississippi. |

EVIDENCE WITH REFERENCE TO MINUTES AND RECORDS.

*October* 18, 1811.—Board met. Present: John B. C. Lucas, Clement B. Penrose, and Frederick Bates, commissioners.

Louis Labeaume, assignee of François Mottier, claiming 600 arpens, and said Mottier claiming 200 arpens of land, situate as above, produces a concession from Charles D. Delassus, L. G., dated 18th April, 1800, a plat of survey as above, a transfer from Mottier to claimant, dated 20th February, 1804.

It is the opinion of the board that this claim ought not to be confirmed. (See book No. 5, page 365.)

*December* 10, 1834.—F. R. Conway, esq., appeared, pursuant to adjournment.

François Mottier, by his legal representatives, claiming 800 arpens of land. (See record-book C, page 343, and minute-book No. 5, page 365.)

Produces a paper purporting to be an original concession from Carlos Dehault Delassus, dated 18th April, 1800.

M. P. Leduc, duly sworn, says that the signature to the concession is in the proper handwriting of the said Don Carlos Dehault Delassus. (See book No. 7, page 81.)

*August* 24, 1835.—The board met, pursuant to adjournment. Present: F. R. Conway, J. H. Relfe, F. H. Martin, commissioners.

François Mottier, claiming 800 arpens of land. (See book No. 7, page 81.)

The board are unanimously of opinion that this claim ought not to be confirmed.   For reasons, see decision in the claim of Louis Lamalice, No. 80.

F. H. MARTIN,
F. R. CONWAY,
JAMES H. RELFE.

Class 2.   No. 82.—François Arnaud, claiming 800 arpens.

To Don CARLOS DEHAULT DELASSUS, <i>Lieutenant Governor of Upper Louisiana:</i>

SIR: Fr. Arnaud has the honor to represent that he would wish to form an establishment in the upper part of this colony, where he has been residing for a number of years; therefore, the petitioner prays you to grant him eight hundred arpens of land, to be taken on the vacant lands of the King's domain, in the place which shall appear most advantageous to the interest of your petitioner, who presumes to expect this favor of your justice.

ST. LOUIS, <i>February</i> 20, 1800.

FRANCOIS ARNAUD.

ST. LOUIS OF ILLINOIS, <i>February</i> 28, 1800.

Whereas it is evident that the petitioner possesses the means necessary to obtain the concession which he solicits, I do grant to him and his heirs the land he solicits, provided it is not prejudicial to any person; and the surveyor, Don Antonio Soulard, shall put the interested in possession of the quantity of land he asks for, in a vacant place of the royal domain; and this being executed, he shall make out a plat, delivering the same to the party, together with his certificate, in order to serve him to obtain the concession and title in form from the intendant general, to whom alone belongs, by royal order, the distributing and granting all classes of land belonging to the royal domain.

CARLOS DEHAULT DELASSUS.

ST. LOUIS, <i>April</i> 14, 1835.—I certify the above to be truly translated from the original.

JULIUS DE MUN, <i>T. B. C.</i>

| No. | Name of original claimant. | Arpens. | Nature and date of claim. | By whom granted. | By whom surveyed, date, and situation. |
|---|---|---|---|---|---|
| 82 | François Arnaud. | 800 | Concession, 28th February, 1800. | Carlos Dehault Delassus. | James S. Rankin, D. S., 20th February, 1801. Certified by A. Soulard, S. G., 24th March, 1804. Sixty-five miles north of St. Louis, and about 17 from the Mississippi. |

EVIDENCE WITH REFERENCE TO MINUTES AND RECORDS.

December 10, 1834.—F. R. Conway, esq., appeared, pursuant to adjournment.

François Arnaud, by his legal representatives, claiming 800 arpens of land.   (See record-book C, page 343, and for survey, page 349.)

Produces a paper purporting to be an original concession from Carlos Dehault Delassus, dated 28th February, 1800.

M. P. Leduc, duly sworn, says that the signature to the concession is in the proper handwriting of the said Carlos Dehault Delassus.   (See book No. 7, page 81.)

August 24, 1835.—The board met, pursuant to adjournment.   Present: F. R. Conway, J. H. Relfe, F. H. Martin, commissioners.

François Arnaud, claiming 800 arpens of land.   (See book No. 7, page 81.)

The board are unanimously of opinion that this claim ought not to be confirmed.   For reasons, see decision in the claim of Louis Lamalice, No. 80.

F. H. MARTIN,
F. R. CONWAY,
JAMES H. RELFE.

Class 2.   No. 83.—François Marechal, claiming 800 arpens.

To Don CHARLES DEHAULT DELASSUS, <i>Lieutenant Governor of Upper Louisiana:</i>

SIR: François Marechal has the honor to represent to you, that, having resided for a long time in this country, he would wish to settle himself in it; therefore he has recourse to your goodness, praying you to be pleased to grant to him a tract of land of 800 arpens in superficie, to be taken on the vacant lands of the King's domain, in the place which shall appear most advantageous and most convenient to the interest of your petitioner, who presumes to expect this favor of your justice.

ST. LOUIS, <i>April</i> 7, 1800.

FRANCOIS ×<sup>his</sup> MARECHAL.
<sub>mark.</sub>

St. Louis of Illinois, *April* 11, 1800.

Whereas we are assured that the petitioner possesses sufficient means to improve the lands which he solicits, I do grant to him and his heirs the land he solicits, provided it is not prejudicial to anybody, and the surveyor, Don Antonio Soulard, shall put the party interested in possession of the quantity of land he asks, in a vacant place of the royal domain ; and this being executed, he shall make out a plat of his survey, delivering the same to the party, with his certificate, in order to enable him to obtain the title in form from the intendant general, to whom alone corresponds, by royal order, the distributing and granting all classes of lands, &c.

CARLOS DEHAULT DELASSUS.

St. Louis, *April* 27, 1833.    Truly translated.

JULIUS DE MUN.

| No. | Name of original claimant. | Arpens. | Nature and date of claim. | By whom granted. | By whom surveyed, date, and situation. |
|---|---|---|---|---|---|
| 83 | François Marechal. | 800 | Concession, 11th April, 1800. | C. Dehault Delassus. | James Rankin, D. S., 20th February, 1804. Certified by Soulard, 28th March, 1804. Sixty - five miles north of St Louis. |

EVIDENCE WITH REFERENCE TO MINUTES AND RECORDS.

*October* 18, 1811.—Board met.    Present : John B. C. Lucas, Clement B. Penrose, and Frederick Bates, commissioners.

Louis Labeaume, assignee of François Marechal, claiming 600 arpens, and said Marechal claiming 200 arpens of land, situate as above, produces a concession from Charles D. Delassus, lieutenant governor, dated 11th April, 1799 ; a plat of survey as above ; a transfer from Marechal to claimant, dated 5th December, 1803. It is the opinion of the board that this claim ought not to be confirmed.    (See book No. 5, page 365.)

*March* 25, 1833.—F. R. Conway, esq., appeared, pursuant to adjournment.

François Marechal, by Louis Labeaume's legal representatives, claiming 800 arpens of land.    (See book C, pages 344 and 349 ; minutes, No. 5, page 365.)    Produces a concession from Carlos Dehault Delassus, dated 11th April, 1800 ; also a plat of survey, part of which is torn and missing, embracing 35 concessions of 800 arpens each, and numbered from 1 to 35 inclusive, on which claimant is No. 5 ; also deeds, dated 5th December, 1803, and July 7, 1804.

M. P. Leduc, duly sworn, says that the signature to the concession is in the proper handwriting of Carlos Dehault Delassus, and that the torn original survey is in the proper handwriting of Antonio Soulard.    (See book No. 6, page 142.)

*August* 24, 1835.—The board met, pursuant to adjournment.    Present : F. R. Conway, J. H. Relfe, and F. H. Martin, commissioners.

François Marechal, claiming 800 arpens of land.    (See book No. 6, page 142.)

The board are unanimously of opinion that this claim ought not to be confirmed.    For reasons, see decision in the claim of Louis Lamalice, No. 80.

F. H. MARTIN,
F. R. CONWAY,
JAMES H. RELFE.

Class 2.    No. 84.—*Auguste Lefevre, claiming 800 arpens.*

To Don CARLOS DEHAULT DELASSUS, *Lieutenant Governor of Upper Louisiana* :

SIR : Auguste Lefevre has the honor to represent to you, that he would wish to form an establishment in this country, wherein he has been residing since a long time ; therefore he has recourse to your goodness, and prays you to grant to him a tract of land of 800 arpens in superficie, to be taken on the vacant lands of the King's domain, in the place which shall be most convenient to the interest of your petitioner, who presumes to expect this favor of your justice.

his
AUGUSTE × LEFEVRE.
mark.

St. Louis, *June* 9, 1800.

St. Louis of Illinois, *June* 11, 1800.

Whereas we are assured that the petitioner possesses sufficient means to improve the lands which he solicits, without prejudice to anybody, I do grant to him and his heirs the land he solicits, and the surveyor, Don Antonio Soulard, shall put the interested (party) in possession of the quantity of land he asks, in a vacant place of the royal domain ; which being executed, he shall make out a plat of his survey, delivering the same to the party, with his certificate, in order to enable him to obtain the title in form from the intendant general, to whom alone corresponds, by royal order, the distributing and granting all classes of lands, &c.

CARLOS DEHAULT DELASSUS.

St. Louis, *April* 29, 1833.    Truly translated.

JULIUS DE MUN.

*Auguste Lefevre, claiming 800 arpens.*

| No. | Name of original claimant. | Arpens. | Nature and date of claim. | By whom granted. | By whom surveyed, date, and situation. |
|---|---|---|---|---|---|
| 84 | Auguste Lefevre. | 800 | Concession, June 11th, 1800. | Carlos Dehault Delassus. | James Rankin, D. S., 20th February, 1804. Certified by Soulard, 28th March, 1804. Sixty-five miles north of St. Louis. |

EVIDENCE WITH REFERENCE TO MINUTES AND RECORDS.

*October* 18, 1811.—Board met.   Present: John B. C. Lucas, Clement B. Penrose, and Frederick Bates, commissioners.

Louis Labeaume, assignee of Auguste Lefevre, claiming 600 arpens of land, and said Lefevre, claiming 200 arpens of land, situate as above, produces a concession from Charles D. Delassus, lieutenant governor, dated 11th June, 1800; a plat of survey, as above; a transfer from Lefevre to claimant, dated 5th December, 1803. It is the opinion of the board that this claim ought not to be confirmed.   (See book No. 5, page 368.)

*March* 25, 1833.—F. R. Conway, esq., appeared, pursuant to adjournment.

Auguste Lefevre, by L. Labeaume's legal representatives, claiming 800 arpens of land.   (See book C, pages 348 and 349; minutes, No. 5, page 368.   Produces a paper, purporting to be an original concession from Carlos D. Delassus, dated June 11, 1800; also a deed to Labeaume; also a plat of survey, part of which is torn and missing, embracing 35 concessions of 800 arpens each, numbered from 1 to 35 inclusive, on which claimant is No. 21.

M. P. Leduc, duly sworn, says that the signature to the concession is in the proper handwriting of said Delassus; and the torn original survey is in the proper handwriting of Antonio Soulard.   (See book No. 6, page 148.)

*August* 24, 1835.—The board met, pursuant to adjournment.   Present: F. R. Conway, J. H. Relfe, and F. H. Martin, commissioners.

Auguste Lefevre, claiming 800 arpens of land.   (See book No. 6, page 148.)

The board are unanimously of opinion that this claim ought not to be confirmed.   For reasons, see decision in the claim of Louis Lamalice, No. 80.

F. H. MARTIN,<br>
JAMES H. RELFE,<br>
F. R. CONWAY.

---

Class 2.   No. 85.—*Jean Baptiste Provencher, claiming 800 arpens.*

To Don CHARLES DEHAULT DELASSUS, *Lieutenant Governor of Upper Louisiana, &c. :*

SIR : Jean Baptiste Provencher has the honor to represent to you that he would wish to establish himself in the upper part of this province, where he has been residing for some time ; therefore he has recourse to the kindness of this government, praying you to be pleased to grant to him a tract of land of 800 arpens in superficie, to be taken on the domain of his Majesty, in the place which will appear most convenient to the interest of your petitioner, who presumes to expect this favor of your justice.

his<br>
J. BTE.   ×   PROVENCHER.<br>
mark.

ST. LOUIS, *January* 13, 1800.

ST. LOUIS OF ILLINOIS, *January* 15, 1800.

Whereas we are assured that the petitioner possesses sufficient means to improve the lands which he solicits, I do grant to him and his heirs the land he solicits, provided it is not prejudicial to anybody, and the surveyor, Don Antonio Soulard, shall put the interested (party) in possession of the quantity of land he asks, in a vacant place of the royal domain ; which being executed, he shall make out a plat (of his survey,) delivering the same to the party, with his certificate, in order to enable him to obtain the title in form from the intendent general, to whom alone corresponds, by royal order, the distributing and granting all classes of lands, &c.

CARLOS DEHAULT DELASSUS.

ST. LOUIS, *April* 26, 1833.   Truly translated.

JULIUS DE MUN.

| No. | Name of original claimant. | Arpens. | Nature and date of claim. | By whom granted. | By whom surveyed, date, and situation. |
|---|---|---|---|---|---|
| 85 | Jean Baptiste Provencher. | 800 | Concession, 15th January, 1800. | Carlos Dehault Delassus. | James Rankin, D. S., 20th February, 1804. Certified by Soulard, 28th March, 1804. Sixty-five miles north of St. Louis. |

EVIDENCE WITH REFERENCE TO MINUTES AND RECORDS.

*October* 18, 1811.—Board met. Present: John B. C. Lucas, Clement B. Penrose, and Frederick Bates, commissioners.

Louis Labeaume, assignee of Jean Baptiste Provencher, claiming 800 arpens of land, situate as above, produces a concession from Charles D. Delassus, lieutenant governor, dated January 15, 1800 ; a plat of survey, as above ; a certified extract of sale made by Provencher to claimant, dated Nov. 7, 1803.

It is the opinion of the board that this claim ought not to be confirmed. (See book No. 5, page 368.)

*March* 25, 1833.—F. R. Conway, esq., appeared, pursuant to adjourn.

Jean Baptiste Provencher, by L. Labeaume's legal representatives, claiming 800 arpens of land. (See book C, pages 348 and 349 ; minutes, No. 5, page 368.) Produces a concession, purporting to be from Carlos D. Delassus, dated January 15, 1800 ; also a certificate of transfer, signed M. P. Leduc, recorder ; also a plat of survey, part of which is torn and missing, embracing 35 concessions of 800 arpens each, numbered from 1 to 35 inclusive, on which claimant is No. 20.

M. P. Leduc, duly sworn, says that the signature to the concession is in the proper handwriting of said Delassus, and the torn original survey is in the proper handwriting of Antonio Soulard. (See book No. 6, page 148.)

*August* 24, 1835.—The board met, pursuant to adjournment. Present: F. R. Conway, J. H. Relfe, and F. H. Martin, commissioners.

Jean Baptiste Provencher, claiming 800 arpens of land. (See book No. 6, page 148.)

The board are unanimously of opinion that this claim ought not to be confirmed. For reasons, see decision in the claim of Louis Lamalice, No. 80.

F. H. MARTIN,<br>
F. R. CONWAY,<br>
JAMES H. RELFE.

---

Class 2. No. 86.—François Paquet, claiming 800 arpens.

To Don CARLOS DEHAULT DELASSUS, *Lieutenant Governor of Upper Louisiana :*

SIR : François Paquet has the honor to represent to you, that, having resided a long time in this province, he would wish to form an establishment ; therefore he prays you to grant to him a concession for a tract of land of eight hundred arpens in superficie, to be taken on the vacant lands of the King's domain, in the place which will appear most advantageous and most convenient to the interest of your petitioner, who presumes to expect this favor of your justice.

his<br>
FRANCOIS × PAQUET.<br>
mark.

St. LOUIS, *April 3, 1800.*

St. LOUIS OF ILLINOS, April 5, 1800.

Whereas we are assured that the petitioner has sufficient means to improve the lands which he solicits, I do grant to him and his heirs the land which he solicits, if it is not prejudicial to any one, and the surveyor, Don A. Soulard, shall put the interested in possession of the quantity of land which he asks, in a vacant place of the royal domain ; and this being executed, he shall draw a plat of his survey, delivering the same to the party, with his certificate, in order to serve him to obtain the title in form, from the intendant general, to whom alone corresponds, by royal order, the distributing and granting all classes of lands, &c.

CARLOS DEHAULT DELASSUS.

St. LOUIS, *December 31, 1832.* Truly translated.

JULIUS DE MUN.

| No. | Name of original claimant. | Arpens. | Nature and date of claim. | By whom granted. | By whom surveyed, date, and situation. |
|---|---|---|---|---|---|
| 86 | François Paquet. | 800 | Concession, April 5, 1800. | Carlos Dehault Delassus. | James Rankin, D. S., 20th February, 1804. Certified by Soulard, 28th March, 1804. On Cuivre river, 65 miles north of St. Louis. |

EVIDENCE WITH REFERENCE TO MINUTES AND RECORDS.

*May* 28, 1806.—The board met, agreeably to adjournment. Present: Hon. Clement B. Penrose.

James St. Vrain, assignee of François Paquet, claiming 600 arpens of land, situate on the river Cuivre, district of St. Charles, produces a concession from Charles D. Delassus for 800 arpens to the said Paquet, dated April 5, 1800 ; a survey of the same, dated February 20th, and certified the 28th March, 1804, and a deed of transfer of the same, dated the 10th January, 1804. The board require further proof of the date of the above concession. The board reject this claim. (See book No. 1, page 303.)

*August* 17, 1811.—Board met. Present: Clement B. Penrose and Frederick Bates, commissioners.

Jacques St. Vrain, assignee of François Paquet, claiming 600 arpens, and François Paquet, claiming 200 arpens of land. (See book No. 1, page 303.) It is the opinion of this board that this claim ought not to be confirmed. (See book No. 5, page 317.)

*December* 19, 1832.—F. R. Conway, esq., appeared, pursuant to adjournment.

François Paquet, by his legal representative, John Mullanphy, claiming 800 arpens of land. (See book C, page 336 ; books No. 1, page 303, No. 5, page 317.) Produces a paper purporting to be an original concession from Carlos Dehault Delassus, dated 5th April, 1800, (also deed of conveyance.)

M. P. Leduc, being duly sworn, saith that the signature to said concession is in the proper handwriting of the said Carlos Dehault Delassus. (See book No. 6, page 86.)

*August* 24, 1835.—The board met, pursuant to adjournment. Present: F. R. Conway, J. H. Relfe, and F. H. Martin, commissioners.

François Paquet, claiming 800 arpens of land. (See book No. 6, page 86.)

The board are unanimously of opinion that this claim ought not to be confirmed. For reasons, see decision in the claim of Louis Lamalice, No. 80.

F. H. MARTIN,<br>F. R. CONWAY,<br>JAMES H. RELFE.

### Class 2. No. 87.—*Joseph Rivet, claiming 800 arpens.*

To Don CARLOS DEHAULT DELASSUS, *Lieutenant Governor of Upper Louisiana:*

SIR : —— Rivet has the honor to represent to you that, residing in the country since a number of years, he wishes to make an establishment; therefore, he has recourse to your goodness, praying you will please to grant to him a tract of land of eight hundred arpens in superficie, to be taken on the vacant lands of the King's domain, in the place which will appear most convenient to the interest of your petitioner, who presumes to expect this favor of your justice.

ST. LOUIS, *February* 21, 1800.

his<br>—— × RIVET.<br>mark.

ST. LOUIS OF ILLINOIS, *February* 28, 1800.

Whereas we are assured that the petitioner has sufficient means to improve the lands which he solicits, I do grant to him and his heirs the lands which he solicits, if it is not prejudicial to any person, and the surveyor, Don Antonio Soulard, shall put the interested in possession of the quantity of land which he asks, on a vacant place of the royal domain; and this being executed, he shall draw a plat of his survey, delivering the same to the party, with his certificate, in order to serve to him to obtain the title in form from the intendant general, to whom alone corresponds, by royal order, the granting and distributing all classes of lands; which he asks, &c.

CARLOS DEHAULT DELASSUS.

ST. LOUIS, *December* 31, 1832. Truly translated.

JULIUS DE MUN, *T. B. C.*

| No. | Name of original claimant | Arpens. | Nature and date of claim. | By whom granted. | By whom surveyed, date, and situation. |
|---|---|---|---|---|---|
| 87 | Joseph Rivet. | 800 | Concession, 28th February, 1800. | Carlos Dehault Delassus. | James Rankin, D. S., 20th February, 1804. Certified by Soulard, 28th March, 1804. On Cuivre river, 65 miles north of St. Louis. |

EVIDENCE WITH REFERENCE TO MINUTES AND RECORDS.

*May* 28, 1806.—The board met, agreeably to adjournment. Present: Hon. Clement B. Penrose.

The same (James St. Vrain) assignee of (Joseph) Rivet, (claiming) 600 arpens of land, situated as aforesaid, produces a concession from Charles D. Delassus to the said Rivet, for 800 arpens, dated 28th February, 1800; survey dated 20th February, and certified 28th March, 1804, and a transfer of the same, dated 12th February, 1804.

The board require further proof of the date of the above concession. Rejected. (See book No. 1, page 303.)

*August* 17, 1811.—Board met. Present: Clement B. Penrose and Frederick Bates, commissioners.

Jaques St. Vrain, assignee of Rivet, claiming 600 arpens, and Rivet, claiming 200 arpens of land. (See book No. 1, page 303.)

It is the opinion of the board that this claim ought not to be confirmed. (See book No. 5, page 317.)

*December* 19, 1832.—F. R. Conway, esq., appeared, pursuant to adjournment.

Joseph Rivet, by his legal representative, John Mullanphy, claiming 800 arpens of land. (See book C, page 333; book No. 1, page 303; No. 5, page 317.)

Produces a paper purporting to be an original concession from Carlos Dehault Delassus, dated 28th February, 1800; also deeds of conveyances.

M. P. Leduc, duly sworn, saith that the signature to the aforesaid concession is in the proper handwriting of the said Carlos Dehault Delassus. (See book No. 7, page 85.)

*August* 24, 1835.—The board met, pursuant to adjournment. Present: F. R. Conway, J. H. Relfe, and F. H. Martin, commissioners.

Joseph Rivet, claiming 800 arpens of land. (See book No. 6, page 85.)

The board are unanimously of opinion that this claim ought not to be confirmed. For reasons, see decision in the claim of Louis Lamalice, No. 80.

F. H. MARTIN,<br>F. R. CONWAY,<br>JAMES H. RELFE.

### Class 2. No. 88.—*Joseph Pressé, claiming 800 arpens.*

To Don CHARLES DEHAULT DELASSUS, *Lieutenant Governor of Upper Louisiana:*

SIR: Joseph Pressé has the honor to represent to you that he would wish to make an establishment in the upper part of this province, where he has been residing for a long time, the petitioner promising to submit to all the taxes and charges which it may please his Majesty to impose; therefore, the petitioner prays you, sir, to grant to him a tract of land of 800 arpens in superficie, to be taken on the vacant lands of the King's domain, in the place which will appear most convenient to his interest; favor which the petitioner presumes to expect of your justice.

St. Louis, *November 10, 1799.*

his  
JOSEPH × PRESSÉ.  
mark.

St. Louis of Illinois, *November 12, 1799.*

Whereas it is notorious that the petitioner possesses more than the means and the number of hands (population) necessary to obtain the concession which he solicits, I do grant to him and his heirs the land he solicits, provided it is not prejudicial to anybody, and the surveyor, Don Antonio Soulard, shall put the (party) interested in possession of the quantity of land he asks, in a vacant place of the royal domain; which being executed, he shall make out a plat of survey, delivering the same to the party, with his certificate, in order to enable him to obtain the concession and title in form from the intendant general, to whom alone corresponds, by royal order, the distributing and granting all classes of lands of the royal domain.

CARLOS DEHAULT DELASSUS.

St. Louis, *April 28, 1833.*  Truly translated.

JULIUS DE MUN.

| No. | Name of original claimant. | Arpens. | Nature and date of claim. | By whom granted. | By whom surveyed, date, and situation. |
|---|---|---|---|---|---|
| 88 | Joseph Pressé. | 800 | Concession, 12th November, 1799. | Carlos Dehault Delassus. | James Rankin, D. S., 20th Feb., 1804. Certified by Soulard, S. Gen., 28th March, 1804. Sixty-five miles N. of St. Louis. |

EVIDENCE WITH REFERENCE TO MINUTES AND RECORDS.

*October* 18, 1811.—Board met.  Present: John B. C. Lucas, Clement B. Penrose, and Frederick Bates, commissioners.

Louis Labeaume, assignee of Joseph Pressé, claiming 800 arpens of land, situated as above; produces a certificate from Carlos Dehault Delassus, lieutenant governor, dated 10th November, 1799; a plat of survey as above; a certified extract of sale made by Pressé to claimant, dated 4th September, 1803.

It is the opinion of the board that this claim ought not to be confirmed.  (See book No. 5, page 367.)

*March* 25, 1833.—F. R. Conway, esq., appeared, pursuant to adjournment.

Joseph Pressé, by Louis Labeaume's legal representatives, claiming 800 arpens of land.  (See book C, pages 344 and 349; minutes, No. 5, page 367.)  Produces a paper purporting to be an original concession from Carlos Dehault Delassus, dated November 12, 1799.  Also a plat of survey, part of the same being torn and missing, embracing thirty-five concessions of 800 arpens each, and numbered from one to thirty-five inclusive, on which claimant is number seventeen; also deeds to Labeaume.

M. P. Leduc, duly sworn, says that the signature to the concession is in the proper handwriting of said Delassus, and that the torn original survey is in the proper handwriting of said Soulard.  (See book No. 6, page 147.)

*August* 24, 1835.—The board met, pursuant to adjournment.  Present: F. R. Conway, J. H. Relfe, F. H. Martin, commissioners.

Joseph Pressé, claiming 800 arpens of land.  (See book No. 6, page 147.)

The board are unanimously of opinion that this claim ought not to be confirmed.  For reasons, see decision in the claim of Louis Lamalice, No. 80.

F. H. MARTIN,  
F. R. CONWAY,  
JAMES H. RELFE.

---

Class 2.    No. 89.—*Michel Vallé, claiming 800 arpens.*

To Don Carlos Dehault Delassus, *Lieutenant Governor of Upper Louisiana :*

Sir: Michel Vallé has the honor to represent to you that, having resided for a long time in this province, he would wish to form an establishment in the same; therefore, he has recourse to your goodness, praying you will be pleased to grant to him a tract of land 800 arpens in superficie, to be taken on the vacant lands of the King's domain, in the place which shall be most convenient to the interest of your petitioner, who presumes to expect this favor of your justice.

his  
MICHEL × VALLÉ.  
mark.

St. Louis, *March 12, 1800.*

St. Louis of Illinois, *March 16, 1800.*

Whereas we are assured that the petitioner possesses sufficient means to improve the lands which he solicits, I do grant to him and his heirs the land which he solicits, provided it is not prejudicial to anybody, and the surveyor, Don Antonio Soulard, shall put the party interested in possession of the quantity of land he asks, in a vacant place of the royal domain; which being executed, he shall make out a plat of his survey, delivering the same to the said party, with his certificate, in order to enable him to obtain the title in form from the intendant general, to whom alone corresponds, by royal order, the distributing and granting all classes of lands, &c.

CARLOS DEHAULT DELASSUS.

St. Louis, *April 17, 1833.*  Truly translated.

JULIUS DE MUN.

*Michel Vallé, claiming 800 arpens.*

| No. | Name of original claimant. | Arpens. | Nature and date of claim. | By whom granted. | By whom surveyed, date, and situation. |
|---|---|---|---|---|---|
| 89 | Michel Vallé. | 800 | Concession, 16th March, 1800. | Carlos Dehault Delassus. | James Rankin, D. S., 20th February, 1804. Certified by Soulard, 28th March, 1804. Sixty-five miles north of St. Louis. |

EVIDENCE WITH REFERENCE TO MINUTES AND RECORDS.

*October* 18, 1811.—The board met. Present: John B. C. Lucas, Clement B. Penrose, and Frederick Bates, commissioners.

Louis Labeaume, assignee of Michel Vallé, claiming 600 arpens, and said Vallé, claiming 200 arpens of land, situated as aforesaid; produces a concession from Charles Dehault Delassus, lieutenant governor, dated 16th March, 1800; a plat of survey, as aforesaid; a transfer from Vallé, to claimant, dated 20th December, 1803.

It is the opinion of the board that this claim ought not to be confirmed. (See book No. 5, page 368.)

*March* 25, 1833.—Michel Vallé, by Louis Labeaume's legal representatives, claiming 800 arpens of land. (See book C, pages 347 and 349; No. 5, page 368.) Produces a paper purporting to be an original concession from Carlos Dehault Delassus, dated March 16, 1800; also deeds to Labeaume; also a plat of survey, part of the same being torn and missing, embracing thirty-five concessions of 800 arpens each, and numbered from one to thirty-five inclusive, on which claimant is No. 18.

M. P. Leduc, duly sworn, says that the signature to the concession is in the proper handwriting of said Delassus, and that the torn original survey is in the proper handwriting of said Soulard. (See book No. 6, page 147.)

*August* 24, 1835.—The board met, pursuant to adjournment. Present: F. R. Conway, J. H. Relfe, and F. H. Martin, commissioners.

Michel Vallé, claiming 800 arpens of land. (See book No. 6, page 147.)

The board are unanimously of opinion that this claim ought not to be confirmed. For reasons, see decision in the claim of Louis Lamalice, No. 80.

F. H. MARTIN,<br>
F. R. CONWAY,<br>
JAMES H. RELFE.

---

Class 2. No. 90.—*Antoine Bizet, claiming 800 arpens of land.*

To Don CARLOS DEHAULT DELASSUS, *Lieutenant Governor of Upper Louisiana:*

SIR: Antoine Bizet has the honor to represent to you, that he would wish to establish himself in the upper part of this province, where he has been residing for a long time; therefore he has recourse to your goodness, and prays you to grant him a tract of land of 800 arpens in superficie, to be taken on the vacant lands of the King's domain, in the place which will appear most convenient to the interest of your petitioner, who presumes to expect this favor of your justice.

his<br>
ANTOINE × BIZET.<br>
mark.

ST. LOUIS, *September* 12, 1800.

ST. LOUIS OF ILLINOIS, *September* 13, 1800.

Whereas we are assured that the petitioner possesses sufficient means to improve the land which he solicits, I do grant to him and to his heirs the land which he solicits, provided it is not prejudicial to anybody, and the surveyor, Don Antonio Soulard, shall put the party interested in possession of the quantity of land he asks, in a vacant place of the royal domain; which being executed, he shall make out a plat of his survey, delivering the same to the party, with his certificate, in order to serve to him to obtain the title in form from the intendant general, to whom alone corresponds, by royal order, the distributing and granting all classes of lands, &c.

CARLOS DEHAULT DELASSUS.

ST. LOUIS, *April* 17, 1833. Truly translated.

JULIUS DE MUN.

| No. | Name of original claimant. | Arpens. | Nature and date of claim. | By whom granted. | By whom surveyed, date, and situation. |
|---|---|---|---|---|---|
| 90 | Antoine Bizet. | 800 | Concession, 13th September, 1800. | C. Dehault Delassus. | James Rankin, D. S., 20th February, 1804. Certified by Soulard, 28th March, 1804. Sixty-five miles north of St. Louis. |

EVIDENCE WITH REFERENCE TO MINUTES AND RECORDS.

*October* 18, 1811.—Board met. Present: John B. C. Lucas, Clement B. Penrose, and Frederick Bates, commissioners.

Louis Labeaume, assignee of Antoine Bizet, claiming 800 arpens of land, situate as above, produces a concession from Charles D. Delassus, lieutenant governor, dated September 13, 1800 ; a plat of survey as above ; a certified extract of sale made by Bizet to claimant, dated 7th November, 1803.

It is the opinion of the board that this claim ought not to be confirmed.  (See book No. 5, page 364.)

*March* 25, 1833.—F. R. Conway, esq., appeared, pursuant to adjournment.

Antoine Bizet, by L. Labeaume's legal representatives, claiming 800 arpens of land.  (See book C, pages 347, 348, and 349 ; minutes, No. 5, page 364.)  Produces a paper purporting to be an original concession from Carlos D. Delassus, dated 13th September, 1800 ; also, a deed to Labeaume, and certificate of transfer, signed M. P. Leduc, recorder ; also, a plat of survey, (part of the same being torn and missing,) embracing 35 concessions of 800 arpens each, on which claimant is No. 19.

M. P. Leduc, duly sworn, says that the signature to the concession is in the proper handwriting of said Delassus, and the torn original survey is in the proper handwriting of Antonio Soulard.  (See book No. 6, page 148.)

*August* 24, 1835.—The board met, pursuant to adjournment.  Present, F. R. Conway, J. H. Relfe, and F. H. Martin, commissioners.

Antoine Bizet, claiming 800 arpens of land.  (See book No. 6, page 148.)

The board are unanimously of opinion that this claim ought not to be confirmed.  For reasons, see decision in the claim of Louis Lamalice, No. 80.

F. R. CONWAY,<br>
F. H. MARTIN,<br>
JAMES H. RELFE.

---

Class 2.    No. 91.—*Louis Boissy, claiming* 800 *arpens.*

To Don Carlos Dehault Delassus, *Lieutenant Governor of Upper Louisiana :*

Sir : Louis Boissy has the honor to represent to you that he would wish to establish himself in the upper part of this province, where he has been residing for some time ; therefore he has recourse to the kindness of this government, praying that you will be pleased to grant to him a tract of land of 800 arpens in superficie, to be taken on the vacant lands of his Majesty's domain, in the place which will appear most convenient to the interest of your petitioner, who presumes to expect this favor of your justice.

LOUIS BOISSY.

St. Louis, *January* 16, 1800.

St. Louis of Illinois, *January* 18, 1800.

Whereas we are assured that the petitioner possesses sufficient means to improve the lands which he solicits, I do grant to him and his heirs the land he solicits, provided it is not prejudicial to any person, and the surveyor, Don A. Soulard, shall put the (party) interested in possession of the quantity of land he asks, in a vacant place of the royal domain ; which being executed, he shall make out a plat of survey, delivering the same to the party, with his certificate, in order to serve him to obtain the title in form from the intendant general, to whom alone corresponds, by royal order, the distributing and granting all classes of lands, &c.

CARLOS DEHAULT DELASSUS.

St. Louis, *April* 25, 1833.    Truly translated.

JULIUS DE MUN.

| No. | Name of original claimant. | Arpens. | Nature and date of claim. | By whom granted. | By whom surveyed, date, and situation. |
|---|---|---|---|---|---|
| 91 | Louis Boissy. | 800 | Concession, 18th January, 1800. | Carlos Dehault Delassus | James Rankin, D. S., 20th February, 1804.  Certified by Soulard, March 28th, 1804.  Sixty-five miles north of St. Louis. |

EVIDENCE WITH REFERENCE TO MINUTES AND RECORDS.

*October* 18, 1811.—Board met.  Present : John B. C. Lucas, Clement B. Penrose, and Frederick Bates, commissioners.

Louis Labeaume, assignee of Louis Boissy, claiming 800 arpens of land, situate as above, produces a concession from Charles D. Delassus, lieutenant governor, dated January 18, 1800 ; plat of survey as above ; a certified extract of sale made by Boissy to claimant, dated 2d November, 1803.  It is the opinion of the board that this claim ought not to be confirmed.  (See book No. 5, page 364.)

*March* 25, 1833.—F. R. Conway, esq., appeared, pursuant to adjournment.

Louis Boissy, by L. Labeaume's legal representatives, claiming 800 arpens of land.  (See book C, pages 346 and 349 ; minutes, No. 5, page 364.)  Produces a paper purporting to be an original concession from Carlos D. Delassus, dated January 18, 1800 ; also a plat of survey, part of the same being torn and missing, embracing 35 concessions of 800 arpens each, and numbered from 1 to 35 inclusive, on which claimant is No. 15.  Also a certificate of transfer signed M. P. Leduc, recorder.

M. P. Leduc, duly sworn, says that the signature to the concession is in the proper handwriting of Carlos D. Delassus, and that the torn original survey is of the proper handwriting of Ant. Soulard.  (See book No. 6, page 146.)

*August* 24, 1835.—The board met, pursuant to adjournment.  Present : F. R. Conway, J. H. Relfe, and F. H. Martin, commissioners.

Louis Boissy, claiming 800 arpens of land.  (See book No. 6, page 146.)

The board are unanimously of opinion that this claim ought not to be confirmed. For reasons, see decision in the claim of Louis Lamalice, No. 80.

F. H. MARTIN,
F. R. CONWAY,
JAMES H. RELFE.

---

Class 2. No. 92.—*Joseph Charleville, claiming 800 arpens.*

To Don CARLOS DEHAULT DELASSUS, *Lieutenant Governor of Upper Louisiana :*

SIR : Joseph Charleville has the honor to represent to you that he would wish to form an establishment in the upper part of this colony, in which he has been residing since his infancy ; therefore the petitioner prays you to grant to him a tract of land of 800 arpens in superficie, to be taken on the vacant lands of his Majesty's domain, in the place which will appear most convenient to the interest of your petitioner. Favor which he presumes to expect of your justice.

ST. LOUIS, *November* 14, 1799.

JOSEPH CHARLEVILLE.

ST. LOUIS OF ILLINOIS, *November* 16, 1799.

Whereas we are assured that the petitioner possesses sufficient means to improve the lands which he solicits, I grant to him and his heirs the land he solicits, provided it is not prejudicial to anybody, and the surveyor, Don Antonio Soulard, shall put the (party) interested in possession of the quantity of land he asks, in a vacant place of the royal domain ; which being executed, he shall make out a plat (of his survey), delivering the same to the party, with his certificate, in order to enable him to obtain the concession and title in form from the intendant general ; to whom alone corresponds, by royal order, the distributing and granting all classes of lands of the royal domain.

CARLOS DEHAULT DELASSUS.

ST. LOUIS, *April* 25, 1833. Truly translated.

JULIUS DE MUN.

| No. | Name of original claimant. | Arpens. | Nature and date of claim. | By whom granted. | By whom surveyed, date, and situation. |
|---|---|---|---|---|---|
| 92 | J. Charleville. | 800 | Concession. 16th November, 1799. | C. Dehault Delassus. | James Rankin, D. S., 20th February, 1804. Certified by Soulard, 28th March, 1804. Sixty-five miles north of St. Louis. |

EVIDENCE WITH REFERENCE TO MINUTES AND RECORDS.

*October* 18, 1811.—Board met. Present : John B. C. Lucas, Clement B. Penrose, and Frederick Bates, commissioners.

Louis Labeaume, assignee of Joseph Charleville, claiming 800 arpens of land, situate as above, produces a concession from Charles Dehault Delassus, lieutenant governor, dated 16th November, 1799 ; a plat of survey as above ; a certified extract of sale made by said Charleville to claimant, dated 7th October, 1803. It is the opinion of the board that this claim ought not to be confirmed. (See book No. 5, page 367.)

*March* 25, 1833.—F. R. Conway esq., appeared, pursuant to adjournment.

Joseph Charleville, by L. Labeaume's legal representatives, claiming 800 arpens of land. (See book C, pages 347 and 349 ; minutes, No. 5, page 367.) Produces a concession purporting to be from Carlos D. Delassus, dated 16th November, 1799 ; also a plat of survey, part of the same being torn and missing, embracing thirty-five concessions of 800 arpens each, and numbered from 1 to 35 inclusive, on which claimant is No. 16 ; also certificate of transfer, signed M. P. Leduc, recorder.

M. P. Leduc, duly sworn, says that the signature to the concession is in the proper handwriting of said Delassus, and that the torn original survey is of the proper handwriting of Antonio Soulard. (See book No. 6, page 146.)

*August* 24, 1835.—The board met, pursuant to adjournment. Present : F. R. Conway, J. H. Relfe, and F. H. Martin, commissioners.

Joseph Charleville, claiming 800 arpens of land. (See book No. 6, page 146.)

The board are unanimously of opinion that this claim ought not to be confirmed. For reasons, see decision in the claim of Louis Lamalice, No. 80.

F. H. MARTIN,
F. R. CONWAY,
JAMES H. RELFE.

---

Class 2. No. 93.—*Baptiste Domine, claiming 800 arpens.*

To Don CARLOS DEHAULT DELASSUS, *Lieutenant Governor of Upper Louisiana, &c. :*

SIR : Baptiste Domine has the honor to represent that he would wish to form an establishment in the upper part of this colony, where he has been residing since a number of years ; therefore the petitioner prays you to grant to him a tract of land of 800 arpens in superficie, to be taken on the lands belonging to the King's domain, in a vacant place, and which he will have surveyed in the manner which shall appear most convenient to his interest ; favor which the petitioner presumes to expect of your justice.

St. Louis, *October* 27, 1799. BAPTISTE x DOMINE.
his
mark.

St. Louis of Illinois, *October* 28, 1799.

Whereas we are assured that the petitioner possesses sufficient means to improve the lands he solicits, I do grant to him and his heirs the land which he solicits, provided it is not prejudicial to anybody, and the surveyor, Don Antonio Soulard, shall put the (party) interested in possession of the quantity of land he asks, in a vacant place of the royal domain ; and this being executed, he shall make out a plat of his survey, delivering the same to the party with his certificate, in order to serve to him to obtain the concession and title in form from the intendant general, to whom alone corresponds, by royal order, the distributing and granting all classes of lands of the royal domain.

CARLOS DEHAULT DELASSUS.

St. Louis, *April* 25, 1833. Truly translated.

JULIUS DE MUN.

| No. | Name of original claimant. | Arpens. | Nature and date of claim. | By whom granted. | By whom surveyed, date, and situation. |
|---|---|---|---|---|---|
| 93 | Baptiste Domine. | 800 | Concession, 28th October, 1799. | Carlos Dehault Delassus. | James Rankin, D. S., 20th February, 1804. Certified by Soulard, 28th March, 1804. Sixty-five miles north of St. Louis. |

EVIDENCE WITH REFERENCE TO MINUTES AND RECORDS.

*October* 18, 1811.—Board met. Present: John B. C. Lucas, Clement B. Penrose, and Frederick Bates, commissioners.

Louis Labeaume, assignee of Baptiste Domine, claiming 600 arpens, and said Domine claiming 200 arpens of land, situate as aforesaid. Produces a paper purporting to be a concession from Charles Dehault Delassus, lieutenant governor, dated 28th October, 1799 ; a plat of survey as aforesaid ; a transfer from Domine to claimant, dated 14th December, 1803.

It is the opinion of the board that this claim ought not to be confirmed. (See book No. 5, page 367.)

*March* 25, 1833.—F. R. Conway, esq., appeared, pursuant to adjournment.

Baptiste Domine, by Louis Labeaume's legal representatives, claiming 800 arpens of land. (See book C, pages 345, 346, and 349 ; minutes, No. 5, page 367.) Produces a paper purporting to be an original concession from Carlos Dehault Delassus, dated October 28, 1799 ; also a plat of survey, part of the same being torn and missing, embracing thirty-five concessions of 800 arpens each, and numbered from 1 to 35 inclusive, on which claimant is No. 12 ; also a certificate.

M. P. Leduc, being duly sworn, says that the signature to the concession is in the proper handwriting of Carlos D. Delassus, and that the torn original survey is in the proper handwriting of Antonio Soulard. (See book No. 6, page 145.)

*August* 24, 1835.—The board met, pursuant to adjournment. Present : F. R. Conway, J. H. Relfe, and F. H. Martin, commissioners.

Baptiste Domine, claiming 800 arpens of land. (See book No. 6, page 145.)

The board are unanimously of opinion that this claim ought not to be confirmed. For reasons, see decision in the claim of Louis Lamalice, No. 80.

F. H. MARTIN,
F. R. CONWAY,
JAMES H. RELFE.

Class 2. No. 94.—*Louis Charleville, claiming* 800 *arpens.*

To Don CARLOS DEHAULT DELASSUS, *Lieutenant Governor of Upper Louisiana :*

SIR : Louis Charleville has the honor to represent to you that he would wish to form an establishment in the upper part of this province, where he has been residing since his infancy ; therefore he has recourse to your kindness, praying you to be pleased to grant to him a concession for 800 arpens of land, in superficie, to be taken on the vacant lands of the King's domain, in the place which shall appear most advantageous to the interest of your petitioner, who presumes to expect this favor of your justice.

St. Louis, *November* 13, 1799. LOUIS x CHARLEVILLE.
his
mark.

St. Louis of Illinois, *November* 14, 1799.

Whereas we are assured that the petitioner possesses sufficient means to improve the lands which he solicits, I do grant to him and his heirs the lands he solicits, provided it is not prejudicial to any person, and the surveyor, Don Antonio Soulard, shall put the party interested in possession of the quantity of land he solicits, in a vacant place of the royal domain ; which being executed, he shall make out a plat of his survey, delivering the same to the party, with his certificate, in order to enable him to obtain the title in form from the intendant general, to whom alone corresponds, by royal order, the distributing and granting all classes of lands.

CARLOS DEHAULT DELASSUS.

St. Louis, *April* 17, 1833. Truly translated.

JULIUS DE MUN.

*Louis Charleville, claiming 800 arpens.*

| No. | Name of original claimant. | Arpens. | Nature and date of claim. | By whom granted. | By whom surveyed, date, and situation. |
|---|---|---|---|---|---|
| 94 | Louis Charleville. | 800 | Concession, 14th November, 1799. | Carlos Dehault Delassus. | James Rankin, D. S., 20th February, 1804. Certified by A. Soulard, 28th March, 1804. Sixty-five miles north of St. Louis. |

EVIDENCE WITH REFERENCE TO MINUTES AND RECORDS.

*October* 18, 1811.—Board met. Present: John B. C. Lucas, Clement B. Penrose, and Frederick Bates, commissioners.

Louis Labeaume, assignee of Louis Charleville, claiming 800 arpens of land situate as above, produces a concession from Charles D. Delassus, lieutenant governor, dated 14th November, 1799, a plat of survey as above, and a certified extract of sale made by Charleville to the claimant, dated 7th October, 1803.

It is the opinion of the board that this claim ought not to be confirmed. (See book No. 5, page 367.)

*March* 25, 1833.—F. R. Conway, esq., appeared, pursuant to adjournment.

Louis Charleville, by L. Labeaume's legal representatives, claiming 800 arpens of land. (See book C, pages 347 and 349; minutes, No. 5, page 367.) Produces a paper purporting to be an original concession from C D. Delassus, dated November 14, 1799; also a plat of survey, part of the same being torn and missing, embracing 35 concessions of 800 arpens each, and numbered from 1 to 35, inclusive, on which claimant is No 13; also certificate of transfer, signed M. P. Leduc, recorder.

M. P. Leduc, duly sworn, says the signature to the concession is in the proper handwriting of Carlos D. Delassus, and that the torn original survey is in the proper handwriting of Soulard. (See book No. 6, page 145.)

*August* 24, 1835.—The board met, pursuant to adjournment. Present: F. R. Conway, James H. Relfe, and F. H. Martin, commissioners.

Louis Charleville, claiming 800 arpens of land. (See book No. 6, page 145.)

The board are unanimously of opinion that this claim ought not to be confirmed. For reasons, see decision in the claim of Louis Lamalice, No. 80.

F. H. MARTIN,
F. R. CONWAY,
JAMES H. RELFE.

Class 2. No. 95.—*François Besnard, claiming 800 arpens.*

To Don CARLOS DEHAULT DELASSUS, *Lieutenant Governor of Upper Louisiana :*

SIR: François Besnard has the honor to represent to you, that, having for a long time resided in this country, he wishes to settle himself and form an establishment in the same; therefore he has recourse to the kindness of this government, praying you to be pleased to grant to him a tract of land of 800 arpens in superficie, to be taken on the lands of the King's domain, in the place which will appear most convenient to the interest of your petitioner, who presumes to expect this favor of your justice.

FRANCOIS $\times$ BESNARD.
his
mark.

ST. LOUIS, *January* 13, 1800.

ST. LOUIS OF ILLINOIS, *January* 16, 1800.

Whereas we are assured that the petitioner possesses sufficient means to improve the lands he solicits, I do grant to him and his heirs the lands he solicits, provided it is not prejudicial to anybody, and the surveyor, Don Antonio Soulard, shall put the interested (party) in possession of the quantity of land he asks, in a vacant place of the royal domain; which being executed, he shall make out a plat of (his) survey, delivering the same to the party, with his certificate, in order to enable him to obtain the title in form from the intendant general, to whom alone corresponds, by royal order, the distributing and granting all classes of land, &c.

CARLOS DEHAULT DELASSUS.

ST. LOUIS, *April* 26, 1833. Truly translated.

JULIUS DE MUN.

| No. | Name of original claimant. | Arpens. | Nature and date of claim. | By whom granted. | By whom surveyed, date, and situation. |
|---|---|---|---|---|---|
| 95 | François Besnard. | 800 | Concession, 16th January, 1800. | Carlos Dehault Delassus. | James Rankin, D. S., 20th February, 1804. Certified by Soulard, 28th March, 1804. Sixty-five miles north of St. Louis |

EVIDENCE WITH REFERENCE TO MINUTES AND RECORDS.

*October* 18, 1811.—Board met. Present: John B. C. Lucas, Clement B. Penrose, and Frederick Bates, commissioners.

Louis Labeaume, assignee of François Besnard, claiming 600 arpens of land, and said Besnard, claiming 200 arpens of land, situate as above, produces concession from Charles Dehault Delassus, lieutenant governor, dated 16th January, 1800 ; a plat of survey as above ; a transfer from Bernard to claimant, dated 10th January, 1804.

It is the opinion of the board that this claim ought not to be confirmed. (See book No. 5, page 364.)

*March* 25, 1833.—F. R. Conway, esq., appeared, pursuant to adjournment.

François Besnard, by Louis Labeaume's legal representatives, claiming 800 arpens of land. (See book C, pages 346 and 349 ; minutes, No. 5, page 364.) Produces a paper purporting to be a concession from Carlos Dehault Delassus, dated January 16th, 1800 ; also a plat of survey, part of the same being torn and missing, embracing 35 concessions of 800 arpens each, and numbered from 1 to 35 inclusive, on which claimant is No. 14 ; also deeds, dated January, August and December, 1804.

M. P. Leduc, duly sworn, says that the signature to the concession is in the proper handwriting of Carlos D. Delassus, and that the torn original survey is in the proper handwriting of Antonio Soulard. (See book No. 6, page 145.)

*August* 24, 1835.—The board met, pursuant to adjournment. Present: F. R. Conway, J. H. Relfe, and F. H. Martin, commissioners.

François Besnard, claiming 800 arpens of land. (See book No. 6, page 145.)

The board are unanimously of opinion that this claim ought not to be confirmed. For reasons, see decision in the claim of Louis Lamalice, No. 80.

F. H. MARTIN,
F. R. CONWAY,
JAMES H. RELFE.

Class 2.   No. 96.—*Baptiste Marle, claiming 800 arpens.*

To Don CARLOS DEHAULT DELASSUS, *Lieutenant Governor of Upper Louisiana :*

SIR : Baptiste Marle has the honor to represent to you, that he wishes to establish himself in this province, in which he has been residing for some time ; therefore he has recourse to the kindness of this government, praying you to be pleased to grant him a concession of 800 arpens of land in superficie, to be taken on the vacant lands of the King's domain, in the place which will appear more convenient to the interest of your petitioner, who presumes to expect this favor of your justice.

BAPTISTE MARLE.

ST. LOUIS, *December* 16, 1799.

ST. LOUIS OF ILLINOIS, *December* 17, 1799.

Whereas we are assured that the petitioner possesses sufficient means to improve the land which he solicits, I do grant to him and his heirs the land he solicits, provided it is not prejudicial to anybody, and the surveyor, Don Antonio Soulard, shall put the (party) interested in possession of the quantity of land he asks, in a vacant place of the royal domain ; which being executed, he shall make out a plat of survey, delivering the same to the party, with his certificate, in order to enable him to obtain the title in form from the intendant general, to whom alone corresponds, by royal order, the distributing and granting all classes of lands, &c.

CARLOS DEHAULT DELASSUS.

ST. LOUIS, *April* 27, 1833.   Truly translated.

JULIUS DE MUN.

| No. | Name of original claimant. | Arpens. | Nature and date of claim. | By whom granted. | By whom surveyed, date, and situation. |
|---|---|---|---|---|---|
| 96 | Baptiste Marle. | 800 | Concession, 17th December, 1799. | Carlos Dehault Delassus. | James Rankin, D. S., 20th February, 1804. Certified by Soulard, 28th March, 1804. Sixty-five miles north of St. Louis. |

EVIDENCE WITH REFERENCE TO MINUTES AND RECORDS.

*October* 18, 1811.—Board met. Present: John B. C. Lucas, Clement B. Penrose, and Frederick Bates, commissioners.

Louis Labeaume, assignee of Baptiste Marle, claiming 800 arpens of land, situate as above, produces a concession from Charles D. Delassus, lieutenant governor, dated 17th December, 1799 ; a plat of survey as above ; a certified extract of sale made by Marle to claimant, dated 31st October, 1803.

It is the opinion of the board that this claim ought not to be confirmed. (See book No. 5, page 366.)

*March* 25, 1833.—F. R. Conway, esq., appeared, pursuant to adjournment.

Baptiste Marle, by Louis Labeaume's legal representatives, claiming 800 arpens of land. (See book C, pages 345 and 349 ; minutes, No. 5, page 366.) Produces a paper purporting to be a concession from Carlos Dehault Delassus, dated December 17, 1799 ; also a plat of survey, part of the same being torn and missing, embracing 35 concessions of 800 arpens each, and numbered from 1 to 35, inclusive, on which claimant's is No. 11.

M. P. Leduc, duly sworn, says that the signature to the concession is in the proper handwriting of Carlos D. Delassus, and that the torn original survey is in the proper handwriting of Antoine Soulard. (See book No. 6, page 144.)

*August* 24, 1835.—The board met, pursuant to adjournment. Present: F. R. Conway, J. H. Relfe, and F. H. Martin, commissioners.

Baptiste Marle, claiming 800 acres of land. (See book No. 6, page 144.)

The board are unanimously of opinion that this claim ought not to be confirmed. For reasons, see decision in the claim of Louis Lamalice, No. 80.

F. H. MARTIN,
F. R. CONWAY,
JAMES H. RELFE.

Class 2.  No. 97.—<i>St. James Beauvais, claiming 800 arpens.</i>

To Don CARLOS DEHAULT DELASSUS, <i>Lieutenant Governor of Upper Louisiana.</i>

SIR: St. James Beauvais has the honor to represent to you, that he would wish to settle himself in the upper part of this province, where he has been residing for some time; therefore he has recourse to your goodness, praying you will please grant to him a tract of land of eight hundred arpens in superficie, to be taken on the vacant lands of the King's domain, in the place which will appear the most convenient to the interest of your petitioner, who presumes to expect this favor of your justice.

St. LOUIS, <i>September 20, 1800.</i>                                    ST. JAMES × BEAUVAIS.
                                                                              his mark.

St. LOUIS OF ILLINOIS, September 23, 1800.

Whereas we are assured that the petitioner has sufficient means to improve the land which he solicits, I do grant to him and his heirs the land which he solicits, in case it is not prejudicial to anybody, and the surveyor, Don Antonio Soulard, shall put the interested in possession of the quantity of land which he asks, in a vacant place of the royal domain; and this being executed, he shall draw a plat of his survey, delivering the same to the party, with his certificate, in order to serve to him to obtain the title in form, from the intendant general, to whom alone corresponds, by royal order, the distributing and granting all classes of land, &c.

CARLOS DEHAULT DELASSUS.

St. LOUIS, <i>January 7, 1833.</i>  Truly translated.

JULIUS DE MUN.

| No. | Name of original claimant. | Arpens. | Nature and date of claim. | By whom granted. | By whom surveyed, date, and situation. |
|---|---|---|---|---|---|
| 97 | St. James Beauvais, | 800 | Concession, 23d September, 1800 | Carlos Dehault Delassus. | James Rankin, D. S., 20th February, 1804. Certified by Soulard, 28th March, 1804. Sixty-five miles north of St. Louis. |

EVIDENCE WITH REFERENCE TO MINUTES AND RECORDS.

October 18, 1811.—Board met. Present: John B. C. Lucas, Clement B. Penrose, and Frederick Bates, commissioners.

Jacques St. Vrain, assignee of St. Gemme Beauvais, claiming 800 arpens of land, situate as above. Produces a concession from Charles Dehault Delassus, L. G., dated 23d September, 1800; a plat of survey as above; a certified extract of sale made by Beauvais to claimant, dated 8th July, 1804. It is the opinion of the board that this claim ought not to be confirmed. (See book No. 5, page 369.)

January 4, 1833.—F. R. Conway, esq., appeared, pursuant to adjournment, having been authorized by a resolution of the board of commissioners, of the 1st of December last, to receive evidence.

St. Gemme Beauvais, by his legal representative, John Mullanphy, claiming 800 arpens of land. (See record-book C, page 332; minutes, No. 5, page 369.)

Produces a paper purporting to be an original concession from Carlos Dehault Delassus, dated 23d September, 1800; also deeds of conveyance.

M. P. Leduc, being duly sworn, saith that the signature to the said concession is in the proper handwriting of the said Carlos Dehault Delassus. (See book No. 6, page 92.)

August 24, 1835.—The board met, pursuant to adjournment. Present: F. R. Conway, J. H. Relfe, and F. H. Martin, commissioners.

St. Gemme Beauvais, claiming 800 arpens of land. (See book No. 6, page 92.)

The board are unanimously of opinion that this claim ought not to be confirmed. For reasons, see decision in the claim of Louis Lamalice, No. 80.

F. H. MARTIN,
F. R. CONWAY,
JAMES H. RELFE.

Class 2.  No. 98.—<i>Pierre Roussel, claiming 800 arpens.</i>

To Don CARLOS DEHAULT DELASSUS, <i>Lieutenant Governor of Upper Louisiana:</i>

SIR: Pierre Roussel has the honor to represent to you, that having for some time resided in this province, he wishes to settle himself in it; therefore, he has recourse to the benevolence of this government, praying you will please to grant to him a tract of land of 800 arpens in superficie, in a vacant part of the King's domain, which will appear most convenient to the interest of your petitioner, who presumes to expect this favor of your justice.

St. LOUIS, <i>January 21, 1800.</i>                                    PIERRE × ROUSSEL.
                                                                              his mark.

St. Louis of Illinois, *January* 25, 1800.

Whereas we are assured that the petitioner has sufficient means to improve the land which he solicits, I do grant to him and his heirs the land which he solicits, in case it is not prejudicial to anybody, and the surveyor, Don Antonio Soulard, shall put the interested in possession of the quantity of land which he asks, in a vacant place in the royal domain; and this being executed, he shall draw a plat of his survey, delivering the same to the party, and his certificate, in order to serve to him to obtain the title in form from the intendant general, to whom alone corresponds, by royal order, the distributing and granting all classes of lands, &c.

CARLOS DEHAULT DELASSUS.

St. Louis, *January* 7, 1833.    Truly translated.

JULIUS DE MUN.

| No. | Name of original claimant. | Arpens. | Nature and date of claim. | By whom granted. | By whom surveyed, date, and situation. |
|-----|---------------------------|---------|---------------------------|------------------|----------------------------------------|
| 98 | Pierre Roussel. | 800 | Concession, 25th January, 1800. | C. Dehault Delassus. | James Rankin, D. S., 20th February, 1804. Certified by Soulard, 28th March, 1804. On Cuivre river, 65 miles north of St. Louis. |

EVIDENCE WITH REFERENCE TO MINUTES AND RECORDS.

*May* 28, 1806.—The board met, agreeably to adjournment.    Present: Hon. Clement B. Penrose.

The same, (Jacques St. Vrain), assignee of Pierre Roussel, claiming 600 arpens of land, situate on the river Cuivre, district of St. Charles, produces a concession from Charles D. Delassus to the said Roussel, for 800 arpens of land, dated 25th January, 1800; a survey, dated 20th February, certified 28th March, 1804, and a deed of transfer of the same, dated 5th of January, 1804.

The board require further proof of the date of the above concession.

*On behalf of the United States.*    Pierre Roussel, being duly sworn, says that, sometime in March, 1804, (as he believes,) he received from Louis Labeaume a concession for which he never had applied; that some time in January or February, of that same year, Labeaume asked him if he wanted land, to which he replied that he would take it if it was given him; that the said concession did not remain in his possession; and further, that in the said month of March, he signed an assignment of 600 arpens of the same to the above claimant, but received nothing for the same; that he has since sold the 200 remaining arpens to another person; was at the time of receiving said concession twenty-five years of age, had a wife and child; never cultivated the same nor inhabited it, and that he claims no other land in his own name in this territory.

The board reject this claim.    (See book No. 1, page 302.)

*August* 17, 1811.—The board met.    Present: Clement B. Penrose and Frederick Bates, commissioners.

Jacques St. Vrain, assignee of Pierre Roussel, claiming 600 arpens, and Pierre Roussel, claiming 200 arpens of land.    (See book No. 1, page 302.)

It is the opinion of the board that this claim ought not to be confirmed.    (See book No. 5, page 317.)

*January* 4, 1833.—F. R. Conway, esq., appeared, pursuant to adjournment.    Having been authorized by a resolution of the board of commissioners of the 1st of December last, to receive evidence:

Pierre Roussel, by his legal representative, John Mullanphy, claiming 800 arpens of land.    (See book C, page 333 and 334; No. 1, page 302; No. 5, page 317.)    Produces a paper purporting to be an original concession from Carlos Dehault Delassus, dated 25th January, 1800; also deeds of conveyance.

M. P. Leduc, being duly sworn, saith that the signature to the said concession is in the proper handwriting of the said Carlos Dehault Delassus.    (See book No. 6, page 93.)

*August* 24, 1835.—The board met, pursuant to adjournment.    Present: F. R. Conway, J. H. Relfe, and F. H. Martin, commissioners.

Pierre Roussel, claiming 800 arpens of land.    (See book No. 6, page 93.)

The board are unanimously of opinion that this claim ought not to be confirmed.    For reasons, see decision in the claim of Louis Lamalice, No. 80.

F. H. MARTIN,
F. R. CONWAY,
JAMES H. RELFE.

Class 2.    No. 99.—*William Clark, claiming 800 arpens.*

To Don CARLOS DEHAULT DELASSUS, *Lieutenant Governor of Upper Louisiana:*

SIR: William Clark has the honor to represent to you, that residing in this province since several years, he wishes to settle himself in it and form an establishment; therefore he has recourse to your goodness, praying that you will please to grant to him a tract of land of 800 arpens in superficie, to be taken on the vacant land of the King's domain, in the place which will appear most convenient to the interest of your petitioner, who presumes to expect this favor of your justice.

WILLIAM CLARK.

St. Louis, *October* 28, 1800.

St. Louis of Illinois, *October* 30, 1800.

Whereas we are assured that the petitioner has sufficient means to improve the lands which he solicits, I do grant to him and his heirs the land which he solicits, if it is not prejudicial to any person, and the surveyor, Don Antonio Soulard, shall put the interested in possession of the quantity of land which he asks, in a vacant place of the royal domain; and this being executed, he shall draw a plat of his survey, delivering the same to the party, with his certificate, in order to serve to him to obtain the title in form from the intendant general, to whom alone corresponds, by royal order, the distributing and granting all classes of lands, &c.

CARLOS DEHAULT DELASSUS.

St. Louis, *January* 1, 1833.   Truly translated.

JULIUS DE MUN.

| No. | Name of original claimant. | Arpens. | Nature and date of claim. | By whom granted. | By whom surveyed, date, and situation. |
|-----|----------------------------|---------|---------------------------|------------------|----------------------------------------|
| 99 | William Clark. | 800 | Concession, 30th October, 1800. | C. Dehault Delassus. | James Rankin, D. S., 20th February, 1804. Certified by Soulard, 28th March, 1804. On Cuivre river, 65 miles north of St. Louis. |

EVIDENCE WITH REFERENCE TO MINUTES AND RECORDS.

*October* 14, 1811.—Board met.   Present: Clement B. Penrose and Frederick Bates, commissioners.

Jacques St. Vrain, assignee of William Clark, claiming 800 arpens of land, situate as above; produces a concession from Charles D. Delassus, lieutenant general, dated October 30, 1800; a plat of survey as above; a certified extract of sale made by Clark to claimant, dated December 3, 1803.

It is the opinion of the board that this claim ought not to be confirmed.   (See book No. 5, page 369.)

*December* 19, 1832.—F. R. Conway, esq., appeared, pursuant to adjournment.

William Clark, by his legal representative, John Mullanphy, claiming 800 arpens of land.   (See book C, pages 332 and 333; book No. 5, page 369.)   Produces a paper purporting to be an original concession from Carlos Dehault Delassus, dated October 30, 1800.

M. P. Leduc, being duly sworn, saith that the signature to said concession is in the proper handwriting of the said Carlos Dehault Delassus.   (See book No. 6, page 86.)

*August* 24, 1835.—The board met, pursuant to adjournment.   Present: F. R. Conway, J. H. Relfe, and F. H. Martin, commissioners.

William Clark, claiming 800 arpens of land.   (See book No. 6, page 86.)

The board are unanimously of opinion that this claim ought not to be confirmed.   For reasons, see decision in the claim of Louis Lamalice, No. 80.

F. H. MARTIN,<br>F. R. CONWAY,<br>JAMES H. RELFE.

---

Class 2.   No. 100.—Dominique Hugé, claiming 800 arpens.

To Don CARLOS DEHAULT DELASSUS, *Lieutenant Governor of Upper Louisiana:*

Sir: Dominique Hugé has the honor of representing to you, that he would wish to form an establishment in this country, which he has been inhabiting from his infancy, therefore he has recourse to your goodness, praying you will please to grant him a concession for eight hundred arpens of land in superficie, to be taken on the vacant lands of the King's domain, in the place which will appear the most convenient to the interest of your petitioner, who presumes to expect this favor of your justice.

St. Louis, *October* 12, 1799.

DOMINIQUE HUGÉ.

St. Louis of Illinois, October 14, 1799.

Whereas we are assured that the petitioner has sufficient means to improve the land which he solicits, I do grant to him and his heirs the land which he solicits, in case it is not prejudicial to anybody, and the surveyor, Don Antonio Soulard, shall put the interested in possession of the quantity of land which he asks, in a vacant place of the royal domain; and this being executed, he shall draw a plat of his survey, delivering the same to the party, with his certificate, in order to serve to him to obtain the title in form from the intendant general, to whom alone corresponds, by royal order, the distributing and granting all classes of lands.

CARLOS DEHAULT DELASSUS.

St. Louis, *December* 31, 1832.   Truly translated.

JULIUS DE MUN.

| No. | Name of original claimant. | Arpens. | Nature and date of claim. | By whom granted. | By whom surveyed, date, and situation. |
|-----|----------------------------|---------|---------------------------|------------------|----------------------------------------|
| 100 | Dominique Hugé. | 800 | Concession, 14th October, 1799. | Carlos Dehault Delassus. | James Rankin, D. S., 20th February, 1804. Certified by Soulard, 28th March, 1804. Situated on Cuivre river, 65 miles north of St. Louis. |

EVIDENCE WITH REFERENCE TO MINUTES AND RECORDS.

*October* 18, 1811.—Board met. Present: John B. C. Lucas, Clement B. Penrose, and Frederick Bates, commissioners.

Jacques St. Vrain, assignee of Dominique Hugé, claiming 800 arpens of land, situate as above, produces a concession from Charles D. Delassus, L. G., dated October 14, 1799 ; a plat of survey as above ; a certified extract of sale made by Hugé to claimant, dated May 4, 1803.

It is the opinion of the board that this claim ought not to be confirmed. (See book No. 5, page 371.)

*December* 19, 1832.—F. R. Conway, esq., appeared, pursuant to adjournment.

Dominique Hugé, by his legal representative, John Mullanphy, claiming 800 arpens of land. (See book C, page 335 ; book No. 5, page 371.) Produces a paper, purporting to be an original concession from Carlos Dehault Delassus, dated October 14, 1799.

M. P. Leduc, duly sworn, saith that the signature to said concession is in the proper handwriting of said Delassus. (See book No. 6, page 85.)

*August* 24, 1835.—The board met, pursuant to adjournment. Present: F. R. Conway, J. H. Relfe, and F. H. Martin, commissioners.

Dominique Hugé, claiming 800 arpens of land. (See book No. 6, page 85.)

The board are unanimously of opinion that this claim ought not to be confirmed. For reasons, see decision in the claim of Louis Lamalice, No. 80.

F. H. MARTIN,
F. R. CONWAY,
JAMES H. RELFE.

---

Class 2.   No. 101.—*Joseph Dequary, claiming 800 arpens.*

To Don CARLOS DEHAULT DELASSUS, *Lieutenant Governor of Upper Louisiana* :

SIR: Joseph Dequary has the honor to represent to you, that wishing to establish himself in the upper part of this province, where he has been residing for several years, therefore he has recourse to your goodness, hoping you will please to grant him a tract of land of eight hundred arpens in superficie, to be taken upon the vacant lands of the King's domain, in the place which will appear most convenient to the interest of your petitioner, who presumes to expect this favor of your justice.

his
JOSEPH × DEQUARY.
mark.

ST. LOUIS, *March* 6, 1802.

ST. LOUIS OF ILLINOIS, *March* 8, 1802.

Whereas we are assured that the petitioner has sufficient means to improve the land which he solicits, I do grant to him and his heirs the land which he solicits, if it does not do prejudice to any one, and the surveyor, Don Antonio Soulard, shall put the interested in possession of the quantity of land which he asks, on a vacant place of the royal domain ; and this being executed, he shall draw a plat of his survey, delivering the same to the party, with his certificate, in order to serve to him to obtain the concession and title in form from the intendant general, to whom alone corresponds, by royal order, the distributing and granting all classes of lands of the royal domain.

CARLOS DEHAULT DELASSUS.

ST. LOUIS, *December* 31, 1832.   Truly translated.

JULIUS DE MUN.

| No. | Name of original claimant. | Arpens. | Nature and date of claim. | By whom granted. | By whom surveyed, date, and situation. |
|-----|----------------------------|---------|---------------------------|------------------|----------------------------------------|
| 101 | Joseph Decarry. | 800 | Concession, 8th March, 1802. | Carlos Dehault Delassus. | James Rankin, D. S., 20th February, 1804. Certified by Soulard, 28th March, 1804. On Cuivre river, 65 miles from St. Louis. |

EVIDENCE WITH REFERENCE TO MINUTES AND RECORDS.

*October* 18, 1811.—Board met. Present: John B. C. Lucas, Clement B. Penrose, and Frederick Bates, commissioners.

Jacques St. Vrain, assignee of John Baptiste (Joseph) Decarry, claiming 800 arpens of land, situate as above, produces a concession from Charles D. Delassus, lieutenant governor, dated 8th March, 1802 ; a plat of survey as above ; a certified extract of sale made by Decarry to claimant, dated 4th June, 1803.

It is the opinion of the board that this claim ought not to be confirmed. (See book No. 5, page 371.)

*December* 19, 1832.—F. R. Conway, esq., appeared, pursuant to adjournment.

Joseph Decarry, by his legal representative, John Mullanphy, claiming 800 arpens of land. (See book C, page 335 ; book No. 5, page 371.) Produces a paper, purporting to be an original concession from Carlos Dehault Delassus, dated 8th March, 1802.

M. P. Leduc, being duly sworn, saith that the signature to the aforesaid concession is in the proper handwriting of the said Carlos Dehault Delassus. (See book No. 6, page 85.)

*August* 24, 1835.—The board met, pursuant to adjournment.  Present: F. R. Conway, J. H. Relfe, and F. H. Martin, commissioners.

Joseph Decarry, claiming 800 arpens of land.  (See book No. 6, page 85.)

The board are unanimously of opinion that this claim ought not to be confirmed.  For reasons, see decisions in the claim of Louis Lamalice, No. 80.

F. H. MARTIN,<br>
F. R. CONWAY,<br>
JAMES H. RELFE.

Class 2.  No. 102.—J. Bte. Dumoulin, claiming 800 arpens.

To Don CARLOS DEHAULT DELASSUS, *Lieutenant Governor of Upper Louisiana:*

SIR: Jno. Bte. Dumoulin, an inhabitant of this town, has the honor to represent to you that he would wish to form a plantation in this province, in which he has been residing several years; and having a numerous family, he claims of the benevolence of this government, and prays you to grant him a tract of land of eight hundred arpens in superficie, to be taken on the vacant lands of the King's domain, in the place which will appear most convenient to his interest.  Favor which the petitioner presumes to hope of your justice.

ST. LOUIS, *November* 3, 1800.

DUMOULIN.

ST. LOUIS OF ILLINOIS, *November* 7, 1800.

Whereas we are assured that the petitioner has sufficient means to improve the land which he solicits, I do grant to him and to his heirs the land which he solicits, if it does prejudice to nobody, and the surveyor, Don Antonio Soulard, shall put the interested in possession of the quantity of land which he asks, in a vacant place of the royal domain; and this being executed, he shall draw a plat of his survey, which he shall deliver to the party, with his certificate, in order to serve to him to obtain the concession and title in form from the intendant general, to whom alone corresponds, by royal order, the distributing and granting all classes of lands of the royal domain.

CARLOS DEHAULT DELASSUS.

ST. LOUIS, *January* 1, 1833.  Truly translated.

JULIUS DE MUN.

| No. | Name of original claimant. | Arpens. | Nature and date of claim. | By whom granted. | By whom surveyed, date, and situation. |
|---|---|---|---|---|---|
| 102 | J. Bte. Dumoulin. | 800 | Concession, 7th November. 1801. | Carlos Dehault Delassus. | James Rankin, D. S., 20th February, 1804. Certified by Soulard, 28th March, 1804. On Cuivre river, 65 miles north of St. Louis. |

EVIDENCE WITH REFERENCE TO MINUTES AND RECORDS.

*October* 18, 1811.—Board met.  Present: John B. C. Lucas, Clement B. Penrose, and Frederick Bates, commissioners.

Jacques St. Vrain, assignee of John Baptiste Dumoulin, claiming 800 arpens of land, situate as above, produces a concession from Charles D. Delassus, L. G., dated 7th November, 1800; a plat of survey as above; a certified extract of sale, made 12th May, 1803, by Dumoulin, to claimant.

It is the opinion of the board that this claim ought not to be confirmed.  (See book No. 5, page 370.)

*December* 19, 1832.—F. R. Conway, esq., appeared, pursuant to adjournment.

John Baptiste Dumoulin, by his legal representative, John Mullanphy, claiming 800 arpens of land.  (See book C, page 334; book No. 5, page 370.)  Produces a paper, purporting to be an original concession from Carlos Dehault Delassus, dated November 7, 1800.

M. P. Leduc, being duly sworn, saith that the signature to the above-mentioned concession is in the proper handwriting of the said Carlos Dehault Delassus.  (See book No. 6, page 87.)

*August* 24, 1835.—The board met, pursuant to adjournment.  Present: F. R. Conway, J. H. Relfe, and F. H. Martin, commissioners.

Jean B. Dumoulin, claiming 800 arpens of land.  (See book No. 6, page 87.)

The board are unanimously of opinion that this claim ought not to be confirmed.  For reasons, see decision in the claim of Louis Lamalice, No. 80.

F. H. MARTIN,<br>
F. R. CONWAY,<br>
JAMES H. RELFE.

Class 2.  No. 103.—Joseph Hebert, claiming 800 arpens.

To Don CARLOS DEHAULT DELASSUS, *Lieutenant Governor of Upper Louisiana:*

SIR: Joseph Hebert has the honor of representing to you, that wishing to form an establishment in the upper part of this province, in which he has been inhabiting since his childhood, therefore he prays you to grant to him a tract of land of 800 arpens in superficie, to be taken on the vacant lands of the King's domain, in the place which will appear the most advantageous and most convenient to the interest of your petitioner, who presumes to expect this favour of your justice.

St. Louis, *April* 14, 1800.

JOSEPH <sup>his</sup> × HEBERT.
mark.

St. Louis of Illinois, *April* 15, 1800.

Whereas we are assured that the petitioner has sufficient means to improve the land which he solicits, I do grant to him and his heirs the land which he solicits, if it is not prejudicial to any person, and the surveyor, Don Antonio Soulard, shall put the interested in possession of the quantity of land which he asks, in a vacant place of the royal domain; and this being executed, he shall draw a plat of his survey, delivering the same to the party, with his certificate, in order to serve to him to obtain the title in form from the intendant general, to whom alone corresponds, by royal order, the distributing and granting all classes of lands, &c.

CARLOS DEHAULT DELASSUS.

St. Louis, *December* 31, 1832.   Truly translated.

JULIUS DE MUN.

| No. | Name of original claimant. | Arpens. | Nature and date of claim. | By whom granted. | By whom surveyed, date, and situation. |
|---|---|---|---|---|---|
| 103 | Joseph Hebert. | 800 | Concession, 15th April, 1800. | Carlos Dehault Delassus. | James Rankin, D. S., 20th Feb., 1804. Certified by Soulard, 28th March, 1804. On Cuivre river, 65 miles north of St. Louis. |

EVIDENCE WITH REFERENCE TO MINUTES AND RECORDS.

*May* 28, 1806.—The board met, agreeably to adjournment.   Present: Hon. Clement B. Penrose.

The same, (Jacques St. Vrain,) assignee of Joseph Hebert, claiming 600 arpens of land, situate as aforesaid, produces a concession from Charles Dehault Delassus to the said Hebert, for 800 arpens, dated April 15, 1800; a survey of the same, dated February 20, and certified March 28, 1804; and a transfer, dated January 10, 1804. The board require further proof of the date of the above concession.   (See book No. 1, page 303.)

*August* 17, 1811.—Board met.   Present: Clement B. Penrose and Frederick Bates, commissioners.

Jacques St. Vrain, assignee of Joseph Hebert, claiming 600 arpens, and Joseph Hebert, claiming 200 arpens of land.   (See book No. 1, page 303.)   It is the opinion of the board that this claim ought not to be confirmed. (See book No. 5, page 317.)

*December* 19, 1832.—F. R. Conway, esq., appeared, pursuant to adjournment.

Joseph Hebert, by his legal representative, John Mullanphy, claiming 800 arpens of land.   (See book C, page 336; book No. 1, page 303; No. 5, page 317.)   Produces a paper purporting to be an original concession from Carlos Dehault Delassus, dated April 15, 1800, (also deed of conveyance.)

M. P. Leduc, being duly sworn, saith that the signature to the above concession is in the proper hand-writing of the said Carlos Dehault Delassus.   (See book No. 6, page 86.)

*August* 24, 1835.—The board met, pursuant to adjournment.   Present: F. R. Conway, J. H. Relfe, and F. H. Martin, commissioners.

Joseph Hebert, claiming 800 arpens of land.   (See book No. 6, page 86.)

The board are unanimously of opinion that this claim ought not to be confirmed.   For reasons, see decision in the claim of Louis Lamalice, No. 80.

F. H. MARTIN,
F. R. CONWAY,
JAMES H. RELFE.

Class 2.   No. 104.—*Regis Vasseur, claiming* 800 *arpens.*

To Don Carlos Dehault Delassus, *Lieutenant Governor of Upper Louisiana* :

Sir : Regis Vasseur, an ancient inhabitant of this town, has the honor to represent to you, that wishing to settle himself in the upper part of this province, therefore he has recourse to your goodness, praying that you will please to grant to him a concession for eight hundred arpens of land in superficie, to be taken on the vacant lands of his Majesty's domain, in the place that will be found the most favorable to the interest of your petitioner, who presumes to expect this favor of your justice.

REGIS <sup>his</sup> × VASSEUR.
mark.

St. Louis, *December* 21, 1799.

St. Louis of Illinois, *December* 23, 1799.

Whereas we are assured that the petitioner has sufficient means to improve the land which he solicits, I do grant to him and his heirs the land which he solicits, if it is not prejudicial to anybody, and the surveyor, Don Antonio Soulard, shall put the interested in possession of the quantity of land which he asks, in a vacant place of the royal domain; and this being executed, he shall draw a plat of his survey, delivering the same to the party, with the certificate, in order to serve to him to obtain the title in form from the intendant general, to whom alone corresponds, by royal order, the distributing and granting all classes of lands.

CARLOS DEHAULT DELASSUS.

St. Louis, *December* 31, 1832.   Truly translated.

JULIUS DE MUN.

*Regis Vasseur, claiming 800 arpens.*

| No. | Name of original claimant. | Arpens. | Nature and date of claim. | By whom granted. | By whom surveyed, date, and situation. |
|---|---|---|---|---|---|
| 104 | Regis Vasseur. | 800 | Concession, December 23, 1799. | Carlos Dehault Delassus. | James Rankin, D. S., February 20, 1804. Certified by Soulard, March 28, 1804. On Cuivre river, sixty-five miles north of St. Louis. |

EVIDENCE WITH REFERENCE TO MINUTES AND RECORDS.

*October* 18, 1811.—The board met. Present: John B. C. Lucas, Clement B. Penrose, and Frederick Bates, commissioners.

Jacques St. Vrain, assignee of Regis Vasseur, claiming 800 arpens of land, situate as above, produces a concession from Charles D. Delassus, L. G., dated September 23, 1799; a plat of survey as above; a certified extract of sale made by Vasseur to claimant, dated August 5, 1803. It is the opinion of the board that this claim ought not to be confirmed. (See page 370, book No. 5.)

*December* 19, 1832.—F. R. Conway, esq., appeared, pursuant to adjournment.

Regis Vasseur, by his legal representative, John Mullanphy, claiming 800 arpens of land. (See book C, pages 334 and 335; book No. 5, page 370.) Produces a paper, purporting to be an original concession from Charles Dehault Delassus, dated December 23, 1799; also deeds of conveyance.

M. P. Leduc, being duly sworn, saith that the signature to the said concession is in the proper handwriting of the above-named Carlos Dehault Delassus. (See book No. 6, page 85.)

*August* 24, 1835.—The board met, pursuant to adjournment. Present: F. R. Conway, J. H. Relfe, and F. H. Martin, commissioners.

Regis Vasseur, claiming 800 arpens of land. (See book No. 6, page 85.)

The board are unanimously of opinion that this claim ought not to be confirmed. For reasons, see decision in the claim of Louis Lamalice, No. 80.

F. H. MARTIN,<br>
F. R. CONWAY,<br>
JAMES H. RELFE.

Class 2. No. 105.—*Jean Louis Marc, claiming 800 arpens.*

To Don CARLOS DEHAULT DELASSUS, *Lieutenant Governor of Upper Louisiana:*

SIR: Jean Louis Marc has the honor to represent to you, that having resided in this province since several years, he would wish to establish himself; therefore he has recourse to your goodness, hoping that you will be pleased to grant to him a tract of land of 800 arpens in superficie, to be taken on the vacant lands of his Majesty's domain, in the place which shall appear most convenient to the interest of your petitioner, who presumes to expect this favor of your justice.

ST. LOUIS, *January* 20, 1800.

JEAN LOUIS MARC.

ST. LOUIS OF ILLINOIS, *January* 24, 1800.

Whereas we are assured that the petitioner possesses sufficient means to improve the land which he solicits, I do grant to him and his heirs the land he solicits, provided that it is not prejudicial to any person, and the surveyor, Don Antonio Soulard, shall put the interested (party) in possession of the quantity of land he asks, in a vacant place of the royal domain; and this being executed, he shall make out a plat of his survey, delivering the same to the said party, with his certificate, in order to enable him to obtain the title in form from the intendant general, to whom alone corresponds, by royal order, the distributing and granting all classes of lands, &c.

CARLOS DEHAULT DELASSUS.

ST. LOUIS, *April* 17, 1833. Truly translated.

JULIUS DE MUN.

| No. | Name of original claimant. | Arpens. | Nature and date of claim. | By whom granted. | By whom surveyed, date, and situation. |
|---|---|---|---|---|---|
| 105 | Jean Louis Marc. | 800 | Concession, 24th January, 1800. | Carlos Dehault Delassus. | James Rankin, D. S., 20th February, 1804. Certified by Soulard. 28th March, 1804. Sixty-five miles north of St. Louis. |

EVIDENCE WITH REFERENCE TO MINUTES AND RECORDS.

*October* 18, 1811.—Board met. Present: John B. C. Lucas, Clement B. Penrose, and Frederick Bates, commissioners.

Louis Labeaume, assignee of Jean Louis Marc, claiming 600 arpens, and said Marc, claiming 200 arpens, situate as above, produces a concession from Charles D. Delassus, L. G., dated 24th January, 1800 ; a plat of survey as above ; a transfer from Marc to claimant, dated 9th January, 1804. It is the opinion of the board that this claim ought not to be confirmed. (See book No. 5, page 366.)

*March* 25, 1833.--F. R. Conway, esq., appeared, pursuant to adjournment.

Jean Louis Marc, by Louis Labeaume's legal representatives, claiming 800 arpens of land. (See book C, pages 345 and 349 ; minutes, No. 5, page 366 ;) produces a paper purporting to be an original concession from Carlos D. Delassus, dated January 24th, 1800 ; also, a plat of survey, part of the same being torn and missing, embracing 35 concessions, of 800 arpens each, and numbered from 1 to 35, inclusive, on which claimant is No. 9 ; also, a deed dated January 9th, 1804.

M. P. Leduc, duly sworn, says that the signature to the concession is in the proper handwriting of Carlos Dehault Delassus, and that the torn original survey is in the proper handwriting of Antonio Soulard. (See book No. 6, page 144.)

*August* 24, 1835.--The board met, pursuant to adjournment. Present : F. R. Conway, J. H. Relfe, and F. H. Martin, commissioners.

Jean Louis Marc, claiming 800 arpens of land. (See book No. 6, page 144.)

The board are unanimously of opinion that this claim ought not to be confirmed. For reasons, see decision in the claim of Louis Lamalice, No. 80.

F. H. MARTIN,<br>
F. R. CONWAY,<br>
JAMES H. RELFE.

Class 2.   No. 106.--*James Haff, claiming 800 arpens.*

To Don CARLOS DEHAULT DELASSUS, *Lieutenant Governor of Upper Louisiana :*

SIR : James Haff has the honor to represent that he would wish to settle himself in the upper part of this province, where he has resided since several years ; therefore he has recourse to the beneficence of this government, praying that you may be pleased to grant him a tract of land of 800 arpens in superficie, to be taken on the domain of his Majesty, in any vacant place which will appear most convenient to the interest of your petitioner, who presumes to expect this favor of your justice.

JAMES $\times$ HAFF.<br>
his   mark.

ST. LOUIS, *November* 14, 1800.

ST. LOUIS OF ILLINOIS, *November* 15, 1800.

Whereas we are assured that the petitioner possesses sufficient means to improve the land which he solicits, I do grant to him and his heirs the land he solicits, provided it is not to the prejudice of any person, and the surveyor, Don Antonio Soulard, shall put the party interested in possession of the quantity of land he asks, in a vacant place of the royal domain ; and this being executed, he shall make out a plat, delivering the same to the party, together with his certificate, in order to serve to him to obtain the title in form from the intendant general, to whom alone belongs, by royal order, the distributing and granting all classes of lands belonging to the royal domain.

CARLOS DEHAULT DELASSUS.

ST. LOUIS, *August* 20, 1834.    Truly translated from record-book C, page 333.

JULIUS DE MUN, *T. B. C.*

| No. | Name of original claimant. | Arpens. | Name and date of claim. | By whom granted. | By whom surveyed, date, and situation. |
|---|---|---|---|---|---|
| 106 | James Haff. | 800 | Concession, 15th November, 1800. | Carlos Dehault Delassus. | James Rankin, D. S., 20th February, 1804. Certified 28th March, 1804, by Soulard, S. G.  On Cuivre river. |

EVIDENCE WITH REFERENCE TO MINUTES AND RECORDS.

*October* 18, 1811.--The board met.    Present : Hon. B. C. Lucas, Clement B. Penrose, and Frederick Bates, commissioners.

Jacques St. Vrain, assignee of James Haff, claiming 800 arpens of land, situate as above, produces a concession from Charles D. Delassus, lieutenant governor, dated 5th November, 1800; a plat of survey as above; a certified extract of sale made by Haff to claimant, dated 3d September, 1803.

It is the opinion of the board that this claim ought not to be confirmed. (See book No. 5, page 370.)

*June* 26, 1834.--The board met, pursuant to adjournment.    Present : J. S. Mayfield and F. R. Conway, commissioners.

James Haff, by his legal representatives, claiming 800 arpens of land. (See record book C, pages 333 and 349 ; minutes, book No. 5, page 370. See book No. 6, page 537.)

*August* 24, 1835.--The board met, pursuant to adjournment. Present : F. R. Conway, James H. Relfe, F. H. Martin, commissioners.

James Haff, claiming 800 arpens of land. (See book No. 6, page 537.)

The board are unanimously of opinion that this claim ought not to be confirmed. For reasons, see decision in the claim of Louis Lamalice, No. 80.

F. H. MARTIN,<br>
F. R. CONWAY,<br>
JAMES H. RELFE.

Class 2.   No. 107.—*Louis Grimard, claiming 800 arpens.*

To Don CHARLES DEHAULT DELASSUS, *Lieutenant Governor of Upper Louisiana :*

SIR : Louis Grimard, alias Charpentier, has the honor to represent that he would wish to make an establishment in the upper part of this province, where he has been residing for some time ; therefore he has recourse to your goodness, praying that you may be pleased to grant him a tract of land of 800 arpens in superficie, to be taken on the vacant lands of the King's domain, in the place which will appear most convenient to the interest of your petitioner, who presumes to expect this favor of your justice.

his<br>
LOUIS × GRIMARD.<br>
mark.

ST. LOUIS, *November* 15, 1799.

ST. LOUIS OF ILLINOIS, November 17, 1799.

Whereas we are assured that the petitioner possesses sufficient means to improve the land which he solicits, I do grant to him and his heirs the land he solicits, provided it is not to the prejudice of any one, and the surveyor, Don Antonio Soulard, shall put the party interested in possession of the quantity of land he asks, in a vacant place of the royal domain ; and this being executed, he shall make out a plat, delivering the same to the said party, together with his certificate, in order to serve to him to obtain the title in form from the intendant general, to whom alone belongs, by royal order, the distributing and granting all classes of lands, &c.

CARLOS DEHAULT DELASSUS.

ST. LOUIS, *August* 20, 1834.   Truly translated from record book C, page 334.

JULIUS DE MUN, T. B. C.

| No. | Name of original claimant. | Arpens. | Nature and date of claim. | By whom granted. | By whom surveyed, date, and situation. |
|---|---|---|---|---|---|
| 107 | Louis Grimar, or Grimaud, alias Charpentier. | 800 | Concession, 17th November, 1799. | Charles Dehault Delassus. | James Rankin, D. S., 20th February, 1804. Certified 28th March, 1804, by A. Soulard, S. G. On Cuivre river. |

EVIDENCE WITH REFERENCE TO MINUTES AND RECORDS.

*October* 18, 1811.—Board met.   Present: John B. C. Lucas, Clement B. Penrose, and Frederick Bates, commissioners.

Jacques St. Vrain, assignee of Louis Grimar, dit Charpentier, claiming 800 arpens of land, situate as above, produces a concession from Charles D. Delassus, L. G., dated 17th of November, 1799 ; a plat of survey as above ; a certified extract of sale made by Grimar to claimant, dated 5th of August, 1803.

It is the opinion of the board that this claim ought not to be confirmed.   (See No. 5, page 570.)

*June* 26, 1834.—The board met, pursuant to adjournment.   Present: J. S. Mayfield, F. R. Conway, commissioners.

Louis Grimar or Grimaud, alias Charpentier, by his legal representatives, claiming 800 arpens of land.   (See record-book C, pages 334 and 349 ; minutes, book No. 5, page 370.   See book No. 6, page 537.)

*August* 24, 1835.—The board met, pursuant to adjournment.   Present: F. R. Conway, James H. Relfe, and F. H. Martin, commissioners.

Louis Grimar or Grimaud, claiming 800 arpens of land.   (See book No. 6, page 537.)

The board are unanimously of opinion that this claim ought not to be confirmed.   For reasons, see decision in the claim of Louis Lamalice, No. 80.

F. H. MARTIN,<br>
F. R. CONWAY,<br>
JAMES H. RELFE.

---

Class 2.   No. 108.—*Jean Godineau, claiming 800 arpens.*

To Don CARLOS DEHAULT DELASSUS, *Lieutenant Governor of Upper Louisiana :*

SIR : Jean Godineau has the honor to represent to you, that residing in this province since several years, he would wish to form in the same an establishment ; in consequence, he has recourse to the kindness of this government, praying that you will be pleased to grant to him a tract of land of 800 arpens in superficie, to be taken on the vacant lands of the King's domain, in the place which will appear most convenient to the interest of your petitioner, who presumes to expect this favor of your justice.

his<br>
JEAN × GODINEAU.<br>
mark.

ST. LOUIS, *May* 5, 1800.

ST. LOUIS OF ILLINOIS, May 7, 1800.

Whereas we are assured that the petitioner possesses sufficient means to improve the land which he solicits, I grant to him and his heirs the land he solicits, provided it is not prejudicial to anybody, and the surveyor, Don Antonio Soulard, shall put the party interested in possession of the quantity of land demanded, in a vacant place of the royal domain ; and this being executed, he shall make out a plat of survey delivering the same to said party, with his certificate, in order to enable him to obtain the title in form from the intendant general, to whom alone corresponds, by royal order, the distributing and granting all classes of lands, &c.

CARLOS DEHAULT DELASSUS.

St. Louis, *April* 11, 1833.   Truly translated.

JULIUS DE MUN.

| No. | Name of original claimant. | Arpens. | Nature and date of claim. | By whom granted. | By whom surveyed, date, and situation. |
|---|---|---|---|---|---|
| 108 | Jean Godineau. | 800 | Concession, 7th May, 1800. | Carlos Dehault Delassus. | James Rankin, D. S., 20th February, 1804. Certified by Soulard, 28th March, 1804 Sixty-five miles north of St. Louis. |

EVIDENCE WITH REFERENCE TO MINUTES AND RECORDS.

*October* 18, 1811.—Board met.   Present: John B. C. Lucas, Clement B. Penrose, and Frederick Bates, commissioners.

Louis Labeaume, assignee of Jean Godineau, claiming 800 arpens of land, situated as above, produces a plat of survey as above.

It is the opinion of the board that this claim ought not to be confirmed.   (See book No. 5, page 369.)

*March* 21, 1833.—F. R. Conway, esq., appeared, pursuant to adjournment, being authorized to receive evidence by a resolution of this board, taken the 9th instant.

Jean Godineau, by his legal representative, J. P. Labanné, claiming 800 arpens of land.   (See book C, page 349.   For survey, see book F, pages 54 and 55 ; minutes, No. 5, page 369.)   Produces a paper purporting to be an original concession from Carlos Dehault Delassus, dated May 7, 1804 ; also, two deeds of conveyance from Godineau to Labeaume ; also, a deed of conveyance from Benoist to Cabanné.

M. P. Leduc, duly sworn, says that the signature to the concession is in the proper handwriting of Carlos Dehault Delassus.   (See book No. 6, page 135.)

*August* 24, 1835.—The board met, pursuant to adjournment.   Present: F. R. Conway, J. H. Relfe, and F. H. Martin, commissioners.

Jean Godineau, claiming 800 arpens of land.   (See book No. 6, page 135.)

The board are unanimously of opinion that this claim ought not to be confirmed.   For reasons, see decision in the claim of Louis Lamalice, No. 80.

F. H. MARTIN,
F. R. CONWAY,
JAMES H. RELFE.

Class 2.   No. 109.—*Antoine Dejarlais, claiming* 800 *arpens.*

To Don CARLOS DEHAULT DELASSUS, *Lieutenant Governor of Upper Louisiana :*

SIR : Antoine Dejarlais has the honor to represent, that having resided for a long time in this country, he wishes to make an establishment in the same, therefore he has recourse to your goodness, praying that you may be pleased to grant to him a tract of land of 800 arpens in superficie, to be taken on the vacant lands of the King's domain, in the place which shall appear most advantageous to the interest of your petitioner, who presumes to expect this favor of your justice.

ANTOINE × DEJARLAIS.
his
mark.

St. Louis, *March* 17, 1800.

St. Louis of Illinois, *March* 19, 1800.

Whereas we are assured that the petitioner possesses sufficient means to improve the land which he solicits, I do grant him and his heirs the land he solicits, provided it is not to the prejudice of any person, and the surveyor, Don Antonio Soulard, shall put the party interested in possession of the quantity of land he asks, in a vacant place of the royal domain ; and this being executed, he shall make out a plat, delivering the same to said party, together with his certificate, in order serve to him to obtain the title in form from the intendant general, to whom alone belongs, by royal order, the distributing and granting all classes of lands, &c.

CARLOS DEHAULT DELASSUS.

St. Louis, *August* 24, 1834.   Truly translated from book C, page 334, of record in the recorder's office.

JULIUS DE MUN, *T. B. C.*

| No. | Name of original claimant. | Arpens. | Nature and date of claim. | By whom granted. | By whom surveyed, date, and situation. |
|---|---|---|---|---|---|
| 109 | Antoine Dejarlais. | 800 | Concession, 19th March, 1800. | Carlos Dehault Delassus. | James Rankin, D. S., 20th February, 1804. Certified 28th March, 1804, by A. Soulard, surveyor general.   On Cuivre river. |

*May* 23, 1806.—The board met, agreeably to adjournment.   Present : Hon. Clement B. Penrose.

The same (Jacques St. Vrain), assignee of Antoine Dejarlais, claiming 600 arpens of land, situated on Cuivre river, district of St. Charles, produces a concession from Charles D. Delassus to the said Dejarlais, for 800 arpens, dated March 19, 1800 ; a survey of the same, taken the 20th February, and certified 28th of March, 1804 ; and a deed of transfer of the same, dated the 10th December, 1803.

The board require further proof of the date of the above concession.

The board reject this claim.   (See book No. 1, page 303.)

*August* 17, 1811.—The board met.   Present : Clement B. Penrose and Frederick Bates, commissioners.

Jacques St. Vrain, assignee of Antoine Dejarlais, claiming 600 arpens, and Antoine Dejarlais, claiming 200 arpens of land.   (See book No. 1, page 303.)

It is the opinion of the board that this claim ought not to be confirmed.   (See book No. 5, page 317.)

*June* 26, 1834.—The board met, pursuant to adjournment.   Present : J. S. Mayfield, F. R. Conway, commissioners.

Antoine Dejarlais, by his legal representatives, claiming 800 arpens of land.   (See record-book C, pages 334 and 349 ; minutes, book No. 1, page 303, and No. 5, page 317.   See book No. 6, page 537.)

*August* 24, 1835.—The board met, pursuant to adjournment.   Present : F. R. Conway, J. H. Relfe, and F. H. Martin, commissioners.

Antoine Dejarlais, claiming 800 arpens of land.   (See book No. 6, page 537.)

The board are unanimously of opinion that this claim ought not to be confirmed.   For reasons, see decision in the claim of Louis Lamalice, No. 80.

F. H. MARTIN,
F. R. CONWAY,
JAMES H. RELFE.

---

Class 2.   No. 110.—*Benjamin Quick, claiming 800 arpens.*

To Don CARLOS DEHAULT DELASSUS, *Lieutenant Governor of Upper Louisiana :*

SIR :  Benjamin Quick has the honor to represent, that he would wish to make an establishment in the upper part of this province, where he has been residing for some time, the petitioner pledging himself to submit to the duties and taxes which it may please his Majesty to establish ; therefore the petitioner prays you, sir, to grant him a tract of land of 800 arpens in superficie, to be taken on the vacant lands of his Majesty's domains, in the place which will appear most advantageous to his interest ; a favor which the petitioner presumes to expect of your justice.

                           his
BENJAMIN ×  QUICK.
                         mark.

ST. LOUIS, *March* 6, 1801.

ST. LOUIS OF ILLINOIS, *March* 10, 1801.

Whereas it is notorious that the petitioner possesses sufficient means to obtain the concession which he solicits, I do grant to him and his heirs the land he solicits, provided it is not to the prejudice of anybody, and the surveyor, Don Antonio Soulard, shall put the party interested in possession of the quantity of land he asks, in a vacant place of the royal domain ; and this being executed, he shall make out a plat, delivering the same to said party, together with his certificate, in order to serve to him to obtain the concession and title in form from the intendant general, to whom alone belongs, by royal order, the distributing and granting all classes of lands, &c.

CARLOS DEHAULT DELASSUS.

ST. LOUIS, *August* 20, 1814.   Truly translated from record-book C, page 335.

JULIUS DE MUN, *T. B. C.*

| No. | Name of original claimant. | Arpens. | Nature and date of claim. | By whom granted. | By whom surveyed, date, and situation. |
|---|---|---|---|---|---|
| 110 | Benjamin Quick. | 800 | Concession, 10th March, 1801. | Carlos Dehault De-lassus. | James Rankin, D. S., 20th Feb., 1804.  Certified 28th March, 1804, by A. Soulard, surveyor general. On Cuivre river. |

*May* 28, 1806.—The board met, agreeably to adjournment.   Present : Hon. Clement B. Penrose.

The same, (Jacques St. Vrain,) assignee of Benjamin Quick, claiming 600 arpens of land, situate as aforesaid, produces a concession from Charles D. Delassus to the said Quick for 800 arpens, dated March 10, 1801 ; a survey of the same, dated 20th February, and certified 28th March, 1804 ; and a transfer, dated December 6, 1803.

The board cannot act.   (See No. 5, page 303.)

*August* 17, 1811.—Board met.   Present : Clement B. Penrose and Frederick Bates, commissioners.

Jacques St. Vrain, assignee of Benjamin Quick, claiming 600 arpens of land, and Benjamin Quick, claiming 200 arpens.   (See book No. 1, page 303.)

It is the opinion of the board that this claim ought not to be confirmed.   (See book No. 5, page 317.)

*June* 26, 1834.—The board met, pursuant to adjournment.   Present : J. S. Mayfield and F. R. Conway, commissioners.

Benjamin Quick, by his legal representatives, claiming 800 arpens of land. (See record-book C, pages 335 and 349; minute-books, No. 1, page 303, and No. 5, page 317. See No. 6, page 538.)

*August 24, 1835.*—The board met, pursuant to adjournment. Present: F. R. Conway, J. H. Relfe, and F. H. Martin, commissioners.

Benjamin Quick, claiming 800 arpens of land. (See book No. 6, page 538.)

The board are unanimously of opinion that this claim ought not to be confirmed. For reasons, see decision in the claim of Louis Lamalice, No. 80.

F. H. MARTIN,
F. R. CONWAY,
JAMES H. RELFE.

---

Class 2. No. 111.—*Jean Derouin, claiming 800 arpens.*

To Don CARLOS DEHAULT DELASSUS, *Lieutenant Governor of Upper Louisiana:*

SIR: John Derouin has the honor to represent to you, that he would wish to establish himself in this Upper Louisiana, where he has been residing since his infancy; therefore he prays you to be pleased to grant to him a tract of land of 800 arpens in superficie, to be taken on the vacant lands of the King's domain, in the place which shall be most convenient to the interest of your petitioner, who presumes to expect this favor of your justice.

his
JEAN x DEROUIN.
mark.

ST. LOUIS, *October 4, 1799.*

ST. LOUIS OF ILLINOIS, *October 5, 1799.*

Whereas we are assured that the petitioner possesses sufficient means to improve the land which he solicits, I do grant to him and his heirs the land he solicits, provided it is not prejudicial to any person, and the surveyor, Don Antonio Soulard, shall put the party interested in possession of the quantity of land he asks, in a vacant place of the royal domain; which being executed, he shall make out a plat of his survey, delivering the same to the party, with his certificate, in order to enable him to obtain the title in form from the intendant general, to whom alone corresponds, by royal order, the distributing and granting all classes of lands, &c.

CARLOS DEHAULT DELASSUS.

ST. LOUIS, *April 27, 1833.* Truly translated.

JULIUS DE MUN.

| No. | Name of original claimant. | Arpens. | Nature and date of claim. | By whom granted. | By whom surveyed, date, and situation. |
|---|---|---|---|---|---|
| 111 | Jean Derouin. | 800 | Concession, October 5, 1799. | Carlos Dehault Delassus. | James Rankin, D. S., 20th February, 1804. Certified by Soulard, 28th March, 1804. Sixty-five miles north of St. Louis. |

EVIDENCE WITH REFERENCE TO MINUTES AND RECORDS.

*October 18, 1811.*—Board met. Present: John B. C. Lucas, Clement B. Penrose, and Frederick Bates, commissioners.

Louis Labeaume, assignee of Jean Derouin, claiming 800 arpens of land, situate as above, produces a concession from Charles Dehault Delassus, lieutenant governor, dated October 5, 1799; a plat of survey as above; a certified extract of sale made by Derouin to claimant, dated September 3, 1803. It is the opinion of the board that this claim ought not to be confirmed. (See book No. 5, page 365.)

*March 25, 1833.*—F. R. Conway, esq., appeared, pursuant to adjournment.

Jean Derouin, by Louis Labeaume's legal representatives, claiming 800 arpens of land. (See book C, pages 343 and 349; minutes, No. 5, page 365.) Produces a paper purporting to be an original concession from Charles D. Delassus, dated October 5, 1799; also a plat of survey (part of said paper torn and missing) embracing 35 concessions of 800 arpens each, numbered from 1 to 35 inclusive, on which claimant is No. 4.

M. P. Leduc, duly sworn, says that the signature to the concession is in the proper handwriting of Charles D. Delassus, and that the torn original survey is in the proper handwriting of Antonio Soulard. (See book No. 6, page 142.)

*August 24, 1835.*—The board met, pursuant to adjournment. Present: F. R. Conway, J. H. Relfe, and F. H. Martin, commissioners.

Jean Derouin, claiming 800 arpens of land. (See book No. 6, page 142.)

The board are unanimously of opinion that this claim ought not to be confirmed. For reasons, see decision in the claim of Louis Lamalice, No. 80.

F. H. MARTIN,
F. R. CONWAY,
JAMES H. RELFE.

---

Class 2. No. 112.—*Joseph Hubert, claiming 800 arpens:*

To Don CARLOS DEHAULT DELASSUS, *Lieutenant Governor of Upper Louisiana:*

SIR: Joseph Hubert has the honor to represent to you that, residing in this country since several years, he wishes to settle himself, and form an establishment in the same; therefore he has recourse to your goodness, praying you to be pleased to grant to him a tract of land of 800 arpens in superficie, to be taken on the vacant lands of the King's domain, in the place which shall appear most convenient to the interest of your petitioner, who presumes to expect this favor of your justice.

St. Louis, *March* 12, 1800.

his<br>
JOSEPH × HUBERT.<br>
mark.

St. Louis of Illinois, March 16, 1803.

Whereas we are assured that the petitioner possesses sufficient means to improve the land which he solicits, I do grant to him and his heirs the land which he solicits, provided it is not prejudicial to anybody, and the surveyor, Don Antonio Soulard, shall put the (party) interested in possession of the quantity of land he asks, in a vacant place of the royal domain; which being executed, he shall make out a plat of (his) survey, delivering the same to the party, with his certificate, in order to enable him to obtain the title in form from the intendant general, to whom alone corresponds, by royal order, the distributing and granting all classes of lands, &c.

CARLOS DEHAULT DELASSUS.

St. Louis, *April* 27, 1833.    Truly translated.

JULIUS DE MUN.

| No. | Name of original claimant. | Arpens. | Nature and date of claim. | By whom granted. | By whom surveyed, date, and situation. |
|---|---|---|---|---|---|
| 112 | Joseph Hubert. | 800 | Conces-ion, 16th March, 1800. | C. Dehault Delassus. | James Rankin, D. S., February 20, 1804. Certi-fied by Soulard, March 28, 1804. Sixty-five miles north of St. Louis. |

EVIDENCE WITH REFERENCE TO MINUTES AND RECORDS.

*October* 18, 1811.—Board met. Present: John B. C. Lucas, Clement B. Penrose, and Frederick Bates, commissioners.

Louis Labeaume, assignee of Joseph Hubert, claiming 600 arpens, and said Hubert, claiming 200 arpens of land, situate as above; produces a concession from Charles D. Delassus, lieutenant governor, dated 16th March, 1800; a plat of survey as above; a transfer from Hubert to claimant, dated 12th December, 1803.

It is the opinion of the board that this claim ought not to be confirmed. (See book No. 5, page 366.)

*March* 25, 1833.—F. R. Conway, esq., appeared, pursuant to adjournment.

Joseph Hubert, by Louis Labeaume's legal representatives, claiming 800 arpens of land. (See book C, pages 344 and 349; minutes, No. 5, page 366.)

Produces a paper purporting to be an original concession from Carlos D. Delassus, dated March 16, 1800; also a plat of survey, part of the same being torn and missing, embraces 35 concessions of 800 arpens each, and numbered from 1 to 35 inclusive, on which claimant is No. 6; also deed, dated December 12, 1803.

M. P. Leduc, being duly sworn, says that the signature to the concession is in the proper handwriting of Carlos D. Delassus, and that the torn original survey is in the proper handwriting of Antonio Soulard. (See book No. 6, page 143.)

*August* 24, 1835.—The board met, pursuant to adjournment. Present: F. R. Conway, James H. Relfe, and F. H. Martin, commissioners.

Joseph Hubert, claiming 800 arpens of land. (See book No. 6, page 143.)

The board are unanimously of opinion that this claim ought not to be confirmed. For reasons, see decision in the claim of Louis Lamalice, No. 80.

F. H. MARTIN,<br>
F. R. CONWAY,<br>
JAMES H. RELFE.

Class 2.   No. 113.—Jean Baptiste Bravier, claiming 800 arpens.

To Don Carlos Dehault Delassus, *Lieutenant Governor of Upper Louisiana:*

Sir: Jean Baptiste Bravier has the honor to represent to you, that having resided in this province for a long time, he wishes to settle himself and make an establishment therein; therefore he has recourse to your goodness, praying that you will be pleased to grant to him a tract of land of 800 arpens in superficie, to be taken on the vacant lands of the King's domain, in the place which will appear most convenient to the interest of your peti-tioner, who presumes to expect this favor of your justice.

St. Louis, *April* 7, 1800.

his<br>
J. B. × BRAVIER.<br>
mark.

St. Louis of Illinois, April 11, 1800.

Whereas we are assured that the petitioner possesses sufficient means to improve the land which he solicits, I do grant to him and his heirs the land he solicits, provided it is not prejudicial to anybody, and the surveyor, Don Antonio Soulard, shall put the (party) interested in possession of the quantity of land he asks, in a vacant place of the royal domain; which being executed, he shall make out a plat (of his survey), delivering the same to the party, with his certificate, in order to enable him to obtain the title in form from the intendant general, to whom alone corresponds, by royal order, the distributing and granting all classes of land, &c.

CARLOS DEHAULT DELASSUS.

St. Louis, *April* 26, 1833.    Truly translated.

JULIUS DE MUN.

*Jean B. Bravier, claiming 800 arpens.*

| No. | Name of original claimant. | Arpens. | Nature and date of claim. | By whom granted. | By whom surveyed, date, and situation. |
|-----|---------------------------|---------|---------------------------|------------------|----------------------------------------|
| 113 | Jean B. Bravier. | 800 | Concession, 11th April, 1800. | C Dehault Delassus. | James Rankin, D. S., 20th February, 1804. Certified by Soulard, 28th March, 1804. Sixty-five miles north of St. Louis. |

EVIDENCE WITH REFERENCE TO MINUTES AND RECORDS.

*October* 18, 1811.—Board met.  Present: John B. C. Lucas, Clement B. Penrose, and Frederick Bates, commissioners.

Louis Labeaume, assignee of Jean Baptiste Bravier, claiming 600 arpens, and said Bravier, claiming 200 arpens of land, situate 65 miles north of St. Louis, district of St. Charles, produces a concession from Charles D. Delassus, dated 11th April, 1800; a plat of survey, dated 20th February, 1804, certified 28th March, 1804; a transfer from Bravier to claimant, dated 12th December, 1803.

It is the opinion of the board that this claim ought not to be confirmed.  (See book No. 5, page 364.)

*March* 25, 1833.—F. R. Conway, esq., appeared, pursuant to adjournment.

Jean Baptiste Bravier, by Louis Labeaume's representatives, claiming 800 arpens of land.  (See book C, pages 345 and 349; minutes, No. 5, page 364.)  Produces a paper purporting to be a concession from Carlos D. Delassus, dated April 11th, 1800; also a plat of the survey, part of the same being torn and missing, embracing 35 concessions of 800 arpens each, and numbered from 1 to 35 inclusive, on which claimant is No. 10; also deeds, dated December 12th, 1803, and July 11th, 1804.

M. P. Leduc, duly sworn, says that the signature to the concession is in the proper handwriting of Carlos D. Delassus, and that the torn original survey is in the proper handwriting of Antonio Soulard.  (See book No. 6, page 144.)

*August* 24, 1835.—The board met, pursuant to adjournment.  Present: F. R. Conway, J. H. Relfe, and F. H. Martin, commissioners.

Jean Baptiste Bravier, claiming 800 arpens of land.  (See book No. 6, page 144.)

The board are unanimously of opinion that this claim ought not to be confirmed.  For reasons, see decision in Louis Lamalice's claim, No. 80.

> F. H. MARTIN,
> F. R. CONWAY,
> JAMES H. RELFE.

---

Class 2.    No. 114.—*Louis Ouvray, claiming 800 arpens.*

To Don CARLOS DEHAULT DELASSUS, *Lieutenant Governor of Upper Louisiana:*

SIR: Louis Ouvray has the honor to represent, that having resided for a long time in this province, he would wish to make an establishment in the same; therefore he has recourse to your goodness, praying that you will please grant him a tract of land of 800 arpens in superficie, to be taken on the vacant lands of the King's domain, in the place which will appear most advantageous to the interest of your petitioner, who presumes to expect this favor of your justice.

ST. LOUIS, *February* 7, 1800.                              his
> LOUIS × OUVRAY.
> mark.

ST. LOUIS OF ILLINOIS, *February* 9, 1800.

Whereas we are assured that the petitioner possesses sufficient means to improve the land he solicits, I do grant to him and his heirs the land he solicits, provided it is not prejudicial to any person, and the surveyor, Don Antonio Soulard, shall put the party interested in possession of the quantity of land he asks, in a vacant place of the royal domain; and this being executed, he shall make out a plat, delivering the same to said party, together with his certificate, in order to serve to him to obtain the title in form from the intendant general, to whom alone belongs, by royal order, the distributing and granting all classes of lands, &c.

> CARLOS DEHAULT DELASSUS.

ST. LOUIS, *July* 22, 1835.  I certify the above to be truly translated from book F, page 54, of record in the recorder's office.

> JULIUS DE MUN, *T. B. C.*

| No. | Name of original claimant. | Arpens. | Nature and date of claim. | By whom granted. | By whom surveyed, date, and situation. |
|-----|---------------------------|---------|---------------------------|------------------|----------------------------------------|
| 114 | Louis Ouvray. | 800 | Concession, 9th February, 1800. | Carlos Dehault Delassus. | James Rankin, D. S., 20th February, 1804. Certified 28th March, 1804, by A. Soulard, S. G.  On Cuivre river, St. Charles. |

EVIDENCE WITH REFERENCE TO MINUTES AND RECORDS.

*October* 18, 1811.—Board met.   Present: John B. C. Lucas, Clement B. Penrose, and Frederick Bates, commissioners.

Louis Labeaume, assignee of Louis Ouvray, claiming 800 arpens of land, situate as above, produces a plat of survey as above.

It is the opinion of the board that this claim ought not to be confirmed.   (See book No. 5, page 369.)

*July* 4, 1835.—F. R. Conway, esq., appeared, pursuant to adjournment.

Louis Ouvray, by his legal representatives, claiming 800 arpens of land, on river Au Cuivre.   (For concession see record-book F, page 54; for survey, book C, page 349; minutes, book No. 5, page 369.)

Charles Sanguinet, duly sworn, says that he, witness, gave the original concession to his brother-in-law, H. Cosin, to have the same recorded in one of the upper counties; that said Cosin died a short time afterward, and since his death, witness has not been able to discover what had become of said paper.   (See book No. 7, page 207.)

*August* 24, 1835.—The board met, pursuant to adjournment.   Present: F. R. Conway, J. H. Relfe, and F. H. Martin, commissioners.

Louis Ouvray, claiming 800 arpens of land.   (See book No. 7, page 207.)

The board are unanimously of opinion that this claim ought not to be confirmed.   For reasons, see decision in the claim of Louis Lamalice, No. 80.

F. H. MARTIN,
F. R. CONWAY,
JAMES H. RELFE.

---

Class 2.   No. 115.—Jacob Eastwood, claiming 800 arpens.

To Don CARLOS DEHAULT DELASSUS, *Lieutenant Governor of Upper Louisiana:*

SIR: Jacob Eastwood has the honor to represent to you, that he would wish to form an establishment in the upper part of this province, where he has been residing for some time, promising (the petitioner) to submit to the taxes and charges which it will please his Majesty to impose; therefore the petitioner prays you, sir, to grant to him a tract of land of 800 arpens in superficie, to be taken on the vacant lands of the King's domain, in the place which will appear most convenient to his interests; favor which the petitioner presumes to expect of your justice.

ST. LOUIS, *February* 5, 1801.					JACOB EASTWOOD.

ST. LOUIS OF ILLINOIS, February 8, 1801.

It being evident that the petitioner has more than the means and number of hands (populacion) necessary to obtain the concession which he solicits, I do grant to him and his heirs the land which he solicits, if it is not prejudicial to any person, and the surveyor, Don Antonio Soulard, shall put the interested in possession of the quantity of land which he asks, in a vacant place of the royal domain; and this being executed, he shall draw out a plat of his survey, delivering the same to the party, with his certificate, in order to serve to him to obtain the concession and title in form from the intendant general, to whom alone corresponds, by royal order, the distributing and granting all classes of lands of the royal domain.

CARLOS DEHAULT DELASSUS.

ST. LOUIS, *December* 28, 1832.   Truly translated.

JULIUS DE MUN.

---

CLASS 2.   SURVEY FOR NOS. 115, 116, 117, 118, AND 119.

Don ANTONIO SOULARD, *Surveyor General of Upper Louisiana:*

I do certify that five tracts of land, of 800 arpens each, (making in all 4,000 arpens, as it is demonstrated in the foregoing figurative plat,) were measured, the lines run, and bounded, in favor of Don Santyago de St. Vrain, in presence of his agent, Albert Tyson; the said five concessions were bought last year, by the said proprietor, from the primitive owners, as it is proven by the deeds of sale recorded in the offices of this government. Each one of the tracts of land is designated, in the said figurative plat, with the name of the vendor; oberving that the dotted lines were not run on the ground, on account of the bad weather which took place, but they shall have to be run at the demand of the interested. These lands have been measured with the perch of Paris, of eighteen French feet, lineal measure of the same city. Said lands are situated at about three miles to the westward of the river Mississippi, and sixty miles to the northwest of this town of St. Louis, and are bounded on the four sides by vacant lands of the royal domain. The said measurement and survey were taken without regard to the variation of the needle, which is of 7° 30′ east, as it is evident by referring to the above figurative plat, on which are noted the dimensions, direction of the lines, other boundaries, &c. Said surveys were taken by virtue of the decrees of the lieutenant governor, Don Carlos Dehault Delassus, as it is proven by the five petitions and decrees here annexed.

In testimony whereof, I do give the present, with the foregoing figurative plat, drawn conformably to the survey executed by the deputy surveyor, Mr. James Rankin, on the 6th and 7th of January of this present year, he having signed on the minutes, which I do certify.

ANTONIO SOULARD, Surveyor General.

ST. LOUIS OF ILLINOIS, *March* 5, 1804.

ST. LOUIS, *January* 1, 1833.   Truly translated.

JULIUS DE MUN.

| No. | Name of original claimant. | Arpens. | Nature and date of claim. | By whom granted. | By whom surveyed, date, and situation. |
|---|---|---|---|---|---|
| 115 | Jacob Eastwood. | 800 | Concession, 8th February, 1801. | Carlos Dehault Delassus. | James Rankin, D. S., 6th and 7th January, 1804. Certified by Soulard, 5th March, 1804. Sixty miles northwest of St. Louis. |

EVIDENCE WITH REFERENCE TO MINUTES AND RECORDS.

*November* 14, 1811.—Board met.    Present: John B. C. Lucas, Clement B. Penrose, and Frederick Bates, commissioners.

Jacques St. Vrain, assignee of Jacob Eastwood, claiming 800 arpens of land, situate as above, produces record of a concession from C. D. Delassus, lieutenant governor, dated 8th February, 1801, and a certificate of survey as above.

It is the opinion of the board that this claim ought not to be confirmed.    (See book No. 5, page 419.)

*December* 19, 1832.—F. R. Conway, esq., appeared, pursuant to adjournment.

Jacob Eastwood, by his legal representative, John Mullanphy, claiming 800 arpens of land.    (See book C, pages 330, 331, and 332 ; book No. 5, page 419.)    Produces a paper purporting to be an original concession from Carlos Dehault Delassus, dated 8th February, 1801 ; also, a plat and certificate of survey, dated 5th March, 1804, by Antonio Soulard ; also, deeds of conveyances.

M. P. Leduc, being duly sworn, saith that the signature to the said concession is in the proper handwriting of Carlos Dehault Delassus, and that the signature to the plat and certificate of survey is in the proper handwriting of Antonio Soulard.    (See book No. 6, page 81.)

*August* 25, 1835.—The board met, pursuant to adjournment.    Present : F. R. Conway, J. H. Relfe, and F. H. Martin, commissioners.

Jacob Eastwood, claiming 800 arpens of land.    (See book No. 6, page 81.)

The board are unanimously of opinion that this claim ought not to be confirmed.    For reasons, see decision in the claim of Louis Lamalice, No. 80.

F. H. MARTIN,
F. R. CONWAY,
JAMES H. RELFE.

---

Class 2.    No. 116.—*T. Todd, claiming 800 arpens.*

To Don CARLOS DEHAULT DELASSUS, *Lieutenant Governor of Upper Louisiana :*

SIR : T. Todd has the honor to represent to you, that he would wish to make an establishment in the upper part of this province, in which he resides since some time ; the petitioner promising to submit himself to all the taxes and charges which his Majesty will be pleased to impose ; therefore, the petitioner prays you to grant to him a tract of 800 arpens of land in superficie, to be taken on the vacant lands of the King's domain, in the place which will appear most convenient to his interest ; favor which, your petitioner presumes to expect of your justice.

ST. LOUIS, *May* 12, 1801.                                                          T. $\overset{\text{his}}{\times}$ TODD.
                                                                                                          mark.

ST. LOUIS OF ILLINOIS, *May* 15, 1801.

Whereas it is evident that the petitioner has more than the means and number of hands (populacion) necessary to obtain the concession which he solicits, I do grant to him and his heirs the land which he solicits, if it is not prejudicial to any person, and the surveyor, Don Antonio Soulard, shall put the interested in possession of the quantity of land which he asks, in a vacant place of the royal domain ; and this being executed, he shall draw a plat of his survey, delivering the same to the party, with his certificate, in order to serve to him to obtain the concession and title in form, from the intendant general, to whom alone corresponds, by royal order, the distributing and granting of all classes of lands of the royal domain.

CARLOS DEHAULT DELASSUS.

ST. LOUIS, *December* 28, 1832.    Truly translated.

JULIUS DE MUN.

| No. | Name of original claimant | Arpens. | Nature and date of claim. | By whom granted. | By whom surveyed, date, and situation. |
|-----|---------------------------|---------|---------------------------|------------------|----------------------------------------|
| 116 | T. Todd. | 800 | Concession, 15th May, 1801. | C. Dehault Delassus. | James Rankin, D. S., 6th and 7th January, 1804. Certified by Soulard, 5th March, 1804.  Sixty miles northwest of St. Louis. |

EVIDENCE WITH REFERENCE TO MINUTES AND RECORDS.

*November* 14, 1811.—Board met.    Present : John B. C. Lucas, Clement B. Penrose, and Frederick Bates, commissioners.

Jacques St. Vrain, assignee of T. Todd, claiming 800 arpens of land, situate as above ; produces the record of a concession from C. D. Delassus, L. G., dated 15th May, 1801.    A plat of survey as above.

It is the opinion of the board that this claim ought not to be confirmed.    (See book No. 5, page 419.)

*December* 19, 1832.—F. R. Conway, esq., appeared, pursuant to adjournment.

T. Todd, by his legal representative, John Mullanphy, claiming 800 arpens of land.    (See book C, pages 330, 331, and 332 ; book No. 5, page 419.)    Produces a paper purporting to be an original concession from Carlos Dehault Delassus, dated 15th May, 1801 ; also, a paper purporting to be a plat and certificate of survey, dated 5th March, 1804, by Antonio Soulard ; also, deed of conveyance.

M. P. Leduc, being duly sworn, saith that the signature to the said concession is in the proper handwriting of Carlos D. Delassus, and the signature to the said plat and certificate of survey is in the proper handwriting of Antonio Soulard. (See book No. 6, page 82.)

*August* 25, 1835.—The board met, pursuant to adjournment. Present: F. R. Conway, J. H. Relfe, and F. H. Martin, commissioners.

T. Todd, claiming 800 arpens of land. (See book No. 6, page 82.)

The board are unanimously of opinion that this claim ought not to be confirmed. For reasons, see decision in the claim of Louis Lamalice, No. 80.

F. H. MARTIN,
F. R. CONWAY,
JAMES H. RELFE.

---

Class 2. No. 117.—*Daniel Hubbard, claiming 800 arpens.*

To Don CARLOS DEHAULT DELASSUS, *Lieutenant Governor of Upper Louisiana :*

SIR: Daniel Hubbard has the honor to represent to you, that he would wish to form an establishment in the upper part of this province, in which he has been residing for some time, promising (the petitioner) to submit himself to all the taxes and charges which it may please his Majesty to impose. Therefore, sir, the petitioner prays you to grant to him a tract of land of eight hundred arpens in superficie, to be taken on the vacant lands of his Majesty's domain, in the place which will appear most convenient to the interest of your petitioner, who presumes to expect this favor of your justice.

ST. LOUIS, *November* 17, 1800.

his
DANIEL × HUBBARD.
mark.

ST. LOUIS OF ILLINOIS, *November* 20, 1800.

Whereas it is notorious that the petitioner has more than the means and number of hands (populacion) necessary to obtain the concession which he solicits, I do grant to him and his heirs the land which he solicits, if it is not prejudicial to any person, and the surveyor, Don Antonio Soulard, shall put the interested in possession of the quantity of land which he asks, in the place indicated; and this being executed, he shall draw a plat of his survey, delivering the same, with his certificate, in order to serve to him to obtain the concession and title in form from the intendant general, to whom alone corresponds, by royal order, the distributing and granting all classes of lands in the royal domain.

CARLOS DEHAULT DELASSUS.

ST. LOUIS, *December* 28, 1832. Truly translated.

JULIUS DE MUN.

| No. | Name of original claimant. | Arpens. | Nature and date of claim. | By whom granted. | By whom surveyed, date, and situation. |
|---|---|---|---|---|---|
| 117 | Daniel Hubbard. | 800 | Concession, 20th November, 1800. | Carlos Dehault Delassus. | James Rankin, D. S., 6th and 7th January, 1804. Certified by Soulard, 5th March, 1804. Sixty miles N. W. of St. Louis. |

EVIDENCE WITH REFERENCE TO MINUTES AND RECORDS.

*November* 14, 1811.—Board met. Present: John B. C. Lucas, Clement B. Penrose, and Frederick Bates, commissioners.

Jacques St. Vrain, assignee of Daniel Hubbard, claiming 800 arpens of land, situate as above, produces record of a concession from C. D. Delassus, L. G., dated 20th November, 1800, and a plat of survey as above.

It is the opinion of the board that this claim ought not to be confirmed. (See book No. 5, page 419.)

*December* 19, 1832.—F. R. Conway, esq., appeared, pursuant to adjournment.

Daniel Hubbard, by his legal representative, John Mullanphy, claiming 800 arpens of land. (See book C, pages 330, 331, and 332 ; book No. 5, page 419.)

Produces a paper purporting to be an original concession from Carlos Dehault Delassus, dated 20th November, 1800 ; also, a plat and certificate of survey, dated 5th March, 1804, by Antoine Soulard ; also, a deed of conveyance.

M. P. Leduc, duly sworn, says that the signature to the said concession is in the proper handwriting of Carlos D. Delassus, and that the signature to the plat and certificate of survey is in the proper handwriting of Antoine Soulard. (See book No. 6, page 82.)

*August* 25, 1835.—The board met, pursuant to adjournment. Present: F. R. Conway, J. H. Relfe, and F. H. Martin, commissioners.

Daniel Hubbard, claiming 800 arpens of land. (See book No. 6, page 82.)

The board are unanimously of opinion that this claim ought not to be confirmed. For reasons, see decision in the claim of Louis Lamalice, No. 80.

F. H. MARTIN,
F. R. CONWAY,
JAMES H. RELFE.

---

Class 2. No. 118.—*Felix Hubbard, claiming 800 arpens.*

To Don CARLOS DEHAULT DELASSUS, *Lieutenant Governor of Upper Louisiana :*

SIR: Felix Hubbard has the honor to represent to you, that he would wish to form an establishment in the upper part of this province, where he has been residing for some time, the petitioner promising to submit to all taxes and charges which his Majesty may think fit to impose; therefore, sir, the petitioner prays you to grant to him a tract of land of eight hundred arpens in superficie, to be taken on the vacant lands of his Majesty's domain, in the place which will appear most convenient to the interest of your petitioner, who presumes to expect this favor of your justice.

FELIX × HUBBARD.
his
mark.

St. Louis, *November* 18, 1800.

St. Louis of Illinois, *November* 20, 1800.

Whereas it is evident that the petitioner has more than the means and the number of hands (populacion) necessary to obtain the concession which he solicits, I do grant to him and his heirs the land which he solicits, if it is not prejudicial to any person; and the surveyor, Don Antonio Soulard, shall put the interested in possession of the quantity of lands which he asks, in the place indicated; and this being executed, he shall draw a plat of his survey, delivering the same to the party, with his certificate, in order to serve to him in obtaining the concession and title in form from the intendant general, to whom alone corresponds the distributing and granting all classes of lands of the royal domain.

CARLOS DEHAULT DELASSUS.

St. Louis, *December* 28, 1832.    Truly translated.

JULIUS DE MUN.

| No. | Name of original claimant. | Arpens. | Nature and date of claim. | By whom granted. | By whom surveyed, date, and situation. |
|-----|---------------------------|---------|---------------------------|------------------|----------------------------------------|
| 118 | Felix Hubbard. | 800 | Concession, 20th November, 1800. | Carlos Dehault Delassus. | James Rankin, D. S., January 6th and 7th, 1804. Certified by Soulard, 5th March 1804. Sixty miles N. W. of St. Louis. |

EVIDENCE WITH REFERENCE TO MINUTES AND RECORDS.

*November* 14, 1811.—Board met.  Present: John B. C. Lucas, Clement B. Penrose, and Frederick Bates, commissioners.

Jacques St. Vrain, assignee of Felix Hubbard, claiming 800 arpens of land, situate as aforesaid, produces record of a concession from C. D. Delassus, L. G., dated November 20, 1800, and a plat of survey as aforesaid.

It is the opinion of this board that this claim ought not to be confirmed.  (See book No. 5, page 418.)

*December* 19, 1832.—F. R. Conway, esq., appeared, pursuant to adjournment.

Felix Hubbard, by his legal representatives, John Mullanphy, claiming 800 arpens of land.  (See book C, pages 330, 331, and 332; book No. 5, page 418.)  Produces a paper purporting to be an original concession from Carlos Dehault Delassus, dated November 20, 1800; also, a plat and certificate of survey, dated March 5, 1804; also, a deed of conveyance.

M. P. Leduc, being duly sworn, saith that the signature to the said concession is in the proper handwriting of said Delassus, and that the signature to plat and certificate of survey is in the proper handwriting of Antonio Soulard.  (See book No. 6, page 83.)

*August* 25, 1835.—The board met, pursuant to adjournment.  Present: F. R. Conway, J. H. Relfe, and F. H. Martin, commissioners.

Felix Hubbard, claiming 800 arpens of land.  (See book No. 6, page 83.)

The board are unanimously of opinion that this claim ought not to be confirmed.  For reasons, see decision in the claim of Louis Lamalice, No. 80.

F. H. MARTIN,
F. R. CONWAY,
JAMES H. RELFE.

Class 2.    No. 119.—*Eusebius Hubbard, claiming 800 arpens.*

To Don CARLOS DEHAULT DELASSUS, *Lieutenant Governor of Upper Louisiana:*

SIR: Eusebius Hubbard has the honor to represent to you, that he would wish to form an establishment in the upper part of this province, where he has been residing for some time; the petitioner promising to submit to all the taxes and charges which it may please his Majesty to impose; therefore, sir, the petitioner prays you to grant to him a tract of land of eight hundred arpens in superficie, to be taken on the vacant lands of his Majesty's domain, in the place which will appear most convenient to the interest of your petitioner, who presumes to expect this favor of your justice.

EUSEBIUS HUBBARD.

St. Louis, *January* 4, 1803.

St. Louis of Illinois, *January* 7, 1803.

Whereas it is notorious that the petitioner has more than the means and number of hands (populacion) necessary to obtain the concession which he solicits, I do grant to him and his heirs the land which he solicits, if it is not prejudicial to any person, and the surveyor, Don Antonio Soulard, shall put the (party) interested in possession of the quantity of land which he asks, in the place indicated; and this being executed, he shall draw a plat of his survey, delivering the same to the party, with his certificate, in order that it shall serve to him to obtain the concession and title in form from the intendant general, to whom alone corresponds, by royal order, the distributing and granting all classes of lands of the royal domain.

CARLOS DEHAULT DELASSUS.

St. Louis, *December* 29, 1832.    Truly translated.

JULIUS DE MUN.

*Eusebius Hubbard, claiming 800 arpens.*

| No. | Name of original claimant. | Arpens. | Nature and date of claim. | By whom granted. | By whom surveyed, date, and situation. |
|---|---|---|---|---|---|
| 119 | Eusebius Hubbard. | 800 | Concession, 7th January, 1803. | Carlos Dehault Delassus. | James Rankin, D. S., 6th and 7th of January, 1804. Certified by Soulard, March 5, 1804. Sixty miles N. W. of St. Louis. |

EVIDENCE WITH REFERENCE TO MINUTES AND RECORDS.

*November* 14, 1811.—Board met. Present: John B. C. Lucas, Clement B. Penrose, and Frederick Bates, commissioners.

Jacques St. Vrain, assignee of Eusebius Hubbard, claiming 800 arpens of land, situate 60 miles northwest of St. Louis, district of St. Charles. Produces a record of concession from Charles D. Delassus, L. G., dated January 7, 1803; a plat of survey, dated 17th (6th and 7th) January, 1804, certified March 5, 1804. It is the opinion of the board that this claim ought not to be confirmed. (See book No. 5, page 418.)

*December* 19, 1832.—F. R. Conway, esq., appeared, pursuant to adjournment.

Eusebius Hubbard, by his legal representative, John Mullanphy, claiming 800 arpens of land. (See book C, pages 330 and 332; book No. 5, page 418.)

Produces a paper purporting to be an original concession from Carlos Dehault Delassus, dated January 7, 1804; also a plat and certificate of survey, dated March 5, 1804, by Antonio Soulard; also, deeds of conveyances.

M. P. Leduc, duly sworn, says that the signature to the above-mentioned papers are in the respective handwriting of Carlos Dehault Delassus and Antonio Soulard. (See book No. 6, page 83.)

*August* 25, 1835.—The board met, pursuant to adjournment. Present: F. R. Conway, J. H. Relfe, and F. H. Martin, commissioners.

Eusebius Hubbard, claiming 800 arpens of land. (See book No. 6, page 83.)

The board are unanimously of opinion that this claim ought not to be confirmed. For reasons, see decision in the claim of Louis Lamalice, No. 80.

> F. H. MARTIN,
> F. R. CONWAY,
> JAMES H. RELFE.

---

Class 2.    No. 120.—*Louis Lajoie, claiming 800 arpens.*

To Don CARLOS DEHAULT DELASSUS, *Lieutenant Governor of Upper Louisiana:*

SIR: Louis Lajoie has the honor to represent to you, that wishing to make an establishment in the upper part of this province, where he has been residing for some time, therefore he has recourse to the benevolence of this government, praying that you may be pleased to grant to him a tract of land of eight hundred arpens in superficie, to be taken on the vacant lands of the King's domain, in the place which will appear the most advantageous and the most convenient to the interest of your petitioner, who presumes to expect this favor of your justice.

ST. LOUIS, *February* 17, 1800.

> his
> LOUIS × LAJOIE.
> mark.

ST. LOUIS OF ILLINOIS, *February* 19, 1800.

Being assured that the petitioner has sufficient means to improve the lands which he solicits, I do grant to him and his heirs the land which he solicits, if it is not prejudicial to any one, and the surveyor, Don Antonio Soulard, shall put the interested in possession of the quantity of land which he asks, in a vacant place of the royal domain; and this being executed, he shall draw a plat of his survey, delivering the same to the party, with his certificate, in order to serve to him in obtaining the title in form from the intendant general, to whom alone corresponds the distributing and granting all classes of land, &c.

> CARLOS DEHAULT DELASSUS.

ST. LOUIS, *December* 27, 1832. Truly translated.

> JULIUS DE MUN.

| No. | Name of original claimant. | Arpens. | Nature and date of claim. | By whom granted. | By whom surveyed, date, and situation. |
|---|---|---|---|---|---|
| 120 | Louis Lajoie. | 800 | Concession, 19th February, 1800. | Carlos Dehault Delassus. | James Rankin, D. S., 19th February, 1804. Certified by Soulard, 20th March, 1804. Seventy-two miles north of St. Louis. |

EVIDENCE WITH REFERENCE TO MINUTES AND RECORDS.

*May* 28, 1806.—The board met, agreeably to adjournment.   Present : Hon. Clement B. Penrose.

Jacques St. Vrain, assignee of Louis Lajoie, claiming 550 arpens of land, situate as aforesaid ; produces a concession from Charles D. Delassus to said Louis Lajoie, dated February 19th, 1800 ; a survey of the same, dated 19th January, 1804, and certified 20th March, 1804 ; together with a deed of transfer of the same, dated 17th December, 1803.

The board require further proof of the date of the above concession.

*On behalf of the United States.*—Louis Lajoie, being duly sworn, says that he never applied for a concession ; that about two years ago, in the winter, Louis Labeaume called on him and informed him that he was ready to give concessions to such as wanted some ; that he, the witness, went to Gregoire Sarpy's where Labeaume lived at that time ; that being there, Labeaume showed him some papers which he deemed to be concessions, but did not give him the same ; that, not knowing how to write, he made his cross to a paper ; that he never received anything for the land he made over to claimant ; and, further, that he does not know where the said land lies ; was, at the time of the above application to him, the said witness, by said Labeaume, of the age of 22 years ; had a wife and child, and claims no other land, in his own name, in this territory.

The board reject this claim.   (See book No. 1, page 302.)

*August* 17, 1811.—Board met.   Present : Clement B. Penrose and Frederick Bates, commissioners.

Jacques St. Vrain, assignee of Louis Lajoie, claiming 550, and Louis Lajoie, claiming 250 arpens of land. (See book No. 1, page 302.)

It is the opinion of the board that this claim ought not to be confirmed.   (See book No. 5, page 316.)

*December* 19, 1832.—F. R. Conway, esq., appeared, pursuant to adjournment.

Louis Lajoie, by his legal representative, John Mullanphy, claiming 800 arpens of land.   (See book C, page 326 ; book No. 1, page 302 ; No. 5, page 316.)

Produces a paper purporting to be an original concession from Carlos Dehault Delassus, dated 19th February, 1800 ; also, a plat and certificate of survey, dated 20th March, 1804, by Antonio Soulard ; also, deeds of conveyances.

M. P. Leduc, duly sworn, saith that the signature to said concession is in the proper handwriting of Carlos Dehault Delassus, and the signature to plat and certificate of survey is in the proper handwriting of Antonio Soulard.   (See book No. 6, page 81.)

*December* 17, 1833.—F. R. Conway, esq., appeared, pursuant to adjournment.

In the case of Louis Lajoie, claiming 800 arpens of land.   (See page 81, of this book, No. 6.)

Louis Lajoie, being duly sworn, says that, under the Spanish government, he asked for a concession of 800 arpens of land ; that on his demand, the said concession was granted to him ; that he asked for said concession through Mr. Labeaume, who drew up the petition ; that, at the time the grant was made, he, the deponent, lived in Florissant, and had a wife and two children ; that he, in company with about 15 others, came to St. Louis for the purpose of asking land of the government ; that he does not recollect of having ever given any testimony before the former board ; that if he has, he must have been drunk at the time ; that then he was oftener drunk than sober ; that previous to obtaining the grant, he had not made any contract with any one for said land ; that he recollects of having sold his interest in the grant to Dejarlais, when in a frolic, for a pint of whiskey ; that he does not recollect of having signed any deeds for said land.   Being asked what was his occupation at that time, he answered, drinking drams.   The witness further says that he supported his family by working by the day, when sober ; that since a few years he has left off drinking ; that at the time the grant was made, the lieutenant governor, Charles Dehault Delassus, lived in a house on Main street, near the market place.   (See book No. 6, page 399.)

*December* 28, 1833.—F. R. Conway, esq., appeared, pursuant to adjournment.

In the case of Louis Lajoie, claiming 800 arpens of land.   (See page 81 of this book, No. 6.)

Benito Vasquez, being duly sworn, and being shown the original deed of sale from Louis Lajoie to Dejarlais, (said deed dated July 10th, 1804,) signed by him, the said Benito, as witness, says that it is his own handwriting and signature.   (See book No. 6, page 423.)

*August* 25, 1835.—The board met, pursuant to adjournment.   Present : F. R. Conway, J. H. Relfe, and F. H. Martin, commissioners.

Louis Lajoie, claiming 800 arpens of land.   (See book No. 6, pages 81, 399, 423.)

The board are unanimously of opinion that this claim ought not to be confirmed.   For reasons, see decision in the claim of Louis Lamalice, No. 80.

F. H. MARTIN,<br>F. R. CONWAY,<br>JAMES H. RELFE.

---

Class 2.   No. 121.—F. Bellanger, claiming 800 arpens.

To Don CHARLES DEHAULT DELASSUS, *Lieutenant Governor of Upper Louisiana* :

SIR : François Bellanger has the honor to represent that he would wish to make an establishment in the upper part of this province ———— (marked on the record illegible) ———— some time, therefore ———— (do, illegible) ————.

his<br>F.  ×  BELLANGER.<br>mark.

*December* 16, 1799.

ST. LOUIS OF ILLINOIS, December 20, 1799.

Whereas we are assured that the petitioner has sufficient means to improve the land he solicits, I do grant to him and his heirs the land he solicits, provided it is not prejudicial to any person, and the surveyor, Don Antonio Soulard, shall put the party interested in possession of the quantity of land he asks, in a vacant part of the royal domain ; and this being executed, he shall make out a plat, delivering the same to said party, together with his certificate, in order to serve him to obtain the title in form from the intendant general, to whom alone belongs, by royal order, the distributing and granting all classes of land on the royal domain.

CARLOS DEHAULT DELASSUS.

ST. LOUIS, *August* 25, 1835.   Truly translated from record-book C, page 325.

JULIUS DE MUN, T. B. C.

*F. Bellanger, claiming 800 arpens.*

| No. | Name of origiual claimant. | Arpens. | Nature and date of claim. | By whom granted. | By whom surveyed, date, and situation. |
|-----|----------------------------|---------|---------------------------|------------------|----------------------------------------|
| 121 | Fran. Bellanger. | 800 | Concession, 20th Dec., 1799. | C. Dehault Delassus. | James Rankin, D. S., 19th January, 1804. Certified by Soulard, 20th March, 1804. Seventy-two miles north of St. Louis. |

EVIDENCE WITH REFERENCE TO MINUTES AND RECORDS.

*May* 28, 1806.—The board met, agreeably to adjournment. Present: Hon. Clement B. Penrose.

The same, (Jacques St. Vrain,) assignee of Francis Bellanger, claiming 550 arpens, situate as aforesaid, produces a concession from Charles Dehault Delassus, for 800 arpens, dated 20th December, 1799; a survey dated 19th January, 1804, and a transfer of the same, dated December 13th, 1803.

The board require further proof of the date of the above concession. The board reject this claim. (See book No. 1, page 301.)

*August* 17, 1811.—Board met. Present: Clement B. Penrose and Frederick Bates, commissioners.

Jacques St. Vrain, assignee of Francis Bellanger, claiming 550 arpens, and Francis Bellanger, claiming 250 arpens of land. (See book No. 1, page 301.)

It is the opinion of the board that this claim ought not to be confirmed. (See book No. 5, pages 316 and 317.)

*December* 19, 1832.—F. R. Conway, esq., appeared, pursuant to adjournment.

François Bellanger, by his legal representative, John Mullanphy, claiming 800 arpens of land. (See book C, pages 325 and 326; book No. 1, page 301; No. 5, pages 316 and 317.) Produces a paper purporting to be a plat and certificate of survey, dated March 20, 1804, by Antoine Soulard.

M. P. Leduc, duly sworn, saith that the signature to said certificate of survey is in the proper handwriting of the said Antoine Soulard. (See book No. 6, page 87.)

*August* 25, 1835.—The board met, pursuant to adjournment. Present: F. R. Conway, J. H. Relfe, and F. H. Martin, commissioners.

François Bellanger, claiming 800 arpens of land. (See book No. 6, page 87.)

The board are unanimously of opinion that this claim ought not to be confirmed. For reasons, see decision in the claim of Louis Lamalice, No 80.

F. H. MARTIN,
F. R. CONWAY,
JAMES H. RELFE.

---

Class 2. No. 122.—*Bte. Joseph Billot, claiming 800 arpens.*

To Don CARLOS DEHAULT DELASSUS, *Lieutenant Governor of Upper Louisiana:*

SIR: Bte. Joseph Billot has the honor to represent to you that, residing in this country since a long time, he wishes to settle himself in it; therefore he has recourse to your goodness, hoping you will please to grant to him a tract of land of eight hundred arpens in superficie, to be taken on the vacant lands of the King's domain, in the place which will appear most convenient to the interest of your petitioner, who presumes to expect this favor of your justice.

ST. LOUIS, *February* 25, 1800.

BTE. JOSEPH  x  BILLOT.
his                        mark.

ST. LOUIS OF ILLINOIS, *February* 29, 1800.

Whereas we are assured that the petitioner has sufficient means to improve the lands which he solicits, I do grant to him and his heirs the land which he solicits, if it is not prejudicial to any person, and the surveyor, Don Antonio Soulard, shall put the interested in possession of the quantity of land which he asks, in a vacant place of the royal domain; and this being executed, he shall draw a plat of his survey, delivering the same to the party, with his certificate, in order that it shall serve to him to obtain the title in form from the intendant general, to whom alone corresponds, by royal order, the distributing and granting all classes of lands, &c.

CARLOS DEHAULT DELASSUS.

ST. LOUIS, *December* 29, 1832. Truly translated.

JULIUS DE MUN.

| No. | Name of original claimant. | Arpens. | Nature and date of claim. | By whom granted. | By whom surveyed, date, and situation. |
|-----|----------------------------|---------|---------------------------|------------------|----------------------------------------|
| 122 | Bte. J. Billot. | 800 | Concession, 29th February, 1800. | C. Dehault Delassus. | James Rankin, D. S., 11th February, 1804. Certified by Soulard, 28th March, 1804. Fifty-five miles north of St. Louis. |

EVIDENCE WITH REFERENCE TO MINUTES AND RECORDS.

*May* 28, 1806.—The board met, agreeably to adjournment.  Present: Hon. Clement B. Penrose.

The same, (Jacques St. Vrain,) assignee of Baptiste Billot, claiming 600 arpens of land, situate as aforesaid, produces a concession from Charles Dehault Delassus to said Billot, for 800 arpens, dated 29th February, 1800, a survey taken the 11th February, and certified 20th (28th) March, 1804 ; and a deed of transfer of the same, dated 10th January, 1804.

The board require further proof of the date of said concession.

*On behalf of the United States.*—Baptiste Billot, being duly sworn, says that, about two years ago, understanding that Louis Labeaume was dealing out concessions, he expressed a wish to have one, if possible to obtain it ; that some days after, one Albert Tyson called on him, the witness, and tendered him a concession ; that he then signed the petition for the same, and at the same time executed a deed of transfer of some part of it, for which he received an iron pot ; and further, that he had then a wife and four children, and claims no other land in his own name in the territory.

The board reject this claim.  (See book No. 1, page 304.)

*August* 17, 1811.—Board met.  Present: Clement B. Penrose and Frederick Bates, commissioners.

Jacques St. Vrain, assignee of Baptiste Joseph Billot, claiming 600 arpens, and Baptiste Joseph Billot, claiming 200 arpens of land.  (See book No. 1, page 304.)

It is the opinion of the board that this claim ought not to be confirmed.  (See book No. 5, page 318.)

*December* 19, 1832.—F. R. Conway, esq., appeared, pursuant to adjournment.

Baptiste Joseph Billot, by his legal representative, John Mullanphy, claiming 800 arpens of land.  (See book C, pages 329 and 330 ; book No. 1, page 304 ; book No. 5, page 318.)  Produces a paper purporting to be an original concession from Carlos Dehault Delassus, dated 29th February, 1800 ; also, a plat of survey and certificate, dated 28th March, 1804 ; also, deed of conveyance.

M. P. Leduc, duly sworn, saith that the signatures to the above-mentioned papers are in the respective handwriting of Carlos Dehault Delassus and Antoine Soulard.  (See book No. 6, page 83.)

*August* 25, 1835.—The board met, pursuant to adjournment.  Present: F. R. Conway, J. H. Relfe, and F. H. Martin, commissioners.

Joseph Billot, claiming 800 arpens of land.  (See book No. 6, page 83.)

The board are unanimously of opinion that this claim ought not to be confirmed.  For reasons, see decision in the claim of Louis Lamalice, No. 80.

F. H. MARTIN,
F. R. CONWAY.
JAMES H. RELFE.

---

Class 2.    No. 123.—*Baptiste Delisle, jr., claiming 800 arpens.*

To Don CARLOS DEHAULT DELASSUS, *Lieutenant Governor of Upper Louisiana :*

SIR : Baptiste Delisle, jr., has the honor to represent to you, that he would wish to establish himself in this country, in which he has been residing for some time ; therefore he has recourse to the benevolence of this government, hoping you will please to grant to him a tract of land of eight hundred arpens in superficie, to be taken on the vacant lands of the King's domain, in the place which shall be most convenient to the interest of your petitioner, who presumes to expect this favor of your justice.

his
BAPTISTE  ×  DELISLE, Jr.
mark.

ST. LOUIS, *April* 21, 1800.

ST. LOUIS OF ILLINOIS, *April* 25, 1800.

Whereas we have been assured that the petitioner has sufficient means to improve the land which he solicits, I do grant to him and his heirs the land which he solicits, if it is not prejudicial to any person, and the surveyor, Don Antonio Soulard, shall put the interested in possession of the quantity of land he petitions for, in a vacant place of the royal domain, and this being executed, he shall draw a plat of his survey, delivering the same to the party, with his certificate, in order to serve to him to obtain the title in form from the intendant general, to whom alone corresponds, by royal order, the distributing and granting all classes of lands, &c.

CARLOS DEHAULT DELASSUS.

ST. LOUIS, *December* 29, 1832.  Truly translated.

JULIUS DE MUN.

| No. | Name of original claimant. | Arpens. | Nature and date of claim. | By whom granted. | By whom surveyed, date, and situation. |
|---|---|---|---|---|---|
| 123 | Baptiste Delisle, junior. | 800 | Concession, 25th April, 1800. | Carlos Dehault Delassus. | James Rankin, D. S., February 11, 1804. Certified by Soulard, March 28, 1804. Fifty-five miles north of St. Louis. |

EVIDENCE WITH REFERENCE TO MINUTES AND RECORDS.

*May* 28, 1806.—The board met, pursuant to adjournment.  Present: Hon. Clement B. Penrose.

The same, (Jacques St. Vrain,) assignee of Baptiste Delisle, jr., claiming 600 arpens of land, situate as aforesaid ; produces a concession from Charles Dehault Delassus to said Delisle for 800 arpens, dated October 9, 1799, (April 25, 1800 ;) a survey of the same, dated February 11, and certified 20th (28th) March, 1804 ; and a deed of transfer of the same, dated January 5, 1804.

The board require further proof of the date of said concession.

The board reject this claim. (See book No. 1, page 304.)

*August* 17, 1811.—Board met. Present : Clement B. Penrose and Frederick Bates, commissioners.

Jacques St. Vrain, assignee of Baptiste Delisle, jr., claiming 600 arpens of land, and Baptiste Delisle, jr., claiming 200 arpens. (See book No. 1, page 304.) It is the opinion of the board that this claim ought not to be confirmed. (See book No. 5, page 318.)

*December* 19, 1832.—F. R. Conway, esq., appeared, pursuant to adjournment. Baptiste Delisle, jr., by his legal representative, John Mullanphy, claiming 800 arpens of land. (See book C, pages 329 and 330 ; book No. 1, page 304 ; No. 5, page 318.) Produces a paper purporting to be an original concession from Carlos Dehault Delassus, dated April 25, 1800 ; also, a plat and certificate of survey, dated March 28, 1804, by Antoine Soulard ; also, deeds of conveyances.

M. P. Leduc, duly sworn, says that the signatures to the above papers are in the proper handwriting of Carlos Dehault Delassus and of Antoine Soulard. (See book No. 6, page 84.)

*August* 25, 1835.—The board met, pursuant to adjournment. Present : F. R. Conway, J. H. Relfe, and F. H. Martin, commissioners.

Baptiste Delisle, jr., claiming 800 arpens of land. (See book No. 6, page 84.)

The board are unanimously of opinion that this claim ought not to be confirmed. For reasons, see decision in the claim of Louis Lamalice, No. 80.

F. H. MARTIN,

F. R. CONWAY.

JAMES H. RELFE.

---

Class 2.  No. 124.—*Baptiste Delisle, sr., claiming 800 arpens.*

To Don CHARLES DEHAULT DELASSUS, *Lieutenant Governor of Upper Louisiana :*

SIR : Baptiste Delisle has the honor to represent to you, that being one of the most ancient inhabitants of this Upper Louisiana, he would wish to form an establishment, therefore he has recourse to the benevolence of this government, hoping you will please to grant to him a tract of land of 800 arpens in superficie, to be taken on the vacant lands of the King's domain, in the place which will appear the most convenient to the interest of your petitioner, who presumes to expect this favor of your justice.

St. Louis, *October* 7, 1799.

his

BAPTISTE  ×  DELISLE.

mark.

St. Louis of Illinois, *October* 9, 1799.

Whereas we have been assured that the petitioner has sufficient means to improve the land which he solicits, I do grant to him and his heirs the land which he solicits, if it is not prejudicial to any person, and the surveyor, Don Antonio Soulard, shall put the interested in possession of the quantity of land which he asks, in a vacant place of the royal domain ; and this being executed, he shall draw a plat of his survey, delivering the same to the party, with his certificate, in order to serve to him to obtain the title in form from the intendant general, to whom corresponds, by royal order, the distributing and granting all classes of lands, &c.

CARLOS DEHAULT DELASSUS.

St. Louis, *December* 29, 1832.  Truly translated.

JULIUS DE MUN.

| No. | Name of original claimant. | Arpens. | Nature and date of claim. | By whom granted. | By whom surveyed, date, and situation. |
|---|---|---|---|---|---|
| 124 | Baptiste Delisle, sr. | 800 | Concession, 9th October, 1799. | Carlos Dehault Delassus. | James Rankin, D. S., 11th February, 1804. Certified by Soulard, 28th March, 1804. Fifty-five miles north of St. Louis. |

EVIDENCE WITH REFERENCE TO MINUTES AND RECORDS.

*May* 28, 1806.—The board met, agreeably to adjournment. Present : Hon. Clement B. Penrose.

The same, (Jacques St. Vrain,) assignee of Baptiste Delisle, sr., claiming 600 arpens of land, situate as aforesaid ; produces a concession from Charles Dehault Delassus to said Delisle for 800 arpens, dated April 25, 1800, (October 9, 1799 ;) a survey of the same, dated February 11, and certified 20th (28th) March, 1804 ; and a deed of transfer, dated 17th December, 1804.

The board require further proof of the date of said concession. The board reject this claim. (See book No. 1, page 304.)

*August* 17, 1811.—Board met. Present : Clement B. Penrose and Frederick Bates, commissioners.

Jacques St. Vrain, assignee of Baptiste Delisle, claiming 600 arpens, and Baptiste Delisle, claiming 200 arpens of land. (See book No. 1, page 304.)

It is the opinion of the board that this claim ought not to be confirmed. (See book No. 5, page 318.)

*December* 19, 1832.—F. R. Conway, esq., appeared, pursuant to adjournment.

Baptiste Delisle, sr., by his legal representative, John Mullanphy, claiming 800 arpens of land. (See book C, pages 328, 329, and 330 ; book No. 1, page 304 ; No. 5, page 318.) Produces a paper, purporting to be an original concession from Carlos Dehault Delassus, dated 9th October, 1799 ; also, a plat and certificate of survey, dated 28th March, 1804, by Antoine Soulard ; also, deeds of conveyance.

M. P. Leduc, duly sworn, saith that the signatures to the above mentioned papers are in the proper hand-writing of the said Carlos Dehault Delassus and Antonio Soulard.  (See book No. 6, page 84.)

*August* 25, 1835.—The board met, pursuant to adjournment.  Present: F. R. Conway, J. H. Relfe, and F. H. Martin, commissioners.

Baptiste Delisle, sr , claiming 800 arpens of land.  (See book No. 6, page 84.)

The board are unanimously of opinion that this claim ought not to be confirmed.  For reasons, see decision in the claim of Louis Lamalice, No. 80.

F. H. MARTIN,
F. R. CONWAY,
JAMES H. RELFE.

---

Class 2.    No. 125.—*Paul Dejarlais, claiming 800 arpens.*

To Don CARLOS DEHAULT DELASSUS, *Lieutenant Governor of Upper Louisiana* :

SIR : Paul Dejarlais has the honor to represent to you, that he would wish to establish himself in this Upper Louisiana, which he has been inhabiting for a long time ; therefore he has recourse to your goodness, hoping that you will please to grant him a tract of land of 800 arpens in superficie, in a vacant place of his Majesty's do-main, praying that you will give him permission to take the said tract of land in the manner which will appear most convenient to the interest of your petitioner, who presumes to expect this favor of your justice.

ST. LOUIS, *July* 9, 1800.

PAUL x DEJARLAIS.
his
mark.

ST. LOUIS OF ILLINOIS, *July* 11, 1800.

Whereas we are assured that the petitioner has sufficient means to improve the land which he solicits, I do grant to him and his heirs the land which he solicits, if it is not prejudicial to any person, and the surveyor, Don Antonio Soulard, shall put the interested in possesion of the quantity of land which he asks, in a vacant place of the royal domain ; and this being executed, he shall draw a plat of his survey, delivering the same to the party, with his certificate, in order to serve to him to obtain the title in form from the intendant general, to whom alone cor-responds, by royal order, the distributing and granting all classes of lands, &c.

CARLOS DEHAULT DELASSUS.

ST. LOUIS, *December* 29, 1832.  Truly translated.

JULIUS DE MUN.

| No. | Name of original claimant. | Arpens. | Nature and date of claim. | By whom granted. | By whom surveyed, date, and situation. |
|---|---|---|---|---|---|
| 125 | Paul Dejarlais. | 800 | Concession, 11th July, 1800. | C. Dehault Delassus. | James Rankin, D. S., 11th February, 1804.  Cer-tified by Soulard, 28th March, 1804.  Fifty-five miles north of St. Louis. |

EVIDENCE WITH REFERENCE TO MINUTES AND RECORDS.

*May* 28, 1806.—The board met, agreeably to adjournment.  Present: Hon. Clement B. Penrose.

The same (Jacques St. Vrain,) assignee of Paul Dejarlais, claiming 600 arpens of land, situate as aforesaid, produces a concession from Charles D. Delassus to said Dejarlais for 800 arpens, dated July 11, 1800 ; a survey of the same, dated 11th February, and certified 20th (28th) March, 1804 ; and a deed of transfer of the same, dated the 13th December, 1803.

The board require further proof of the date of said concession.

*On behalf of the United States.*  Paul Dejarlais, being duly sworn, says that some time in the spring of 1804, Labeaume called on him and told him that if he wanted lands he might have some ; to which he, the witness, replied, that if he was to pay nothing for the same, he would like to have it ; that accordingly, some time in June of that year (as he believes), Labeaume gave him a concession for 800 arpens of land ; that the Spanish officers had not then left the country ; and that when the said concession was given to him, he gave an assign-ment of 600 arpens of the same, for which he did not receive any thing ; and further, that he had then a wife and children, and claims no other lands, in his own name, in the territory.

The board reject this claim.  (See book No. 1, page 304.)

*August* 17, 1811.—Board met.  Present: Clement B. Penrose and Frederick Bates, commissioners.

Jacques St. Vrain, assignee of Paul Dejarlais, claiming 600 arpens, and Paul Dejarlais, claiming 200 arpens of land.  (See book No. 1, page 304.)

It is the opinion of the board that this claim ought not to be confirmed.  (See book No. 5, page 318.)

*December* 19, 1832.—F. R. Conway, esq., appeared, pursuant to adjournment.

Paul Dejarlais, by his legal representative, John Mullanphy, claiming 800 arpens of land.  (See book C, pages 328 and 330 ; book No. 1, page 304 ; No. 5, page 318.)  Produces a paper purporting to be an original concession from Carlos Dehault Delassus, dated 11th July, 1800 ; also, a plat and certificate of survey, dated 28th March, 1804, by Antonio Soulard ; also, deeds of conveyance.

M. P. Leduc, duly sworn, says that the signatures to the aforesaid papers are in the proper handwriting of Carlos Dehault Delassus and of Antonio Soulard. (See book No. 6, page 84.)

*August* 25, 1835.—The board met, pursuant to adjournment. Present: F. R. Conway, J. H. Relfe, and F. H. Martin, commissioners.

Paul Dejarlais, claiming 800 arpens of land. (See book No. 6, page 84.)

The board are unanimously of opinion that this claim ought not to be confirmed. For reasons, see decision in the claim of Louis Lamalice, No. 80.

F. H. MARTIN,<br>F. R. CONWAY,<br>JAMES H. RELFE.

---

Class 2. No. 126.—*Baptiste Marion, claiming* 800 *arpens.*

To Don CARLOS DEHAULT DELASSUS, *Lieutenant Governor of Upper Louisiana* .

SIR: Baptiste Marion has the honor to represent to you, that wishing to form an establishment in the upper part of this province, where he has been residing for a long time, therefore the petitioner has recourse to your goodness, praying that you may be pleased to grant to him a tract of land of 800 arpens in superficie, to be taken on the vacant lands of the King's domain, in the place which will appear most convenient to the interest of your petitioner, who presumes to hope this favor of your justice.

ST. LOUIS, *February* 17, 1800.

his<br>BAPTISTE × MARION.<br>mark.

ST. LOUIS OF ILLINOIS, *February* 21, 1800.

Being assured that the petitioner has means sufficient to improve the lands which he solicits, I do grant to him the land which he solicits, for him and his heirs, if it is not prejudicial to any person, and the surveyor, Don Antonio Soulard, shall put the interested in possession of the quantity of land solicited, in a vacant part of the royal domain ; and this being executed, he shall draw out a plat of survey, delivering the same to said party, with his certificate, in order to serve to him in obtaining the title in form from the intendant general, to whom alone corresponds the distributing and granting all classes of lands, &c.

CARLOS DEHAULT DELASSUS.

ST. LOUIS, *December* 13, 1832.   Truly translated.

JULIUS DE MUN.

| No. | Name of original claimant. | Arpens. | Nature and date of claim. | By whom granted. | By whom surveyed, date, and situation. |
|---|---|---|---|---|---|
| 126 | Baptiste Marion. | 800 | Concession, 21st Feb , 1800. | C. Dehault Delassus. | James Rankin, D. S., 11th February, 1804. Certified by Antoine Soulard, surveyor general, January 9, 1806. |

EVIDENCE WITH REFERENCE TO MINUTES AND RECORDS.

*November* 27, 1811.—The board met. Present: John B. C. Lucas, Clement B. Penrose, and Frederick Bates, commissioners.

Edward Hempstead, assignee of the sheriff of St. Charles district, who sold the same as the property of John Campbell and White Matlock, assignees of Jacques St. Vrain, assignee of Baptiste Marion, claiming 600 arpens of land, and the said Marion claiming 200 arpens of land, situate in the district of St. Charles, produces record of concession from Charles D. Delassus, L. G., dated February 21, 1800 ; record of a plat of survey, dated March 28, 1804, certified January 9, 1806 ; record of a transfer from Marion to St. Vrain, dated January 10, 1804 ; record of a transfer from St. Vrain to Campbell and Matlock, dated August 29, 1805 ; record of a transfer from sheriff to claimant, dated June 29, 1808.

It is the opinion of this board that this claim ought not to be confirmed. (See book No. 5, page 455.) ·

*November* 29, 1832.—The board met, pursuant to adjournment. Present: L. F. Linn and F. R. Conway, commissioners.

Baptiste Marion, by his legal representatives, Edward Hempstead's heirs and devisees, claiming 800 arpens of land. (See record-book C, page 423 ; book No. 5, page 455.) Produces a paper purporting to be an original concession from Carlos Dehault Delassus, dated February 21, 1800 ; also, deeds of conveyance.

M. P. Leduc, duly sworn, saith that the signature to the aforesaid concession is in the proper handwriting of said Carlos Dehault Delassus. (See book No. 6, page 66.)

*August* 25, 1835.—The board met, pursuant to adjournment. Present: F. R. Conway, J. H. Relfe, and F. H. Martin, commissioners.

Baptiste Marion, claiming 800 arpens of land. (See book No. 6, page 66.)

The board are unanimously of opinion that this claim ought not to be confirmed. For reasons, see decision in the claim of Louis Lamalice, No. 80.

F. H. MARTIN,<br>F. R. CONWAY,<br>JAMES H. RELFE.

Class 2.   No. 127.—*Toussaint Tourville, claiming 800 arpens.*

To Don CARLOS DEHAULT DELASSUS, *Lieutenant Governor of Upper Louisiana:*

SIR: Toussaint Tourville has the honor to represent to you, that having resided, since a long time, in this country, and wishing to form a plantation, therefore he has recourse to your goodness, that you may be pleased to grant to him a tract of land of eight hundred arpens in superficie, to be taken upon the vacant lands of the King's domain, in the place which may appear most convenient to the interest of your petitioner, who presumes to hope to obtain this favor from your justice.

ST. LOUIS, *January* 14, 1800.

his
TOUSSAINT × TOURVILLE.
mark.

ST. LOUIS OF ILLINOIS, *January* 18, 1800.

Being assured that the petitioner has means sufficient to improve the land which he solicits, I do grant to him and his heirs the land which he solicits, if it is not prejudicial to any person, and the surveyor, Don Antonio Soulard, shall put the interested party in possession of the quantity of land solicited, in a vacant place of the royal domain ; and this being executed, he shall draw a plat of survey, delivering the same to the party, with his certificate, in order that it may serve to him in obtaining the title in form from the intendent general, to whom alone corresponds, by royal order, the distributing and granting all classes of lands, &c.

CARLOS DEHAULT DELASSUS.

ST. LOUIS, *December* 13, 1832.   Truly translated.

JULIUS DE MUN.

| No. | Name of original claimant. | Arpens. | Nature and date of claim. | By whom granted. | By whom surveyed, date, and situation. |
|---|---|---|---|---|---|
| 127 | Toussaint Tourville. | 800 | Concession, 18th January, 1800. | Carlos Dehault Delassus. | James Rankin, D. S, February 11, 1804. Certified by Antoine Soulard, S. G., January 9, 1806. |

EVIDENCE WITH REFERENCE TO MINUTES AND RECORDS.

*December* 10, 1811.—Board met.   Present : John B. C. Lucas, Clement B. Penrose, and Frederick Bates, commissioners.

Edward Hempstead, assignee of the sheriff of St. Charles district, who sold the same as the property of John Campbell and White Matlock, assignees of Jacques St. Vrain, assignee of Toussaint Tourville, claiming 600 arpens, and said Tourville, claiming 200 arpens of land, situate district of St. Charles.   Produces record of a concession from Charles D. Delassus, L. G., dated 18th January, 1800 ; record of a plat of survey, dated 11th February, 1804, certified 9th January, 1806 ; record of a transfer from Tourville to St. Vrain, dated 12th February, 1800 ; record of a transfer from St. Vrain to Campbell and Matlock, dated 29th August, 1805 ; record of a transfer from sheriff to claimant, dated 29th January, 1808.   It is the opinion of the board that this claim ought not to be granted.   (See book No. 5, page 505.)

*November* 29, 1832.—The board met, pursuant to adjournment.   Present : L. F. Linn and F. R. Conway, commissioners.

Toussaint Tourville, by his legal representatives, claiming 800 arpens of land.   (See record-book C, page 423 ; book No. 5, page 505.)   Produces a paper purporting to be an original concession from Carlos Dehault Delassus, dated 18th January, 1800 ; also, deeds of conveyance.

M. P. Leduc, duly sworn, saith that the signature to said concession is in the proper handwriting of the said C. D. Delassus.   (See book No. 6, page 67.)

*August* 25, 1835.—The board met, pursuant to adjournment.   Present : F. R. Conway, J. H. Relfe, and F. H. Martin, commissioners.

Toussaint Tourville, claiming 800 arpens of land.   (See book No. 6, page 67.)

The board are unanimously of opinion that this claim ought not to be confirmed.   For reasons, see decision in the claim of Louis Lamalice, No. 80.

F. H. MARTIN,
F. R. CONWAY,
JAMES H. RELFE.

Class 2.   No. 128.—*Gabriel Constant, claiming 800 arpens.*

To Don CARLOS DEHAULT DELASSUS, *Lieutenant Governor of Upper Louisiana:*

SIR; Gabriel Constant has the honor to represent to you, that residing in this province since several years, he wishes to settle himself in it, and make a farm ; therefore he has recourse to the goodness of the government, hoping that you will be pleased to grant to him a tract of land of 800 arpens in superficie, to be taken out of the vacant lands of the King's domain, in the place which will appear most advantageous to the interest of your petitioner, who presumes to hope this favor of your justice.

ST. LOUIS, *March* 20, 1800.

his
GABRIEL × CONSTANT.
mark.

ST. LOUIS OF ILLINOIS, *March* 24, 1800.

Being assured that the petitioner has sufficient means to improve the land which he solicits, I do grant to him and his heirs the land which he solicits, if it is not prejudicial to any person, and the surveyor, Don Antonio

Soulard, shall put the interested in possession of the land solicited, in a vacant place of the royal domain; and this being done, he shall make out a plat of survey, delivering the same to the party, with his certificate, in order to serve to obtain the title in form from the intendant general, to whom alone corresponds, by royal order, the distributing and granting all classes of lands of the royal domain.

CARLOS DEHAULT DELASSUS.

St. Louis, *December 26, 1832.*   Truly translated.

JULIUS DE MUN.

CLASS 2. SURVEY FOR NOS. 128, 129, 130, 131, 132, 133, 134, 135, 136, AND 137.

Don Antonio Soulard, *Surveyor General of Upper Louisiana:*

I do certify that ten tracts of land, of 800 arpens (each) in superficie, were measured, the lines run and bounded, in favor and in presence of Don Alberto Tyson, as it is demonstrated in the foregoing figurative plat; the said proprietor having acquired those ten concessions, as well in the last, as in the present year, from the primitive owners, as it is notorious by referring to the extra-judicial deeds of sale annexed to the petitions and decrees of the primitive owners.

Each of the tracts of land is designated, in the said figurative plat, with the name of the vendor, and with the number corresponding to that which is put on the margin of each petition, in order to fix, clearly, the situation of the respective tracts ceded by each vendor, and to facilitate, to the one and the others, the knowledge of the conditions contained in the different deeds of sale—observing, that the dividing lines could not be run on the ground, on account of the bad weather which took place, and they shall have to be run at the demand of the interested.

Said lands were measured with the perch of the city (of Paris, omitted) of eighteen French feet, lineal measure of the same city, according to the agrarian measure in this province, and are situated at about nine miles to the west of the bank of the river Mississippi, and at fifty-one miles to the north of this town of St. Louis; bounded on its four sides as follows: to the N. N. W. by lands of Don Santyago St. Vrain, Alberto Tyson, and of Don Francisco Janin; to the S. S. E. in part by vacant lands of the royal domain, and by lands of various proprietors; to the E. S. E. and W. N. W., by vacant lands of the royal domain. Said survey and measurement was done without having regard to the variation of the needle, which is 7° 30′ E.; as is evident by referring to the foregoing figurative plat, on which are noted the dimensions, directions of the lines, and other boundaries, &c. Said survey was executed by virtue of the decrees of Don Carlos Dehault Delassus, as it is obvious by the ten petitions and decrees here annexed.

In testimony whereof, I do give the present, with the figurative plat here above, drawn conformably to the survey executed by the deputy surveyor, James Rankin, on the 13th of February of this present year, who signed on the minutes, which I certify.

St. Louis of Illinois, *March 20, 1804.*

ANTONIO SOULARD, *Surveyor General.*

St. Louis, *December 27, 1832.*   Truly translated.

| No. | Name of original claimant. | Arpens. | Nature and date of claim. | By whom granted. | By whom surveyed, date, and situation. |
|-----|---------------------------|---------|---------------------------|------------------|----------------------------------------|
| 128 | Gabriel Constant. | 800 | Concession, March 24, 1800. | C. Dehault Delassus. | James Rankin, D. S., 11th February, 1804. Certified by Soulard, 20th March, 1804. Fifty-one miles north of St. Louis, on Cuivre river. |

EVIDENCE WITH REFERENCE TO MINUTES AND RECORDS.

*May 8, 1806.*—The board met, agreeably to adjournment. Present: Hon. Clement B. Penrose, and James L. Donaldson, esq.

The same, (Albert Tyson,) assignee of Gabriel Constant, (claiming) 600 arpens of land, situate as aforesaid, produces a concession from Charles D. Delassus to said Constant, for 800 arpens, dated 24th of March, 1800; a survey, plat, and certificate, dated as aforesaid; and a deed of transfer, dated 5th January, 1804.

The board require further proofs.

*Witness on the part of the United States.* Gabriel Constant, being duly sworn, says that he never applied for the aforesaid concession; that the above claimant offered him one, but cannot tell when. The board reject this claim. The said concession is not duly registered. (See book No. 1, page 286.)

*August 27, 1810.*—Board met. Present: John B. C. Lucas, Clement B. Penrose, and Frederick Bates, commissioners.

Albert Tyson, assignee of Gabriel Constant, claiming 800 arpens of land. (See book No. 1, page 286.)

It is the opinion of the board that this claim ought not to be confirmed. (See book No. 4, page 474.)

*November 27, 1832.*—The board met, pursuant to adjournment. Present: L. F. Linn, and F. R. Conway, commissioners.

Gabriel Constant, by Albert Tyson, claiming 800 arpens of land. (See book C, pages 436, 438, and 439; book No. 1, page 286; No. 4, page 474.) Produces a concession dated 24th March, 1800, from Carlos Dehault Delassus; also, a deed of conveyance from said Constant to said Tyson; also, a plat and certificate of survey as above, (same produced by Toussaint Gendron, ten claims in one survey.)

M. P. Leduc, being duly sworn, saith that the signature to said concession is in the proper handwriting of Carlos Dehault Delassus. (See book No. 6, page 57.)

*August 25, 1835.*—The board met, pursuant to adjournment. Present: F. R. Conway, J. H. Relfe, and F. H. Martin, commissioners.

Gabriel Constant, claiming 800 arpens of land. (See book No. 6, page 57.)

The board are unanimously of opinion that this claim ought not to be confirmed. For reasons, see decision in the claim of Louis Lamalice, No. 80.

F. H. MARTIN,
F. R. CONWAY,
JAMES H. RELFE.

Class 2.  No. 129.—*Antoine Desnoyers, by Albert Tyson, claiming 800 arpens.*

To Don CARLOS DEHAULT DELASSUS, *Lieutenant Governor of Upper Louisiana:*

SIR : Antoine Desnoyers has the honor to represent to you, that residing in this province since several years, he would wish to settle himself in it, and establish a farm ; for these motives, he has recourse to the benevolence of this government, hoping that you may be pleased to grant to him a tract of land of eight hundred arpens in superficie, to be taken upon the vacant lands of the King's domain, in the place which will appear most convenient to the interest of your petitioner, who presumes to hope this favor of your justice.

ST. LOUIS OF ILLINOIS, *February 3,* 1800.

his<br>
ANTOINE × DESNOYERS.<br>
mark.

ST. LOUIS OF ILLINOIS, *February* 7, 1800.

Being assured that the petitioner has sufficient means to improve the land which he solicits, I do grant to him and his heirs the land which he solicits, if it is not prejudicial to any one, and the surveyor, Don Antoine Soulard, shall put the interested in possession of the quantity which he asks, in a vacant place of the royal domain ; and this being executed, he shall draw out a plat of survey, delivering the same to the party, with his certificate, in order to serve to obtain the title in form from the intendant general, to whom alone corresponds, by royal order, the distributing and granting all classes of lands, &c.

CARLOS DEHAULT DELASSUS.

ST. LOUIS, *December* 26, 1832.  Truly translated.

JULIUS DE MUN.

| No. | Name of original claimant. | Arpens. | Nature and date of claim. | By whom granted. | By whom surveyed, date, and situation. |
|---|---|---|---|---|---|
| 129 | Antoine Desnoyers, by Albert Tyson. | 800 | Concession, 7th February, 1800. | Carlos Dehault Delassus. | James Rankin, D. S., 13th February, 1804. Certified by Soulard, 20th March, 1804.  On Cuivre river. |

EVIDENCE WITH REFERENCE TO MINUTES AND RECORDS.

*May* 8, 1806.—The board met, agreeably to adjournment.  Present : Hon. Clement B. Penrose and James L. Donaldson, esq.

The same, (Albert Tyson,) assignee of Antoine Desnoyers, claiming 600 arpens of land, situate as foresaid, produces a concession from Charles D. Delassus, to said Desnoyers, for 800 arpens, dated 7th February, 1800 ; survey, plat, and certificate of the same, as aforesaid, and a deed of transfer of the same, dated 5th January, 1804.

The board require further proofs.

*Witness on the part of the United States.*  Antoine Desnoyers, being duly sworn, says that he is about twenty-one years of age ; that he never applied for a concession ; and that about three years ago claimant offered him one.

The board reject this claim, with the remark on the other side, (to wit : the said concession is not duly registered.)  (See book No. 1, page 286.)

*August* 27, 1810.—Board met.  Present : John B. C. Lucas, Clement B. Penrose, and Frederick Bates, commissioners.

Albert Tyson, assignee of Antoine Desnoyers, claiming 800 arpens of land.  (See book No. 1, page 286.)

It is the opinion of the board that this claim ought not to be confirmed.  (See book No. 4, page 475.)

*November* 27, 1832.—Board met, pursuant to adjournment.  Present : L. F. Linn and F. R. Conway, commissioners.

Antoine Desnoyers, by Albert Tyson, claiming 800 arpens of land.  (See book C, pages 437, 438, and 439 ; book No. 1, page 286 ; No. 4, page 475.)  Produces a paper purporting to be an original concession from Carlos Dehault Delassus, dated 7th February, 1800, and a deed of conveyance from said Desnoyers to said Tyson ; survey as above.

M. P. Leduc, duly sworn, says that the signature to the said concession is in the proper handwriting of Carlos Dehault Delassus.  (See book No. 6, page 57.)

*August* 25, 1835.—The board met, pursuant to adjournment.  Present : F. R. Conway, J. H. Relfe, and F. H. Martin, commissioners.

Antoine Desnoyers, claiming 800 arpens.  (See book No. 6, page 57.)

The board are unanimously of opinion that this claim ought not to be confirmed.  For reasons, see decision in the claim of Louis Lamalice, No. 80.

F. H. MARTIN,<br>
F. R. CONWAY,<br>
JAMES H. RELFE.

Class 2.  No. 130.—*Gabriel Hunaut, claiming 800 arpens.*

To Don CARLOS DEHAULT DELASSUS, *Lieutenant Governor of Upper Louisiana:*

SIR : Gabriel Hunaut has the honor to represent to you, that having resided in this province several years, he wishes to make an establishment in it ; therefore he has recourse to your goodness, hoping you will be pleased to grant to him a tract of land of 800 arpens in superficie, to be taken on the vacant lands of the King's domain, in the place which will appear most convenient to the interest of your petitioner, who presumes to hope this favor of your justice.

his<br>
GABRIEL + HUNAUT.<br>
mark.

ST. LOUIS, *May* 5, 1800.

St. Louis of Illinois, *May* 9, 1800.

Being assured that the petitioner has sufficient means to improve the land which he solicits, I do grant to him and his heirs the land which he solicits, if it is not prejudicial to anybody, and the surveyor, Don Antonio Soulard, shall put the interested in possession of the quantity of land which he asks, in a vacant place of the royal domain ; and this being done, he shall draw a plat of survey, delivering the same to the party, with his certificate, in order to serve to obtain the title in form from the intendant general, to whom alone corresponds, by royal order, the distributing and granting all classes of lands, &c.

CARLOS DEHAULT DELASSUS.

St. Louis, *December* 26, 1832.   Truly translated.

JULIUS DE MUN.

| No. | Name of original claimant. | Arpens. | Nature and date of claim. | By whom granted. | By whom surveyed, date, and situation. |
|-----|----------------------------|---------|---------------------------|------------------|----------------------------------------|
| 130 | Gabriel Hunaut. | 800 | Concession, 9th May, 1800. | C. Dehault Delassus. | James Rankin, D. S., 13th February, 1804. Certified by Soulard, 20th March, 1804. On Cuivre river. |

EVIDENCE WITH REFERENCE TO MINUTES AND RECORDS.

*May* 8, 1806.—The board met, agreeably to adjournment.   Present: Hon. Clement B. Penrose, and James L. Donaldson, esq.

The same, assignee of Gabriel Hunaut (Albert Tysón), claiming 600 arpens of land, situate as aforesaid, produces a concession from Charles D. Delassus for 800 arpens, dated 9th May, 1800 ; survey, plat, and certificate, as aforesaid, and a transfer of the same, dated December 3d, 1803.

The board require further proofs.

*Witness on the part of the United States.*   Gabriel Hunaut, being duly sworn, says that he never applied for a concession ; that the claimant offered him one, but cannot tell when.

The board reject this claim.   Remark as above, to wit: The said concession is not duly registered.   (See book No. 1, page 286.)

*August* 27, 1810.—Board met.   Present: John B. C. Lucas, Clement B. Penrose, and Frederick Bates, commissioners.

Albert Tyson, assignee of Gabriel Hunaut, claiming 800 arpens of land.   (See book No. 1, page 286.)

It is the opinion of the board that this claim ought not to be confirmed.   (See book No. 4, page 475.)

*November* 27, 1832.—The board met, pursuant to adjournment.   Present: L. F. Linn and F. R. Conway, commissioners.

Gabriel Hunaut, by Albert Tyson, claiming 800 arpens of land.   (See record-book C, pages 437, 438, and 439 ; book No. 1, page 286 ; No. 4, page 475.)   Produces a paper purporting to be an original concession from Carlos Dehault Delassus, dated 9th May, 1800 ; also, deeds of conveyance of the same ; also, plat and certificate of survey as above.

M. P. Leduc, duly sworn, says that the signature to the above-mentioned concession is in the proper handwriting of said Carlos Dehault Delassus.   (See book No. 6, page 58.)

*August* 25, 1835.—The board met, pursuant to adjournment.   Present: F. R. Conway, J. H. Relfe, and F. H. Martin, commissioners.

Gabriel Hunaut, claiming 800 arpens of land.   (See book No. 6, page 58.)

The board are unanimously of opinion that this claim ought not to be confirmed.   For reasons, see decision in the claim of Louis Lamalice, No. 80.

F. H. MARTIN,<br>F. R. CONWAY,<br>JAMES H. RELFE.

---

Class 2.   No. 131.—*Charles Tibeaux, claiming* 800 *arpens.*

To Don Carlos Dehault Delassus, *Lieutenant Governor of Upper Louisiana :*

Sir: Charles Baptiste Tibeaux has the honor to represent to you, that he would wish to form an establishment in the upper part of this province, which he has been inhabiting for a long while ; therefore he has recourse to your goodness, praying that you will be pleased to grant to him a tract of land of 800 arpens in superficie, to be taken on the vacant lands of the King's domain, in the place which will appear most advantageous to the interest of your petitioner, who presumes to hope this favor of your justice.

St. Louis, *December* 4, 1799.

CHARLES <sup>his</sup> × TIBEAUX.<br>mark.

St. Louis of Illinois, *December* 7, 1799.

Being assured that the petitioner has sufficient means to improve the lands which he solicits, I do grant to him and his heirs the land which he solicits, if it is not prejudicial to any one, and the surveyor, Don Antonio Soulard, shall put the interested in possession of the quantity of land asked by him, in a vacant place of the royal domain ; and this being done, he shall draw out a plat of his survey, delivering the same to the party, with his certificate, in order to serve to him to obtain the title in form from the intendant general, to whom alone corresponds, by royal order, the distributing and granting all classes of lands, &c.

CARLOS DEHAULT DELASSUS.

St. Louis, *December* 26, 1832.   Truly translated.

JULIUS DE MUN.

*Charles Baptiste Thibault, claiming 800 arpens.*

| No. | Name of original claimant | Arpens. | Nature and date of claim. | By whom granted. | By whom surveyed, date, and situation. |
|---|---|---|---|---|---|
| 131 | Charles Baptiste Thibault. | 800 | Concession, 7th December, 1799. | Carlos D. Delassus. | James Rankin, D. S., Feb. 13, 1804. Certified by Soulard, March 20, 1804. On Cuivre river. |

EVIDENCE WITH REFERENCE TO MINUTES AND RECORDS.

*May* 8, 1806.—The board met, agreeably to adjournment. Present: Hon. Clement B. Penrose, and James L. Donaldson, esq.

The same (Albert Tyson,) assignee of Charles B. Thibault, claiming 600 arpens of land, situate as aforesaid, produces a concession from Charles D. Delassus to said Thibault, for 800 arpens, dated December 7th, 1799; survey, plat, and certificate of the same, dated as aforesaid, and a deed of a transfer of the same, dated January 10, 1804.

The board require further proofs. The board reject this claim. Remark as above, (to wit: "The said concession is not duly registered.") (See book No. 1, page 287.)

*August* 27, 1810.—Board met. Present: John B. C. Lucas, Clement B. Penrose, and Frederick Bates, commissioners.

Albert Tyson, assignee of Charles B. Thibault, claiming 800 arpens of land. (See book No. 1, page 287.)

It is the opinion of the board that this claim ought not to be confirmed. (See book No. 4, page 475.)

*November* 27, 1832.—The board met, pursuant to adjournment. Present: L. F. Linn and F. R. Conway, commissioners.

Charles B. Thibault, by Albert Tyson, claiming 800 arpens of land. (See book C, pages 438 and 439; book No. 1, page 287; No. 4, page 475.)

Produces a paper purporting to be a concession from Carlos Dehault Delassus, dated 7th December, 1799; also, a deed of conveyance for the same. Plat and certificate as above.

M. P. Leduc, duly sworn, says that the signature to said concession is in the proper handwriting of the said Carlos Dehault Delassus. (See book No. 6, page 58.)

*August* 25, 1835.—The board met, pursuant to adjournment. Present: F. R. Conway, J. H. Relfe, and F. H. Martin, commissioners.

Charles B. Thibault, claiming 800 arpens of land. (See book No. 6, page 58.)

The board are unanimously of opinion that this claim ought not to be confirmed. For reasons, see decision in the claim of Louis Lamalice, No. 80.

F. H. MARTIN,<br>F. R. CONWAY,<br>JAMES H. RELFE.

---

Class 2.    No. 132.—*Joseph Desnoyers, claiming 800 arpens.*

To Don CARLOS DEHAULT DELASSUS, *Lieutenant Governor of Upper Louisiana:*

SIR: Joseph Desnoyers has the honor to represent to you, that residing in this country since a long while, he would wish to make an establishment in it; therefore he has recourse to your goodness, praying you will be pleased to grant to him a tract of land of 800 arpens in superficie, to be taken on the vacant lands of the King's domain, in a place which will appear the most convenient to the interests of your petitioner, who presumes to hope this favor of your justice.

ST. LOUIS, *January* 13, 1800.

JOSEPH <sup>his</sup> × <sub>mark.</sub> DESNOYERS.

ST. LOUIS OF ILLINOIS, *January* 15, 1800.

Being assured that the petitioner has sufficient means to improve the land which he solicits, I do grant to him and his heirs the land which he solicits, if it is not prejudicial to anybody, and the surveyor, Don Antonio Soulard, shall put the interested in possession of the quantity of land he asks, in a vacant place of the royal domain; and this being executed, he shall draw out a plat of his survey, delivering the same to the party, with his certificate, in order to serve to him to obtain the title in form from the intendant general, to whom alone corresponds, by royal order, the distributing and granting all classes of lands, &c.

CARLOS DEHAULT DELASSUS.

ST. LOUIS, *December* 26, 1832. Truly translated.

JULIUS DE MUN.

| No. | Name of original claimant. | Arpens. | Nature and date of claim. | By whom granted. | By whom surveyed, date, and situation. |
|---|---|---|---|---|---|
| 132 | Joseph Desnoyers. | 800 | Concession, January 15, 1800. | Carlos Dehault Delassus. | James Rankin, D. S., 13th February, 1804. Certified by Soulard, 20th March, 1804. On Cuivre river. |

EVIDENCE WITH REFERENCE TO MINUTES AND RECORDS.

*May* 8, 1806.—The board met, agreeably to adjournment.  Present: Hon. Clement B. Penrose, and James L. Donaldson, esq.

The same, (Albert Tyson,) assignee of Joseph Desnoyers, (claiming) 600 arpens of land, situate as aforesaid, produces a concession from Charles Dehault Delassus to said Desnoyers for 800 (arpens), dated January 15, 1800; a survey, plat, and certificate of the same, dated as aforesaid; and a transfer of said land, dated as aforesaid.

The board require further proofs.

*Witness on the part of the United States.*  Joseph Desnoyers, being duly sworn, says that he never applied for a concession; and that about two years ago he had one offered to him by claimant.

The board reject this claim, with the above remark, (to wit: the said concession is not duly registered.)  (See book No. 1, page 286.)

*August* 27, 1810.—The board met.  Present: John B. C. Lucas, Clement B. Penrose, and Frederick Bates, commissioners.

Albert Tyson, assignee of Joseph Desnoyers, claiming 800 arpens of land.  (See book No. 1, page 286.)

It is the opinion of the board that this claim ought not to be confirmed.  (See book No. 4, page 474.)

*November* 27, 1832.—The board met, pursuant to adjournment.  Present: L. F. Linn, and F. R. Conway, commissioners.

Joseph Desnoyers, by Albert Tyson, claiming 800 arpens of land.  (See book C, pages 437, 438 and 439; No. 1, page 286; and No. 4, page 474.)  Produces a paper purporting to be an original concession from Carlos Dehault Delassus, dated January 15, 1800; also, deeds of conveyance for same; also, plat and certificate as above.

M. P. Leduc, duly sworn, says that the signature to said concession is in the proper handwriting of said Carlos Dehault Delassus.  (See book No. 6, page 58.)

*August* 25, 1835.—The board met, pursuant to adjournment.  Present: F. R. Conway, J. H. Relfe, and F. H. Martin, commissioners.

Joseph Desnoyers, claiming 800 arpens of land.  (See book No. 6, page 58.)

The board are unanimously of opinion that this claim ought not to be confirmed.  For reasons, see decision in the claim of Louis Lamalice, No. 80.

F. H. MARTIN,
F. R. CONWAY,
JAMES H. RELFE.

---

### Class 2.  No. 133.—*Augustin Langlois, claiming 800 arpens.*

To Don CARLOS DEHAULT DELASSUS, *Lieutenant Governor of Upper Louisiana:*

SIR: Augustin Langlois has the honor of representing to you, that having for a long time been a resident in this province, and wishing to form an establishment in it, he has recourse to the benevolence of this government, praying that you may be pleased to grant to him a tract of land of 800 arpens in superficie, to be taken on the vacant lands of the King's domain, in the place which will appear most convenient to the interest of your petitioner, who presumes to expect this favor of your justice.

AUGUSTIN LANGLOIS.

ST. LOUIS, *June* 2, 1800.

ST. LOUIS OF ILLINOIS, *June* 4, 1800.

Being assured that the petitioner has sufficient means to improve the land which he solicits, I do grant to him and his heirs the land which he solicits, if it is not prejudicial to any person, and the surveyor, Don A. Soulard, shall put the interested in possession of the quantity of land which he asks, in a vacant place of the royal domain; and this being executed, he shall draw out a plat of his survey, delivering the same to the party, with his certificate, in order to serve to him to obtain the title in form from the intendant general, to whom corresponds, by royal order, the distributing and granting all classes of lands, &c.

CARLOS DEHAULT DELASSUS.

ST. LOUIS, *December* 26, 1832.  Truly translated.

JULIUS DE MUN.

| No. | Name of original claimant. | Arpens. | Nature and date of claim. | By whom granted. | By whom surveyed, date, and situation. |
|-----|---------------------------|---------|---------------------------|------------------|----------------------------------------|
| 133 | Augustin Langlois. | 800 | Concession, 4th June, 1800. | Carlos Dehault Delassus. | James Rankin, D. S., 13th February, 1804.  Certified by Soulard, 20th March, 1804.  On Cuivre river. |

EVIDENCE WITH REFERENCE TO MINUTES AND RECORDS.

*May* 8, 1806.—The board met, agreeably to adjournment.  Present: Hon. Clement B. Penrose and, J. L. Donaldson, esq.

The same, (Albert Tyson,) assignee of Augustin Langlois, claiming 600 arpens of land, situate as aforesaid, produces a concession from Carlos Dehault Delassus to the said Langlois for 800 arpens, dated June 4, 1800, with a survey, plat, certificate, and deed of transfer of the same, dated as aforesaid.  The board require further proofs.

*Witness on the part of the United States.* Augustin Langlois, being duly sworn, says that he never applied for a concession, and that about three or four years ago, claimant offered him one. The board reject this claim. Remark as aforesaid, (to wit: that this claim is not duly registered.) (See book No. 1, page 287.)

*August* 27, 1810.—Board met. Present: John B. C. Lucas, Clement B. Penrose, and Frederick Bates, commissioners.

Albert Tyson, assignee of Augustin Langlois, claiming 800 arpens of land. (See book No. 1, page 287.) It is the opinion of the board that this claim ought not to be confirmed. (See book No. 4, page 475.)

*November* 27, 1832.—The board met, pursuant to adjournment. Present: L. F. Linn and F. R. Conway, commissioners.

Augustin Langlois, claiming 800 arpens of land. (See book C, pages 438 and 439; book No. 1, page 287; No. 4, page 475.) Produces a paper purporting to be an original concession from Carlos Dehault Delassus, dated June 4, 1800, and deeds of conveyance for same. Plat as above.

M. P. Leduc, duly sworn, saith that the signature to said concession is in the proper handwriting of said Carlos Dehault Delassus. (See book No. 6, page 59.)

*August* 25, 1835.—The board met, pursuant to adjournment. Present: F. R. Conway, J. H. Relfe, and F. H. Martin, commissioners.

Augustin Langlois, claiming 800 arpens of land. (See book No. 6, page 59.)

The board are unanimously of opinion that this claim ought not to be confirmed. For reasons, see decision in the claim of Louis Lamalice, No. 80.

F. H. MARTIN,
F. R. CONWAY,
JAMES H. RELFE.

---

Class 2. No. 134.—*Louis Desnoyers, claiming 800 arpens.*

To Don CARLOS DEHAULT DELASSUS, *Lieutenant Governor of Upper Louisiana:*

SIR: Louis Desnoyers has the honor to represent to you, that residing in this province since a long time, he wishes to settle himself and make an establishment in it; therefore he has recourse to your goodness, praying you will be pleased to grant to him a tract of land of eight hundred arpens in superficie, to be taken on the vacant lands of the King's domain, in the place which will appear most convenient to the interest of your petitioner, who presumes to expect this favor of your justice.

ST. LOUIS, *January* 13, 1800.

LOUIS × DESNOYERS.
his mark.

ST. LOUIS OF ILLINOIS, *January* 15, 1800.

Being assured that the petitioner has sufficient means to improve the land which he solicits, I do grant to him and his heirs the land which he solicits, if it is not prejudicial to any one, and the surveyor, Don Antonio Soulard, shall put the interested in possession of the quantity of land he asks, in a vacant place of the royal domain; and this being executed, he shall draw a plat of his survey, which he shall deliver to the party, with his certificate, in order to serve to him to obtain the title in form from the intendant general, to whom alone corresponds, by royal order, the distributing and granting of all classes of lands, &c.

CARLOS DEHAULT DELASSUS.

ST. LOUIS, *December* 27, 1832. Truly translated.

JULIUS DE MUN.

| No. | Name of original claimant. | Arpens. | Nature and date of claim. | By whom granted. | By whom surveyed, date, and situation. |
|---|---|---|---|---|---|
| 134 | Louis Desnoyers. | 800 | Concession, 15th January, 1800. | Carlos Dehault Delassus. | James Rankin, D. S., 13th February, 1804. Certified by Soulard, 20th March, 1804. Fifty-one miles north of St. Louis. On Cuivre river. |

EVIDENCE WITH REFERENCE TO MINUTES AND RECORDS.

*May* 8, 1806.—The board met, agreeably to adjournment. Present: Hon. Clement B. Penrose, and James L. Donaldson, esq.

The same, (Albert Tyson,) assignee of Louis Desnoyers, claiming 800 arpens of land, situate as aforesaid, produces a concession from Charles D. Delassus to the said Louis Desnoyers, for 800 arpens, dated January 15, 1800; a survey, plat, certificate, and transfer of the same, dated as aforesaid. The board require further proofs.

*Witness as aforesaid on the part of the United States.* Louis Desnoyers, being duly sworn, says, that he never applied for a concession, and that claimant did, about three years ago, offer him one. The board reject this claim. Remark as aforesaid, (to wit: the said concession is not duly registered.) (See book No. 1, page 287.)

*August* 27, 1810.—Board met. Present: John B. C. Lucas, Clement B. Penrose, and Frederick Bates, commissioners.

Albert Tyson, assignee of Louis Desnoyers, claiming 800 arpens of land. (See book No. 1, page 287.) It is the opinion of the board that this claim ought not to be confirmed. (See book No. 4, page 475.)

*November* 27, 1832.—The board met, pursuant to adjournment. Present: L. F. Linn, F. R. Conway, commissioners.

Louis Desnoyers, by Albert Tyson, claiming 800 arpens of land. (See book C, pages 437, 438 and 439; book No. 1, page 287; No. 4, page 475. Produces a paper purporting to be an original concession from Carlos Dehault Delassus, dated January 15, 1800; also, deeds of conveyance for same, and plat and certificate.

M. P. Leduc, duly sworn, says that the signature to said concession is in the proper handwriting of said Carlos D. Delassus. (See book No. 6, page 59.)

*August* 25, 1835.—The board met, pursuant to adjournment. Present: F. R. Conway, J. H. Relfe, and F. H. Martin, commissioners.

Louis Desnoyers, claiming 800 arpens of land. (See book No. 6, page 59.)

The board are unanimously of opinion that this claim ought not to be confirmed. For reasons, see decision in the claim of Louis Lamalice, No. 80.

F. H. MARTIN,<br>F. R. CONWAY,<br>JAMES H. RELFE.

---

Class 2. No. 135.—Amable Chartran, claiming 800 arpens.

To Don CARLOS DEHAULT DELASSUS, *Lieutenant Governor of Upper Louisiana:*

SIR: Amable Chartran has the honor to represent to you, that residing since a long time in this province, he wishes to make an establishment in it; therefore he has recourse to your goodness, praying that you will be pleased to grant to him a tract of land of eight hundred arpens in superficie, to be taken on the vacant land of the King's domain, in the place which will appear most convenient to the interest of your petitioner, who presumes to hope this favor of your justice.

ST. LOUIS, *June* 16, 1800.

AMABLE × CHARTRAN.<br>mark.

ST. LOUIS OF ILLINOIS, June 18, 1800.

Being assured that the petitioner has sufficient means to improve the land which he solicits, I do grant to him and his heirs the lands which he solicits, provided it is not prejudicial to any one, and the surveyor, Don Antonio Soulard, shall put the interested in possession of the quantity of land he asks, in a vacant place in the royal domain; and this being executed, he shall draw a plat of his survey, delivering the same to the party, with his certificate, in order to obtain the title in form from the intendant general, to whom alone corresponds, by royal order, the distributing and granting all classes of land, &c.

CARLOS DEHAULT DELASSUS.

ST. LOUIS, *December* 27, 1832. Truly translated.

JULIUS DE MUN.

| No. | Name of original claimant. | Arpens | Nature and date of claim. | By whom granted. | By whom surveyed, date, and situation. |
|---|---|---|---|---|---|
| 135 | Amable Chartran. | 800 | Concession, 18th June, 1800. | Carlos Dehault Delassus. | James Rankin, D. S., 13th February, 1804. Certified by Soulard, 20th March, 1804. Fifty-one miles north of St. Louis, on Cuivre river. |

EVIDENCE WITH REFERENCE TO MINUTES AND RECORDS.

*May* 8, 1802.—The board met, agreeably to adjournment. Present: Hon Clement B. Penrose, and James L. Donaldson, esq.

Albert Tyson, assignee of Amable Chartran, claiming 800 arpens of land, situated on the waters of the river Cuivre, district of St. Charles. Produces a concession from Charles Dehault Delassus for 800 arpens, dated June 8, 1800; a survey and plat taken February 13, and certified March 20, 1804; and a deed of transfer for the same, dated January 3, 1804.

The board require further proof. Witness on the part of the United States absent.

The board reject this claim, and observe that the concession or warrant of survey is not duly registered. (See book No. 1, page 285.)

*August* 27, 1810.—Board met. Present: John B. C. Lucas, Clement B. Penrose, and Frederick Bates, commissioners.

Albert Tyson, assignee of Amable Chartran, claiming 800 arpens of land. (See book No. 1, page 285.)

It is the opinion of the board that this claim ought not to be confirmed. (See book No. 4, page 474.)

*November* 27, 1832.—The board met, pursuant to adjournment. Present: L. F. Linn and F. R. Conway, commissioners.

Amable Chartran, by Albert Tyson, claiming 600 arpens, and said Chartran 200 arpens of land. (See book C, pages 436, 438, and 439; book No. 1, page 285; No. 4, page 474.) Produces a paper purporting to be an original concession from Carlos Dehault Delassus, dated 18th June, 1800; also plat and certificate as above.

M. P. Leduc, duly sworn, says that the signature to said concession is in the proper handwriting of the said Carlos Dehault Delassus. (See book No. 6, page 59.)

*August* 25, 1835.—The board met, pursuant to adjournment. Present: F. R. Conway, J. H. Relfe, and F. H. Martin, commissioners.

Amable Chartran, claiming 800 arpens of land. (See book No. 6, page 59.)

The board are unanimously of opinion that this claim ought not to be confirmed. For reasons, see decision in the claim of Louis Lamalice, No. 80.

F. H. MARTIN,<br>F. R. CONWAY,<br>JAMES H. RELFE.

Class 2.    No. 136.—*François Desnoyers, claiming 800 arpens.*

To Don Carlos Dehault Delassus, *Lieutenant Governor of Upper Louisiana :*

Sir : François Desnoyers has the honor to represent to you, that residing in this province since a long time, he wishes to settle himself in it and improve a farm ; therefore he has recourse to your goodness, praying that you will be pleased to grant to him a tract of land of 800 arpens in superficie, to be taken on the vacant lands of the King's domain, in the place which will appear most convenient to the interests of your petitioner, who presumes to expect this favor of your justice.

St. Louis, *January* 13, 1800.    FRANCOIS × DESNOYERS.
his
mark.

St. Louis of Illinois, *January* 15, 1800.

Being assured that the petitioner has sufficient means to improve the land which he solicits, I do grant to him and his heirs the land which he solicits, if it does not prejudice any one, and the surveyor, Don Antonio Soulard, shall put the interested in possession of the quantity of land which he asks, in a vacant place of the royal domain ; and this being executed, he shall draw a plat of his survey, delivering the same to the party, with his certificate, in order to serve to him to obtain the title in form from the intendant general, to whom alone corresponds, by royal order, the distributing and granting all classes of lands, &c.

CARLOS DEHAULT DELASSUS.

St. Louis, *December* 27, 1832.    Truly translated.

JULIUS DE MUN.

| No. | Name of original claimant. | Arpens. | Nature and date of claim. | By whom granted. | By whom surveyed, date, and situation. |
|---|---|---|---|---|---|
| 136 | François Desnoyers. | 800 | Concession, 15th Jan , 1800. | Carlos Dehault Delassus. | James Rankin, D. S., 13th February, 1804. Certified by Soulard, 20th March, 1804. Fifty-one miles north of St. Louis. On Cuivre river. |

EVIDENCE WITH REFERENCE TO MINUTES AND RECORDS.

*May* 8, 1806.—The board met, pursuant to adjournment.  Present : Hon. Clement B. Penrose, and James L. Donaldson, esq.

The same, (Albert Tyson,) assignee of Francis Desnoyers, claiming 600 arpens of land, situate as aforesaid, produces a concession from Charles D. Delassus to the said Francis Desnoyers, dated as aforesaid, for 800 arpens ;  a survey, plat, certificate, and transfer of the same, dated as aforesaid.  The board require further proofs.

The board reject this claim, remarks as aforesaid (to wit : the said concession is not duly registered.)  (See book No. 1, page 287.)

*August* 27, 1810.—Board met.  Present : John B. C. Lucas, Frederick Bates, and Clement B. Penrose, commissioners.

Albert Tyson, assignee of Francois Desnoyers, claiming 800 arpens of land.  (See book No. 1, page 287.)

It is the opinion of the board that this claim ought not to be confirmed.  (See book No. 4, page 475.)

*November* 27, 1832.—The board met, pursuant to adjournment.  Present : L. F. Linn and F. R. Conway, commissioners.

Francis Desnoyers, by Albert Tyson, claiming 800 arpens of land.  (See book C, pages 438 and 439 ;  book No. 1, page 287 ; No. 4, page 475.)  Produces a paper, purporting to be an original concession from Carlos Dehault Delassus, dated 15th January, 1800 ; also, deeds of conveyance for the same ; plat and certificate as above, (produced by Toussaint Gendron, ten claims in one survey.)

M. P. Leduc, duly sworn, saith that the signature to said concession is in the proper handwriting of said Carlos Dehault Delassus.  (See book No. 6, page 59.)

*August* 25, 1835.—The board met, pursuant to adjournment.  Present : F. R. Conway, J. H. Relfe, F. H. Martin, commissioners.

François Desnoyers, claiming 800 arpens of land.  (See book No. 6, page 59.)

The board are unanimously of opinion that this claim ought not to be confirmed.  For reasons, see decision in the claim of Louis Lamalice, No. 80.

F. H. MARTIN,
F. R. CONWAY,
JAMES H. RELFE.

Class 2.    No. 137.—*Toussaint Gendron, claiming 800 arpens.*

To Don Carlos Dehault Delassus, *Lieutenant Governor of Upper Louisiana :*

Sir : Toussaint Gendron has the honor to represent that he would wish to establish himself in the upper part of this province, where he has been residing for some time ; therefore he has recourse to your goodness, praying that you will please grant him a tract of land of 800 arpens in superficie, to be taken on the vacant lands of his Majesty's domain, in the place which will appear most favorable to the interest of your petitioner, who presumes to expect this favor of your justice.

TOUSSAINT × GENDRON.
his
mark.

St. Louis, *April* 3, 1800.

St. Louis of Illinois, *April 5, 1800.*

Whereas we are assured that the petitioner possesses sufficient means to improve the land which he solicits, I do grant to him and his heirs the land he solicits, provided it is not prejudicial to any person, and the surveyor, Don Antonio Soulard, shall put the party interested in possession of the quantity of land he asks, in a vacant place of the royal domain; and this being executed, he shall make out a plat, delivering the same to said party, together with his certificate, in order to serve to him to obtain the title in form from the intendant general, to whom alone belongs, by royal order, the distributing and granting all classes of lands.

CARLOS DEHAULT DELASSUS.

St. Louis, *August 25, 1835.*

I certify the above to be truly translated from book A, pages 31 and 32 of record in this office.

JULIUS DE MUN, *T. B. C.*

| No. | Name of original claimant. | Arpens. | Nature and date of claim. | By whom granted. | By whom surveyed, date, and situation. |
|---|---|---|---|---|---|
| 137 | Toussaint Gendron. | 800 | Concession, 5th April, 1800. | C. Dehault Delassus. | James Rankin, D. S., Feb., 13, 1804. Certified by Soulard, March 20, 1804. Fifty-one miles north of St. Louis. On Cuivre river. |

EVIDENCE WITH REFERENCE TO MINUTES AND RECORDS.

*November* 15, 1809.—Board met. Present: John B. C. Lucas and Clement B. Penrose, commissioners.

John Mullanphy, assignee of Toussaint Gendron, claiming 800 arpens of land, situate on the river Cuivre, in the district of St. Charles, produces to the board a concession from Don Carlos Dehault Delassus, lieutenant governor, dated the 5th of April, 1800, to the said Toussaint Gendron; also a conveyance from the said Gendron to claimant, dated the 5th of September, 1803.

It is the opinion of the board that this claim ought not to be confirmed. (See book No. 4, page 193.)

*November* 27, 1832.—The board met, pursuant to adjournment. Present: L. F. Linn and F. R. Conway, commissioners.

Toussaint Gendron, by Albert Tyson, claiming 800 arpens of land. (See book C, pages 438 and 439; book No. 4, page 193.) Produces a paper, purporting to be the original survey for 800 arpens of land, taken on the 13th of February, and certified 20th March, 1804: said plat of survey comprising 10 concessions of 800 arpens each.

M. P. Leduc, being duly sworn, saith that the signature to said plat of survey is in the proper handwriting of Antonio Soulard, surveyor general. (See book No. 6, page 57.)

*August* 25, 1835.—The board met, pursuant to adjournment. Present: F. R. Conway, J. H. Relfe, and F. H. Martin, commissioners.

Toussaint Gendron, claiming 800 arpens of land. (See book No. 6, page 57.)

The board are unanimously of opinion that this claim ought not to be confirmed. For reasons, see decision in the claim of Louis Lamalice, No. 80.

F. H. MARTIN,
F. R. CONWAY,
JAMES H. RELFE.

Class 2.   No. 138.—*Daniel Quick, claiming* 800 *arpens.*

To Don CARLOS DEHAULT DELASSUS, *Lieutenant Governor of Upper Louisiana:*

SIR: Daniel Quick has the honor to represent, that wishing to establish himself in the upper part of this province, where he has been residing for some time, he promises to submit to the duties and taxes which it may please his Majesty to establish; therefore, the petitioner prays you, sir, to grant him a tract of land of 800 arpens in superficie, to be taken in the King's domain, at the place which will appear the most advantageous to the interest of the petitioner, who presumes to expect this favor of your justice.

St. Louis, *February 3, 1801.*

DANIEL × QUICK.
his
mark.

St. Louis of Illinois, *February 5, 1801.*

Whereas it is notorious that the petitioner possesses more than the means and number of hands (population) necessary to obtain the concession which he solicits, I do grant to him and his heirs the land he solicits, provided it is not to the prejudice of any person, and the surveyor, Don Antonio Soulard, shall put the party interested in possession of the quantity of land he asks, in a vacant place of the royal domain; and this being executed, he shall make out a plat, delivering the same to said party, together with his certificate, in order to serve to him to obtain the concession and title in form from the intendant general, to whom alone belongs, by royal order, the distributing and granting all classes of lands belonging to the royal domain.

CARLOS DEHAULT DELASSUS.

St. Louis, *August 21, 1834.* Truly translated from record book C, pages 324 and 325.

JULIUS DE MUN, *T. B. C.*

*Daniel Quick, claiming 800 arpens.*

| No. | Name of original claimant. | Arpens. | Nature and date of claim. | By whom granted. | By whom surveyed, date, and situation. |
|-----|---------------------------|---------|---------------------------|------------------|----------------------------------------|
| 138 | Daniel Quick. | 800 | Concession, 5th February, 1801. | Carlos Dehault Delassus. | James Rankin, D. S., January 2, 1804. Certified 5th March, 1804, by A. Soulard, surveyor general. One hundred and thirty miles N. W. of St. Louis. |

EVIDENCE WITH REFERENCE TO MINUTES AND RECORDS.

*May* 28, 1806.—The board met, agreeably to adjournment.  Present : Hon. Clement B. Penrose.

Jacques St. Vrain, assignee of Daniel Quick, claiming 550 arpens of land, situate in the district of St. Charles, produces a concession from Charles Dehault Delassus for 800 arpens to the said Daniel Quick, dated February 5, 1801, a certificate of survey of the same, dated 5th March, 1804, and a deed of transfer, dated December 5, 1803.

The board cannot act on this claim.  (See book No. 1, page 301.)

*August* 17, 1811.—Board met.  Present : Clement B. Penrose and Frederick Bates, commissioners.

Jacques St. Vrain, assignee of Daniel Quick, claiming 550 arpens, and Daniel Quick, claiming 250 arpens of land.  (See book No. 1, page 301.)

It is the opinion of the board that this claim ought not to be confirmed.  (See book No. 5, page 316.)

*June* 26, 1834.—The board met, pursuant to adjournment.  Present : J. S. Mayfield and F. R. Conway, commissioners.

Daniel Quick, by his legal representatives, claiming 800 arpens of land.  (See record-book C, page 324 ; minutes, book No. 1, page 301 ; No. 5, page 316.  See book No. 6, page 538.)

*August* 25, 1835.—The board met, pursuant to adjournment.  Present : F. R. Conway, J. H. Relfe, and F. H. Martin, commissioners.

Daniel Quick, claiming 800 arpens of land.  (See book No. 6, page 538.)

The board are unanimously of opinion that this claim ought not to be confirmed.  For reasons, see decision in the claim of Louis Lamalice, No. 80.

F. H. MARTIN,
F. R. CONWAY,
JAMES H. RELFE.

Class 2.    No. 139.—*Joseph Jamison, claiming 800 arpens.*

To Don CARLOS DEHAULT DELASSUS, *Lieutenant Governor of Upper Louisiana :*

SIR : Jos. Jamison has the honor to represent to you, that he would wish to form a plantation in the upper part of this province, in which he has been residing for some time ; the petitioner engaging himself to submit to all the taxes and charges which his Majesty will please to impose ; therefore he supplicates you to grant to him a tract of land of eight hundred arpens in superficie, to be taken on the vacant lands of his Majesty, in the place which will appear most convenient to the interest of your petitioner ; favor which the petitioner presumes to expect of your justice.

JOSEPH JAMISON.

ST. LOUIS, *February* 8, 1802.

ST. LOUIS OF ILLINOIS, *February* 9, 1802.

Whereas it is notorious that the petitioner has more than the means and the number of hands (populacion) necessary to obtain the concession which he solicits, I do grant to him and his heirs the land which he solicits, if it is not prejudicial to anybody, and the surveyor, Don Antonio Soulard, shall put the interested in possession of the quantity of land which he asks, in the place indicated ; and this being executed, he shall draw a plat of his survey, which he shall deliver to the party, with his certificate, in order to serve to him to obtain the concession and title in form from the intendant general, to whom alone corresponds, by royal order, the distributing and granting all classes of lands of the royal domain.

CARLOS DEHAULT DELASSUS.

ST. LOUIS, *January* 1, 1833.  Truly translated.

JULIUS DE MUN.

Don ANTONIO SOULARD, *Surveyor General of the settlements of Upper Louisiana :*

I do certify that a tract of land of eight hundred arpens in superficie was measured, the lines run and bounded, in favor and in presence of Joseph Jamison ; said measurement was done with the perch of the city of Paris, of eighteen French feet in length, lineal measure of the same city, conformably to the agrarian measure of this province, which land is situated at about 130 miles to the northwest of this town, and 13 miles to the west of the river Mississippi ; bounded to the north and east by vacant lands of the royal domain ; to the south by lands of Dorresto Flubbert, and to the west by lands of Daniel Quick.  Which surveys and measurements were executed without regard to the variation of the needle, which is 7° 30′ east, as can be verified by referring to the foregoing figurative plat, on which are noted the dimension, direction of the lines, and other boundaries, &c.  Said survey was taken by virtue of the decree of the lieutenant governor and sub-delegate of the royal Fiscal, Don Carlos Dehault Delassus, dated December 1, 1800, here annexed.  In testimony whereof, I do give the present, with the foregoing figurative plat, drawn conformably to the survey executed by the deputy surveyor, Mr. James Rankin, on the 2d of January, 1804, who has signed on the minutes, which I do certify.

ANTONIO SOULARD, *Surveyor-General.*

St. Louis of Illinois, *February 10, 1804.*

| No. | Name of original claimant. | Arpens. | Nature and date of claim. | By whom granted. | By whom surveyed, date, and situation. |
|---|---|---|---|---|---|
| 139 | Joseph Jamison. | 800 | Concession, 9th February, 1802. | Carlos Dehault Delassus. | James Rankin, D. S., 2d Jan., 1804. Certified by Soulard, 10th Feb., 1804. One hundred and thirty miles N. W. of St. Louis. |

EVIDENCE WITH REFERENCE TO MINUTES AND RECORDS.

*May 28, 1806.*—The board met, agreeably to adjournment. Present : Hon. Clement B. Penrose.

The same, (Jacques St. Vrain,) assignee of Joseph Jamison, 600 arpens of land, situate as aforesaid, produces a concession from Charles D. Delassus, dated February 9, 1802 ; a survey of the same, dated 10th February, 1804 ; and a deed of transfer, dated December 5, 1803.

The board cannot act. (See book No. 1, page 304.)

*August 17, 1811.*—Board met. Present : Clement B. Penrose and Frederick Bates, commissioners.

Jacques St. Vrain, assignee of Joseph Jamison, claiming 600 arpens, and Joseph Jamison, claiming 200 arpens of land. (See book No. 1, page 304.)

It is the opinion of the board that this claim ought not to be confirmed. (See book No. 5, page 318.)

*December 19, 1832.*—F. R. Conway, esq., appeared, pursuant to adjournment.

Joseph Jamison, by his legal representative, John Mullanphy, claiming 800 arpens of land. (See book C, pages 327 and 328 ; books No. 1, page 304 ; No. 5, page 318.) Produces a paper purporting to be an original concession from Carlos Dehault Delassus, dated 9th February, 1802 ; also, a plat and certificate of survey, dated 10th February, 1804, by Antonio Soulard ; also, deed of conveyance.

M. P. Leduc, being duly sworn, saith that the signatures to the above-mentioned concession and certificate of survey are in the proper handwriting of said Delassus and Soulard. (See book No. 6, page 87.)

*August 25, 1835.*—The board met, pursuant to adjournment. Present : F. R. Conway, J. H. Relfe, and F. H. Martin, commissioners.

Joseph Jamison, claiming 800 arpens of land. (See book No. 6, page 87.)

The board are unanimously of opinion that this claim ought not to be confirmed. For reasons, see decision in the claim of Louis Lamalice, No. 80.

F. H. MARTIN,
F. R. CONWAY,
JAMES H. RELFE.

---

Class 2. No. 140.—*Charles Miville, claiming 800 arpens.*

To Don CARLOS DEHAULT DELASSUS, *Lieutenant Governor of Upper Louisiana :*

SIR : Charles Miville has the honor to represent to you, that he would wish to obtain a concession, in order to form an establishment in the upper part of this province, which he has been inhabiting for a long while ; the petitioner promising to submit himself to the taxes and charges which it may please his Majesty to impose ; therefore the petitioner prays you to grant to him a tract of land of eight hundred arpens in superficie, to be taken on the vacant lands of his Majesty's domain, in the place which will appear most advantageous to his (the petitioner's) interest ; favor which the petitioner presumes to expect of your justice.

St. Louis, *November 16, 1799.*

his<br>CHS. × MIVILLE.<br>mark.

St. Louis of Illinois, *November 18, 1799.*

Whereas it is notorious that the petitioner possesses more than the means and the number of hands (population) necessary to obtain the concession which he solicits, I do grant to him and his heirs the land he solicits, provided it is not prejudicial to anybody, and the surveyor, Don Antonio Soulard, shall put the interested (party) in possession of the quantity of land he asks, in a vacant place of the royal domain ; which being executed, he shall make out a plat of (his) survey, delivering the same to said party, with his certificate, in order to serve him to obtain the concession and title in form from the intendant general, to whom alone corresponds, by royal order, the distributing and granting all classes of lands of the royal domain.

CARLOS DEHAULT DELASSUS.

St. Louis, *April 29, 1833.* Truly translated.

JULIUS DE MUN, *T. B. C.*

Don ANTONIO SOULARD, *Surveyor General of Upper Louisiana :*

I do certify that two tracts of land, of 800 arpens each, making the quantity of 1,600 arpens in superficie, as it is evinced by the foregoing figurative plat, have been measured, the lines run and bounded, in favor of Don Louis Labeaume, and in presence of his agent, Albert Tyson ; which two concessions have been purchased last year by the said proprietor from the original owners, as can be seen by the deed of sale, recorded in this government, and by another deed (*familiar*) inserted below one of the petitions here annexed. Each of the tracts of land are designated in the said figurative plat by the name of the vendor ; observing that the dotted line could not be run on the spot on account of the bad weather which occurred, and it shall be run whenever the interested (party) shall require it. The said lands were measured with the perch of the same city, according to the agrarian measure of this province, and are situated at about 100 miles north of this town of St. Louis; bounded north by the banks of Salt river; south by the lands of William Jamison; east by vacant lands of the royal domain, and west by other lands of Carlos Fremon Delauriere. The said survey and measurement were executed without regard to the variation of the needle, which is of 7° 30' E., as is evinced by the foregoing figurative plat, on which is noted the dimensions and courses of the lines, and other boundaries, &c. This survey was executed by virtue of the decree of Don Carlos Dehault Delassus, as it is proven by the petitions and decrees here annexed. And in order that the whole be available, according to law, I do give the present, with the foregoing figurative plat, drawn conformably to the operations executed by the deputy surveyor, James Rankin, under date of January 4, of this present year, and who signed on the minutes, to which I certify.

St. Louis of Illinois, *March* 5, 1804.

ANTONIO SOULARD, *Surveyor General.*

Truly translated.

JULIUS DE MUN.

| No. | Name of original claimant. | Arpens. | Nature and date of claim. | By whom granted. | By whom surveyed, date, and situation. |
|---|---|---|---|---|---|
| 140 | Charles Miville. | 800 | Concession, 18th November, 1799. | Carlos Dehault Delassus. | James Rankin, D. S., 4th January, 1804. Certified by Soulard, 5th March, 1804. One hundred miles north of St. Louis. |

EVIDENCE WITH REFERENCE TO MINUTES AND RECORDS.

*November* 27, 1811.—Board met. Present: John B. C. Lucas, Clement B. Penrose, and Frederick Bates, commissioners.

Louis Labeaume, assignee of Charles Miville, claiming 600 arpens of land, and said Miville, claiming 200 arpens of land, situate on Salt river, district of St. Charles, produces record of a concession from Delassus, lieutenant governor, dated 18th November, 1799; record of a plat of survey, dated 4th January, and certified 5th March, 1804; record of a transfer from Miville to claimant, dated 9th December, 1803.

It is the opinion of the board that this claim ought not to be confirmed. (See book No. 5, page 456.)

*March* 25, 1833.—F. R. Conway, esq., appeared, pursuant to adjournment.

Charles Miville, by Louis Lebeaume's representatives, claiming 800 arpens of land. (See book C, pages 341 and 342; minutes, No. 5, page 456.) Produces a paper, purporting to be an original concession from Carlos Dehault Delassus, dated November 18, 1799; also, a plat and certificate of survey, taken January 4th, and certified by Soulard, March 5, 1804; also, a deed dated December 20, 1811.

M. P. Leduc, duly sworn, says that the signature to the concession and to the plat of survey are in the respective handwriting of Carlos Dehault Delassus and Antonio Soulard. (See book No. 6, page 141.)

*August* 25, 1835.—The board met, pursuant to adjournment. Present: F. R. Conway, J. H. Relfe, and F. H. Martin, commissioners.

Charles Miville, claiming 800 arpens of land. (See book No. 6, page 141.)

The board are unanimously of opinion that this claim ought not to be confirmed. For reasons, see decision in the claim of Louis Lamalice, No. 80.

F. H. MARTIN,
F. R. CONWAY,
JAMES H. RELFE.

---

Class 2.    No. 141.—*Joseph Marié, claiming 800 arpens.*

To Don Carlos Dehault Delassus, *Lieutenant Governor of Upper Louisiana:*

Sir: Joseph Marié has the honor to represent to you, that he would wish to establish himself in the upper part of this province, where he has been residing for several years; therefore, he has recourse to your goodness, praying that you will be pleased to grant to him a tract of land of 800 arpens in superficie, to be taken on the vacant lands of the King's domain, in the place which shall be most convenient to the interest of your petitioner, who presumes to expect this favor of your justice.

St. Louis, *January* 8, 1801.

JOSEPH x MARIÉ.
his
mark.

St. Louis of Illinois, *January* 10, 1801.

Whereas we are assured that the petitioner possesses sufficient means to improve the lands which he solicits, I do grant to him and his heirs the land which he solicits, provided it is not prejudicial to anybody, and the surveyor, Don Antonio Soulard, shall put the interested in possession of the quantity of land he asks, in a vacant place of the royal domain; and this being executed, he shall draw a plat of his survey, delivering the same to the party, with his certificate, in order to serve him to obtain the concession and title in form from the intendant general, to whom alone corresponds, by royal order, the distributing and granting all classes of lands of the royal domain.

CARLOS DEHAULT DELASSUS.

Registered at the desire of the interested. (Book No. 2, page 48, No. 34.)

SOULARD.

St. Louis, *March* 28, 1833. Truly translated.

JULIUS DE MUN.

*Joseph Marié, claiming 800 arpens.*

| No. | Name of original claimant. | Arpens. | Nature and date of claim. | By whom granted. | By whom surveyed, date, and situation. |
|---|---|---|---|---|---|
| 141 | Joseph Marié. | 800 | Concession, January 10, 1801. | Carlos Dehault Delassus. | James Rankin, D. S. Certified, November 15, 1807, by A. Soulard, ex-surveyor general. On Salt river. |

EVIDENCE WITH REFERENCE TO MINUTES AND RECORDS.

*November* 27, 1811—Board met. Present: John B. C. Lucas, Clement B. Penrose, and Frederick Bates, commissioners.

Charles Fremon Delauriere, assignee of Joseph Marié, claiming 800 arpens of land, situate on Salt river, district of St. Charles. Produces record of a concession from Delassus, lieutenant governor, dated January 10, 1801; record of a certified extract of sale made by Marié to claimant, dated the 1st of March, 1804.

It is the opinion of the board that this claim ought not to be confirmed. (See book No. 5, page 458.)

*March* 12, 1833.—The board met, pursuant to adjournment. Present: L. F. Linn, A. G. Harrison, commissioners.

Joseph Marié, by his legal representatives, claiming 800 arpens of land. (Book D, page 291; minutes, No. 5, page 458.) Produces a paper, purporting to be a concession from Carlos Dehault Delassus, dated January 10, 1801; also an affidavit, by Antoine Soulard.

M. P. Leduc, duly sworn, says that the signature to the concession is in the proper handwriting of said Carlos Dehault Delassus. (See book No. 6, page 116.)

*June* 26, 1834.—The board met, pursuant to adjournment. Present: J. S. Mayfield and F. R. Conway, commissioners.

In the case of Joseph Marié, claiming 800 arpens of land. (See No. 6, page 116.) Claimant produces a certified plat of survey by A. Soulard, dated November 15, 1807.

M. P. Leduc, duly sworn, says that the signature to the said plat and certificate of survey is in the proper handwriting of Antoine Soulard, surveyor general. (See No. 6, page 536.)

*August* 25, 1835.—The board met, pursuant to adjournment. Present: F. R. Conway, J. H. Relfe, F. H. Martin, commissioners.

Joseph Marié, claiming 800 arpens of land. (See book No. 6, pages 116 and 536.)

The board are unanimously of opinion that this claim ought not to be confirmed. For reasons, see decision in the claim of Louis Lamalice, No. 80.

                                                    F. H. MARTIN,
                                                    F. R. CONWAY,
                                                    JAMES H. RELFE.

---

Class 2. No. 142.—*Jean Baptiste Geffré, claiming 800 arpens.*

To Don CARLOS DEHAULT DELASSUS, *Lieutenant Governor of Upper Louisiana:*

SIR: Jean Baptiste Geffré, alias Gascon, has the honor to represent that, wishing to form an establishment in the upper part of this province, where he has been residing since a number of years; therefore, sir, the petitioner prays that you will grant him a piece of land of 800 arpens in superficie, to be taken on the vacant lands of the King's domain, in the place which will appear most suitable to the interest of your petitioner, who presumes to expect this favor of your justice.

                                                    JEAN BAPTISTE × GEFFRÉ.
                                                                   his mark.
ST. LOUIS, *October* 7, 1800.

                                        ST. LOUIS OF ILLINOIS, *October* 9, 1800.

Whereas we are assured that the petitioner possesses sufficient means to improve the lands which he solicits, I do grant to him and his heirs the land which he solicits, if it is not prejudicial to any person; and the surveyor, Don Antonio Soulard, shall put the interested party in possession of the quantity of land which he asks, in a vacant place of the royal domain; and this being executed, he shall draw a plat of his survey, delivering the same to said party, with his certificate, in order to serve to him to obtain the concession and title in form from the intendant general, to whom alone corresponds, by royal order, the distributing and granting all classes of lands of the royal domain.                    CARLOS DEHAULT DELASSUS.

Recorded at the desire of the interested. (Book No. 2, folio 47, No. 33.)

                                                    SOULARD.
ST. LOUIS, *March* 20, 1833.  Truly translated.
                                        JULIUS DE MUN, *T. B. C.*

| No. | Name of original claimant. | Arpens. | Nature and date of claim. | By whom granted. | By whom surveyed, date, and situation. |
|---|---|---|---|---|---|
| 142 | Jean B. Geffré. | 800 | Concession, 9th October, 1800. | C. Dehault Delassus. | James Rankin, D. S. Certified November 9th, 1807, by A. Soulard, ex-surveyor general. On Salt river. |

*November* 20, 1811.—Board met.  Present: John B. C. Lucas, Clement B. Penrose, and Frederick Bates commissioners.

Charles Fremon Delauriere, assignee of Jean Baptiste Geffré, claiming 800 arpens of land, situate on Salt river, district of St. Charles.  Produces record of a concession from Charles D. Delassus, lieutenant governor, dated 9th October, 1800; record of a plat of survey, certified by A. Soulard, 15th November, 1807; record of a certified extract of sale made by Geffré to claimant, dated 10th May, 1805.

It is the opinion of the board that this claim ought not to be confirmed.  (See book No. 5, page 438.)

*March* 12, 1833.—The board met, pursuant to adjournment.  Present: L. F. Linn and A. G. Harrison, commissioners.

Baptiste Geffré, (Jean Baptiste Geffré,) by his legal representative, Henry Vouphul, claiming 800 arpens of land.  (See book D. page 290; minutes, No. 5, page 438.)  Produces a paper purporting to be a concession from C. Dehault Delassus, dated 9th October, 1800; also, an affidavit of Antonio Soulard.

M. P. Leduc, duly sworn, says that the signature to the concession is in the proper handwriting of said Carlos Dehault Delassus.  (See book No. 6, page 116.)

*June* 26, 1834.—The board met, pursuant to adjournment.  Present: J. S. Mayfield and F. R. Conway, commissioners.

In the case of Baptiste Geffré, claiming 800 arpens of land, (see No. 6, page 116,) claimant produces a certified plat of survey, by A. Soulard, dated 15th November, 1807.

M. P. Leduc, duly sworn, says that the signature to the said plat and certificate of survey is in the proper handwriting of said Antonio Soulard.  (See book No. 6, page 536.)

*August* 25, 1835.—The board met, pursuant to adjournment.  Present: F. R. Conway, J. H. Relfe, and F. H. Martin, commissioners.

Jean Baptiste Geffré, claiming 800 arpens of land.  (See book No. 6, pages 116 and 536.)

The board are unanimously of opinion that this claim ought not to be confirmed.  For reasons, see decision in the claim of Louis Lamalice, No. 80.

F. H. MARTIN,<br>F. R. CONWAY,<br>JAMES H. RELFE,

---

Class 2.  No. 143.—*André Pelletier, claiming 800 arpens.*

To Don CARLOS DEHAULT DELASSUS, *Lieutenant Governor of Upper Louisiana:*

SIR: André Pelletier has the honor to represent to you, that wishing to settle himself in the upper part of this province, where he has been residing for some time, therefore he has recourse to the benevolence of this government, praying that you may be pleased to grant to him a tract of land of 800 arpens in superficie, to be taken on the vacant lands of the King's domain, in the place which will appear most convenient to the interest of your petitioner, who presumes to hope this favor of your justice.

his<br>ANDRE × PELLETIER.<br>mark.

ST. LOUIS, *May* 13, 1800.

ST. LOUIS OF ILLINOIS, *May* 15, 1800.

Being assured that the petitioner has sufficient means to improve the land which he solicits, I do grant to him and his heirs the land which he solicits, if it is not prejudicial to any person, and the surveyor, Don Antonio Soulard, shall put the interested in possession of the quantity of land solicited, in a vacant place of the royal domain; which being executed, he shall draw a plat of survey, delivering the same to the party, with his certificate, in order to serve to him to obtain the title in form from the intendant general, to whom alone corresponds, by royal order, the distributing and granting all classes of lands, &c.

CARLOS DEHAULT DELASSUS.

ST. LOUIS, *December* 13, 1832.  Truly translated.

JULIUS DE MUN.

| No. | Name of original claimant. | Arpens. | Name and date of claim. | By whom granted. | By whom surveyed, date, and situation. |
|---|---|---|---|---|---|
| 143 | André Pelletier. | 800 | Concession, May 15, 1800. | Carlos Dehault Delassus. | |

*December* 6, 1811.—Board met.  Present: John B. C. Lucas, Clement B. Penrose, and Frederick Bates, commissioners.

Edward Hempstead and Claibourne Rhodes, assignee of Antoine Dejarlais, assignee of Andrew Pelletier, claiming 800 arpens of land, situate in the district of St. Charles.  Produces record of a concession, not signed, dated May 15, 1800; record of a transfer from Pelletier to Dejarlais, dated January 14, 1804; record of a transfer from Dejarlais to Rhodes, without date; record of a transfer from Rhodes to Hempstead for one half of this tract, dated June 25, 1803.

It is the opinion of the board that this claim ought not to be confirmed.  (See book No. 5, page 480.)

*November* 29, 1832.—The board met, pursuant to adjournment.  Present: L. F. Linn and F. R. Conway, commissioners.

André Pelletier, by his legal representatives, claiming 800 arpens of land.  (See book D, pages 258 and 259; book No. 5, page 480.)  Produces a paper purporting to be an original concession from Carlos Dehault Delassus, dated May 15, 1800, and deed of conveyance.

M. P. Leduc, duly sworn, saith that the signature to said concession is in the proper handwriting of Carlos Dehault Delassus. (See book No. 6, page 66.)

*August* 25, 1835.—The board met, pursuant to adjournment. Present: F. R. Conway, J. H. Relfe, and F. H. Martin, commissioners.

André Pelletier, claiming 800 arpens of land. (See book No. 6, page 66.)

The board are unanimously of opinion that this claim ought not to be confirmed. For reasons, see decision in the claim of Louis Lamalice, No. 80.

F. H. MARTIN,<br>
F. R. CONWAY,<br>
JAMES H. RELFE.

---

Class 2. No. 144.—Pierre Lord, claiming 800 arpens.

To Don CARLOS DEHAULT DELASSUS, *Lieutenant Governor of Upper Louisiana :*

SIR: Pierre Lord has the honor of representing to you, that wishing to make an establishment in the upper part of this province, where he resides since several years, the petitioner having a numerous family, has recourse to your goodness, praying that you may be pleased to grant to him a concession of 800 arpens of land in superficie, to be taken upon the vacant lands of his Majesty's domain, in the place which will appear most convenient to the interest of your petitioner ; favor which he presumes to hope of your justice.

PIERRE <sup>his</sup> × LORD.<br>
<sup>mark.</sup>

ST. LOUIS, *December* 9, 1799.

ST. LOUIS OF ILLINOIS, December 14, 1799.

Being assured that the petitioner has sufficient means to improve the land which he solicits, I do grant to him and his heirs the land which he solicits, if it is not prejudicial to any person, and the surveyor, Don Antonio Soulard, shall put the interested party in possession of the quantity of land solicited, in a vacant place of the royal domain ; and this being executed, he shall draw a plat of survey, which he shall deliver to the said party, with his certificate, in order to serve to him to obtain the concession and title in form from the intendant general, to whom alone corresponds, by royal order, the distributing and granting all classes of lands of the royal domain.

CARLOS DEHAULT DELASSUS.

ST. LOUIS, *December* 18, 1832. Truly translated.

JULIUS DE MUN.

| No. | Name of original claimant. | Arpens. | Nature and date of claim. | By whom granted. | By whom surveyed, date, and situation. |
|---|---|---|---|---|---|
| 144 | Pierre Lord. | 800 | Concession, 14th December, 1799. | Carlos Dehault Delassus. | |

EVIDENCE WITH REFERENCE TO MINUTES AND RECORDS.

*November* 23, 1811.—Board met. Present: John B. C. Lucas, Clement B. Penrose, and Frederick Bates, commissioners.

Edward Hempstead, assignee of sheriff of St. Charles district, who sold the same as the property of John Campbell and White Matlock, assignees of Louis Labeaume, assignee of Pierre Lord, claiming 800 arpens of land, situate in Bay de Roy, district of St. Charles. Produces record of a concession from Charles D. Delassus, lieutenant governor, dated 9th (14th) December, 1799 ; record of a plat of survey, dated 8th February, and certified 15th April, 1803 ; record of a transfer from Labeaume to Campbell and Matlock, dated 20th April, 1805 ; record of a transfer from sheriff of St. Charles district to claimant, dated 29th June, 1808.

It is the opinion of the board that this claim ought not to be confirmed. (See book No. 5, page 445.)

*November* 29, 1832.—The board met, pursuant to adjournment. Present: L. F. Linn and F. R. Conway, commissioners.

Pierre Lord, by his legal representatives, Edward Hempstead's heirs and devisees, claiming 800 arpens of land. (See book C. page 424 ; book No. 5, page 445.) Produces a paper, purporting to be an original concession from Carlos Dehault Delassus, dated 14th December, 1799 ; also, deeds of conveyance.

M. P. Leduc, duly sworn, saith that the signature to said concession is in the proper handwriting of said Carlos Dehault Delassus. (See book No. 6, page 67.)

*August* 25, 1835.—The board met, pursuant to adjournment. Present: F. R. Conway, J. H. Relfe, and F. H. Martin, commissioners.

Pierre Lord, claiming 800 arpens of land. (See book No. 6, page 67.)

The board are unanimously of opinion that this claim ought not to be confirmed. For reasons, see decision in the claim of Louis Lamalice, No. 80.

F. H. MARTIN,<br>
F. R. CONWAY,<br>
JAMES H. RELFE.

---

Class 2. No. 145.—Joseph Lafleur, claiming 800 arpens.

To Don CARLOS DEHAULT DELASSUS, *Lieutenant Governor of Upper Louisiana :*

SIR: Joseph Lafleur has the honor to represent to you, that wishing to form an establishment in the upper part of this province, where he has been residing for some time, therefore he prays you to grant to him a tract of land of eight hundred arpens in superficie, to be taken on the vacant lands of the King's domain, in the place which will appear most advantageous to the interest of your petitioner.

St. Louis, *September* 16, 1800.          JOSEPH $\times$ LAFLEUR.
                                          his
                                          mark.

St. Louis of Illinois, *September* 18, 1800.

Being assured that the petitioner has sufficient means to improve the land which he solicits, I do grant to him and his heirs the land he solicits, if it is not prejudicial to any one, and the surveyor, Don Antonio Soulard, shall put the interested in possession of the quantity of land petitioned for, in a vacant place of the royal domain; and this being executed, he shall draw a plat of his survey, delivering the same to the party, with his certificate, in order to serve to him to obtain the title in form from the intendant general, to whole alone corresponds, by royal order, the distributing and granting all classes of lands, &c.

CARLOS DEHAULT DELASSUS.

St. Louis, *December* 24, 1832. Truly translated from a copy certified by A. Soulard, on the 10th January, 1805.

JULIUS DE MUN.

| No. | Name of original claimant. | Arpens. | Nature and date of claim. | By whom granted. | By whom surveyed, date, and situation. |
|---|---|---|---|---|---|
| 145 | Joseph Lafleur. | 800 | Concession, 18th September, 1800. | Carlos Dehault Delassus. | |

EVIDENCE WITH REFERENCE TO MINUTES AND RECORDS.

*November* 19, 1808.—Board met. Present: Hon. Clement B. Penrose and Frederick Bates.

Edward Hempstead, assignee of Albert Tyson and wife, assignee of Joseph Lafleur, claiming 800 arpens of land unlocated. Produces to the board a certified copy of the concession, said to have been dated 18th September, 1800, certified 11th January, 1805; a deed of conveyance from said Lafleur to Albert Tyson, dated 11th January, 1805; and a deed of conveyance from Albert Tyson and wife to claimant, dated 21st September, 1807.

Antoine Soulard, duly sworn, says that he had the original concession in this claim in his hands in 1805, and that the copy produced and written by him is a true copy; says that he knows Louis Lafleur, and that he was in the country at the time the concession bears date.

Albert Tyson sworn, says that he had the said original concession in his possession in 1805, and lost it with other papers that year; that he has it not in his possession, nor does he know what has become of it. Laid over for decision. (See book No. 3, page 360.)

*July* 9, 1810.—Board met. Present: John B. C. Lucas, Clement B. Penrose, and Frederick Bates, commissioners.

Edward Hempstead, assignee of Albert Tyson, assignee of Louis Lafleur, claiming 800 arpens of land. (See book No. 3, page 360.) It is the opinion of the board that this claim ought not to be confirmed. (See book No. 4, page 420.)

*November* 29, 1832.—The board met, pursuant to adjournment. Present: L. F. Linn and F. R. Conway, commissioners.

Joseph Lafleur, by same as above (Edward Hempstead), claiming 800 arpens of land. (See book D, pages 225 and 226; book No. 3, page 360; No. 4, page 420.) Produces a paper purporting to be a copy of a concession from Carlos Dehault Delassus, dated September 18, 1800; said copy certified by Antoine Soulard on the 10th January, 1805; also, a deed of conveyance.

M. P. Leduc, duly sworn, saith that the signature to said copy of concession is in the proper handwriting of said Antoine Soulard. (See book No. 6, page 68.)

*August* 25, 1835.—The board met, pursuant to adjournment. Present: F. R. Conway, J. H. Relfe, and F. H. Martin, commissioners.

Joseph Lafleur, claiming 800 arpens of land. (See book No. 6, page 68.)

The board are unanimously of opinion that this claim ought not to be confirmed. For reasons, see decision in the claim of Louis Lamalice, No. 80.

F. H. MARTIN,
F. R. CONWAY,
JAMES H. RELFE.

Class 2. No. 146.—*Joseph P. Lamarche, sr., claiming* 800 *arpens.*

To Don CARLOS DEHAULT DELASSUS, *Lieutenant Governor of Upper Louisiana:*

Sir: Joseph Philip Lamarche has the honor to represent to you, that wishing to establish himself in the upper part of this province, where he has resided for some time, therefore he has recourse to the benevolence of this government, praying that you will be pleased to grant to him a tract of land of 800 arpens in superficie, to be taken on the vacant lands of the royal domain, in the place which will appear most convenient to the interest of your petitioner, who presumes to expect this favor of your justice.

St. Louis, *February* 8, 1800.          JOSEPH PH. $\times$ LAMARCHE.
                                        his
                                        mark.

St. Louis of Illinois, *February* 10, 1800.

Whereas we are assured that the petitioner possesses sufficient means to improve the lands which he solicits, I do grant to him and his heirs the land which he solicits, if it is not prejudicial to anybody, and the surveyor, Don Antonio Soulard, shall put the interested in possession of the quantity of land he asks, in a vacant place of the royal domain ; and this being executed, he shall draw a plat of his survey, delivering the same to the party, with his certificate, in order to serve to him to obtain the title in form from the intendant general, to whom alone corresponds, by royal order, the distributing and granting all classes of lands, &c.

CARLOS DEHAULT DELASSUS.

St. Louis, *March* 25, 1833. Truly translated.

JULIUS DE MUN.

| No. | Name of original claimant. | Arpens. | Nature and date of claim. | By whom granted. | By whom surveyed, date, and situation. |
|---|---|---|---|---|---|
| 146 | Joseph Philip Lamarche. | 800 | Concession, 10th February, 1800. | Carlos Dehault Delassus. | James Rankin, D. S. Certified by Soulard, 15th November, 1807. On the waters of Salt river. |

EVIDENCE WITH REFERENCE TO MINUTES AND RECORDS.

*November* 25, 1811.—Board met. Present: John B. C. Lucas, Clement B. Penrose, and Frederick Bates, commissioners.

Charles Fremon Delauriere, assignee of Joseph P. Lamarche, claiming 800 arpens of land, situate on Salt river, district of St. Charles. Produces record of concession from Delassus, L. G., dated 10th February, 1800 ; record of a plat of survey, dated 15th November, 1807, signed Soulard ; record of transfer from Lamarche to claimant, dated 25th May, 1805.

It is the opinion of the board that this claim ought not to be confirmed. (See book No. 5, page 449.)

*March* 12, 1833.—The board met, pursuant to adjournment. Present: L. F. Linn and A. G. Harrison, commissioners.

Joseph Philip Lamarche, by his legal representative, Henry Vouphul, claiming 800 arpens of land. (See book D, page 292 ; No. 5, page 449.)

Produces a paper, purporting to be an original concession, dated 10th February, 1800, from Carlos Dehault Delassus.

Albert Tyson, duly sworn, says that the signatures to the concession are in the proper handwriting of said Delassus and Soulard. (See book No. 6, page 116.)

*June* 26, 1834.—The board met, pursuant to adjournment. Present: J. S. Mayfield and F. R. Conway, commissioners.

In the case of Joseph Philip Lamarche, claiming 800 arpens of land. (See No. 6, page 116.) Claimant produces a paper purporting to be a certified plat of survey, dated November 15th, by A. Soulard.

M. P. Leduc, duly sworn, says that the signature to the said plat and certificate of survey is in the proper handwriting of Antoine Soulard, surveyor general. (See book No. 6, page 535.)

*August* 24, 1835.—The board met, pursuant to adjournment. Present: F. R. Conway, J. H. Relfe, and F. H. Martin, commissioners.

Joseph Philip Lamarche, claiming 800 arpens of land. (See book No. 6, pages 116 and 535.)

The board are unanimously of opinion that this claim ought not to be confirmed. For reasons, see decision in the claim of Louis Lamalice, No. 80.

F. H. MARTIN,<br>F. R. CONWAY,<br>JAMES H. RELFE.

Class. 2. No. 147.—François Lami Duchouquet, claiming 800 arpens.

To Don Carlos Dehault Delassus, *Lieutenant Governor of Upper Louisiana :*

Sir : François Lami Duchouquet, for a long time inhabitant of this town, has the honor to represent to you that he would wish to form an establishment in the upper part of this province ; therefore he prays you to grant to him a tract of land of 800 arpens in superficie, on the vacant lands of his Majesty's domain, in the place which will appear most convenient to the interest of your petitioner, who presumes to expect this favor of your justice.

F. DUCHOUQUET.

St. Louis, *October* 12, 1799.

St. Louis of Illinois, October 14, 1799.

Whereas we are assured that the petitioner possesses sufficient means to improve the lands which he solicits, I do grant to him and his heirs the land which he solicits, provided it is not prejudicial to any person, and the surveyor, Don Antonio Soulard, shall put the interested in possession of the quantity of land he asks, in a vacant place of the royal domain ; and this being executed, he shall draw a plat of his survey, delivering the same to the party, with his certificate, in order to serve to him to obtain the title in form from the intendant general, to whom alone corresponds, by royal order, the distributing and granting all classes of lands, &c.

CARLOS DEHAULT DELASSUS.

Registered at the desire of the interested. (Book No. 2, page 49, No. 35.)

SOULARD.

St. Louis, *March* 28, 1833. Truly translated.

JULIUS DE MUN.

*François Lami Duchouquet, claiming 800 arpens.*

| No. | Name of original claimant. | Arpens. | Nature and date of claim. | By whom granted. | By whom surveyed, date, and situation. |
|-----|---------------------------|---------|---------------------------|------------------|----------------------------------------|
| 147 | F. L. Duchouquet. | 800 | Concession, 14th October, 1799. | C. Dehault Delassus. | |

EVIDENCE WITH REFERENCE TO MINUTES AND RECORDS.

*November* 14, 1811.—Board met.  Present: John B. C. Lucas, Clement B. Penrose, and Frederick Bates, commissioners.

Charles Fremon Delauriere, assignee of Louis Labeaume, assignee of François Duchouquet, claiming 400 arpens, and said Duchouquet claiming 400 arpens of land, situate on Salt river, district of St. Charles.  Produces the record of a concession from Charles D. Delassus, lieutenant governor, dated 14th October, 1799 ; a plat of survey signed Fremon Delauriere, deputy surveyor, dated 27th September, 1805 ; a transfer from Duchouquet to Labeaume, dated 7th December, 1803 ; a transfer from Labeaume to claimant, dated 15th July, 1806.

It is the opinion of the board that this claim ought not to be confirmed.  (See book No. 5, page 412.)

*March* 12, 1833.—The board met, pursuant to adjournment.  Present : L. F. Linn, A. G. Harrison, commissioners.

François Lami Duchouquet, by his legal representative, Henry Vouphul, claiming 800 arpens of land.  (See book D, pages 293 and 294 ; minutes, No. 5, page 412.)

Produces a paper purporting to be an original concession from Carlos Dehault Delassus, dated 14th October, 1799.

M. P. Leduc, being duly sworn, says that the signature to the concession is in the proper handwriting of C. D. Delassus.  (See book No. 6, page 117.)

*June* 26, 1834.—The board met, pursuant to adjournment.  Present : J. S. Mayfield and F. R. Conway, commissioners.

In the case of François Lami Duchouquet, claiming 800 arpens of land, (see No. 6, page 117), claimant produces a plat and certificate of survey, signed by Fremon Delauriere, deputy surveyor, dated 27th December, 1807.

M. P. Leduc, duly sworn, says that the signature to the said plat and certificate of survey is in the proper handwriting of said Fremon Delauriere, deputy surveyor, whose commission as such has already been filed before this board.  (See book No. 6, page 536.)

*August* 25, 1835.—The board met, pursuant to adjournment.  Present : F. R. Conway, J. H. Relfe, and F. H. Martin, commissioners.

François Lami Duchouquet, claiming 800 arpens of land.  (See book No. 6, pages 117 and 536.)

The board are unanimously of opinion that this claim ought not to be confirmed.  For reasons, see decision in the claim of Louis Lamalice, No. 80.

F. H. MARTIN,<br>
F. R. CONWAY,<br>
JAMES H. RELFE.

---

Class 2.  No. 148.—*Joseph Fenwick, claiming 20,000 arpens.*

*To the Lieutenant Governor of Upper Louisiana :*

Joseph Fenwick, a Roman Catholic, father of ten children, owner of a number of slaves, and of a great number of cattle of all kind, has the honor to represent that, having come from the United States to these parts, with the consent and recommendation of his excellency the governor general, the Baron de Carondelet, in order to form an extensive establishment, as well for agricultural purposes as for raising horses, cattle, and (*parcherie*— supposed to mean *tanyard*), he has made choice, on the waters of the river St. Francis, of a tract of land suitable for the above-mentioned purposes, containing twenty thousand arpens, on his Majesty's domain, and which cannot be prejudicial to any person, on account of its remoteness from all other settlements.  Therefore, may it please you to grant to him, his heirs or assigns, a concession for the said twenty thousand arpens of land, to be taken in the aforesaid place.  The petitioner shall never cease to pray for the preservation of your days.

St. Genevieve, *August* 10, 1796.

JOSEPH FENWICK.

Don Zenon Trudeau, *Lieutenant Governor of the western part of Illinois, &c. :*

Don Antonio Soulard, surveyor of this jurisdiction of Illinois, shall survey, in favor of the party interested, the twenty thousand arpens of land in superficie, in the place where he solicits the same, provided it belongs to his Majesty's domain ; and he shall deliver to him the plat and certificate of survey, in order that, together with this decree, it will serve to the said party as a title to his property, until one in better form shall be delivered to him by the general government of the province, to which he shall have to apply in due time.

St. Louis, *August* 18, 1796.

ZENON TRUDEAU.

St. Louis, *September* 4, 1834.  Truly translated from the original.

JULIUS DE MUN, *T. B. C.*

| No. | Name of original claimant. | Arpens. | Nature and date of claim. | By whom granted. | By whom surveyed, date, and situation. |
|-----|---------------------------|---------|---------------------------|------------------|----------------------------------------|
| 148 | Joseph Fenwick. | 20,000 | Concession, 18th August, 1796. | Z. Trudeau. | On the St. Francis river. |

*November* 14, 1811.—Board met.　Present: John B. C. Lucas, Clement B. Penrose, and Frederick Bates, commissioners.

John Smith T., assignee of Joseph Fenwick, claiming 20,000 arpens of land, situate on the river St. Francis, district of St. Genevieve.　Produces the record of a concession from Zenon Trudeau, L. G., dated 18th of August, 1796.

It is the opinion of the board that this claim ought not to be confirmed.　(See minutes, book No. 5, page 421.)

*June* 12, 1833.—F. R. Conway, esq., appeared, pursuant to adjournment.

Joseph Fenwick, by his legal representatives, John Smith T., claiming 20,000 arpens of land, situated on the waters of St. Francis river.　(See minutes, No. 5, page 421; record-book C, page 504.)　Produces a paper purporting to be an original concession granted by Zenon Trudeau, dated 18th August, 1796.　(See minutes, No. 6, page 175.)

*October* 29, 1834.—The board met, pursuant to adjournment.　Present: F. R. Conway, J. S. Mayfield, and J. H. Relfe, commissioners.

In the case of Joseph Fenwick, claiming 20,000 arpens of land.　(See book No. 6, page 175.)

M. P. Leduc, duly sworn, says that the concession and signature affixed to it is in the proper handwriting of Zenon Trudeau, who was, at the time of the date of said concession, lieutenant governor of Upper Louisiana. (See book No. 7, page 58.)

*August* 26, 1835.—The board met, pursuant to adjournment.　Present: F. R. Conway, J. H. Relfe, and F. H. Martin, commissioners.

Joseph Fenwick, claiming 20,000 arpens of land.　(See book No. 6, page 175; No. 7, page 58.)

A majority of the board are of opinion that this claim ought not to be confirmed, F. R. Conway, commissioner, voting for the confirmation.　(See book No. 7, page 243.)

F. H. MARTIN,
JAMES H. RELFE,
F. R. CONWAY.

The majority of the board who rejected the claim of Joseph Fenwick to 20,000 arpens of land on the St. Francis river, and numbered 148 in the report, offer the following reasons for the grounds of their opinion : The claimant was an emigrant from the State of Kentucky, and proposed to establish himself in Upper Louisiana, and make certain improvements, if a grant of land should be given to him of 20,000 arpens, on the river St. Francis. His proposition, as set forth in his petition, was acceded to.　The following year, viz.: on 26th May, 1797, as a citizen of the United States and an inhabitant of Kentucky, he makes a similar proposition, asking for 3,000 arpens between the mouth of Apple creek and the river St. Côme, promising to remove to, settle, and cultivate the same, if it should be granted.　Lieutenant Governor Trudeau made the grant on the 10th of June, 1797, and, from the records of this office, it appears that Joseph Fenwick complied with the conditions set forth in his petition, and this government has confirmed to said Fenwick the claim of 3,000 arpens ; but there is no evidence of his having made any improvement, or establishment, as promised in his petition for the 20,000 arpens on the river St. Francis.

---

Class 2.　No. 149.—*James Clamorgan, claiming 536,904 arpens.*

To Don CHARLES DEHAULT DELASSUS, *Lieutenant Colonel of the stationary regiment of Louisiana, and Lieutenant Governor of New Madrid and dependencies, &c. :*

James Clamorgan, merchant, residing in the town of St. Louis, has the honor to represent that he has been strongly encouraged by his excellency, the governor general of this province, to establish a rope manufactory, for the purpose of making cordage for the use of his Majesty's ships, and especially to supply the Havana, at which place his excellency desires that the petitioner should send the cordage under his protection, conformably to the notice he has given to you on that subject, in order that, in all cases, the petitioner should have recourse to your goodness, so as to be favored by all your power, particularly in this undertaking, which may become very important to the prosperity of this dependency, and very profitable, in time, to all the inhabitants of this Upper Louisiana, so much the more, as the petitioner is connected in correspondence and matters of interest with a powerful house in Canada, which can procure hereafter a sufficient number of farmers to come to this country to teach the cultivation of hemp, and its fabrication into different kinds of cordage in the most perfect manner, thereby fulfilling the views of the general government, which desires this undertaking to succeed by all just and honest means which it will be possible to use, in order to exempt his Majesty from drawing, henceforth, from foreign countries, an article so important to the fitting out of his navy.　In hopes of obtaining this end, the petitioner has made the most pressing demands to obtain from his correspondents in Montreal a considerable number of people fit for this cultivation, whom we are compelled by necessity to attract to this country, although, for the present, political circumstances in Canada appear opposed to it, but in more peaceful times, this object may indubitably be obtained.

Meanwhile, the petitioner is obliged to secure beforehand a title from you, sir, which will guaranty to him the property of a quantity of arable land, proportionate to his views, in order to form an extensive establishment, as soon as circumstances will appear favorable to his undertaking, and when his correspondents will be able to cause to emigrate to this country, without hurting their feelings, the number of people necessary to give a start to this culture, so much desired by the government.

The petitioner hopes, sir, that, in consideration of the above statement, and of the particular recommendations of his excellency, the governor general of the province, you will be pleased to grant him the quantity of land he wishes to obtain, as much in order to favor him in all that may contribute to the execution and future prosperity of his undertaking, as it will also facilitate to him the means of drawing from foreign parts an emigration of cultivators, who, perhaps, cannot be obtained but after a considerable lapse of time, and under promises of rewards which the petitioner shall be obliged to fulfil.　Therefore, he supplicates you to grant him, in the name of his Majesty, the tract of land lying on the western side of the river Mississippi, to begin from the place opposite the head of an island situated at about one hundred arpens below the little prairie, which is distant about thirty miles from the village of New Madrid, in descending the current, and continuing to follow said current, until one is placed on the same western side, right opposite the mouth of the river commonly called river à *Carbono*, which is on the eastern side of the Mississippi.  So that, from the said place, situated opposite the mouth of the aforesaid river Carbono, a line be drawn toward the interior, running southwest or thereabout; said line shall be prolonged parallel to the one which will have to be drawn from the place situated opposite the head of the island lying as here above stated, at about one hundred arpens below the said little prairie; these two said lines shall run in the depth, in a southwestern direction or thereabout, and shall be the boundaries of each of those two opposite sides, until the extremities of the said two lines be sufficiently prolonged in the said direction, so as to reach the banks of the branches of the river St. Francis, the most distant from the Mississippi; which banks (of said branches) of the river St. Francis, shall be the boundary and limit to the third side of the land demanded, and the banks of the Mississippi shall be the fourth (side of the same,) to begin from the head of the aforesaid island of the little prairie, and descending the current on the western side, till the place situated opposite the said river, called river Carbono; in order that as soon as it is in the power of the petitioner, he may select and improve, in the said tract demanded, the land which is most suitable for the cultivation of hemp; a great part of this same tract being overflowed by ponds and impracticable low swamps, which will prevent the improving of the whole in all its extent. And the petitioner to enjoy and dispose of the same for ever, as if a thing to him belonging, and to his heirs or assigns; and even to distribute the said lands, or part of them, if he thinks proper, in favor of such person or persons whom he may judge fit, in order to attain, as much as in his power lies, the accomplishment of his project. And the petitioner shall never cease to render thanks to your goodness.

Done at New Madrid, this 1st day of August, 1796.

J. CLAMORGAN.

New Madrid, *August 9, 1796.*

Having examined the statement contained in this petition; being satisfied as to the means of the petitioner, and of his late partnership with the house of Todd, which may facilitate to him the accomplishments of the undertaking he proposes, the profits of which, if it succeeds, will devolve in part to the benefit of this remote country, so miserable on account of the actual want of population; due attention being paid to the particular recommendations made to me by the Baron de Carondelet, governor general of these provinces: (*Attando ha tenido a bien el nombrar de comandante de est puesto y dependencias de huscar.*)  Supposed meaning: *Considering that he thought fit to recommend to the commandant of this post and dependencies,* "*to seek,* by all possible means, the mode of increasing the population and of encouraging agriculture in all its branches, and particularly that of hemp."  It appearing to me that what the petitioner proposes will contribute to the attainment of this last recommendation, I do grant to him and his heirs the land which he solicits, in the place where, and in the same terms as, he asks the same, provided it is not prejudicial to any person.  And when he establishes the said land, he shall have it surveyed, not compelling him to have it done immediately, as its extent is so considerable that it would occasion a ruinous expense to him if he was to execute said survey before the arrival of the families which he must send for to Canada; but as soon as they arrive, and he settles them on said land, he shall have to secure his property by having the same surveyed, in order afterward to have recourse to the governor general to obtain the approbation and the title in form for this, his concession.

CARLOS DEHAULT DELASSUS.

St. Louis, *September 9, 1834.*  Truly translated from the original.

JULIUS DE MUN, *T. B. C.*

| No. | Name of original claimant. | Arpens. | Nature and date of claim. | By whom granted. | By whom surveyed, date, and situation. |
|---|---|---|---|---|---|
| 149 | James Clamorgan. | 536,904 | Concession, 9th August, 1796. | Carlos Dehault Delassus. | R. A. Nash, D. S., from January 30, to February 12.  Received for record by Soulard, 28th of February, 1806.  Below New Madrid. |

EVIDENCE WITH REFERENCE TO MINUTES AND RECORDS.

*June 21, 1833.*—The board met, pursuant to adjournment.  Present: A. G. Harrison and F. R. Conway, commissioners.

James Clamorgan, by his legal representative, Pierre Chouteau, claiming 536,904 arpens, being 458, 963 acres of land.  (See record-book C, page 31; Spanish records of concessions, book No. 3, page 7, No. 7.)  Produces a paper purporting to be an original concession, dated August 9, 1796, by Carlos Dehault Delassus, commandant of New Madrid; also, a plat of survey made from the 30th of January to the 12th of February, 1806, certified by Soulard (to have been received for record) February 28, 1806; also, an original deed of conveyance from Clamorgan to Chouteau.

M. P. Leduc, being duly sworn, says that the decree of concession, and the signature affixed to it, are in the proper handwriting of Carlos Dehault Delassus; that the petition and signature to the same are in the proper handwriting of James Clamorgan; and that the signature to the record of survey is in the proper handwriting of Soulard.  (See minutes, No. 6, page 179.)

*August 26, 1835.*—The board met, pursuant to adjournment.  Present: F. R. Conway, J. H. Relfe, and F. H. Martin, commissioners.

James Clamorgan, claiming 536,904 arpens of land.  (See book No. 6, page 179.)

The board are unanimously of opinion that this claim ought not to be confirmed, the conditions not having been complied with.  (See book No. 7, page 244.)

F. H. MARTIN,
JAMES H. RELFE,
F. R. CONWAY.

Class 2.   No. 150.—*John Godfrey, claiming* 640 *acres.*

| No. | Name of original claimant. | Acres. | Nature and date of claim. | By whom granted. | By whom surveyed, date, and situation. |
|-----|----------------------------|--------|---------------------------|------------------|----------------------------------------|
| 150 | John Godfrey. | 640 | Settlement right. | | |

EVIDENCE WITH REFERENCE TO MINUTES AND RECORDS.

*July* 1, 1835.—F. H. Martin, esq., appeared, pursuant to adjournment.

John Godfrey, assignee of John Coleman, who was assignee of Jacob Swaney, claiming 640 acres of land on the Marameck.   (See record-book E, page 317, and Bates's decisions, page 91, where the same is " not granted." See book No. 7, page 203.)

*September* 19, 1835.—The board met, pursuant to adjournment.   Present : F. R. Conway, J. H. Relfe, and F. H. Martin, commissioners.

John Godfrey, claiming 640 acres of land.   (See book No. 7, page 203.)

The board are unanimously of opinion that this claim ought not to be granted.   (See book No. 7, page 246.)

F. R. CONWAY,
JAMES H. RELFE,
F. H. MARTIN.

Class 2.   No. 151.—*Martin Fenwick, claiming* 500 *arpens.*

To Don ZENON TRUDEAU, *Lieutenant Governor of the western part of Illinois, and Commandant of St. Louis:*

Martin Fenwick, of the State of Kentucky, professing the Catholic and Roman religion, has the honor to represent to you, that having determined to come and settle himself in these parts, he supplicates you to grant him a concession for five hundred arpens in superficie, situated between Apple river and *riviere à la Viande,* (Meat river,) alias river of Cape St. Côme, the said Fenwick promising to build on and cultivate the same, in the time prescribed by the ordinances, and to conform himself to the laws and constitution of the kingdom, as a good, faithful, and loyal subject.

MARTIN FENWICK.

NEW BOURBON, *May* 26, 1797.

ST. LOUIS, *June* 10, 1797.

The surveyor, Don Antonio Soulard, shall put this party in possession of the five hundred arpens of land he solicits, and his survey being executed, he shall deliver it (the plat and certificate) to him, in order to enable him to solicit the concession from the governor general of these provinces, who is, by these presents, informed that the petitioner is a son of Don Joseph Fenwick, the same whom his lordship has recommended in order that lands should be granted to him, his family, and to the Catholic and Roman settlers he would bring with him, to establish themselves in this western part of Illinois.

ZENON TRUDEAU.

OFFICE OF THE RECORDER OF LAND TITLES, *St. Louis, May* 4, 1835.

I certify the foregoing to be a true translation of the original filed in this office.

JULIUS DE MUN, *T. B. C.*

| No. | Name of original claimant. | Arpens. | Nature and date of claim. | By whom granted. | By whom surveyed, date, and situation. |
|-----|----------------------------|---------|---------------------------|------------------|----------------------------------------|
| 151 | Martin Fenwick. | 500 | Concession, 10th June, 1797. | Z. Trudeau. | |

EVIDENCE WITH REFERENCE TO MINUTES AND RECORDS.

*November* 14, 1811.—Board met.   Present: John B. C. Lucas, Clement B. Penrose, and Frederick Bates, commissioners.

Martin Fenwick, claiming 500 arpens of land, situate as aforesaid (Apple creek, district of St. Genevieve). Produces record of a concession from Zenon Trudeau, lieutenant governor, dated 10th June, 1797.

It is the opinion of the board that this claim ought not to be confirmed.   (See minutes, book No. 5, page 422.)

*April* 24, 1835.—The board met, pursuant to adjournment.   Present : F. R. Conway and James H. Relfe, commissioners.

Martin Fenwick, claiming 500 arpens of land.   (See record-book D, page 44 ; minutes, No. 5, page 422.) Produces a paper purporting to be an original concession from Zenon Trudeau, dated 10th June, 1797.

The following testimony was taken before James H. Relfe, one of the commissioners, at St. Genevieve, on the 22d of April, 1825 :

Barthelmi St. Gemme, aged about sixty years, being duly sworn, deposeth and saith that he was well acquainted with Zenon Trudeau, and he was lieutenant governor in Upper Louisiana, in the year 1797.   He further says, that the signature to the concession is in the proper handwriting of the said Zenon Trudeau, that he has often seen him write.   Witness further says that he knew the claimant, and he was the son of Joseph

Fenwick; that there was a large and respectable family of them; and that the claimant, at the date of the grant, was a citizen and resident in the then province of Upper Louisiana, and continued so until long after the change of government.     BARTHELMI ST. GEMME.

(See book No. 7, page 129.)

*September* 15, 1835.—The board met, pursuant to adjournment.  Present: F. R. Conway, J. H. Relfe, and F. H. Martin, commissioners.

Martin Fenwick, claiming 500 arpens of land.  (See book No. 7, page 129.)

The board are unanimously of opinion that this claim is destitute of merit, an alteration being apparent in the original petition on file, as noted in the translation; the name of a river *à Brazeau* having been altered into that of a river *à la Viande,* alias St. Côme, thus increasing the distance, for location of grant, several miles; and the conditions not having been complied with.  (See book No. 7, page 246.)

F. R. CONWAY,
JAMES H. RELFE,
F. H. MARTIN.

Class 2.     No. 152.—*Jacques Clamorgan, claiming* 500,000 *arpens.*

To Don ZENON TRUDEAU, *Lieutenant Governor of Upper Louisiana:*

Nothing has made the petitioner so proud as the encouragement and emulation you have given to his industry, for the purpose of accomplishing the discovery of the Indian nations extending themselves to the Pacific ocean.  The petitioner being charged with that mission by the general government, you condescended to give him hopes that he would have the honor of your protection and support; you did more, you solicited from the general government the aid claimed by the petitioner, in order to proceed with vigor, in an enterprise in which his Majesty himself appeared to be occupied.  In fact, his Majesty granted to the petitioner an exclusive privilege for trading ten whole years with the nations of Upper Missouri, not only in order to open a new branch of commerce in furs, but also to get information about, and topographical knowledge of, the immense territory which was to be explored.  Those objects could not be attained but by making great sacrifices among the Indian nations, in order to conciliate to us their esteem and friendship.  In consequence of your recommendations, sir, his excellency, the Baron de Carondelet, laid before his Majesty an account of the excessive expenses to which the petitioner had been subjected in this arduous enterprise of facilitating communications then so extensive.  His Majesty, in his goodness, determined, in favor of the petitioner, that a sum of ten thousand dollars should be paid annually to him, in order to contribute to the expenses occasioned by the discovery of the nations and territories of Upper Missouri, as also in keeping away foreigners, who, from Hudson's bay and Lake Superior, transported their goods, in order to bribe the credulous natives inhabiting the said Upper Missouri.  His excellency, the Baron de Carondelet, as well as you, sir, communicated immediately, by official letters to the petitioner, the generosity of his Majesty in his favor; but it had not its intended effect, on account of the impediments thrown in the way by the intendant Morales, who pretended at the time to have in the King's coffers no funds appropriated to that object!  In consequence of that state of contradiction between the two powers, the petitioner has remained a victim of his zeal and activity in rendering himself useful in compliance to the wishes of the general government and to the intentions of his Majesty.

In these unfortunate circumstances, the petitioner presumes to claim of your goodness that you will be pleased to grant to him, on the western side of the river Mississippi, some leagues above the mouth of the Missouri, the tract of land bounded on one side by the little river called Lacharette, alias Dardenne, and on the other by the little river called Au Cuivre, one on the south the other on the north, will serve as boundaries to those two sides.  The petitioner wishes, moreover, that you would be pleased to grant to him sixty arpens of land in front, on the banks of the Mississippi, immediately adjoining the mouth of the first above-named river Lacharette, in descending the current of the Mississippi; and again, sixty arpens in front, also on the banks of the Mississippi, adjoining immediately to the upper side of the mouth of the second above-named river Au Cuivre, and ascending the current of the Mississippi.  The depth of the three different above-described tracts of land to be extended by two lines, starting from the banks of the Mississippi, one from the most southern, and the other from the most northern point (of the front) of the above-demanded tracts, which two lines shall be run parallel, on each side, in a westerly direction, until they reach the top of the high hills in the rear, and from there, the said two lines to be continued and prolonged in the same westerly direction, until they reach a point at the distance of about two hundred arpens from the foot of said hills; and then those two extreme points shall be connected together by a straight line which shall be run so as to form the fourth side of the said three tracts here above demanded.  The said lines encompassing in their extent all the waters of the above-mentioned rivers Lacharette, alias Dardenne, and Au Cuivre, in order that, hereafter, the petitioner may erect saw and grist mills thereon, also place there a number of cattle, have slaughter-houses, and send salt meat to the capital.  And the petitioner shall render thanks to your goodness.

J. CLAMORGAN.

ST. LOUIS, *March* 1, 1797.

Don ZENON TRUDEAU, *Captain in the regiment of Louisiana, Lieutenant Colonel by brevet, and Lieutenant Governor of the western part of Illinois:*

Cognizance being taken of the statement made by Don Santyago Clamorgan, and the governor general, the Baron de Carondelet having particularly recommended to me to facilitate and protect the discovery and commerce of Upper Missouri, in which the above-named Clamorgan has engaged in my entreaties; considering the losses which said enterprise has occasioned to him, and the new expenses to which he shall have to contribute on account of the same undertaking, and how important it is to favor and extend the discoveries here before mentioned, without prejudice to the royal treasury, and to the interest and welfare of these settlements, but on the contrary, in contributing to their prosperity, by drawing new inhabitants:  For these considerations, and on account of the said Clamorgan having rendered himself worthy and deserving of the favors of the government, the surveyor of this jurisdiction (as soon as the occupations of his place will permit) shall survey, in favor of the party interested, the extent of land he solicits, in the way and manner described in the foregoing document, which, together with the plat and certificate of survey, and of the boundaries which shall be set (to said land) will form the title of concession, which, in due time, he shall have to lay before the general government of the province, in order to get its approbation and record.

ZENON TRUDEAU.

St. Louis, *March* 3, 1797.

St. Louis, *August* 16, 1834. Truly translated from record book D, pages 314 and 315.

JULIUS DE MUN, *T. B. C.*

---

### No. 1.

New Orleans, *May* 26, 1794.

I have read, sir, with much interest, the memorial you have addressed to me. It contains political views which do honor to your understanding, and are in accordance with the ideas I have laid before the court two years ago. We are, perhaps, very near the moment when we shall see them realized, but time and pains are needed to convince the ministers of their utility. The grand objects which for the present absorb all the attention of the different powers will, perhaps, delay for some months the approbation of this plan, but I do not despair to see it adopted before the end of the year.

Some errors have crept in among your details, which the enthusiasm for what is good, and too full conviction of your own ideas, have hidden from you; but in the main they are just, and the means of execution well combined.

I have the honor to be, with the most perfect consideration, sir, your very humble and very obedient servant,

LE BARON DE CARONDELET.

Mons. Clamorgan.

---

### No. 2.

New Orleans, *July* 22, 1794.

Sir: I have, indeed, received the political memorial you directed to me under the double cover which you mention. The letter annexed to it, for Mr. Delassus, was also received at the same time, and suspecting some mistake, and also conjecturing what might be the contents of it, I threw it into the fire.

I have already had the honor to tell you my sentiments on one part of the contents of your memorial, which I have read with the greatest interest. Let us wait till the storm which agitates the political atmosphere be somewhat dissipated, and then we shall see what the future situation of Europe will permit us to do for the welfare of Louisiana, which, I hope, will advance more in the last five years of this century, than it has done ever since the beginning of it, up to the period of my coming into the province.

Your views, sir, are in perfect accordance with mine. True wealth is to be found only in agriculture, and this requires a competent population and easy outlets. Louisiana is susceptible of all these advantages, but present circumstances are not favorable to our views. Let us then have patience for awhile, and, by remaining attentive spectators of passing events, we may seize on the first opportunity of success.

I have the honor to be, with the most perfect consideration, sir, your very humble and very obedient servant,

LE BARON DE CARONDELET.

Mons. De Clamorgan.

---

### No. 3.

New Orleans, *May* 11, 1796.

Sir: In consequence of what you wrote to me in your letter of 10th April, I send to Mr. Trudeau some medals for the company, and among them a very fine gilt one, which I intend for the great Maha chief, in order to flatter him most. I also send several commissions, leaving a blank for the names, so that Mr. Trudeau may have them filled up; but it is to be wished, as much for the company as for the King, that there should be but one single chief decorated with a great medal, one with a small one, and two captains in each nation; for hereafter, those chiefs will require compensations adequate to their grades. I send also five flags by Mr. Chouteau, and when, in execution of the treaty concluded with the United States, we shall abandon the bluffs, the commandant will send to Mr. Trudeau ten swivels for the service of the company's forts.

Mr. Chouteau is also bearer of a commission, such as you desired, for Mr. Mackay. Finally, I send to Mr. Trudeau the order that Mr. Todd may take an interest in the order of discoveries.

There are no objections to Mr. Todd having the exclusive trade of the Sac and Fox nations in the country east of the Missouri, and even on the said Missouri, during the term of his contract; but it would not be proper to have it extended to the western side before we positively know and are perfectly acquainted with the force and situation of the nations situated on the (last) above-mentioned side of said river. Besides, I must avoid to have those nations at variance with the Osages, whom Messrs. Chouteau are beginning to keep in subjection, and who will be an impediment to the aggrandizement of our settlements, as long as we cannot keep them in peace.

I am concerned to see that our settlers of Upper Mississippi, who might acquire true wealth by agriculture, prefer to devote themselves to the fur trade, which is as dangerous as it is precarious. The working of the lead mines would also afford great profits, because we might furnish the Havana with this article, and yet we are constantly destitute of it, for want of labor; at this moment there is none, either in the king's or in private warehouses.

I have the honor to be, with the most perfect consideration, sir, your very humble and very obedient servant,

LE BARON DE CARONDELET.

Mons. De Clamorgan.

No. 4.

NEW ORLEANS, *July* 9, 1796.

SIR: I have received the account of Mr. Mackay's travel to the Maha nation, as also his instructions given to the party going to the discovery of the South sea. I would be so much the more flattered, should this last (expedition) succeed, as it is confidently reported that a Spanish squadron has sailed from Europe, in order to go and dislodge the English from Nootka sound, and it would be a curious fact if our people were to reach the same point at the same time.

I thought that I had written to you that the establishment of a fort at the river St. Peter had already been proposed to the court, which is occupying itself of the means required to put Louisiana in a respectable state of defence; but time is needed, for everything remains yet to be done, and the political circumstances of Europe attract all the attention.

I have the honor to be, with the most perfect consideration, sir, your very humble and very obedient servant,

LE BARON DE CARONDELET.

Mons. DE CLAMORGAN.

ST. LOUIS, *August* 26, 1834.   The above letters are truly translated from the original.

JULIUS DE MUN, *T. B. C.*

No. 5.

NEW ORLEANS, *September* 18, 1796.

SIR: I have just received the agreeable news of the approval of the "Spanish company formed in 1794, (these are the proper words of the royal decree made in the council of state held on the 27th of last May"), for the purpose of making discoveries to the westward of the Missouri, as also of the regulations and instructions under which your lordship has sanctioned and granted to the said company the exclusive privilege of the fur trade with all the nations of Indians on said Missouri, who inhabit beyond the nation of Poncas, offering three thousand dollars as a reward to the first who will reach the South sea.

2d. The permission granted to the said company to arm and maintain armed in the forts which it has or may have hereafter, at the expense of his Majesty, the one hundred men who are thought to be necessary; the whole being under your lordship's orders, for the end designated, which you will watch with the greatest care, &c.

I hope, sir, that, in consequence of these favors and privileges, the company will derive new vigor, and will make the greatest efforts in order to correspond to the intentions of his Majesty, and exclude the English from those parts.

The house of Todd is also approved of by the King, who has added to all these favors, that of the reduction of the duties, from fifteen to six per cent. for all the colony.

We will see if Leglise gets the prize of $3,000.

I have the honor to be, with the most perfect consideration, sir, your very humble and obedient servant,

LE BARON DE CARONDELET.

Mons. CLAMORGAN.

The above letter, No. 5, is truly translated from record-book D, page 316.

JULIUS DE MUN, *T. B. C.*

No. 6.

NEW ORLEANS, *October* 26, 1796.

In a royal order, under date of the 11th of June of this year, the most excellent Sor. Don Diego de Gardoqui, Secretary of State, and of the Universal Despacho, &c., among other things, tells me the following:

"In the council of state, held on the 27th of last month, extracts of your lordship's last letters, up to the 10th of February, were laid before the King, together with the topographical plat of the rivers Mississippi and Missouri, on which are demonstrated the progress of the Spanish company of discoveries, to the westward of this last river, established on the 12th of May, 1794, as also the encroachments of the English companies upon the Spanish possessions. His Majesty being well informed of all the occurrences in that province, and of the means which your lordship has proposed, with the advice of the intendant and of the English merchant, Don Andrew Todd, of Michilimackinac, his Majesty has condescended to grant, with the unanimous accordance of the said council, the following points and favors:

1st. The approval of the Spanish company formed in 1794, for the purpose of making discoveries to the westward of the river Missouri, under the instructions and regulations with which your lordship has permitted, and granted to said company the exclusive privilege of the trade with all the nations of the Indians on the said Missouri, who inhabit beyond the nation of Poncas, offering a reward of $3,000 to the first who reaches the South sea.

2d. The permission that the company may arm at its own expense, and maintain armed in the forts which said company has or may have hereafter, the one hundred men who are considered necessary; the whole to be under your lordship's orders for the purpose indicated, the accomplishment of which your lordship shall have to watch with the greatest care.

3d. That all the duties on imports and exports shall be reduced, for the present, to six per cent., as your lordship and the intendant have proposed, both taking care, with the greatest exactness possible, to observe and lay before his Majesty, at the end of the first year, the results which are expected from so munificent a disposition.

Finally, that your lordship give to understand to all the magnitude of these concessions, and the immense benefits which the sovereign munificence has condescended to accumulate in the treaty of amity, limits and navigation ; benefits which are of reciprocal utility to his beloved subjects, to the United States, and to the Indian nations allied and friendly to the two contracting parties ; and that your lordship shall so order, that all the important objects which are expected from these dispositions shall be duly executed. All which I do communicate to your lordship, by order of his Majesty, for your intelligence and for their execution.

I forward the same to you for your satisfaction and government.

May God have you in his keeping many years.

EL BARON DE CARONDELET.

Sor. Don. SANTYAGO CLAMORGAN.

---

### No. 7.

NEW ORLEANS, *November* 5, 1796.

Under date of the 3d instant, the intendant of these provinces writes to me what follows :

" The meaning which I give to the article in the royal order of the 11th June of this year, upon which Don Santyago Clamorgan, director of the Spanish company of discoveries to the westward of the Missouri, has founded the demand which your lordship has been pleased to enclose in your official note of 31st ultimo, is, that the cost of arming, and the maintenance of the one hundred men whom the company wants for the forts it has or may have hereafter, must be on its own account, and in this opinion, besides the literal interpretation of said article, to wit, *the permission that the company may arm at its own expense, and maintain armed, &c.*, I am, moreover, confirmed, 1st, by the circumstance of the permission of arming having ever been granted, for, it appears to me that, had it been intended to be on the King's account, it would only have been necessary to notify that the one hundred men were to be furnished to the company ; 2d, by said royal order not mentioning any sum, as it would have been indispensable in order to enable the royal treasury to make the disbursement ; and, finally, by his Majesty not having appropriated funds for this no small expenditure, which cannot be supported by his royal coffers in this province, particularly in their present state of scarcity and embarrassment, without being deprived of the means necessary to maintain the troops, the civil officers, the squadron of galleys, the works at Pensacola, and other extraordinary contingencies which occur every day. In consequence of all this, I find myself under the obligation to oppose the delivery of the said sum of ten thousand dollars, and to beg of your lordship, that, in case my reasons should not appear well founded, to consult his Majesty on this matter, and in order that, by his royal declaration, I shall be sheltered from the responsibility which would result to me were I to accede to the demand of Mr. Clamorgan on the terms he has established it."

I transmit the same to you for your knowledge and government.

May God have you in his keeping many years.

EL BARON DE CARONDELET.

Sor. Don SANTYAGO CLAMORGAN.

The above two letters, Nos. 6 and 7, are truly translated from the originals.

JULIUS DE MUN, *T. B. C.*

---

### No. 8.

NEW ORLEANS, *November* 8, 1796.

I see no objection to your levying in the country of Illinois the one hundred militia-men whom his Majesty has granted for the forts of the Missouri company, but I cannot answer for the reimbursement of the ten thousand dollars, because it depends on his Majesty's decision, although I am confident that when he sees my representation he will order it to be made, since I have solicited and supported the same.

It is all I have at present to answer to your official letter on this subject.

May God our Lord have you in his keeping many years.

EL BARON DE CARONDELET.

Sor. Don SANTYAGO CLAMORGAN.

---

### No. 9.

NEW ORLEANS, *May* 24, 1797.

SIR : I have received the letter you directed to me under date of the 15th of last April.

Your claim is accompanied by the best reasons possible, and would not suffer any difficulties, were it not for the obligation I am under to take all the sureties necessary to the responsibility of my place, in order to justify, in the clearest manner, the extraordinary use made of the funds confided to me by his Majesty. Therefore, I have written on this subject to Mr. Dehault Delassus, and according to the explicit answer which I expect of him, I will order what shall appear to me most advisable.

I have the honor to be, sir, your very humble and very obedient servant,

JUAN VENTURA MORALES.

Mr. CLAMORGAN.

---

### No. 10.

ST. LOUIS, *July* 3, 1797.

Under date of April 5 of this current year, the governor general, Baron de Carondelet, writes to me as follows :

" I have read your official note dated 11th of last March, in which you state the motives which have induced you to grant to Mr. Clamorgan the tract of land situated between the two rivers Charette and Cuivre, both emptying into the Mississippi; also sixty arpens to the north and sixty arpens to the south of said rivers, which serve to determine the situation of said land, having the Mississippi in front. Two parallel lines are to be drawn, running in the interior of the country until they reach at the distance of two hundred arpens beyond the foot of the first hills, conformably to the solicitation of the party interested. All which I do approve, Clamorgan having deserved this favor from the government."

I transmit the same to you for your knowledge and government.

May God have you in his keeping many years.

ZENON TRUDEAU.

Sor. Don Santyago Clamorgan.

St. Louis, *August* 28, 1834. The three last letters, Nos. 8, 9, 10, are truly translated from record-book D, pages 315 and 316.

JULIUS DE MUN, *T. B. C.*

B.

| No. of survey and certificate of confirmation. | To whom confirmed or granted. | Area of survey. |
|---|---|---|
| 10 | Isaac Hosteller | 400 arpens |
| 11 | John Wealthy | 400 do. |
| 16 | William Stewart | 400 do. |
| 23 | Toussaint Cerré | 400 do. |
| 29 | James Green | 800 do. |
| 30 | Antoine Janis and Peter Chouteau, under Jos. Langlois and Joseph Generaux | 240 do. |
| 53 | Peter Sommalt, son of Christopher | 300 do. |
| 54 | Christopher Sommalt, sr | 550 do. |
| 55 | Jacob Sommalt | 450 do. |
| 56 | Perry Brown | 300 do. |
| 57 | Peter Hoffman | 300 do. |
| 58 | Nicholaus Coontz | 400 do. |
| 60 | Squire Boone | 700 do. |
| 61 | Comod, *alias* Leonard Price | 650 do. |
| 63 | Andrew Sommalt, son of Jacob | 200 do. |
| 64 | James Flaugherty | 600 do. |
| 67 | John Walker, under Henry Groff, *alias* Groves | 400 do. |
| 127 | Thomas Caulk, under Peter Valigne | 300 do. |
| 165 | George R. Spencer, under Michael Prybolt | 450 do. |
| 205 | John Tayon | 400 do. |
| 280 | Isaac Welden, or his legal representatives | 400 do. |
| 284 | Francis Hosteller's representatives | 500 do. |
| 285 | John Coontz's legal representatives | 600 do. |
| 287 | Jacob Zoomalt, under Angus Gillis | 350 do. |
| 289 | Francis Smith | 250 do. |
| 290 | George Gatty | 450 do. |
| 291 | John Cook | 600 do. |
| 292 | William McConnell | 800 do. |
| 293 | George Hoffman, jr | 400 do. |
| 294 | Adam Zoomalt | 600 do. |
| 296 | Andrew Zoomalt, sr | 580 do. |
| 297 | James Baldridge | 400 do. |
| 304 | Warren Cottle | 650 do. |
| 306 | Robert Burns | 600 do. |
| 308 | Francis Duquette | 260 do. |
| 312 | Thomas Caulk | 400 do. |
| 353 | Ira Cottle | 400 do. |
| 354 | Warren Cottle, jr | 640 acres. |
| 417 | John Parkett | 650 arpens. |
| 418 | Daniel Kiesler | 600 do. |
| 424 | Godfrey Kroh (or Crow) | 600 do. |
| 453 | John Howell | 404 arp. 50 p's. |
| 456 | George Fallis | 350 do. |
| 460 | Jeremiah Grojean, under Louis Crow | 200 do. |
| 462 | Christian Denni's legal representatives | 400 do. |
| 469 | Christopher Clark, under Richard Taylor | 240 do. |
| 524 | Ira Cottle, under William Hays | 600 do. |
| 657 | Elisha Goodrich | 400 do. |
| 731 | Louis Jeanett's representatives | 640 acres. |
| 735 | John A. Smith | 640 do. |
| 737 | Henry Zoomalt, jr | 640 do. |
| 739 | Jacob Coontz | 640 do. |
| 743 | John Tourney | 600 arpens. |
| 749 | John B. Belland, under Louis Marchant | 160 do. |

B.—*Continued.*

| No. of survey and certificate of confirmation. | To whom confirmed or granted | Area of survey. |
|---|---|---|
| 754 | William Farnsworth.................................... | 640 acres. |
| 755 | Isaac Cottle........................................ | 640   do. |
| 756 | Sylvanus Cottle..................................... | 500 arpens. |
| 757 | Jonathan Woods..................................... | 640 acres. |
| 765 | Noel Herbert....................................... | 640   do. |
| 762 | Etienne Bernard, under Lauren Deraucher................ | 500 arpens. |
| 825 | Robert Baldridge.................................... | 640 acres. |
| 885 | Jonathan Cottle..................................... | 640   do. |
| 887 | Francis Howell...................................... | 640   do. |
| 888 | Angus Gillis, under Jacob Sommalt..................... | 640   do. |
| 891 | William Crow....................................... | 640   do. |
| 929 | Martrom Lewis, or his representatives.................. | 650 arpens. |
| 931 | Melkiah Baldridge................................... | 640 acres. |
| 935 | Benjamin Jones's heirs............................... | 640   do. |
| 947 | Daniel Kichelie..................................... | 640   do. |
| 948 | Christian Wolf...................................... | 640   do. |
| 979 | Michael Reybold's representatives..................... | 640   do. |
| 991 | James Beatty....................................... | 640   do. |
| 1198 | Jacques Clamorgan, for use of Edward Hempstead, under Jacques Eglise.................................... | 1066 arpens. |
| 1640 | Noel A. Prieur..................................... | 400   do. |
| 1641 | James Kerr........................................ | 1200   do. |
| 1652 | Baptiste Roy....................................... | 800   do. |
| 1653 | Joseph Roy........................................ | 800   do. |
| 1654 | Toussaint Cerré .................................... | 1000   do. |
| 1655 | Toussaint Cerré .................................... | 160   do. |
| 1669 | Arend Rutgers .................................... | 7056   do. |
| 1687 | Bernard Pratte and Joseph Beauchemin.................. | 1600   do. |
| 1696 | John Scott, under Thomas Johnson..................... | 500   do. |
| 1704 | Peter Chouteau, under Charles Tayon................... | 510   do. |
| 1719 | Charles Tayon, under Baptiste Belland.................. | 160   do. |
| 1731 | Pelagie Labbadie, under Etienne Bernard................ | 160   do. |
| 1738 | James Morrison, under Joseph Beauchamp................ | 240   do. |
| 1742 | James W. Cochran .................................. | 800   do. |
| 1754 | Antoine Janis...................................... | 160   do. |
| 1756 | Paul Lacroix....................................... | 1600   do. |
| 1757 | Widow Labbadie.................................... | 160   do. |
| 1771 | Milton Lewis....................................... | 352   do. |
| 1773 | Thomas Howell..................................... | 350   do. |
| 1776 | Nathaniel Simonds, or Marshal Cottle's representatives....... | 300   do. |
| 1777 | Lewis Crow........................................ | 640 acres. |
| 1778 | Andrew Walker .................................... | 640   do. |
| 1779 | Peter Chouteau, or P. Dessonet's representatives........... | 640   do. |
| 1780 | Christopher Soomalt................................. | 640   do. |
| 1781 | Abraham Keithley................................... | 300 arpens. |
| 1782 | Samuel Lewis...................................... | 640 acres. |
| 1783 | David Conrad...................................... | 640   do. |
| 1784 | Peter Teague. ..................................... | 640   do. |
| 1785 | John McConnell.................................... | 640   do. |
| 1786 | Joseph Voisard..................................... | 640   do. |
| 1787 | George Hoffmann................................... | 640   do. |
| 1788 | Arthur Burns...................................... | 640   do. |
| 1790 | Henry Stephenson.................................. | 640   do. |
| 1795 | Nathaniel Simonds.................................. | 640   do. |
| 1796 | John Weldon....................................... | 500 arpens. |
| 1798 | Thomas Howell. ................................... | 640 acres. |
| 1799 | Robert Spencer..................................... | 640   do. |
| 1801 | Daniel Baldridge................................... | 640   do. |
| 1807 | David Edwards..................................... | 640   do. |
| 1808 | Etienne Bernard, assignee of Mary Ann, widow of Jos. Violet. | 400   do. |
| 205 | Joseph St. Mary (New-Madrid claim).................... | 160   do. |
| 253 | Baptiste Chartier (New-Madrid claim).................. | 250 arpens. |
| 149 | John Baker, sr. (New-Madrid claim)..................... | 250   do. |

## C.

*Abstract of lands sold within and conflicting with the claim of J. Clamorgan, situated and embracing parts of townships Nos. 46, 47, 48, ranges 2, 3, and 4, east of 5th principal meridian.*

### Township 46. Range 2, east.

All the land within said claim sold.

### Township 47. Range 2, east.

| Sec. | | Acres sold. |
|---|---|---|
| 1. | S. W. quarter | 208.32 |
| 2. | S. E. quarter | 160.00 |
| 10. | S. fractional half and N. E. quarter | 376.00 |
| 11. | N. half and S. W. quarter | 480.00 |
| 12. | W. half of N. E. quarter, W. half of N. W. quarter, and S. W. quarter | 406.18 |
| 14. | S. half of S. E. fractional quarter | 38.52 |
| 21. | N. fractional half | 285.21 |
| 22. | W. half of S. W. quarter | 80.00 |
| 25. | West fractional half | 104.07 |
| 26. | S. W. fractional quarter and N. half of N. E. quarter | 97.44 |
| 27. | S. half | 145.56 |
| 28. | N. E. fractional quarter and S. fractional half | 201.57 |
| 29. | | 399.03 |
| 32. | S. fractional half | 123.72 |
| 33. | N. W. quarter of N. W. quarter | 40.00 |
| 34. | E. fractional half | 87.61 |
| 35. | E. fractional half and N. W. fractional quarter | 364.80 |
| 36. | W. half S. E. quarter and E. half of N. E. quarter | 535.41 |

### Township 48. Range 2, east.

| | | |
|---|---|---|
| 25. | All sold except 120 acres (viz. S. E. qr. of N. E. qr. and West half of S. W. qr. | 378.25 |
| 35. | N. E. quarter of S. E. quarter, W. half of N. E. quarter, and E. half of N. W. quarter | 200.00 |
| 36. | N. E. fractional quarter and N. E. quarter of N. W. quarter | 92.30 |

### Township 46. Range 3, east.

| | | |
|---|---|---|
| 1. | All sold except E. half of N. E. quarter (80 acres) | 344.73 |
| 4. | Reserved for 16th section (school land). | |
| 5. | S. W. fractional quarter and S. E. quarter of S. E. quarter | 61.66 |
| 6. | | 449.90 |
| 7. | | 44.66 |
| 8. | N. fractional half | 176.94 |
| 9. | S. E. fractional quarter | 47.95 |
| 12. | | 105.15 |
| 15. | E. fractional half of N. W. quarter | 78.57 |
| 26. | S. E. fractional quarter | 103.52 |

### Township 47. Range 3, east.

| | | |
|---|---|---|
| 7. | E. half of S. E. quarter | 80.00 |
| 8. | S. fractional half | 163.22 |
| 16. | | 272.24 |
| 17. | | 432.21 |
| 22. | | 473.25 |
| 25. | N. fractional half | 13.72 |
| 26. | S. W. fractional quarter | 133.35 |
| 27. | S. E. fractional quarter and E. fractional half of N. W. quarter | 219.47 |
| 30. | N. E. fractional quarter | 153.19 |
| 31. | E. half W. half of N. W. quarter and N. W. quarter of S. W. quarter | 232.84½ |
| 32. | N. W. fractional quarter, S. E. quarter, E. half of S. W. quarter, and S. W. qr. of S. W. qr. | 400.44 |
| 33. | N. W. fractional quarter | 48.37 |
| 34. | N. E. fractional quarter | 144.02 |
| 35. | N. W. fractional quarter and S. E. fractional quarter | 110.22 |

### Township 48. Range 3, east.

| | | |
|---|---|---|
| 31. | W. fractional half of S. W. quarter | 41.58 |

### Township 46. Range 4, east.

| | | |
|---|---|---|
| 5. | | 252.09 |
| 6. | N. E. fr. qr. N. W. qr. S. E. qr. E. half of S. W. qr. and S. W. fr. qr. of S. W. qr. | 532 34 |
| 7. | N. W. fr. qr. S. E. fr. qr. E. half of N. E. qr. and S. W. qr. of N. E. qr. | 263.31 |
| 8. | S. W. fractional quarter and W. half of N. W. quarter | 166.07 |

*Township 47. Range 4, east.*

| Sec. | | Acres sold. |
|---|---|---|
| 19. | .................................................................................................. | 76.66 |
| 28. | .................................................................................................. | 82.19 |
| 29. | S. E. fractional quarter ..................................................................... | 70.64 |
| 31. | W. fractional half............................................................................ | 176.82 |
| 32. | N. E. fractional quarter...................................................................... | 80.95 |
| 33. | N. W. fractional quarter...................................................................... | 89.60 |

*Township 48. Range 4, east.*

| 25. | S. E. fractional quarter (S. of Mississippi river).......................................... | 3.39 |
|---|---|---|
| 36. | N. E. fractional quarter (S. of Mississippi river)......................................... | 101.95 |

U. S. REGISTER'S OFFICE, *at St. Louis, Missouri, September* 4, 1835.

I certify that the foregoing abstract, as far as it purports, is correctly copied from the files in this office.

N. P. TAYLOR, *Clerk Register's office.*

---

*By Trudeau, prior to date of Clamorgan's grant of 3d March, 1797.*

| | Arpens. |
|---|---|
| Antonio Janis, under Langlois, 1st December, 1796................................... | 240 |
| Jno. Howell, 22d February, 1797..................................................... | 404 50 per. |
| Toussaint Cerré, 1st July, 1796 ...................................................... | 160 |
| Charles Tayon, under Belland, 7th March, 1796....................................... | 160 |
| Palazie Labbadie, under Bernard, 7th March, 1796................................... | 160 |
| J. Morrison, under Beauchamp, 18th June, 1796...................................... | 240 |
| Antonio Janis, 15th January, 1796.................................................... | 160 |
| | 1,524 50 per. |

---

*By Trudeau, subsequent to Clamorgan's grant. Surveyed 19th December, 1799.*

| | Arpens. |
|---|---|
| William Stewart, 4th February, 1798................................................. | 400 |
| Toussaint Cerré, 30th May, 1798..................................................... | 400 |
| James Green, 14th January, 1799..................................................... | 800 |
| T. Caulk, under P. Valigne, 15th December, 1797..................................... | 300 |
| C. Clark, under Taylor, 17th June, 1797.............................................. | 240 |
| Ira Cottle, under Hays, 24th January, 1798........................................... | 600 |
| Elisha Goodrich, 23d August, 1799................................................... | 400 |
| J. B. Belland, under Marchant, 1st July, 1798......................................... | 160 |
| James Kerr, 4th March, 1798 ......................................................... | 1,200 |
| Arend Rutgers, 14th April, 1799...................................................... | 7,056 |
| P. Chouteau, under Tayon, 28th January, 1798......................................... | 500 |
| | 12,066 |

---

*By Carlos Dehault Delassus.*

| | Arpens. |
|---|---|
| John Wealthy, 2d April, 1799......................................................... | 400 |
| Peter Sommalt, son of Christopher, 9th November, 1799............................... | 300 |
| Christopher Sommalt, sr., 9th November, 1799........................................ | 550 |
| Jacob Sommalt, 9th November, 1799.... ............................................. | 450 |
| Perry Brown, 26th October, 1799..................................................... | 300 |
| Peter Hoffman, 29th November, 1799................................................. | 300 |
| Nicholas Coontz, 29th August, 1799.................................................. | 400 |
| Squire Boon, 10th November, 1799................................................... | 700 |
| Coonrod, alias Leonard Price, 9th November, 1799.................................... | 650 |
| Andrew Sommalt, 9th November, 1799................................................ | 200 |
| James Flaugherty, 25th October, 1799................................................ | 600 |
| J. Walker, under Groff, 20th November, 1799......................................... | 400 |
| G. R. Spencer, under Ribault, 5th December, 1799.................................... | 450 |
| John Tayon, 5th October, 1799....................................................... | 400 |
| Isaac Weldons, rep., 21st September, 1799 ........................................... | 400 |
| Francis Smith, 6th November, 1799................................................... | 250 |
| George Getty, 8th September, 1799................................................... | 450 |
| John Cook, 28th December, 1799..................................................... | 600 |
| Warren Cottle, 8th October, 1799.................................................... | 650 |
| Robert Burns, 11th December, 1801.................................................. | 600 |
| John Parkett, 9th November, 1799 ................................................... | 650 |

*By Carlos Dehault Delassus*—Continued.

|  | Arpens. |
|---|---|
| Daniel Keesleler, 26th November, 1799 | 600 |
| Godfrey Crow, 7th November, 1799 | 600 |
| George Fallis, 15th January, 1800 | 350 |
| J. Grossjean, under Crow, 9th November, 1799 | 200 |
| Christian Dennis, rep., 16th June, 1800 | 400 |
| Noel A. Prieur, 3d February, 1801 | 400 |
| Baptist Roy, 29th December, 1799 | 800 |
| Joseph Roy, 29th December, 1799 | 800 |
| Toussaint Cerré, 28th October, 1799 | 1,000 |
| B. Pratt and J. Beachemin, 30th January, 1800 | 1,600 |
| John Scott, under Johnson, 20th October, 1799 | 500 |
| James W. Cochran, 5th July, 1800 | 800 |
| Paul La Croix, 15th December, 1799 | 1,600 |
| Widow Labbadie, 8th December, 1802 | 160 |
| Milton Lewis, 15th December, 1800 | 352 |
| Thomas Howell, 10th October, 1799 | 350 |
| John Weldon, 20th December, 1803 | 500 |
|  | 20,912 |
| E. Hempstead, under J. Eglise, survey 20th January, 1798 | 1.066 |
|  | 21,978 |

*By the original Board of Commissioners and Recorder Bates, under second section act of Congress.*

|  | Arpens. |
|---|---|
| Isaac Hosteller | 400 |
| Francis Hosteller, representative | 500 |
| John Coontz, representative | 600 |
| J. Zoomalt, under Gillis | 350 |
| William McConnell | 800 |
| George Hoffman, jr | 400 |
| Adam Zoomalt | 600 |
| Andrew Zoomalt, sr | 580 |
| James Baldridge | 400 |
| Francis Duquette (ten years' possession) | 260 |
| Thomas Caulk | 400 |
| Ira Cottle | 400 |
| John Tourney | 600 |
| Sylvanus Cottle | 500 |
| E. Bernard, under Derocher | 500 |
| Malthom Lewis | 650 |
| N. Simons | 300 |
| Mary Ann, widow of J. Violet | 400 |
|  | 8,640 |

*By original Board of Commissioners and Commissioner Bates, under the second section of act of Congress.*

|  | Acres. |
|---|---|
| Warren Cottle, jr | 640 |
| Louis Zeanetts, representative | 640 |
| John A. Smith | 640 |
| Henry Zoomalt | 640 |
| Jacob Coontz | 640 |
| William Fairnsworth | 640 |
| Isaac Cottle | 640 |
| Jonathan Woods | 640 |
| Noel Hebert | 640 |
| Robert Baldridge | 640 |
| Jonathan Cottle | 640 |
| Francis Howell | 640 |
| A. Gillis, under Sumalt | 640 |
| William Crow | 640 |
| Mekia Baldridge | 640 |
| Benjamin Jones (heirs) | 640 |
| Daniel Kichlie | 640 |
| Christian Wolf | 640 |
| Michael Reybolds, representative | 640 |
| James Beatty | 640 |
| Lewis Crow | 640 |
| Andrew Walker | 640 |
| P. Chouteau, or Dessonnets, representative | 640 |
| Christopher Zumalt | 640 |

*By the original Board, &c.*—Continued.

|                                   | Acres. |
|-----------------------------------|-------:|
| Abraham Keithley                  | 300    |
| Samuel Lewis                      | 640    |
| David Conrad                      | 640    |
| Peter Teague                      | 640    |
| John McConnell                    | 640    |
| Joseph Voisard                    | 640    |
| George Hoffman                    | 640    |
| Arthur Burns                      | 640    |
| Henry Stephenson                  | 640    |
| Nathaniel Simonds                 | 640    |
| Thomas Howell                     | 640    |
| Robert Spencer                    | 640    |
| Daniel Baldridge                  | 640    |
| David Edwards                     | 640    |
|                                   | 23,980 |
| Joseph St. Mary, New-Madrid claim | 160    |
|                                   | 24,140 |

|                                        | Arpens. |
|----------------------------------------|--------:|
| B. Chartier, New-Madrid claim          | 250     |
| John Baker, sr., New-Madrid claim      | 250     |
|                                        | 500     |

RECAPITULATION.

|                                                                                | Arpens. |
|--------------------------------------------------------------------------------|--------:|
| Granted by Trudeau, prior to 3d of March, 1797                                 | 1,524 50 per. |
| Granted by Trudeau, subsequent to March, 1797                                  | 12,066  |
| Granted by C. D. Delassus                                                      | 21,978  |
| Granted by commissioner and recorder under second section                     | 8,640   |
| Two New-Madrid claims located                                                  | 500     |
|                                                                                | 44,708 50 per. |

|                                                                                                    | Acres. |
|----------------------------------------------------------------------------------------------------|-------:|
| One New-Madrid claim located                                                                       | 160    |
| Granted by commissioners and recorder under the second section of the act of Congress              | 23,980 |
|                                                                                                    | 24,140 |

Of the claims granted by Zenon Trudeau and C. D. Delassus, in the above list, in almost every instance the survey took place prior to the change of government.

*James Clamorgan, claiming 500,000 arpens.*

| No. | Name of original claimant. | Arpens. | Nature and date of claim. | By whom granted. | By whom surveyed, date, and situation. |
|-----|----------------------------|---------|---------------------------|------------------|----------------------------------------|
| 152 | James Clamorgan.           | Not ascertained. | Concession, March 3d, 1797. | Z. Trudeau. | On Cuivre and Dardenne, on the Mississippi. |

EVIDENCE WITH REFERENCE TO MINUTES AND RECORDS.

*November* 14, 1811.—Board met. Present: John B. C. Lucas, Clement B. Penrose, and Frederick Bates, commissioners.

James Clamorgan, claiming 500,000 arpens of land, situate on rivers Mississippi, Dardenne, and Cuivre, district of St. Charles. Produces a concession from Zenon Trudeau, L. G., dated 3d March, 1797; also, four letters to claimant from Zenon Trudeau, Juan Ventura Morales, and Baron de Carondelet.

It is the opinion of the board that this claim ought not to be confirmed.

James Clamorgan, claiming 60 arpens, front on the Mississippi, Chorette, and Dardenne, back to the hills, about 200 arpens, district of St. Charles. Produces same concession and papers as in the preceding claim.

It is the opinion of the board that this claim ought not to be confirmed.

James Clamorgan, claiming 60 arpens of land, front on the Mississippi, commencing above the mouth of Cuivre, up the Mississippi, and back to the hills. Produces same concession and papers as in the foregoing claim.

It is the opinion of the board that this claim ought not to be confirmed. (See minutes, No. 5, page 417.)

*June* 21, 1833.—The board met, pursuant to adjournment. Present: A. G. Harrison and F. R. Conway, commissioners.

James Clamorgan, by his legal representatives, claiming a tract of land on the Cuivre and Dardenne;

quantity not ascertained. (See record book D, page 314; minutes, No. 5, page 417; Spanish record of conces-sion, No. 3, page 21, No. 13.)

Produces in evidence six letters, purporting to be original letters from Baron de Carondelet to James Cla-morgan; also, a certificate of James Mackay, and one of Charles Sanguinette, both sworn to before a magistrate; also, a paper purporting to be a translation from Spanish into French of a letter from Baron de Carondelet to Clamorgan, translated by M. P. Leduc, and certified by him to have been so translated from the original letter in the proper handwriting of the said Carondelet; also, a paper purporting to be a receipt from Risdon H. Price for two original letters from Baron de Carondelet to James Clamorgan.

M. P. Leduc, duly sworn, says that the signatures to the six above-mentioned letters are in the proper handwriting of Baron de Carondelet, and that the translation here above produced, is a faithful translation made by him from the original letter written in Spanish, in the proper handwriting of said Baron de Carondelet.

L. E. Lawless, agent of claimants, being duly sworn, says that the two original letters described in the receipt were delivered by him to said R. H. Price, on the day of the date of said receipt signed by said Price. To the best of deponent's belief, the concession, as recorded, was, at same date, in the possession of said Price, and that said Price is at present out of this State. Deponent further thinks that said documents have remained in the possession of said Price, and are now out of the reach of the present claimants. Deponent further states that said Price obtained said documents for the purpose of laying the same before Congress, in order to obtain the confirmation of said claim. (See minutes, book No. 6, page 179.)

*June* 29, 1833.—The board met, pursuant to adjournment. Present: L. F. Linn and F. R. Conway, commissioners.

In the case of James Clamorgan, claiming lands on Cuivre and Dardenne, (see page 179, No. 6,) the fol-lowing testimony was taken:

Pascal Cerré, being duly sworn, deposes and says, that he was well acquainted with Charles Sanguinette, sr., who died some twelve or fifteen years ago; that he was a man of probity, and in every way to be relied on; likewise he was a man of considerable property. The deponent further states that he was acquainted with James Mackay, and that he was a man of respectability and property; that, about forty years since, Mackay made a voyage of discovery and trading up the Missouri river. The deponent knows the outfit was made at Clamorgan's house, and believes that Mackay was concerned and interested with Clamorgan in the enterprise.

Jesse Richardson, being duly sworn, says that he is 57 years of age; that he has lived in the now State of Missouri, and in that vicinity, since 1799. This deponent says he knew James Clamorgan, deceased, and always understood, among the old inhabitants of the country, that the said Clamorgan had been in the employ-ment of the Spanish government, and that the Spanish government was largely indebted to said Clamorgan, and that by way of remunerating said Clamorgan for his services, and compensating him for what the government owed him, large grants of land were made to said Clamorgan, particularly a large tract lying on the Mississippi, and on the rivers Dardenne and Cuivre. This tract was looked upon by the old inhabitants under the Spanish government, as said Clamorgan's property. Deponent says that he knew James Mackay; he was a man of pro-bity and of high standing under the Spanish government. Charles Sanguinette, deceased, was a man of good reputation, and this affiant believes that the statements of said Mackay and Sanguinette are entitled to full credit, any statements they made in relation to this claim, or on any other subjects.

*Question by commissioners.* Do you know the quantity and boundaries of said tract?

*Answer.* I do not know the boundaries of said tract. I understood it was very large, embracing a great por-tion of the lands lying in the fork of the Missouri and Mississippi. This affiant has always heard the people ex-pressing their fears that this claim would be confirmed, and deprive those settled on it of their possessions. This affiant understood the land was about 500,000 arpens; that it lies on the Mississippi, extending from above the mouth of the Cuivre to below the mouth of the Dardenne and back, for quantity.

*Question by commissioners.* Did you ever hear of this claim spoken of as fraudulent?

*Answer.* Never; but on the contrary. I always understood that it was made to Clamorgan, to pay him what the Spanish government owed him as a reward for his services. I never heard any person who was inter-ested against this claim pretend that it was fraudulent, or any person whatever.

*Question by commissioners.* Have you any interest in this claim?

*Answer.* No. I have feared that it would interfere with a claim I have, not confirmed, but, on inquiry, I believe there is no danger. (See minutes, No. 6, page 205.)

*July* 16, 1833.—The board met, pursuant to adjournment. Present: L. F. Linn and F. R. Conway, commissioners.

In the case of James Clamorgan, claiming land on Cuivre and Dardenne. (See page 179 of this book, No. 6.)

Jean Elie Tholozan, being duly sworn, says that he believes it was about the year 1816, that he gave to Risdon H. Price the concession and all the papers he had in his possession relating to this claim, in order to have said claim presented to Congress for confirmation; that he has heard that said Price is now out of this State, and does not know where those papers are, and neither to whom to apply for them. (See No. 6, page 234.)

*September* 26, 1835.—The board met, pursuant to adjournment. Present: F. R. Conway, J. H. Relfe, and F. H. Martin, commissioners.

In the case of James Clamorgan, claiming land on Dardenne and Cuivre. (See book No. 6, pages 179 and 234.)

The board are unanimously of opinion that this claim ought not to be confirmed, believing it to have been disregarded by both Trudeau, the lieutenant governor, who made the grant, and by his successor, Delassus. For a full opinion and notice of interferences, see the report of the board to commissioner of the General Land Office. (See book No. 7, p. 249.)

JAMES H. RELFE,
F. R. CONWAY,
F. H. MARTIN.

244

248

254

FRANCOIS, 58, 59,
60, 143, 144, 145
FRANCOIS, JR., 144,
145, 146
FRANCOIS, SR., 144,
145
J. BAPTISTE, 45,
107, 123, 143
J.B., 30, 58, 60,
73, 101, 119,
137, 144, 145
J.B., JR., 145
JEAN B., 101
JEAN BAPTISTE, 45,
143, 144
JOHN B., 58, 60, 73,
102, 137, 144
JOHN B., JR., 145
JOHN B., SR., 118
JOHN BAPTISTE, 30,
101
JOHN BAPTISTE, SR.,
107, 121, 145
MICHEL, 179, 180
MR., 74
VANBIBBER
ISAAC, SR., 159
VASQUEZ
BENITO, 205
VASSEUR
REGIS, 191, 192
VIENENTENDRE
P., 171
VINCENT
ANTONIO, 53
VINEYARD
JONATHAN, 164, 165
VIOLET
J., 241
JOS., 238
MARY ANN, 238, 241
VOISARD
JOSEPH, 238, 242
VOISIN
JOSEPH, 142
VOUPHUL
HENRY, 225, 228, 229

-W-

WALKER
ANDREW, 238, 241
J., 240
JOHN, 237
WALLER
RICHARD, 44, 155
WASHINGTON, 97, 165
WATKINS
DOCTOR, 74
SAMUEL, 25, 26
WEALTHY
JOHN, 237, 240
WEAVER
JOHN, 33
WELDEN
ISAAC, 237
WELDON
JOHN, 163, 164, 238,
241
WELDONS
ISAAC, 240
WHITE OX PRAIRIE, 62
WHITE WATER, 67
WHITE-WATER, 83
WHITEOAK RUN, 160
WHITEWATER, 137
WICKERS
JULIUS, 34, 35

WIDEMAN
JOHN, 75
WILBORN
JAMES, 38
WILBOURN
CURTIS, 47
JAMES, 48, 49
JOHN, 37
WILKINSON
GEN., 109
JAMES, 73
WILLIAMS
JOSEPH, 53, 54,
55
LEWIS, 80
SALLY, 161
WILLIAM, 44, 68, 69
WILSON
SAMUEL, 100
WISE
JACOB, 32, 33
WOLF
CHRISTIAN, 238, 241
WOODS
JONATHAN, 238, 241
ZADOCK, 146

-X-

XIMENES
CARLOS, 89, 90

-Y-

YOSTI
EMILIAN, 54, 61
YOSTY
EMILIAN, 53
MR., 60, 65
YOUNG
JOSEPH, 151
MORRIS, 150, 151
PHILIP, 47
ROBERT, 53, 161

-Z-

ZEANETTS
LOUIS, 241
ZOOMALT
ADAM, 237, 241
ANDREW, SR., 237,
241
HENRY, 241
HENRY, JR., 237
J., 241
JACOB, 237
ZUMALT
ANDREW, 142, 143
CHRISTOPHER, 241

www.ingramcontent.com/pod-product-compliance
Lightning Source LLC
Chambersburg PA
CBHW080418270326
41929CB00018B/3077